Kitchen & Bath Source Book 1998/99

Sweet's Group
McGraw·Hill Construction Information Group

A Division of The **McGraw·Hill** Companies

1221 Avenue of the Americas
New York, New York 10020-1095

1221 Avenue of the Americas
New York, NY 10020-1095
Tel 212 512 4216
Fax 212 512 3441

Steve Fan
Vice President
Product Management

McGraw-Hill Construction Information Group
A Division of The **McGraw-Hill** Companies

April 1998

Welcome to the *Kitchen & Bath Source Book!*

As you create your new kitchen or bath, you'll be drawing on your own imagination and common sense. But you need more—you need product information and design guidelines to develop your ideas.

That's where Sweet's *Kitchen & Bath Source Book* comes in. It's brimming with product, color and design ideas all in one handy reference guide. Published by **McGraw-Hill**, this easy-to-use book is composed of manufacturers' catalogs offering all the information you need to plan your dream kitchen or bathroom.

Forget those piles of brochures and individual catalogs that are so easily misplaced. You'll find all the best information and ideas between the covers of the *Kitchen & Bath Source Book!*

For more than 90 years, Sweet's has provided designers, builders and consumers with the best resources for planning construction and renovation projects. The secret to our success is listening to our customers, and finding out what they need to help make the construction process go smoothly. I welcome your questions and suggestions on how to improve the *Kitchen & Bath Source Book* or other Sweet's products and services.

In the meantime, I hope you'll take full advantage of everything the *Kitchen & Bath Source Book* has to offer. Your new kitchen or bath should be everything you dreamed it would be. The *Kitchen & Bath Source Book* can help you make that happen.

Sincerely,

Sweet's Group
McGraw-Hill Construction Information Group

Contact our Customer Service Hotline if you are a construction professional with inquiries regarding Sweet's products and services:
1-800-442-2258 or
fax 212-512-2348

Contact our Sales Hotline if you are a building product manufacturer interested in participating in Sweet's:
1-800-421-9330 or
fax 212-512-6774

Look for Sweet's on the World Wide Web at http://www.sweets.com

Sweet's Consultants

Cynthia Belisle, AIA, CSI
Robert C. Boettcher, AIA, CSI
Donna Burns, AIA, CSI
Robert C. Chandler, AIA
Dorothy H. Cox, AIA, CSI
John W. Embler, AIA, CSI
Raymond M. Hennig, AIA, CSI
E. Michael Hollander, AIA
Richard J. Mazzuca, AIA, CSI
Wayne W. Puchkors, AIA, CSI
Barbara Ruppel, AIA, CSI
Peter G. Schramm, AIA
G. Robert Steiner, S.E., ASCE, CSI
Albert J. Thomas, AIA, CSI
John S. Vaci, AIA
William E. White, AIA, CSI

Regional Offices

Atlanta, GA 30319
4170 Ashford Dunwoody Road, Suite 275
404-843-4787 • 404-843-4795 - fax
Regional Director of Sales – Christopher J. Noble

Chicago, IL 60601
Two Prudential Plaza
180 North Stetson Avenue, Suite 700
312-616-3213 • 312-616-4554 – fax
Regional Director of Sales – Kevin J. Glynn

Dallas, TX 75247
1341 West Mockingbird, Suite 1103E
214-688-5152 • 214-688-5157 – fax
Regional Director of Sales – Bret A. Ronk

New York, NY 10019
1633 Broadway, 13th Floor
212-512-3181 • 212-512-6831 – fax
Regional Director of Sales – Douglas Runner

Pittsburgh, PA 15219
411 Seventh Avenue, Suite 1100
412-227-3610 • 412-281-7051 – fax
Regional Director of Sales – Elizabeth F. Hazlett

San Francisco, CA 94105
221 Main Street, Suite 800
415-882-2885 • 415-882-2824 – fax
Regional Director of Sales – Nancy E. Harmon

Canadian Offices

Montreal, QC H3G 2A5 Canada
3495 de la Montagne, Suite 11
514-842-9573 • 514-843-3166 – fax
Regional Manager – Pierre Savoie

North York, ON M2J 1R8 Canada
270 Yorkland Boulevard
416-496-3100 • 416-496-3104 – fax
Director of Manufacturing – Bruce Irish

Cover Photos:
Top left: Courtesy of Gerard Valentini.
Top right and bottom: Images © 1996 PhotoDisc, Inc.

Kitchen & Bath Source Book

Table of Contents

To Find Information Quickly 4

Sweet's BuyLine® 5

Sweet's Customer Service 6

Selected Articles from the *National Kitchen & Bath Association* (NKBA) 7

- A Space for Everyone
- Get Off to a Good Start
- Universal Design: Planning Kitchens That Last a Lifetime
- Kitchen/Bathroom Remodeling - Needs vs. Wants
- Creating your Dream Kitchen or Bathroom
- From Inspiration to Sensation

Firms Index 37

Products Index 38

Trade Names Index 60

To Find Information Quickly

The *Kitchen & Bath Source Book* is organized in an easy-to-use format. Catalogs are grouped by similar product type to help you quickly locate information on manufacturers and products for your kitchen and bath projects.

Coding System

Catalogs are assigned a four-character code indicating their position in the *Kitchen & Bath Source Book.*

As an example: C123

In addition, each catalog displays a unique BuyLine® number for use when calling Sweet's BuyLine® service (see page 5). You will find a two-tiered code on Kitchen & Bath catalog covers:

C123
BuyLine 1234

Refer to the Indexes

The *Kitchen & Bath Source Book* contains complete Firms, Products and Trade Name indexes:

The **Firms** index is an alphabetical list of manufacturers and their catalog codes.

The **Products** index is an alphabetical list of all products within the book. Manufacturers and their catalog codes appear for each product heading.

The **Trade Names** index contains an alphabetical list of trade names accompanied by a brief product description and the catalog code.

Sweet's BuyLine® 1-888-280-9950

Toll-free throughout the U.S., including Alaska and Hawaii.

Sweet's BuyLine is a service for kitchen & bath professionals. It does NOT provide information of use to consumers.

Attention Kitchen & Bath Professionals:
Need to contact the local sales representative for any manufacturer in Sweet's *Kitchen & Bath Source Book*? **Call Sweet's BuyLine®**.

Here's how to use BuyLine

1. Dial 1-888-280-9950. If you are using a touch-tone line, you will be greeted by an automated voice response from the Sweet's computer. If your telephone uses a rotary line, an operator will assist you (between 8 AM and 9 PM Eastern Time).
2. You will be asked to enter your telephone number using the numbers on your telephone keypad.
3. The system will then instruct you to enter the four-digit BuyLine code assigned to the manufacturer you have selected. The BuyLine code may be found on the front cover of the manufacturer's catalog (upper right-hand corner).
4. The BuyLine system will respond with the name, telephone and fax number (if provided by the manufacturer) of the manufacturer's sales representative serving your area.

When you call the sales representative, let him or her know you found them through Sweet's BuyLine. It's the best way to make sure manufacturers continue to provide you with valuable information in Sweet's.

Sweet's Customer Service

Call 1-800-442-2258

Sweet's wants to provide you with the quickest and easiest access to the wealth of information within the *Kitchen & Bath Source Book*. This guide outlines several of the special services we offer.

To answer any questions you may have regarding the *Kitchen & Bath Source Book*, our Customer Service representatives are available Monday through Friday from 8:30 AM to 6:00 PM (Eastern Time). Use our toll-free number for any of the following.

Shipping Inquiries

Please call us if your book arrives damaged or if you have received a duplicate copy.

Qualification or Additional Orders

If you have any questions concerning your qualification for the *Kitchen & Bath Source Book*, or any of Sweet's Catalog Files, please call. You will be immediately directed to the proper individual for assistance.

Change of Address

Please let us know if you have moved recently or plan to move in the near future. We need to keep our address records current to make sure you continue to receive the *Kitchen & Bath Source Book*.

If you wish to contact Sweet's Group in writing, please send correspondence to:

Sweet's Group
A Division of The McGraw-Hill Companies
1221 Avenue of the Americas
Room 2040
New York, New York 10020
USA

Selected Articles from the National Kitchen & Bath Association (NKBA)

If you're building or remodeling your home, the bathroom is one space you can't afford to overlook. When you consider how much time you spend in this room, you realize that this is one space you definitely want to be comfortable and functional, as well as good looking.

The bathroom is more than a space for three necessary fixtures; it's the place where you can relax after a long day, change your clothes, mend your wounds, apply your make up, comb your hair and take care of a multitude of other grooming and hygiene needs. It's probably the first room you visit in the morning, and the last room you visit at night.

But, how do you begin to make it the luxury room of your dreams? The National Kitchen & Bath Association (NKBA) recommends beginning by assessing your needs for the space.

"First, you must determine who will use the bathroom," says NKBA Director of Societies John Spitz, CBD, CKD. "This will affect the mood of the space as well as the features included in it."

According to Spitz, bathrooms should be designed around the users - a family bathroom, a children's bathroom, an adult's or master suite bathroom, a powder room or guest bathroom.

Each of these types of spaces has its own specific needs and concerns.

The Family Bathroom

"Traditionally, all of the fixtures in the bathroom are placed in one open space," adds Spitz. "But, for a family of four or more who is sharing one bathroom, zoning the fixtures would work much better."

By separating the fixtures into individualized compartments, several family members can use the space together while retaining some privacy. For example, the tub/shower and toilet could be placed in one space and a single- or double-bowl vanity in a second area. This would allow one person to use the vanity area while someone else was using the tub/shower area. Dividing the space into three separate areas may be the best approach for a larger family - one long vanity with the toilet and tub/shower in their own nooks allows three people to use the space concurrently.

The Children's Bathroom

"Small children always pose unique concerns in the home," Spitz says. "They require more safety features and lower heights, but also adaptability as they grow."

According to Spitz, some features which should be included for children are safety latches on drawers and cabinets; door locks which can be opened from outside the space; above-floor storage for cleaning supplies; shower valves which balance water pressure and temperature; pull-out step under the vanity; and adjustable pole-mounted showerheads or hand-held showerheads.

"Many of the safety features listed for a child's bath can and should be included in all bathrooms," notes Spitz.

The Adult's Bathroom or Master Bath Suite

When planning a bathroom for adults only, or a master bath suite, it is important to note the reasons for the space - privacy, relaxation, efficiency. Again, the reason will affect the fixtures, the lighting, etc.

"When space is limited, but you want a large private bathroom, the master bath suite is the answer," Spitz adds. "By 'stealing' space from the bedroom, the master bathroom can be enlarged creating a private retreat."

According to Spitz, adult baths may also incorporate added amenities such as whirlpool tubs, saunas and bidets, which increase the level of relaxation and luxury for the user. And for those who dream of a more efficient place to dress and groom, Spitz suggests improving the storage and closet area.

"Adequate cabinets with interior storage are a must in the adult bath," says Spitz. "Built-in drawers, racks, and hooks should be added for clothing storage, and divided, shallow drawers as well as deeper drawers and adjustable shelves should be added for grooming supplies in the bathroom area."

The Powder Room or Guest Bath

This specialized space is also known as the "half bath" because it does not include the tub/shower fixture. This is the bathroom that is typically used by guests.

"Obviously this type of bathroom requires less space than a full bath; however, comfort is still important and should not be overlooked," Spitz adds.

According to Spitz, the powder room should incorporate enough space for the fixtures as well as for storage, and enough room for the user to comfortably enter and exit the space.

It is also important that the room include proper soundproofing and ventilation.

As you can see, a bathroom remodel, no matter what style, is a major undertaking. Beyond planning the type of bathroom it will be and the users it will serve, there are electrical, plumbing and clearance considerations which must also be carefully planned. With all these things to consider, it's easy to see that this is not a do-it-yourself project. Spitz recommends working with a bathroom specialist, or a Certified Bathroom Designer (CBD). These are professionals who know the ins and outs of bathroom planning and can make your dreams become reality.

The National Kitchen & Bath Association offers a complete planning kit for $5 to help you get started. This kit includes a list of specialists in your area. To order your kit call 1-800-401-NKBA, ext. 600.

Get Off to a Good Start

The decision has been made! You've decided that the time has come to turn your dream kitchen or bathroom into a reality. Great! Now what?

The Beginning

Your first step should be locating and hiring a professional kitchen/bathroom designer. What can a professional do for you? Plenty!

A kitchen/bathroom specialist can guide you through every phase of your project — decorating, design, construction, and plumbing and electrical systems.

Specifically, kitchen/bathroom specialists are able to:

- work with contractors, electricians and plumbers
- answer any questions you have about design, products and colors, as well as anticipate and prevent problems that you may not have considered.
- create designs that reflect your individual personality through color, style and pattern selection

"To ensure a successful project, it is important to find a kitchen or bathroom professional who is right for you," explains Doris Lacroix, CKD, CBD, NKBA's 1997 President. "Similar to finding a doctor or dentist, you need to locate someone who is capable of completing the job, but who also meshes with your personality."

The National Kitchen & Bath Association (NKBA) provides a list of its retail members, including Certified Kitchen and Bathroom Designers (CKDs and CBDs), in your area who can help you with your project.

The Middle

"Once you have found the kitchen/bathroom planners near you, it is a good idea to visit them in person," says Lacroix. "This gives you the opportunity to see kitchens and bathrooms on display and to talk with designers about products, materials and colors. This will help you discover which designer is right for you."

Lacroix also suggests that you prepare for your visit. Here's how:

- Collect and clip photographs of kitchens or bathrooms that appeal to you. Examining these with the designers during your visits will give them a good idea of the styles to which you are attracted.
- Evaluate your current kitchen or bathroom to find out what works and what doesn't.

For example, is there enough cabinet shelf space? Is there enough counter space? Is there adequate task lighting above the countertop? In the bathroom, is the bathtub big enough? Is the showerhead at a comfortable height for all users? Is the bathroom safe — does it include grab bars and non-slip flooring?

- Write down the answers to these questions and bring them with you when you visit the kitchen/bathroom planners. They will play an important role in the design of your new space.

The Completion

After you choose a firm, a designer will visit your home to take precise measurements. He or she will also spend a great deal of time interviewing you to discover the exact type and style of kitchen or bathroom you desire. Then, a plan, which includes material costs, specifications and design details, will be prepared. When the design is approved and the budget is set, a payment schedule will be arranged. Typically, a schedule is set up where 50% of the total is paid at the signing of the contract, 40% upon start of installation and the remaining 10% when the job is completed. NKBA member firms will usually offer a contract that outlines project responsibilities and a payment schedule.

The time frame for completion of projects will vary. Generally, kitchen and bathroom projects take two weeks to several months to complete. Although living with construction is not easy, it will all seem worth it once your new kitchen or bathroom is complete.

To obtain a list of NKBA member firms in your area, and a remodeling organizer kit for $5, call (800) 401-NKBA, ext. 600.

People come in all sizes, shapes and varieties. So do their kitchens. But this space should do more than just reflect personal tastes in regard to color and style. The kitchen must be functional, and it must be designed to suit the needs of all users throughout their lifecycles. This is the basis of universal design.

"When planning a new kitchen, it is just as important to consider who will use the space and how they will use it as it is to choose colors, appliances and styles," explains Mary Jo Peterson, CKD, CBD, Mary Jo Peterson Design Consultants, Brookfield, Conn.

For example, the kitchen is no longer the sole domain of the female of the household. According to the National Kitchen & Bath Association (NKBA), men, women and children are sharing in kitchen activities such as cooking, doing homework, paying the bills, entertaining, etc., and this has an effect on how the space is designed.

Another aspect to consider when conducting a kitchen project is aging. According to the American Association of Retired Persons (AARP), by the year 2020, over 20 percent of the population will be over 65 years old. A survey completed by the AARP shows that a majority of these people wish to stay in their homes and age in place.

"In order to achieve this, it is essential to plan kitchens that allow for independent living," Peterson says. "Although you may not currently need special features, it is a strong possibility that you will someday. So why not plan for it now?"

Planning a universally designed kitchen requires special consideration of every aspect of the space: countertops, cabinets, appliances, etc.

Countertops and Cabinets

Countertops, for example, must be designed within easy reach of the user. Therefore, countertop height must be carefully considered.

A standard countertop is 36″ high, but this height is often uncomfortable for children or adults who are shorter or taller than average or for those who prefer to work while seated. For a universally designed kitchen, NKBA recommends including some countertops that are 28″ - 32″ high. This height is appropriate for seated or shorter users and for use as a chopping or baking center. For taller users, countertops that are 42″ - 45″ high are suitable. This height will work well as a snack bar also. The space should also include some countertops at 36″ high for general use by standing users. In addition, adjustable countertops can be incorporated into the space. By doing so, the kitchen becomes functional for all who will use it, both now and in the future.

NKBA also offers the following suggestions for cabinets:

- Lowering wall cabinets via motorized or mechanical system
- Interior storage systems such as divider drawers, roll-out shelves and tray dividers to provide clear accessibility and easy retrieval of items
- Open shelves for quick detection of items and to eliminate the hazard of open doors
- Drawers instead of doors to eliminate the need to get around the open door
- Lever handles as opposed to knobs to allow easier opening of doors

Appliances

As more and more manufacturers become aware of universal design, more appliance options become available. This allows universally designed appliances to be incorporated into the space without sacrificing aesthetics.

Consider the following items when planning a universal kitchen:

- Side-by-side refrigerators or bottom freezer models provide ideal access for all users — young and old
- Separate cooktop and oven accommodate height differences
- Appliance controls placed at the front allow easy access
- Easy-to-read numbers and touch-pad controls rather than knobs are easier to see and use
- Microwave placement within reach and sight of the individuals who will use it

By including these items in the kitchen and considering carefully their placement in the design, you ensure that the space can be used by everyone, regardless of their abilities or stage of life.

Hiring a Professional

Peterson cautions that the above suggestions are just that — suggestions. And they only scratch the surface.

"Each kitchen is unique — a reflection of the person who uses it," she says.

To be certain that your kitchen suits your needs, it is a good idea to consult with a professional. NKBA provides a list of its retail members, including Certified Kitchen and Bathroom Designers (CKDs and CBDs), in your area who can help you with your project. These professionals will work with you to plan a space that is right for you.

"Your new kitchen should last a lifetime," Peterson says. "A professional kitchen designer will help see that it does."

For a list of designers in your area, contact NKBA at (800) 401-NKBA, ext. 600.

Kitchen/Bathroom Remodeling - Needs vs. Wants

Remodeling can be an overwhelming process, whether you're remodeling your kitchen, bathroom or any room in your home. It's easy to build an idea file that is overflowing with products and styles that you like. But, how do you turn your idea file into your dream kitchen or bath?

The National Kitchen & Bath Association (NKBA) recommends making two lists to narrow your options:

1. what you need for your new space to be functional
2. things you want, if budget permits

Some things you'll need to consider for the kitchen include:

	Need	Want
cabinets	_____	_____
countertops	_____	_____
flooring	_____	_____
oven/range/cooktop	_____	_____
refrigerator/freezer	_____	_____
dishwasher	_____	_____
sink	_____	_____
lighting	_____	_____
waste disposal	_____	_____
recycling bins	_____	_____
desk area	_____	_____

For the bathroom, the following should be considered:

vanity	_____	_____
separate tub/shower	_____	_____
whirlpool tub	_____	_____
toilet	_____	_____
sink	_____	_____
faucets	_____	_____
storage	_____	_____
flooring	_____	_____
countertops	_____	_____

Keep in mind that the way you use the space(s) should also be a determining factor in the amenities that you choose for you new kitchen or bath. For example, is there one primary cook in the household, or do all family members share in the cooking process? Do you normally make heat-and-serve meals, or full-course "from scratch" meals? Is the kitchen a socializing place? Who will use the bathroom - children, guests? How many people will use the bathroom at one time? What activities will take place in the bathroom - make up application, dressing, laundry?

Since the kitchen and bath pose their own unique remodeling challenges, the NKBA recommends working with a kitchen and bathroom specialist to help you plan your new space. He/she will look at your idea file and talk with you in depth about your needs and wants. A kitchen or bathroom specialist can make recommendations for your new space based on the way you live that will save you time and money before, during and after the remodeling process. And, he/she can help you choose products and colors to fit your individual style.

To receive a list of NKBA members in your area, and a kitchen and bathroom planning kit for $5, call 1-800-401-NKBA, ext. 600.

Creating Your Dream Kitchen or Bathroom

Millions of kitchens will be built or remodeled in 1998. Some of the projects will be dreams come true. Some others could be nightmares.

When you stop and think about the effects that every alteration has on a room, you realize just how complicated remodeling or building can be. Besides the logistical questions, many decisions must be made in terms of color, hardware, appliances, lighting, plumbing fixtures, countertops, and the overall style of your new room.

"With so many decisions to make and so much to think about, the average consumer needs a professional to organize this project — someone who understands all of the complexities involved," said Doris Y. Miller, 1998 President of the *National Kitchen & Bath Association*. "Kitchen and bathroom design is a specialized trade. It requires a good deal of experience and know-how to accomplish successful projects."

The first step in creating a successful new room is a simple one — find an NKBA member to design and coordinate the construction of your room.

"Someone remodeling a kitchen or bathroom wants the project to get off to a good start, and a kitchen and bath professional is definitely the way to go," said Miller. "An NKBA member will coordinate every aspect of the design and installation. They are experienced at working with contractors, electricians, plumbers, etc., and can efficiently schedule the jobs involved. And, most important, they are experts at working with the client. They listen to client needs and translate them into the kind of rooms they want."

To help consumers get ready for a remodeling and help them work with a kitchen or bathroom designer, the NKBA offers a complete planning kit, including a listing of kitchen and bathroom designers, to consumers for $5. **Contact NKBA at 1-800-401-NKBA, ext. 600.**

A105

BuyLine 8665

NATIONAL KITCHEN
NKBA
& BATH ASSOCIATION

FROM INSPIRATION TO SENSATION

Creating Your Dream Kitchen Or Bathroom

OFF TO A GOOD START

So, you've decided to create your dream kitchen or bathroom. Great idea. You'll finally be able to apply all of those wishes you've collected on your list over the years, like that kitchen island with a cooktop (and more of that invaluable countertop and cabinet space), or maybe you've always wanted a bathtub-for-two. Whether it's the kitchen or bathroom (or both), you can look forward to an exciting transformation into the room you've always wanted.

But when you stop and think about the effects that every alteration has on a room, you realize just how complicated remodeling or building can be. Take, for instance, the kitchen island with a cooktop. Where there's a cooktop, there's smoke and steam. And where there's smoke and steam, there has to be ventilation. So an overhead hood must be added, unless you have a downventing cooktop. Also, any time you have work space like the added countertop, you need electrical outlets. So wiring will be necessary for the outlets, as well as the cooktop and vent hood. And that's just the beginning.

Besides the logistical questions, many decisions must be made in terms of color, hardware, appliances, lighting, plumbing fixtures, countertops, and the overall style of your new room.

With so many decisions to make and so much to think about, you need a professional to organize this project — someone who understands all of the complexities involved. That's where the National Kitchen and Bath Association (NKBA) comes in.

FINDING THE NKBA MEMBER FOR THE JOB

The first step in creating your new room is a simple one — find an NKBA member to design and coordinate the construction of your room. You want your project to get off to a good start, and a kitchen and bath professional is definitely the way to go.

WHY?

The National Kitchen & Bath Association is an organization of professionals who focus specifically on kitchens and bathrooms. When you deal with an NKBA member, you'll benefit from specialized expertise, years of experience, a commitment to quality, and a high degree of professionalism. They maintain showrooms with products and complete designs on display so you can get a feel for the type and quality of work they can do.

A kitchen and bath professional can offer sound advice and suggest solutions to any problems that may arise, or, better yet, prevent problems from occurring. They also understand the ways families and individuals relate to their surroundings, and therefore may be able to troubleshoot and meet needs in ways that may not occur to those who don't specialize in kitchens and bathrooms.

An NKBA member will coordinate every aspect of the design and installation. They are experienced at working with contractors — electricians, plumbers, etc. — and can efficiently schedule the jobs involved. And, most important, they are expert at working with you, the client. They listen to your needs and translate them into the kind of room you want.

Don't take chances with your investment. When you make the decision for a new kitchen or bathroom, make the decision to find an NKBA member.

HOW?

NATIONAL KITCHEN
NKBA
& BATH ASSOCIATION

It's easy to find an NKBA member, if you know what to look for. And easy identification begins with the NKBA logo, a symbol of quality, dedication and expertise in kitchens and bathrooms.

When visiting kitchen and bath showrooms, look for the logo in windows or on the counter.

If you know anyone who has recently remodeled, talk with them. Ask them who they used and if he or she is associated with the NKBA. Referrals are an excellent source for finding an industry professional, but be sure you're dealing with someone qualified in kitchens and bathrooms specifically — an NKBA member.

You can find all of the NKBA members in your area by contacting the National Kitchen and Bath Association at 687 Willow Grove Street, Hackettstown, New Jersey 07840, **1-800-401-NKBA, Ext. 600.** They will provide you with a directory of NKBA firms who design, supply and install residential kitchens and bathrooms.

HAVE YOU FINISHED YOUR HOMEWORK?

Now that you have a name in mind (or possibly more than one — you may want to talk with several NKBA professionals to find the one with whom you feel most comfortable), you can go ahead and set up an appointment to discuss your project. But before you actually sit down with the designer, there are several things you should do in preparation. (This is the fun part.)

Chances are you've been thinking about this for a while, but if not, start reading magazines geared toward the home, remodeling, architecture, and especially those that focus on kitchens and bathrooms. Clip out pictures of kitchens or bathrooms that interest you — this will help the designer get a feel for the styles you like. You may even find features that would work in your new room.

Visit kitchen and bath showrooms to see the many options for new countertops and other surfaces, and to collect brochures on fixtures, cabinets, appliances and any other items or materials that interest you.

As you visit different showrooms in your search for ideas and NKBA designers, you should make notes on each one. The best way to find the NKBA member with whom you're most comfortable is to evaluate the designers and their showrooms. Use the following checklist to help you in your decision:

Evaluating the kitchen and bath dealership

	Showrooms #1	Showrooms #2	Showrooms #3
Showroom Clean and Neat	____	____	____
Displays Highlight Interesting Design	____	____	____
Displays Well-Constructed and Presented	____	____	____
Broad Range of Styles Offered	____	____	____
Staff Friendly and Helpful	____	____	____
Staff Knowledgeable About Products and Design	____	____	____

	Showrooms #1	Showrooms #2	Showrooms #3
Designers Ask Questions About Your Project	____	____	____
NKBA Membership Identified	____	____	____
Firm Has Been In Business for at Least Two Years	____	____	____
Firm Provides Complete Design and Installation Services	____	____	____
Referrals Provided	____	____	____

As you visit showrooms and gather notes, clippings, photographs, brochures and samples, you may want to organize them into an "idea file." As your file grows, you'll see a definite style emerge from the decorating trends you've chosen — *your* style.

KITCHEN PLANNING WITH YOUR NKBA SPECIALIST

You can save a lot of time and money, and greatly reduce guesswork by first evaluating your needs. Before even your initial consultation, write down some basic lifestyle facts.

Simple facts, like how many hours a week you work, will affect how often you cook and what appliances you use. If you work a lot of hours out of the home, you may cook less often, opting instead for microwave meals, in which case you'd need your microwave in a convenient location and a lot of freezer space.

Who uses your kitchen? Is it a setting for family gatherings, or the private domain of a gourmet chef? Will it function well with two or more cooks? Do you entertain often? All of these answers will affect the size, layout and type of equipment you need for your kitchen.

When preparing your evaluation, first consider your normal cooking habits. For instance, if your family shares in the meal preparation, you may need two sinks and built-in cutting and chopping boards strategically placed throughout the kitchen to maximize food preparation areas.

Will children be active in the kitchen? If so, easy-to-clean surfaces are a must. You may also want to consider a desk or counter setup for homework and after-school snacks.

If you like to entertain, often cooking for large groups of guests, you may need two ovens and a wide-shelved refrigerator.

Do you recycle? You'll need the separating and storage space, depending on your involvement and the requirements in your area.

All of the variables mentioned here (and others your designer will pose) will affect the layout of your kitchen. Each shape — U-shaped, L-shaped, Corridor, Island, One-Wall, or Peninsula — has its own functionality and advantages. Once the NKBA kitchen specialist has laid out your kitchen, he or she will guide you in selecting components. With all of the advances in materials, appliances and designs, this selection process would be overwhelming without the help of a professional.

Your decision-making becomes much easier once you have related your needs to your lifestyle. By providing your NKBA professional with a clear picture of what works best for your family, you'll be off to a head start.

BATHROOM PLANNING WITH YOUR NKBA SPECIALIST

Do you look forward to spending time in your bathroom? Sounds like a strange question to most people. Most bathrooms are cold and claustrophobic, places where comfort is either kept to a bare minimum, or simply not an option. But with the shift in society back toward the home also come changes in the bathroom.

Bathrooms have become more than a necessity. Their role has now expanded to that of "bodyroom," incorporating such amenities as whirlpool tubs, exercise equipment, dual-head showers, heat lamps and entertainment systems.

Before you talk to an NKBA professional about your new bathroom, evaluate your needs by first looking at who will use it, and how. The best way to do that is to examine present bathroom usage. Some NKBA members suggest taking notes as you use the room on a typical weekday and weekend. By mapping out your routine, you and your bath designer will be better-equipped to create a floorplan that is efficient and incorporates the features you need.

For example, you may think the first thing you do when you step out of the shower is to reach for your towel. Keeping a diary, however, might reveal that oftentimes the first move after exiting the shower is to drip, drip, drip across the hall to the linen closet. So, by simply focusing on details and making note of them, you've discovered the need for bathroom towel storage.

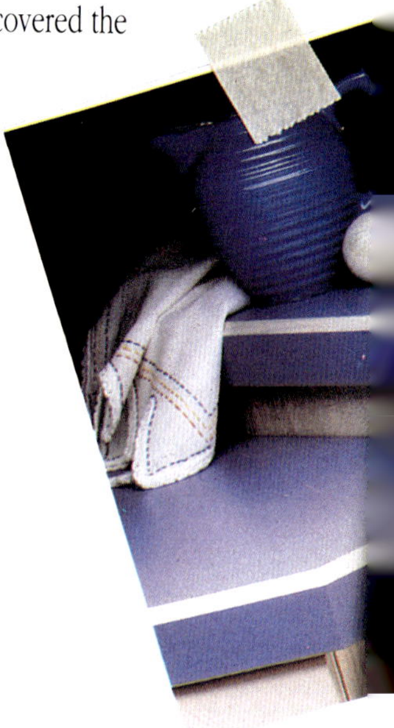

If several girls or women use the bathroom, adequate circuits and outlets are necessary for hair dryers and curling irons, as well as appropriate lighting for makeup application.

Special safety and convenience features should be considered for elderly, very young and handicapped family members. High water closet seats, grab bars and locking cabinets are practical options, and your designer will likely have other suggestions.

For family bathrooms which are shared by several people, privacy zones isolating the shower, tub, lavatory and water closet will allow simultaneous use.

Your NKBA bathroom specialist will take into consideration all of these factors and more. They have the experience to anticipate potential problems and point out options that may help you with your choices.

SETTING PRIORITIES

When your idea file is overflowing with clippings and photographs, you've thought about style and color, and evaluated your needs, there is one final step that will really help your NKBA professional: your "must-have" and "want" lists. You simply make two lists which include:

1) features you consider essential for your new room, and
2) features you'd like to have, if possible and if budget permits.

It sounds easy, right? Well, this one may force you to make some tough decisions and possibly even some sacrifices, but it is a very valuable step. Just listing and distinguishing the "must-haves" from the "wants" will help you focus on the features most important to you and your family. In fact, you may want to let each member of the family make their own lists. When you can actually see them on paper, it puts your needs into better perspective.

KITCHEN CHECKLIST AND WORKSHEET

Needs and Wants

Check the items you feel your kitchen must have in the "need" column, and the items you would like, if the budget and design allow, in the "want" column. (This should be used as a preliminary guideline; they may change along the way.)

	Need	Want		Need	Want
New cabinets	____	____	Recycling bins	____	____
New countertop	____	____	More workspace	____	____
New floor	____	____	More storage	____	____
New oven(s)	____	____	Pantry	____	____
New refrigerator/freezer	____	____	Wet bar	____	____
New cooktop	____	____	New window(s)	____	____
New microwave	____	____	Desk area	____	____
New dishwasher	____	____	Eating area	____	____
New sink(s)	____	____	Media/TV center	____	____
New light fixtures	____	____	Others ____________	____	____
Cutting/chopping surfaces	____	____	________________	____	____
Waste disposal	____	____	________________	____	____
Trash compactor	____	____	________________	____	____

Lifestyle/Room Use

This worksheet will give you some things to think about in your initial planning, but it's only the beginning. Your NKBA kitchen specialist will conduct an in-depth interview with you in order to create a design that suits your lifestyle and satisfies your needs and wants.

Who is the primary cook? ______________

How many other household members cook? _________

Do any of these members have physical limitations? _________

What type of cooking do you normally do?

____ Heat and serve meals
____ Full-course, "from scratch" meals
____ Bulk cooking for freezing/leftovers
____ Other ____________________________

Do you entertain frequently? ____ Formally ____ Informally

Is the kitchen a socializing place? __________

Where do you plan to sort recyclables?

___ Kitchen ___ Laundry ___ Garage ___ Other

What type of feeling would you like your new kitchen space to have?

___ Sleek/Contemporary ___ Warm & Cozy Country
___ Traditional ___ Open & Airy
___ Strictly Functional ___ Formal
___ Family Retreat ___ Personal Design Statement

BATHROOM CHECKLIST AND WORKSHEET

Needs and Wants

Check the items you feel your bathroom must have in the "need" column, and the items you would like, if the budget and design allow, in the "want" column. (This should be used as a preliminary guideline; they may change along the way.)

	Need	Want		Need	Want
New vanity	____	____	Heat lamp	____	____
Separate shower	____	____	Bidet	____	____
New lavatory (sink)	____	____	New floor/wall surfaces	____	____
Tub for two	____	____	New countertops	____	____
Whirlpool tub	____	____	Customized storage	____	____
New water closet (toilet)	____	____	Others ____________	____	____
Exercise area	____	____	________________	____	____
Entertainment center	____	____	________________	____	____
Linen storage	____	____	________________	____	____
Lighting fixtures	____	____	________________	____	____

Lifestyle/Room Use

This worksheet will give you some things to think about in your initial planning, but it's only the beginning. Your NKBA bathroom specialist will conduct an in-depth interview with you in order to create a design that suits your lifestyle and satisfies your needs and wants.

Who will use this bathroom (i.e., client, spouse, child, guests)?

____

Type of bathroom?

___ Powder ___ Children's ___ Mastersuite ___ Hall

How many will use it at one time? ____________________

What activities will take place in the bathroom?

___ Makeup application
___ Hair care
___ Exercising
___ Laundering
___ Bathing
___ Dressing
___ Lounging
___ Other ____________

Would you like his and hers facilities? __________

Do you prefer the water closet and/or bidet to be isolated from the other fixtures? __________

Would you like a closet planned as part of your new bathroom?

___ Yes ___ No

What type of feeling would you like your new bathroom to have?

___ Sleek/Contemporary
___ Traditional
___ Personal Design Statement
___ Warm/Country
___ Open & Airy

THE DESIGN CONFERENCE

O.K., you've done your homework — you stand ready with your ideas, lists, samples, photographs, maybe even rough plans. And now it's time to meet with your designer.

You may first meet with the NKBA member at the showroom to look over samples and displays, but then he or she will come out to your house and really get to work. Here's where you'll begin to see what sets NKBA specialists apart from other designers. The NKBA member will take careful and thorough measurements, right down to locating the pipes in the walls (something often overlooked by those who do not specialize in kitchen and bathroom planning).

He or she will look at your idea file and talk with you in depth about your needs. This is an opportunity for both of you to discuss thoughts and opinions, ask questions and determine a direction for your room design. Think of it as an exchange of ideas, a "design conference." This is another advantage of working with an NKBA member. He or she will work *with you* to achieve the best results, instead of simply dictating a design.

One very important determinant for your new room design is your budget. You should have a figure established as you go into this — one that's realistic for your situation. And the initial design conference is the time to talk budgets. Your NKBA specialist will let you know what can be achieved — in the way of materials, construction, appliances, etc. — for what you want to spend. And together, you can set priorities for your design that will allow your new dream room to stay within your budget.

When you both agree on a general direction and a budget, you can make arrangements for payment.

With many firms, payment begins with 50% at the signing of the contract, then 40% when installation begins, and the remaining 10% upon completion of the job. Financing can be arranged through a home improvement loan, or you may be able to negotiate the price into the mortgage when purchasing a home. Remember, your new room is an investment in your home's equity. It increases with the value of your home, and may be recovered when the home is sold.

LET THE TRANS-FORMATION BEGIN

From the first meeting, you'll begin to see how working with an NKBA member will make the project easier, and the results, better. When you've got the knowledge and experience of an NKBA professional on your side, you can rest assured that your new room will be everything you dreamed it would be, and more.

First, your NKBA specialist will design the complete layout, choose the final materials, and begin coordinating the contractors — all with your approval, of course. Then, the construction begins.

Living under construction is never easy, but your NKBA professional will do everything possible to minimize the inconvenience for you. Ask him or her for tips on living under construction. For example, setting up temporary facilities for cooking and cleanup. Your NKBA designer has experience in these matters and will undoubtedly have ideas to make you more comfortable during this phase.

And now it's only a matter of time before you see your dream room become a reality. Exactly how long depends on many variables (whether or not you are having cabinets custom-designed, for example), but in somewhere between two weeks and several months, you'll see the results.

You'll soon see your room taking shape. The ideas you've envisioned, the style you've developed, the colors you've decided upon, you'll see it all materialize at the hands of the craftsmen.

ANOTHER HAPPY ENDING

It's evening, you're dining in your new kitchen, or soaking in your new whirlpool tub. You proudly gaze around the room. For the next few weeks you'll have to open an extra drawer or two looking for the silverware. Or you may catch yourself walking across the room to where the towels *used to* be. But you'll enjoy getting to know your new room and growing with it. After all, you created it (with a little help from NKBA).

NATIONAL KITCHEN
NKBA
& BATH ASSOCIATION

National Kitchen & Bath Association
687 Willow Grove St.
Hackettstown, New Jersey 07840
1-800-401-NKBA, Ext. 600.

CON1-9/92-10K-RA

Catalogs are coded by position within the volume in numerical sequence, e.g., C345.

A

Acme Brick Co., Innovative Building Products, Inc.
glass masonry units B667
showers C565A

B

Broan Mfg. Co., Inc.
indoor air quality systems C915
medicine cabinets C587
range hoods C485
residential appliances ii
Bruce Floors, Bruce Hardwood Floors, Triangle Pacific Corp. C310
Bruce Hardwood Floors, Triangle Pacific Corp.
wood flooring C246
Triangle Pacific Corp., Bruce Floors
laminate flooring C310
Triangle Pacific Corp., Premier Wood Floors
wood flooring C247

C

Clarion Bathware C566B

D

Dodge-Regupol, Inc. C285
DuPont Co. C474

E

Echeguren Slate, Inc. A651
Eldorado Stone Corp. A663

G

Gerbert, Ltd.
resilient flooring C290; C291

I

Innovative Building Products, Inc., Acme Brick Co.
glass masonry units B667
showers C565A
Interceramic, Inc. C180

J

JADO C588
Jeld-Wen, Pozzi Window Co. B303
Jenn-Air Corp. C502

K

Kestrel Mfg. C845
Kohler Co., Plumbing Div. C574
KraftMaid Cabinetry, Inc. C529

M

Maytag Co. C507
Moen Incorporated C564B

N

Nevamar Corp. C467
NuTone C509

O

O'Hagin's, Inc. A741
Opella, Inc. C561

P

Pozzi Window Co., Jeld-Wen B303
Praxis Industries, Inc., PRC, Inc. C575
PRC, Inc., Praxis Industries, Inc. C575
Premier Wood Floors, Bruce Hardwood Floors, Triangle Pacific Corp. C247

S

Sharp Electronics Corp. C512
Sign of the Crab, Strom Plumbing C584
Strom Plumbing, Sign of the Crab C584
Sub-Zero Freezer Co., Inc.
refrigerators/freezers C514; C515; C515A

T

Task Lighting Corp. C950
Triangle Pacific Corp., Bruce Hardwood Floors
wood flooring C246
Bruce Hardwood Floors, Bruce Floors
laminate flooring C310
Bruce Hardwood Floors, Premier Wood Floors
wood flooring C247

W

Wellborn Cabinet, Inc. C536
White River Hardwood Products C464
Wilsonart International, Inc. C478

Z

Zoeller Co. C908

Products

Catalogs are coded by position within the volume in numerical sequence, e.g., C345.

A

Accessible products for the disabled
see
bathroom accessories: —grab bars—specific material
kitchen or kitchenette units—disabled persons' use
plumbing fittings and trim
showers: —disabled persons' use
showers: —seats for—wall-mounted

Acoustical products
see
acoustical products—form
specific products

Acoustical products—form
tile or tile form
Dodge-Regupol, Inc. C285

Acoustic isolation and control
see
acoustical products
partitions—properties: —sound-insulating or retarding—specific type

Acrylic products
see
sinks—residential: —bathroom—acrylic, composite—specific type: —kitchen—acrylic, composite—specific type

Address systems—public
see
intercommunicating systems—specific type

Adhesives for
see
specific products: —adhesives for

Aerators
see
liquid waste disposal or treatment equipment: —filters, strainers, aerators, interceptors
water conditioning equipment: —filters, aerators, deodorizers, hydrators, strainers

Air conditioners
see
blowers—centrifugal or axial

packaged—unitary
see
heaters—unit

Air-conditioning equipment
see
blowers—centrifugal or axial

Air distribution equipment
see
blowers—centrifugal or axial
dampers
ducts and duct assemblies
fans
louvers
ventilators
vents

Air/liquid treatment equipment
see
liquid waste disposal or treatment equipment
waste handling equipment and systems
water conditioning equipment

Air pollution, quality control equipment
see
blowers—centrifugal or axial
dampers: —air pollution control
vacuum cleaning systems
ventilators: —grease containment/extractor—food service equipment

Alarms and alarm systems
horns, bells, chimes, sirens
see
bells, buzzers, chimes (entrance and alarm)

Aluminum products
see
skylights—framing: —aluminum or aluminum alloy
windows—wood-aluminum/operation

Appliances—residential—kitchen
see
dishwashers—residential
kitchen or kitchenette units
kitchen or kitchenette units—disabled persons' use
ranges and ovens—residential
refrigerator-freezer combination: —residential—specific type
refrigerators: —residential—specific type

Architectural artwork
cornices
see
lath and plasterwork accessories and trim: —cove moldings

Architectural artwork *cont.*
cornices *cont.*
see cont.
moldings and cornices
surfacing and paneling—interior—materials: —moldings and trim for—specific material

ironwork—ornamental
see
specific products

mantels
see
mantels

moldings and cornices
see
moldings and cornices

mosaics
see
ceramic or clay tile: —ceramic mosaic
glass—form: —patterned, carved, decorative, etched, mosaic, sandblasted or textured: —stained—specific type

niche caps, casings
White River Hardwood Products C464

Architectural woodwork
see
woodwork

Art and decorative objects
see
architectural artwork
ceramic or clay tile: —ceramic mosaic
glass—form: —patterned, carved, decorative, etched, mosaic, sandblasted or textured: —stained—specific type

Ash handling equipment
see
vacuum cleaning systems

Association catalogs
see
specific products

Athletic equipment and facilities
see
bathtubs: —hydro-massage combination
consultants and services
dance floors
flooring—gymnasium
steam bath rooms and equipment

Audio and visual equipment
see
- *intercommunicating systems*

Auditorium equipment
see
- *dance floors*
- *flooring—stage, studio, theater*

B

Badminton courts
see
- *flooring—gymnasium*

Barbecue grills
see
- *grills—barbecue*

Bar furniture and equipment
elbow rests, bar tops
- Nevamar Corp. C467
- Wilsonart International, Inc. C478

sinks
- Kohler Co., Plumbing Div. C574
- Nevamar Corp. C467
- Opella, Inc. C561

Barrier-free design products
see
- *bathroom accessories: —grab bars—specific material*
- *kitchen or kitchenette units—disabled persons' use*
- *plumbing fittings and trim*
- *showers: —disabled persons' use: —seats for—wall-mounted*

Bars
see
- *bar furniture and equipment*
- *bathroom accessories: —grab bars—specific material*

Bases
see
- *flooring—specific material*
- *lath and plasterwork accessories and trim: —bases and fittings*
- *showers: —stalls and receptors for—specific material*

Basketball equipment
see
- *flooring—gymnasium*

Bathroom accessories
see also
- *washroom accessories*

cabinets and mirrors
see also
- *cabinets: —medicine*
- *mirrors*
- Broan Mfg. Co., Inc. C587
- NuTone C509

cabinets and mirrors—with lighting fixtures
see also
- *lighting—application: —accent and display —cabinets and mirrors*
- Broan Mfg. Co., Inc. C587
- NuTone C509

dispensers—facial tissue
- JADO C588

Bathroom accessories *cont.*
dryers—hand or hair
see
- *washroom accessories: —dryers—specific type—hand or hair*

fans
see
- *fans: —kitchen or bathroom*

fittings
see
- *plumbing fittings and trim*

grab bars—plastic
- Praxis Industries, Inc., PRC, Inc. C575

grab bars, safety toilet seats, safety towel bars—metal
see also
- *plumbing fittings and trim: —toilet seats*
- Praxis Industries, Inc., PRC, Inc. C575

heaters
see
- *heaters—unit*

holders—toothbrush and/or tumbler—metal
- JADO C588

hooks—coat or robe
- JADO C588

lighting—accent
see
- *lighting—application: —accent and display*

mirrors
see
- *mirrors*

partitions
see
- *partitions—shower, toilet, urinal*

shelves
see
- *shelving: —bathroom or washroom—specific material*

sinks
see
- *sinks—residential: —bathroom—specific material—specific bowl*

toilet paper holders, soap dishes—metal
- JADO C588

towel holders
- JADO C588
- Kohler Co., Plumbing Div. C574
- Strom Plumbing, Sign of the Crab C584

vanity cabinets
see
- *cabinets: —bathroom vanity*

water closets
see
- *toilets*

Bathroom planning and design
see
- *consultants and services: —kitchen and bath planning and design*

Baths
see
- *bathtubs: —hydro-massage combination*
- *steam bath rooms and equipment*

Bathtubs
accessories for
- Clarion Bathware C566B
- Kohler Co., Plumbing Div. C574
- Strom Plumbing, Sign of the Crab C584

Bathtubs *cont.*
ceramic
- Kohler Co., Plumbing Div. C574

enclosures for
- DuPont Co. C474
- Kohler Co., Plumbing Div. C574
- Nevamar Corp. C467
- Praxis Industries, Inc., PRC, Inc. C575
- Strom Plumbing, Sign of the Crab C584
- Wilsonart International, Inc. C478

enclosures for—sliding door
- Kohler Co., Plumbing Div. C574

fiberglass, fiberglass-reinforced, plastic
- Clarion Bathware C566B
- Kohler Co., Plumbing Div. C574
- Praxis Industries, Inc., PRC, Inc. C575
- Wilsonart International, Inc. C478

fittings for
see
- *faucets—application: —bathtub*
- *plumbing fittings and trim*

hydro-massage combination
- Clarion Bathware C566B
- Kohler Co., Plumbing Div. C574
- Praxis Industries, Inc., PRC, Inc. C575

iron
- Kohler Co., Plumbing Div. C574

porcelain enamel, vitreous china
- Kohler Co., Plumbing Div. C574

surrounds, wall liners for
see
- *bathtubs: —enclosures for*

whirlpools
see
- *bathtubs: —hydro-massage combination*

Bathtub/shower—prefabricated units
- Clarion Bathware C566B
- Kohler Co., Plumbing Div. C574
- Praxis Industries, Inc., PRC, Inc. C575

Beads
see
- *flooring—specific material*

Bells, buzzers, chimes (entrance and alarm)
- Broan Mfg. Co., Inc. ii
- NuTone C509

Bicycle equipment
see
- *toppings—traffic-bearing*

Bidets
see also
- *faucets—application: —bidet*
- Kohler Co., Plumbing Div. C574

Blinds—venetian
door—built-in
see
- *doors—swinging—by materials/construction: —specific material—frame and glass—built-in venetian blind*

Blocks—glass
see also
- *flooring—glass block*

Blocks—glass *cont.*
see also cont.
glass—form: —block
partitions—materials: —glass block
paving: —glass block
skylights—materials: —glass—block, corrugated, plain or wired
windows—replacement: —glass blocks for

curved
Innovative Building Products, Inc., Acme Brick Co. B667

decorative
Innovative Building Products, Inc., Acme Brick Co. B667

framing for
Innovative Building Products, Inc., Acme Brick Co. B667

structural
Innovative Building Products, Inc., Acme Brick Co. B667

Blowers—centrifugal or axial
see also
fans
ventilators

ventilating or exhaust
Broan Mfg. Co., Inc. C915

Bluestone
see
specific products—flagstone

Bookcases
residential
Wellborn Cabinet, Inc. C536

Bookstacks
see
bookcases

Brick face—simulated/manufactured
panels—prefabricated
Eldorado Stone Corp. A663

Brick products
see
fascias—materials: —panels—stone—simulated/manufactured or brick
fireplaces: —hearths—brick or simulated/manufactured brick

Brick—simulated/manufactured
Eldorado Stone Corp. A663

Brick—simulated/manufactured products
see
fireplaces: —facings for—simulated/manufactured stone or brick: —hearths—brick or simulated/manufactured brick
siding—materials: —brick—simulated/manufactured
walls—exterior insulation and finish systems—materials: —brick, stone—simulated/manufactured

Bridges
nosings for
see
toppings—traffic-bearing

Broilers
residential
see also
ranges and ovens—residential —ranges—griddle/broiler/oven combination
Jenn-Air Corp. C502

Brownstone—simulated/manufactured products
see
walls—exterior insulation and finish systems—materials: —brick, stone—simulated/manufactured

Building panels
see
panels—building
siding
walls—exterior insulation and finish systems

Bumpers
door
see
hardware—door: —holders and stops—specific type

Burners
range
see
ranges and ovens—residential: —cooktops—specific type

Butt hinges
see
hardware—door: —hinges—specific type

Buzzers
see
bells, buzzers, chimes (entrance and alarm)

C

Cabinets
bathroom vanity
see also
bathroom accessories: —cabinets and mirrors: —cabinets and mirrors—with lighting fixtures
lighting—application: —cabinets and mirrors
Broan Mfg. Co., Inc. . . . . ii; C587
KraftMaid Cabinetry, Inc. C529
Wellborn Cabinet, Inc. C536

custom-designed
Broan Mfg. Co., Inc. C587
KraftMaid Cabinetry, Inc. C529
Wellborn Cabinet, Inc. C536
Wilsonart International, Inc. C478

doors for
see
doors—application: —cabinet

equipment cabinets, racks, consoles—electrical, electronic
see
storage equipment: —cabinets—specific type

kitchen—residential
KraftMaid Cabinetry, Inc. C529
Wellborn Cabinet, Inc. C536

lavatory
see
cabinets: —washroom vanity
lavatories and accessories: —cabinets for

lighting for
see
lighting—application: —accent and display: —cabinets and mirrors
luminaires—types —undercabinet

Cabinets *cont.*
medicine
see also
bathroom accessories: —cabinets and mirrors—specific type
Broan Mfg. Co., ... ii; C587
NuTone C509

residential
Broan Mfg. Co., Inc. C587
KraftMaid Cabinetry, Inc. C529
Wellborn Cabinet, Inc. C536

shower
see
showers: —cabinets and enclosures for—specific type

storage
see
storage equipment: —cabinets—specific type

tops for
DuPont Co. C474
Wellborn Cabinet, Inc. C536
Wilsonart International, Inc. C478

wall storage
see
wall storage units: —shelf/cabinet units

washroom vanity
Broan Mfg. Co., Inc. C587
Wilsonart International, Inc. C478

wood
see
woodwork

Canopies
inserts for
see
glass
plastic

Caps
see
architectural artwork: —niche caps, casings

Carvings—wood
see
woodwork

Casework
see
cabinets

Casing
see
architectural artwork: —niche caps, casings
lath and plasterwork accessories and trim: —casings and corner guards

Castings
see
specific products

Ceilings—general
fans for
see
fans: —wall, ceiling or pedestal

moldings—ornamental
White River Hardwood Products C464

ventilators for
see
ventilators: —ceiling, wall, window

Ceilings—panels and tiles for
glass
Innovative Building Products, Inc., Acme Brick Co. B667

Ceramic or clay tile
ceramic mosaic
Interceramic, Inc. C180
glazed
Interceramic, Inc. C180
unglazed
Interceramic, Inc. C180

Ceramic products
see
bathtubs: —ceramic
ceramic or clay tile
flooring—clay or ceramic tile
shelving: —bathroom or washroom—ceramic or clay tile
showers: —stalls and receptors for—ceramic or clay tile
sinks—residential: —bathroom—ceramic—specific type: —kitchen—ceramic—specific type
surfacing and paneling—interior—materials

Chairs
rails for
see
lath and plasterwork accessories and trim: —rails—chair, display or map
woodwork: —rails—chair or plate

Chimes
see
bells, buzzers, chimes (entrance and alarm)

Church equipment
windows—inserts for
see
glass
plastic

Chutes
rubbish and waste
see
waste handling equipment and systems

Cladding
see
siding

Clay products
see
ceramic or clay tile
flooring—clay or ceramic tile
shelving: —bathroom or washroom—ceramic or clay tile
showers: —stalls and receptors for—ceramic or clay tile
surfacing and paneling—interior—materials: —ceramic or clay tile—specific type: —clay tile—quarry

Cleaning systems
see
vacuum cleaning systems

Closers—door
see
hardware—door —holders and stops—specific type

Closets
accessories for
see
shelving
water
see
toilets

Clothes racks, hooks, hook panels
see
washroom accessories: —hooks—coat or robe—specific type

Clothes washers
see
laundry equipment—specific use

Coatings and toppings—concrete or masonry
see
toppings—traffic-bearing
walls—exterior insulation and finish systems

Coatings—roof
see
roofing
toppings—traffic-bearing

Coatings—slip-resistant
see
flooring—specific material

Communicating systems
see
intercommunicating systems—specific type
wiring devices—electrical

Communication shelters
see
specific products

Compact kitchens
see
kitchen or kitchenette units

Compactors—waste
see
waste handling equipment and systems

Concrete
floor
see
toppings—traffic-bearing
roof
see
toppings—traffic-bearing

Consultants and services
kitchen and bath planning and design
Maytag Co. C507

Controls
air volume
see
dampers: —air volume control or duct
damper
see
dampers: —regulators for
electric, electronic—centralized
Broan Mfg. Co., Inc. C915

Controls *cont.*
lighting
see
controls—lighting
transformers
wiring devices—electrical
pest
see
specific products
rodent
see
specific products
time
Broan Mfg. Co., Inc. C915
vermin
see
specific products

Controls—lighting
see also
transformers
wiring devices—electrical
dimmers—manual
Task Lighting Corp. C950
sensors—occupancy—infrared, ultrasonic
Task Lighting Corp. C950

Cooktops
see
ranges and ovens—residential: —cooktops: —cooktops/grills—convertible

Copings
flagstone
Echeguren Slate, Inc. A651
slate
Echeguren Slate, Inc. A651

Cork products
see
flooring—cork or cork composition

Cornices
see
moldings and cornices
surfacing and paneling—interior: —moldings and trim for—specific material
woodwork: —moldings, cornices, door and window trim

Counters
custom-designed
Wilsonart International, Inc. C478
lighting for—accent
see
lighting—application: —accent and display
tops for
DuPont Co. C474
Interceramic, Inc. C180
Nevamar Corp. C467
Wilsonart International, Inc. C478

Coves
see
flooring—specific material
lath and plasterwork accessories and trim: —cove moldings
luminaires—types: —cove

Curtain walls
see
panels—building
storefronts

Curtain walls—window framing systems
panels for
see
panels—building
siding

Cushions
see
flooring—gymnasium: —shock-cushioning
surfacing—recreational, athletic, sport—properties: —shock-cushioning, safety

D

Dampers
see also
louvers: —adjustable—manual or power-operated

air pollution control
Broan Mfg. Co., Inc. C915

air volume control or duct
Broan Mfg. Co., Inc. C915

moderate-pressure and temperature
Broan Mfg. Co., Inc. C915

regulators for
Broan Mfg. Co., Inc. C915

Dance floors
see also
flooring—stage, studio, theater

fixed
Dodge-Regupol, Inc. C285

Decking
see
toppings—traffic-bearing

Decks—patio and pool
see
toppings—traffic-bearing

Dentils
see
moldings and cornices

Detectors—intrusion
see
luminaires—types: —motion detector combination

Detention equipment
see
glass—properties —burglar-resistant
hardware—door

Diffusers—air distribution
see
louvers
ventilators
vents

Dimmers—light
see
controls—lighting: —dimmers—specific type

Disabled persons' products
see
bathroom accessories: —grab bars—specific material
kitchen or kitchenette units—disabled persons' use
plumbing fittings and trim

Disabled persons' products *cont.*
see cont.
showers: —disabled persons' use: —seats for—wall-mounted

Dishes
see
bathroom accessories: —toilet paper holders, soap dishes—specific material

Dishwashers—residential
built-in
Jenn-Air Corp. C502
Maytag Co. C507

energy-saving
Jenn-Air Corp. C502

free-standing or mobile
Jenn-Air Corp. C502
Maytag Co. C507

kitchenette combination
Maytag Co. C507

undersink
Jenn-Air Corp. C502
Maytag Co. C507

Dispensers
facial tissue, lotion, paper cup, soap
see
washroom accessories: —dispensers—specific type

Display equipment
see
shelving

cabinets and cases
see
cabinets

lighting for
see
lighting—application: —accent and display

Display rails
see
lath and plasterwork accessories and trim: —rails—chair, display or map

Disposers—liquid/solid waste
see
food waste disposers
liquid waste disposal or treatment equipment
waste handling equipment and systems

Dividers
see
flooring—specific material
partitions

Door entrance trim
see
woodwork: —moldings, cornices, door and window trim

Door hardware
see
hardware—door

Doors
see
doors—application
doors—frames for
doors—properties
doors—swinging—by materials/construction

Doors—application
balcony
see
doors—application: —patio/terrace—specific operation

bathtub enclosure
see
bathtubs: —enclosures for—specific type

cabinet
Broan Mfg. Co., Inc. C587
KraftMaid Cabinetry, Inc. C529

entrance
see
doors—swinging—by materials/construction
storefronts

inserts for
see
glass
plastic

lights for
see
glass
plastic

patio/terrace—sliding
Pozzi Window Co., Jeld-Wen B303

patio/terrace—swinging
Pozzi Window Co., Jeld-Wen B303

shutters
see
shutters: —door—specific type

vision lights
see
glass
plastic

Doors—frames for
wood or plywood
Pozzi Window Co., Jeld-Wen B303

Doors—operation
swinging
see
doors—swinging—by materials/construction

Doors—properties
insulating—thermal—wood or wood-faced
Pozzi Window Co., Jeld-Wen B303

Doors—swinging—by materials/construction
french type
see
doors—application: —patio/terrace—specific operation

inserts for
see
glass
plastic

lights for
see
glass
plastic

louvered
see
shutters: —door—specific type

wood-clad—frame and glass
Pozzi Window Co., Jeld-Wen B303

wood—frame and glass
Pozzi Window Co., Jeld-Wen B303

Drainboards
see
laboratory equipment: —sinks, drainboards, troughs
sinks—residential: —kitchen—drainboard combination

Drains
see
strainers

Drawers
hardware for
see
hardware—drawer

storage
see
storage equipment: —cabinets with drawers

Dressing rooms, booths
see
showers: —dressing rooms, compartments for

Driveways
see
toppings—traffic-bearing

Dryers
clothing
see
laundry equipment—residential: —dryers—specific type

hand or hair
see
washroom accessories: —dryers—specific type—hand or hair

residential
see
laundry equipment—residential: —dryers—specific type

Ducts and duct assemblies
see
ducts and duct assemblies—types

Ducts and duct assemblies—general
dampers for
see
dampers

Ducts and duct assemblies—types
air
see also
vents: —duct or sleeve extensions for
Broan Mfg. Co., Inc. C915

Dust collectors
see
vacuum cleaning systems

E

Edgings
see
flooring—clay or ceramic tile: —bases, dividers, edgings and inserts for
landscape accessories: —walk edgings, perimeter strips

Educational equipment
see
intercommunicating systems

Efficiency kitchens
see
kitchen or kitchenette units—specific type

EIFS
see
walls—exterior insulation and finish systems

Electrical equipment
see
controls
heaters—unit
lighting—application
luminaires—specific types
piping and tubing—application: —gas, electrical, sewer or water system
transformers
wiring devices—electrical

Enclosures
see
bathtubs: —enclosures for—specific type
showers: —cabinets and enclosures for—specific type

Energy conservation
see
dishwashers—residential: —energy-saving
plumbing fittings and trim: —shower or spray—water-saving
specific products
ventilators: —heat recovery, air filtering

Entrances
see
doors—application
doors—frames for
doors—properties
doors—swinging—by materials/construction
hardware—door
storefronts

Etching
see
glass—form: —patterned, carved, decorative, etched, mosaic, sandblasted or textured
plastic—form: —engraved, etched

Exhaust systems
air
see
blowers—centrifugal or axial
fans
ventilators

louvers for
see
louvers

Extractors
see
ventilators: —grease containment/extractor—food service equipment

F

Faceted or stained glass windows
see
windows—specific material/operation

Facings, refacings or veneers
see
panels—building
siding
surfacing and paneling—interior
veneers

Fans
see also
blowers—centrifugal or axial
ventilators

fan-light combination—air-circulating
Broan Mfg. Co., Inc. C915
NuTone C509

fan-light combination—exhaust
Broan Mfg. Co., Inc. C915

kitchen or bathroom
Broan Mfg. Co., Inc. C915
NuTone C509

ventilating or exhaust
Broan Mfg. Co., Inc. C915
NuTone C509

wall, ceiling or pedestal
Broan Mfg. Co., Inc. . . . . ii; C915
NuTone C509

Fascias—materials
see also
walls—exterior insulation and finish systems

panels—brick
see
fascias—materials: —panels—stone—simulated/manufactured or brick

panels—plastic or vinyl
Wilsonart International, Inc. C478

panels—stone—simulated/manufactured or brick
Eldorado Stone Corp. A663

Fascias—properties
fire-resistant
Eldorado Stone Corp. A663

Fasteners
see
flooring—specific material

Faucets
see
faucets—application
faucets—types

Faucets—application
bathtub
JADO C588
Kohler Co., Plumbing Div. C574
Moen Incorporated C564B
Strom Plumbing, Sign of the Crab C584

bidet
JADO C588

exterior hose bibb
Moen Incorporated C564B

lavatory
JADO C588
Kohler Co., Plumbing Div. C574
Moen Incorporated C564B
Strom Plumbing, Sign of the Crab C584

sink—kitchen
JADO C588
Kohler Co., Plumbing Div. C574
Moen Incorporated C564B
Opella, Inc. C561

Faucets—application *cont.*

sink—kitchen *cont.*
Strom Plumbing, Sign of the Crab C584

Faucets—types

mixing—pressure-balancing, thermostatic
JADO C588
Kohler Co., Plumbing Div. C574
Opella, Inc. C561

single-supply
JADO C588
Kohler Co., Plumbing Div. C574
Moen Incorporated C564B
Opella, Inc. C561
Strom Plumbing, Sign of the Crab C584

swivel spout
JADO C588
Kohler Co., Plumbing Div. C574
Moen Incorporated C564B
Opella, Inc. C561
Strom Plumbing, Sign of the Crab C584

wall-mounted
JADO C588
Kohler Co., Plumbing Div. C574
Strom Plumbing, Sign of the Crab C584

water-saving
JADO C588

Fiberglass products

see
bathtubs: —fiberglass, fiberglass-reinforced, plastic
showers: —stalls and receptors—fiberglass, plastic

Fillers

see
plastic—form: —corrugated or flat sheet—filler strips for

Filters

water
see
water conditioning equipment: —filters, aerators, deodorizers, hydrators, strainers

Filters—industrial processing

liquid
see
liquid waste disposal or treatment equipment: —filters—specific type
water conditioning equipment: —filters—specific type

Fireplaces

facings for—simulated/manufactured stone or brick
Eldorado Stone Corp. A663

hearths—brick or simulated/manufactured brick
Eldorado Stone Corp. A663

hearths—simulated/manufactured stone
Eldorado Stone Corp. A663

mantels for
see
mantels

Fire protection equipment and systems

partitions
see
partitions—properties: —fire-rated: —fire-resistant—specific type

Fitness equipment

see
bathtubs: —hydro-massage combination
steam bath rooms and equipment

Fittings

see
lath and plasterwork accessories and trim: —bases and fittings
plumbing fittings and trim

Flagging

flagstone
Echeguren Slate, Inc. A651

slate
Echeguren Slate, Inc. A651

Flagstone products

see
copings: —flagstone
flagging: —flagstone
flooring—flagstone
paving: —flagstone
stair treads, risers: —flagstone

Flitches

see
woodwork

Floor cleaning and maintenance equipment

vacuum cleaning systems
see
vacuum cleaning systems

Flooring

see
flooring—clay or ceramic tile
flooring—cork or cork composition
flooring—flagstone
flooring—glass block
flooring—gymnasium
flooring—linoleum
flooring—marble
flooring—properties
flooring—seamless, monolithic
flooring—slate
flooring—stage, studio, theater
flooring—vinyl
flooring—wood

Flooring—acrylic

see
flooring—seamless, monolithic

Flooring—athletic

see
flooring—gymnasium

Flooring—bridge

surfacing, toppings for
see
toppings—traffic-bearing

Flooring—clay or ceramic tile

adhesives for
Interceramic, Inc. C180

Flooring—clay or ceramic tile *cont.*

bases, dividers, edgings and inserts for
Interceramic, Inc. C180

custom-designed
Interceramic, Inc. C180

glazed
Interceramic, Inc. C180

grouting or mortar for
Interceramic, Inc. C180

patterned, decorative or textured
Interceramic, Inc. C180

Flooring—cork or cork composition

sheet or tile
Dodge-Regupol, Inc. C285
Gerbert, Ltd. C290

Flooring—epoxy—seamless

see
flooring—seamless, monolithic

Flooring—flagstone

Echeguren Slate, Inc. A651
Interceramic, Inc. C180

Flooring—glass block

Innovative Building Products, Inc., Acme Brick Co. B667

Flooring—gymnasium

fixed
Dodge-Regupol, Inc. C285

shock-cushioning
Dodge-Regupol, Inc. C285

Flooring—linoleum

Gerbert, Ltd. C290

Flooring—marble

panel or tile
Interceramic, Inc. C180

Flooring—plastic

see
flooring—seamless, monolithic

Flooring—properties

acid or alkali-resistant—commercial or institutional use
Gerbert, Ltd. C290; C291
Interceramic, Inc. C180

acid or alkali-resistant—industrial use
Gerbert, Ltd. C290; C291

acid or alkali-resistant—residential use
Gerbert, Ltd. C291
Interceramic, Inc. C180

antimicrobial
see
flooring—properties: —fungus, decay, insect, rot, vermin-resistant

corrosion-resistant
Gerbert, Ltd. C290; C291
Interceramic, Inc. C180

fire-resistant
Bruce Hardwood Floors, Triangle Pacific Corp. C246
Bruce Hardwood Floors, Triangle Pacific Corp., Bruce Floors C310
Echeguren Slate, Inc. A651
Gerbert, Ltd. C290; C291

Flooring—properties *cont.*

frostproof
Interceramic, Inc. C180

fungus, decay, insect, rot, vermin-resistant
Gerbert, Ltd. C290

grease-resistant—commercial or institutional use
Bruce Hardwood Floors, Triangle Pacific Corp., Bruce Floors C310
Gerbert, Ltd. C290

grease-resistant—industrial use
Gerbert, Ltd. C290

slip-resistant—commercial or institutional use
Bruce Hardwood Floors, Triangle Pacific Corp. C246
Bruce Hardwood Floors, Triangle Pacific Corp., Bruce Floors C310
Interceramic, Inc. C180

slip-resistant—residential use
Bruce Hardwood Floors, Triangle Pacific Corp. C246
Bruce Hardwood Floors, Triangle Pacific Corp., Bruce Floors C310
Interceramic, Inc. C180

static-dissipating, conductive—commercial or institutional use
Gerbert, Ltd. C290; C291

static-dissipating, conductive—industrial use
Gerbert, Ltd. C290; C291

static-dissipating, conductive—residential use
Gerbert, Ltd. C291

Flooring—resilient
see
flooring—gymnasium
surfacing—recreational, athletic, sport

Flooring—seamless, monolithic
Bruce Hardwood Floors, Triangle Pacific Corp., Bruce Floors C310

Flooring—slate
Echeguren Slate, Inc. A651

Flooring—sport
see
flooring—gymnasium

Flooring—stage, studio, theater
Dodge-Regupol, Inc. C285

Flooring—stone
see
flooring—specific stone

Flooring—treatments, maintenance and resurfacing
see
toppings—traffic-bearing
wax—floor or wall

Flooring—vinyl

bases, coves for
Gerbert, Ltd. C291

borders for—ornamental
Gerbert, Ltd. C291

Flooring—vinyl *cont.*

reducer strips for
Gerbert, Ltd. C291

sheet or roll
Gerbert, Ltd. C291

strips
Gerbert, Ltd. C291

tile
Gerbert, Ltd. C291

Flooring—wood

adhesives for
Bruce Hardwood Floors, Triangle Pacific Corp. C246
Bruce Hardwood Floors, Triangle Pacific Corp., Bruce Floors C310
Bruce Hardwood Floors, Triangle Pacific Corp., Premier Wood Floors C247

blocks—residential (parquet)
Bruce Hardwood Floors, Triangle Pacific Corp. C246
Bruce Hardwood Floors, Triangle Pacific Corp., Premier Wood Floors C247

borders, inlays, inserts for—ornamental design
Bruce Hardwood Floors, Triangle Pacific Corp. C246
Bruce Hardwood Floors, Triangle Pacific Corp., Premier Wood Floors C247

cherry
Bruce Hardwood Floors, Triangle Pacific Corp., Premier Wood Floors C247

coatings for—slip-resistant
Bruce Hardwood Floors, Triangle Pacific Corp. C246

hickory
Bruce Hardwood Floors, Triangle Pacific Corp. C246

installation systems
Bruce Hardwood Floors, Triangle Pacific Corp. C246

maple or elm
Bruce Hardwood Floors, Triangle Pacific Corp. C246
Bruce Hardwood Floors, Triangle Pacific Corp., Premier Wood Floors C247

oak
Bruce Hardwood Floors, Triangle Pacific Corp. C246
Bruce Hardwood Floors, Triangle Pacific Corp., Premier Wood Floors C247

parquet
see
flooring—wood: —blocks—residential (parquet)

pecan
Bruce Hardwood Floors, Triangle Pacific Corp., Premier Wood Floors C247

planks
Bruce Hardwood Floors, Triangle Pacific Corp. C246
Bruce Hardwood Floors, Triangle Pacific Corp., Bruce Floors C310
Bruce Hardwood Floors, Triangle Pacific Corp., Premier Wood Floors C247

plastic-impregnated
Bruce Hardwood Floors, Triangle Pacific Corp. C246

Flooring—wood *cont.*

prefinished
Bruce Hardwood Floors, Triangle Pacific Corp. C246

simulated/manufactured
Bruce Hardwood Floors, Triangle Pacific Corp., Bruce Floors C310

strips
Bruce Hardwood Floors, Triangle Pacific Corp. C246
Bruce Hardwood Floors, Triangle Pacific Corp., Bruce Floors C310
Bruce Hardwood Floors, Triangle Pacific Corp., Premier Wood Floors C247

unfinished
Bruce Hardwood Floors, Triangle Pacific Corp. C246

walnut, cedar, mahogany or teak
Bruce Hardwood Floors, Triangle Pacific Corp., Premier Wood Floors C247

Floor proximity egress path-marking systems
see
lighting—application: —stair, aisle, path

Floor toppings
see
toppings—traffic-bearing

Food service equipment—commercial or institutional

compactors—waste
see
waste handling equipment and systems

dispensers
see
washroom accessories

grease containment/extractors
see
ventilators: —grease containment/extractor—food service equipment

ventilators
see
ventilators

waste handling equipment
see
waste handling equipment and systems

water conditioning equipment
see
water conditioning equipment

Food waste disposers
see also
waste handling equipment and systems

residential
Opella, Inc. C561

Frames
see
doors—frames for

Framing
see
blocks—glass: —framing for

Freezers—residential
see also
refrigerator-freezer combination: —residential—specific type

Freezers—residential *cont.*

built-in
Jenn-Air Corp. C502
Sub-Zero Freezer Co., Inc. C514; C515; C515A

energy-saving
Jenn-Air Corp. C502
Sub-Zero Freezer Co., Inc. C514; C515; C515A

free-standing
Jenn-Air Corp. C502
Sub-Zero Freezer Co., Inc. C514; C515

undercounter
Sub-Zero Freezer Co., Inc C514; C515; C515A

Fume control
see
ventilators

Furnaces
see
heaters—unit

Furniture
see
bar furniture and equipment
bookcases
cabinets
laboratory equipment
shelving
tables
wall storage units

G

Gable vents
see
louvers
vents

Garbage disposal equipment
see
food waste disposers
waste handling equipment and systems

Garden equipment
see
landscape accessories
lighting—application: —landscape—deck, garden, patio/terrace, walk

Gas equipment and products
see
piping and tubing—application: —gas, electrical, sewer or water system
ranges and ovens—residential: —gas

Generators
steam
see
steam bath rooms and equipment

Generic information
see
specific products/materials

Glass block products
see
blocks—glass
flooring—glass block
glass—form: —block
partitions—materials: —glass block
paving: —glass block

Glass block products *cont.*
see cont.
skylights—materials: —glass—block, corrugated, plain or wire
storefronts: —structural frames, mullions for—glass, glass block
windows—replacement: —glass blocks for

Glass—film finish for
see
glass—properties

Glass—form
block
see also
blocks—glass
Innovative Building Products, Inc., Acme Brick Co. B667

patterned, carved, decorative, etched, mosaic, sandblasted or textured
Innovative Building Products, Inc., Acme Brick Co. B667

structural
see
storefronts: —structural frames, mullions for—glass, glass block

Glass mullion glazing
see
storefronts: —structural frames, mullions for—glass, glass block

Glass products
see
ceilings—panels and tiles for: —glass
mirrors: —glass
shelving: —bathroom or washroom—glass
skylights—materials: —glass—block, corrugated, plain or wire

Glass—properties
anti-glare/shading
Innovative Building Products, Inc., Acme Brick Co. B667

burglar-resistant
Innovative Building Products, Inc., Acme Brick Co. B667

diffusing
see
glass—form: —patterned, carved, decorative, etched, mosaic, sandblasted or textured

heat-absorbing
Innovative Building Products, Inc., Acme Brick Co. B667

insulating panel
Innovative Building Products, Inc., Acme Brick Co. B667

security and detention
see
glass—properties

sound-resistant
Innovative Building Products, Inc., Acme Brick Co. B667

Glassware washers
see
dishwashers—specific application

Glazing compounds or accessories
glass blocks
see
blocks—glass —framing for

Glazing, glazing film
see
glass—form
glass—properties
plastic—form
plastic—properties

Golf paths
see
toppings—traffic-bearing

Grab bars
see
bathroom accessories: —grab bars—specific material

Graphics
see
architectural artwork

Grease containment/extractors
see
ventilators: —grease containment/extractor—food service equipment

Greenhouses
see
heaters—unit

Griddles
see
ranges and ovens—residential: —ranges—griddle/broiler/oven combination

Grilles or screens
see
partitions

wood—fixed units
see
woodwork: —decorative grillework

Grills—barbecue
see also
ranges and ovens—residential: —cooktops/grills—convertible

indoor—built-in or portable
Jenn-Air Corp. C502

Grout—application
see
flooring—clay or ceramic tile: —grouting or mortar for

Guards
corner—metal
see
lath and plasterwork accessories and trim: —casings and corner guards

wall
see
lath and plasterwork accessories and trim: —casings and corner guards

Gymnasium equipment
flooring
see
flooring—gymnasium
surfacing—recreational, athletic, sport

H

Hangers—clothing
see
bathroom accessories: —hooks—coat or robe—specific type
washroom accessories: —hooks—coat or robe—specific type

Hardware—bathroom, washroom
shower
see
showers: —rods, hardware and tracks for

Hardware—door
handles—flat, half round, round
JADO C588
handles—lever
JADO C588
hinges
JADO C588
hinges—pins, tips for
JADO C588
holders and stops
JADO C588
knobs
JADO C588
latches
JADO C588
locksets
see
hardware—door: —locks, locksets
locks, locksets
JADO C588
locks—narrow stile
JADO C588
lock trim
JADO C588
pulls
JADO C588

Hardware—drawer
knobs, pulls and slides
JADO C588

Hardware—shower
see
showers: —rods, hardware and tracks for

Heads—shower
see
plumbing fittings and trim: —shower or spray—specific type

Health club equipment
see
steam bath rooms and equipment

Hearths
see
fireplaces: —hearths—specific material

Heaters—unit
electric
NuTone C509
electric—with lighting
NuTone C509

Heat reclamation equipment
see
ventilators: —heat recovery, air filtering

High-voltage power distribution equipment
see
transformers

Hinges
see
hardware—door: —hinges—specific type

Holders
door
see
hardware—door —holders and stops—specific type
washroom, bathroom
see
bathroom accessories
washroom accessories: —holders—specific type

Hoods
see
ventilators: —hood—specific type

Hooks—clothing
see
bathroom accessories: —hooks—coat or robe—specific type
washroom accessories: —hooks—coat or robe—specific type

Hose
bibbs for
see
faucets—application: —exterior hose bibb
shower
see
plumbing fittings and trim: —shower or spray—hoses for

Hospital equipment
communication systems
see
intercommunicating systems—specific type
grab bars, safety toilet seats, safety towel bars
see
bathroom accessories: —grab bars—specific material
plumbing fittings and trim: —toilet seats
laboratory
see
laboratory equipment
plumbing fittings for
see
plumbing fittings and trim

Hotel, motel equipment
appliances—compact
see
kitchen or kitchenette units—specific type
bathroom
see
bathroom accessories
washroom accessories
lighting for
see
lighting—application

HVAC terminal units
see
dampers
heaters—unit

I

Intercommunicating systems
NuTone C509

Ironing boards
see also
laundry equipment—specific type: —ironing boards—built-in
NuTone C509

Iron products
see
bathtubs: —iron
sinks—residential: —bathroom—iron—specific type: —kitchen—iron—specific type

J

Jail equipment
see
specific products

K

Kitchen equipment—commercial or institutional
see
ventilators
waste handling equipment and systems

Kitchen equipment—residential
see
cabinets: —kitchen—residential—specific type
consultants and services: —kitchen and bath planning and design
dishwashers—residential
fans: —kitchen or bathroom
faucets—application: —sink—kitchen
food waste disposers: —residential
freezers—residential
grills—barbecue
kitchen or kitchenette units
kitchen or kitchenette units—disabled persons' use
kitchen planning
ranges and ovens—residential
refrigerator-freezer combination: —residential—specific type
refrigerators: —residential—specific type
sinks—residential
ventilators: —hood—residential kitchen—specific type
waste handling equipment and systems: —compactors—residential or institutional

Kitchen or kitchenette units
Maytag Co. C507

Kitchen or kitchenette units—disabled persons' use
Maytag Co. C507

Kitchen planning
see also
consultants and services: —kitchen and bath planning and design
Maytag Co. C507

Knobs
see
hardware—door: —knobs
hardware—drawer: —knobs, pulls and slides

L

Laboratory equipment
plumbing fittings for
see
plumbing fittings and trim
sinks, drainboards, troughs
Nevamar Corp. C467
sinks—strainers for
see
strainers
work surfaces for
DuPont Co. C474
Nevamar Corp. C467
Wilsonart International, Inc. C478

Laminates
see
plastic laminate sheets
veneers

Landscape accessories
lighting
see
lighting—application: —landscape—deck, garden, patio/terrace, walk
walk edgings, perimeter strips
Echeguren Slate, Inc. A651

Latches
see
hardware—door: —latches

Lath and plasterwork accessories and trim
bases and fittings
White River Hardwood Products C464
casings and corner guards
White River Hardwood Products C464
cove moldings
White River Hardwood Products C464
rails—chair, display or map
White River Hardwood Products C464

Laundry equipment—commercial or institutional
ironing boards—built-in
see
ironing boards

Laundry equipment—residential
dryers
Maytag Co. C507
ironing boards—built-in
see also
ironing boards
Broan Mfg. Co., Inc. ii
Maytag Co. C507
NuTone C509
washer/dryer combination
Maytag Co. C507
washers—top-loading
Maytag Co. C507

Lavatories and accessories
cabinets for
Wellborn Cabinet, Inc. C536

Lavatories and accessories *cont.*
fittings and trim for
see
faucets—application: —lavatory
plumbing fittings and trim
lavatories
DuPont Co. C474
Nevamar Corp. C467
Strom Plumbing, Sign of the Crab C584
tops for
DuPont Co. C474
Nevamar Corp. C467
Wilsonart International, Inc. C478
vanity top and bowl—molded—one-piece
see also
sinks—residential
DuPont Co. C474
Nevamar Corp. C467

Learning systems
see
intercommunicating systems—specific type

Lift stations
see
pumps: —grinder—sewage

Lighting
see
controls—lighting
fans: —fan-light combination—specific type
heaters—unit: —electric—with lighting
lighting—application
luminaires—components for
luminaires—types
wiring devices—electrical

Lighting—application
see also
luminaires—types
accent and display
Task Lighting Corp. C950
cabinets and mirrors
see also
bathroom accessories: —cabinets and mirrors—with lighting fixtures
Broan Mfg. Co., Inc. .... ii ; C587
NuTone C509
Task Lighting Corp. C950
display
see
lighting—application: —accent and display
floor proximity egress path-marking system
see
lighting—application: —stair, aisle, path
landscape—deck, garden, patio/terrace, walk
Task Lighting Corp. C950
railing
see
luminaires—types: —railing
showcase
see
lighting—application: —accent and display
stair, aisle, path
Task Lighting Corp. C950
street
see
lighting—application: —landscape—deck, garden, patio/terrace, walk
walkway
see
lighting—application: —landscape—deck, garden, patio/terrace, walk: —stair, aisle, path

Lights
window
see
glass
plastic

Linoleum floors
see
flooring—linoleum

Liquid waste disposal or treatment equipment
see also
waste handling equipment and systems
water conditioning equipment
filters, strainers, aerators, interceptors
Opella, Inc. C561
piping for
see
piping and tubing—application: —gas, electrical, sewer or water system

Locks
door
see
hardware—door

Locksets
see
hardware—door: —locks, locksets

Louvers
see also
ventilators
vents
adjustable—manual or power-operated
see also
dampers
Kestrel Mfg. C845
attic
see
vents: —attic—louvered
door vent
Kestrel Mfg. C845
stationary
Kestrel Mfg. C845

Luminaires—components for
controls
see
controls—lighting
housings—reflector
Task Lighting Corp. C950

Luminaires—types
see also
lighting—application
cove
Task Lighting Corp. C950
fan
see
fans: —fan-light combination—specific type
heater combination
see
heaters—unit: —electric—with lighting
incandescent
Task Lighting Corp. C950
incandescent—indirect
Task Lighting Corp. C950
incandescent—recessed
Task Lighting Corp. C950
incandescent—surface
Task Lighting Corp. C950

Luminaires—types *cont.*

low-voltage
Task Lighting Corp. C950

motion detector combination
Task Lighting Corp. C950

railing
Task Lighting Corp. C950

task
Task Lighting Corp. C950

tube lighting
Task Lighting Corp. C950

undercabinet
Task Lighting Corp. C950

xenon
Task Lighting Corp. C950

M

Mantels

wood
White River Hardwood Products C464

Marble

counter tops
see
counters: —tops for

Marble products

see
flooring—marble
surfacing and paneling—interior—materials: —marble—specific type

Material handling equipment/ systems

see
storage equipment

Measurement devices

see
controls

Medical equipment

see
laboratory equipment

Merchandising equipment

see
lath and plasterwork accessories and trim: —rails—chair, display or map
lighting—application: —accent and display
storage equipment

Metalwork—ornamental

see
architectural artwork
consultants and services
shutters

Microphones and accessories

see
intercommunicating systems—specific type

Microwave ovens

see
ranges and ovens—residential: —ovens—microwave—specific type
ranges and ovens—residential: —ranges—microwave/conventional oven combination

Millwork

see
woodwork

Mirrors

see also
bathroom accessories: —cabinets and mirrors—specific type

glass
Broan Mfg. Co., Inc. C587
JADO C588

Moldings and cornices

hardboard
see
surfacing and paneling—interior—materials: —moldings and trim for—hardboard

lighting for
see
luminaires—types: —cove

plaster
see
lath and plasterwork accessories and trim: —cove moldings

plastic, composite
see also
surfacing and paneling—interior—materials: —moldings and trim for—plastic, composite
DuPont Co. C474

simulated/manufactured stone
see also
surfacing and paneling—interior—materials: —moldings and trim for—simulated/ manufactured stone
DuPont Co. C474

woodwork
see
surfacing and paneling—interior—materials: —moldings and trim for—wood—specific type
woodwork: —moldings, cornices, door and window trim

Mortar

see
flooring—clay or ceramic tile: —grouting or mortar for

Mosaics

see
ceramic or clay tile: —ceramic mosaic
glass—form: —patterned, carved, decorative, etched, mosaic, sandblasted or textured

Mosaic tile

ceramic
see
ceramic or clay tile: —ceramic mosaic

glass
see
glass—form: —patterned, carved, decorative, etched, mosaic, sandblasted or textured

O

Office equipment

see
storage equipment

appliances—compact
see
kitchen or kitchenette units—specific type

shelving
see
shelving

Operators—powered door

see
hardware—door

Ovens

see
kitchen or kitchenette units
kitchen or kitchenette units—disabled persons' use
ranges and ovens—specific type

P

Paging or signaling systems

see
intercommunicating systems—specific type

Paneling—interior

see
surfacing and paneling—interior

Panels—building

see
panels—building—materials
panels—building—properties
siding

Panels—building—materials

brick face—simulated/manufactured
see
brick face—simulated/manufactured: —panels—prefabricated
walls—exterior insulation and finish systems—materials: —brick, stone—simulated/ manufactured

granite—simulated/manufactured
see
panels—building—materials: —stone—simulated/manufactured
walls—exterior insulation and finish systems—materials: —brick, stone—simulated/ manufactured

limestone—simulated/manufactured
see
panels—building—materials: —stone—simulated/manufactured
walls—exterior insulation and finish systems—materials: —brick, stone—simulated/ manufactured

marble—simulated/manufactured
see
panels—building—materials: —stone—simulated/manufactured
walls—exterior insulation and finish systems—materials: —brick, stone—simulated/ manufactured

slate—simulated/manufactured
see
panels—building—materials: —stone—simulated/manufactured
walls—exterior insulation and finish systems—materials: —brick, stone—simulated/ manufactured

stone—simulated/manufactured
Eldorado Stone Corp. A663

Panels—building—properties

fire-resistant
Eldorado Stone Corp. A663

insulating
see
walls—exterior insulation and finish systems

Panels—ceiling
see
ceilings—panels and tiles for

Park equipment
see
consultants and services
landscape accessories
surfacing—recreational, athletic, sport

Partitions
see
partitions—materials
partitions—properties
partitions—shower, toilet, urinal

Partitions—application
shower
see
partitions—shower, toilet, urinal

toilet, urinal
see
partitions—shower, toilet, urinal

Partitions—general
blocks for
see
blocks—specific material
partitions—materials: —glass block

Partitions—materials
glass block
see also
blocks—glass
Innovative Building Products, Inc., Acme Brick Co. B667

plastic
Wilsonart International, Inc. C478

plastic laminate-faced
Wilsonart International, Inc. C478

shoji
see
plastic—form: —patterned or textured

Partitions—properties
fire-rated
Wilsonart International, Inc. C478

fire-resistant
Wilsonart International, Inc. C478

sound-insulating or retarding—floor-to-ceiling
Innovative Building Products, Inc., Acme Brick Co. B667

Partitions—shower, toilet, urinal
shower—plastic
Wilsonart International, Inc. C478

toilet, urinal—plastic
Wilsonart International, Inc. C478

Patio equipment
see
doors—application: —patio/terrace—specific operation
lighting—application: —landscape—deck, garden, patio/terrace, walk

Pavers
see
paving

Paving
see also
toppings—traffic-bearing

flagstone
Echeguren Slate, Inc. A651

glass block
Innovative Building Products, Inc., Acme Brick Co. B667

slate
Echeguren Slate, Inc. A651

Photographic artwork
see
architectural artwork

Physical fitness equipment
see
bathtubs: —hydro-massage combination
showers: —hydro-massage combination

Piping and tubing
see
piping and tubing—application

Piping and tubing—accessories for
see
plumbing fittings and trim

strainers
see
strainers

Piping and tubing—application
gas, electrical, sewer or water system
Zoeller Co. C908

Planning services—manufacturers
see
kitchen planning

Planning services—professional consultants
see
consultants and services

Planting accessories
see
landscape accessories

Plaster
accessories for
see
lath and plasterwork accessories and trim

trim for
see
lath and plasterwork accessories and trim

Plastic
see
plastic—form
plastic laminate sheets
plastic materials—custom-molded
plastic—properties

Plastic—form
colored
DuPont Co. C474
Nevamar Corp. C467
Wilsonart International, Inc. C478

corrugated or flat sheet
DuPont Co. C474
Nevamar Corp. C467

Plastic—form *cont.*
corrugated or flat sheet *cont.*
Wilsonart International, Inc. C478

corrugated or flat sheet—filler strips for
Wilsonart International, Inc. C478

engraved, etched
Nevamar Corp. C467

patterned or textured
DuPont Co. C474
Nevamar Corp. C467

sheet, coil
DuPont Co. C474
Nevamar Corp. C467

Plastic laminate products
see
partitions—materials: —plastic laminate-faced
plastic laminate sheets
surfacing and paneling—interior—materials: —plastic laminate-faced

Plastic laminate sheets
DuPont Co. C474
Nevamar Corp. C467

Plastic materials—custom-molded
DuPont Co. C474
Nevamar Corp. C467

Plastic products
see
bathroom accessories: —plastic—specific type
fascias—materials: —plastic—specific type
flooring—wood: —plastic-impregnated
moldings and cornices: —plastic, composite
partitions—materials: —plastic—specific type
partitions—shower, toilet, urinal: —shower—plastic: —toilet, urinal—plastic
plastic materials—custom-molded
shelving: —bathroom or washroom—plastic
showers: —stalls and receptors for—fiberglass, plastic
surfacing and paneling—interior—materials: —moldings and trim for—plastic, composite: —plastic—specific type

Plastic—properties
chemical-resistant
DuPont Co. C474
Nevamar Corp. C467

fire-resistant
DuPont Co. C474
Nevamar Corp. C467
Wilsonart International, Inc. C478

moldable
Nevamar Corp. C467
Wilsonart International, Inc. C478

safety
Nevamar Corp. C467
Wilsonart International, Inc. C478

Plates
wall
see
wiring devices—electrical: —wall plates

Plumbing fittings and trim
faucets, fixture trim
see
faucets

shower or spray
JADO C588
Kohler Co., Plumbing Div. C574

Plumbing fittings and trim *cont.*

shower or spray *cont.*
Strom Plumbing, Sign of the Crab C584

shower or spray—hoses for
JADO C588

shower or spray—water-saving
JADO C588

thermostatic
see
plumbing fittings and trim: —valves—mixing—pressure-balancing, thermostatic

toilet seats
Kohler Co., Plumbing Div. C574

toilet seats—child training
Kohler Co., Plumbing Div. C574

valves—diverter
JADO C588

valves—mixing—pressure-balancing, thermostatic
JADO C588

Plumbing fixtures
see
bar furniture and equipment: —sinks
bathtubs
bidets
faucets
laboratory equipment: —sinks, drainboards, troughs
lavatories and accessories
piping and tubing
plumbing fittings and trim
showers
sinks—commercial or institutional
sinks—residential
toilets

Plywood products
see
doors—frames for: —wood or plywood
shelving: —wood, plywood, wood fiber

Pollution control equipment and systems
see
fans
liquid waste disposal or treatment equipment
pumps: —grinder—sewage
vacuum cleaning systems
ventilators
waste handling equipment and systems
water conditioning equipment

Porcelain or baked enamel products
see
bathtubs: —porcelain enamel, vitreous china
sinks—residential: —bathroom—porcelain or baked enamel—specific type: —kitchen—porcelain or baked enamel—specific type

Power supplies, protection/conditioning equipment
see
transformers
wiring devices—electrical

Precast brick products
see
walls—exterior insulation and finish systems—materials: —brick—specific type

Prison equipment
see
specific products

Product information—associations
see
specific products

Product information—general
see
specific products

Pulls
see
hardware—door: —pulls—specific type: —push and pull bars
hardware—drawer: —knobs, pulls and slides

Pumps
sewage ejector or sump
Zoeller Co. C908

R

Railings—types
handrails—illuminated
see
luminaires—types: —railing

Rails
chair
see
lath and plasterwork accessories and trim: —rails—chair, display or map
woodwork: —rails—chair or plate

display and map
see
lath and plasterwork accessories and trim: —rails—chair, display or map

Ranges and ovens—commercial or institutional
see
kitchen or kitchenette units

Ranges and ovens—residential
accessories for
Jenn-Air Corp. C502

broiler combination
see
broilers: —residential
ranges and ovens—residential —ranges—griddle/broiler/oven combination

cooktops
Jenn-Air Corp. C502
Maytag Co. C507

cooktops/grills—convertible
see also
grills—barbecue
Jenn-Air Corp. C502

electric
Jenn-Air Corp. C502
Maytag Co. C507

gas
Jenn-Air Corp. C502
Maytag Co. C507

kitchenette combination
see also
kitchen or kitchenette units
Maytag Co. C507

ovens—built-in
Jenn-Air Corp. C502
Maytag Co. C507

ovens—built-in—double
Jenn-Air Corp. C502
Maytag Co. C507

Ranges and ovens—residential *cont.*

ovens—energy-saving
Jenn-Air Corp. C502

ovens—microwave
Jenn-Air Corp. C502
Maytag Co. C507
Sharp Electronics Corp. C512

ovens—microwave/conventional combination
Jenn-Air Corp. C502
Sharp Electronics Corp. C512

ovens—microwave—kitchenette units
Jenn-Air Corp. C502
Maytag Co. C507

ovens—self-cleaning
Jenn-Air Corp. C502

ranges—built-in
Jenn-Air Corp. C502
Maytag Co. C507

ranges—energy-saving
Jenn-Air Corp. C502

ranges—griddle/broiler/oven combination
see also
broilers: —residential
Jenn-Air Corp. C502

ranges—microwave/conventional oven combination
Jenn-Air Corp. C502
Maytag Co. C507

ranges—rotisserie combination
Jenn-Air Corp. C502

ventilating hoods for
see
ventilators: —hoods—residential kitchen—specific type

Receptors—shower
see
showers: —stalls and receptors for—specific material

Recreational equipment
see
bathtubs: —hydro-massage combination
dance floors
flooring—gymnasium
steam bath rooms and equipment

Refacings or facings
see
fascias
panels—building
siding
surfacing and paneling—interior
veneers
walls—exterior insulation and finish systems

Reflectors—electrical
see
luminaires—components for: —housings—reflector—specific type

Refrigerator-freezer combination
residential
Jenn-Air Corp. C502
Maytag Co. C507
Sub-Zero Freezer Co., Inc. C514; C515; C515A

residential—built-in
Jenn-Air Corp. C502
Maytag Co. C507
Sub-Zero Freezer Co., Inc. C514; C515; C515A

Refrigerator-freezer combination
cont.

residential—energy-saving
Jenn-Air Corp. C502
Sub-Zero Freezer Co., Inc. C514; C515; C515A

Refrigerators
see also
refrigerator-freezer combination

commercial or institutional
see
kitchen or kitchenette units

residential
Jenn-Air Corp. C502
Maytag Co. C507
Sub-Zero Freezer Co., Inc. C514; C515; C515A

residential—built-in
Jenn-Air Corp. C502
Maytag Co. C507
Sub-Zero Freezer Co., Inc. C514; C515; C515A

residential—energy-saving
Jenn-Air Corp. C502
Sub-Zero Freezer Co., Inc. C514; C515; C515A

residential—ice, chilled water dispensers
Jenn-Air Corp. C502
Sub-Zero Freezer Co., Inc. C514; C515

residential—kitchenette combination
see also
kitchen or kitchenette units
Maytag Co. C507

residential—undercounter
Sub-Zero Freezer Co., Inc. C514; C515; C515A

water cooler combination
see
refrigerators: —residential—ice, chilled water dispensers

Registers and grilles
see
louvers
ventilators
vents

Regulators
air volume
see
dampers: —regulators for

Rehabilitation equipment
see
bathtubs: —hydro-massage combination

Renovation—building
see
consultants and services

Reroofing
see
roofing

Restaurant equipment and furniture
see
refrigerator-freezer combination
waste handling equipment and systems

Risers
see
stair treads, risers

Roadway construction
see
paving
toppings—traffic-bearing

Rods and bars
see
bathroom accessories: —grab bars—specific material
showers: —rods, hardware and tracks for

Roof assemblies
see
skylights

Roofing
see
roofing—form
roofing—materials
roofing—properties

Roofing—form
tile or tile form
Echeguren Slate, Inc. A651

Roofing—materials
slate
Echeguren Slate, Inc. A651

Roofing—properties
fire-resistant
Echeguren Slate, Inc. A651

traffic-bearing—automobile, vehicular
see
toppings—traffic-bearing

traffic-bearing—pedestrian
see
toppings—traffic-bearing

Roofing specialties and construction products
coatings
see
roofing
toppings—traffic-bearing

copings
see
copings

fascias
see
fascias

traffic-bearing
see
toppings—traffic-bearing

ventilators
see
ventilators: —roof—specific type

vents
see
vents

walkways, vehicular pathways
see
toppings—traffic-bearing

Roof windows
see
skylights

Room assemblies
dressing
see
showers: —dressing rooms, compartments for

Room assemblies *cont.*
partitions for
see
partitions

showers
see
showers: —dressing rooms, compartments for

steam
see
steam bath rooms and equipment

Room dividers
see
partitions

Rotisseries
see
ranges and ovens—residential: —ranges—rotisserie combination

S

Saddles
see
sills and stools

Safety equipment
plastic
see
plastic—properties: —safety

Sandwich panels or walls
see
panels—building

Scale control—water treatment
see
water conditioning equipment

School equipment
display and map rails
see
lath and plasterwork accessories and trim: —rails—chair, display or map

intercommunicators
see
intercommunicating systems—specific type

laboratories
see
laboratory equipment

partitions
see
partitions

storage
see
storage equipment

Screens
partition
see
partitions

space dividers
see
partitions

vision
see
louvers

Seats—shower, toilet
see
bathroom accessories: —grab bars—specific material
plumbing fittings and trim: —toilet seats

Seats—shower, toilet *cont.*
see cont.
showers: —seats for—specific type

Security and bullet-resistant equipment
see
consultants and services
glass—properties —burglar-resistant
hardware—door
luminaires—types: —motion detector—specific type
shutters

Sensors—light
see
controls—lighting: —sensors—occupancy—infrared, ultrasonic
luminaires—types: —motion detector combination

Septic tanks and accessories
see
liquid waste disposal or treatment equipment
waste handling equipment and systems

Service basins
see
sinks—commercial or institutional

Sewage treatment equipment and systems
see
liquid waste disposal or treatment equipment
piping and tubing—application: —gas, electrical, sewer or water system
pumps: —grinder—sewage
waste handling equipment and systems
water conditioning equipment

Shades—window—properties
protective, security
see
shutters: —window—specific type

Sheets, strips, plates, coils
glass
see
glass—form

plastic
see
plastic—form

Shelving
see also
storage equipment
wall storage units: —shelf/cabinet units

bathroom or washroom—ceramic or clay tile
Kohler Co., Plumbing Div. C574

bathroom or washroom—glass
JADO C588
NuTone C509

bathroom or washroom—metal
Kohler Co., Plumbing Div. C574

bathroom or washroom—plastic
Kohler Co., Plumbing Div. C574

filing and storage—high-density
see
specific equipment: —filing and storage—high-density

wood, plywood, wood fiber
Wellborn Cabinet, Inc. C536

Shingles—general
wood—roof ridge vent for
see
vents: —roof—louvered, continuous ridge

Shingles—materials
see
roofing
siding

Showcases
see
lighting—application: —accent and display

Shower heads
see
plumbing fittings and trim: —shower or spray—specific type

Showers
see also
bathtub/shower—prefabricated units

cabinets and enclosures for
Acme Brick Co., Innovative Building Products, Inc. C565A
Clarion Bathware C566B
DuPont Co. C474
Innovative Building Products, Inc., Acme Brick Co. B667
Kohler Co., Plumbing Div. C574
Nevamar Corp. C467
Strom Plumbing, Sign of the Crab C584

disabled persons' use
Praxis Industries, Inc., PRC, Inc. C575

dressing rooms, compartments for
Wilsonart International, Inc. C478

fittings, levers, valves for
see
plumbing fittings and trim

hydro-massage combination
Clarion Bathware C566B
Kohler Co., Plumbing Div. C574

partitions for
see
partitions—shower, toilet, urinal

rods, hardware and tracks for
Praxis Industries, Inc., PRC, Inc. C575
Strom Plumbing, Sign of the Crab C584

seats for—wall-mounted
Praxis Industries, Inc., PRC, Inc. C575

stalls and receptors for—ceramic or clay tile
Kohler Co., Plumbing Div. C574

stalls and receptors for—composition
DuPont Co. C474
Kohler Co., Plumbing Div. C574

stalls and receptors for—fiberglass, plastic
Kohler Co., Plumbing Div. C574

systems
Kohler Co., Plumbing Div. C574
Praxis Industries, Inc., PRC, Inc. C575

Shutters—application, type
door—folding or sliding type
Kestrel Mfg. C845

door—side-hinged type
Kestrel Mfg. C845

Shutters—application, type *cont.*
window—folding or sliding type
Kestrel Mfg. C845

window—side-hinged type
Kestrel Mfg. C845

Siding
see
siding—materials
siding—properties

Siding—materials
brick face—simulated/manufactured
see
brick face—simulated/manufactured: —panels—prefabricated

brick—simulated/manufactured
see also
walls—exterior insulation and finish systems—materials: —brick, stone—simulated/manufactured
Eldorado Stone Corp. A663

stone
see
specific type

stone—simulated/manufactured
see also
walls—exterior insulation and finish systems—materials: —brick, stone—simulated/manufactured
Eldorado Stone Corp. A663

Siding—properties
fire-resistant
Eldorado Stone Corp. A663

Signaling systems
see
bells, buzzers, chimes (entrance and alarm)

Sills and stools
slate
Echeguren Slate, Inc. A651

Sinks—commercial or institutional
fittings and trim for
see
plumbing fittings and trim

laboratory
see
laboratory equipment: —sinks, drainboards, troughs

tops for
DuPont Co. C474

Sinks—residential
see also
bar furniture and equipment: —sinks
lavatories and accessories

bathroom—accessories for
Kohler Co., Plumbing Div. C574

bathroom—acrylic, composite—double bowl
DuPont Co. C474
Nevamar Corp. C467

bathroom—acrylic, composite—single bowl
DuPont Co. C474
Kohler Co., Plumbing Div. C574
Nevamar Corp. C467

bathroom—ceramic—single bowl
Kohler Co., Plumbing Div. C574

Sinks—residential *cont.*

bathroom—iron—double bowl
Kohler Co., Plumbing Div. C574

bathroom—iron—single bowl
Kohler Co., Plumbing Div. C574

bathroom—porcelain or baked enamel—single bowl
Kohler Co., Plumbing Div. C574

bathroom—stainless steel—single bowl
Kohler Co., Plumbing Div. C574

faucets for
see
faucets—application: —sink—specific type

fittings for
see
plumbing fittings and trim

food waste disposers for
see
food waste disposers

kitchen—accessories for
Kohler Co., Plumbing Div. C574

kitchen—acrylic, composite—double bowl
Kohler Co., Plumbing Div. C574
Nevamar Corp. C467

kitchen—acrylic, composite—single bowl
Kohler Co., Plumbing Div. C574
Nevamar Corp. C467

kitchen—acrylic, composite—triple bowl
Kohler Co., Plumbing Div. C574

kitchen—ceramic—double bowl
Kohler Co., Plumbing Div. C574

kitchen—ceramic—single bowl
Kohler Co., Plumbing Div. C574

kitchen—ceramic—triple bowl
Kohler Co., Plumbing Div. C574

kitchen—drainboard combination
Kohler Co., Plumbing Div. C574
Nevamar Corp. C467

kitchen—iron—double bowl
Kohler Co., Plumbing Div. C574

kitchen—iron—single bowl
Kohler Co., Plumbing Div. C574

kitchen—oversize
Kohler Co., Plumbing Div. C574
Nevamar Corp. C467

kitchen—porcelain or baked enamel—double bowl
Kohler Co., Plumbing Div. C574

kitchen—porcelain or baked enamel—triple bowl
Kohler Co., Plumbing Div. C574

kitchen—stainless steel—double bowl
Kohler Co., Plumbing Div. C574

kitchen—stainless steel—single bowl
Kohler Co., Plumbing Div. C574

kitchen—stainless steel—triple bowl
Kohler Co., Plumbing Div. C574

tops for
DuPont Co. C474
Nevamar Corp. C467

Skirting
see
fascias

Skylights
see
skylights—form
skylights—framing
skylights—materials
skylights—properties

Skylights—form

flat panel
Innovative Building Products, Inc., Acme Brick Co. B667

Skylights—framing

aluminum or aluminum alloy
Innovative Building Products, Inc., Acme Brick Co. B667

Skylights—materials

glass—block, corrugated, plain or wired
Innovative Building Products, Inc., Acme Brick Co. B667

Skylights—operation

ventilators for—power-driven
see
ventilators: —adjustable—manual or power-operated

Skylights—properties

heat and glare-retarding
Innovative Building Products, Inc., Acme Brick Co. B667

insulating
Innovative Building Products, Inc., Acme Brick Co. B667

Slate
Echeguren Slate, Inc. A651

Slate products
see
copings: —slate
flagging: —slate
flooring—slate
paving —slate
roofing—materials: —slate
sills and stools: —slate
stair treads, risers: —slate
surfacing and paneling—interior—materials: —slate

Slides

drawer
see
hardware—drawer: —knobs, pulls and slides

Soap, soap dispensers and holders
see
bathroom accessories: —toilet paper holders, soap dishes—specific materials

Soffits—exterior
see
walls—exterior insulation and finish systems

Solar energy conversion—components for—passive

glazing—insulating
see
glass—properties: —insulating—specific type
windows—properties

Solar screens
see
shutters: —door—specific type
shutters: —window—specific type

Sound control products
see
acoustical products
partitions—properties: —sound-insulating or retarding—specific type

Space dividers—interior
see
partitions

Spandrel panels
see
panels—building—materials

Sports training equipment
see
bathtubs: —hydro-massage combination
steam bath rooms and equipment
surfacing—recreational, athletic, sport

Stage, theater and cinema equipment

flooring
see
dance floors
flooring—stage, studio, theater

Stained or faceted glass
see
windows—specific material/operation

Stainless steel products
see
sinks—residential: —bathroom—stainless steel—specific type: —kitchen—stainless steel—specific type

Stairs—concrete

treads and risers for
see
stair treads, risers

Stairs—metal

treads and risers for
see
stair treads, risers

Stairs—wood

treads and risers for
see
stair treads, risers

Stair treads, risers

flagstone
Echeguren Slate, Inc. A651

lighting for
see
lighting—application: —stair, aisle, path

slate
Echeguren Slate, Inc. A651

Stalls—shower
see
showers

Steam bath rooms and equipment
Kohler Co., Plumbing Div. C574

Stone
see
specific products

Stone *cont.*
see cont.
specific types

Stone—simulated/manufactured products
see
fascias—materials: —panels—stone—simulated/manufactured or brick
moldings and cornices: —simulated/manufactured stone
panels—building—materials: —stone—simulated/manufactured
siding—materials: —stone—simulated/manufactured
surfacing and paneling—interior—materials: —moldings and trim for—simulated/manufactured stone: —stone—simulated/manufactured
veneers: —stone—simulated/manufactured
walls—exterior insulation and finish systems—materials: —brick, stone—simulated/manufactured

Stools
see
sills and stools

Stops—door
see
hardware—door: —holders and stops—specific type

Storage and retrieval systems
see
shelving
specific equipment/products
storage equipment

Storage equipment
see also
shelving

cabinets with doors
Wellborn Cabinet, Inc. C536

cabinets with drawers
Wellborn Cabinet, Inc. C536

wall storage units
see
wall storage units

Storefronts
structural frames, mullions for—glass, glass block
Innovative Building Products, Inc., Acme Brick Co. B667

Stoves
see
ranges and ovens—residential

Strainers
see also
liquid waste disposal or treatment equipment: —filters, strainers, aerators, interceptors
water conditioning equipment: —filters, aerators, deodorizers, hydrators, strainers

basket type
Opella, Inc. C561

Street, outdoor equipment
lighting
see
lighting—application: —landscape—deck, garden, patio/terrace, walk

Sun controls
see
glass
louvers
plastic
shutters
skylights

Surfacing and paneling—exterior
see
panels—building
siding
walls—exterior insulation and finish systems

Surfacing and paneling—interior
see
surfacing and paneling—interior—general
surfacing and paneling—interior—materials
surfacing and paneling—interior—properties

Surfacing and paneling—interior—general
custom-designed
Wilsonart International, Inc. C478

Surfacing and paneling—interior—materials
brick face—simulated/manufactured
see
brick face—simulated/manufactured: —panels—prefabricated

ceramic or clay tile—glazed
Interceramic, Inc. C180

ceramic or clay tile—patterned, sculptured or textured
Interceramic, Inc. C180

ceramic or clay tile—unglazed
Interceramic, Inc. C180

marble tile
Interceramic, Inc. C180

moldings and trim for—hardboard
White River Hardwood Products C464

moldings and trim for—plastic, composite
see also
moldings and cornices: —plastic, composite
DuPont Co. C474

moldings and trim for—simulated/manufactured stone
see also
moldings and cornices: —simulated/manufactured stone
DuPont Co. C474

moldings and trim for—wood or plywood
see also
woodwork: —moldings, cornices, door and window trim
White River Hardwood Products C464

moldings and trim for—wood or plywood—simulated/manufactured
DuPont Co. C474
White River Hardwood Products C464

plastic laminate-faced
see also
plastic laminate sheets
Wilsonart International, Inc. C478

plastic—sheet or tile
DuPont Co. C474
Wilsonart International, Inc. C478

slate
Echeguren Slate, Inc. A651

stone—simulated/manufactured
DuPont Co. C474

Surfacing and paneling—interior—materials *cont.*
stone—simulated/manufactured *cont.*
Eldorado Stone Corp. A663

wood—simulated/manufactured
DuPont Co. C474

Surfacing and paneling—interior—properties
acoustical
see
acoustical products

fire-resistant
DuPont Co. C474
Eldorado Stone Corp. A663
Wilsonart International, Inc. C478

Surfacing—recreational, athletic, sport—application
see
dance floors
flooring—gymnasium
flooring—stage, studio, theater

Surfacing—recreational, athletic, sport—properties
shock-cushioning, safety
Dodge-Regupol, Inc. C285

Surveillance equipment and systems
see
luminaires—types: —motion detector combination

Swimming pool equipment
chlorination
see
water conditioning equipment

filters
see
water conditioning equipment: —filters, aerators, deodorizers, hydrators, strainers

flooring—safety
see
surfacing—recreational, athletic, sport
toppings—traffic-bearing

pumps
see
pumps

safety decking, flooring
see
surfacing—recreational, athletic, sport
toppings—traffic-bearing

water treatment apparatus
see
water conditioning equipment

Switches
dimmer
see
controls—lighting

T

Tables
tops for
DuPont Co. C474
Nevamar Corp. .C467
Wilsonart International, Inc. C478

Tambour
see
surfacing and paneling—interior—materials
veneers

Telephone equipment
see
intercommunicating systems

Tessera
see
ceramic or clay tile
glass

Testing equipment
water
see
water conditioning equipment

Theatrical equipment
see
flooring—stage, studio, theater

Theft detection/protection equipment and systems
see
consultants and services
glass—properties —burglar-resistant
hardware—door
luminaires—types: —motion detector combination
shutters

Therapeutic equipment
see
bathtubs: —hydro-massage combination
showers: —hydro-massage combination

Thresholds
see
sills and stools

Time systems
sequence control
see
controls: —time

Toilets
compartments for
see
partitions—shower, toilet, urinal

paper, dispensers for
see
washroom accessories —holders—toilet paper

partitions for
see
partitions—shower, toilet, urinal

seats for
see
plumbing fittings and trim: —toilet seats—specific type

sewage removal pump compartments
Zoeller Co. C908

unit
Kohler Co., Plumbing Div. C574

Toppings—traffic-bearing
tile or tile form
Bruce Hardwood Floors, Triangle Pacific Corp., Bruce Floors C310

Tops
see
bar furniture and equipment: —elbow rests, bar tops
cabinets: —tops for
counters: —tops for
laboratory equipment: —work surfaces for
lavatories and accessories: —tops for
sinks—commercial or institutional: —tops for
sinks—residential: —tops for
tables: —tops for

Towel bars—safety
see
bathroom accessories: —grab bars—specific material

Towels
see
bathroom accessories: —towel holders

Track and field equipment
running surface
see
surfacing—recreational, athletic, sport

Tracks
shower cubicle
see
showers: —rods, hardware and tracks for

Traffic accessories, equipment and products
see
toppings—traffic-bearing

Transformers
power and distribution
Task Lighting Corp. C950

Treads—stair
see
stair treads, risers

Trim
see
hardware—door: —lock trim
lath and plasterwork accessories and trim
moldings and cornices
surfacing and paneling—interior—materials: —moldings and trim for—specific material
woodwork: —moldings, cornices, door and window trim

Troughs
see
laboratory equipment: —sinks, drainboards, troughs

Tubing
see
piping and tubing

Tubs
see
bathtubs
bathtub/shower—prefabricated units

U

Universal design products
see
bathroom accessories: —grab bars—specific material

Universal design products *cont.*
see cont.
kitchen or kitchenette units—disabled persons' use
plumbing fittings and trim
showers: —disabled persons' use: —seats for—wall-mounted

Urinals
fittings, levers, valves for
see
plumbing fittings and trim

partitions for
see
partitions—shower, toilet, urinal

Utility line accessories
see
wiring devices—electrical

V

Vacuum cleaning systems
accessories
NuTone C509

centralized, automatic operation
Broan Mfg. Co., Inc. ii
NuTone C509

Valves
see
plumbing fittings and trim

mixing
see
plumbing fittings and trim: —valves—mixing—pressure-balancing, thermostatic

Vanities
see
cabinets: —bathroom vanity: —washroom vanity
lavatories and accessories: —vanity top and bowl—molded—one-piece

Veneers
see also
walls—exterior insulation and finish systems

stone—simulated/manufactured
Eldorado Stone Corp. A663

Ventilators
see also
blowers—centrifugal or axial
fans
louvers

adjustable—manual or power-operated
Broan Mfg. Co., Inc. C485; C915
NuTone C509

ceiling, wall, window
Broan Mfg. Co., Inc. C485; C915
NuTone C509

grease containment/extractor—food service equipment
Broan Mfg. Co., Inc. C485

heat recovery, air filtering
Broan Mfg. Co., Inc. C485; C915

hood—food service equipment
Broan Mfg. Co., Inc. C485

hood—residential kitchen
Broan Mfg. Co., Inc. . . . . ii; C485; C915
NuTone C509

hood—residential kitchen—fan and light combination
Broan Mfg. Co., Inc. C485
NuTone C509

Ventilators *cont.*
hood—residential kitchen—plate warmer
Broan Mfg. Co., Inc. C485
kitchen fan
see
fans: —kitchen or bathroom
make-up air unit—food service equipment
Broan Mfg. Co., Inc. C485
roof
see also
vents
O'Hagin's, Inc. A741
roof—continuous ridge
O'Hagin's, Inc. A741

Vents
see also
louvers
attic—louvered
NuTone C509
O'Hagin's, Inc. A741
dampers for
see
dampers
duct or sleeve extensions for
see also
ducts and duct assemblies—types: —air
Broan Mfg. Co., Inc. C915
roof, hatches—fire and smoke
see
ventilators: —roof—specific type
roof—louvered, continuous ridge
O'Hagin's, Inc. A741
roof—natural pressure-release
see also
ventilators: —roof—specific type
O'Hagin's, Inc. A741

Vinyl products
see
fascias—materials: —panels—plastic or vinyl
flooring—vinyl

Vision screens or barriers
see
louvers

Voltage regulators
see
controls

W

Wainscoting
see
surfacing and paneling—interior
veneers

Walkways
see
toppings—traffic-bearing

Wallboard
strip channels and corner lath for
see
lath and plasterwork accessories and trim

Wall coverings—flexible
see
surfacing and paneling—interior

Wall coverings—rigid
see
surfacing and paneling—interior

Walls—exterior insulation and finish systems
see
walls—exterior insulation and finish systems—materials
walls—exterior insulation and finish systems—properties

Walls—exterior insulation and finish systems—general
see
veneers

Walls—exterior insulation and finish systems—materials
brick, stone—simulated/manufactured
see also
siding—materials: —brick—simulated/manufactured
Eldorado Stone Corp. A663

Walls—exterior insulation and finish systems—properties
fire-resistant
Eldorado Stone Corp. A663

Wall storage units
shelf/cabinet units
KraftMaid Cabinetry, Inc. C529

Washers
clothes
see
laundry equipment—residential: —washers—specific type

Washroom accessories
see also
bathroom accessories
cabinets
see
cabinets: —washroom vanity
dispensers—lotion
Opella, Inc. C561
dryers—electric—hand or hair
Broan Mfg. Co., Inc. ii
holders—toilet paper
JADO C588
holders—toothbrush and/or tumbler—metal
JADO C588
hooks—coat or robe
JADO C588
partitions
see
partitions—shower, toilet, urinal
shelving
see
shelving: —bathroom or washroom—specific material
sinks
see
sinks—residential: —bathroom—specific material—specific bowl

Waste handling equipment and systems
see also
food waste disposers

Waste handling equipment and systems *cont.*
see also cont.
liquid waste disposal or treatment equipment
water conditioning equipment
compactors—residential or institutional
Broan Mfg. Co., Inc. ii
piping for
see
piping and tubing—application

Water closets
see
toilets

Water conditioning equipment
see also
liquid waste disposal or treatment equipment
waste handling equipment and systems
filters, aerators, deodorizers, hydrators, strainers
see also
strainers
Moen Incorporated C564B
filters—cartridges for—special applications
Moen Incorporated C564B
piping for
see
piping and tubing—application: —gas, electrical, sewer or water system

Water conservation equipment
see
plumbing fittings and trim

Waterproofing membranes
protection for
see
toppings—traffic-bearing

Water supply and treatment equipment
see
liquid waste disposal or treatment equipment
strainers
waste handling equipment and systems
water conditioning equipment

Water testing equipment
see
water conditioning equipment

Wax—floor or wall
Bruce Hardwood Floors, Triangle Pacific Corp. C246

Whirlpools
see
bathtubs: —hydro-massage combination

Windows
see
windows—properties
windows—replacement
windows—wood-aluminum/operation
windows—wood/operation

Windows—aluminum/operation
insulating
see
windows—properties —insulating—thermal—specific type

Windows—aluminum/operation
cont.

low-emissivity
see
windows—properties: —low-emissivity

Windows—aluminum-vinyl combination/operation

insulating
see
windows—properties —insulating—thermal—specific type

low-emissivity
see
windows—properties: —low-emissivity

Windows—bronze/operation

insulating
see
windows—properties —insulating—thermal—specific type

low-emissivity
see
windows—properties: —low-emissivity

Windows—composite—wood and metal—non-clad/operation

insulating
see
windows—properties

low-emissivity
see
windows—properties: —low-emissivity

Windows—general

church
see
glass
plastic

industrial
see
windows—properties

inserts for
see
glass
plastic

monumental
see
windows—specific material/operation: —monumental

overglazing
see
glass
plastic

shutters for
see
shutters: —window—specific type

sills and stools for
see
sills and stools

stained or faceted glass
see
glass
plastic
windows—specific material/operation

ventilators for
see
ventilators: —ceiling, wall, window

Windows—overglazing for
see
glass
plastic

Windows—properties

insulating—thermal—add-on-glazing
see
glass
plastic

insulating—thermal sash
Pozzi Window Co., Jeld-Wen B303

low-emissivity
Pozzi Window Co., Jeld-Wen B303

Windows—replacement

glass blocks for
Innovative Building Products, Inc., Acme Brick Co. B667

Windows—stainless steel/operation

insulating
see
windows—properties —insulating—thermal—specific type

low-emissivity
see
windows—properties: —low-emissivity

Windows—steel/operation

insulating
see
windows—properties —insulating—thermal—specific type

low-emissivity
see
windows—properties: —low-emissivity

Windows—vinyl/operation

insulating
see
windows—properties —insulating—thermal—specific type

low-emissivity
see
windows—properties: —low-emissivity

Windows—wood-aluminum/operation

casement
Pozzi Window Co., Jeld-Wen B303

circular, octagonal, half or quarter-round
Pozzi Window Co., Jeld-Wen B303

corner
Pozzi Window Co., Jeld-Wen B303

curved
Pozzi Window Co., Jeld-Wen B303

custom-designed
Pozzi Window Co., Jeld-Wen B303

double-hung
Pozzi Window Co., Jeld-Wen B303

fixed
see
windows—wood-aluminum/operation: —picture

insulating
see
windows—properties —insulating—thermal—specific type

low-emissivity
see
windows—properties: —low-emissivity

picture
Pozzi Window Co., Jeld-Wen B303

rolling or sliding—horizontal
Pozzi Window Co., Jeld-Wen B303

single-hung
Pozzi Window Co., Jeld-Wen B303

Windows—wood-aluminum/operation *cont.*

sliding
see
windows—wood-aluminum/operation: —rolling or sliding—horizontal

Windows—wood-copper/operation

insulating
see
windows—properties —insulating—thermal—specific type

low-emissivity
see
windows—properties: —low-emissivity

Windows—wood/operation

casement
Pozzi Window Co., Jeld-Wen B303

circular, octagonal, half or quarter round
Pozzi Window Co., Jeld-Wen B303

corner
Pozzi Window Co., Jeld-Wen B303

curved
Pozzi Window Co., Jeld-Wen B303

custom-designed
Pozzi Window Co., Jeld-Wen B303

double-hung
Pozzi Window Co., Jeld-Wen B303

fixed
see
windows—wood/operation: —picture

insulating
see
windows—properties —insulating—thermal—specific type

low-emissivity
see
windows—properties: —low-emissivity

picture
Pozzi Window Co., Jeld-Wen B303

rolling or sliding—horizontal
Pozzi Window Co., Jeld-Wen B303

single-hung
Pozzi Window Co., Jeld-Wen B303

sliding
see
windows—wood/operation: —rolling or sliding—horizontal

Windows—wood-stainless steel/operation

insulating
see
windows—properties —insulating—thermal—specific type

low-emissivity
see
windows—properties: —low-emissivity

Windows—wood-vinyl/operation

insulating
see
windows—properties —insulating—thermal—specific type

low-emissivity
see
windows—properties: —low-emissivity

Wiring devices—electrical

wall plates
NuTone C509

Wood products

see

doors—frames for: —wood—specific type
doors—swinging—by materials/construction: —wood—specific type
flooring—wood
mantels: —wood
shelving
surfacing and paneling—interior—materials: —wood—specific type
windows—wood-aluminum/operation
windows—wood/operation

Wood—simulated/manufactured products

see

surfacing and paneling—interior—materials: —wood—simulated/manufactured—specific type

Woodwork

custom-built

KraftMaid Cabinetry, Inc. C529
Wellborn Cabinet, Inc. C536
White River Hardwood Products C464

decorative grillework

White River Hardwood Products C464

mantels

see

mantels: —wood

moldings, cornices, door and window trim

see also

surfacing and paneling—interior—materials: —moldings and trim for—wood or plywood

White River Hardwood Products C464

rails—chair or plate

White River Hardwood Products C464

stock

White River Hardwood Products C464

Woodwork—simulated/ manufactured

moldings, cornices, door and window trim

see also

moldings and cornices: —plastic, composite
surfacing and paneling—interior—materials: —moldings and trim for—wood or plywood—simulated/manufactured

White River Hardwood Products C464

Trade Names

Catalogs are coded by positions within the volume in numerical sequence, e.g., C345

NOTE: Sweet's has been requested by manufacturers to include the following trade names and trademarks in this index. Sweet's makes no representations or warranties as to the rights of any manufacturer to any trade name or trademark listed in this index.

A

ACME (showers) C565A
ANTELL (oak planks) C246

B

BAYPORT (oak strips) C246
BENCHMARK (wood flooring collection) C246
BLUE CREEK (cooking systems) C502
BRANDON (oak planks) C246
BROAN (indoor air quality systems) C915
BROAN (range hoods) C485
BROAN (residential appliances) ii
BROAN (toilet & bath accessories) C587
BROOKHOLLOW (oak strips) C246
BROOKSIDE (oak planks) C246
BRUCE (hardwood flooring products) C246
BRUCE (laminate flooring) C310
BRUCE (wood flooring) C247

C

CAMBRIDGE (oak planks) C246
CAROUSEL (convection & microwave ovens) C512
CARUTH (maple planks) C246
CATHEDRAL (oak planks) C246
CATHEDRAL (MOEN's dramatic high-arc spouts on MONTICELLO kitchen & lavatory faucets) C564B
CHAPARRAL (oak flooring) C247
CHARLEMONT (oak planks) C246
CHERRY ROYALE (cherry flooring) C247
CLARION (whirlpools) C566B
CLASSIC (oak planks) C246
CLEAN 'N' STRIP (cleaner for wood flooring) C246
COASTAL WOODLANDS (floating varietal planks) C246
COLORJET INFUSION (color process) C246
COMFORTGUARD (foam/poly underlayments) C246
COMFORTGUARD (underlayments) C310
COMPUCOOK (convection & microwave ovens) C512
CORIAN (plastic material) C474
COUNTRY OAK (oak planks) C246
CREATED FOR LIFE (plastic sheets, precast shapes) C474
CRYSTALGUARD (finish for laminate floors) C310

D

DAKOTA (oak planks) C246
DARK 'N' RICH (wax for wood flooring) C246
DEBUT (custom wood tiles) C246
DESIGNER LINE (cooking systems) C502
DEVON (oak planks) C246
DIAMOND ACCENTS (maple flooring accents) C246
DLW (linoleum flooring) C290; C291
DLW COLORETTE (resilient flooring—linoleum) C290
DLW CONTOUR (resilient, homogenous vinyl flooring) C291
DLW IKADUR (non-PVC polyolefin tiles) C291
DLW IMPACT (resilient, homogenous vinyl flooring) C291
DLW LINODUR (resilient flooring—linoleum) C290
DLW LINOKETT (resilient flooring—linoleum) C290
DLW LINORETTE (resilient flooring—linoleum) C290
DLW MARKA (resilient flooring—linoleum) C290
DLW MARMORETTE (resilient flooring—linoleum) C290
DLW MERIT (resilient, homogenous vinyl flooring) C291
DLW OPAC (resilient, homogenous vinyl flooring) C291
DLW ORBIT (resilient, homogenous vinyl flooring) C291
DLW PASTELL (resilient, homogenous vinyl flooring) C291
DLW ROYAL CLASSIC (resilient, homogenous vinyl flooring) C291
DLW SCALA (100% vinyl in wood, stone, marble & metallic designs) C291
DLW UNI WALTON (resilient flooring—linoleum) C290
DODGE CORK TILE (natural cork floor tiles) C285
DUPONT (plastic sheets, precast shapes) C474
DURA-LUSTER (cleaner for laminate floors) C310
DURA-LUSTER (cleaner for urethane floors) C246
DURA-LUSTER (urethane finish for wood flooring) C246
DURA-SATIN (wax finish for wood flooring) C246
DURANGO (oak planks) C246

E

ECHEGUREN (slate) A651
ELDORADO STONE (landscape stepstones & pavers) A663
ELDORADO STONE (manufactured stones & brick veneers) A663
EVER-ROLL (resilient rubber flooring) C285
EVER-SEAL (adhesives) C310
EVERBOND LP ADHESIVE (adhesives) C246
EVERGUARD (no-wax finish for wood flooring) C247
EVERLAST (rubber floor tiles) C285
EXPRESSIONS COLLECTION (cooking systems) C502

F

FIRESIDE (oak planks) C246
FLEXFORM (milling systems) C247
FOUNDERS (wood flooring) C247

G

GERBERT (resilient flooring) C290; C291
GLASS BLOCK GRID SYSTEM-IBP (aluminum frames & sealants for installing glass blocks without mortar) B667
GLEN COVE (oak planks) C246

H

HALLMACK (bath hardware) C509
HANCOCK (oak planks) C246
HEAT-A-VENTLITE (fan/heaters) C509
HERITAGE SQUARE (oak parquet) C246
HERRINGSTRIP (custom wood tiles) C246
HOMESTEAD (oak planks) C246

I

IBP (glass blocks for grid systems) B667
IBP GLASS BLOCK GRID SYSTEM (aluminum frames & sealants for installing glass blocks without mortar) B667
IBP GLASS BLOCK GRID SYSTEM (shower enclosures & windows) B667
INNOVATIVE (showers) C565A
INTERCERAMIC (ceramic tiles) C180

J

JADO (faucets, bath accessories, door & cabinet hardware) C588
JEFFERSONIAN II (custom wood tiles) C246
JEWELS OF NATURE (wood flooring) C247

K

KENNEDALE (maple strips) C246
KENSINGTON COLLECTION (wood flooring) C246
KESTREL (wood shutters) C845
KOHLER (leading mfr. of plumbing fixtures & faucets) C574
KRAFTMAID (kitchen cabinets) C529

L

LA MARQUE DIGNE DE CONFIANCE (laminate floors) C310
LANDMARK (oak flooring) C247
LAUREL (oak strips) C246
LECLAIRE (oak planks) C246
LIFESHINE (non-tarnish plumbing fixture finish) C564B
LITE N NATURAL (wax for wood flooring) C246
LUCHE LX (low-voltage task/accent lights) C950
LUMERE (12-volt lighting systems) C950
LUMERE MODULAR SYSTEM (indoor/outdoor accent & task lighting fixtures) C950

M

MADISON PLANK (oak planks) C246
MANCHESTER (oak planks) C246
MAPLE TREASURES (maple flooring) C247
MAYTAG (residential appliances) C507
MERIDIAN STONE (maple custom wood tiles) C246

MICROTECH (replacement filters for PURETOUCH water filtering faucet systems) C564B
MILAN (cabinets) C536
MOEN (mfr. of faucets, sinks & related plumbing products) C564B
MOISTURE GUARD (moisture protection for laminate floors) C310
MONTEREY (cabinets) C536
MONTEREY (oak planks) C246
MONTGOMERY (oak strips) C246
MONTICELLO (custom wood tiles) C246
MONTICELLO (MOEN brand kitchen & bath faucets) C564B

N

NATURAL CHOICE (tag line) C246
NATURAL REFLECTIONS (oak strips) C246
NAUTILUS (residential appliances) ii
NAUTILUS (toilet & bath accessories) C587
NEVAMAR (plastic fabrications) C467
NEW ORLEANS (oak flooring) C247
NOBLE (pecan flooring) C247
NUTONE (built-in home products) C509

O

OAKBOND (adhesives) C246
OAKMONT (oak parquet) C246
O'HAGIN'S (vent tiles) A741
OLYMPIC (oak flooring) C247
1225 (MOEN's 1-piece cartridge for single-handle faucets) C564B
OPELLA (kitchen faucets) C561
ORNAMENTAL (walnut flooring) C247
OVER THE RANGE (convection & microwave ovens) C512

P

PAVESAFE (pavers & tiles) C285
PLANTATION (oak flooring) C247
POZZI (wood windows & doors) B303
PRAXIS (bath units) C575
PRC (bath units) C575
PRE-FINISHED STRIP (oak strips) C246
PREMIER (wood flooring) C247
PRO STYLE (cooking systems) C502
PURETOUCH (filtering water faucet systems) C564B

Q

QUIETTEST (bath ventilating fans) C509
QWIK JON (waste water & sewage removal systems) C908

R

RANCH PLANK (oak planks) C246
REGUPOL (recycled rubber membranes) C285
REGUPOL (rubber flooring for commercial & sports applications/multipurpose sports flooring) C285
REUNION (oak planks) C246
RIDGESIDE (oak strips) C246
RIDGEWOOD (oak parquet) C246
RIVERSIDE (oak planks) C246

S

SANTA FE SQUARE (custom wood tiles) C246
SENSONIC (speaker systems) C509
SHARP (appliances & microwave ovens) C512
SHILOH (oak flooring) C247
SIERRA PLANK (oak planks) C246
SIGN OF THE CRAB (fittings, trim & accessories) C584
SKYWALK (rooftop walkway rubber membranes) C285
SMART & EASY (convection & microwave ovens) C512
SMARTSENSE (bath ventilating fans) C509
SOFTSTONE (commercial rubber flooring) C285
SONATA (custom wood tiles) C246
SORRENTO (oak parquet) C246
SPRINGDALE (oak planks) C246
STAFFORD (oak strips) C246
STERLING (oak strips) C246
STERLING ENCORE PLANK (oak planks) C246
STERLING PRESTIGE PLANK (oak planks) C246
STROM (fittings, trim & accessories) C584
SUB-ZERO (refrigerators/freezers) C514; C515; C515A
SUMMERSIDE (oak strips) C246
SUMMIT HILL (oak planks) C246
SUTTON (oak planks) C246

T

TARA (oak flooring) C247
THE BRAND YOU CAN TRUST (laminate floors) C310
TOPLINE (faucets, bath accessories & door hardware) C588
TRAFFIC ZONE (laminate flooring) C310
TRIANGLE PACIFIC (laminate flooring) C310
TRIANGLE PACIFIC (wood flooring) C247

U

UNFINISHED STRIP (oak strips) C246
UNIT BLOCK (oak parquet) C246

V

VALLEY VIEW (oak planks) C246
VALUETEST (ventilating fans & heaters) C509
VAPOR-LOCK (moisture barriers) C246
VILLA NOVA PLANK (oak planks) C246
VILLAGE PLANK (oak planks) C246

W

WEARMASTER 3.0 (hickory, oak, maple & basswood planks) C246
WELLBORN (kitchen & bath cabinets) C536
WESTMINSTER (oak planks) C246
WHITE RIVER (architectural wood moldings, hardwoods, ornamentals, millwork, embossed moldings) C464
WILSONART (solid polymer fabrications) C478
WINDWARD STRIP (oak strips) C246

Z

ZOELLER (pumps) C908

A651
04415/ECH
BuyLine 6459

Echeguren Slate, Inc.

1495 Illinois St., San Francisco, CA 94107 • Phone: 415-206-9343, 800-992-0701 • Fax: 415-206-9353
Internet: http://www.echeguren.com • E-Mail: slate@echeguren.com

Echeguren Slate, Inc.

Slate Roofing

UA/Uses & Applications

The classic, elegant and prestigious way to roof. The beauty of a slate roof is enhanced over time, adds value to your project and lasts generations.

In addition to distributing the standard high grade slates of Vermont and New York, Echeguren Slate, Inc. imports and stocks a large array of attractively colored slates from China, Europe and Africa. Besides being economical, some of the foreign slates are thick with rough textured surfaces which can add eye pleasing substance to a building. To accommodate classical European architecture, we also offer the refined smaller sized slates of Spain.

The architectural versatility of slate, in combination with its durable, low-maintenance and fire-resistant qualities, make it a top quality roofing material of unmatched value.

Classic Elegant Prestigious

AI/Assembly & Installation

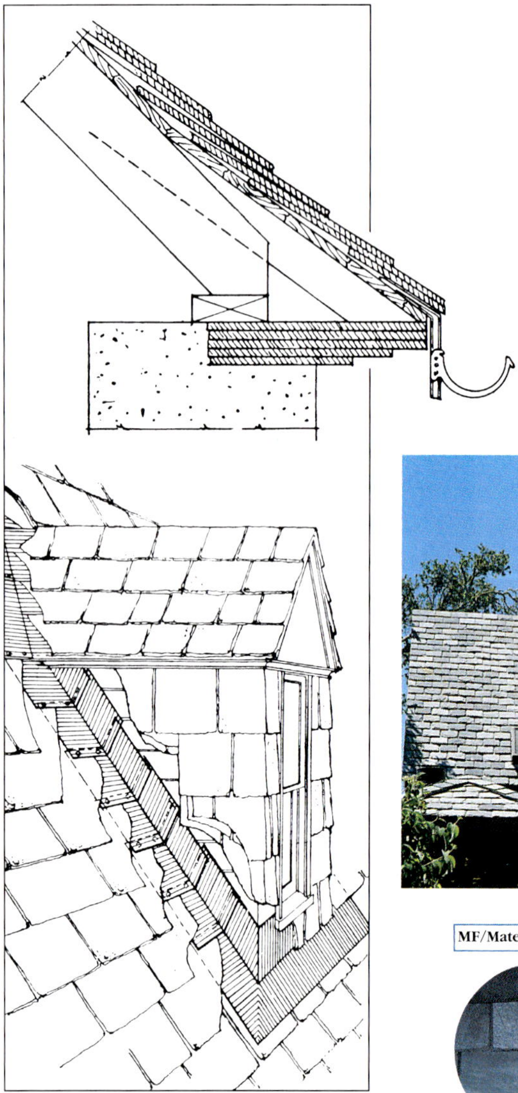

Drawings from National Slate Association "Slate Roofs" published 1926

OP/Overall Product-in-Place

Grey, Green, Imperial Blend

Green

Green (detail)

MF/Materials & Finishes

Silver Blue

China Green

Grey-Green

Imperial Blend

Uniform Grey

Vermont Salvage

African Blend

African Multicolor

Spanish Black

Plum

UA/Uses & Applications

An elegant yet economical and resistant interior and exterior flooring application.

Echeguren Slate, Inc. imports and stocks an extensive line of slate, sandstone and quartzite from China, Brazil, India, Africa, Europe and the U.S. New slates of striking color and exotic beauty are being introduced into the American market. The many shapes, textures and colors being offered are enhancing the architectural palette. A slate floor will enliven your project and give it a finished look of unique character.

In addition to tile, pavers, dimensional slabs and flagging, we offer slate for walls, treads and risers, sills and coping.

Slate Flooring

Custom Versatile Handsome

OP/Overall Product-in-Place

Jade

Imperial Blend

Yosemite

Lotus

AI/Assembly & Installation

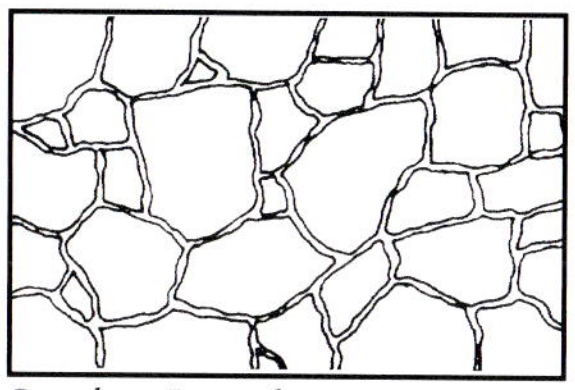
Random Irregular

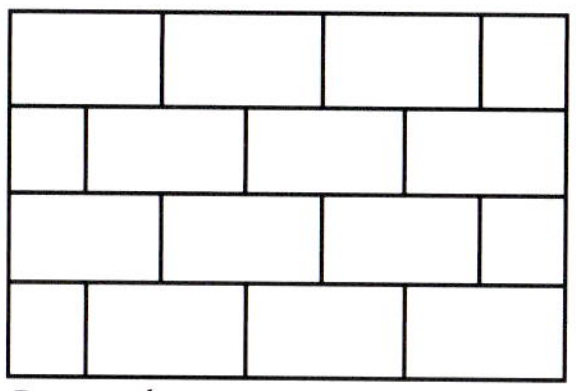
Rectangles

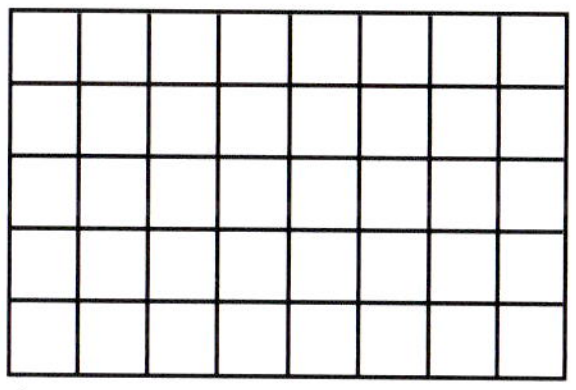
Squares

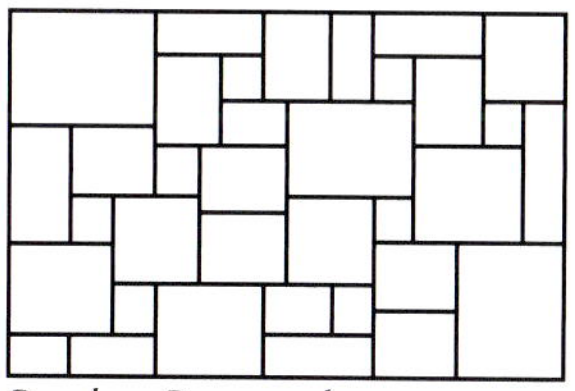
Random Rectangular

Coursed

MF/Materials & Finishes

Rainbow Teak

Multi-Red

Aqua Rose

Autumn

Raja

White Mara

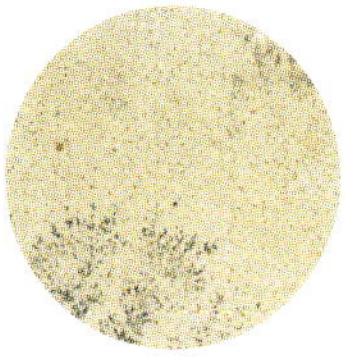
Fossil

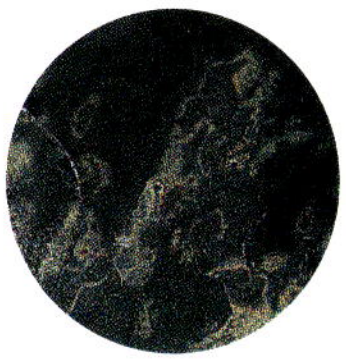
Westcountry

India Pink

Red Rose

Specifications

PART 1 General

1.01 Summary

Section Includes: Echeguren slate flooring and flagstone paving installations with accessories, as required for complete installation. Coordinate installation with waterproofing membrane at setting beds.

Related Sections:

Division 7: Waterproofing membrane at slate setting beds.

1.02 References

ANSI A 108.1: Installation of Tile with Portland Cement Mortar.

ANSI A 108.5: Installation of Tile with Latex-Portland Cement Mortar.

ANSI A 108.10: Installation of Grout in Tilework.

Tile Council of America (TCA): Handbook for Ceramic Tile Installation.

1.03 Submittals

Product Data: Furnish manufacturer's literature for each manufactured material.

Shop Drawings: Provide pattern drawings indicating field and edge conditions for each area of stone flooring. Indicate locations and widths of expansion, contraction, control, and isolation joints in slate flooring substrates and finished surfaces.

Samples: Furnish samples of each type, color, grade, and finish of slate and each color of grout required for Project.

Color Charts: Show full range of colors, textures and patterns available for each type of slate.

Full Size Samples: Prepare sample panels consisting of not less than four slate units with grout mounted on plywood, clearly indicating pattern, coloration, and joints.

Certification: Furnish manufacturer certification materials comply with Contract Documents for each shipment and type of slate, signed by supplier and installer.

Maintenance Instructions: Furnish maintenance instructions including information regarding recommended materials and methods for cleaning and maintaining slate flooring systems.

1.04 Quality Assurance

Source: Obtain each stone from single quarry source, with consistent color range and texture throughout work; do not change sources or kinds of materials during course of work.

Installer Qualifications: Firm with minimum five years successful experience completing installation similar to that required.

Preinstallation Conference: Conduct meeting at site prior to commencing work related to slate flooring installation.

Require attendance of parties directly affecting installation.

For full specifications, please contact Echeguren Slate or Sweet's.

Installation

Slate Flooring

Autumn Ashlar

- Marin Performing Arts Center, *Mill Valley, CA*
- Industrial Indemnity, *San Francisco, CA*
- Nordstrom, *Nationwide*
- Bank of America, *Stanford, CA*
- Splendido's Restaurant, *San Francisco, CA*
- Singleton Residence, *Santa Fe, NM*
- Academy of Motion Pictures, *Beverly Hills, CA*

Slate Roofing

Black

- Chalk Hill Winery, *Healdsburg, CA*
- Colman Residence, *Lake Geneva, WI*
- Grace Cathedral, *school and administration buildings San Francisco, CA*
- Marsh Commons, *Kirkland, WA*
- Hearst Residence, *Honolulu, HI*
- Hockley Residence, *Calgary, Canada*
- Tito Residence, *Pacific Palisades, CA*

For complete slate flooring and roofing specifications, installation details and additional information, see the Echeguren Slate, Inc. program in SweetSource, or contact Echeguren Slate, Inc. directly at below:

Echeguren Slate, Inc.

1495 Illinois Street
San Francisco, CA 94107
Phone: 415-206-9343
800-992-0701
Fax: 415-206-9353
Internet: http://www.echeguren.com
E-Mail: slate@echeguren.com

ELDORADO STONE®

A663

04730/ELD

BuyLine 5250

MANUFACTURED

BUILDING STONE

VENEER

ELDORADO STONE®

Buff Shadow Rock

Standard Cobblestone

ELDORADO STONE Corporation was formed to supply the building industry with a manufactured stone of unmatched quality. Since its founding in 1969, millions of square feet of Eldorado Stone have been sold. We believe Eldorado Stone is aesthetically and technically the best manufactured building stone available on the market today.

Eldorado Stone is manufactured and sold by local Eldorado Stone Franchisees in all parts of the United States and in many other parts of the world. Since we have more stone manufacturing facilities than anyone else, we are always nearby to help with any problem you might encounter. By manufacturing Eldorado Stone locally, we not only give you faster service, but we are also more responsive to the demands of your particular market area.

Product Presentation

Eldorado Stone is a manufactured building stone veneer offering excellent durability and the authentic beauty of natural stone at a fraction of the cost of natural stone. A unique molding method allows us to replicate the actual shape and texture of any natural stone. Eldorado Stone offers you the largest variety of manufactured stone available anywhere. With thousands of individually molded stones, repetition is negligible.

Eldorado Stone is made from portland cement, mineral oxide colors and lightweight aggregates (all of which are basic components of natural stone). Eldorado Stone is in essence natural stone re-formed. The light weight permits easy installation over nearly any existing or new surface. The color is permanent. In fact, weathering actually enhances the stone appearance, thus virtually eliminating maintenance (and maintenance costs).

Northwest River Rock

Sandstone Monarch

Standard Cobblestone

Ohio Limestone

Uses, Applications

Eldorado Stone fits nearly any building plan, large or small, interior or exterior, residential or commercial, remodel or new. The light weight and low cost make stone installation feasible where it otherwise would not have been. No wall ties, footings or special structural support are needed, as Eldorado Stone carries only a minimal shearing force.

Assembly, Installation

Eldorado Stone is easy to install. No special tools or elaborate procedures are necessary. Due to its light weight, no footings are required. Eldorado Stone can be applied to nearly any structurally sound surface. On clean (unpainted and untreated) brick, block or concrete, install stone directly to the surface. On all other surfaces, use metal lath. Outside, on wood surfaces, apply a moisture barrier such as building paper before lathing. Detailed installation instructions are available.

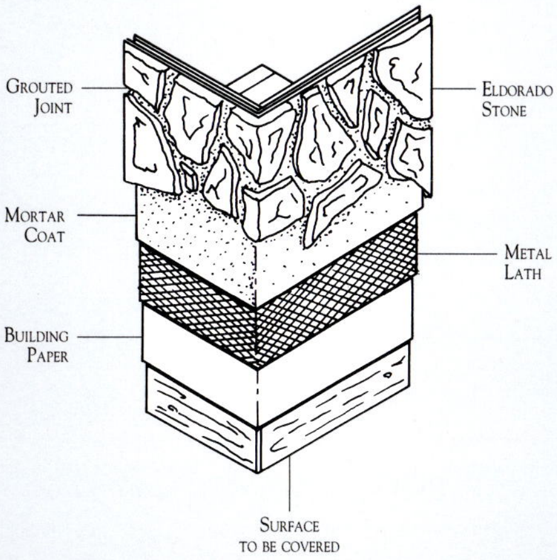

Technical Support

The best test of Eldorado Stone veneers can be found in the performance record of the millions of square feet in service. In support of this excellent record is the following data from current independent laboratory tests:

Compressive Strength: 2000+psi

Splitting Tensile Strength: 590 psi

Absorption: 13.3%

Thermal Resistance: R=.60

Shear Strength: 115 psi

Fire Rating: UL classification #546T shows zero flame spread, zero fuel contributed, and zero smoke developed.

Durability: Numerous installations in Alaska, Canada, and the Northern United States are successful tests in themselves of the durability and freeze-thaw resistance of Eldorado Stone.

Repetition: Eldorado Stone is manufactured in thousands of different molds and each stone is individually colored, so the chances of repetition on any surface are negligible.

Dimensions: Stones vary in thickness from 3/4 inch to 3 1/2 inches, and in size from 8 square inches to 4 square feet.

Color Retention: Only permanent mineral oxide colors are used. No detectable color change can be observed even after years of weathering.

Detailed technical data is available upon request.

ELDORADO STONE®

Wisconsin Weather-Edge

Pennsylvania Weather-Edge

Red Lion

Driftstone

Cascade Shadow Rock

Gray Shadow Rock

Gray Quartz

Glacier Gold Quartz

Mountain Blend Quartz

Code Acceptability, Certification

Eldorado Stone complies with major building codes and other building requirements as follows:

- ICBO Evaluation Report No. 3568 • Underwriters' Laboratories Classification No. 546T
- FHA/VA Materials Release No. 910 • Canadian Central Mortgage & Housing Corporation Acceptance No. 8183

Ocala

Buff Ledgestone

English Castle Stone

Berkshire Castle Stone

Lava

Moss Rock

Top Rock

Ohio Limestone

Splitface Granite

Availability, Cost

Eldorado Stone is available from franchised Eldorado Stone manufacturers and Eldorado dealers worldwide.

If you would like more information on prices, availability of stone or stone installers, or answers to any questions not covered in this brochure, please contact us. We would like to help you with your stone building plans.

ELDORADO STONE®

Stacked Stone

Stacked Stone with Jumpers

Mountain Blend River Rock

Northwest River Rock

White Monarch

Limestone Gray Monarch

Canyon Gray Monarch

Mountain Stone Monarch

Sandstone Ridge Rock

• LIGHTWEIGHT • DURABLE • INEXPENSIVE • EASY TO INSTAL

Canyon Gray Cobblestone

Standard Cobblestone

Buff Cobblestone

Icicle Creek Cobble

Used Brick

Clinker Brick

Sierra Brick

Mountain Brick

Antique Buff Brick

ELDORADO STONE®

Flagstone/Hearthstone

Mica Slate

Copper Mountain Ledge

Flagstone Slate

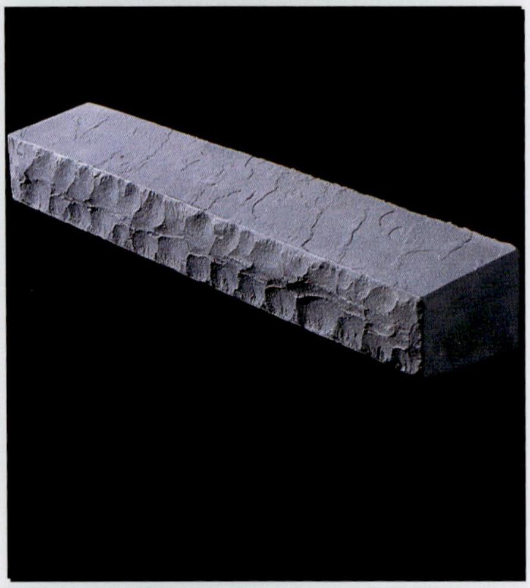

Wainscot Cap

Keystone

Quoin

Corners

Styles, Textures and Colors

Eldorado Stone is available in additional styles, textures and colors not shown here.

Corners are available for most stone types.

Home Office

Eldorado Stone Corporation
P.O. Box 489
Carnation, Washington 98014
800-925-1491 • 425-333-6722
Fax: 425-333-4755

Although colors in this brochure are as close to the actual stone color as possible, variations can be expected.

Ask your local dealer which types of Eldorado Stone are available in your area.

Eldorado Stone - don't settle for less

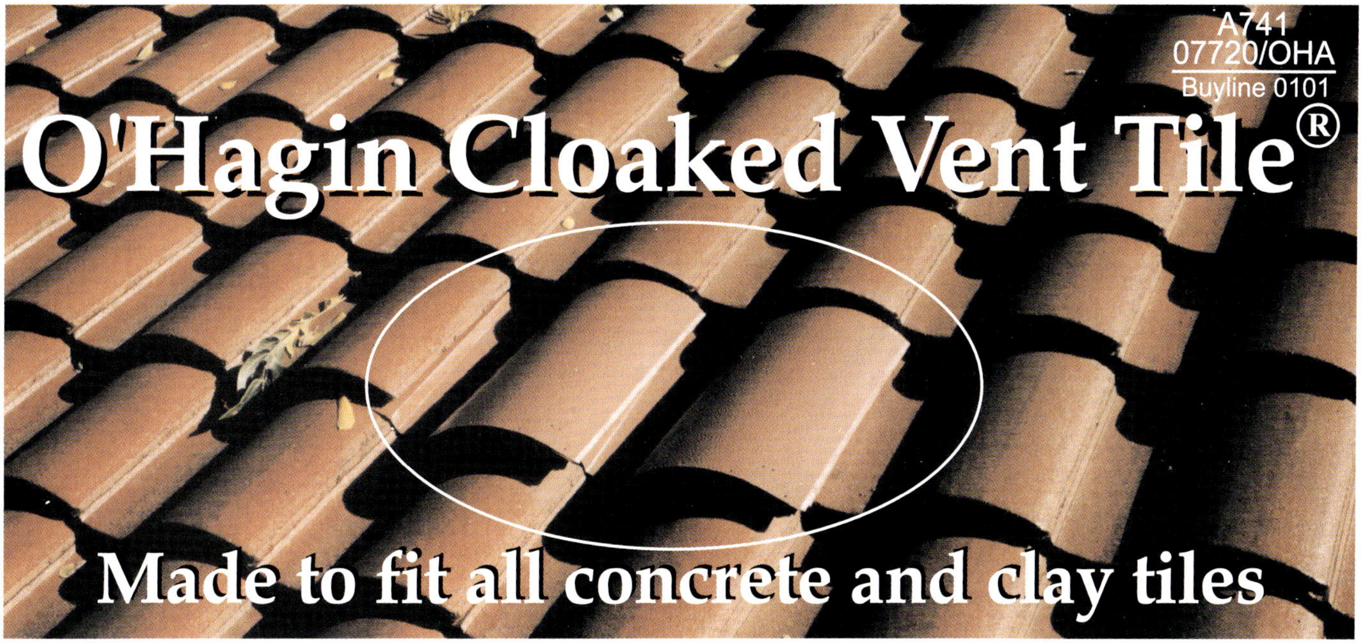

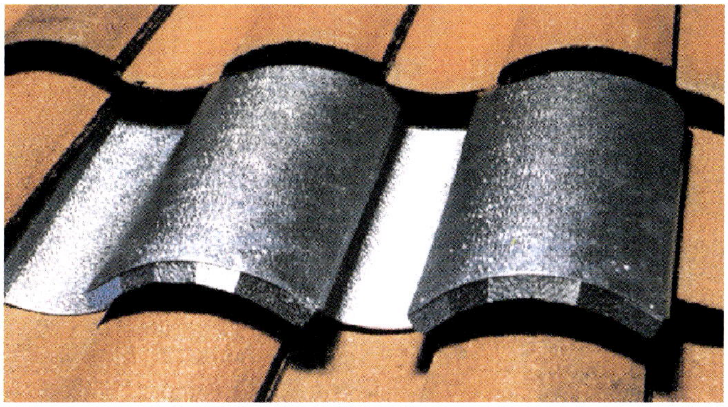

Concrete "S" Model 50046

Clay "S" Model 50037

Concrete "M" Model 50044

Clay "M" Model 50035

Concrete Flat Model 50043

Clay Flat Model 50056

THE O'HAGIN VENTILATION SYSTEM

The O'Hagin Ventilation System for roofing utilizes the only true, all metal, profile specific ventilators on the market today. O'Hagin vents are rapidly becoming THE CHOICE for superior passive air venting for concrete and clay tile roofs. The O'Hagin vent is a 95 square inch NFVA two piece vent with no other vent required. It is easy to install, wind resistant, fire retardant with spark arrester, has no toxic lead or plastic materials and blends beautifully with the tile of choice. It is a complete eave to ridge ventilation system, tested and approved by ICBO No. 5214, SBCCI No. 9650 and Dade County FL. Product Control No. 96-0830.02. It is available in aluminum, galvanized steel or copper at a competitive price. With the increasing need and requirements for home ventilation it is by far the most efficient vent in the tile market.

The illustration below depicts the placement of O'Hagin vents on a gabled structure with an attic on one side and a cathedral ceiling on the other. With the O'Hagin vents strategically placed in the eave and ridge positions, ventilation will occur naturally on either side by air pressure (wind passing over the structure drawing out hot air) or by convection (hot air rising and exiting the ridge with cool air entering the eaves).

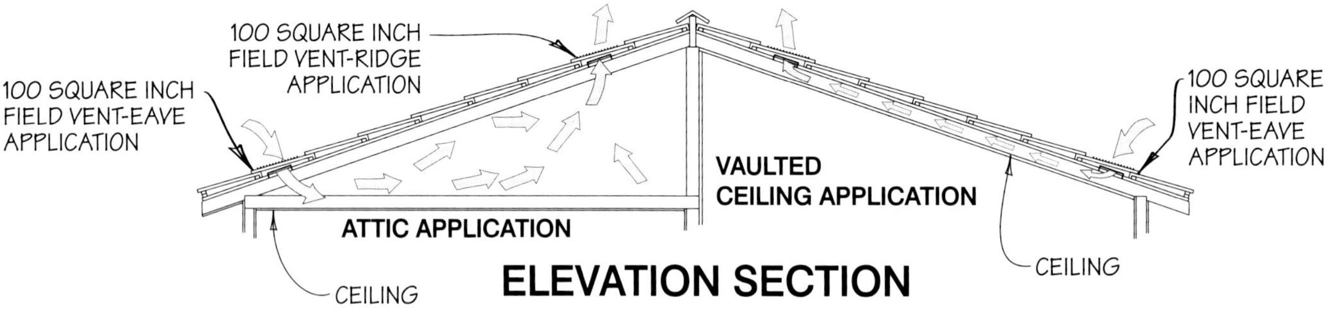

ELEVATION SECTION

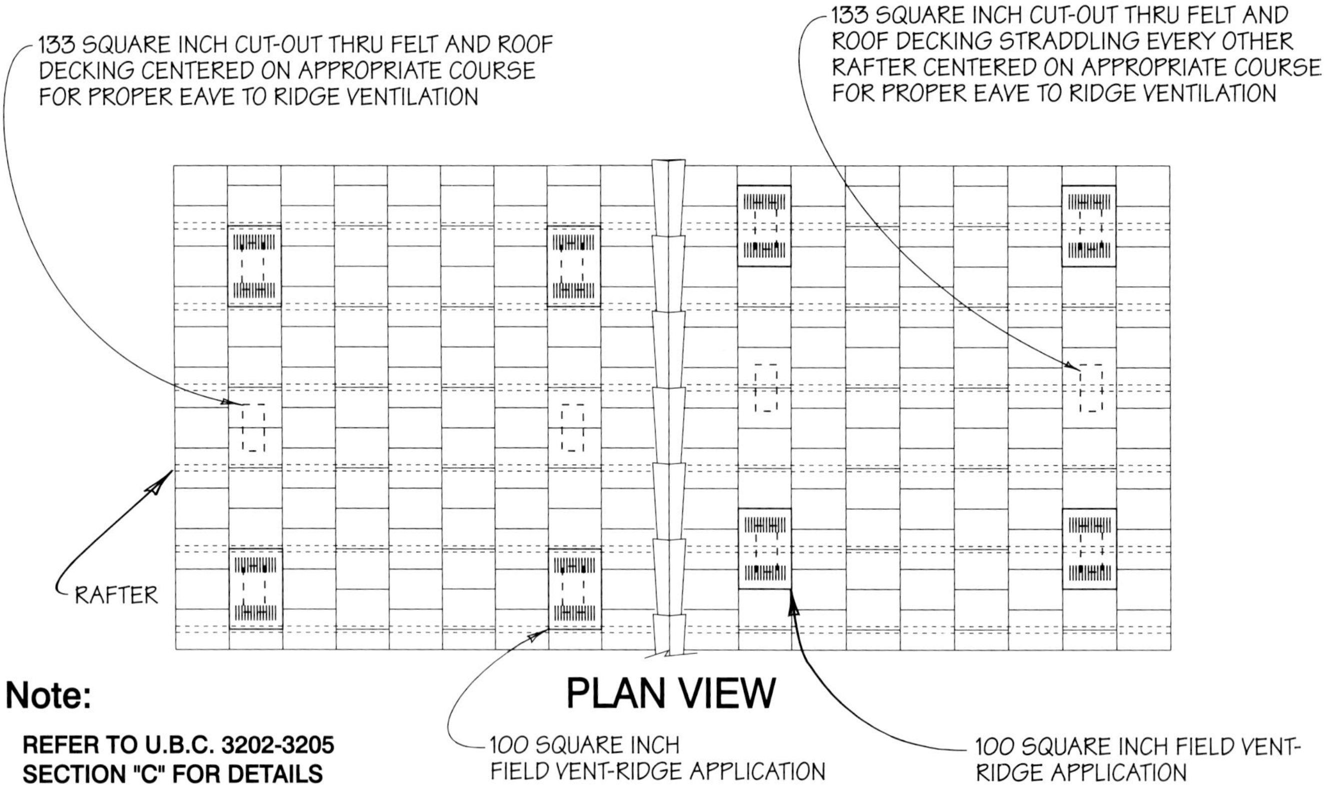

PLAN VIEW

Note:

REFER TO U.B.C. 3202-3205 SECTION "C" FOR DETAILS

SCALE: NONE

O'HAGIN VENTILATION SYSTEM

A741
07720/OHA
Buyline 0101

50 YEAR LIMITED WARRANTY

VENTS FOR CONCRETE TILE APPLICATIONS

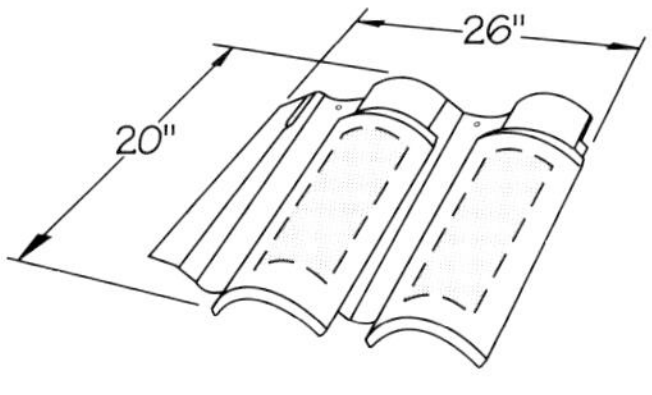

MODEL "S" #50046
100 SQUARE INCH OPENING

ACTUAL OUTSIDE SIZE	26" X 20"
PERIMETER OPENING	103.75 SQ IN
SCREEN OPENING	97.50 SQ IN

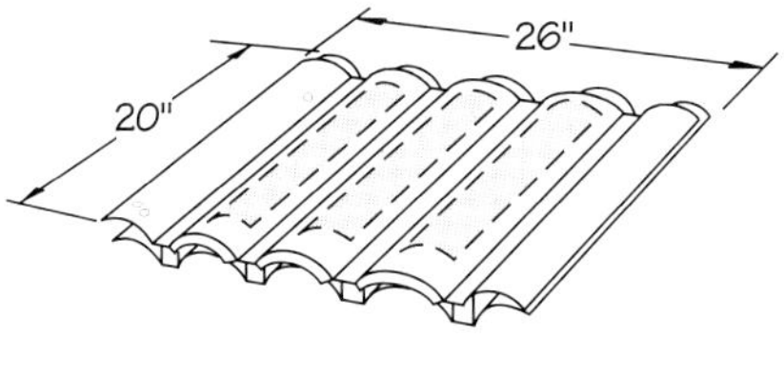

MODEL "M" #50044
100 SQUARE INCH OPENING

ACTUAL OUTSIDE SIZE	26" X 20"
PERIMETER	85.25 SQ IN
SCREEN OPENING	86.25 SQ IN

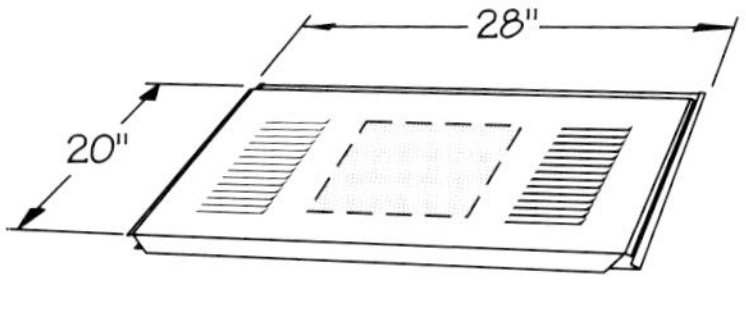

MODEL "FLAT" #50043
100 SQUARE INCH OPENING

ACTUAL OUTSIDE SIZE	28" X 20"
PERIMETER	123.25 SQ IN
SCREEN OPENING	98.75 SQ IN

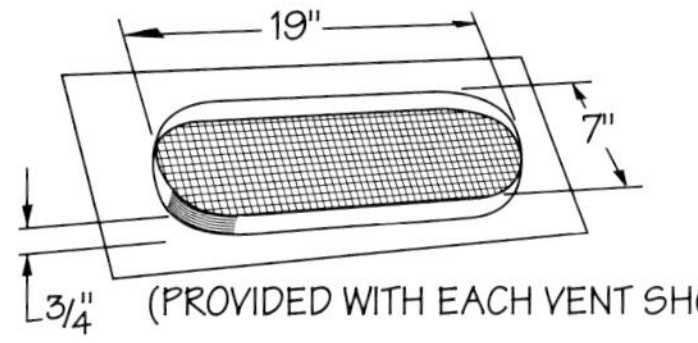

(PROVIDED WITH EACH VENT SHOWN)

PRIMARY VENT - SUB FLASHING #PV50002
133 SQUARE INCH OPENING

ACTUAL OUTSIDE SIZE	24" X 11"
ACTUAL SCREEN SIZE	19" X 7"
NET FREE VENT AREA	112.25 SQ IN

DESCRIPTION:

THE O'HAGIN VENTILATION SYSTEM is a way of venting homes and structures that was developed over a long period of time. The concept of venting the area under the roof sheathing, without the noticeable clutter that comes with roof jacks and wind driven turbines, had long been a goal for O'Hagin's Inc. The idea was simple, however, designing and developing a vent that is unobtrusive, easy to install, and leak proof was another matter. The end result is a product that does the job intended and looks beautiful doing it.

MATERIALS:

Galvanized hardware cloth; Size #4 mesh, .023 thick. Material must meet or exceed ASTM B-250

Copper: 16 ounce, .0216 thick. 20 ounce, .0270 thick. Material meets or exceeds ATSM A-219 and A-239

Aluminum: .032 thick. .0270 thick. Material meets or exceeds ASTM A-219 and A-239

Galvanized Flat Sheet: .019 thick. Material meets or exceeds ASTM A-219 and A-239

Adhesive: Must be a structural adhesive. Material meets or exceeds ASTM D-1002

Accessory items including, but not necessarily limited to:

- Flange sealant equal to APOC No. 100, complying with ASTM D-2822-75, Type 1
- Peel and stic flashing equal to Polyken 660, complying with ASTM D-570
- Fasteners, non corrosive, of same material as subflashing and vent tiles being fastened.
- Paint designed specifically for sheet metal to match the color of the chosen tile (to be specified by the architect or building owner) for galvanized metal vents. Aluminum and copper vents do not require painting but may be painted, if so desired.

VENTS FOR CLAY TILE APPLICATIONS

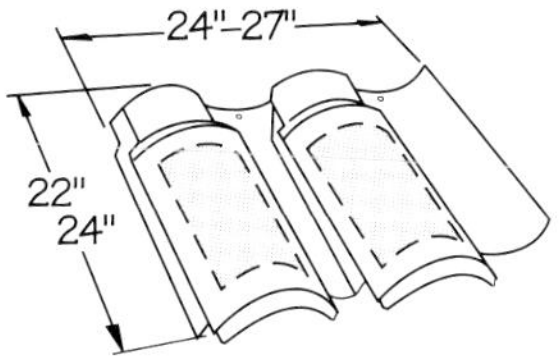

MODEL "S" #50037
18"
100 SQUARE INCH OPENING

ACTUAL OUTSIDE SIZE	24" X 22"
PERIMETER OPENING	101.25 SQ IN
SCREEN OPENING	99.75 SQ IN

MODEL "S" #50042
20"
100 SQUARE INCH OPENING

ACTUAL OUTSIDE SIZE	27" X 24"
PERIMETER OPENING	109.25 SQ IN
SCREEN OPENING MCA	120.00 SQ IN

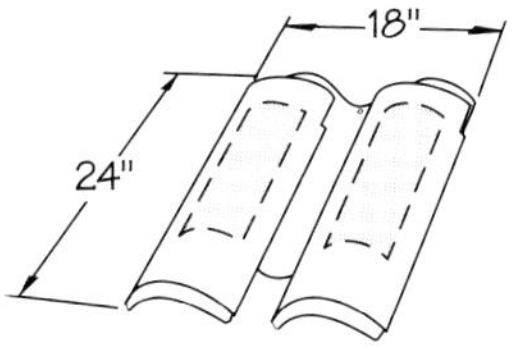

MODEL "M" #50035
18"
100 SQUARE INCH OPENING

ACTUAL OUTSIDE SIZE	18" X 24"
PERIMETER OPENING	105.56 SQ IN
SCREEN OPENING	80.50 SQ IN

MODEL "M" #50052
20"
100 SQUARE INCH OPENING

ACTUAL OUTSIDE SIZE	24" X 26"
PERIMETER OPENING	124.50 SQ IN
SCREEN OPENING MCA	120.00 SQ IN

RETROFITTING:

When an existing roof lacks proper ventilation, the O'HAGIN VENT is easily installed. Remove the field tile directly above the point where the opening will be cut into the roof sheathing. The PRIMARY VENT (sub flashing) is installed and the SECONDARY VENT replaces the tiles removed. No cutting of roofing tile is necessary. The SECONDARY VENT can be painted or otherwise fused with color to match the surrounding tiles.

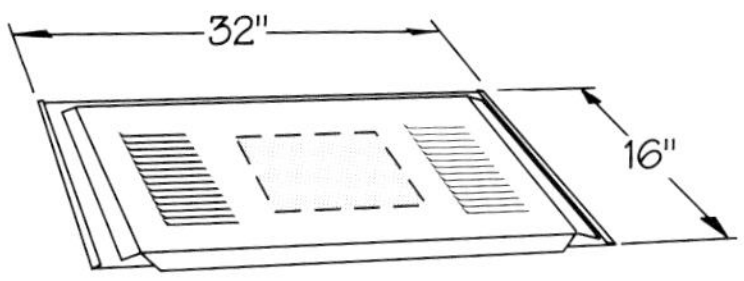

MODEL "FLAT" #50056
100 SQUARE INCH OPENING

ACTUAL OUTSIDE SIZE	32" X 16"
PERIMETER OPENING	110.75 SQ IN
SCREENED OPENING	100.00 SQ IN

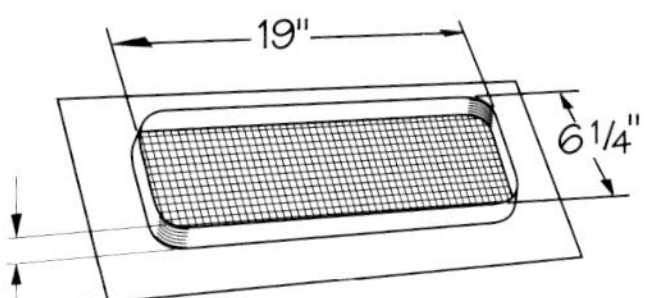

(PROVIDED WITH EACH VENT SHOWN)

PRIMARY VENT - SUB FLASHING #PV50001
118 SQUARE INCH OPENING

ACTUAL OUTSIDE SIZE	23" x 10.25"
ACTUAL SCREEN SIZE	19" x 6.25"
NET FREE VENT AREA	104.50 SQ IN

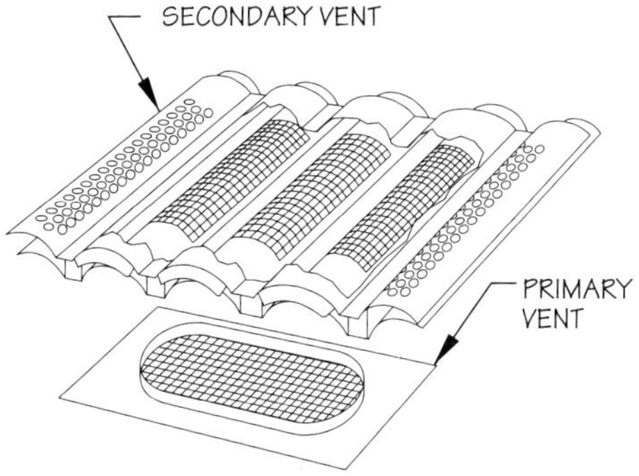

CONCRETE VILLA STYLE SECONDARY VENT SHOWN WITH CONCRETE STYLE PRIMARY VENT

O'HAGIN VENTILATION SYSTEM

INSTALLATION INSTRUCTIONS

MODEL "S" CONCRETE TILE - 100 SQ. INCH VENT

MARK CENTERED BETWEEN LAYOUT LINES AND ALIGNED APPROXIMATELY AS SHOWN ON EXPOSURE LINES

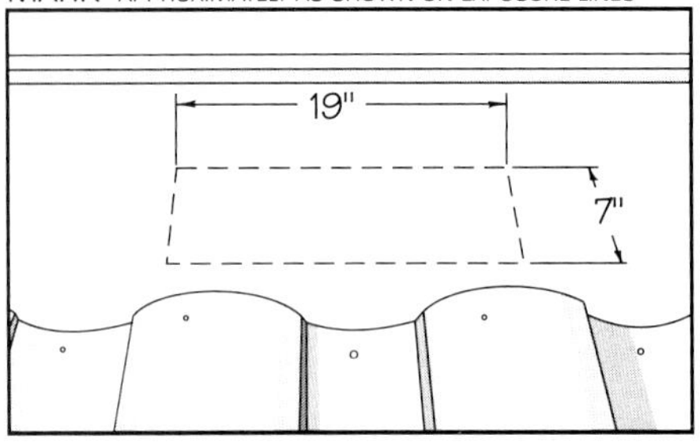

CUT SET BLADE TO THICKNESS OF SHEATHING

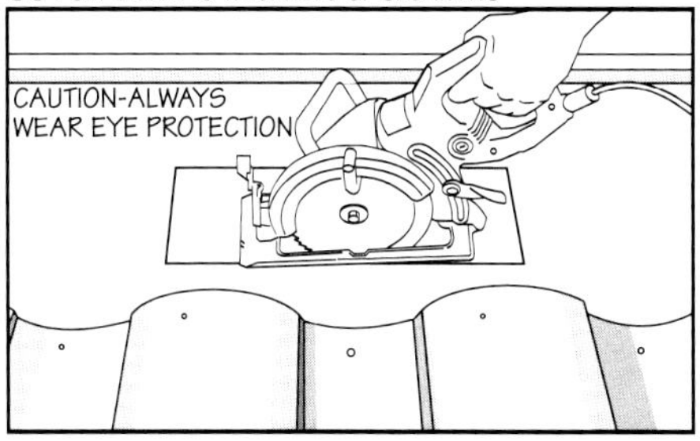

SEAL FLANGES WITH MASTIC APOC No. 100 - ASTM D2822-75 TYPE 1 WITH CAULKING GUN OR TROWEL

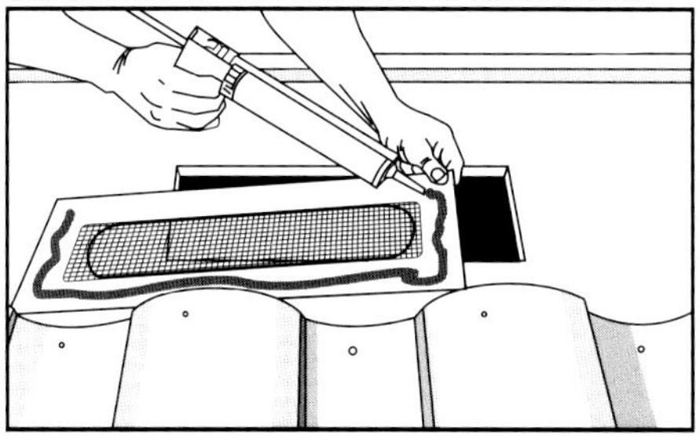

SECURE WITH ROOFING NAILS OF SUFFICIENT LENGTH TO PENETRATE SHEATHING ON 4 INCH CENTERS

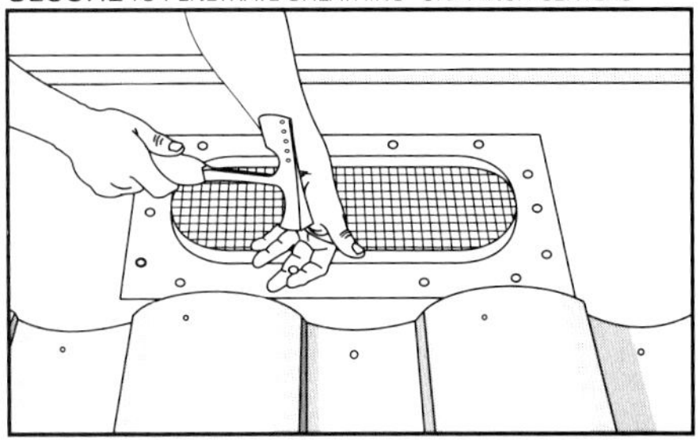

FLASH WITH PEEL AND STICK OR SLIP UNDER FELT (SEE NOTE 1 BELOW)

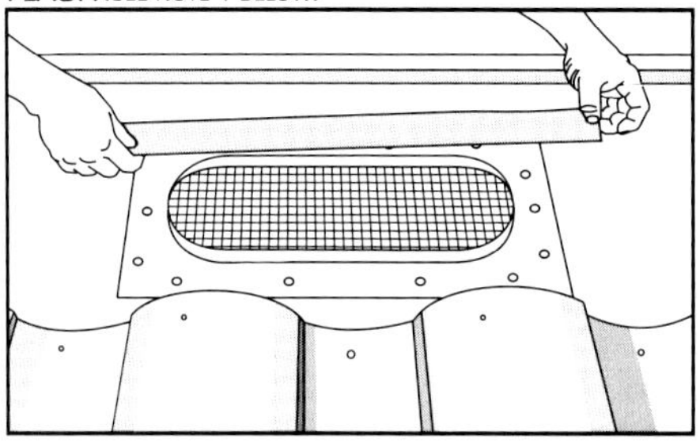

INSTALL AND SECURE VENT COVER WITH ROOFING NAILS OF SUFFICIENT LENGTH TO PENETRATE SHEATHING

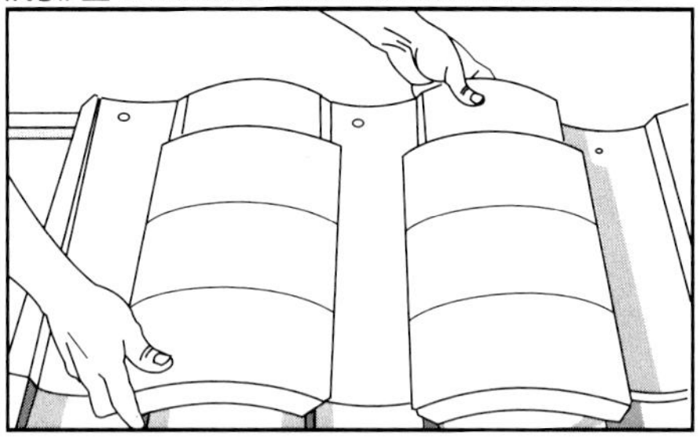

MODEL "M" CLAY TILE - 100 SQ. INCH VENT

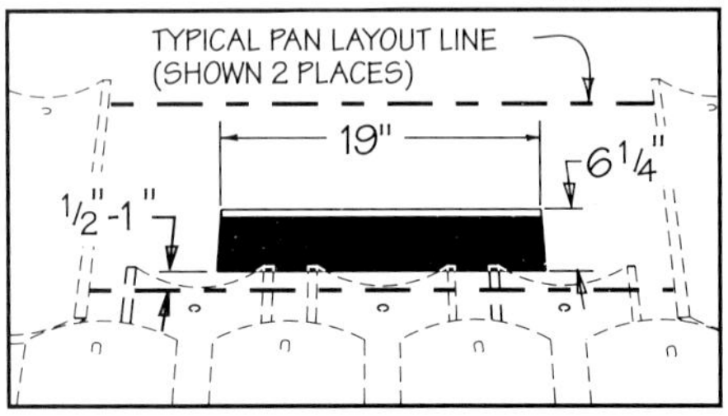

MARK AND CUT VENT OPENING AS SHOWN ABOVE FOR THE CONCRETE TILE VENT. ALIGN THE BOTTOM OF THE CUTOUT 1/2" TO 1" ABOVE THE PAN TILE LAYOUT LINE AS SHOWN

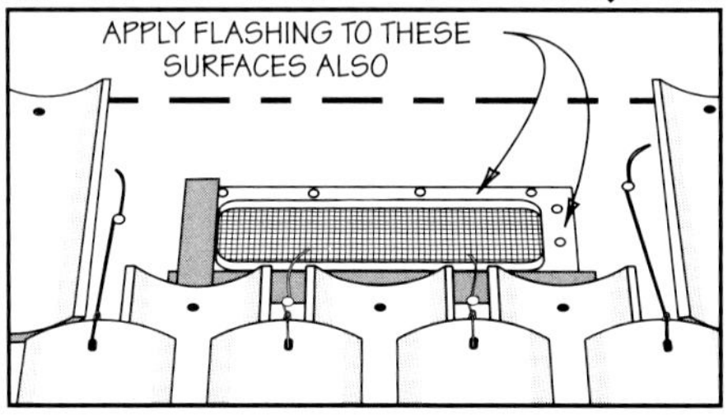

SEAL, SECURE AND FLASH (SEE NOTE 1 BELOW) AS SHOWN FOR THE CONCRETE TILE VENT. APPLY THE FIELD TILE UP TO THE PRIMARY VENT NAILING TILE WIRE INTO PLACE AS SHOWN. (PEEL AND STICK FLASHING SHOWN PARTIALLY APPLIED TO SHOW NAILS SECURING PRIMARY VENT TO ROOF DECK FOR CLARITY)

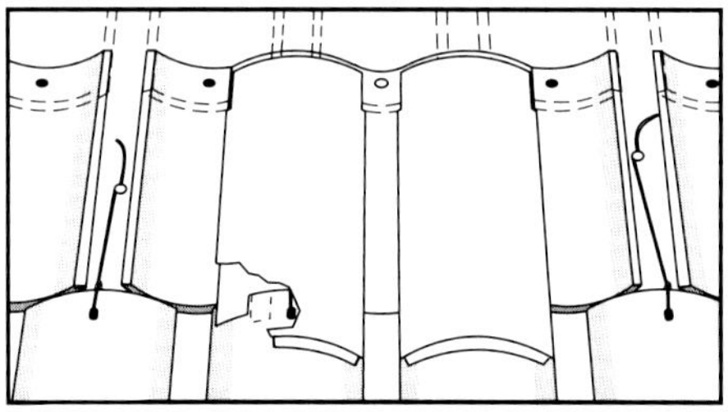

APPLY FIELD TILE AROUND THE PRIMARY VENT AND INSTALL THE VENT TILE (THE VENT TILE TAKES THE PLACE OF ONE CAP TILE AND TWO PAN TILES) AND SECURE INTO PLACE WITH A NAIL (SEE NOTE 2 BELOW) OF SUFFICIENT LENGTH TO PENETRATE TILE TO SHEATHING. INSTALLATION IS NOW COMPLETE AND THE REMAINING PORTION OF THE ROOF CAN BE FINISHED.

SCALE: NONE

NOTES: 1. PEEL AND STICK POLYKEN 660 - ASTM D 570
2 STRIPS 24" x 3" (TOP AND BOTTOM)
2 STRIPS 11" x 3" (SIDES)

2. LIKE MATERIALS MUST BE USED, I.E. COPPER VENT MUST USE COPPER WIRE AND NAILS

SQUARE INCHES OF NET FREE VENT AREA (NFVA)

MINIMUM 1/300 FOR 1000 SQUARE FEET
240 INCHES OF RIDGE VENT 50% REQUIRED
240 INCHES OF EAVE VENT 50% REQUIRED

BETTER 1/150 FOR 1000 SQUARE FEET
480 INCHES OF RIDGE VENT 50% REQUIRED
480 INCHES OF RIDGE VENT 50% REQUIRED

SUPERIOR 1/100 FOR 1000 SQUARE FEET
576 INCHES OF RIDGE VENT 40% REQUIRED
864 INCHES OF EAVE VENT 60% REQUIRED

BASIC BUILDING CODE REQUIREMENTS FOR ATTIC VENTILATION

MINIMUM 1/300

ONE SQUARE FOOT OF NFVA FOR EACH 300 SQUARE FEET OF AREA TO BE VENTILATED PROVIDED A VAPOR BARRIER IS USED, OR 50% OF NFVA IS LOCATED AT EAVES AND ROOF VENTS ARE AT LEAST 3 FEET OR MORE ABOVE THE VENTS.

BETTER 1/150 (ONE TO ONE RULE)

WHEN MINIMUM REQUIREMENTS ABOVE ARE NOT MET-CODE REQUIREMENTS ARE DOUBLED TO ONE SQUARE FOOT OF EACH NFVA FOR EACH 150 SQUARE FEET OF AREA TO BE VENTILATED.

SUPERIOR 1/100 (ONE PERCENT RULE)

SUPERIOR VENTILATION REQUIRES CONTINUOUS RIDGE VENTILATION THE ENTIRE LENGTH OF THE ROOF WITH MATCHING LENGTHS OF VENT IN EAVE.

NUMBER OF VENTS REQUIRED FOR PROPER VENTILATION USING O'HAGIN CLOAKED VENT TILE®

SQUARE FEET OF ROOF AREA	1000	1500	2000	2500	3000	3500	4000	4500	5000
1/300									
50% ridge	2	6	7	8	9	10	11	12	13
50% eave	3	6	7	8	9	10	11	12	13
1/150									
50% ridge	5	8	10	13	15	18	20	23	26
50% eave	5	8	10	13	15	18	20	23	26
1/100									
40% ridge	6	9	12	15	18	21	25	28	31
60% eave	9	14	18	23	27	32	36	41	46

O'HAGIN'S, INC.
2661 Gravenstein Hwy. South • Sebastopol California 95472

1-800-394-3864
FAX 1-707-823-5208

B303
08550/POZ
BuyLine 5539

wood windows and patio doors

timeless beauty...

Wood.

Timeless beauty. Warmth and integrity. Architects and builders alike know the value of wood and appreciate its beauty and performance. That's why they choose Pozzi® wood windows and patio doors, year after year.

Pozzi products are handcrafted in the Pacific Northwest by artisans who understand that creating a beautiful window means more than beautiful wood. We are experts at combining new technology and manufacturing systems with architecturally sound design to create the finest windows and doors available.

You can choose from 4,000 standard designs, or we will gladly take your design and create an extraordinary window or patio door that meets all your expectations—including energy efficiency, structural integrity and thoughtful beauty.

Pozzi designs and builds beautiful windows to meet your needs. We also have the tools to help you fit them into your plans. Take a look inside to find out more about our tools for the trade and how they can make your job easier.

POZZI
WOOD WINDOWS®
OUTSTANDING. OUT PERFORMING.™
1-800-257-9663 ext. S98
http://www.pozzi.com

POZZI WOOD WINDOWS®

POZZI WOOD WINDOWS®

Tools for the trade.

Our all new 1997-1998 Pozzi Architecture Reference Manuals are now available from your local Pozzi® distributor. They include three different manuals to serve your particular needs:

Pozzi's Product Line Manual includes our full line of windows and patio doors, including complete specifications and details.

Epic Commercial Manual covers our products for commercial construction.

Builder Series Manual includes designs for lower cost residential casement and awning windows.

All our reference manuals are also available on our new **1997-1998 Architectural Reference CD-ROM.** It contains all the technical drawings in an electronic format compatible with most CAD software and makes it easy to produce your plans with accurate renderings.

We choose only the most qualified window and door specialists to become Pozzi distributors. You can be assured that each one is dedicated to working—sleeves-up—with builders, architects, designers and homeowners, giving you information and on-site expertise that make your job run smoothly.

Pozzi also makes ordering easier with our new **1997-1998 Fast Track™** software. This custom-designed program lets your Pozzi distributor obtain quotes and specifications on nearly every product we manufacture. And by using our **ROE** (Remote Order Entry) mechanism, your distributor can streamline the ordering and purchasing process by going directly to the plant—electronically. This makes it simple to design and order a window and patio door package without confusion. All the information the distributor needs is on **Fast Track.**

Welcome to www.pozzi.com

Our Web site at **http://www.pozzi.com** is continually updated to bring you instant information on the whole range of Pozzi products and services, including a complete listing of North American distributors and specification and warranty details. We'll answer your questions within one working day. Log on and see how Pozzi's tools for the trade help meet your design and building needs.

POZZI WOOD WINDOWS®

B303
08550/POZ
BuyLine 5539

Performance, style and service.

Pozzi wood windows and patio doors are different. Not only in the way they're made, but in the way they perform. Pozzi makes certain all window components work together to deliver the best overall thermal and moisture protection available. And Pozzi continually develops features guaranteed to keep its windows functioning perfectly for the life of the home.

Creating your own style is easy with Pozzi's 4,000 standard window and door designs. They include casement windows, double-hung windows, horizontal sliders, French and center swing patio doors, gliding patio doors, transoms and accent windows, operating geometric windows and straight-line and radius geometric windows. Should your home require one of our standard windows in a special size, it's not a problem. We simply go to the next larger size and reduce it in increments until we have just the size you need.

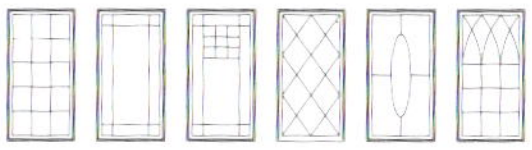

We have taken the tradition of divided lites, and modified it to meet the needs of today's architecture. We have designed and perfected techniques such as our thermal bar system, which solves many of the maintenance needs of divided lites. All our "lite" solutions, including thermal bar, full-surround interior wood grilles, and between-the-glass muntins, are available with custom breaks to complement any design.

Custom windows to order.

Pozzi specializes in one-of-a-kind masterpieces. In fact, 40% of the windows we build are special orders. We believe the innovation and creative thinking needed to build the finest custom-order windows are the same skills needed to build the finest standard ones. So, when you choose Pozzi, you can be assured we deliver the same high quality and expert craftsmanship for our standard line as our custom orders.

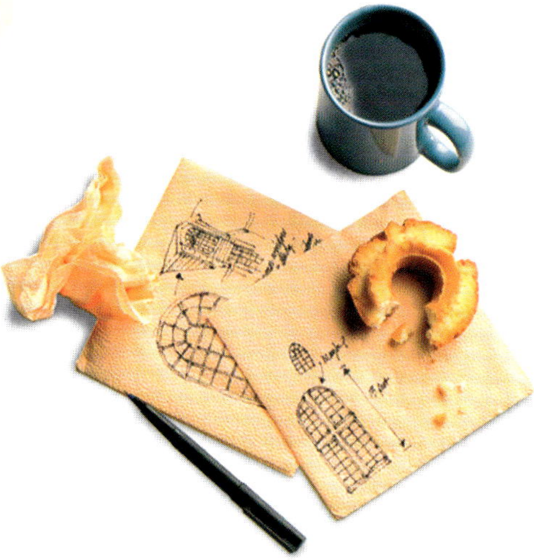

Thermal Bar Divided Lite

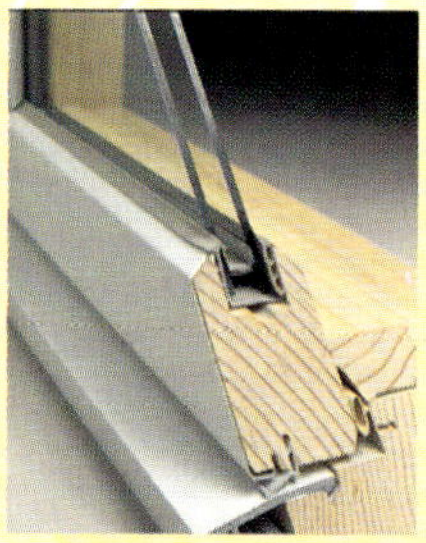

Our boot glazing system is standard on all one-lite windows. It's a commercial-grade vinyl that cushions the glass against environmental stress.

Mix and match our standard windows to create endless possibilities.

POZZI WOOD WINDOWS®

Exterior finishes.

At Pozzi, we construct the interior of every window and patio door with fine-grained, precision-milled Western Pine. This makes it easy to achieve the color and finish you want with stains and coatings. We also construct the exteriors from the same Western Pine, then treat it with a high-performance, water-repellent preservative, allowing you the flexibility to create the exact exterior finish you need.

Standard finishes.

Many builders and homeowners paint window and patio door exteriors as part of a home's overall color scheme, so our standard exterior finish is primed wood. We carefully prepare the wood for painting and apply a high-quality primer. That way, the window is protected against the elements during shipment and installation.

There has also been a trend toward clear wood sidings and the use of natural materials in building. Pozzi makes staining these types of exteriors easy with our optional clear, unprimed finish.

Clads.

Our aluminum-clad exterior delivers all the superior insulation of wood, plus the added protection of a weather-proof, low-maintenance aluminum "shell." We have perfected the cladding technology that best suits each specific part of the window.

Pozzi clad products are available in four standard colors: White, Bronze, Champagne and Hunter Green. You can also explore a palette of 27 Designer Choice™ colors that include hues as rich as Buckskin, as warm as Garnet or as tailored as Capri Blue. Plus, thanks to our Color Endurance System,™ we offer a 10-year warranty that guarantees you'll enjoy years of vibrant color.

Warranty.

All Pozzi products are warranted for a full 10 years against defects in workmanship and materials. If something isn't right, it's repaired or replaced at no charge. Our insulated glass warranty is even better, extending to 20 years from date of manufacture.

Outstanding performance and beauty. If that's what you're looking for, the natural choice is Pozzi.

Pozzi
WOOD WINDOWS®
OUTSTANDING. OUT PERFORMING.™
1-800-257-9663 ext. S98
http://www.pozzi.com

B667
04270/INN
Buyline 6535

IBP glass block grid system™

WINDOWS SKYLIGHTS • FLOORS SHOWERS WALLS

ACME BRICK
Since 1891

IBP glass block grid system™

WINDOWS SKYLIGHTS • FLOORS SHOWERS WALLS

The IBP Glass Block Grid System™ combines a strong, lightweight aluminum frame with glass block and weatherproof sealant, to provide cost-effective glass block installation without mortar. Applications of the IBP Grid System are limited only by the imagination. Over sixty thousand successful installations worldwide include store fronts, windows, curtain walls, mosaics, shower enclosures, floors, retail displays, signage, furniture, and sun spaces.

Installation

IBP grid assemblies are available in many standard sizes, and can be custom-manufactured to meet your specifications. Installers simply nail or screw the grid assembly into place. Glass block are then wrapped with insulating foam tape, inserted into the grid, and sealed. A frame can be assembled and installed either by professionals or by do-it-yourselfers.

Durability

The IBP Glass Block Grid System, unlike mortar installations, allows both for building movement and for expansion/contraction of glass block and surrounding materials. The result is a glass block installation that retains its beauty and integrity over time.

Appearance

Gray mortar joints tend to limit the aesthetic appeal of traditional glass block installations. IBP assemblies replace the mortar look with a variety of grid colors which harmonize well with any building design. A wide array of Trimline glass block patterns and colors add further design choices.

Versatility

With the IBP grid system, it's easy to achieve a new effect simply by replacing existing glass block with a new pattern or color. Again, this replacement process takes only minutes and requires no special tools or labor.

Design Assistance

IBP offers free professional design services for all customers. Details are also available on all IBP products in AutoCAD® Release 12 format. To inquire about this service, or to ask for any additional information on the IBP Glass Block Grid System, please call Acme Brick Company at **1-800-932-2263**. Outside the US dial 010-817-820-2532.

Security

The IBP Glass Block Grid System offers the same advantage as security bars, making it one of the most secure components of any building structure. Even if block are broken and removed, the grid system performs like burglar bars and impedes entry.

Sound Transmission

Traditional windows and skylights transmit more than light. They also transmit or possibly amplify sounds from raindrops, hailstones, traffic, and aircraft. When the IBP Glass Block Grid System is utilized, sounds are subdued and muted by the mass of the block. Light passes freely, but sound doesn't.

Cost

Because skilled labor is generally not required, an IBP grid system can cost less to install than traditional mortared glass block or glass pavers.

Insulation

The acceptable U-value standard, according to the American Architectural Manufacturers Association (AAMA), for a double-pane window is .69. The IBP Glass Block Grid System has a U-value of .49, more than 25 percent better than the accepted standard. Additionally, this system has an air and water infiltration rate of 0.00.

Repair

To replace a damaged block, a maintenance person simply cuts away the sealant, removes the block from the grid, inserts the new block, and reseals. Skilled labor and special tools aren't required, and the repair process takes only a few minutes. To replace a damaged block in a mortar installation, a skilled mason must carefully chip out the mortar and replace the block. When the new mortar dries, it may or may not match the existing mortar.

WINDOWS AND WALLS

IBP window and wall grids enhance the appearance of glass block installations. The IBP system assures a proper, uniformly spaced glass block installation without using the time-consuming method of mortar and spacers. IBP window performance factors such as thermal efficiency, air infiltration, water penetration, and security surpass most competing window installations.

The versatility of the IBP Glass Block Grid System™ extends far beyond the standard grid sizes depicted on the project to the right. Stair-stepped windows and the service island counter pictured below are just two examples of the infinite number of design possibilities. Other applications include work space enclosures, interior partitions, curtain walls, and room dividers

New York, NY; New York City Transit Authority

Designed by Boyer Glass & Mirror

Krebs, OK; Terry D. Miller, Designer

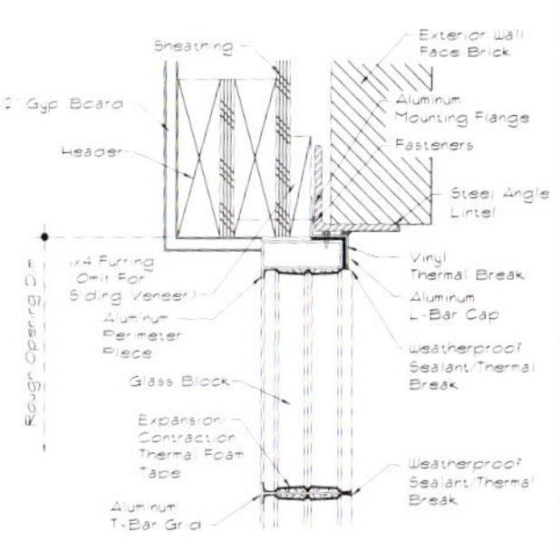
WINDOW HEAD
WOOD STUD / BRICK VENEER

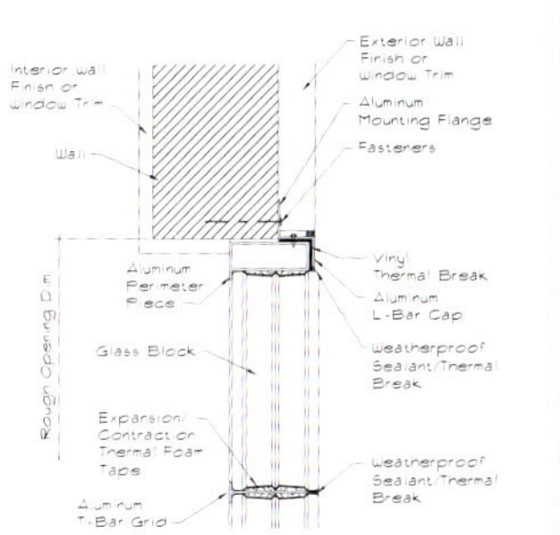
WINDOW HEAD
(Jamb Similar)
Mounting Flange Installation

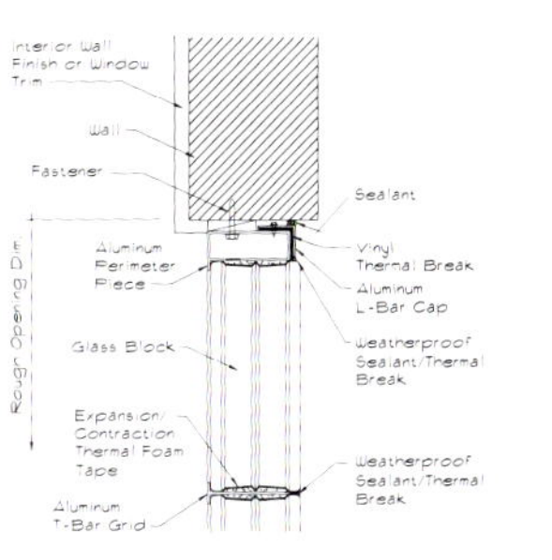
WINDOW HEAD
(Jamb Similar)
Flushmount Installation

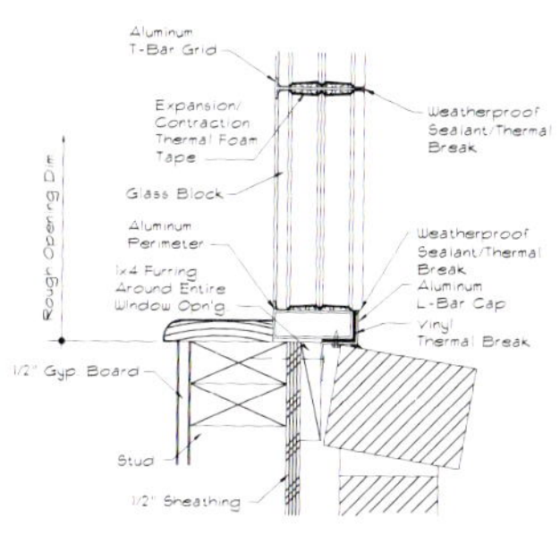
WINDOW SILL
WOOD STUD / BRICK VENEER

Standard grid colors are shown below. Silver and Gold are anodized. Custom colors are available.

White	Bronze	Taupe	Black	Red	Silver	Gold
Interior/Exterior	*Interior/Exterior*	*Interior/Exterior*	*Interior Grid*	*Interior Grid*	*Interior Grid*	*Interior Grid*

SKYLIGHTS

IBP *glass block* skylights provide features unavailable in conventional *plastic* skylights. By selecting various block patterns and colors, designers can customize an IBP skylight to meet the aesthetic, energy efficiency, and lighting requirements of a project. Because security is always important, the grid system serves as security bars even if block are broken and removed. IBP skylights provide greater sound insulation qualities than conventional skylights. Additionally, the durability and beauty of aluminum and of glass block make this a superior skylight.

IBP skylights accommodate typical curb and flashing construction as detailed. Standard skylight models span areas up to 49" x 80" (six block wide by ten block long) without additional support. Custom skylights can be designed to span larger areas.

Louisville, KY; Designed by Rodney Wells

Bonita Springs, FL; Bonita Springs Medical Center

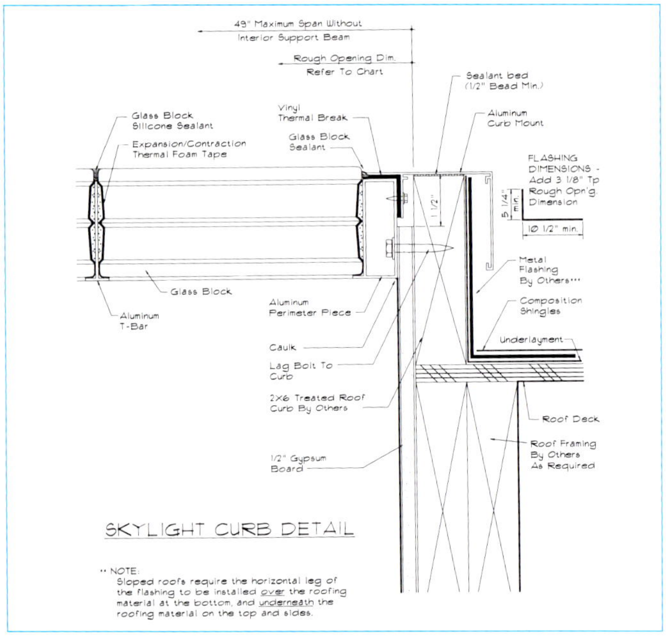

Bonita Springs, FL; Bonita Springs Medical Center

Skylight grid with curb mount.

Installation of glass block

Application of the sealant

SHOWER ENCLOSURES

Today's most beautiful shower enclosures are fashioned from glass block, and IBP's new shower enclosure system renders glass block showers practical for the first time. Aluminum extrusions link together in 22.5° increments to turn corners as shown below. A flush aluminum finishing piece easily attaches the grid panels to adjoining walls and to the shower base. To prevent leaks, the interior side of the shower is sealed with a mildew-resistant silicone. IBP offers a self-supporting glass block door header frame to further enhance the shower's aesthetic appeal.

IBP shower enclosures can be designed to fit your specific requirements. Examples shown at right are just a few of the many design configurations available. Many shower designs are installed within two hours, and usually at less cost than traditional glass block shower installations.

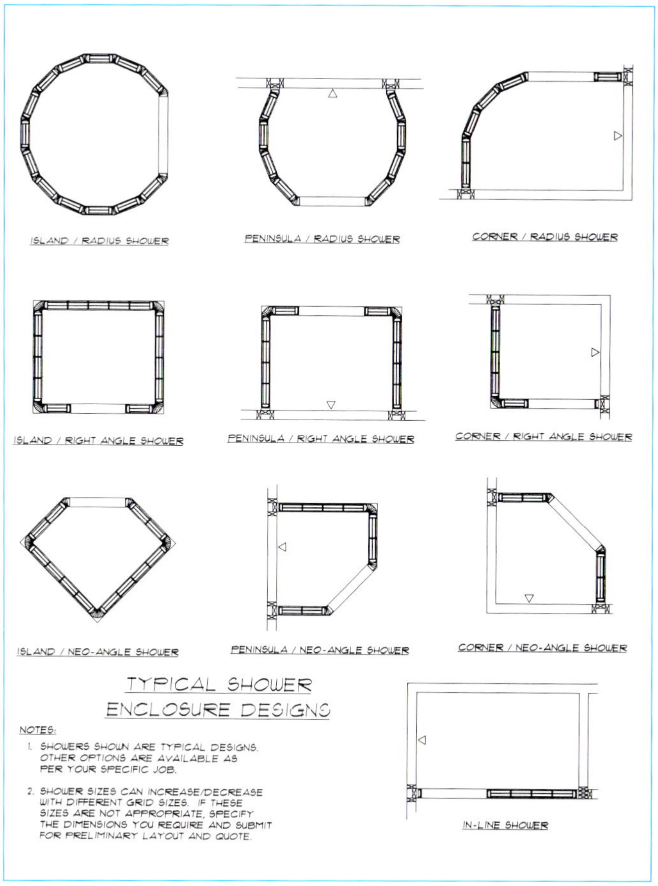

Fort Worth, TX; Custom Unique Homes

Austin, TX; Newmark Homes

FLOORS AND CEILINGS

IBP's engineered grid system assures easy installation of glass paver floors and ceilings. The lightweight structural aluminum grid, which is assembled on site, can span up to 7'6" without additional reinforcement. In the pedestrian bridge application pictured below, the floor also serves as a large skylight. Durability and beauty make IBP grids and glass pavers a logical choice for floors and ceilings.

The IBP grid system for floors was developed to provide an alternative method for installing glass paver units. This system eliminates the problems associated with conventional glass paver installations. Before the IBP system was available, glass paver units were set in grout within heavy and cumbersome prefabricated floor panels. The inflexibility of the typical concrete paver system can result in cracked or broken pavers. To prevent this problem, the IBP aluminum grid system utilizes a neoprene boot which encases the sides and bottom edges of each glass paver unit. The boot creates a cushion between the glass and the aluminum. A silicone sealant is applied to a narrow channel around each paver unit. The completed IBP floor system is beautiful and cost effective. Additionally, the IBP system circumvents the limitations of prefabricated concrete floor panels.

J. Wise Smith Associates, Inc.

Wm. Graves, Inc. Architects

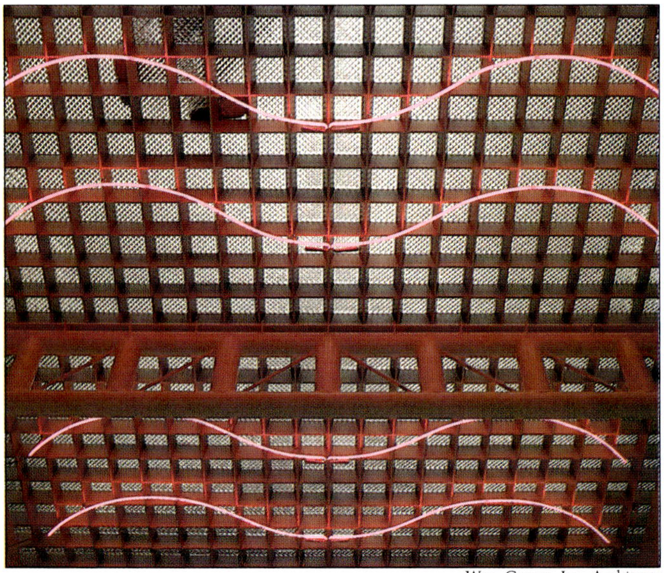

Wm. Graves, Inc. Architects

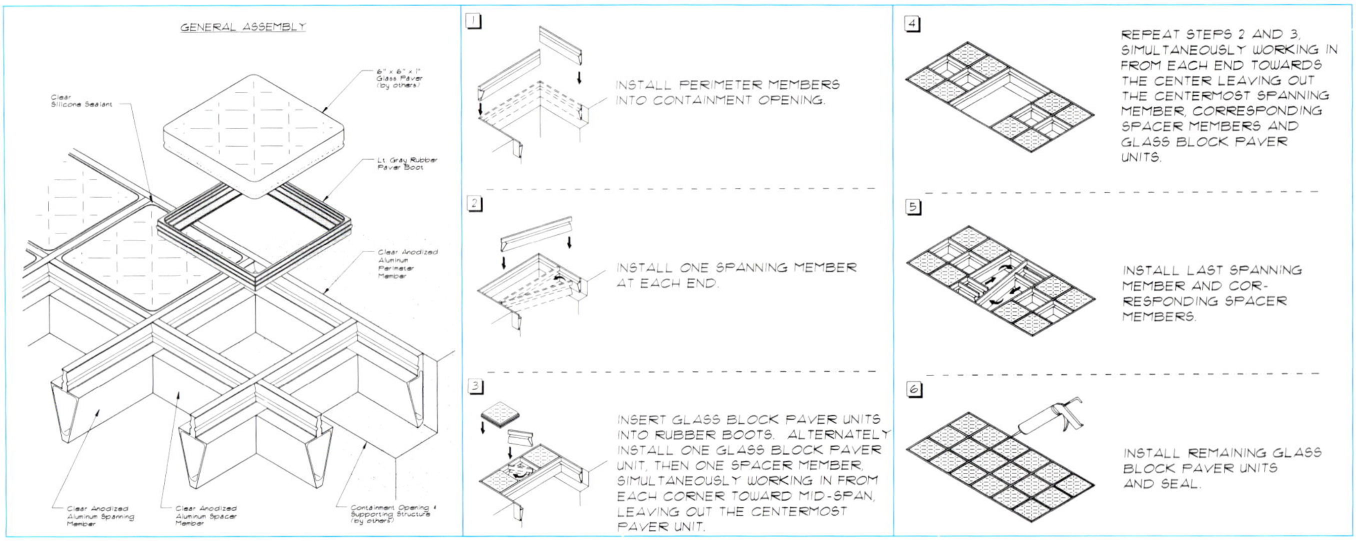

PHOTO GALLERY

Spokane, Washington; Law/Kingdon, Inc., Architects

Seattle, Washington; Seattle Glass Block

Baton Rouge, LA; Roy Hendrick, Architect

Dallas, TX

Richmond American Homes

San Antonio, TX; Rita Heck, Designer

GUIDE SPECIFICATION: IBP WINDOWS AND WALLS

PART 1 - GENERAL

1.1. SCOPE

1.1.1. Furnish and install all window perimeter frame pieces, T-Bar grid members, glazing materials, expansion-contraction thermal foam tape, sealants, framing, flashings, and other items necessary for complete window installation as indicated on the Drawings and specified herein.

1.1.2. Related work specified elsewhere: 1.1.2.1. Glass and Glazing 1.1.2.2. Sealants 1.1.2.3. Flashings

1.2. Guarantee

1.2.1. Window manufacturer shall guarantee for a period of one year from the date of purchase that the windows will be free of defects in materials and factory workmanship, and that defective materials will be repaired or replaced immediately, after proper notification.

1.2.2. The installing contractor shall guarantee for a period of one year against faulty installation workmanship or water leakage due to on-site errors.

1.3. Submittals

1.3.1. Submit assembly instructions and installation drawings as required to indicate methods on construction, location and spacing of anchorage, joinery, finishes, sizes, shape, thickness and alloy materials, glazing materials, and relationship to the adjoining work.

1.4. Material Storage and Handling

1.4.1. Store material in dry place, off the ground, where temperature will not exceed 90 degrees Fahrenheit.

1.4.2. Handle material to prevent damage to finished surfaces. Do not install scratched or damaged components.

1.4.3. After installation, protect finished surfaces from damage caused by ensuing work.

PART 2 - PRODUCTS

2.1. Materials

2.1.1. IBP Glass Block Grid System: Extruded aluminum Glass Block Grid System for Windows as manufactured by Innovative Building Products, Inc., 2917 W. 7th Street, Fort Worth, TX 76107.

2.1.2. Expansion-Contraction Thermal Foam tape: Adhesive backed, closed cell foam, 1/16" or 3/32" thick, furnished.

2.1.3. Sealant: TradeMate Glass Block Sealant, furnished.

2.1.4. Finish: Selected from manufacturer's standard finishes and colors.

2.1.5. Glass block units: 7 3/4" x 7 3/4" x 3 1/8" thick, partially evacuated hollow units, made of clear or colored glass as manufactured by Pittsburgh Corning, Solaris, or Weck.

PART 3 - EXECUTION

3.1. Field Conditions

3.1.1. Verify all applicable field dimensions and adjust as necessary to accommodate window frame.

3.1.2. Examine supporting frame to which window will be attached. Correct any conditions which are not constructed according to installation instructions furnished by window manufacturer.

3.2. Installation

3.2.1. Assemble and seal glass block grid system for window according to instructions furnished by manufacturer.

3.2.2. Apply continuous sealant bead to back of window Z-bar. Place assembled glass block grid system frame into properly prepared and sized rough opening and adjust until plumb and level. Screw or nail grid system in place utilizing all predrilled holes in nailing flange.

3.2.3. Adhere foam tape gasket to each glass block according to instructions furnished by glass block grid system manufacturer. Carefully insert glass blocks into grid system from exterior side of window so that each block is pressed against T-Bar and foam tape does not roll back.

3.2.4. Apply sealant to completely fill channel around each glass block and wipe flush with surface. Apply sealant to exterior frame corners according to instructions furnished by grid system manufacturer.

3.3. Cleanup

3.3.1. Clean all exposed surfaces of aluminum glass block grid system with clean, soft cloth and mild hand soap using gentle rubbing action. Do not use abrasive or solvent-type cleaners, detergents or paint removers.

3.3.2. Remove all labels from glass block and clean with soft cloth and water.

GUIDE SPECIFICATION: IBP GRID SYSTEM FOR SKYLIGHTS

PART 1 - GENERAL

1.1. SCOPE

1.1.1. Furnish and install all skylight perimeter frame pieces, T-Bar grid members, glazing materials, expansion-contraction thermal foam tape, sealants, curbs, flashings, and other items necessary for complete skylight installation as indicated on the Drawings and specified herein.

1.1.2. Related work specified elsewhere: 1.1.2.1. Glass and Glazing 1.1.2.2. Sealants 1.1.2.3. Flashings

1.2. Guarantee

1.2.1. Skylight manufacturer shall guarantee for a period of one year from the date of purchase that the skylights will be free of defects in materials and factory workmanship, and that defective materials will be repaired or replaced immediately, after proper notification.

1.2.2. The installing contractor shall guarantee for a period of three years against faulty installation workmanship or water leakage due to on-site errors.

1.3. Submittals

1.3.1. Submit assembly instructions and installation drawings as required to indicate methods on construction, location and spacing of anchorage, joinery, finishes, sizes, shape, thickness and alloy materials, glazing materials, and relationship to the adjoining work.

1.4. Material Storage and Handling

1.4.1. Store material in dry place, off the ground, where temperature will not exceed 90 degrees Fahrenheit.

1.4.2. Handle material to prevent damage to finished surfaces. Do not install scratched or damaged components.

1.4.3. After installation, protect finished surfaces from damage caused by ensuing work.

PART 2 - PRODUCTS

2.1. Materials

2.1.1. IBP Glass Block Grid System: Extruded aluminum Glass Block Grid System for Skylights as manufactured by Innovative Building Products, Inc., 2917 W. 7th Street, Fort Worth, TX 76107.

2.1.2. Expansion-contraction thermal foam tape: Adhesive backed, closed cell foam, 1/16" or 3/32" thick, furnished.

2.1.3. Sealant: TradeMate Glass Block Sealant, furnished.

2.1.4. Fasteners: Tamper-proof cadmium plated steel for attaching skylight perimeter frame to curb.

2.1.5. Finish: Selected from manufacturer's standard finishes and colors.

2.1.6. Glass block units: 7 3/4" x 7 3/4" x 3 1/8" thick, partially evacuated hollow units, made of clear or colored glass as manufactured by Pittsburgh Corning, Solaris, or Weck.

PART 3 - EXECUTION

3.1. Field Conditions

3.1.1. Verify all applicable field dimensions and adjust as necessary to accommodate skylight frame.

3.1.2. Examine supporting curb and structural support to which skylight frame will be attached. Correct any conditions which are not constructed according to installation instructions furnished by skylight manufacturer.

3.2. Installation

3.2.1. Assemble and seal glass block grid system for skylight according to instructions furnished by manufacturer.

3.2.2. Apply continuous sealant bead around top of skylight supporting curb. Place assembled glass block grid system frame on curb and press down to seat properly and overlap flashings. Attach frame to curb with specified fasteners and tighten.

3.2.3. Adhere foam tape gasket to each glass block according to instructions furnished by glass block grid system manufacturer. Carefully insert glass blocks into grid system from exterior side of skylight so that each block is pressed against T-Bar and foam tape does not roll back.

3.2.4. Apply sealant to completely fill channel around each glass block and wipe flush with surface. Apply sealant to frame caps according to instructions furnished by grid system manufacturer.

3.3. Cleanup

3.3.1. Clean all exposed surfaces of aluminum glass block grid system with clean, soft cloth and mild hand soap using gentle rubbing action. Do not use abrasive or solvent-type cleaners, detergents, or paint removers.

3.3.2. Remove all labels from glass block and clean with soft cloth and water.

GUIDE SPECIFICATION: IBP GRID SYSTEM FOR FLOORS

PART 1 - GENERAL

1.1. SCOPE

1.1.1. Furnish all floor system perimeter pieces, spanning members, spacer members, paver boots, paver units, sealants, all other materials and labor necessary for complete floor system installation as indicated on the Drawings and specified herein.

1.1.2. Related work specified elsewhere: 1.1.2.1. Glass and Glazing 1.1.2.2. Sealants 1.1.2.3. Containment Opening

1.2. Guarantee

1.2.1. Floor system manufacturer shall guarantee for a period of five years from the date of purchase that the floor system will be free of defects in materials and factory workmanship, and that defective materials will be repaired or replaced immediately, after proper notification.

1.2.2. The installing contractor shall guarantee for a period of five years against faulty installation workmanship due to on-site errors.

1.3. Submittals

1.3.1. Submit assembly instructions and shop drawings as required to indicate methods of construction, location and spacing of anchorage, joinery, finishes, sizes, shape, thickness and alloy materials, paver units, and relationship to the adjoining work.

1.4. Material Storage and Handling

1.4.1. Store material in dry place, off the ground, where temperature will not exceed 90 degrees Fahrenheit.

1.4.2. Handle material to prevent damage to finished surfaces. Do not install scratched or damaged components.

1.4.3. After installation, protect finished surfaces from damage caused by ensuing work.

PART 2 - PRODUCTS

2.1. Materials

2.1.1. IBP Glass Block Grid System for Floors: Extruded aluminum Glass Block Grid System for Floors as manufactured by Innovative Building Products, Inc., 2917 W. 7th Street, Fort Worth, TX 76107.

2.1.2. Paver Unit Boots: EPDM Ethylene Propylene Diene Terpolymer, a man-made, UV and oil resistant compound furnished with IBP Glass Block Grid System.

2.1.3. Sealant: TradeMate Glass Block Sealant, furnished with IBP Glass Block Grid System.

2.1.4. Finish: Clear anodized matte finish.

2.1.5. Glass block paver units: Nominal 6" x 6" x 1" thick, solid glass paver units, in color and pattern as selected.

PART 3 - EXECUTION

3.1. Field Conditions

3.1.1. Verify all applicable field dimensions and adjust as necessary to accommodate floor system.

3.1.2. Examine supporting structure and containment opening to which floor system will be installed. Correct any conditions which are not constructed according to installation instructions and approved shop drawings furnished by floor system manufacturer.

3.2. Installation

3.2.1. Insert each paver unit into paver boot.

3.2.2. Assemble glass block grid floor system according to instructions furnished by manufacturer into prepared containment opening. Top surface of glass pavers shall finish flush with adjoining surface and exposed aluminum surface joints unless shown otherwise on the drawings.

3.2.3. Apply sealant to completely fill channel around each glass block paver unit and joints between aluminum grid members and wipe flush with top surface. Perform all sealant work in accord with the requirements of the Sealant Section of the specifications.

3.3. Cleanup

3.3.1. Clean all exposed surfaces of aluminum glass block grid system with clean, soft cloth and mild hand soap using gentle rubbing action. Do not use abrasive or solvent-type cleaners, detergents, or paint removers.

3.3.2. Remove all labels from glass block and clean with soft cloth and water.

www.ibpglassblock.com

IBP-SWT-A1-11/97

C180
09300/INT
BuyLine 4860

COMMERCIAL

floor & wall tile

Interceramic® USA

THE BEST THE WORLD HAS TO OFFER.

IC BRITES & IC MATTES

- Deep, rich, high-gloss finish on brites
- Non-reflective, satin-like finish on mattes
- Single tone
- Coordinates with most name brand fixtures
- Coordinating trim
- Spacer lugs
- Beveled edge

SIZES: 4 1/4 x 4 1/4 & 6 x 6
Thickness: 7.5 mm

RECOMMENDED APPLICATION:

	COMMERCIAL	RESIDENTIAL
FLOORS		• bathroom (IC Mattes)
WALLS	•	•
COUNTERS	•	•

Meets All Recommended Specifications for ANSI - A 137.1

PEARL BRITES / PEARL MATTES

- Undulated, slate-like surface
- Rich, high-gloss finish on brites
- Non-reflective, pearl-like finish on mattes
- Single tone
- Coordinating trim
- Spacer lugs
- Beveled edge

SIZES: 4 1/4 x 4 1/4 & 6 x 6
Thickness: 7.5 mm

RECOMMENDED APPLICATION:

	COMMERCIAL	RESIDENTIAL
FLOORS		• bathroom (P Mattes)
WALLS	•	•
COUNTERS	•	•

Meets All Recommended Specifications for ANSI - A 137.1

BOLD TONES

- Deep, rich, high-gloss, smooth finish
- Single tone
- Coordinating trim
- Spacer lugs
- Beveled edge

SIZES: 4 1/4 x 4 1/4 (6 x 6 by special order)
Thickness: 7.5 mm

RECOMMENDED APPLICATION:

	COMMERCIAL	RESIDENTIAL
FLOORS WALLS COUNTERS	•	•

Meets All Recommended Specifications for ANSI - A 137.1

IC BRITES / MATTES

• IC Ultra White • IC White • IC Bone

• IC Almond • Smoke Harbor

Mint Blossom Sunrise

• Available in IC Brites & IC Mattes. All others are IC Brites.

(High-gloss finishes may show scratches)

PEARLS

IC Ultra White IC White IC Bone

BOLD TONES

Absolute Black Teal Antique Red

Pure Cobalt Classic Navy Colonial Blue

Evergreen Yellow Jacket Dusty Rose

IC CRYSTALS

IC Ultra White | IC White | IC Bone | IC Almond | Smoke

EGYPTIAN SLATE

Cairo | Pyramid | Sphinx

Oasis | Pharaoh

ASTRATTO

Blanco | Negro | Gris

CLASS

Blanco | Azul | Amarillo

IC CRYSTALS

- Finely textured crystalline surface
- Single tone
- Coordinates with most name brand fixture colors
- Coordinating trim
- Spacer lugs
- Beveled edge

SIZES: 4 1/4 x 4 1/4
Thickness: 7.5 mm

RECOMMENDED APPLICATION:

	COMMERCIAL	RESIDENTIAL
FLOORS		• (bathrooms)
WALLS	•	•
COUNTERS	•	•

Meets All Recommended Specifications for ANSI - A 137.1

EGYPTIAN SLATE

- Sculptured stone surface, matte finish
- Coordinates with Interceramic floor tile
- Coordinating trim
- Spacer lugs
- Beveled edge

SIZES: 4 1/4 x 4 1/4 & 6 x 6
Thickness: 7.5 mm

RECOMMENDED APPLICATION:

	COMMERCIAL	RESIDENTIAL
FLOORS		• (bathrooms)
WALLS	•	•
COUNTERS	•	•

Meets All Recommended Specifications for ANSI - A 137.1

ASTRATTO / CLASS

- Deep, rich, high-gloss smooth finish on Astratto
- High-gloss, undulated surface on Class
- Single tone
- Coordinating decorative listels
- Coordinating trim
- Easy to clean

SIZES: 8 x 8 (8 x 12 Class Blanco only)

RECOMMENDED APPLICATION:

	COMMERCIAL	RESIDENTIAL
FLOORS		
WALLS	•	•
COUNTERS		

SHADE & TEXTURE SPECTRUM

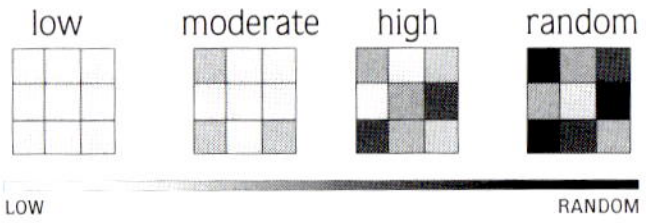

Low STS - Least amount of shade and texture variation attainable in naturally fired clay products.

Moderate STS - Moderate shade and texture variation within each carton.

High STS - High shade and texture variation within each carton.

Random STS - Very high shade and texture variation within each carton.

MAXIMA / ACCENTS

GROUP V, (IV Accents)

Moderate

- Skid inhibiting surface
- Decorative inserts available
- Coordinating trim
- Maxima 20 year wear warranty
- Impact & acid resistant
- Frost resistant

SIZES: 8 x 8, 12 x 12

• Design Folder and Technical Sheet Available.

Group V (Accents Group IV)
Heavy plus traffic: All residential and all commercial where extra heavy duty wearability is required.

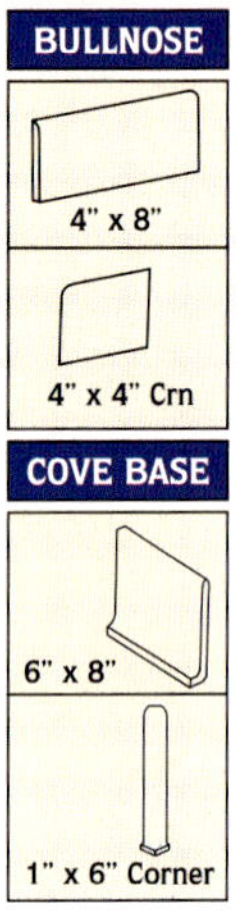

METALLIC

GROUP IV

Moderate

- Cut granite finish, 10 solid colors
- Skid inhibiting surface
- Coordinating trim
- Impact & acid resistant
- Frost resistant

SIZES: 8 x 8, 12 x 12

• Design Folder and Technical Sheet Available.

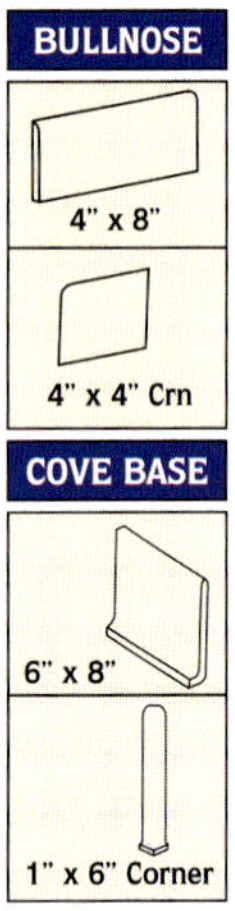

ELEMENT / ROCA II

GROUP IV

Moderate

- Granite-like finish
- Skid inhibiting surface
- Coordinating trim
- Impact & acid resistant
- Frost resistant

SIZES: 12 x 12

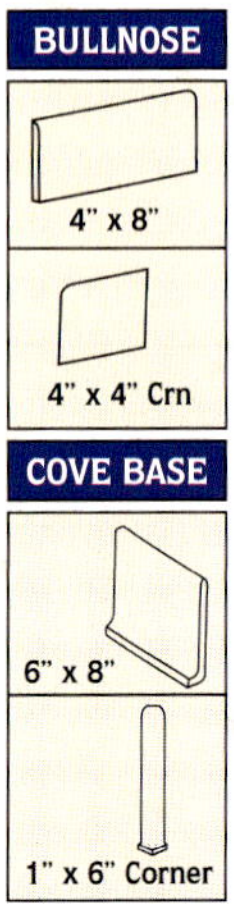

RECOMMENDED APPLICATION:
GROUP IV PRODUCTS

Heavy traffic: All residential and most commercial applications. Shopping malls & most public areas.

MAXIMA / ACCENTS

Cobalt Center/Insert — Plata Border/Corner — Niquel Border/Runner — Topaz Corner/Accent

Jade Accent — Zafiro Accent — Terra Accent — Diamante Accent — Obsidiana Accent

METALLIC

Aluminum — Lead — Steel — Zinc — Alloy

Copper — Brass — Ore — Pewter — Iron

ELEMENT

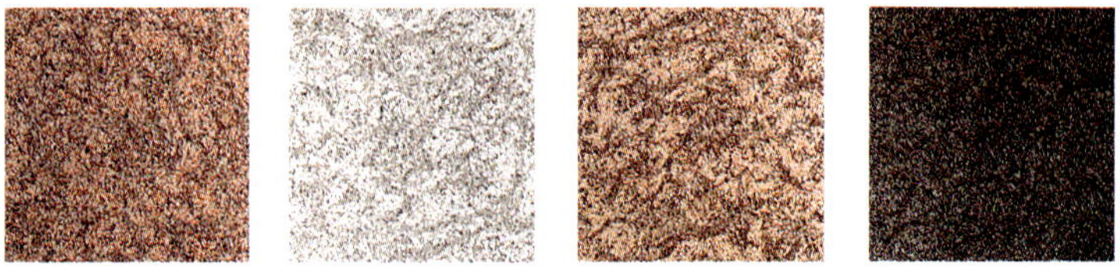

Fiero — Aqua — Tierra — Viento

ROCA II

Granate II — Zirconio II — Amatista II

FLAGSTONE

Empress Green | Serengeti | Blue Ridge

Corinthian | Angel Fire | Rajah

DAKOTA

Bismarck | Prairie | Bison | Custer | Tioga

ALASKA

Timberline | Kodiak | Tundra | Gold Rush | Yukon

CONQUEST

Trojan Gray | Titan Green | Samurai Beige | Spartan White | Viking Blue

MEDITERRANEAN

Marsala | Valencia | Crete | Palermo

FLAGSTONE

BULLNOSE

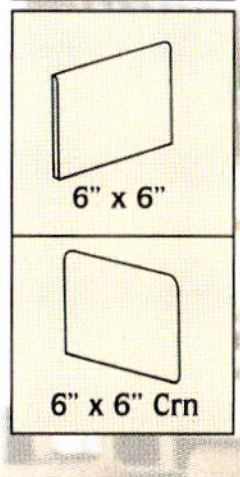

GROUP IV

Random

- Natural slate-like surface
- Skid inhibiting
- Coordinating 6 x 6 bullnose trim
- Impact & acid resistant
- Frost resistant

SIZES: 6 x 6, 6 x 12, 12 x 12

• Design Folder and Technical Sheet Available.

DAKOTA

BULLNOSE

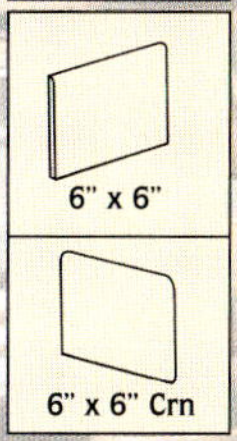

GROUP IV

Moderate

- Rustic stone surface
- Skid inhibiting
- Coordinating 6 x 6 bullnose trim
- Impact & acid resistant
- Frost resistant

SIZES: 6 x 6, 12 x 12, 18 x 18

• Design Folder and Technical Sheet Available.

ALASKA

BULLNOSE

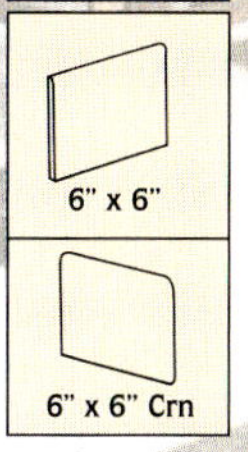

GROUP IV

High

- Light grain, stone surface
- Skid inhibiting
- Coordinating 6 x 6 bullnose trim
- Impact & acid resistant
- Frost resistant

SIZES: 6 x 6, 6 x 12, 12 x 12

• Design Folder and Technical Sheet Available.

CONQUEST

BULLNOSE

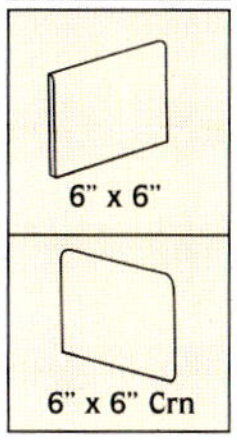

GROUP IV

High

- Natural weathered slate surface
- Skid inhibiting
- Coordinating 6 x 6 bullnose trim
- Impact & acid resistant
- Frost resistant

SIZES: 6 x 6, 6 x 12, 12 x 12

• Design Folder and Technical Sheet Available.

MEDITERRANEAN

BULLNOSE

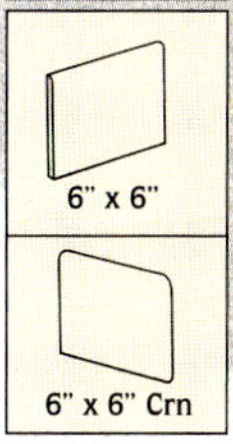

GROUP IV

High

- Old World look, worn stone surface
- Skid inhibiting
- Coordinating 6 x 6 bullnose trim
- Impact & acid resistant
- Frost resistant

SIZES: 6 x 6, 6 x 12, 12 x 12, 12 x 18, 18 x 18

• Design Folder and Technical Sheet Available.

RECOMMENDED APPLICATION:
GROUP IV PRODUCTS

Heavy traffic: All residential and most commercial applications. Shopping malls & most public areas.

MONTANA

GROUP IV

Moderate

- Light grain texture
- Skid inhibiting surface
- Eight solid colors
- Coordinating trim
- Impact & acid resistant
- Frost resistant

SIZES: 8 x 8, 12 x 12

• Design Folder and Technical Sheet Available.

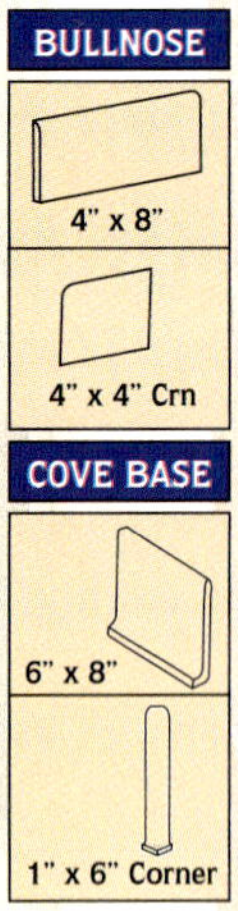

RECOMMENDED APPLICATION:
GROUP IV PRODUCTS

Heavy traffic: All residential and most commercial applications. Shopping malls & most public areas.

For more information on our complete line of floor and wall tile products, as well as our architectural design program,
call:
800 365-6733
or visit us at:
www.interceramicusa.com

MONTANA

FLOOR TILE TECHNICAL DATA

COEFFICIENT OF FRICTION (Avg. Results)

	Skid-inhibiting
Dry Leather	0.82
Dry Rubber	0.80
Dry Neolite	0.78
Wet Leather	0.63
Wet Rubber	0.67
Wet Neolite	0.72

Smooth surface tiles are not recommended for areas exposed to direct outside traffic. Skid-inhibiting surfaces are inherently more difficult to clean. Attention to this characteristic should be noted when product is specified.

Meets Recommended Guidelines for Americans With Disabilities Act for Horizontal Surfaces.

ADA

TECHNICAL DATA+	Interceramic Tile	ANSI/ASTM Tests
Water Absorption	3% or less	ASTM C-373
Abrasive Hardness Index Number	170 Avg.	ASTM C-501
Breaking Strength	390 lbs. Avg.	ASTM C-648
Thermal Shock	Resistant	ASTM C-484
Scratch Hardness of Glaze	5.0-9.0	MOHS Scale
Frost Resistance	Resistant	Hobert-Goodrich
Bonding Strength	Over 147 p.s.i.	ASTM C-482

+These test results vary by item. Detailed information may be obtained from Interceramic. 800-365-6733

MAINTENANCE
Interceramic tile is vitreous with a hard-glaze surface. Normal precautions should be observed during setting and grouting, and the grout manufacturer's instructions should be carefully followed. The characteristics of skid-inhibiting tile, while providing greater safety, will require more extensive cleaning procedures than the smooth finish tiles.

VARIATIONS IN SHADE OR COLOR
Variations in shade or color are inherent in all fired clay products and are one of the natural qualities which help create the beautiful effect characteristic of tile. Blending of tiles from at least six different boxes during installation is recommended to achieve best results. This is especially important when installing skid-inhibiting tiles, as shine can differ under certain lighting conditions.

SIZES
All sizes are sold on a nominal (approximate) basis. Size tolerance: plus or minus 1.5%. Exact measurements are available from Interceramic.

COLOR ILLUSTRATIONS AND SAMPLES
Color charts, color illustrations, and reproduction in catalogs and other publications of Interceramic are not represented to match the exact color or shade of the tile represented. Color illustrations of tile are offered at approximations only. All samples are submitted as representative of a type of tile, a color, a shade, or a kind of finish; and the tile furnished in a shipment may vary from such samples.

LIMITS OF LIABILITY
Tests are performed on random samples of Interceramic tile by an independent testing laboratory and are believed to be representative of the general quality of the tile. There is no guarantee by Interceramic that these exact results will be guaranteed on every tile. Interceramic extends no guarantees, expressed or implied, as to glaze slipperiness, wear-time periods, gloss or maintenance procedures. Test procedures and individual results are available from Interceramic.

ANSI A-137.1
Interceramic tile achieves the necessary values for the ANSI A 137.1-P188 (American National Standards Institute) requirement. This is the most complete testing done on ceramic tile and includes tests on thickness, facial dimension, warpage, wedging, water absorption, crazing, thermal shock, bonding strength and breaking strength.

ANSI A137.1 TESTING AS APPLIED TO INTERCERAMIC WALL TILE

Interceramic wall tile is available in a beautiful assortment of sizes, colors and textures to meet all of your design needs. From deep, rich, high-gloss bright glaze finishes, low-sheen matte finishes, durable crystalline glazes, to beautiful bold, designer colors, Interceramic wall tile is ideal for almost any interior application. Our tile features a non-vitreous dry clay body with pressed spacer lugs for joint space and alignment uniformity.

WARPAGE

ASTM C 485 The warpage of each tile shall not exceed 1 % along any edge or .75% on either diagonal.

Requirements: Minimum warpage edge 1%
Results: Interceramic warpage edge .23%
Requirements: Minimum warpage diagonal .75%
Results: Interceramic warpage edge .22%
INTERCERAMIC MEETS AND EXCEEDS ALL WARPAGE REQUIREMENTS.

THICKNESS

ASTM C 499 The range of average thickness of each tile shall not exceed .40 inches.

Requirements: Minimum thickness range .40 in.
Results: Interceramic thickness range .16 in.
INTERCERAMIC MEETS AND EXCEEDS ALL THICKNESS REQUIREMENTS.

THERMAL SHOCK RESISTANCE

ASTM C 484 The glaze shall show no failure and the body shall show no evidence of disintegration.

Requirements: No glaze failure
Results: Interceramic has no glaze failure
Requirements: No body disintegration
Results: Interceramic has no body disintegration
INTERCERAMIC MEETS AND EXCEEDS ALL THERMAL SHOCK REQUIREMENTS.

SCRATCH HARDNESS SURFACE (MOHS Scale)

MOHS Test. The highest hardness number with which no scratches are visible to the naked eye.

Requirements: None
Results: Interceramic scratch hardness on MOHS scale - 5
INTERCERAMIC MEETS AND EXCEEDS ALL INDUSTRY GUIDELINES.

BREAKING STRENGTH

ASTM C 648 The average breaking strength from wall tile shall be 90 lbs. or greater.

Requirements: Average breaking strength 90 lbs. or greater
Results: Interceramic breaking strength - 141 lbs.
INTERCERAMIC MEETS AND EXCEEDS ALL WALL TILE BREAKING STRENGTH REQUIREMENTS.

WEDGING

ASTM C 502 The percent wedging of each tile shall not exceed more than 1%.

Requirements: Minimum wedging 1%
Results: Interceramic wedging edge .75%
INTERCERAMIC MEETS AND EXCEEDS ALL WEDGING REQUIREMENTS.

FACIAL DIMENSION

ASTM C 499 The average facial dimensions of each tile shall not vary more than 3% from the nominal dimension. The ranges of average facial dimensions shall not exceed 1.5% of the largest value in range.

Requirements: Minimum facial dimensions variation from nominal dimensions 3%
Results: Interceramic facial dimensions variation from nominal dimension .98%.
Requirements: Minimum facial dimension range requirements 1.5%
Results: Interceramic facial dimensions range requirements .38%.
INTERCERAMIC MEETS AND EXCEEDS ALL FACIAL DIMENSION REQUIREMENTS.

BOND STRENGTH

ASTM C 482 The average bond strength shall be 50 PSI or greater.

Requirements: Average bond strength is 50 PSI or greater
Results: Interceramic average bond strength is 110 PSI
INTERCERAMIC MEETS AND EXCEEDS ALL BOND STRENGTH REQUIREMENTS.

CRAZING RESISTANCE

ASTM C 424 The tile should show no evidence of crazing.

Requirements: No Crazing
Results: Interceramic showed no evidence of crazing
INTERCERAMIC MEETS AND EXCEEDS ALL CRAZING RESISTANCE REQUIREMENTS.

WATER ABSORPTION

ASTM C 373 The bisque wall tile should not attain 20% water absorption.

Requirements: Water absorption less than 20%
Results: Interceramic water absorption is 17.7%
INTERCERAMIC MEETS AND EXCEEDS ALL WATER ABSORPTION REQUIREMENTS.

PACKAGING INFORMATION

- Sq. Ft. per Carton: 4 1/4 - 10 Sq. Ft.
  6 x 6 - 10 Sq. Ft.
- Pcs. per Carton: 4 1/4 - 80 Pcs.
  6 x 6 - 40 Pcs.
- Weight per Carton: 4 1/4 - 27 lbs.
  6 x 6 - 27 lbs.

PRODUCT FEATURES:

- Size Available: 4 1/4 x 4 1/4 and 6 x 6
- Coordinates with Interceramic Floor Tile
- Single Tone and Single Size
- Coordinating Trim Package Available
- Coordinates with Name Brand Fixture Colors
- Easy to Clean and Maintain
- Spacer Lugs for Easy Installation
- Manufactured in USA

INTERCERAMIC TILE MEETS ALL RECOMMENDED AMERICAN NATIONAL STANDARD SPECIFICATIONS FOR CERAMIC TILE.

ARCHITECTURAL SPECIFICATION - SECTION 09300

PART I-GENERAL

A. Related Work Specified Elsewhere

1. Lathing and cement scratch coat — Section____________
2. Waterproof membranes or wallboard — Section____________
3. Handrails in bathroom areas — Section____________
4. This section should include all work required before the installation of the tile.

B. Description of Work

1. This is to include all work and materials required to furnish and install ceramic tile as indicated on the drawings.

C. Quality Assurance

1. Provide Interceramic samples as well as samples of the grout and thinset as approved by the architect.
2. Use quality and skilled tile installers who are thoroughly trained and experienced in the installation methods being specified.
3. Work shall be executed and tested in accordance with current editions of the following standards:
   (a) ANSI A108.1 - Installation of Ceramic Tile with Portland Cement
   (b) ANSI A108.4 - Installation of Ceramic Tile with Water Resistant Organic Adhesives
   (c) ANSI A108.5 - Installation of Ceramic Tile with Dry Set Portland Cement Mortar
   (d) ANSI A108.6 - Installation of Ceramic Tile with Chemical Resistant
   (e) Consult the Tile Council of America's Handbook for Ceramic Tile Installation for other types of specifications.

D. Submittals

1. The manufacturer shall assure that all the tile being used is in compliance with ANSI A 137.1-1988.
2. If applicable, a Master Grade certificate may be required with both the signature of the manufacturer and the tile contractor.
3. Submit a 12" square sample of each color, pattern and type of tile being specified.

E. Product Handling

1. The cartons should be delivered to the job site unopened and undamaged with all labels intact.
2. Keep tile cartons dry.
3. An additional 2% of each tile used should be ordered for the owner's emergency use.

F. Environmental Project Conditions

1. Maintain environmental conditions during and after the installation in accordance with reference standards and accordance with manufacturer's printed recommendations.

PART II - PRODUCTS

A. Tile

1. The tile shall be manufactured by Interceramic, Inc. in accordance with the published specification of ANSI A 137.1-1988.
2. The tile shall be:
   (a) Wall tile Series ____________ Color ____________ Size ____________
   (b) Floor tile Series ____________ Color ____________ Size ______________
3. Provide the pattern to be used for the installation
4. Provide the trims of the same or coordinating colors, size and finish of the adjacent flat tile. Check the Interceramic product catalogs for a description of the trims available.

B. Setting Materials

1. Consult the Tile Council of America's Handbook for Ceramic Tile Installation or the Ceramic Tile Institute for the specifications to properly install ceramic tile. Consult the manufacturer of premixed setting materials for correct installation procedures.
   (a) Portland cement mortar
   (b) Metal lathe
   (c) Membrane
   (d) Dry set mortar
   (e) Latex mortar
   (f) Epoxy mortar

C. Grouting Materials

1. The grout chosen should conform to the Group Specification Guide published on Page 9 of the Tile Council of America's Handbook for Ceramic Tile Installation. Refer to the grout manufacturer for more specific information regarding the grout and method chosen for the installation.
   (a) Commercial cement grout
   (b) Dry set grout
   (c) Sand-Portland cement grout
   (d) Latex Portland cement grout
   (e) Epoxy grout

D. Sealants

1. Use sealants in control joints, tub and showers, etc... that meet FSTT-S-001543 Class A or B (COM-NBS).

E. Thresholds and Edge Strips

1. Provide thresholds or edge strips to provide for a proper transition between the tile and other adjacent surfaces.

PART III - INSTALLATION

A. Acceptability of Surface

1. Before installation of ceramic tile, the substrate surface cannot show variations in excess of:

	Floor	Wall
Dry set mortar	1/8" in 10'	1/8" in 8'
Latex Portland cement mortar	1/8" in 10'	1/8" in 8'
Epoxy	1/8" in 10'	1/8" in 8'
Organic Adhesives	1/16" in 3'	1/8" in 8'

2. The substrate surface must be free of all loose dirt, oil, grease, wax, dust, or curing compounds. If the substrate contains these materials, sand blast, grind or sand to remove the materials and scarify the surface.

B. Layout

1. Locate all movement or expansion joints prior to determining the layout of the tile.
2. Layout all tile work so as to minimize cuts less than one-half tile in size.
3. Layout all tile work so that cuts in both walls and floors are to be least conspicuous.
4. Align all floor and wall joints to give straight and uniform grout lines.

C. Setting Materials

(Methods shown are only examples. Specify method that is required).

1. On Dimensionally Stable Concrete Subfloor: ANSI A108.1 (Reference TCA Method F112, Cement Mortar, Bonded)
2. On Non-Dimensionally Stable Concrete Subfloor: ANSI A108.1 (Reference TCA Method F111, Cement Mortar, Cleavage Membrane)
3. On Wood Subfloor: ANSI A108.1 (Reference TCA Method F141, Cement Mortar)
4. See TCA Handbook for Ceramic Tile Installation for other methods for installing ceramic tile.

D. Grouting

1. Follow grout manufacturer's recommendations as to grouting procedures and precautions.
2. Remove all grout haze, observing grout manufacturer's recommendations as to the use of various cleaners.
3. Thoroughly rinse all tile work before and after the use of cleaners and chemicals, if required.

E. Protection of Tile Surface

1. Finished installation should be free of all chipped, cracked, defective or unbonded tile.
2. Cover all tile floors with heavy duty construction or kraft paper masked in place to avoid stains or damage from construction traffic.
3. No foot and wheel traffic can use the floor for a minimum of 3 days, preferable 7 days.
4. Place large, flat sheets of wood in high traffic areas to protect newly tiled floor.

This specification is designed for your use as a helpful guide. You should modify it if job requirements deem it necessary.
If you require Interceramic samples for architectural color boards or client submittals, please contact your local Interceramic distributor or call 800-365-6733.

Printed in USA

C246
09640/BRU
Buy Line 4923

Factory Finished and Contract Unfinished Hardwood Floors

Photo by Michael Lowry, Southern Living Magazine
WearMaster® Maple EWM-3200 Maize color floor with EWM-3101 Mocha Glaze feature strip

Bruce®
hardwood floors
A division of Triangle Pacific Corp.

The Natural Choice®

SUPERIOR

WearMaster®

Universal Studios retail store — Orlando International Airport
WearMaster Oak EWM-3100 Golden Wheat

Introduction:

Bruce Hardwood Floors, a division of Triangle Pacific Corporation, is America's largest manufacturer of hardwood floors. Since 1884, architects, builders and consumers have trusted Bruce to provide the best quality and value in hardwood floors.

With manufacturing facilities in Center, Texas; Nashville and Jackson, Tennessee; West Plains, Missouri; Port Gibson, Mississippi; and Beverly, West Virginia, Bruce provides our national and international, independent distributor network with a complete line of hardwood flooring products.

Contents:

WearMaster® Acrylic Impregnated Hardwood Floors . . . . .2 - 5
Benchmark™ Collection —
Dura-Luster® Urethane Finish Floors . . . . .6 - 9
Benchmark™ Collection —
Dura-Satin® Wax Finish Floors . . . . .10 - 11
Kensington™ Collection —
Dura-Luster® Urethane Finish Floors .12 - 13
Kensington™ Collection —
Dura-Satin® Wax Finish Floors 14
Contract Unfinished Floors 15
Accessories/Installation Supplies 16

The photography featured in this catalog is provided as a visual guide to the product pattern, not as an actual representation of the floor color itself.

Acrylic Impregnated Hardwood Floors

WearMaster
Maple Hardwoods

EWM-3200 Maize

EWM-3202 Classic Cocoa

EWM-3209 Berry

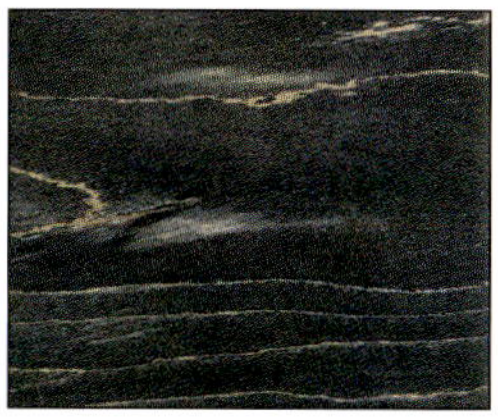

EWM-3210 Galaxy

EWM-3213 Canyon

WearMaster
Basswood

EWM-3411 Midnight

EWM-3412 Empire

Description:

WearMaster floors are designed, engineered and manufactured specifically for commercial applications. Every WearMaster performance feature represents state-of-the-art technology.

WearMaster floors are manufactured using a perfected acrylic impregnation process that makes them the toughest, most durable hardwood floors ever made. They are almost 50% harder than standard, unimpregnated hardwood floors.

WearMaster floors also feature a unique, pressurized ColorJet Infusion™ process that results in stain penetration through the entire surface layer.

WearMaster floors have a low gloss, urethane surface that assures easy-care and superior stain resistance.

WearMaster floors are backed by the most comprehensive warranty in the hardwood flooring industry...your assurance of lasting beauty and durability in any commercial or residential application.

Technical Information:

WearMaster floors are factory-finished, 3-ply engineered plank floors. The planks are 3/8" thick (10 mm), 3" wide (76 mm) and are random in length ranging from 12" to 60" (305 - 1527 mm). WearMaster has tongue-and-groove construction, square end and side surface edges, and a smooth low gloss, commercial finish. WearMaster also carries a Class C Flame Spread rating, and exceeds the American's With Disabilities Act Recommendations for slip resistance. The impregnated wood surface and color layer is available in four hardwood species (oak, maple, hickory, and basswood).

Testing Standards:

ASTM D 2394-83, Sections 18-22 - Test Method for Indentation Resistance Using a Falling Ball. Indent depth (inches) Oak: 0.012 Maple: 0.011 Hickory: 0.0095 Basswood: 0.005

ASTM D 2394-83, Sections 33-37 - Test Method for Static Slip Resistance. Oak: 0.70 Maple: 0.072 Hickory: 0.069 Basswood: 0.66 Exceeds American's With Disabilities Acts Recommendations

ASTM D 4060-95 - Test Method for Abrasion Resistance of Organic Coatings by the Taber Abrader. Abrasion depth (inches) Oak: 0.011 Maple: 0.013 Hickory: 0.010 Basswood: 0.048

ASTM E 648-94a - Test Method for Critical Radiant Flux of Floor-Covering Systems Using a Radiant Heat Energy Source. Oak: 0.52 Maple: 0.50 Hickory: 0.52 Basswood: 0.80

ASTM E 84-95 - Test Method for Surface Burning Characteristics of Building Materials. Oak: Class C Maple: Class C Hickory: Class C Basswood: Class C

Product Usage:

WearMaster acrylic impregnated hardwood floors are designed for use in heavy and light commercial applications as well as residential use. WearMaster floors can be installed on, above, or below grade. They carry a Class C Flame Spread Rating and exceed the Americans With Disabilities Act Recommendations for slip resistance.

Note: WearMaster floors are not recommended for use in areas with high humidity, excessive moisture, or on concrete with compressive strength of less than 2000 psi.

WearMaster®

"Store of the Future," featuring WearMaster, designed by Chute Gerdeman, Columbus, OH

Installation:

WearMaster floors can be installed on, above or below grade level, and over most existing SOUND, DRY AND LEVEL SUBFLOORS including; solid wood, exterior rated 5/8" (15.88mm) plywood or greater; underlayment grade particle board, wafer or chip board, and OSB; concrete - minimum 90 lb. density reinforced; resilient and sheet vinyl, VCT, terrazzo, or ceramic tile.

WearMaster can be installed over all radiantly heated concrete floors providing the concrete meets the requirements listed above.

- Bruce does not recommend installation over lightweight or acoustical concrete subfloors.
- All subfloors should be sound, clean, thoroughly dry, smooth, and level/flat within 3/16" (4.763mm) in a 10' (3m) span.
- For a copy of WearMaster installation instructions, call toll free 1-800-722-4647.
- Bruce Adhesive is required for warranted installations. Trowel shall be pyramid notched 1/4" X 1/2" X 3/16" (6.350 X 12.70 X 4.763 mm) as required by Bruce Hardwood Floors.

WearMaster

Oak Hardwood

EWM-3100 Golden Wheat

EWM-3101 Mocha Glaze

Acrylic Impregnated Hardwood Floors

WearMaster

Hickory Hardwoods

EWM-3301 Sierra Brown

EWM-3302 Cordovan Brown

EWM-3304 Rustic Wood

EWM-3305 Violet Mist

EWM-3308 Cayenne

WearMaster Oak EWM-3101 Mocha Glaze

Maintenance: WearMaster Acrylic Impregnated Products

WearMaster floors provide unprecedented ease of maintenance. The acrylic impregnated surface layer features a tough, low gloss, commercial urethane finish that practically takes care of itself. It resists damage from most spills and stains. With prompt attention, most spills and stains wipe perfectly clean.

WearMaster floors require no special cleaning equipment or procedures. Routine maintenance is simply vacuuming to remove dirt and grit...and occasional light cleaning with Dura-Luster® Commercial Cleaner Concentrate.

Availability:

Bruce Hardwood Floors are sold through an international distribution network including; the United States, Canada, Mexico, Europe and Japan. For further information, please call the Sweet's BuyLine at 1-800-892-1165 or Bruce Hardwood Floors at 1-800-722-4647.

Warranty:

Bruce WearMaster products carry a Full Lifetime Warranty on Structural Integrity, Adhesive Bond and Subfloor Moisture Protection. Bruce includes a 25 Year Warranty on the acrylic impregnated wood layer in that it will not wear through or separate from its multi-ply, laminated construction. For complete details of Bruce product warranties, call toll-free 1-800-722-4647.

How to Specify WearMaster Acrylic Impregnated Floors:

A. Flooring shall be Bruce 3/8" X 3" (10 mm X 76 mm) WearMaster flooring (specify product item number) in the (specify wood species) grade of wood as manufactured by Bruce Hardwood Floors, a division of Triangle Pacific Corporation.

B. Flooring shall be manufactured in a 3-ply, engineered construction that utilizes the Bruce ColorJet Infusion™ process to create a minimum 1/12" thick, pressurized wood color layer in the color (specify color name and number).

C. Flooring shall feature a minimum 1/12" thick acrylic impregnated wear surface utilizing the patented Bruce WearMaster impregnation process. U.S. Patent Nos. 5,609,915 and 5,605,767.

D. Factory finished, engineered WearMaster flooring shall be sanded to a smooth surface and provide a stain resistant, ultra-violet cured, low gloss, commercial urethane surface.

E. Factory finished, acrylic impregnated wood flooring will have no less than a Class C Flame Spread Rating (ASTM Test E-84-95).

F. Installed product will meet the Fuel Contribution and Smoke Density standards established for a product with a Class C Flame Spread Rating by the American Society for Testing and Materials (ASTM Test E-84-95).

G. Product to be installed will pass the Critical Radiant Flux test with a minimum Class I rating (ASTM Test E-648-94a).

H. Installed flooring material will have a finish that exceeds the American's With Disabilities Act Recommendations of a minimum .692 coefficient of friction (slip resistance) rating (ASTM Test D-2394-83).

I. Installation of WearMaster floors shall be made in accordance with instructions provided in each carton.

J. Use Bruce Tribond™ Adhesive and a notched trowel for WearMaster glue-down installations as required by Bruce Hardwood Floors.

Benchmark™ Collection:

Meridian Stone® Custom Crafted Wood Tile —
H-4020 Sedona with H-316 Creme Diamond Accents

Description:

The Bruce Benchmark Collection features the widest assortment of colors, styles, and patterns in the hardwood flooring industry. Benchmark floors are manufactured from the finest, premium-grade hardwoods to assure an outstanding consistency of grain pattern and texture. Benchmark products are available in the Bruce Dura-Luster® urethane finish and the Dura-Satin® wax finish.

Dura-Luster urethane finish products are recommended for all phases of residential areas, including kitchens.

Dura-Satin wax finish products are recommended for light commercial and residential use, including high traffic areas.

Maintenance: Dura-Luster® Urethane Finish Products

For the Dura-Luster urethane finish, Bruce recommends good general maintenance practices that include sweeping or vacuuming to remove dirt and grit. For a more thorough cleaning, simply clean with Bruce Dura-Luster Cleaner. The Bruce Dura-Luster finish is a no-wax finish and does not require buffing. However, if buffing is desired after cleaning, use only a soft polishing attachment such as a lamb's wool pad.

Dura-Luster Urethane Finish

09640/BRU
Buy Line 4923

3/4" Solid Oak Strip and Planks

Sterling® Strip
Random lengths and a standard 2 1/4" width. Square edges and ends. Tongue and groove. Size: 3/4" X 2 1/4"

C-720 Natural	C-7220 Auburn
C-721 Gunstock	C-7222 Vintage Brown
C-722 Spice	C-7223 Glacial White
C-723 Winter White	

Sterling Encore Plank®
Random lengths and alternate widths. Square edges and ends. Tongue and groove. Size: 3/4" X 2 1/4" - 3 1/4"

B-740 Natural	B-741 Gunstock

Devon® Plank
Random lengths and alternate widths. Eased edges and square ends. Tongue and groove. Size: 3/4" X 2 1/4" - 3 1/4"

B-640 Natural	B-642 Spice
B-641 Gunstock	B-643 Winter White

Windward® Strip
Random lengths and a standard 2 1/4" width. Eased edges and square ends. Tongue and groove. Size: 3/4" X 2 1/4"

C-620 Natural	C-623 Winter White
C-621 Gunstock	C-6220 Auburn
C-622 Spice	C-6224 Driftwood

Sterling Prestige Plank®
Random lengths and a standard 3 1/4" width. Square edges and ends. Tongue and groove. Size: 3/4" X 3 1/4"

C-730 Natural	C-732 Spice
C-731 Gunstock	C-733 Winter White

American Maple COLLECTION

Kennedale™ Strip
Random lengths and a standard 2 1/4" width. Slightly eased edges and ends. Tongue and groove. Size: 3/4" X 2 1/4"

CM-700 Natural	CM-728 Cherry
CM-710 Country Natural	CM-733 Cinnamon

5/16" Solid Oak Strip

Natural Reflections™
Random lengths and a standard 2 1/4" width. Square edges and ends. Tongue and groove. Size: 5/16" X 2 1/4"

C-5010 Natural	C-5021 Quartz
C-5011 Gunstock	C-5028 Cherry
C-5012 Spice	C-5029 Mink Grey
C-5013 Ivory White	C-5030 Prairie
C-5014 Mellow	C-5031 Walnut
C-5016 Butterscotch	

3/8" Engineered Strip and Planks

Reunion® Flank
Random lengths and a standard 3" width. 5-ply engineered oak. Square edges and ends. Tongue and groove. Size: 3/8" X 3"

E-710 Toast	E-7120 Auburn
E-711 Gunstock	E-7122 Vintage Brown
E-712 Mellow	E-7123 Glacial White
E-713 Ivory White	

LeClaire® Plank
Random lengths and a standard 3" width. 3-ply engineered oak with eased edges and ends. Tongue and groove.

E-820 Toast	E-823 Ivory White
E-821 Gunstock	E-824 Spice

Charlemont® Plank
Random lengths and widths. 3-ply engineered oak with eased edges and ends. Tongue and groove. Size: 3/8" X 3" - 5" - 7"

E-840 Toast	E-841 Gunstock

Caruth® Plank
Random lengths and a standard 3" width. 5-ply engineered maple with square edges and ends. Tongue and groove. Size: 3/8" X 3"

E-910 Toast	E-913 Creme
E-911 Caramel	E-920 Sedona

Antell® Plank
Random lengths and alternate widths. 3-ply engineered oak with eased edges and ends. Tongue and groove. Size: 3/8" X 3" - 5"

E-830 Toast	E-831 Gunstock

Hancock™ Plank
Factory installed pegs. Random lengths and widths. 3-ply engineered oak with eased edges and ends. Tongue and groove. Size: 3/8" X 3" - 5" - 7"

E-851 Gunstock	E-854 Spice

Stafford® Strip
Random lengths and a standard 2 1/4" width. 3-ply engineered oak with square edges and ends. Tongue and groove. Size: 3/8" X 2 1/4"

E-410 Toast	E-416 Butterscotch
E-410U Unfinished	E-417 Saddle
E-411 Gunstock	E-420 Auburn
E-413 Ivory White	E-421 Quartz

Installation:

Bruce Dura-Luster urethane products are recommended for all phases of residential areas, including the kitchen.

Solid oak products can be installed on or above grade. Engineered products can be installed on, above or below grade level, including basements.

Detailed installation instruction sheets are provided in every product carton.

Benchmark™ Collection:

3/8" Engineered Custom Wood Tile and Parquet

Debut®
3-ply engineered oak, single unit. Eased edges, tongue and groove. Size: 3/8" X 9" X 9"
K-2010 Toast   K-2011 Gunstock

Sonata™
3-ply engineered maple center/oak pickets, five piece construction. Eased, butt edges.
Size: 3/8" X 12" X 12"
H-4621 Creme Center/Quartz Pickets
H-4625 Creme Center/Peachtree Pickets

Meridian Stone®
3-ply engineered maple, one unit with eased, butt edges. Four corners diagonally cut to accept diamond inserts. Diamond inserts ordered separately. Size: 3/8" X 12" X 12"
H-4010 Toast   H-4020 Sedona
H-4016 Creme

Herringstrip™
3-ply engineered oak, one unit with eased edges. Variety of pattern/design options. Tongue and groove. Size: 3/8" X 3" X 15"
H-1010 Toast   H-1022 Vintage Brown
H-1011 Gunstock

Jeffersonian™ II
3-ply engineered oak, three piece construction. Eased, butt edges. Size: 3/8" X 8" X 8"
H-1710 Toast   H-1711 Gunstock

Santa Fe Square
3-ply engineered oak, one unit with one diagonally cut corner to accept diamond insert. Eased edges, tongue and groove. Diamond inserts ordered separately. Size: 3/8" X 9" X 9"
K-2110 Toast   K-2111 Gunstock

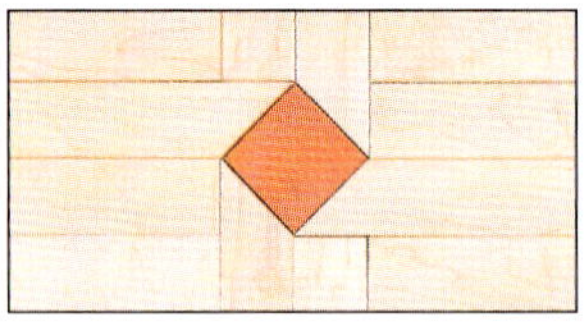

Diamond Accents
3-ply engineered maple, one unit with eased, butt edges. For use with Santa Fe Square and Meridian Stone only. Size: 2 7/8" X 2 7/8"
H-310U Unfinished   H-325 Parchment
H-316 Creme   H-326 Sherwood
H-320 Sedona   H-327 Wood Violet
H-322 Espresso   H-328 Sahara
H-324 Charcoal

5/16" Solid Oak Custom Wood Tile and Parquet

Oakmont®
Single unit contains oak fillets joined with a soft metal spline. Square edges. Tongue and groove.
Size: 5/16" X 12" X 12"
L-70 Desert   L-77 Tudor
L-71 Chestnut   L-720 Auburn
L-72 Mellow   L-721 Quartz
L-76 Ivory White   L-724 Driftwood

Dura-Luster Testing Standards:

ASTM D 968 - The falling sand test. Results represent the amount, in milliliters, of sand that falls on a controlled area before the finish is worn away. The higher the number, the better the finish.

Bruce Dura-Luster urethane finish - 88,000 milliliters per mil of finish.

Competitive urethane finish - 48,000 milliliters per mil of finish.

ASTM D 2394-83, Sections 33-37 - Test Method for Static Slip Resistance. Oak and Maple: Exceeds 0.60

Exceeds the American's With Disabilities Act Recommendations for slip resistance.

ASTM E 648-94a - Test Method for Critical Radiant Flux of Floor Covering Systems Using a Radiant Heat Energy Source. Oak: 0.48

Color Fastness: Results represent in numerical value, the amount of shift from the original color toward a yellow coloration. The lower the number the better the color/finish.

Raw Oak Test Score: 8.055

Bruce Ivory White Test Score: 4.919

Bruce Desert/Natural Test Score: 3.003

Note: Bruce parquet products with a self-stik foam backing are available on a select basis. For acoustical rating data on these self-stik, foam backed hardwood floors, call: 1-800-722-4647.

Warranty:

All Bruce products carry a Full Lifetime Warranty on Structural Integrity, Adhesive Bond, and Subfloor Moisture Protection.

Benchmark Collection Dura-Luster urethane products carry a Full Five Year Finish Wear Layer Warranty for residential applications. For complete details of Bruce product warranties, call toll-free 1-800-722-4647.

Dura-Luster Urethane Finish (continued)

09640/BRU
Buy Line 4923

Coastal Woodlands™
International Benchmark™ Collection

1/2" Engineered Plank

ECW-124 Oak Nutmeg

ECW-126 Oak Butterscotch

ECW-121 Oak Natural

ECW-200 Plantation Beech

ECW-161 Beech

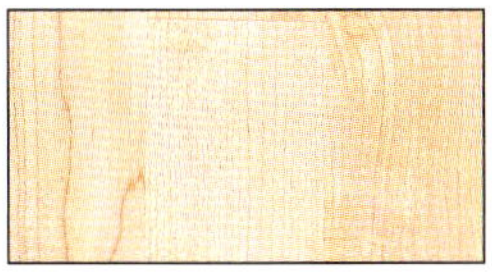
ECW-171 Maple Natural

ECW-170 Country Maple

ECW-131 Asian Pine

ECW-141 Iroko

ECW-151 Kempas

ECW-181 Cherry Natural

ECW-188 Country Cherry

ECW-191 Nyatoh

ECW-211 Merbau Natural

Description:

Designed for floating floor installations, Coastal Woodlands products consist of three strips of hardwoods pre-assembled on 1/2" thick, 7 11/16" wide and 86 5/8" long planks. Precision tongue and groove construction and true square edges combine for a flat, smooth surface.

Installation:

Coastal Woodlands products are installed over Bruce ComfortGuard™ underlayment as a floating floor. The rolled foam underlayment provides a cushioning effect, sound absorption and moisture protection.

Coastal Woodlands™ — Kempas floor — ECW-151

How to Specify Benchmark Products:

A. Flooring shall be Bruce (state name, size and/or width) strip, plank, custom wood tile or parquet in the grade of (specify wood species) with a surface color/finish of (state color item number) as manufactured by Bruce Hardwood Floors, a division of Triangle Pacific Corporation.

B. Factory finished engineered strip, plank, or parquet and solid strip, plank or parquet shall be sanded for a smooth finish and have a (specify desired finish) Dura-Luster ultra-violet cured urethane finish or Dura-Satin baked-in wax finish that includes a soya and linseed penetrating stain and carnauba wax.

C. Installation must be made in accordance with the installation instruction sheets provided in each carton.

D. Installation of all 3/8", 3-ply products can be either nailed, stapled, or glued using properly recommended tools.

E. Use Bruce Tribond Adhesive for glue-down installation. Bruce Tribond Adhesive shall be used for all 3/8" strip, plank, and parquet (5/16" and 3/4"). Adhesive for end fastening 3/4" random planks shall be Bruce Oakbond or PL-400 as recommended by Bruce Hardwood Floors.

F. Trowel for spreading Bruce Tribond Adhesive shall be notched as required by Bruce Hardwood Floors.

G. Nailing Machines: 2" barbed fasteners or approved staples should be used for installing Bruce 3/4" strip or plank flooring, and nailing machines with 1 1/4" cleats should be used for nail-down installation of 3/8" strip or plank as required by Bruce Hardwood Floors. One inch or longer glue-coated staples should be used with Stanley LHF #S3297 stapler for 3/8", 3-ply products as recommended.

Benchmark™ Collection:

Dillard's Department Store — Little Rock, Arkansas — Monterey Plank E-20 Gunstock

Description:

Bruce Dura-Satin® wax finish floors are specifically designed for light commercial and residential use, including high traffic areas. The Dura-Satin finish epitomizes the old-world richness and patina of soft, baked-in stain and wax. The exclusive Bruce 13-step penetrating stain and wax finish creates a protective barrier that provides lasting durability against traffic, wear, soil and stains. The Bruce Dura-Satin wax finish is an outstanding choice for beauty and durability in light commercial applications.

Maintenance:

Bruce recommends good general maintenance practices for Dura-Satin® wax finish products.

Commercial Maintenance

- Sweep or vacuum daily to remove grit.
- Using a commercial floor buffer, buff daily with a fiber bristle polishing brush.
- Using a lamb's wool applicator or equivalent, apply Bruce floor care products once every two weeks or as required in extreme traffic areas. Follow with buffing.

Residential Maintenance

- Use quality solvent-based cleaners and waxes.
- Buffing between waxing will restore the floor's sheen.
- High traffic areas can be waxed without waxing the entire floor.
- Waxing too often may cause a wax build-up and dull the finish.
- Do not use water base waxes. Water may dull the finish and cause additional maintenance problems.

Dura-Satin® Testing Standards:

ASTM D 4060-95 - Test Method for Abrasion Resistance of Organic Coatings by the Taber Abrader. Oak: 0.011 Maple: 0.010

ASTM E 84-95 - Test Method for Surface Burning Characteristics of Building Materials. Oak: Class C Maple: Class C

Warranty:

All Bruce products carry a Full Lifetime Warranty on Structural Integrity, Adhesive Bond, and Subfloor Moisture Protection.

Benchmark Collection Dura-Satin wax products carry a Full Five Year Finish Wear Layer Warranty for residential applications and Full One Year Finish Wear Layer Warranty in approved commercial applications. For complete details of Bruce product warranties, call toll-free 1-800-722-4647.

Dura-Satin Wax Finish

09640/BRU

Buy Line 4923

3/4" Solid Oak Strip and Planks

Westminster® Plank
Wrought iron nails for end fastening. Random lengths and widths. Beveled edges and ends. Tongue and groove. Size: 3/4" X 3" - 5" - 7"
A-3 Mellow Textured

Ranch® Plank
Factory installed pegs. Random lengths and alternate widths. Beveled edges and ends. Tongue and groove. Size: 3/4" X 2 1/4" - 3 1/4"
B-3 Gunstock

Fireside® Plank
Random lengths and alternate widths. Beveled edges and ends. Tongue and groove.
Size: 3/4" X 2 1/4" - 3 1/4"
B-4 Gunstock B-8 Toast

Homestead® Plank
Textured finish. Random lengths and alternate widths. Beveled edges and ends. Tongue and groove. Size: 3/4" X 2 1/4" - 3 1/4"
B-5 Mellow Textured

Cathedral® Plank
Factory installed pegs. Random lengths and widths. Beveled edges and ends. Tongue and groove. Size: 3/4" X 3" - 5" - 7"
A-5 Toast A-7 Gunstock

Cambridge® Plank
Random lengths and widths. Beveled edges and ends. Tongue and groove. Size: 3/4" X 3" - 4" - 6"
A-20 Toast A-21 Gunstock

Country Oak® Plank
Factory installed pegs. Random lengths and widths. Beveled edges and ends. Tongue and groove. Size: 3/4" X 3" - 4" - 6"
A-25 Rustic

Prefinished Strip
Random lengths, standard 2 1/4" width. Beveled edges and ends. Tongue and groove.
Size: 3/4" X 2 1/4"
C-1 Natural C-4 Gunstock
C-3 Bronzetone

3/4" Solid Oak Parquet

Unit Block
Single unit with 6 tongue and groove fillets joined with a soft metal spline. Beveled edges.
Size: 3/4" X 9" X 9"
G-7 Natural G-8 Gunstock

3/8" Engineered Plank

Village Plank®
Factory installed pegs. 3-ply engineered plank. Random lengths and widths. Beveled edges and ends. Tongue and groove. Size: 3/8" X 3" - 5" - 7"
E-1 Mellow E-11 Gunstock

Sierra Plank®
3-ply engineered plank. Random lengths and alternating widths. Beveled edges and ends. Tongue and groove. Size: 3/8" X 3" - 5"
E-30 Gunstock

Classic™ Plank
5-ply engineered plank. Square edges, random lengths and standard 3" width. Square edges and ends. Tongue and groove. Size: 3/8" X 3"
E-510 Toast E-511 Gunstock

Villa Nova Plank®
3-ply engineered plank. Random lengths and widths. Beveled edges and ends. Tongue and groove. Size: 3/8" X 3" - 5" - 7"
E-12 Gunstock

Monterey™ Plank
3-ply engineered plank. Random lengths and standard 3" width. Beveled edges and ends. Tongue and groove. Size: 3/8" X 3"
E-20 Gunstock

3/8" Engineered Parquet

Heritage Square®
3-ply engineered oak. One unit, with beveled edges. Tongue and groove. Size: 3/8" X 9" X 9"
K-25-TG Gunstock K-27-TG Mellow Textured
K-26-TG Toast

BETTER

Kensington™ Collection:

Glen Cove Plank — EB-880 Toast

Description:

Kensington Collection products are manufactured from specially selected hardwoods chosen with natural characteristics for a more rustic, casual style. Kensington products are available in the Bruce Dura-Luster urethane finish and the Dura-Satin wax finish.

Dura-Luster urethane finish floors receive multiple coats of urethane cured with ultraviolet light between each coat. This produces a tough, durable finish that repels most household spills, never requires waxing, and is very easy to maintain. Dura-Luster finish products are recommended for all phases of residential areas, including kitchens.

Dura-Satin wax finish products are the result of a 13-step penetrating stain and wax finish that creates a protective barrier that provides lasting durability against traffic, wear, soil and stains. Dura-Satin wax finish products are specifically designed for light commercial and residential use, including high traffic areas.

Installation:

Bruce Dura-Luster urethane products are recommended for all phases of residential areas, including the kitchen.

Solid oak products can be installed on or above grade. Engineered products can be installed on, above or below grade level, including basements.

Detailed installation instruction sheets are provided in every product carton.

Dura-Luster Testing Standards:

Refer to the Dura-Luster testing standards on page 8.

Dura-Luster Urethane Finish

09640/BRU
Buy Line 4923

3/4" Solid Oak Strip and Plank

Laurel™ Strip
Random lengths and a standard 2 1/4" width. Eased edges with square ends. Tongue and groove. Size: 3/4" X 2 1/4"

CB-910 White Oak Natural	CB-924 Gunstock
CB-921 Natural	CB-926 Butterscotch
CB-922 Spice	CB-927 Saddle
CB-923 Winter White	

Bayport™ Strip
Random lengths and a standard 2 1/4" width. Square edges and ends. Tongue and groove. Size: 3/4" X 2 1/4"

CB-820 Auburn	CB-824 Gunstock
CB-821 Natural	CB-826 Butterscotch
CB-822 Spice	CB-827 Saddle

Valley View™ Plank
Random lengths and a standard 3 1/4" width. Eased edges with square ends. Tongue and groove. Size: 3/4" X 3 1/4"

CB-931 Natural	CB-934 Gunstock

5/16" Solid Oak Parquet

Sorrento® Parquet
Single unit contains oak fillets joined with a soft metal spline. Square edges.
Size: 5/16" X 12" X 12"

L-92 Mellow	L-94 Chestnut
L-93 Desert	L-95 Quartz

3/8" Engineered Oak Strip and Planks

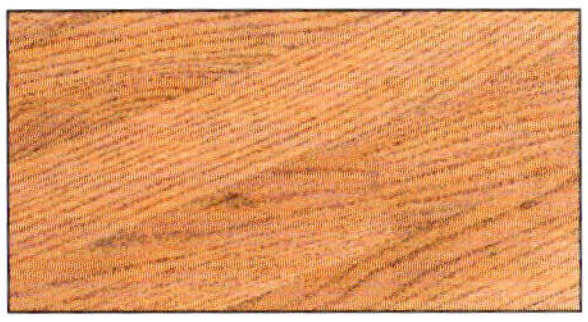

Riverside™ Plank
Random lengths with a standard 3" width. 5-ply engineered oak with square edges and ends. Tongue and groove. Size: 3/8" X 3"

EB-720 Toast	EB-724 Spice
EB-721 Gunstock	EB-726 Butterscotch
EB-723 Ivory White	EB-727 Saddle

Springdale™ Plank
Random lengths with a standard 3" width. 3-ply engineered oak with square edges and ends. Tongue and groove. Size: 3/8" X 3"

EB-520 Toast	EB-526 Butterscotch
EB-521 Gunstock	EB-527 Saddle
EB-525 Mellow	

Glen Cove™ Plank
Random lengths and a standard 3" width. 3-ply engineered oak with eased edges and ends. Tongue and groove. Size: 3/8" X 3"

EB-880 Toast	EB-884 Spice
EB-881 Gunstock	EB-886 Butterscotch
EB-883 Ivory White	EB-887 Saddle

Summerside™ Strip
Random lengths and a standard 2 1/4" width. 3-ply engineered oak with square edges and ends. Tongue and groove. Size: 3/8" X 2 1/4"

EB-620 Toast	EB-626 Butterscotch
EB-621 Gunstock	EB-627 Saddle
EB-625 Mellow	

Warranty:

All Bruce products carry a Full Lifetime Warranty on Structural Integrity, Adhesive Bond, and Subfloor Moisture Protection.

Kensington Collection Dura-Luster urethane products carry a Full Three Year Finish Wear Layer Warranty for residential applications. For complete details of Bruce product warranties, call toll-free 1-800-722-4647.

How to Specify Kensington Collection Products:

A. Flooring shall be Bruce (state name, size and/or width) strip, plank, custom wood tile or parquet in the grade of (specify wood species) with a surface color/finish of (state color item number) as manufactured by Bruce Hardwood Floors, a division of Triangle Pacific Corporation.

B. Factory finished engineered strip, plank, or parquet and solid strip, plank or parquet shall be sanded for a smooth finish and have a (specify desired finish) Dura-Luster ultra-violet cured urethane finish or Dura-Satin baked-in wax finish that includes a soya and linseed penetrating stain and carnauba wax.

C. Installation must be made in accordance with the installation instruction sheets provided in each carton.

D. Installation of all 3/8", 3-ply products can be either nailed, stapled, or glued using properly recommended tools.

E. Use Bruce Tribond Adhesive for glue-down installation. Bruce Tribond Adhesive shall be used for all 3/8" strip, plank, and parquet (5/16" and 3/4"). Adhesive for end fastening 3/4" random planks shall be Bruce Oakbond or PL-400 as recommended by Bruce Hardwood Floors.

F. Trowel for spreading Bruce Tribond Adhesive shall be notched as required by Bruce Hardwood Floors.

G. Nailing Machines: 2" barbed fasteners or approved staples should be used for installing Bruce 3/4" strip or plank flooring, and nailing machines with 1 1/4" cleats should be used for nail-down installation of 3/8" strip or plank as required by Bruce Hardwood Floors.
One inch or longer glue-coated staples should be used with Stanley LHF S3297 stapler for 3/8", 3-ply products as recommended.

Kensington™ Collection: Dura-Satin Wax Finish

3/4" Solid Oak Strip and Planks

Madison™ Plank
Random lengths and widths. Beveled edges and ends. Tongue and groove. Size: 3/4" X 3" - 4" - 6"
A-51 Gunstock A-52 Toast

Manchester® Plank
Random lengths and alternating widths. Beveled edges and ends. Tongue and groove.
Size: 3/4" X 2 1/4" - 3 1/4"
B-11 Toast B-14 Gunstock

Prefinished Strip
Random lengths and standard 2 1/4" width. Beveled edges and ends. Tongue and groove.
Size: 3/4" X 2 1/4"
CB-21 Toast CB-24 Gunstock

Brookhollow™ Strip
Random lengths and standard 2 1/4" width. Eased edges and square ends. Tongue and groove. Size: 3/4" X 2 1/4"
CB-91 Natural CB-94 Gunstock

3/8" Engineered Oak Planks

Brookside™ Plank
Factory installed pegs. Random lengths and widths. Beveled edges and ends. Tongue and groove. Size: 3/8" X 3" - 5" - 7"
E-50 Gunstock Textured

Brandon™ Plank
Random lengths and widths. Beveled edges and ends. Tongue and groove. Size: 3/8" X 3" - 5" - 7"
E-52 Gunstock Textured

Sutton™ Plank
Random lengths and standard 3" width. Beveled edges and ends. Tongue and groove.
Size: 3/8" X 3"
E-51 Gunstock Textured E-55 Toast

3/8" Engineered Oak Parquet

Ridgewood® Parquet
3-ply engineered oak. Center unit surrounded with 2 pickets. Beveled, butt edges.
Size: 3/8" X 8" X 8"
H-84 Gunstock Textured

Heritage Square®
3-ply engineered oak. One unit with beveled edges. Tongue and groove. Size: 3/8" X 9" X 9"
K-28-TG Gunstock Textured

Installation:

Bruce Dura-Satin wax finish products are recommended for both residential and light commercial applications, including high traffic areas.

Solid oak products can be installed on or above grade. Engineered oak products can be installed on, above or below grade level, including basements.

Detailed installation instruction sheets are provided in every product carton.

Dura-Satin Testing Standards:

Refer to the Dura-Satin testing standards on page 10.

Warranty:

All Bruce products carry a Full Lifetime Warranty on Structural Integrity, Adhesive Bond, and Subfloor Moisture Protection.

Kensington Collection Dura-Satin wax products carry a Full Three Year Finish Wear Layer Warranty in residential applications and a One-Year Finish Wear Layer Warranty in approved commercial applications. For complete details of Bruce product warranties, call toll-free 1-800-722-4647.

Maintenance: Dura-Satin Wax Finish Products

Bruce recommends good general maintenance practices for Dura-Satin wax finish products.

Commercial Maintenance

- Sweep or vacuum daily to remove grit.
- Using a commercial floor buffer, buff daily with a fiber bristle polishing brush.
- Using a lamb's wool applicator or equivalent, apply Bruce floor care products once every two weeks or as required in extreme traffic areas. Follow with buffing.

Residential Maintenance

- Use quality solvent-based cleaners and waxes.
- Buffing between waxings will restore the floor's sheen.
- High traffic areas can be waxed without waxing the entire floor.
- Waxing too often may cause a wax build-up and dull the finish.
- Do not use water base waxes. Water may dull the finish and cause additional maintenance problems.

GOOD

Contract Unfinished Products

09640/BRU
Buy Line 4923

Contract Unfinished CU-740. Custom finished in a Gunstock color.

3/4" Signature Series Solid Oak Plank

Available with square ends. Side edges may be square or beveled. The 3/4" solid oak series is available in red or white oak, and in 3", 4", 5", 6" or 7" widths in random lengths. Sizes can be mixed to achieve alternate or random patterns.

Installation: Nail down, on or above grade level.

3" Plank	4" Plank	5" Plank	6" Plank	7" Plank
Item#				
CU-3RB	CU-4RB	CU-5RB	CU-6RB	CU-7RB
CU-3RS	CU-4RS	CU-5RS	CU-6RS	CU-7RS
CU-3WB	CU-4WB	CU-5WB	CU-6WB	CU-7WB
CU-3WS	CU-4WS	CU-5WS	CU-6WS	CU-7WS

R = Red Oak W = White Oak B = Beveled Edges S = Square Edges

Engineered Flooring

Engineered oak construction with square ends and edges and tongue and groove milling. Traditional red and white oak boards available in 2 1/4" and 3" widths and random lengths.

Installation: Glue down, on above or below grade level.

1/2" Strip and Plank

Size	Select & Better Red Oak	Select & Better White Oak	#1 Common Red Oak	#1 Common White Oak
1/2" X 2 1/4"	CU-600	CU-610	CU-615	CU-625
1/2" X 3"	CU-640	CU-650	CU-635	CU-645

3/8" Strip and Plank

Size	Select & Better Red Oak	Select & Better White Oak	#1 Common Red Oak	#1 Common White Oak
3/8" X 2 1/4"	CU-700	CU-710	CU-715	CU-725
3/8" X 3"	CU-740	CU-750	CU-735	CU-745

Description:

Bruce manufactures a complete line of contract unfinished products for job site finishing. These products are kiln dried prior to milling and go through the identical manufacturing process as all other Bruce products with the exception of finishing. Contract unfinished floors are available in both solid and engineered oak.

Warranty:

Bruce Contract Unfinished products carry a Full Lifetime Warranty on Structural Integrity, Adhesive Bond, and Subfloor Moisture Protection. For complete details of Bruce product warranties, call toll-free 1-800-722-4647.

How to Specify Contract Unfinished Floors:

A. Flooring shall be Bruce (state name, size and/or width) strip or plank in the species of oak or maple (state item number) as manufactured by Bruce Hardwood Floors, a division of Triangle Pacific Corporation.

B. Bruce CU unfinished strip or plank shall be installed and job site sanded and finished according to the job specification. Engineered strip and plank shall be presanded at the factory for minimum job site sanding.

C. Installation must be completed in accordance with the installation instruction sheets provided in each carton.

D. Installation of all Contract Unfinished 3/8", 3-ply products can be either nailed, stapled, or glued using properly recommended tools.

E. Use Bruce Tribond Adhesive for glue-down installation. Bruce Tribond Adhesive shall be used for all 1/2" and 3/8" thick strip and plank. Adhesive for end fastening of 3/4" random strip or planks shall be Bruce Oakbond or PL-400 as recommended by Bruce Hardwood Floors.

F. Trowel for spreading Bruce Tribond Adhesive shall be notched as required by Bruce Hardwood Floors.

G. Nailing Machines: 2" barbed fasteners or approved staples should be used for installing Bruce 3/4" strip or plank flooring, and nailing machines with 1 1/4" cleats should be used for nail-down installation of 3/8" strip or planks as required by Bruce Hardwood Floors. One inch or longer glue-coated staples should be used with Stanley LHF #S3297 stapler for 3/8", 3-ply products as recommended.

al Dente Restaurant featuring WearMaster — Bally's Las Vegas

Installation Products:

- **Adhesives.** Bruce Tribond Adhesive is used for installation of all 3/8" strip, plank and custom wood tile or parquet (5/16" and 3/4") except when the parquet is self-stick, dry foam back or a vapor barrier is involved. Check adhesive label for trowel specifications.

  Bruce Oakbond Adhesive is required for end fastening some of the solid oak, random width nail-down strip or plank floors.
- **Trim and Molding.** Bruce's complete line of trim and molding products are available either factory-finished or unfinished for job site finishing.
- **Installation Accessories.** Bruce offers specially notched trowels for spreading adhesives to the proper specifications, cork expansion products, nails and other installation products to complete the job.
- **Nailing machines.** Recommended nailers and staplers, along with proper fasteners are available through your Bruce Distributor. Follow required nailing schedules and subfloor recommendations.

Maintenance/Repair Products

Bruce offers a complete line of maintenance products formulated specifically for each individual Bruce finish. In addition, a full line of repair products such as stains, fillers and finishes are available for routine maintenance and repair.

Sales and Specifier Support

Bruce has a complete library of sales and specifier support materials available, and a nationwide network of distributor representatives ready to assist you at the local level.

To order support materials, or for the name of the Bruce distributor in your area, call toll free: 1-800-722-4647.

Wood is a natural material containing distinctive differences in color and grain configuration. It is these differences caused by nature that create the warmth, beauty, and individuality of each hardwood floor. The printed room scenes in this catalog are intended as a visual guide for product pattern, not as an actual representation of the floor itself.

Bruce® hardwood floors
A division of Triangle Pacific Corp.
The Natural Choice®
16803 Dallas Parkway Dallas, Texas 75248

Sweets brochure #102 9/97

Maple Treasures™, shown in Natural.

Chaparral™ Strip, shown in Brandywine.

C247
09640/BRV
BuyLine 0105

PREMIER
WOOD FLOORS

A division of Triangle Pacific Corp.

For All The Favorite Rooms In Your Life™

Plantation™ Strip shown in Natural

Founder's™ Collection

The Founder's Collection is a superior line of flooring exclusively milled from premium-grade American hardwoods. The Founder's Collection features Premier's durable Everguard™ no-wax finish.

Plantation™ Strip & Plank Engineered Oak

- 3/8" thick, 2 1/4" wide (strip) or 3/8" thick, 3" wide (plank) cross-ply engineered oak, three ply
- Random lengths of 10" to 48"
- Patented Flexform™ milling system
- Available in square edges and ends (plank & strip) and eased edges and ends (plank only)
- Tongue and groove side construction with Level-Lock end system
- Available in all Founder's Collection stain choices
- Install on, above or below grade

New Orleans™ Strip Solid Oak

- 3/4" thick, 2 1/4" wide solid oak
- Random lengths of 9" to 84"
- Square edges and ends
- Tongue and groove construction
- Available in Natural, Autumn, Brandywine and Golden Oak
- Install on or above grade only

Founder's Collection Colors

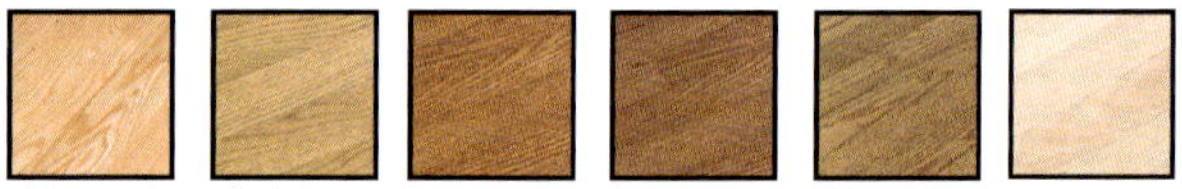

	Natural	*Sable*	*Autumn*	*Brandy-wine*	*Golden Oak*	*Dove White*
Plantation™ Plank EE*	14111	14611	14711	14811	14911	14511
Plantation™ Plank SE**	13111	13611	13711	13811	13911	13511
Plantation™ Strip SE	15121	15621	15721	15821	15921	15521
New Orleans™ Strip SE	03121		03721	03821	03921	

* Eased Edges ** Square Edges

Noble™ Pecan shown in Amber.

Jewels of Nature™

In this rare collection you'll find Cherry, Maple, Pecan and Walnut hardwoods. And as part of the Founder's Collection, the same five year warranty applies. Cherry Royale™, 3/8" x 3"; Maple Treasures™, 3/8" x 2 1/4"; Noble™ Pecan, 3/8" x 3"; and an Ornamental™ Walnut Feature Strip, 3/8" x 1 1/2".

- 3/8" thick, cross-ply engineered hardwoods, 3-ply
- Random lengths of 10" to 48"
- Square edges and ends
- Tongue and groove side construction with Level-Lock end system
- Patented Flexform™ milling system
- Install on, above or below grade

Jewels of Nature™ Collection Colors:

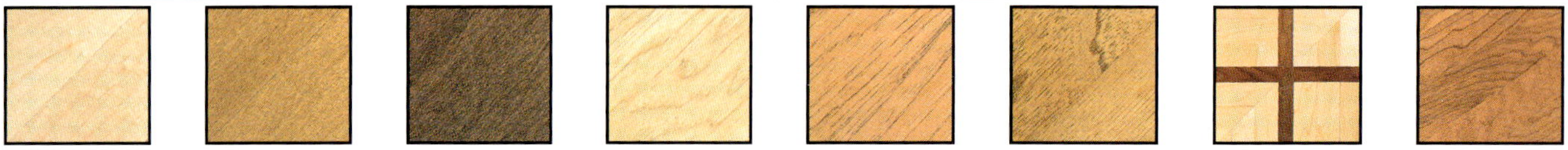

Maple			Pecan			Walnut	Cherry
Natural 27121	*Cinnabar* 27721	*Garnet* 27421	*Natural* 23111	*Amber* 23211	*Smokey Topaz* 23911	*Walnut* 23391	*Cherry Royale* 23411

For additional product and warranty information, please call 1-800-588-1707.

Landmark™ Collection

09640/BRV
BuyLine 0105

Landmark Collection floors are manufactured from American oak hardwoods that are specially chosen for their distinctive natural characteristics. Landmark Collection floors feature the Premier Everguard™ no-wax finish.

Olympic™ Plank shown in Sable

Olympic™ Strip & Plank Engineered Oak

- 3/8" thick, 2 1/4" wide (strip) or 3/8" thick, 3" wide (plank) cross-ply engineered oak, three ply
- Random lengths of 10" to 48"
- Patented Flexform™ milling system
- Available in square edges and ends (plank & strip) and eased edges and ends (plank only)
- Tongue and groove side construction with Level-Lock end system
- Available in all Landmark Collection stain choices
- Install on, above or below grade

Tara™ Oak Parquet Solid Oak

- 5/16" thick, 12" x 12" solid oak
- Square edges
- Tongue and groove construction
- Available in Natural, Autumn, Brandywine and Golden Oak
- Install on or above grade only

Chaparral™ Strip & Shiloh® Strip Solid Oak

- 3/4" thick, 2 1/4" wide solid oak
- Random lengths of 9" to 84"
- Square edges and ends (Chaparral Strip), or eased edges and ends (Shiloh Strip)
- Tongue and groove construction
- Available in Natural, Autumn, Brandywine and Golden Oak
- Install on or above grade only

Landmark™ Collection Colors

	Natural	*Sable*	*Autumn*	*Brandy-wine*	*Golden Oak*
Olympic™ Plank EE	14112	14612	14712	14812	14912
Olympic™ Plank SE	13112	13612	13712	13812	13912
Olympic™ Strip SE	15122	15622	15722	15822	15922
Shiloh™ Strip EE	02122		02722	02822	02922
Chaparral™ Strip SE	03122		03722	03822	03922
Tara™ Oak Parquet	01102		01702	01802	01902

For additional product and warranty information, please call 1-800-588-1707.

Premier General Information

Founder's Collection

Warranty: All Premier wood floors first quality products have a full lifetime construction warranty and all Premier engineered products have a full lifetime adhesive and subfloor moisture protection warranty. Founder's Collection products with the Everguard urethane wear surface are guaranteed not to wear through or separate from the wood for a full five years from the date of purchase when used in normal residential traffic conditions.

Landmark Collection

Warranty: All first quality Landmark Collection floors have a full lifetime construction warranty and all Premier engineered products have a full lifetime adhesive and subfloor moisture protection warranty. Landmark Collection products with the Everguard urethane wear surface are guaranteed not to wear through or separate from the wood for a full three years from the date of purchase when used in normal residential traffic conditions.

Premier's Patented Flexform™ Milling System

The Flexform milling system is a standard feature on all Premier engineered products, and insures that the floor will lay flat, even when installed over subfloors with slight irregularities.

The Flexform construction process starts with 3 layers of solid hardwoods glued together in a cross-ply process. Premier then applies a tongue and groove interlocking system and the Flexform milling process of tension relief grooves with computer aided manufacturing techniques. This results in the Level Lock end system, whereby ends are locked in position by the precision tongue and groove side construction. This combination dramatically improves the floors ability to remain stable under normal seasonal humidity changes and to conform to irregular subfloors.

Premier floors with the patented Flexform milling system help eliminate the popping sound often encountered when hardwood floors bridge depressions in the subfloor.

Easy Care Everguard™ Finish

The Premier Everguard finish consists of multiple layers of tough, durable urethane resins cured by ultra-violet light between each layer. The result is a hard, durable shell that forms a traffic-resistant shield and protects the wood from wear and spills. The Everguard finish resists most household spills and stains. Maintenance is as simple as vacuuming and cleaning occasionally with Premier Spray-N-Wipe™.

How to Specify Premier Wood Floors:

A. Premier products are designed for residential and light commercial use.

B. Flooring shall be Premier (specify name, size and/or width) strip, plank or parquet in the grade of (specify wood species) with a surface color/finish of (state color item number) as manufactured by Premier Wood Floors, a division of Triangle Pacific Corporation.

C. Factory finished engineered strip or plank and solid strip or parquet shall be sanded for a smooth finish and have an ultra-violet cured urethane finish.

D. Installation must be made in accordance with the installation instruction sheets provided in each carton.

E. Installation of 3/8", 3-ply products can be glued using properly recommended tools.

F. Use Premier Adhesive for glue-down installation. Premier Adhesive shall be used for all 3/8" strip, plank and 5/16" parquet.

G. Trowel for spreading Premier Adhesive shall be notched as required by Premier Wood Floors.

H. Nailing machines: 2" barbed fasteners or approved staples should be used for installing Premier 3/4" strip flooring as required by Premier Wood Floors.

I. For additional product information, please call **1-800-588-1707.**

PREMIER™ WOOD FLOORS

A division of Triangle Pacific Corp.

16803 Dallas Parkway, Dallas, TX 75248

Sweet's brochure # PRMSWT ©1997 Premier™ Wood Floors 7/97
a division of Triangle Pacific Corp. Printed in U.S.A.

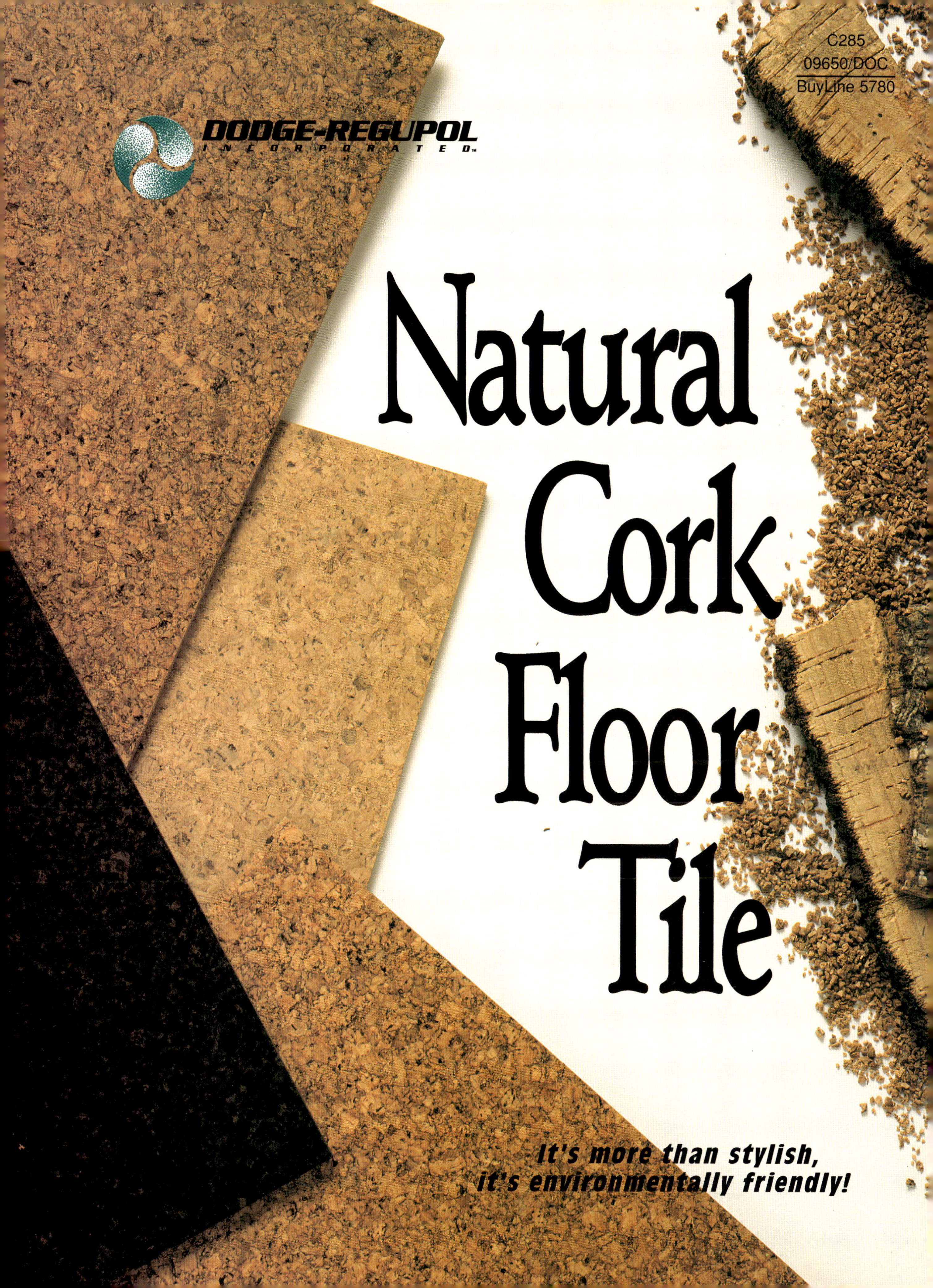

C285
09650/DOC
BuyLine 5780

DODGE-REGUPOL
INCORPORATED™

Natural Cork Floor Tile

It's more than stylish, it's environmentally friendly!

DODGE CORK TILE™

C285
09650/DOC
BuyLine 5780

The original non-laminate tile consisting of 100% natural cork.

Outstanding features

For over one hundred years, cork flooring has proven to be one of the most resilient and durable natural flooring materials available. It combines excellent aesthetic and performance features in one beautiful product. The unique molecular structure of 100% compounded cork particles provides unprecedented properties in recovery, shock absorption and acoustic and thermal insulation.

DODGE CORK TILE™ is available in a variety of high quality finishes for an attractive appearance as well as protection against moisture and indentation. DODGE CORK TILE™ can be used for almost any residential or commercial installation.

Naturally warm, shock proof and practical

Medium

Light

Ideal for:

- KITCHENS
- BATHROOMS
- FAMILY ROOMS
- HALLWAYS
- LIBRARIES
- CHURCHES
- STAGES
- MUSIC ROOMS
- DANCE FLOORS
- GYMNASIUMS
- TV STUDIOS

Time tested & proven

From Frank Lloyd Wright's Falling Water to Mayo Clinic in Rochester, MN, innovators continue to choose DODGE CORK TILE™ for dramatic interior flooring solutions. Commercial and prestigious residential installations span the country: Harry S. Truman Memorial, Independence, MO., St. Andrews School, Middleton, DE., Historic Williamsburg, the Federal Court Building, Chapels at both Stanford and Colgate Universities, the National Archives Building, York Community College, homes of celebrities and hundreds more. From the turn of the century until as recently as today, DODGE CORK TILE™ continues to shine in such notable places while remaining stylish and popular.

Absorbs heavy traffic in quiet places

PHOTOS:
(left) kitchen and bathroom in private residence, Lancaster, Pennsylvania
(right) chapel at Colgate University, Hamilton, New York
(below) integrating dual shades of cork flooring in Japanese public library

Medium Dark **Natural**

Finishes

- Unfinished (for natural only)
- Waxed
- Polyurethane Satin
- Polyurethane Gloss

Shades

Recommended Sizes

RESIDENTIAL	COMMERCIAL
12″ x 12″ x 3/16″	12″ x 12″ x 5/16″

Installation, Finishing & Maintenance

Preparation of Subfloors

All subfloors should be thoroughly cleaned, filled and primed. Remove paint, varnish, oil, grease and wax. On wood floors, use a chemical paint or varnish remover. On concrete, use solution of trisodium phosphate (or xylol for rubber based paint). For oil, grease, or wax, scrub with trisodium phosphate or machine sand. In all cases, complete with thorough washing and rinsing. • Concrete floors must be made even with latex floor fill. Fill cracks with latex crack filler. If floor is new, be sure it is completely dry (several months curing is preferred). Sweep clean. • In wood floors, fill cracks with plastic wood, sand uneven boards, renail loose boards, or replace where necessary. If needed, floor may be covered with 5-ply 5/8 in. plywood or hardboard, or covered with latex floor fill. Single wood floors of tongue and groove construction should be completely covered with latex fill or hardboard or plywood.

Laying the Tile

After the subfloor has been properly prepared, laying the floor tile may begin. • Mark the floor into quarters with chalk and lay tile a quarter at a time. Start from center and work to borders. Follow lines of permanent fixtures. For protective edges use bevelled edging. • Spread Ever-Grip™ adhesive in accordance with instructions provided with the adhesive. Press tile firmly to adhesive and butt to adjacent tile. • DO NOT FORCE OR COMPRESS TILE. Roll with 100 lb. roller. Remove excess adhesive. When floor is completed, roll again.

Applying the Finish

Series No. 6300 is an unfinished tile and will require a protective coating. DO NOT START the finish process for at least 5 days. You have a choice of using paste wax or polyurethane. • A light sanding may be required if you have any uneven areas. It should not be necessary to sand the entire floor as No. 6300 is factory sanded. Any uneven or high edges can be corrected by light sanding with No. 80 Mesh Disc Sander - 3M or equal and a very light sanding with No. 150 fine sandpaper. • Apply your finish. If you use wax, you can use any paste wax that is recommended for use with wood floors, as cork is a natural wood product. Follow the same for polyurethane finish. Always follow the recommendations of the finish manufacturer. When applying urethane, 3 or 4 coats may be required to obtain the finish you desire. Use any commercial grade polyurethane that is recommended for Unfinished Hardwood Flooring Systems.

Caution

1. MOISTURE CAN CAUSE PROBLEMS. (a) Moisture in the slab cannot exceed 2% max. (b) Airborne moisture cannot exceed 65% R.H. 2. Avoid abrasive alkaline or cheap cleaners. 3. Keep surface free from grit, sand and cinders. 4. Avoid flooding the floor with water. 5. Protect against indentation with furniture rests. 6. Cork is a natural wood product and may have some shade variation from photograph to tile. 7. CORK FLOOR TILE MUST BE ACCLIMATIZED PRIOR TO INSTALLATION. We recommend the tile be removed from the cartons and plastic sleeves at least 72 hours prior to installation, and the temperature should be maintained between minimum 60°F and maximum 85°F. The relative humidity should be maintained between 50% and 65%.

DODGE-REGUPOL
INCORPORATED™

PO Box 989 • 715 Fountain Avenue
Lancaster, PA 17608-0989
Telephone 717-295-3400 • Fax 717-295-3414
TOLL FREE 800-322-1923
www.Regupol.com

Architectural Specifications

Nature of Product

DODGE CORK TILE™ is derived from the bark of a cork oak tree found primarily in Portugal, Spain and Tunisia. Cork bark is harvested every nine years during the summer when trees dehydrate, and the bark becomes easier to remove. Cork bark then regrows completely with no harm to the tree.

Composition

DODGE CORK TILE™ consists of 100% natural granulated cork particles and non-toxic resin binders.

Technical Data

Density: 30 lbs/cu ft
Indentation & Recovery: ASTM F 36
Indent = 6% Unfinished, 4.1% Waxed
Recovery = 82.6% Unfinished, 87.5% Waxed
Acoustical Rating: Superior
Weight: 18 lbs/carton
New York State Fire Gas Toxicity:
#0300-900216-4005
Federal Specification:
LLL-T-431b Type I and II, Class I

Product Identification

FINISH	SHADE	NUMBER
Unfinished	Natural	# 6300
Waxed	Light Medium Med. Dark	# 200 # 202 # 201
Polyurethane Satin	Light Medium Med. Dark	# 800 # 802 # 801
Polyurethane Gloss	Light Medium Med. Dark	# 700 # 702 # 701

PRINTED IN USA

C290
09650/GER

BuyLine 1361

DLW **LINOLEUM**

Linoleum - A Trend Setter Once Again

Over its history of more than 100 years linoleum has always proven to be a superior floor covering.

Leading architects from the Bauhaus Era were particularly partial to the use of linoleum as an outstanding interior design medium.

Generations of Architects have specified linoleum flooring. Generations of people have used, lived and worked with linoleum. The close relationship between man and material is the secret of linoleum.

Today, a broad and much-varied range of DLW linoleum is available; from the pure simple form of a monochromatic design to designs exemplifying the joy of creating with color.

Highly expressive colors, natural earthy tones, sophisticated design patterns and custom inlays create unlimited design possibilities.

DLW Linoleum Today is known by generations as dependable and modern floor covering. As an element of interior design it is refreshingly young. Due to its natural ingredients, it fulfills the social and ecological demands of today's environment.

DLW linoleum offers solutions for the exacting demands of today's architecture offering purity and simplicity in design.

09650/GER
BuyLine 1361

Marmorette - classical elegance
Marbled linoleum
Available in 35 colors. **2.0-2.5-3.2mm.** Sheet width 79".

Uni-Walton - understated elegance
Monochrome linoleum
Available in 12 colors. **2.0-2.5-3.2mm.** Sheet width 79".

Colorette - refreshingly colorful
Finely textured linoleum
Available in 12 colors. **2.0-2.5-3.2mm.** Sheet width 79".

Linorette - dynamic structure
Heavily marbled linoleum
Available in 7 colors. **2.5-3.2mm.** Sheet width 79". Available in tile.

Linodur - indestructible
Heavy duty linoleum
Available in 12 colors. **4.0mm.**
Available in tile.

Linokett
Available in 8 Marmorette colors.
9.0mm. Plank size only.

Granette - expressive
A design with tradition which has been given a new look. The geometric, marbled structure in an interesting color range and suitable for any application.
Available in 12 colors. **3.2mm.** Sheet width 79".

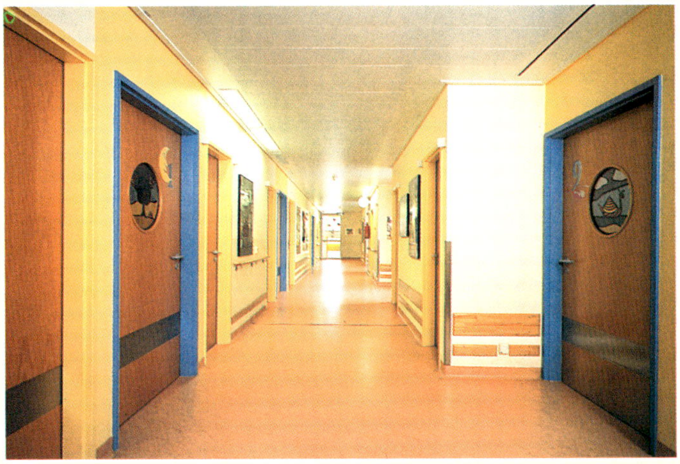

Marka - traditional design
Soft colors-uncomplicated striated patterns and natural ingredients resulting in a durable, budget-oriented linoleum.
Available in 12 colors. **2.0-25mm.** Sheet width 79".

Linoleum Special - conductive
DLW offers conductive floor coverings for a wide variety of applications where demands are made on the material's conductivity.
Available in Marmorette **2.5-3.2mm.**
Available in Linodur **4.0mm.**
Available in sheet and tile.

C291
09650/GER
BuyLine 7601

THE DLW DELIPLAN COLLECTION

offers solutions to many design problems.

Each individual design in the Collection speaks its own, independent language of colors and shapes. The designs are of unique brilliance and are executed using complex manufacturing processes.

DLW Deliplan floors can be used in all heavy-traffic industrial, commercial, and residential areas and due to its hygienic and antistatic properties DLW Deliplan is well suited for hospital and health care installations.

DLW Deliplan floorings are made of homogeneous plastic materials and therefore fully recyclable.

DLW DELIPLAN

is a Collection with a range of applications that goes far beyond the job of solving ordinary, everyday problems. The scope and diversity of the Collection will help the architect with his planning work. Modern cutting technology makes is possible to integrate logos, lettering or individualized designs into the Deliplan flooring.

A wide selection of flooring accessories complete the DLW Deliplan range.

DELIPLAN **CONTOUR**

DELIPLAN **IMPACT**

DELIPLAN **ROYELL**

DELIPLAN **PASTELL**

DELIPLAN **ORBIT**

DELIPLAN **OPAC**

DELIPLAN **SPECIAL**

Safety first

DLW Deliplan Special LG is the conductive variant in the DLW Deliplan Collection. This quality grade ensures a high and durable level of safety in rooms in which there is any risk of electrostatic charges, e.g. operation rooms or electronic workshops. DLW Deliplan Special LG is available in Royal, Contour, and Pastel.

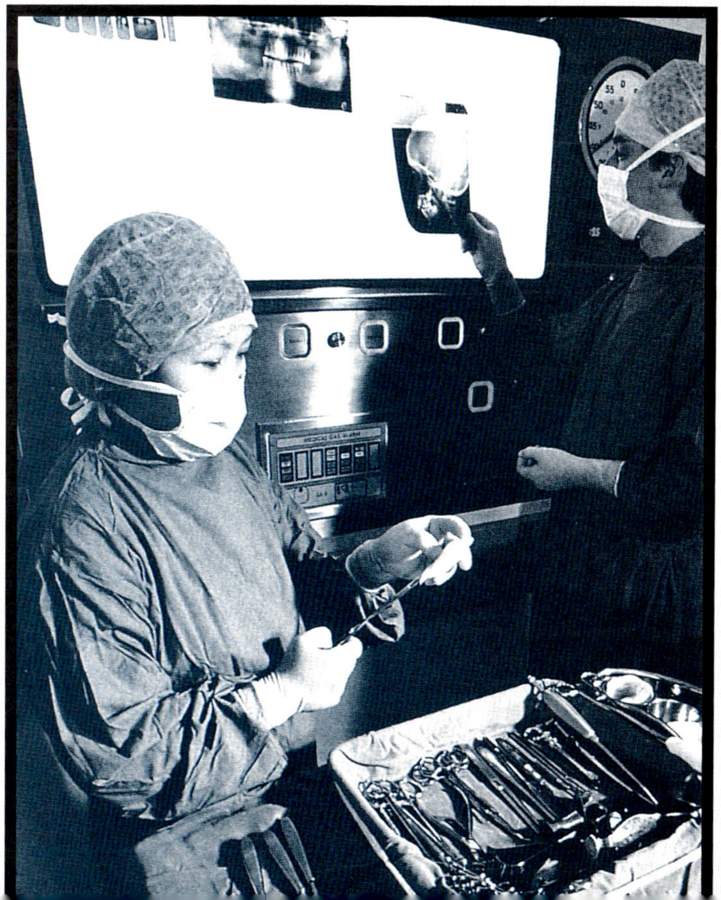

C310

09652/BRU

BuyLine 0106

TRAFFIC ZONE™ by Bruce® Floors

A Business Unit of Triangle Pacific Corp.

The Brand You Can Trust™

High-Performance Laminate Floors

Dent Resistant

Wear Resistant

Stain Resistant

Fade Resistant

Slip Resistant

Ecologically Friendly No VOC's

Description:

Traffic Zone high performance laminate floors are precision engineered in a 4-ply construction that is fused together under tremendous heat and pressure to form a single plank of unprecedented strength and durability.

CrystalGuard™ Finish
A durable wear and stain resistant finish with superior resilience.

Image Design Paper Layer
Product patterns are printed on this layer in various styles including wood, stone and contemporary designs.

Magnum HDF Core
A moisture resistant, high-density fiberboard core that maintains the structural integrity of each precision engineered plank.

Moisture Guard™ Backer
Seals the bottom of each plank for additional stability and moisture protection.

Installation:

Installation Type: Floating Floor Suspension System. Traffic Zone products are glued to each other, not directly to the floor.

Subfloor: Must be smooth, clean, level, dry and structurally sound.

Level: Subfloor surface should be level within 3/16" per ten foot span.

Grade: Install on, above and below ground level.

Surfaces: Old floor coverings (except carpet), concrete, metal, wood and radiant heated surfaces (operating below 85° F).

Underlayment: ComfortGuard™ open cell foam with poly moisture barrier.

Traffic Zone Cherry and Alder color planks.

Traffic Zone Planks:

5/16" x 7 5/8" x 50 5/8" (8 mm x 19.3 cm x 128.5 cm). These versatile planks are available in richly grained wood, granite and marble patterns. Traffic Zone planks can be combined with tiles, blocks or designer squares to create an endless array of patterns and designs.

Color	Pattern	Item#	Color	Pattern	Item#
Ash	3 Strip	Z00321	Cranberry*	3 Strip	Z00342
Beech	3 Strip	Z00324	Forest*	3 Strip	Z00343
Maple	3 Strip	Z00325	Indigo*	3 Strip	Z00344
Cherry	3 Strip	Z00327	Grey*	3 Strip	Z00345
Red Oak Natural	3 Strip	Z00331	Pearl*	3 Strip	Z00346
Red Oak Honey	3 Strip	Z00332	Autumn	3 Strip	Z00347
Red Oak Chestnut	3 Strip	Z00333	Mahogany	3 Strip	Z00348
Autumn Maple	3 Strip	Z00334	Pine	2 Strip	Z00222
Summer Maple	3 Strip	Z00335	Apple	2 Strip	Z00238
Natural Cherry	3 Strip	Z00336	Alder	1 Strip	Z00126
Royal Cherry	3 Strip	Z00337	Birch	1 Strip	Z00128
White Oak	3 Strip	Z00339	Antique Birch	1 Strip	Z00130
Seafoam	3 Strip	Z00341	Granite*	Stone	Z02001
			Marble	Stone	Z02102

*These products also available in 5/16" x 7 5/8" x 7 5/8" Designer Feature Squares.

Monét tiles in the Orchard color.

Traffic Zone Tiles:

5/16" x 15 3/16" x 15 3/16" (8 mm x 38.6 cm x 38.6 cm). Traffic Zone tiles are available in marble, stone and abstract patterns and can be utilized in conjunction with blocks and planks to create an endless number of floor fashions.

Name	Color	Item #
Imagery	Moonstone	Z39003
Imagery	Mocha	Z39004
Chalet	Crystal Ice	Z39005
Chalet	Winter Moss	Z39006
Adobe	Spanish Clay	Z39007
Adobe	Sandstone	Z39008
Dynasty	Pewter	Z39009
Dynasty	Silver Mist	Z39010
Monét	Orchard	Z39011
Monét	Desert	Z39012
Monét	Sierra	Z39013

Traffic Zone Blocks:

5/16" x 15 3/16" x 25 1/4" (8 mm x 38.6 cm x 64.25 cm). Traffic Zone blocks create bold patterns of slate, ceramic and marble, and can be combined with other Traffic Zone products for custom patterns.

Name	Color	Item #
Niagara	Fossil White	Z48014
Empress	Nordic	Z48015
Empress	Sunset	Z48016
Imperial Slate	Brushed Beige	Z48017

Empress blocks in the Sunset color.

Maintenance:

Preventive Maintenance: The use of walk-off mats, proper casters, normal humidity levels, floor protectors, etc, can reduce long term floor care.

Daily or as needed - Remove dust, grit, spills, and organic materials with an untreated (dry) dust mop or vacuum.

Monthly or as needed - Remove surface films by spraying Bruce Dura-Luster® Cleaner on a cloth or sponge mop and wipe the floor. Do not spray Dura-Luster directly on the floor.

Caution: Never wax or apply any surface finish to Traffic Zone floors. Never use steel wool or abrasive cleaners.

Availability: Service & Support

Bruce Floors offers a complete line of installation and maintenance products for Traffic Zone floors.

Traffic Zone products are available through a nationwide network of floor covering distributors. For the name of the Bruce Floors distributor in your area, or to order support materials, call 1-800-722-4647 or write Bruce Floors, P.O. Box 660100, Dallas TX 75266-0100.

Warranty:

Bruce Floors warrants Traffic Zone for light and medium commercial applications. The 15-Year Warranty covers the surface wear layer against stains and fading when used as directed. See the Traffic Zone Buyer Protection Brochure for complete information.

How to Specify Traffic Zone High Performance Laminate Floors:

A. Flooring shall be Bruce (state name, pattern and/or size) plank, block, tile or designer square as manufactured for Bruce Floors, a business unit of Triangle Pacific Corp.

B. Factory finished laminate planks, blocks, tiles or designer squares shall have a CrystalGuard finish constructed of aluminum oxide crystals set into a cellulosic web and fused with a melamine thermosetting resin.

C. Installation must be made in accordance with the installation instruction sheets provided in each carton.

D. Adhesive for joining planks, blocks, tiles or designer squares shall be Bruce Ever-Seal™ adhesive utilizing the top-of-tongue adhesive system as required by Bruce Floors.

E. Underlayment shall be a 1/16" thick open cell foam ComfortGuard with a poly moisture barrier lining one side as required by Bruce Floors.

At Bruce Floors we know what it takes to meet the challenge designers face in their very competitive markets. We can satisfy your floor covering challenges with:

- Service
- Local Factory Representative
- 1-800-722-4647 Help Line
- Wide Range of Consistent Color Choices
- One Cost Effective Flooring System
- Complete Warranty Coverage

TRAFFIC ZONE™ by Bruce® Floors

A Business Unit of Triangle Pacific Corp.

The Brand You Can Trust™

16803 Dallas Parkway ▼ Dallas, Texas 75248

Sweet's brochure # TZSWT

CORNICE MOULDINGS

C464
06400/WHI
BuyLine 9696

SCALE: 1/4"=1"

SPECIES:
Poplar   Red Oak

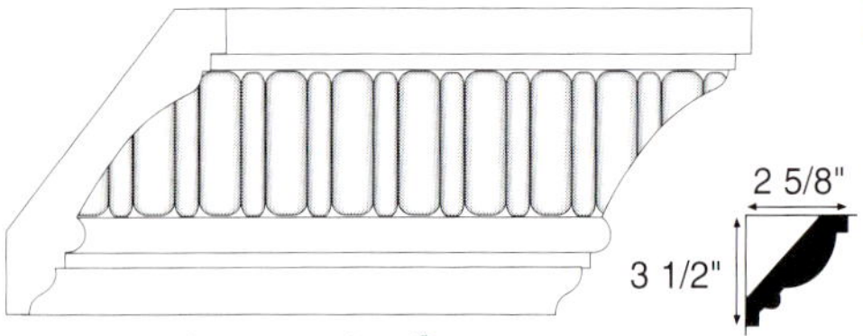

CM70 13/16" x 4 3/8"

CM71 13/16" x 4 1/2"

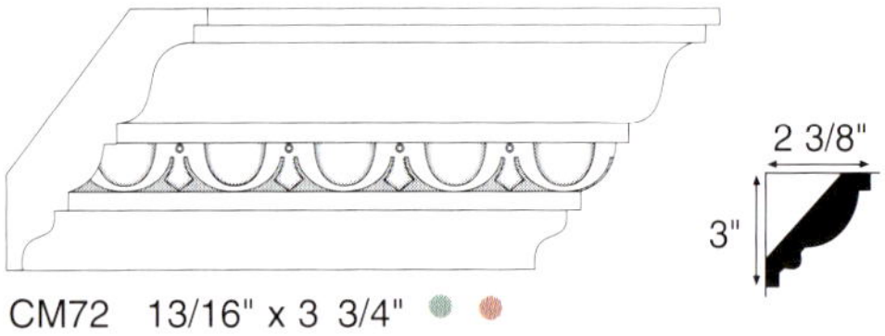

CM72 13/16" x 3 3/4"

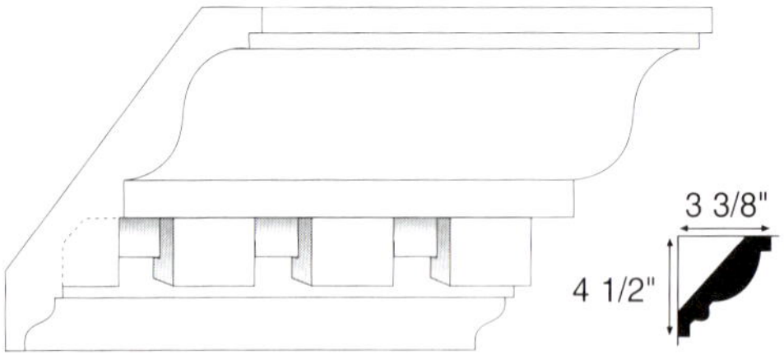

CM73 13/16" x 5 1/2"

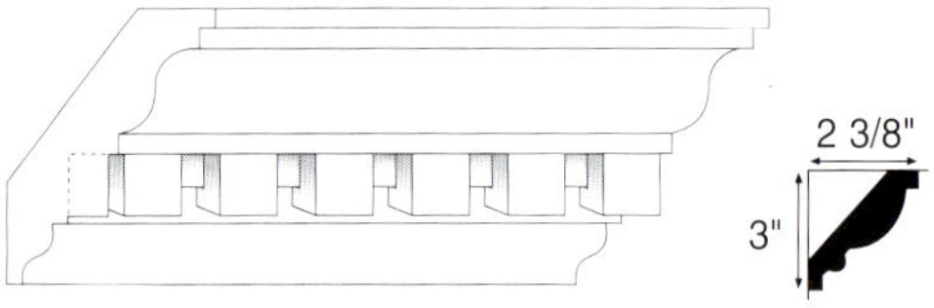

CM74 13/16" x 3 3/4"

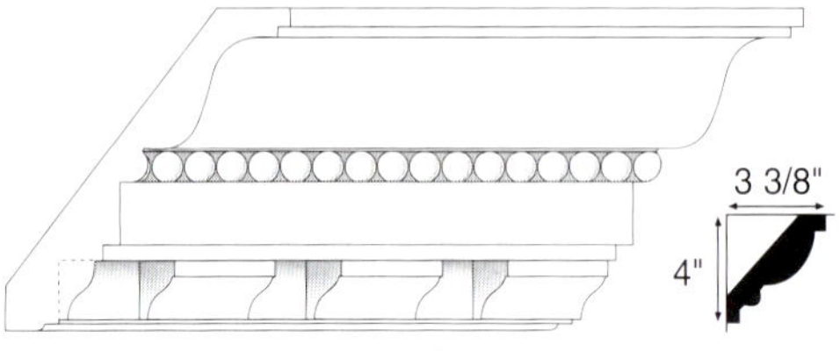

CM75 13/16" x 5 3/16"

CM76 13/16" x 5 1/2"

CM77 13/16" x 4"

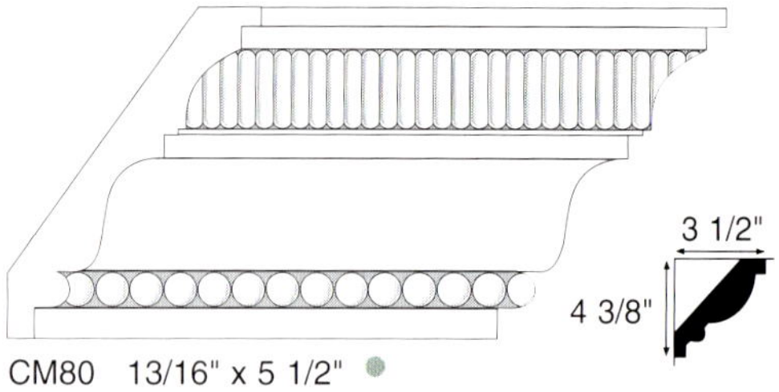

CM80 13/16" x 5 1/2"

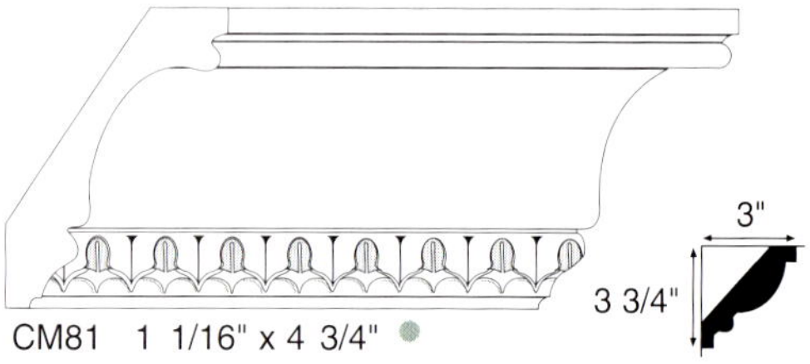

CM81 1 1/16" x 4 3/4"

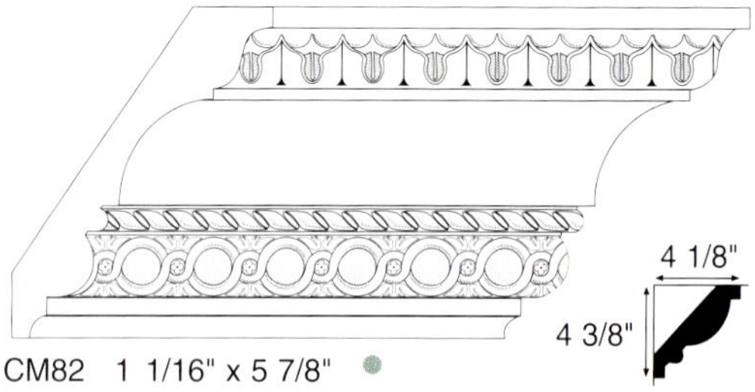

CM82 1 1/16" x 5 7/8"

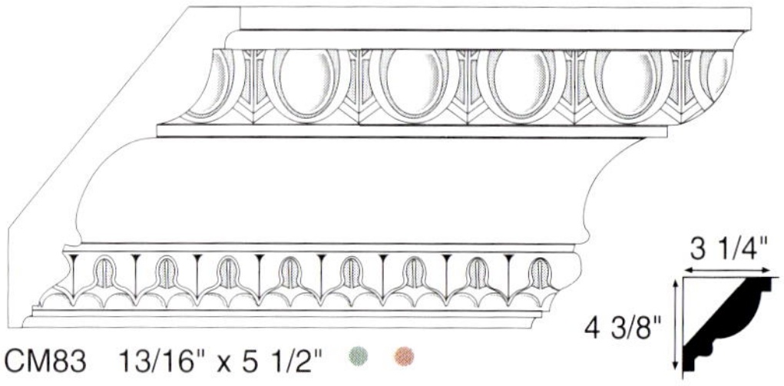

CM83 13/16" x 5 1/2"

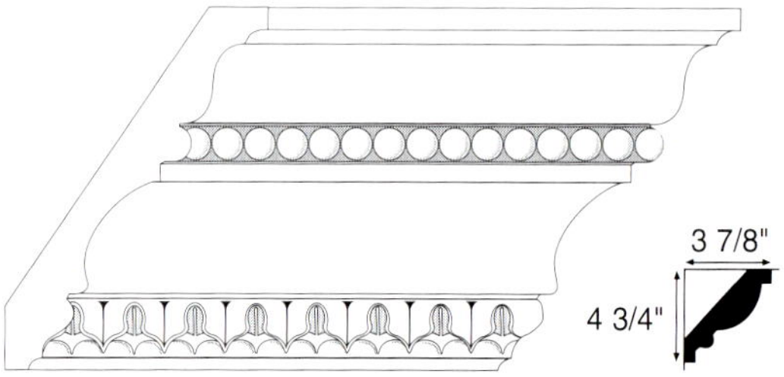

CM84 13/16" x 6 1/4"

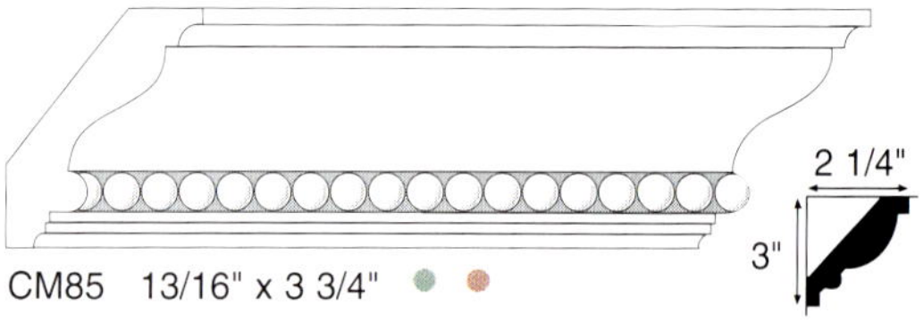

CM85 13/16" x 3 3/4"

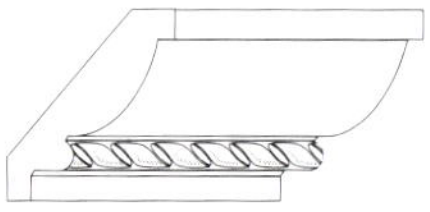

CM88 3/4" x 2 3/4"

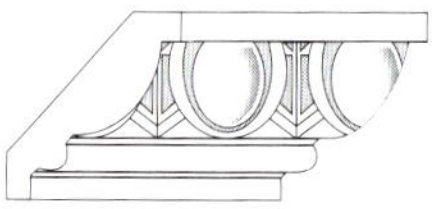

CM89 3/4" x 2 3/4"

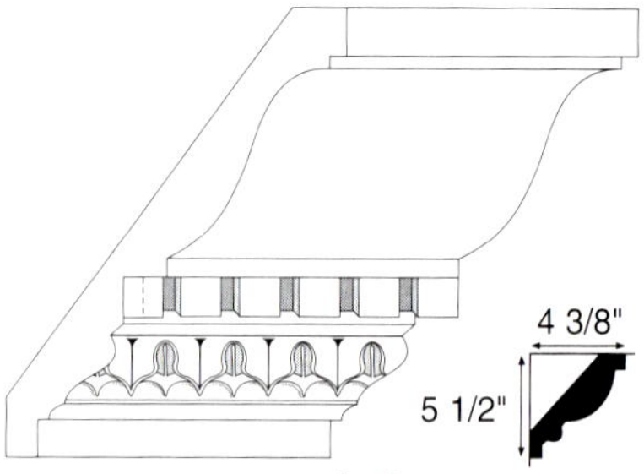

CM86 13/16" x 7"

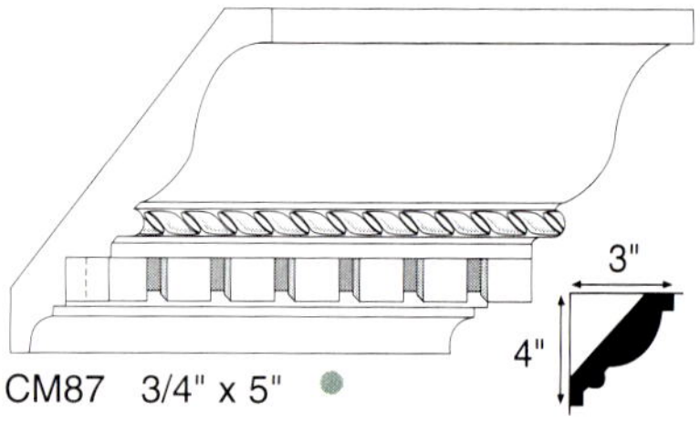

CM87 3/4" x 5"

White River Ornamentals
...are offered in Poplar in all patterns
...are offered in Red Oak where specified
...are all full-sized & full-thickness
...come in long lengths
...meet or exceed A.W.I. standards & specifications
...are shipped unfinished for staining & painting

CURVED APPLICATIONS:
"UltraFlex" curved parts are available for all patterns shown.

WHITE RIVER ORNAMENTALS
MFG. BY:
WHITE RIVER HARDWOODS WOODWORKS, INC.
1-800-558-0119

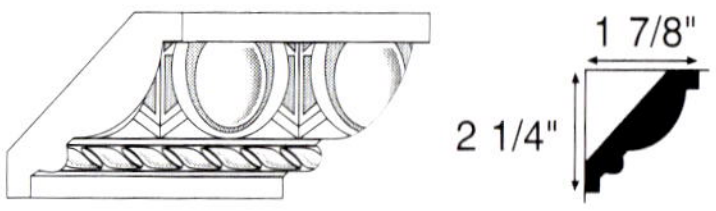

CM69 3/4" x 2 3/4"

CROWN & COVE MOULDINGS...

C464
06400/WHI
BuyLine 9696

SPECIES:
● Poplar
● Red Oak

SCALE: 1/4"=1"

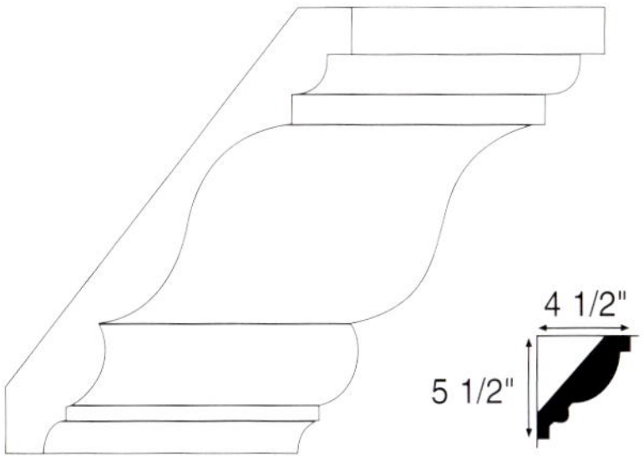

CR800 13/16" x 7" ● ●

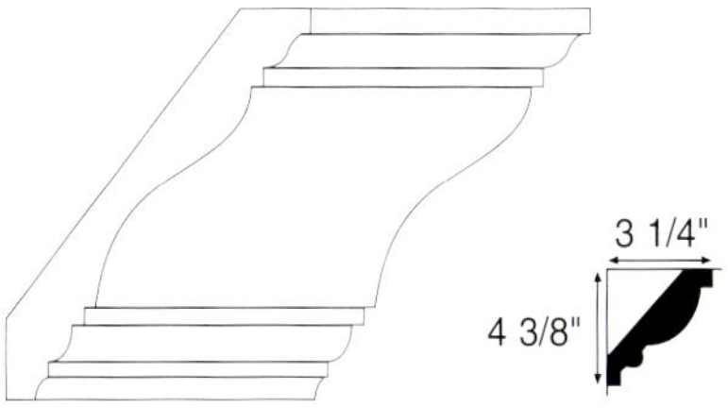

CR806 13/16" x 5 1/2" ●

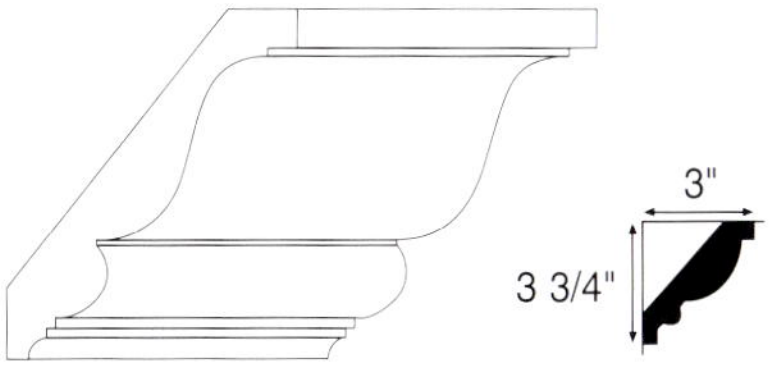

CR810 3/4" x 4 3/4" ● ●

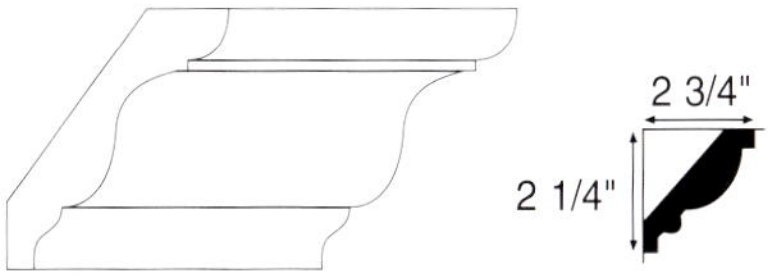

CR820 3/4" x 3 1/2" ● ●

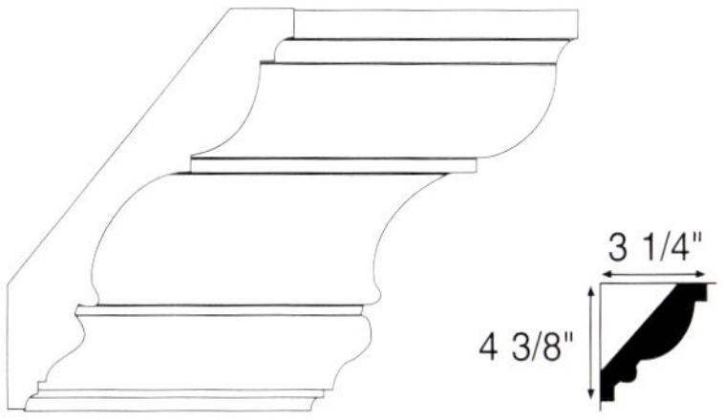

CR830 13/16" x 5 1/2" ● ●

CR840 11/16" x 1 3/4" ● ●

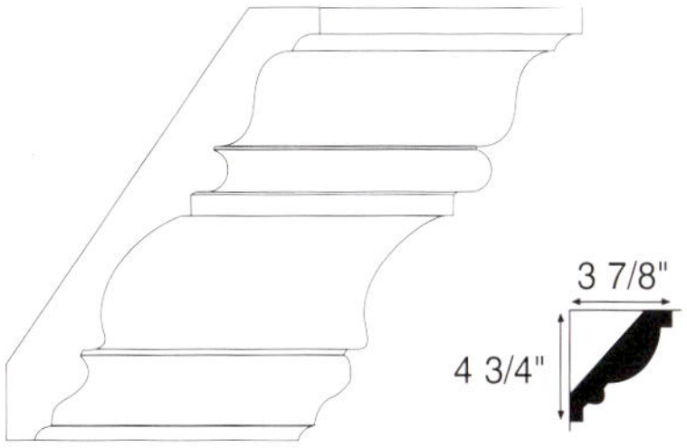

CR841 13/16" x 6 1/4" ●

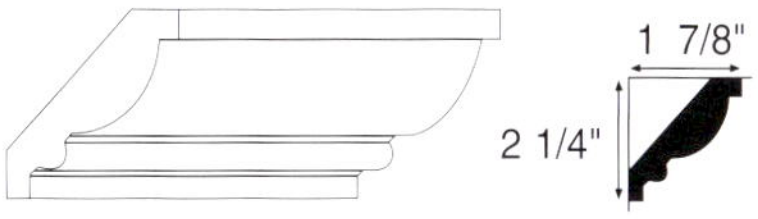

CR850 3/4" x 2 3/4" ● ●

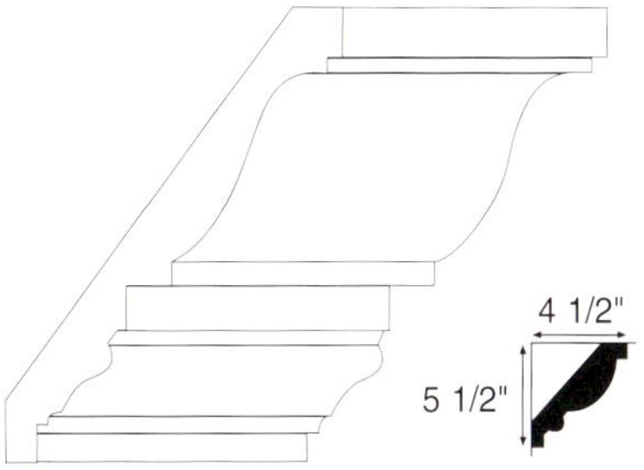

CR860 13/16" x 7" ●

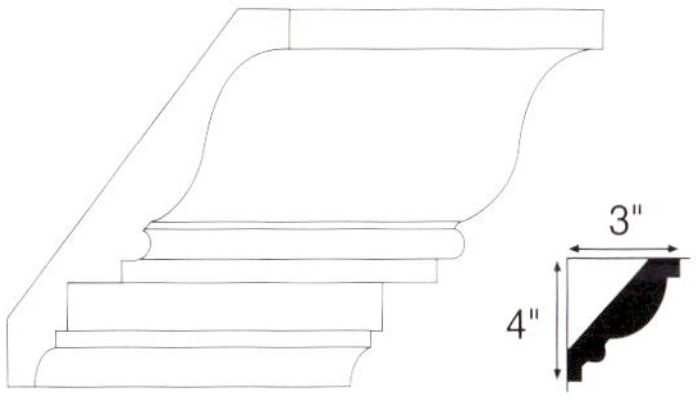

CR866 3/4" x 5" ●

● ● MM187 1 1/4" x 4 3/8"

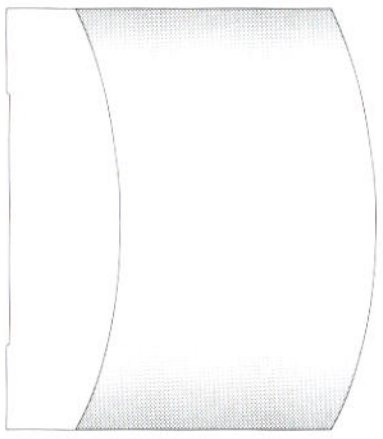

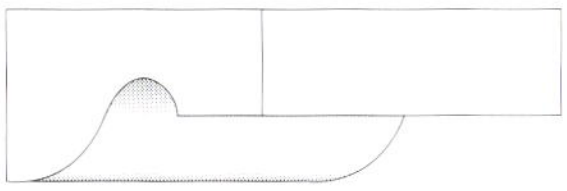

MM189 1 3/4" x 2 3/4" ● ●
(Can be cut to size for Dentil Blocks)

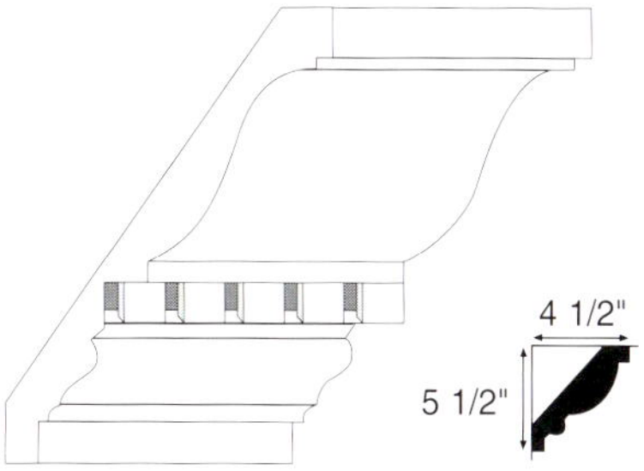

CR862 13/16" x 7" ● ●

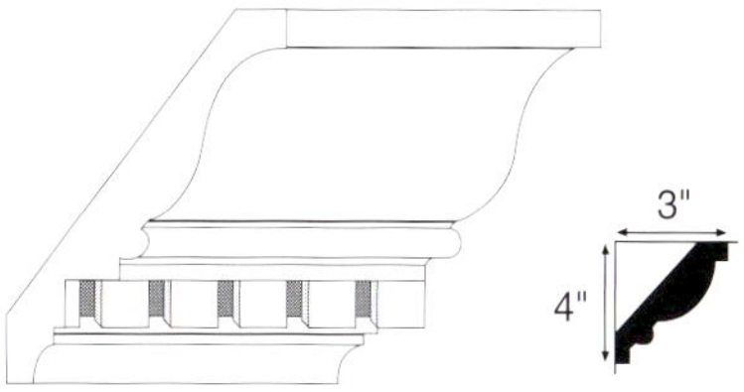

CR864 3/4" x 5" ● ●

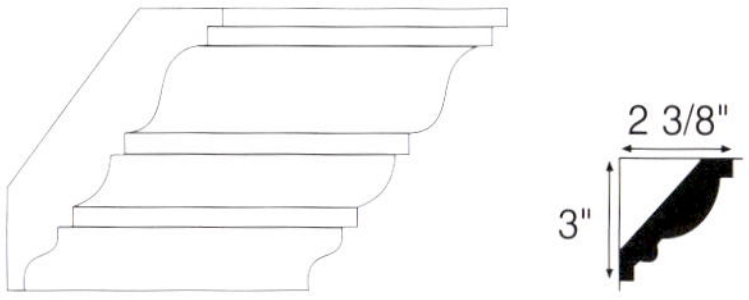

CR872 13/16" x 3 3/4" ●

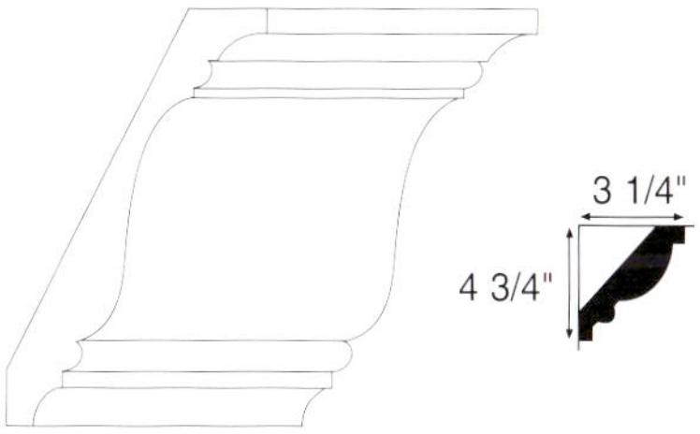

CR880 13/16" x 5 1/2" ● ●

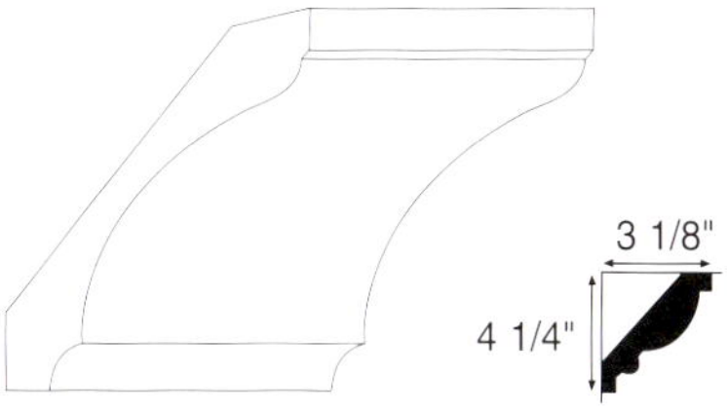

CO705 13/16" x 5 1/4" ●

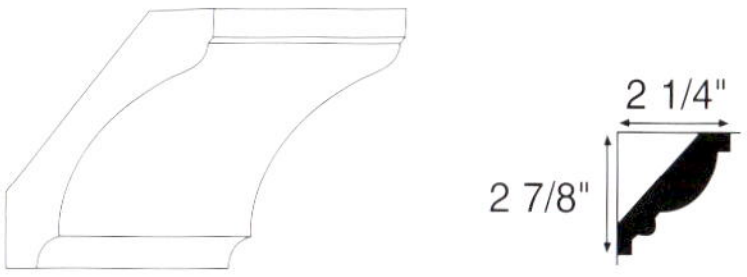

CO707 3/4" x 3 1/2" ●

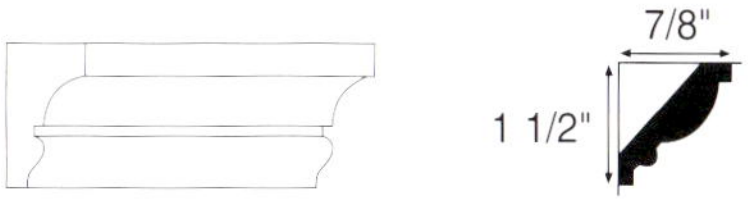

CO730 7/8" x 1 1/2" ●

CURVED APPLICATIONS:

"UltraFlex" curved parts are available for all patterns shown.

WHITE RIVER ORNAMENTALS MFG. BY:
WHITE RIVER HARDWOODS / WOODWORKS, INC.
1-800-558-0119

CHAIRRAILS & PANEL MOULDINGS

C464
06400/WHI
BuyLine 9696

SCALE: 1/4"=1"

SPECIES:
- Poplar
- Red Oak

Item	Size	Species
PM08	5/8" x 1 1/4"	Poplar
PM09	5/8" x 1 1/4"	Poplar
PM10	5/8" x 1 1/4"	Poplar, Red Oak
PM11	7/16" x 5/8"	Poplar
PM12	5/8" x 1 1/8"	Poplar
PM14	1/2" x 1"	Poplar, Red Oak
PM20	13/16" x 2"	Poplar
PM22-pl *(lips 1/4")*	11/16" x 1 3/4"	Poplar
PM22	11/16" x 1 3/4"	Poplar
PM24	3/4" x 2"	Poplar
PM27	3/4" x 2"	Poplar
PM28	3/4" x 1 1/2"	Poplar
PM70 *(lips 1/2"-3/4")*	3/4" x 2 3/8"	Poplar
PM52	13/16" x 1 3/4"	Poplar, Red Oak
PM54	11/16" x 1 1/2"	Poplar
PM55	13/16" x 1 1/4"	Poplar
PM57	5/8" x 1 1/4"	Poplar
PM59	5/8" x 3/4"	Poplar, Red Oak
PM500 *(lips 3/4")*	5/8" x 2 1/4"	Poplar
PM511	13/16" x 1 3/4"	Poplar, Red Oak
PM520 *(lips 1/4")*	11/16" x 1 3/4"	Poplar, Red Oak
PM527	1" x 2 1/2"	Poplar
PM535	5/8" x 1 1/4"	Poplar, Red Oak
PM540	5/8" x 1"	Poplar
PM539	1/2" x 5/8"	Poplar, Red Oak
PM560	3/4" x 1"	Poplar, Red Oak
PM569	3/4" x 1"	Poplar, Red Oak
PM570	3/4" x 2"	Poplar, Red Oak
PM577 *(lips 1/2"-3/4")*	3/4" x 2 3/8"	Poplar, Red Oak
PM580 *(lips 3/4")*	3/4" x 1 3/4"	Poplar, Red Oak
PM582 *(lips 3/4")*	3/4" x 1 3/8"	Poplar
PM590	1 1/2" x 2 1/2"	Poplar, Red Oak
CH610 *(lips 1/2"-3/4")*	3/4" x 3"	Poplar, Red Oak
CH640	1 1/16" x 3"	Poplar
CH690	11/16" x 3"	Poplar, Red Oak
CA324	3/4" x 4"	Poplar, Red Oak
CR61	13/16" x 2 1/2"	Poplar
CR63-A	1 1/16" x 3 1/4"	Poplar
CR64	1 1/16" x 3"	Poplar
CR65	13/16" x 2 1/2"	Poplar, Red Oak
CR66	1" x 3 1/2"	Poplar
CR67	13/16" x 2 1/8"	Poplar, Red Oak
CR68 *(May also be used as Backband)*	1 3/4" x 2 1/2"	Poplar
CR69	1 1/8" x 2 1/4"	Poplar
RE104	9/16" x 1 5/8"	Poplar
OS101 *(Inside covers 5/8" x 5/8")*	13/16" x 13/16"	Poplar, Red Oak
DS110	1/2" x 1 1/2"	Poplar, Red Oak
RE107	3/8" x 3/4"	Poplar

WHITE RIVER ORNAMENTALS MFG. BY:
WHITE RIVER HARDWOODS / WOODWORKS, INC.
1-800-558-0119

Casings & Baseboards, Rosettes & Plynths...

Shown in complimentary application.

SPECIES:
- Poplar
- Red Oak

C464
06400/WHI
BuyLine 9696

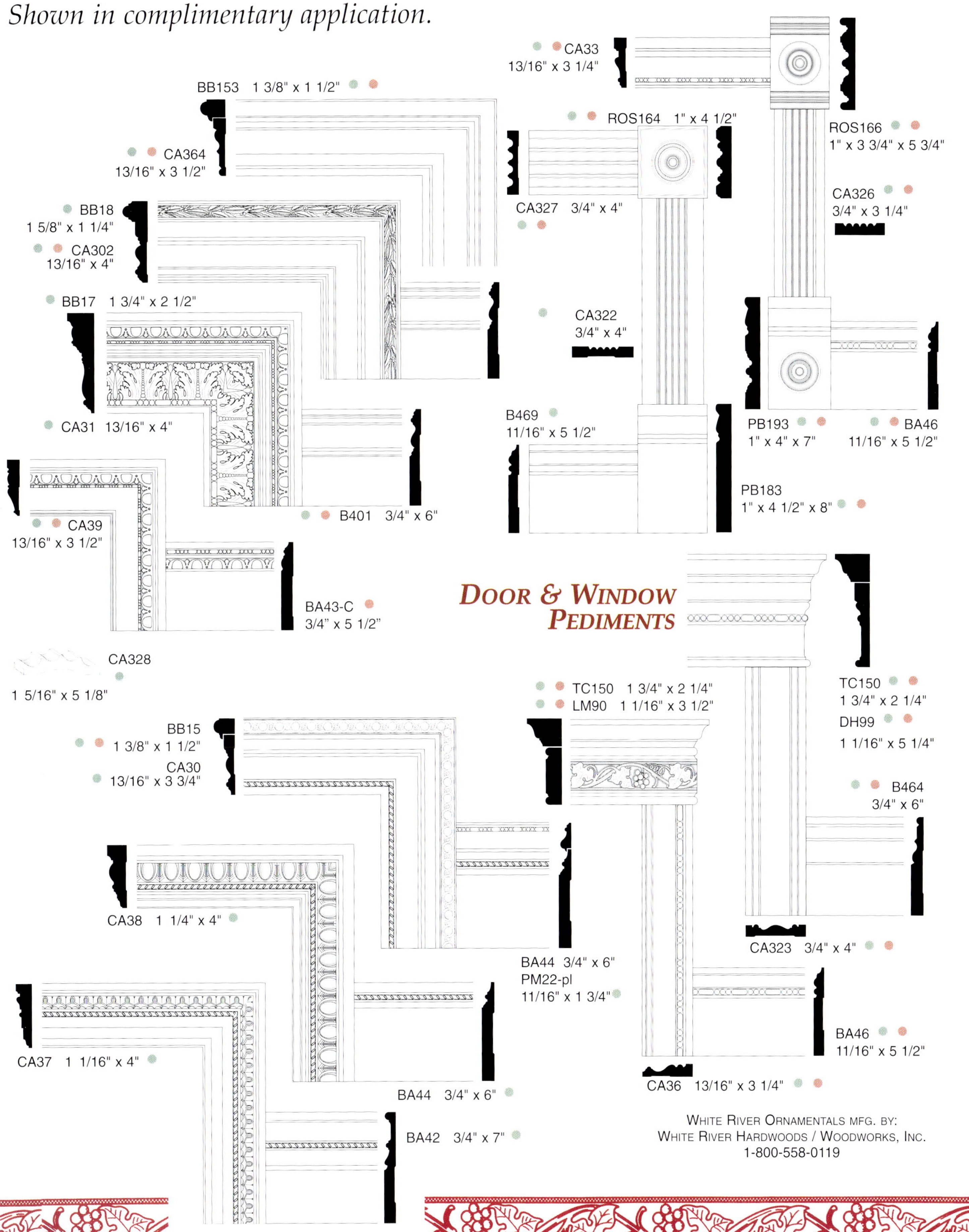

White River Ornamentals mfg. by:
White River Hardwoods / Woodworks, Inc.
1-800-558-0119

LINEAL MOULDINGS...

Used as Casings, Chairrails or as parts of Crown assembly.

SPECIES:
- Poplar
- Red Oak

C464
06400/WHI
BuyLine 9696

LM90
1 1/16" x 3 1/2"

LM91
1 1/16" x 3 1/2"

LM92
1 1/16" x 3 1/2"

LM93-A
1 1/16" x 3 1/2"

(Lineal Mouldings shown 1/4 scale)

Curved Casings are available in stainable solid hardwoods or *"UltraFlex"* curved parts.

KEYSTONES

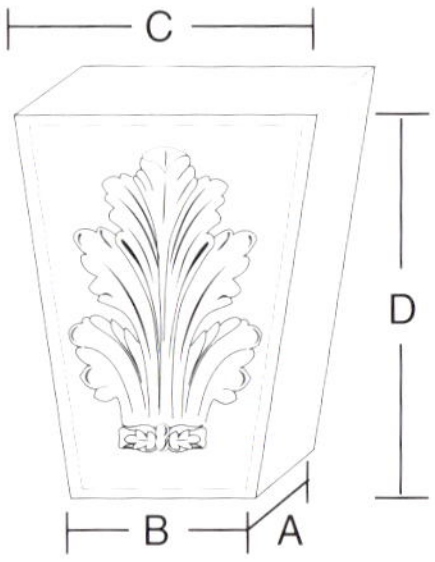

Key 034 (1/8th scale)

	A	B	C	D	Fits Casings up to
Key 031	1"	2"	4"	4 1/2"	13/16" x 2 1/2"-3 1/2"
Key 032	1"	2 1/2"	4 1/2"	5"	13/16" x 3 1/2"-4"
Key 033	1 3/4"	3"	5 1/2"	6"	1 1/2" x 4"-5 1/2"
Key 034	1 3/4"	4"	6 1/2"	8"	1 1/2" x 4 1/2"-7"

Key 031, 032, 033 available in plain face only.
Key 034 (shown) cast as *"UltraFlex" Red Oak & Poplar.*

Curved Crowns, Baseboards, Chairrails and Panel Moulds are available in *"UltraFlex"* curved parts.

ROSETTES & PLYNTH BLOCKS

27/32" THICK
ROS161
2 3/4" x 2 3/4"
ROS159
3 1/2" x 3 1/2"
ROS163
3 3/4" x 3 3/4"

1" THICK
ROS162
2 3/4" x 2 3/4"
ROS169
3 1/2 X 3 1/2"
ROS160
3 3/4" x 3 3/4"
ROS164
4 1/2" X 4 1/2"
ROS165
5 1/2" X 5 1/2"

1" THICK
ROS166
3 3/4" x 5 3/4"
ROS167
4 1/2" x 6 1/2"
ROS168
5 1/2" x 7 1/2"

1" THICK
PB171
3" x 5"
PB170
4" x 7"
PB183
4 1/2" x 8"

1" THICK
PB192
3" x 5"
PB193
4" x 7"
PB185
4 1/2" x 8"

Crown Corners add style while eliminating hard-to-fit miters.

Rosettes should be 1/4"-1/2" wider than casing.
Plynth Block should be 1/4"-3/4" wider than casing.
Plynth Block should be 1"-3" taller than base.

WHITE RIVER ORNAMENTALS MFG. BY:
WHITE RIVER HARDWOODS / WOODWORKS, INC.
1-800-558-0119

Ornate Poplar Mouldings are complemented by a variety of finishes that are sure to inspire you!

CM82

Painted | *Pickled (White Stain)* | *Glazed* | *Fruitwood Stain* | *Walnut Stain*

NOTE: All mouldings shipped unfinished for staining or painting.

New Product!

C464
06400/WHI
BuyLine 9696

Elegant Additions™

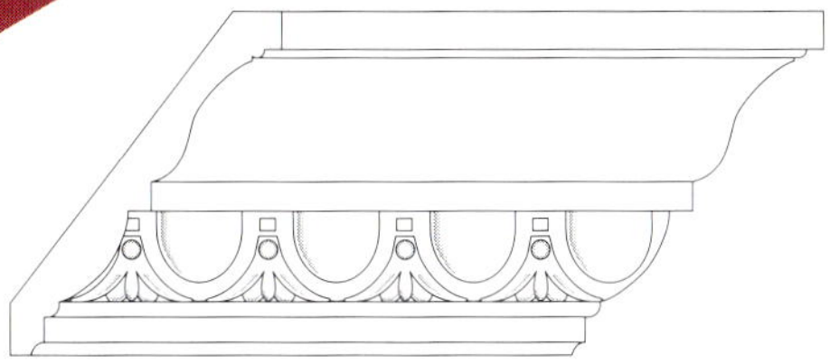

Crown CR8
$\frac{5}{8}$ x $4\frac{1}{4}$

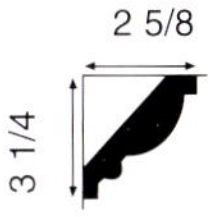

Crown CR7
$\frac{5}{8}$ x 3

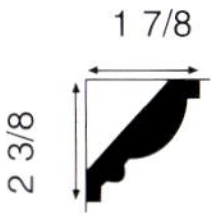

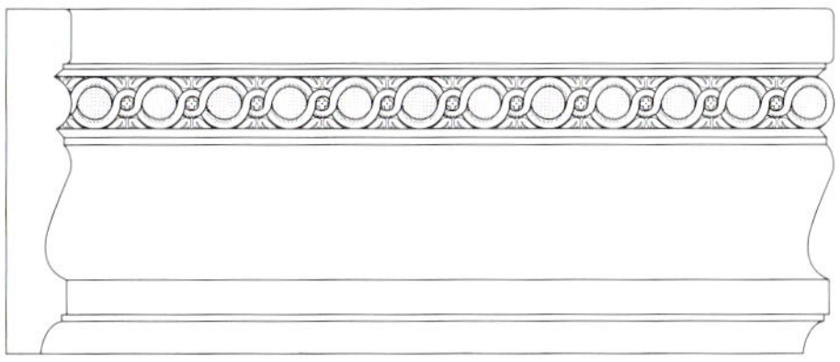

Case CA5
5/8 x 3 1/4

Panel Mould PM4
5/8 x 2

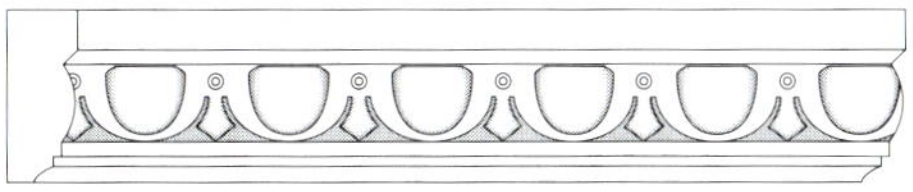

Panel Mould PM3
5/8 x 1 1/2

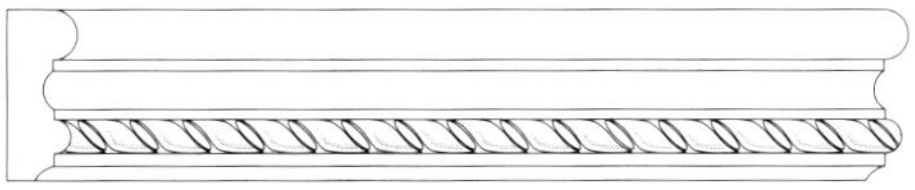

Panel Mould PM2
5/8 x 1 1/2

Panel Mould PM1
5/8 x 2 1/2

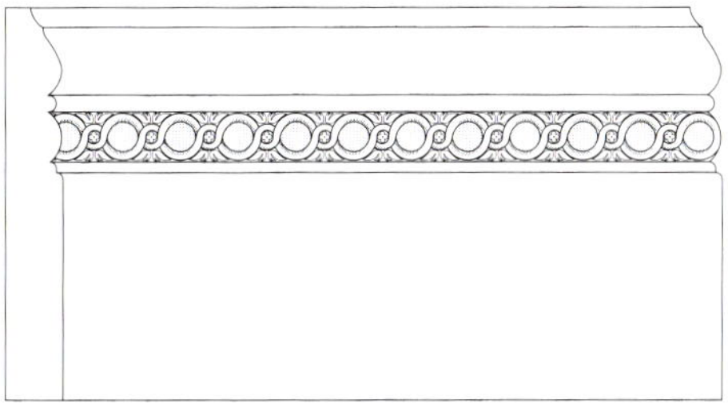

Base BA6
5/8 x 4 1/4

New Embossed MDF (fine-grained Medium Density Fiberboard) is an Elegant Addition to any project. The warmth of wood at a fraction of the cost!

- *Make Projects Beautiful & Simple*
- *Installs and Finishes Just Like Wood*
- *Mix & Match*
- *Can be used Alone or Combined Together for a Larger Architectural Look*
- *Manufactured from Double-Processed Pine Fibers that Create a Smoothly Machined Moulding*
- *Available in Ultra-Flex for Curved & Radius Applications*

CR7 combined with embossed hardwoods

New–High-Relief Wood Mouldings!

C464
06400/WHI
BuyLine 9696

MON REALE

Mon Reale is an opulent new line of 80 profiles...the newest offering from White River Hardwoods–Woodworks, Inc. of Fayetteville, Arkansas. The line complements White River's smooth and embossed hardwoods mouldings with its classic design. Mon Reale will grace the appearance of any room and achieve dimensions never before possible with precision machined wood mouldings.

The process produces a fine-grained overlay material contoured to traditional hardwood mouldings. This procedure results in depth of detail with a much greater degree of definition like that found in plaster, carved wood and hand-laid composition ornament. The extra detail will give architects, designers and decorators more options when creating rooms of lasting beauty. Skilled trim carpenters can easily install Mon Reale; no special installation crews are required. Mon Reale paints and stains just like hardwood mouldings. The mouldings are available for curved application in Ultra-Flex.

Phase I, the first fifty profiles, have been released for National Distribution and are now ready for your inspection and purchase. The completion of the line is expected by the end of 1997. Additional literature will be available in the near future.

Mon Reale is available only from White River, the innovator in hardwood mouldings. Please call to request more information.

for further information:

White River
HARDWOODS • WOODWORKS, INC.
1-800-558-0119
http://www.mouldings.com

1197 Happy Hollow Road
Fayetteville, Arkansas 72701 U.S.A.
Phone (501) 442-6986
Fax: (501) 444-0406

Fountainhead by Nevamar®

C467
06600/NEV
BuyLine 7632

NEVAMAR®
DECORATIVE SURFACES

As tough as they are beautiful.

INTERNATIONAL PAPER
DECORATIVE PRODUCTS DIVISION
8339 TELEGRAPH ROAD
ODENTON MD 21113-1397

The solid surface alternative

Elegant Fountainhead by Nevamar® solid surfacing is a wise investment that can increase the value of your home now and at resale. Extremely durable and easy to care for, Fountainhead is available in a wide range of colors and patterns. Fountainhead sinks and bowls complete the look in bath or kitchen. A 10-year limited warranty is standard on all Fountainhead products when installed by a Nevamar accredited fabricator.

*Because it's non-porous, most spills can simply be wiped away from Fountainhead with a damp cloth or sponge. Stains from wine, vinegar, coffee, even grape juice can be removed, although some may require more aggressive cleaning with household bleach.**

When properly fabricated, Fountainhead's outstanding heat resistance makes it ideal for use around rangetops.

Fountainhead resists most household chemicals.

Fountainhead resists the impact of falling objects.

Fountainhead will not burn. Brown nicotine stains or scorch marks can be removed from the matte finish by using an abrasive cleanser or buffing with a wet Scotch Brite® pad.

*Because the color runs throughout, scuffs, scratches and even accidental cuts can be easily repaired on the matte finish by buffing with a Scotch Brite pad or 320-350 grit sandpaper. If your countertop has a polished (gloss) appearance which requires more complicated finishing techniques, damage must be repaired by a professional.**

*Please refer to the Fountainhead care and cleaning guide for additional information.

Fountainhead offers a wide selection of kitchen and bar/utility sinks and vanity bowls. These products provide all the beauty and performance of Fountainhead sheet goods. Fountainhead sinks and bowls have been tested and approved by IAPMO/UPC. They are also certified by the National Association of Home Builders Research Foundation, Inc. Color choices include a range of solid colors (for kitchen sinks, vanity bowls and the bar/utility sink) as well as Nevamar's exclusive Matrix pattern on vanity bowls. An extra deep (9-1/2") kitchen sink is available to accommodate large pots and pans.

Mounting Options and Installation

Fountainhead kitchen and bar/utility sinks offer three mounting options: Flush,* Seamed,* and Undermount. All three options are installed level with or below the counter surface, facilitating easy cleanup. Fountainhead vanity bowls can be seamed or undermounted.

The monolithic* appearance of an integral bowl can be achieved by seaming sinks or bowls to sheet goods of the same color. Thanks to their unique design, all Fountainhead sinks and bowls can be positioned on the sheet anywhere the installation requires. Two or more bowls can even be installed in the same sheet. The special design also makes installation faster and easier than most other solid surface sinks and bowls to save time and money!

* When selecting the same color for sink and countertops, Seam and Flush mount options are not recommended unless a contrasting color strip or inlay is used at the seam line, as slight color variations could occur.

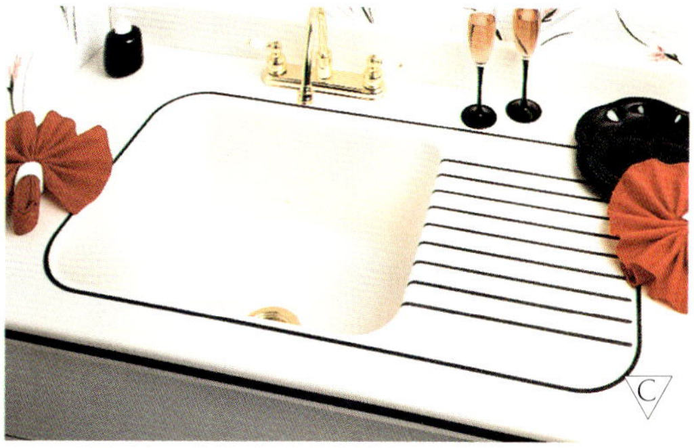

A. **Material Used:** *Winter White Fountainhead double kitchen sink (K020-Seam mount) in Fawn Mist Fountainhead countertop*

B. **Material Used:** *Medium Gray Matrix Fountainhead vanity bowl (B022-Seam mount) in Architectural White Fountainhead top*

C. **Material Used:** *Classic White Fountainhead sink (K013-Seam mount) in Classic White Fountainhead top with Black Matrix accents and drainboard inlay*

D. **Material Used:** *Sand Beige Fountainhead bar/utility sink (B031- Flush mount) in Verde Matrix Fountainhead top*

Edges for a customized look

Fountainhead can be fabricated to give your designs a truly personalized effect. Edges can be left at just the thickness of the Fountainhead sheet or built up to create a greater thickness and unique edge appearance. These edges represent just a few of the looks which can be achieved.

Fountainhead has met the requirements for a Class I fire rating. It has been classified by Underwriters Laboratories (UL) as safe for use in all public and private spaces. Fountainhead sheets have met all requirements of and been certified by NSF International.

A: **Material Used:** *Linen combined with Fawn Mist*
B: **Material Used:** *Mystic White Matrix with routed grooves*
C: **Material Used:** *Architectural White with quarter round Verde Matrix accent*
D: **Material Used:** *Federal Cornerstone Fountainhead countertop with Linen sandwich edge and Alabaster Vitricor backsplash*

C474
06650/DUP
Buy Line 0665

Corian®

Only by DuPont

Baths and kitchens—
Created for the way you live.

Life is good.

With CORIAN® in the kitchen and bath, it gets better.

Life revolves around the surfaces in the home. Especially in the kitchen and bath.

So it makes sense to choose surfaces people can enjoy living with year after year. Surfaces that can stand up to wear and tear. Children. Pets. Guests. Relatives. The inevitable spills. The unavoidable accidents. The hard knocks life can dish out.

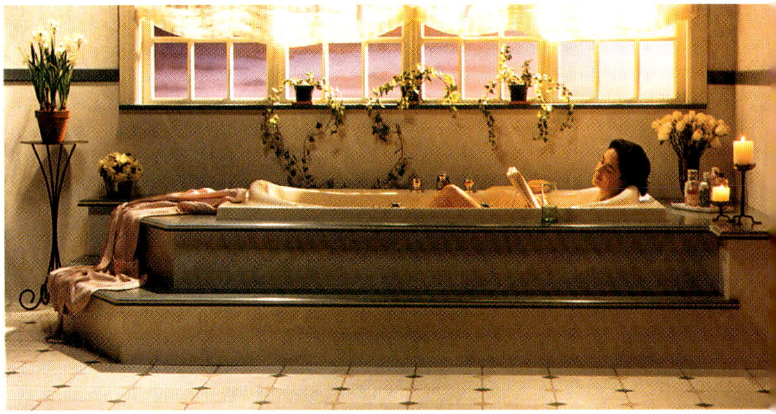

That's why DuPont created CORIAN®. **For the way you live.**

The more people live, **the more CORIAN® forgives.**

Whatever the spill, CORIAN® is *easy to clean*. CORIAN® *resists stains* because *liquids can't penetrate*.

CORIAN® resists the mold, mildew, scratches and stains that may harm other surfaces.

CORIAN® *keeps its good looks longer.* It survives the impacts, nicks and cuts that can mar most surfaces. Everyday spills clean up with just soapy water or cleanser. Scratches and stubborn stains that can ruin other surfaces can be removed easily by scouring or lightly sanding.*

What is CORIAN®?

More than 30 years ago, DuPont discovered a way to blend natural minerals with pure acrylic resin to create an ideal surface for living. Ever since then, we've been hard at work creating new colors, patterns and innovative CORIAN® products.

We must be doing something right. Because other companies have been working just as hard, trying to duplicate CORIAN®.

That won't be easy: The solid beauty of CORIAN® goes all the way through. So the possibilities for patterns, colors and shapes are just about unlimited. And if the surface is damaged, there's plenty more renewable beauty underneath.

98% of people who have CORIAN® surfaces in their homes today say they'd buy it again.

CORIAN® has a rich, natural translucence, and it's inviting to touch.

And only CORIAN® has DuPont and the exclusive CORIAN® warranty to stand behind you after the sale.

Every inch of **CORIAN®** is backed by **a 10-year limited product warranty from DuPont.**

And when a DuPont Certified Fabricator/Installer puts in CORIAN®, *the entire job is warranted for 10 years against fabrication and installation defects.* It's the only warranty in the industry that's transferable when a home is sold. For details, see CORIAN® warranty literature.

10 YEAR DUPONT WARRANTY

*For more information, refer to the *DuPont CORIAN® Care & Maintenance Tips Card* (H-56461)

C474
06650/DUP
Buy Line 0665

In the kitchen.

CORIAN® gives you more possibilities than any other surface material. Start with CORIAN® countertops. Add a custom inlay or edge treatment. Choose a CORIAN® sink from the many styles and colors offered. Create a one-of-a-kind kitchen with the rich, natural colors and textures of CORIAN® bringing warmth and style to any decor.

◀ *SIGNATURE style: CORIAN® sweeps across this connoisseur's kitchen from coved backsplashes to counters to sinks to inlaid bullnose edges.*

▲ *CLASSIC value: With just a plain edge treatment, square backsplash and a drop-in sink, a CORIAN® countertop makes an ordinary kitchen extraordinary.*

◀ *CUSTOM touches: A CORIAN® countertop flows gracefully into a CORIAN® sink. A simple edge treatment and inlay add depth, drama and a unique twist.*

In the bath.

With CORIAN®, a simple bathroom can become simply elegant. Whether you choose a custom-fabricated or a Ready-To-Install application, CORIAN® is a pleasure to live with. No surface in your bathroom is easier to clean or looks new longer. CORIAN® survives the impacts, scratches and scrubbings that can wreck cultured marble, ceramic tile and fiberglass.

▶ *SIGNATURE style: CORIAN® comes to life in the hands of a craftsman. Intricate inlays mix rich colors and textures. Graceful, continuous waves of CORIAN® flow across walls, trim, tops and sinks.*

▶ *CUSTOM touches: Coordinated colors and textures tie together a bathroom, complete with a custom CORIAN® Vanity Top & Bowl and custom shower wall.*

▲ *CLASSIC value: Add luxury and value to your home with a coordinated bathroom. It's easy and affordable when you combine a CORIAN® Ready-To-Install Tub and Shower Wall Kit with a matching CORIAN® One-Piece Vanity Top & Bowl.*

the *Living* Colors of CORIAN®

GENESIS
- Glacier White
- Cameo White
- Bisque
- Bone
- Peach
- Champagne
- Tea Rose
- Dusty Rose
- Pearl Gray
- Seagrass

VENARO
- Venaro White
- Venaro Gray
- Dawn Beige
- Venaro Champagne
- Venaro Peach
- Venaro Rose

SIERRA
- Dusk
- Midnight
- Eclipse
- Burnt Amber
- Aurora
- Sandstone
- Beach
- Primrose
- Pink Coral
- Sunset
- Tarragon
- Evergreen
- Malachite
- Oceanic
- Lavender

JEWEL
- Black Quartz
- Black Pearl
- Garnet
- Azure
- Sapphire
- Jade

SUMMIT
- Everest
- Mont Blanc
- Matterhorn
- Kilimanjaro
- Sequoia
- Vesuvius
- Blue Ridge
- Pyrenees
- Spruce

MAGNA
- Rosetta
- Platinum
- Sahara
- Mediterranean
- Rain Forest

See your retailer for the latest available colors. Actual colors may vary. Photography of Venaro colors is not large enough to represent full veining pattern. For actual samples or color options for sinks, countertops, tubs, shower walls and bowls, see your retailer.

Because of their dark colors, jewel tones may require more maintenance.

Look beyond **the surface.**

Compare CORIAN® to other materials. CORIAN® gives you all their **advantages** with none of their **disadvantages**.

Material	Advantages	Disadvantages
CORIAN®	• All of the below	• None of the below
GRANITE	• Rich visual texture • Elegance	• Porous surface can stain • Cold to touch • Scratches hard to remove • Lack of design flexibility • Must be resealed occasionally
MARBLE	• Dramatic beauty • Luxurious color and texture	• Cracks and stains easily • Cold to touch • Scratches hard to remove
CERAMIC TILE	• Versatile styling • Heat resistance • Durability	• Grout lines are hard to clean, support growth of mold and mildew • Cracks and chips • Uneven surfaces • Replacement grout is difficult to color-match
LAMINATE	• Cleanability • Styling flexibility	• Thin surface color can chip or wear away • Conspicuous seams/edges • Scorches, cuts easily • Excess water can cause delamination
CULTURED MARBLE	• Rich visual texture	• Thin gel coat can chip or wear away • Cracks and chips • Nicks and scratches are difficult to repair
STAINLESS STEEL	• Practicality • Efficiency • Durability	• Sterile, institutional look • Cold to touch • Scratches, dents and water spots easily
PORCELAIN & & ENAMELED IRON/STEEL	• Rich color • Scrubbable	• Cracks and chips • Cold to touch • Sink lip/caulk line traps water, dirt
FIBERGLASS	• No grout lines to clean	• Scratches easily • Thin surface color and gloss can wear away with normal scrubbing • Shows water spots • Nicks and scratches very difficult to repair
WOOD	• Warmth • Charm • Rich visual texture	• Fragile…scratches very easily • Unsanitary • Very susceptible to heat and water damage
CORIAN®	• All of the above	• None of the above

HOW TO SPECIFY CORIAN®

The following suggested write-ups are included to assist you when specifying CORIAN®.

One-Piece Vanity Tops & Bowls

Vanity bowls and tops shall be of a one-piece, monolithic design, made of CORIAN® (methyl methacrylate binder) manufactured by DuPont. Color and pattern shall be selected by the architect and physical properties shall conform to the manufacturer's standard specifications. The material shall be homogenous, not coated or laminated. Installation shall be in a workmanlike manner, in accordance with the manufacturer's instructions.

Surfaces

Surfaces shall be CORIAN®. Color and pattern shall be selected by the architect. CORIAN® sheets shall be ½″ (13mm) or ¾″ (19mm) for countertops. Backsplashes, where specified, shall be ¼″ (6mm), ½″ (13mm) or ¾″ (19mm). Wall coverings shall be ¼″ (6mm) unless otherwise specified. Physical properties shall conform to the manufacturer's standard specifications. The material shall be homogenous, not coated or laminated. Installation shall be in a workmanlike manner, in accordance with the manufacturer's instructions.

When specifying CORIAN® for applications that are wider then 30″ (760mm) or require a seam, specify DuPont Joint Adhesive for CORIAN®. It can be used to form a smooth, inconspicuous seam. DuPont Silicone Sealant for CORIAN® should be used for caulking tub and shower wall seams and edges.

Generic specifications that can be customized for your CORIAN® applications are available from your local CORIAN® Distributor. Both electronic and hard copy versions are available in several of the most popular specification formats.

FOR MORE INFORMATION…

For technical data, please refer to Sweet's C474/06650/DUP.

For the latest information regarding sizes, shapes, colors and engineered products, contact your CORIAN® Distributor or Retailer.

Or call DuPont, toll-free:
1-800-4-CORIAN (1-800-426-7426).

DUPONT®

Corian®
Only by DuPont

C952-H59411 (Rev. 9/96) Printed in the U.S.A.

WILSONART INTERNATIONAL

C478
06650/WIL
BuyLine 6889

Wilsonart® Laminate

You want a broad range of choices. You want a surface that lasts. Yet, you have a budget you must maintain. Relax. Wilsonart Laminate combines the best of design, durability, and value in a surfacing material that looks great in any setting.

Choose from our unique palette of over 250 colors and patterns, ranging from solid tones to woodgrains and marbles or patterns. A designer finish, such as Crystal, may be added. And, as always, a matching edge treatment lends dimension and flair to any decor. No matter what your budget, Wilsonart Laminate has the right combination for you.

Wilsonart® Custom Edges

Nothing sets off the look of your countertop like a well-chosen edge treatment. Available in a wide variety of durable, affordable surfacing materials, Wilsonart Custom Edges add expression to your interior decor. All colors and patterns have been thoughtfully designed to coordinate with our complete line of laminate and SSV materials. And when matched with any of our various profiles and styles, there's no limit to the effects a Custom Edge can achieve.

On the lower end of the cost spectrum, choose a beveled edge in any of our 250 laminate designs. Or move up to our more traditional Red Oak or Hard Maple wood moldings, available in three styles and numerous profiles. For a more modern look, consider one of our Acrylic, SSV, or Gibraltar moldings, with over 32 complementary colors and patterns available for your choosing. Single-color moldings are standard. Mixed designs are slightly more.

For a surface that adds style to any decor, nothing completes a Wilsonart countertop better than Wilsonart Custom Edges. Our edges carry a 10-year warranty against delamination.

For information on product, samples or literature, call toll free (800) 433-3222.

Wilsonart® SSV™ Solid Surfacing

Until now, the price of solid surfacing has been as upscale as the look. Wilsonart SSV Solid Surfacing provides the style so many homeowners admire, at a cost approximately one-third less than traditional solid surfacing. And SSV is still backed by a 10-year installed, transferable, limited warranty when installed by a certified fabricator.

Wilsonart SSV Solid Surfacing is a one-eighth-inch-thick solid surfacing material that is entirely renewable. Slight scratches and burns can be buffed away with a Scotch-Brite® pad. And the look is simply sophisticated.

Choose from 32 solid colors and stone-like patterns in all, each designed to complement our full line of integrated sinks and bowls. Wilsonart SSV Solid Surfacing also coordinates with a broad range of standard and upgrade edges to create the perfect countertop look or style. For elegant durability at a reasonable price, consider SSV from Wilsonart.

Wilsonart® Gibraltar® Solid Surfacing

Few materials of any sort command the attention or create the mystique of stone-like, premium-grade Wilsonart Gibraltar Solid Surfacing. Its beautiful, sculpted appearance affirms its underlying strength and durability, plus it's backed by a 10-year installed, transferable, limited warranty when installed by a certified fabricator. Its half-inch-thick substance lends a wood-like workability to its form. Scratch it or burn it, and it buffs back to "like new" condition under the stroke of a Scotch-Brite® pad. Match any of 32 solid colors and stone-like patterns with a coordinating sink, bowl, or edge and you'll create a showcase countertop.

Starting with solid colors, and moving up to the slightly higher-priced stone-like patterns, Wilsonart Gibraltar Solid Surfacing looks spectacular when matched with a standard one-color or premium two-color edge profile.

Wilsonart® SSV™ Solid Surfacing & Wilsonart® Gibraltar® Solid Surfacing

C478
06650/WIL
BuyLine 6889

Solid Colors (standard)

● SSV only
▲ Gibraltar only

Designer White	Frosty White	Ivory	Antique White	Natural Almond	Bone	Orchid Glow
D354-SL*	1573-SL*	9076-SL*	1572-SL*	D30-SL*	9035-SL●	9011-SL*●

Patterns — Mirage and Tempest Groups (upgrade)

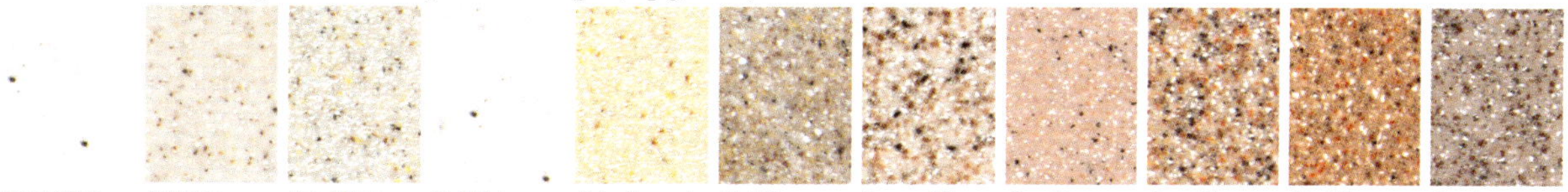

Frosty White Mirage	Alabaster Mirage	Grey Mirage	Light Beige Mirage	Beige Tempest	Khaki Brown Tempest	Pawnee Mirage	Rose Stone Mirage	Fawn Mirage	Clay Mirage	Raspberry Mirage
1573-MG	D431-MG	1500N-MG	1531-MG*	1530-TM	D50-TM	D396-MG	9052-MG▲	D309-MG	9050-MG●	9051-MG▲

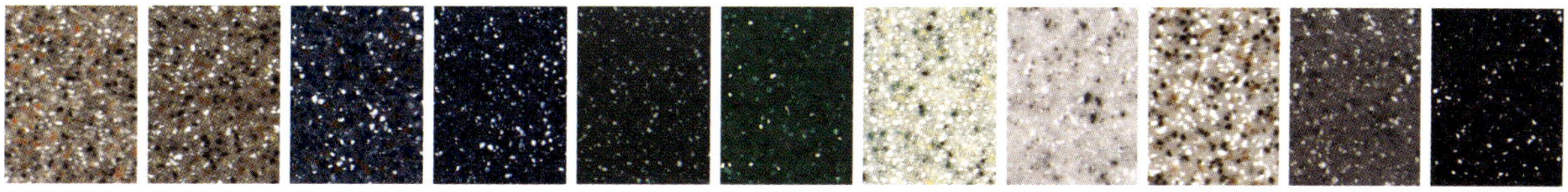

Taupe Mirage	Burnt Amber Mirage	Atlantis Mirage	Sapphire Mirage	Jade Mirage	Hunter Green Mirage	Seacrest Mirage	Platinum Tempest	Moonstruck Mirage	Raven Mirage	Graphite Mirage
D368-MG	9040-MG●	9022-MG	9020-MG▲	9080-MG	D79-MG▲	9081-MG●	D315-TM*	9010-MG▲	D426-MG	9021-MG

Patterns — Melange Group (premium)

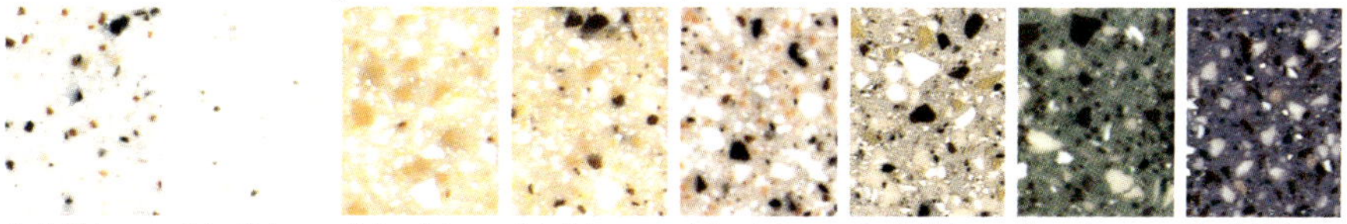

Arctic Melange	Alpine Melange	Mojave Melange	Baja Melange	Adirondack Melange	Eureka Melange	Cascades Melange	Acadia Melange
9070-ML	9071-ML	9031-ML	9030-ML	9012-ML	9090-ML	9082-ML	9023-ML

Wilsonart® SSV™ Solid Surfacing

Standard Edge — Upgrade Edges

Self Edge — *Gibraltar Edge* — *SE Molding* — *XP Molding* — *Wood Edge*

Wilsonart® Gibraltar®

Standard Edges — Upgrade Edges

Roundover — *Bevel/Chamfer* — *Ogee* — *Bullnose* — *Inlay* — *Insert*

Wilsonart® Laminate

Standard Edges — Upgrade Edges

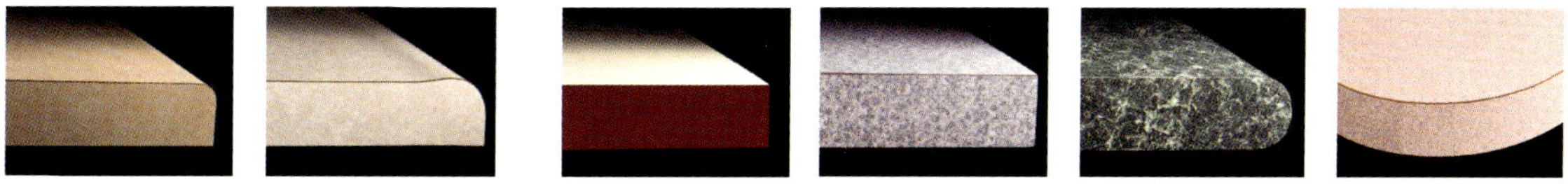

Waterfall — *No Drip* — *Accent Color* — *Self Edge* — *Bullnose* — *Rounded Edge*

*Kitchen sinks and vanity bowls available to match. Platinum Tempest and Light Beige Mirage available in coordinating solid colors only.

Wilsonart® Laminate

Manufacturer

Wilsonart International
2400 Wilson Place
P.O. Box 6110
Temple, Texas 76503-6110
Phone: (254) 207-7000
FAX: (254) 207-2384

For more information and delivery of samples, just call: (800) 433-3222.

Short Specification Form

Type:	(specify 107, 335 or 350)	
Surface:	Color Number:	
	Color Name:	
Finish:	Number:	Name:
Edge Trim:	Color Number:	
	Color Name:	
Adhesive:	Name:	
	Grade/Type:	
	Brand: Lokweld®	

Care and Maintenance

1. To clean the surface, use a damp cloth or sponge and a mild soap or detergent.
2. Difficult stains such as coffee or tea can be removed using a mild household cleaner/detergent and a soft bristle brush, repeating as necessary.
3. If a stain persists, use a paste of baking soda and water and apply with a soft bristled brush. Light scrubbing for 10 to 20 strokes should remove most stains. Although baking soda is a low abrasive, excessive scrubbing or exerting too much force could damage the decorative surface, especially if it has a gloss finish.
4. Stubborn stains that resist any of the above cleaning methods may require the use of undiluted household bleach or nail polish remover. Apply the bleach or nail polish remover to the stain and let stand no longer than two minutes. Rinse thoroughly with warm water and wipe dry. This step may be repeated if the stain appears to be going away and the color of the laminate has not been affected. WARNING: Prolonged exposure of the laminate surface to bleach will cause discoloration.

Your area sales representative will provide free copies of the "Care and Maintenance Guide," which covers care and maintenance of most Wilsonart products, for your own information, for project manuals and for provision to clients and contractors involved with interior construction and finishing.

Limited Warranty

Wilsonart International warrants that, under normal use and service, the material and workmanship of its products shall conform to the standards set forth on the applicable technical data sheets for a period of twelve (12) months from the date of sale to the first consumer purchaser. Dealers and distributors are provided with the technical data sheets which contain specific standards of performance for the products. In the event that a Wilsonart International product does not perform as warranted, the first purchaser's sole remedy shall be limited to repair or replacement of all or any part of the product which is defective, at the manufacturer's sole discretion.

This warranty applies only to product:

1. In its original installation; and
2. Purchased by the first consumer purchaser.

This warranty is not transferable, and expires upon resale or transfer by the first consumer purchaser.

This warranty shall not apply to defects or damage arising from any of the following:

1. Accidents, abuse or misuse;
2. Exposure to extreme temperature;
3. Improper fabrication or installation; or
4. Improper maintenance.

No other warranties, expressed or implied, are made. Under no circumstances shall the manufacturer be liable for any loss or damage arising from the purchase, use or inability to use this product, or for any special, indirect, incidental or consequential damages. No fabricator, installer, dealer, agent or employee of Wilsonart International has the authority to modify the obligations or limitation of this warranty.
This warranty gives you specific legal rights, and you may also have other rights which vary from state to state; therefore, some of the limitations stated above may not apply to you. It is to your benefit to save your documentation upon purchase of a product.

Availability Summary

Sheet Widths:	30", 36", 48", 60" (762mm, 914mm, 1219mm, 1524mm)	
Sheet Lengths:	96", 120", 144" (2438mm, 3048mm, 3658mm)	
Sheet Thicknesses:		
	General Purpose Type 107:	0.048" ± 0.005" (1.219mm ± 0.127mm)
	Vertical Surface Type 335:	0.028" ± 0.004" (0.711mm ± 0.101mm)
	Postforming Type 350:	0.039" ± 0.005" (.990mm ± 0.127mm)

For information on product, samples or literature, call toll free (800) 433-3222.

Sinks and Bowls (limited colors)

BD321 Offset Double Sink

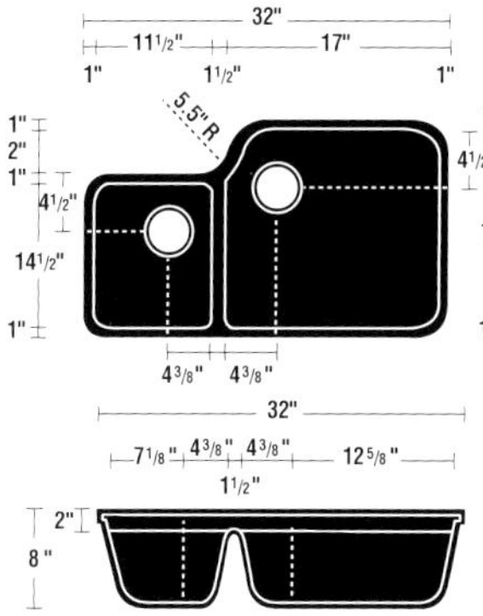

BD322 Double Sink

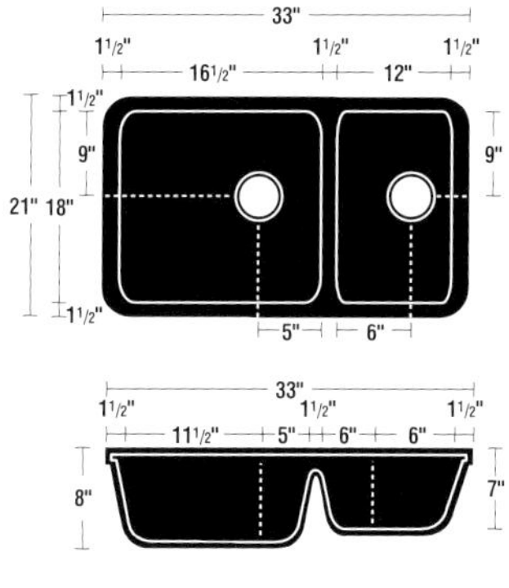

BD323 Double Sink

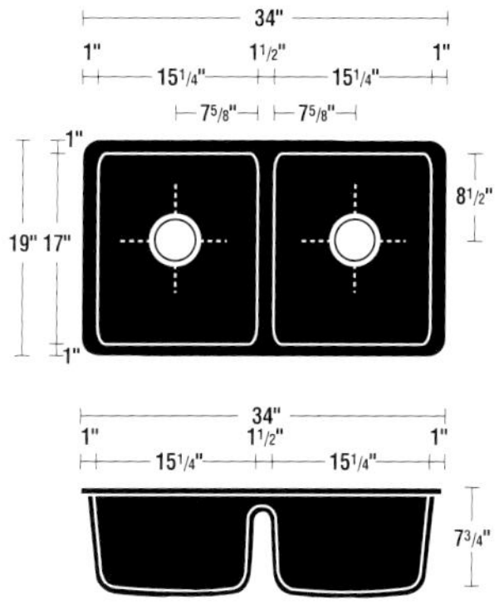

BD324 Double Sink

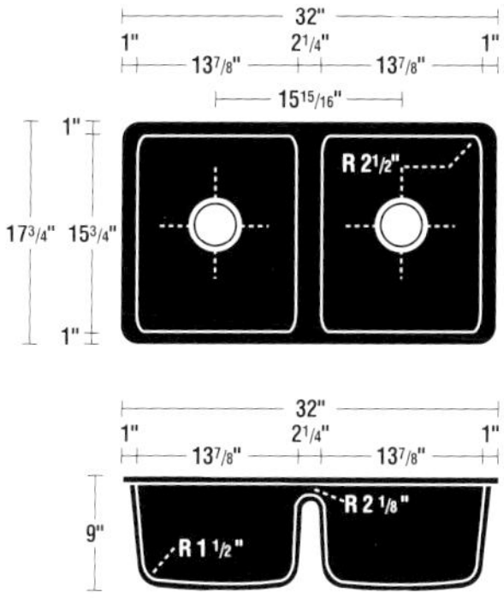

BV123 Vanity Bowl

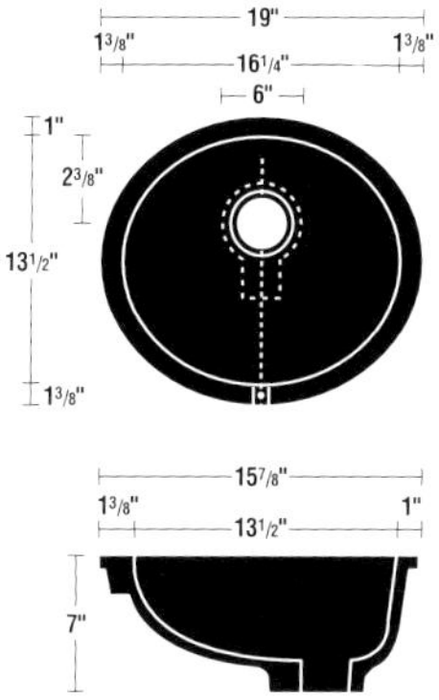

BV121/111 Vanity Bowl

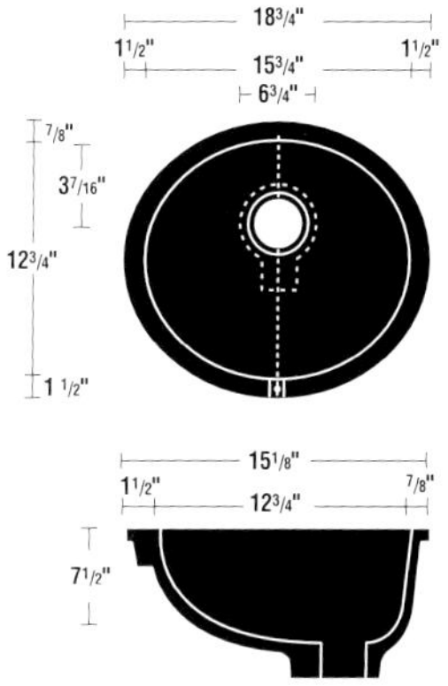

Edge Diagrams

Bevel Edge Style - FE, SE

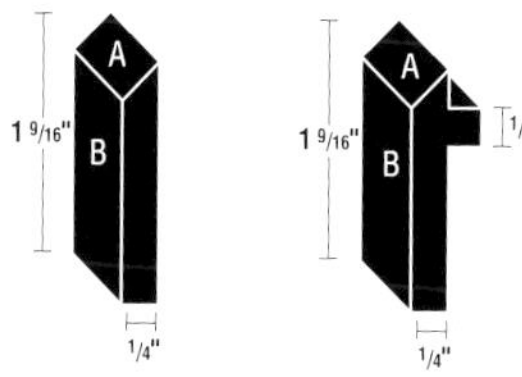

Lengths: 144"
Profile (FE)

Lengths: 144"
Profile (SE)

Available Patterns/Finishes: All Wilsonart Laminate, Chemsurf, Colorthrough Laminate, and SSV

Bevel Edge Style - XP, L

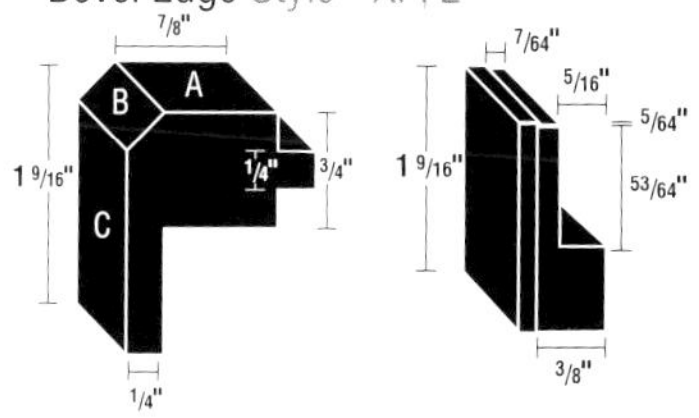

Lengths: 144"
Profile (XP)

Lengths: 144"
Profile (L)

Available Patterns/Finishes: All Wilsonart Laminate, Chemsurf, Colorthrough Laminate, and SSV

Acrylic Style - AT -1, AT-2

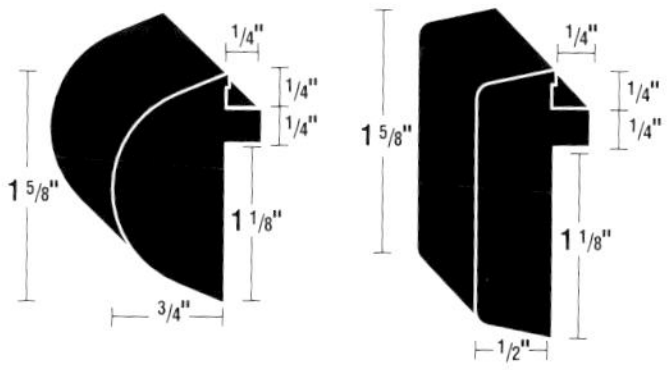

Lengths: 144"
Profile (AT-1)
1 5/8" Bullnose

Lengths: 144"
Profile (AT-2)
1 5/8" Roundover

Gibraltar Style - GB -11, GB-12

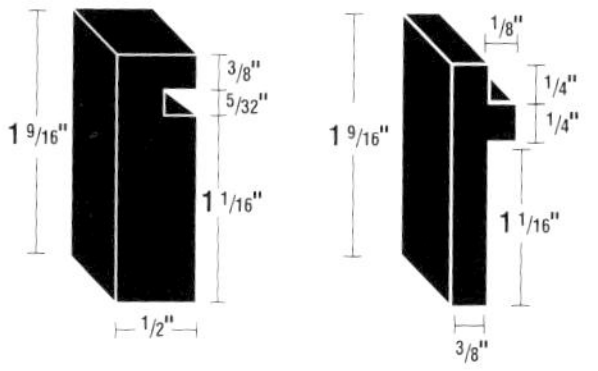

Lengths: 144"
Profile (GB-11: 1/2")

Lengths: 144"
Profile (GB-12: 3/8")

Wood Style - HT-1, HT-11, KT-1

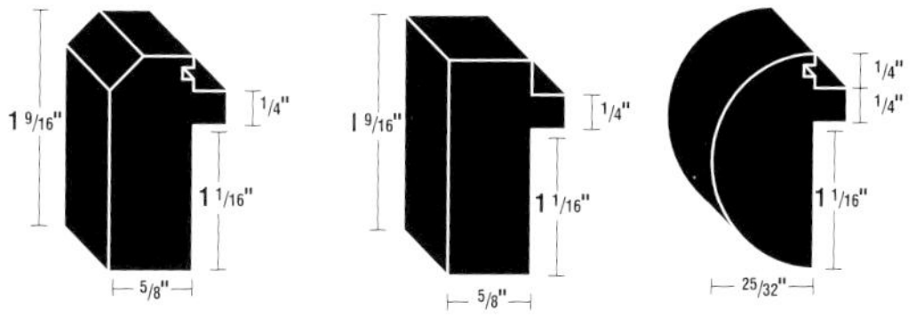

Lengths: 96", 120", 144"
Profile (HT-1) 3/8" Bevel Top

Lengths: 96", 120", 144"
Profile (HT-11) Square

Lengths: 96", 120", 144"
Profile (KT-1)
1 9/16" Half Round

*Available Species: Red Oak, Hard Maple**

Backsplash Style - SS, BS

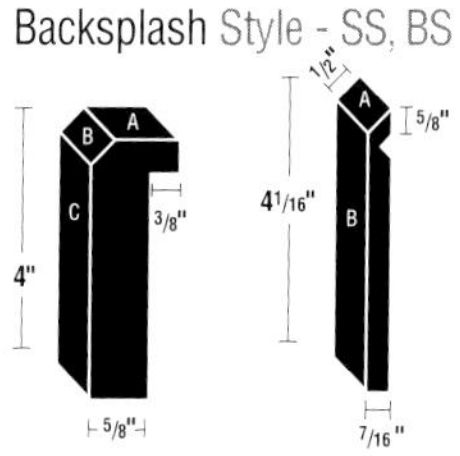

Lengths: 144"
Profile (SS)

Lengths: 144"
Profile (BS)

Available Patterns/Finishes: All Wilsonart Laminate, Chemsurf, Colorthrough Laminates, and SSV

Recommended Uses

Wilsonart® Laminate is suitable for use on fine quality residential and contract furniture and casework; and for architectural application on columns, wainscoting, valances, cornices, interior doors and divider systems.

General Purpose Type 107 is most frequently used for work surfaces on counters, islands, vanities, desks and tables. Typical vertical uses include surfacing for wall panels, teller cages and the front panels of work stations, such as those in hospitals, airports and restaurants.

Vertical Surface Type 335 is the usual choice to surface cabinet walls, doors and drawer panels. It often appears on the vertical surfaces of desks, restaurant booths and maitre d' stations, and as architectural cladding.

Postforming Type 350 adds the decorative capability of the soft edge to any typical laminate use. Formed edges for counters and desk tops and for cabinet doors and drawer panels are familiar applications of postforming laminates.

Basic Limitations

Wilsonart Laminate is for interior use only, and is not recommended for direct application to plaster or concrete walls or gypsum wallboard. This laminate is not a structural material, and must be bonded to a suitable substrate.

Do not subject these laminates to extremes in humidity, or to temperatures of over 275°F (135°C) for sustained periods of time, or to intense, continuous, direct sunlight.

Fabrication and Assembly

Wilsonart Laminate must be bonded to a substrate of reliable quality, such as particleboard, medium-density fiberboard, or plywood with one A face. Recommended substrate material is 45-lb. industrial-grade particleboard. High pressure laminate, plaster, concrete and gypsum board should not be considered suitable substrates. Basic Types laminate may not be used as structural members.

Bond with adhesives and follow the techniques recommended by the adhesive manufacturer.

Recommended adhesives are permanent types, such as urea and polyvinyl acetate (PVA); and contact types. Lokweld® Adhesives are recommended for most bonding conditions.

Take care to ensure an appropriate moisture balance between the laminate and the substrate prior to fabrication. The face and backing laminates and the substrate should be conditioned in the same environment for 48 hours before fabrication.

Recommended conditioning temperature is about 75°F (24°C). Laminates should be conditioned at about 45% relative humidity.

With postforming machinery, a sheet will form, throughout its thickness, at a nominal temperature of 325°F (163°C) in 20 ± 5 seconds.

Tools: Carbide-tipped saw and router blades should be used for cutting. High tool speed and low feed speed are advisable. Cutting blades should be kept very sharp, and use a hold-down to prevent any vibration.

Methods: Fabrication should follow approved methods. Assembled pieces should meet the specifications of DLPA (Decorative Laminate Products Association), ANSI A-161.2-1995, and "Architectural Woodwork Quality Standards, Guide Specifications and Quality Certification Program" guidelines of the Architectural Woodwork Institute where applicable.

To avoid stress cracking, do not use square-cut inside corners. All inside corners should have a minimum of 1/8" (3.175mm) radius and all edges should be routed smooth.

Drill holes for bolts or screws oversized. Screws or bolts should be slightly countersunk into the face side of a laminate-clad substrate.

Optional Finishes

Wilsonart Laminate may be specified in other optional designer finishes. Contact your local representative for availability.

#1 High Gloss. A mirror sheen finish which gives a smooth, brilliant appearance.

Glossometer reading: MD and CD 90 minimum.

#7 Textured Gloss. A textured finish which reproduces the high sheen of waxed wood furniture.

Glossometer reading: MD and CD 36 ± 3.

#41 Gloss Diagonal. Semigloss diagonal finish.

Glossometer reading: MD and CD 75 ± 5.

#50 Touchstone. A pebbled texture with the look and feel of coarse-grained sand.

Glossometer reading: MD and CD 10 ± 2.

#60 Matte. A textured finish with a moderate reflective quality.

Glossometer reading: MD and CD 10 ± 1.

#81 Cathedral Grain. An embossed finish that offers the look and feel of true flatcut wood.

Glossometer reading: MD and CD 25 ± 6.

#90 Crystal. A very finely beaded texture which minimizes smudges and finger marks and improves scratch resistance.

Glossometer reading: MD and CD 13 ± 3.

NOTE: Glossometer readings made at 60° angle of incidence. MD means the machine direction of a laminate sheet, and CD refers to the cross direction.

For information on product, samples or literature, call toll free (800) 433-3222.

Wilsonart® SSV™ Solid Surfacing & Wilsonart® Gibraltar® Solid Surfacing

Care And Maintenance

1. Wilsonart Gibraltar Solid Surfacing and SSV Solid Surfacing offer exceptional beauty and durability. Routine care is as simple as wiping the surface with a damp cloth.
2. Most stains will wash away with soap and water. For tougher stains (on a matte finish*), apply an abrasive cleanser and buff with a Scotch-Brite® pad using a circular motion.
3. Minor burns (on a matte finish*) may also be removed using an abrasive cleanser and buffing the surface with a Scotch-Brite pad.
4. Hot pans and heat-producing appliances should be placed on heat shields or hot pads.

* If you have a high-gloss finish, contact your dealer or fabricator before attempting repairs.

Recommended Uses

Wilsonart SSV and Gibraltar Solid Surfacing panels are recommended for interior and exterior decorative and functional applications where a prestigious appearance, high stain resistance, ease of maintenance and extensive customizing capabilities are beneficial.

Wilsonart SSV is also fire-rated to a code compliance Class II per ASTM-E-84.

Gibraltar Solid Surfacing panels are Class 1 (A) fire-rated, which further enhances their usefulness in high-end contract, commercial and institutional applications.

Appropriate horizontal applications include tops for counters, tables, vanities, bars and laboratory work surfaces.

These materials may also be used to create windowsills and store fixtures, as well as fine custom furniture.

Typical vertical applications include paneling for walls, elevators, counter facades; partitions for toilets and dressing rooms; and interior signage.

Because of their chemical makeup, panels are appropriate for many hospital surfaces. Gibraltar Solid Surfacing panels may be bonded to each other with watertight seals.

Watertight seals can be created with Wilsonart SSV by using Lokweld® 8215 Adhesive (see corresponding tech data).

Basic Limitations

Gibraltar Solid Surfacing sheet goods are designed for interior and exterior use. When specifying Gibraltar Solid Surfacing for exterior applications, the design, fabrication and installation procedures must consider extreme concurrent temperature contrasts which could result in seam failure. Gibraltar Solid Surfacing is not recommended for building facade and facia applications.

Wilsonart SSV is designed for interior use. It should be bonded to particleboard, medium-density fiberboard or plywood (please refer to Fabrication Manual for details regarding substrate selection).

Gibraltar Solid Surfacing panels do not require bonding to substrates, and should not be bonded to solid wood, plaster, concrete, gypsum wallboard or other brands of solid surfacing. They do, however, require a supporting material or framework.

Wilsonart® SSV™ Solid Surfacing

Availability Summary

Panel Widths:	30", 36", 48"*, 60"*	(762mm, 914mm, 1219.2mm*, 1524mm*)
Panel Lengths:	60"*, 72"*, 96", 144"	(1524mm*, 1829mm*, 2438mm, 3658mm)
Thickness:	Product Type 013	0.115" ± 0.010"

*Available in limited colors

Wilsonart® Gibraltar® Solid Surfacing

Short Specification Form

Type:	See specific types under Product Description/Product Definition
Surface:	Color/Design Number:
	Color/Design Name:
Finish:	(specify desired texture of completed application)
Sink Type:	Color/Design Name/Model Number:
Decorative Functional Treatments:	
Adhesive:	Gibraltar Seam Kit Adhesive, color-matched to panels to be seamed.
	Color/Design Number:
	Color/Design Name:
Caulk/Sealant:	Gibraltar Color-Matched Silicone Sealant
	Color/Design Number:
	Color/Design Name:
	Fastening System:
Certification:	Surface shall be UL rated, Class 1 (A)

Availability Summary

Panel Widths:	30", 36"*	(762mm, 914mm*)
Panel Lengths:	96", 144"	(2438mm, 3658mm)
Thickness:	Product Type 051	1/2" (13mm) Nominal
Strips:	Width - 1 3/4", 5 3/4"	(44mm, 146mm)
	Length - 144"	(3658mm)

*Available in limited colors

Shaped Goods: (inside dimensions only)	
BK128-Round Sink	16 3/4" x 16 3/4" x 7 1/2"
BK222-Square Sink	16 3/4" x 16 3/4" x 8"
BK323-Rectangle Sink	10 1/4" x 16 3/4" x 8"
BK324-Rectangle Sink	21" x 15 3/4" x 7 1/2"
BK325-Bar Sink	9" x 12" x 5 1/2"
BK327-Disposal Sink	8" x 15 3/4" x 5 1/2"
BK426-D Bowl	21" x 16 3/4" x 7 1/2"
BV111, BV121-Vanity Bowl (BV111 is a drop-in)	12 3/4" x 15 3/4" x 7 1/2"
BV122-Vanity Bowl (ADA)	12 3/4" x 15 3/4" x 5 1/4"
BV123-Vanity Bowl	13 1/2" x 16 1/4" x 7"
BD321-Offset Double Sink	30" x 16" x 8"
BD322-Double Sink	30" x 18" x 8"
BD323-Double Sink	32" x 17" x 7 3/4"

Wilsonart® Gibraltar® Solid Surfacing

Warranty Information

Wilsonart International warrants to the consumer in the U.S. and Canada that Gibraltar Solid Surfacing, when installed by a recognized Gibraltar Solid Surfacing fabricator in the Gibraltar Fabricators Guild program, shall be free from defects in material, workmanship, fabrication and installation under normal use and service, for a period of ten years from date of sale to the consumer.

This warranty shall not apply to damage arising from any of the following:

1. Accidents, abuse or misuse;
2. Exposure to extreme heat;
3. Improper maintenance; or
4. Alteration or repair by anyone other than a recognized Gibraltar Solid Surfacing fabricator.

This warranty applies only to installations in which the Gibraltar Solid Surfacing product is affixed to the location (e.g. kitchen and bath countertops, vanity tops). This warranty extends to the original purchaser and may be transferred to the new purchaser of the location, provided the new purchaser submits a warranty registration card and provides proof of purchase. A warranty registration card can be obtained by notifying the manufacturer at the address listed below. The transferred warranty shall apply only for the remainder of the original ten year period.

No other warranties, expressed or implied, are made, including merchantability or fitness for a particular purpose. Under no circumstances shall Wilsonart International be liable for any loss or damage arising from the purchase, use or inability to use this product, or for any special, indirect or consequential damages.

To make a claim under this warranty, the consumer must contact Wilsonart International at the following address:
2400 Wilson Place, P.O. Box 6110, Temple, Texas 76503-6110.

This warranty gives you specific legal rights, and you may also have other rights which may vary from state to state. Some states do not allow the exclusion of implied warranties or of incidental or consequential damages, so the above limitation or exclusion may not apply to you. Return of owner registration card is not a condition precedent to warranty coverage. No fabricator, installer, dealer, agent or employee of Wilsonart International has the authority to increase or alter the obligation or limitation of this warranty.

Wilsonart® SSV™ Solid Surfacing

Warranty Information

Wilsonart International, Inc., warrants that, under normal use and service, installed Wilsonart® SSV™ Solid Surfacing products shall be free from defects in material and workmanship for a period of ten (10) years from the date of sale to the consumer purchaser. In the event that the product does not perform as warranted, the consumer purchaser's sole remedy shall be limited to repair or replacement, at manufacturer's discretion, of all or any part of the product which is defective. This warranty applies only to product that is attached to the building (such as kitchen or bathroom countertops) and was purchased by the original consumer purchaser.

This warranty shall not apply to any defects or damages arising from any of the following:

1. Accidents, abuse or misuse
2. Exposure to extreme temperatures
3. Improper installation or fabrication
4. Improper maintenance
5. Improper adhesive, grout, or caulk
6. Alteration or repair by anyone other than an authorized Smart Source Fabricator

This warranty applies only to product which has been fabricated and installed by an authorized Smart Source Fabricator and is in its original installation location. This warranty extends to the original purchaser and may be transferred to the new purchaser of the location, provided the new purchaser submits a warranty registration card and provides proof of purchase.

No other warranties, express or implied, are made, including merchantability or fitness for a particular purpose. Under no circumstances shall the manufacturer be liable for any loss or damage arising from the purchase, use or inability to use this product, or for any special, indirect, incidental, or consequential damages. No fabricator, installer, dealer, agent or employee of Wilsonart International has the authority to modify the obligations or limitations of this warranty.

This warranty gives you specific legal rights, and you may also have other rights which may vary from state to state. Some states do not allow the exclusion of implied warranties or of incidental or consequential damages, so the above limitation or exclusion may not apply to you. Return of owner registration card is not a condition precedent to warranty coverage.

To receive a warranty registration form, call toll free (800) 433-3222.

Corporate Headquarters
2400 Wilson Place
P.O. Box 6110
Temple, TX 76503-6110
Toll Free: (800) 433-3222
Mon.-Fri. 7:00 am-7:00 pm CST
Phone: (254) 207-7000
Fax: (254) 207-2384
Internet: www.wilsonart.com

THE SMART SOURCE

WILSONART INTERNATIONAL

C485
11452/BRQ
Buyline 3727

BROAN®

Range Hoods

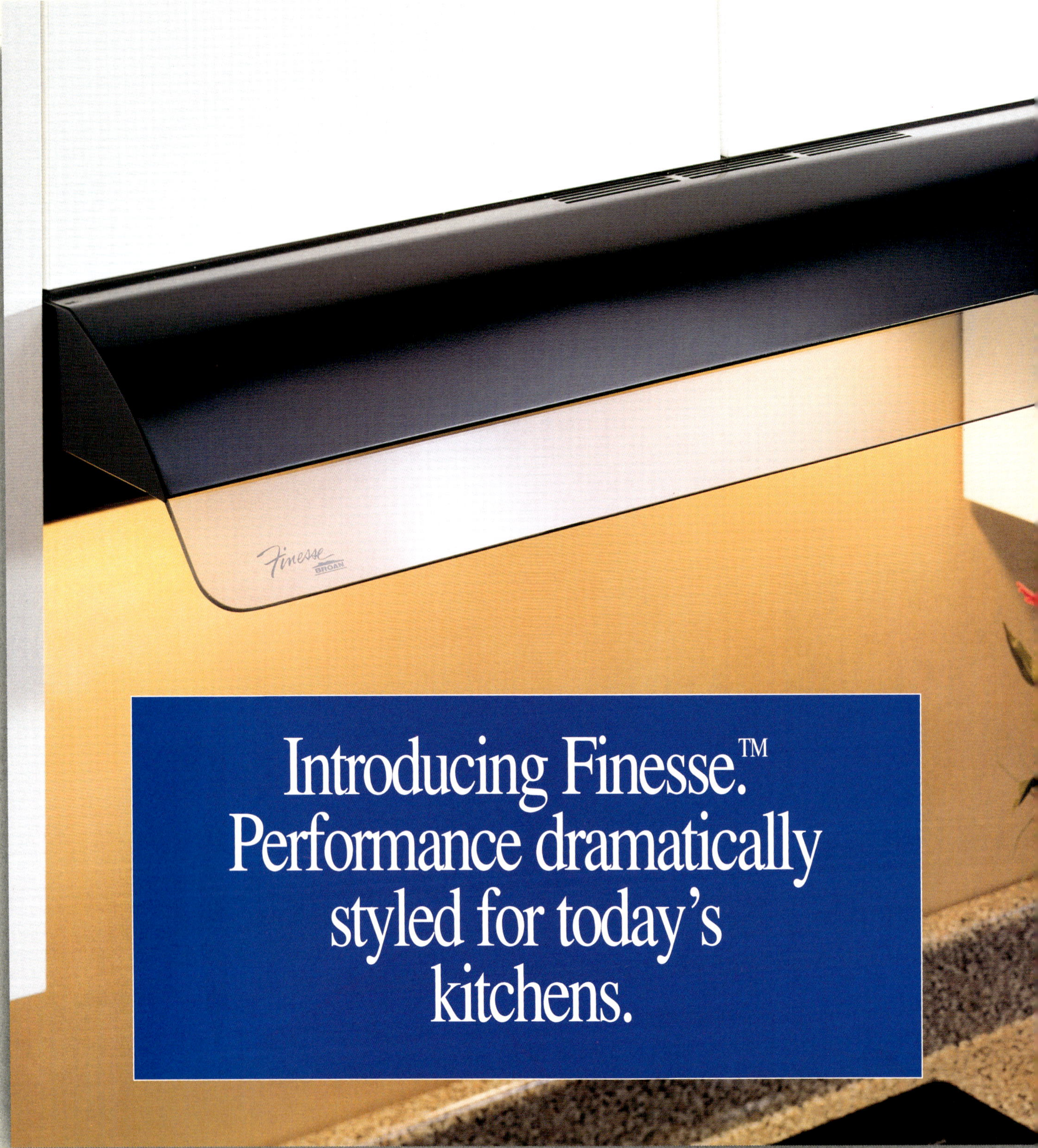

See page 15 for all performance specifications and installation requirements.

Finesse

By BROAN

Finesse is an innovative vision of what range hoods are meant to be. Graceful, contoured lines beautifully complement today's popular new range and cooktop designs. Yet its form follows function.

- Powerful, quiet dual centrifugal blower — 250 CFM (81000 Series) and 400 CFM (83000 Series) models available.
- Select horizontal or vertical exhausting.
- Convertible to vent-free operation with exclusive Microtek® System filters that are 25 times more effective than vent-free filters of other manufacturers (available separately).
- Smoked, tempered-glass visor elegantly accentuates the clean, sweeping lines of this range hood, while improving overall performance.
- Infinite-speed touch controls are color-matched to the hood and form-fitted for a clean, stylish appearance.
- Indicator light lets you know the blower is on.
- Dual 75-watt lights provide 150-watts of illumination (bulbs not included); dual prismatic lenses help eliminate harsh glare.
- Fully enclosed underside is easy to keep clean.
- Dishwasher-safe filters run the full width of the range hood; filters lift out easily with no tools necessary.
- Duct connector with built-in damper included (vented models only).
- Available in 30" and 36" widths.
- Choose white, almond, black or stainless steel finish.

Broan's commercial quality Rangemaster Series.

When your customers step beyond simple "remodeling" to dream kitchens with facilities for serious cooking... Rangemaster® by Broan.

High-performance, restaurant ranges are one of the hottest trends in kitchen remodeling today. When your customers select one of these commercial-look, high B.T.U. units, show them the range hood designed for these ranges: Rangemaster.

Top line features in all Rangemaster hoods include:

- Heavy-gauge, double-wall steel construction for years of service.
- Easy-to-clean stainless steel interior with no sharp edges.
- Two, 15" fluorescent tubes for two-level, cooktop lighting (bulbs not included).
- Two, 250-watt infrared food warming lamps "hold" one dish while you finish preparing others (bulbs not included).
- Extra large, easily removable, dishwasher-safe grease filters.
- Exclusive Heat Sentry™ automatically turns blower to high speed when excess heat is detected.
- Infinite, solid-state speed control with blower memory "remembers" last setting selected.

Custom options fit Rangemaster to any range; any kitchen.

- Select eight sizes (widths) from space-saving 30" to spacious 72".
- Select HVI-certified 600 CFM or 1200 CFM interior blowers, or 600 CFM or 900 CFM exterior blowers for maximum ventilation performance. See page 14 for blower choices.
- Restaurant quality stainless steel backsplash with fold-down food warming shelves provides the ultimate in "commercial" looks and ease of cleaning.
- Matching soffit chimneys for kitchens with higher "cathedral" ceilings; vertical ducting only, two soffit maximum.
- Select horizontal or vertical exhausting.
- Select stainless steel, white, almond or black.

Optional backsplash with condiment shelves that fold down for food warming.

When customers demand a hood with a disappearing act ... show them our Eclipse® or Silhouette® Series.

Eclipse downdraft ventilator.

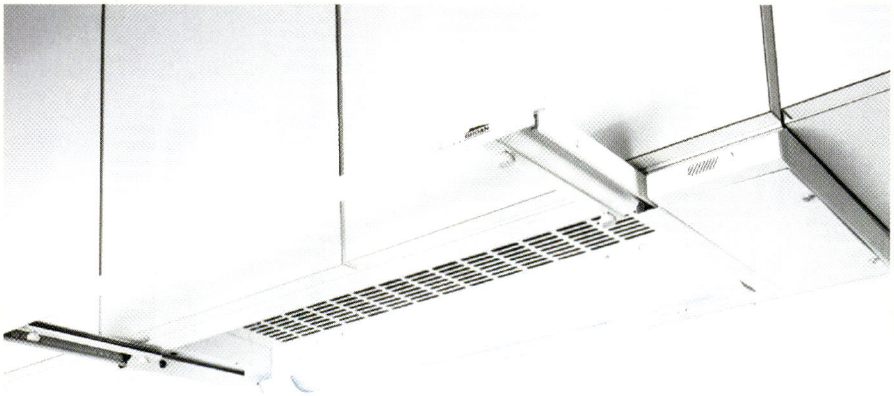

Silhouette slide-out range hood.

See page 14 for all performance specifications and installation requirements.

Eclipse downdraft system for island and peninsula cooking where updraft venting is impractical.

Features of all Eclipse ventilators:

- Sleek, trim line styling complements any cooktop style or color.
- Compatible with virtually all cooktops.
- Discreet, integral, easy-to-reach blower control.
- Blower discharges to right, left or down and side-to-side to avoid floor joists.
- Space-saving design saves valuable under-counter cabinet space.
- Access panel allows easy cleaning.

Eclipse options to suit any kitchen layout:

- Select 30" or 36" wide models (fits all standard kitchen cabinets).
- Powerful, quiet 500 CFM internal or 900 CFM external blower.
- Stainless steel cover standard. White or black optional.

Silhouette hoods fit under kitchen cabinets, and slide out of sight when not in use.

Features found in all Silhouette Series range hoods:

- Powerful performance – HVI- certified 300 CFM. For vented installations only.
- Ultra-quiet performance – HVI-certified 4.5 Sones.
- Compact, trim line styling maximizes kitchen cabinet space.
- Dramatic glass visor slides out to turn on blower; slides in to turn off.
- 24" fluorescent light with prismatic glass lens provides bright cooktop lighting (bulb not included).
- Easy to reach, "up-front" infinite blower control.
- Exclusive Heat Sentry automatically turns blower to high speed when excess heat is detected.
- Dual connector with built-in damper.

Options available in Silhouette Series:

- 30" or 36" width hoods (fits all standard kitchen cabinets).
- Available in white or black. Fits any contemporary kitchen decor.

90000 Series deluxe hood.

Industry-leading, exclusive features make Broan Deluxe Range Hoods the obvious choice for your preferred customers.

Heat Sentry™, Auto Temp, Blower Memory, Microtek® System filters…they're the features that define deluxe range hoods today and only Broan has them.

Broan 90000 Series. Take control of every cooking task with the most technologically advanced conventional range hood in North America.

Deluxe features in all 90000 Series range hoods:

- Powerful, quiet 360 CFM / 5.5 Sone (vertical discharge) or 350 CFM / 6.0 Sone (horizontal discharge) performance (HVI certified).
- Also available vent-free with exclusive Microtek System filter that's 65 times more effective than vent-free filters of other manufacturers (available separately).
- Popular 30", 36" and 42" widths.

- Advanced function electronic touchpad controls, flush-mounted for easy cleaning.
- LED indicators signal all operating functions whenever hood is operating.
- Exclusive Heat Sentry automatically turns blower to high speed when excess heat is detected.
- Auto Temp continuously monitors cooking conditions; automatically adjusting blower to appropriate ventilation levels.
- High Heat Signal sounds alarm whenever overheating occurs on cook-top (Heat Sentry and High Heat Signal activate at all times; even when blower is off).
- Two 75-watt bulbs offer three light settings, including "night light" (bulbs not included).
- Test function enables monitoring of all features.
- Broan's dual blower system is the quietest, high-performance system available in a conventional range hood.
- Choose white-on-white, white, almond, black or stainless steel finish.

88000 Series deluxe hood.

89000 Series deluxe hood.

Broan 88000 Series. A top-performing, great-looking hood that would be the top of anyone else's line.

These features are found in all Broan 88000 Series range hoods:

- Powerful, quiet 360 CFM/5.5 Sone (vertical discharge) or 350 CFM/6.0 Sone (horizontal discharge) performance (HVI certified).
- Convertible to vent-free operation with exclusive Microtek® System filter that's 65 times more effective than vent-free filters of other manufacturers (available separately).
- Popular 30", 36" and 42" widths.
- Convenient, contemporary slide controls.
- Exclusive Blower Memory automatically returns to last setting selected.
- Exclusive Heat Sentry automatically turns blower to high speed when excess heat is detected.
- Two 75-watt bulbs offer bright cooktop lighting and night-light settings (bulbs not included).
- Infinite blower controls.
- Choose white-on-white, white, almond, black or stainless steel finish.

Broan 89000 Series. Perfect for high-performance cooktops or indoor gas or electric grilles.

Same great feature complement as Broan 88000 Series, plus:

- Super-performing 460 CFM/6.0 Sone (vertical discharge) or 440 CFM/7.0 Sone (horizontal discharge) dual centrifugal blowers (HVI certified).
- Available in 30", 36", 42" and 48" widths (and additional special order sizes).
- Choose white, almond, black, or stainless steel finish (additional special order colors available).

See page 14 for all performance specifications and installation requirements.

76000 Series intermediate hood.

Broan offers more intermediate hoods than anyone because step-up sales come in all shapes, sizes and colors.

Broan 76000 Series. More performance, quality and value than any hood in its class.

All these great features are found in every 76000 Series hood:

- Powerful, quiet 200 CFM/5.5 Sone (vertical discharge) or 200 CFM/6.0 Sone (horizontal discharge) performance (HVI certified).
- Convertible to vent-free operation with exclusive Microtek® System filter that's 25 times more effective than vent-free filters of other manufacturers.
- 11-5/8" by 6-5/8" dishwasher safe aluminum grease filters (vented models).
- Popular 24", 30", 36" and 42" widths.
- Infinite rotary blower speed control.
- 75-watt cooktop lighting with polymeric lens.
- Duct connector with built-in damper.
- Choose white-on-white, white, almond, black or stainless steel finish.

75000 Series intermediate hood.

68000 Series intermediate hood.

48000 Series intermediate hood.

Broan 75000 Series. Same great features as 76000 Series with more powerful blowers.

- Powerful, quiet 250 CFM/6.5 Sone (vertical discharge) or 250 CFM/6.0 Sone (horizontal discharge) performance (HVI certified).
- Popular 30", 36" and 42" widths.
- Choose white-on-white, white, almond, black or stainless steel finish.

Broan 68000 and 67000 Series. Simple, understated elegance in range hood design.

Features common to 68000 (7" round vented) and 67000 (vent-free) Series range hoods:

- 230 CFM/7.0 Sone (vertical discharge) performance (68000 only) (HVI certified).
- Simple, elegant, easy-to-clean black or white "glass look" styling.
- Popular 30", 36" and 42" widths.
- Two-speed control inside hood presents clean, uncluttered front.
- 75-watt cooktop lighting with lens (bulb not included).
- Dishwasher safe aluminum grease filter and damper (68000 only).
- Combination vent-free filter (67000 only).
- Choose monochromatic white or black finish.

Broan 48000 and 47000 Series. Straight side styling offers that subtle difference preferred by many consumers.

Features common to 48000 (7" round vented) and 47000 (vent-free) Series range hoods:

- 230 CFM/7.0 Sone (vertical discharge) performance (HVI certified).
- Popular 30", 36" and 42" widths.
- 75-watt cooktop lighting with lens (bulb not included).
- Dishwasher safe aluminum grease filter and damper (48000 only).
- Combination vent-free filter (47000 only).
- Choose white, almond or stainless steel finish.

See pages 14 and 15 for all performance specifications and installation requirements.

46000 Series with optional, matching backsplash.

Simple. Dependable. Affordable. No wonder Broan economy range hoods lead the category.

Broan 46000 Series. When performance, profits and value are critical, you can rely on this great, step-up economy model.

Standard features of 46000 Series include:

- 180 CFM/7.0 Sone (vertical discharge) and 180 CFM/6.5 (horizontal discharge) performance (HVI certified).
- Convertible to vent-free operation with exclusive Microtek® System filter that's 10 times more effective than vent-free filters of other manufacturers.
- Microtek System filter included.
- Popular 30", 36" and 42" widths.
- Infinite rotary fan speed control.
- 75-watt cooktop lighting with polymeric lens (bulb not included).
- Duct connector with built-in damper included (vented models).
- Choose white, almond or stainless steel finish.

41000 Series economy hood with optional, matching backsplash.

40000/42000 Series economy hood with optional, matching backsplash.

Broan 42000, 41000 and 40000 Series. The industry's best-featured economy hoods.

Standard features of 42000, (7" round vented) 41000 (vent-free) and 40000 (vented) Series range hoods:

- 190 CFM/5.5 Sone (vertical discharge) performance (42000 Series) (HVI certified).
- 160 CFM/5.5 Sone (vertical discharge) or 160 CFM/6.5 Sone (horizontal discharge) performance (40000 Series) (HVI certified).
- 10-1/2" diameter dishwasher safe aluminum grease filter (42000 Series).
- Requires Broan #87 damper (available separately) (42000 Series).
- Microtek® System filter included that's 9 times more effective than vent-free filters of other manufacturers (41000 Series).
- 75-watt cooktop lighting with polymeric lens (bulb not included).
- Duct connector with built-in damper included (40000 Series).
- 10-1/2" by 8-3/4" dishwasher safe aluminum grease filter (40000 Series).
- Popular 24", 30" and 36" widths (41000 and 40000 Series); 30" and 36" widths (42000 Series).
- Choose white, almond or stainless steel finish.

See page 15 for all performance specifications and installation requirements.

For customers who want a custom look in kitchen ventilation, look to Broan.

Hideaway Hood (inside cabinets)-Model 113023.

Hideaway...great ventilation performance. Great flush look.

- Expandable 24"-30" height accommodates 30" face frame with cabinet doors.
- Powerful, quiet 360 CFM/4.5 Sone (vertical or horizontal discharge) performance (HVI certified).
- Blower and light automatically turn on when hood is pulled out.
- Exclusive Heat Sentry™ automatically turns blower to high speed when excess heat is detected.
- Bright cooktop lighting (bulb not included).
- For vented installations only; not available vent-free.
- Requires rough-in kit Model 113123.

Wood Hood Kit-Model 103023.

Wood Hood...high-performance ventilation in a rich, traditional look.

- Fits into wood hoods from 28-1/4" to 28-7/8" wide (and adapts to hoods up to 42" in width).
- Powerful, quiet 360 CFM/5.0 Sone (vertical discharge) or 360 CFM/4.5 Sone (horizontal discharge) performance (HVI certified).
- Exclusive Heat Sentry automatically turns blower to high speed when excess heat is detected.
- 24" fluorescent tube lighting (bulb not included).
- Duct connector with built-in damper for 3-1/4" by 10" vents.
- For vented installations only; not available vent-free.
- Requires rough-in kit Model 103123.

See page 15 for all performance specifications and installation requirements.

Micromate™. A powerful range hood. A place for your microwave. In one unit.

- Accommodates virtually any brand microwave oven.
- Installs vented or vent-free (Microtek® filter sold separately).
- Powerful, quiet 300 CFM/4.5 Sone (vertical discharge) performance (HVI certified).
- Bright cooktop lighting (bulb not included).

Micromate-120000 Series.

Canopy Hood. A warm, traditional, "heart-of-the-home" look.

- 190 CFM/6.0 (vertical discharge) or 200 CFM/6.5 Sone (horizontal discharge) performance (HVI certified).
- Convertible to vent-free operation with exclusive Microtek System filter that's 10 times more effective than vent-free filters of other manufacturers (available separately).
- Cooktop lighting with your choice of 100-watt bulb or 150-watt flood lamp (lamps sold separately).
- Textured, hammered finish in white, almond, harvest, avocado and coffee.

11000 Series Wall Canopy Hood.

Range Hood Accessories and Blower Systems

Accessories

Model #	Description
634	Roof cap with backdraft damper and safety screen, 3-1/4" x 10" or up to 8" round duct
644	Aluminum roof cap with backdraft damper and safety screen, 3-1/4" x 10" or up to 8" round duct
639	Wall cap 3-1/4" x 10" duct with backdraft damper with safety screen
641	Aluminum wall cap with backdraft damper with safety screen fits 6" round duct
643	Aluminum wall cap fits 8" round duct
647	Aluminum wall cap fits 7" round duct
649	Aluminum wall cap fits 3-1/4" x 10" duct with backdraft damper with safety screen
87	7" vertical discharge damper
97	7" spring-loaded, in-line damper
99	9" spring-loaded, in-line damper
401	3-1/4" x 10" duct, 2' section
406	6" round duct, 2' section
407	7" round duct, 2' section
410	10" round duct, 2' section
411	3-1/4" x 10" to 6" round transition
412	3-1/4" x 10" to 7" round transition
413	3-1/4" x 10" to 8" round transition
414	8" to 10" expander
415	7" adjustable elbow (carton of four)
418	10" adjustable elbow (individual)
419	6" adjustable elbow (individual)
421	10" round section with in-line damper
423	Vertical transition, 4-1/2" x 18-1/2" to 10" round
424	Rear transition, 4-1/2" x 18-1/2" to 10" round
425	Horz. left transition, 4-1/2" x 18-1/2" to 10" round
426	Horz. right transition, 4-1/2" x 18-1/2" to 10" round
453	Right end boot
454	Left end boot
428	3-1/4" x 10" vertical elbow
429	3-1/4" x 10" horizontal elbow
430	Short eave elbow for 3-1/4" x 10" duct with backdraft damper and grille
431	Long eave elbow for 3-1/4" x 10" duct with backdraft damper and grille
437	High capacity roof cap – up to 1200 CFM exhaust
441	Wall cap with gravity damper, 13-1/8" sq. fits 10" round duct
35	Wall hanging kit (for mounting hoods to wall when not hung from overhead cabinets)

Broan 331 (600 CFM) and 332 (900 CFM) exterior blowers.

Broan's new 600 CFM and 900 CFM exterior blowers offer your customers powerful ventilation performance with all the benefits of exterior mounting (roof or wall), and one benefit they won't find anywhere else... Broan quality.

- Reduce kitchen noise by locating range hood blowers on roof or outside walls.
- Select either Model 331 or the 332 exterior blower with 332K rough-in kit for Rangemaster® depending on cooking style and ventilation needs; the 332 is recommended for the Eclipse® downdraft.
- New, low-profile design fits unobtrusively with all home exterior styles.
- Durable, weather-resistant all aluminum construction.
- Safety screen keeps small animals and debris away from blower and motor.

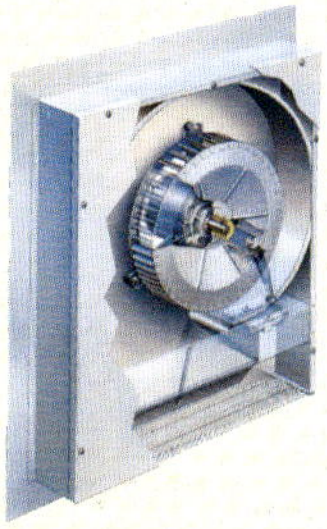

Broan splash plates.

Stock and display splash plates for add-on sales:

- Durable 19-gauge enamel finish (appliance colors) or 24-gauge stainless steel.
- Select white, almond, black, stainless steel, avocado, coffee or harvest wheat.
- Available in 24", 30", 36" or 42" widths; all 24" high.
- Simplifies kitchen clean-up.
- Easily installed with four screws.
- See Broan price list for colors, models and prepacked display/dispenser.

SPECIALTY RANGE HOODS AND ACCESSORIES

See page 15 for all performance specifications and installation requirements.

RANGEMASTER®...see page 4

Width	Stainless Steel	White	Black	Almond
30"	603004	603001	603023	603008
36"	603604	603601	603623	603608
42"	604204	604201	604223	604208
48"	604804	604801	604823	604808
54"	605404	+	+	+
60"	606004	+	+	+
66"	606604	+	+	+
72"	607204	+	+	+

Options Selection Table

	Backsplash	Soffit Chimney			
Width	Stainless Steel	Stainless Steel	White	Black	Almond
30"	RP3004	RN3004	RN3001	RN3023	RN3008
36"	RP3604	RN3604	RN3601	RN3623	RN3608
42"	RP4204	RN4204	RN4201	RN4223	RN4208
48"	RP4804	RN4804	RN4801	RN4823	RN4808
54"	RP5404	RN5404	+	+	+
60"	RP6004	RN6004	+	+	+
66"	RP6604	RN6604	+	+	+
72"	RP7204	RN7204	+	+	+

+ Available as special order

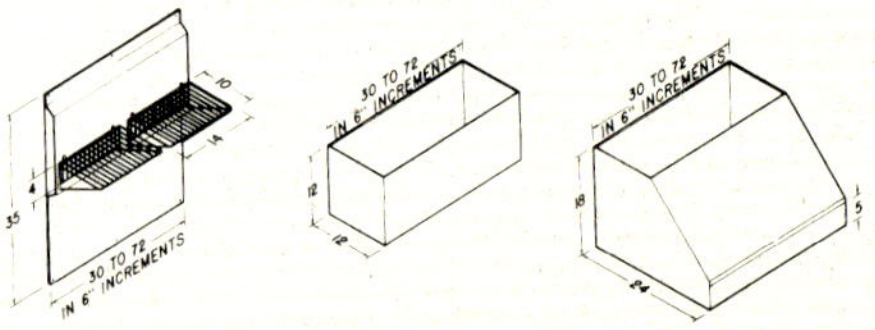

Blower Selection Table and Specifications

Model	Mounting	CFM	Volts	Hz	Amps*	Vent Size
325	Interior	600	120	60	7.6	7" Round
326	Interior	1200	120	60	8.1	4-1/2" x 18-1/2" **
331	Exterior	600	120	60	2.3	10" Round
332++	Exterior	900	120	60	5.8	10" Round

++ Model 332K rough-in kit required for mounting. Model no. 421 10" in-line damper recommended.
* Includes 4.5 Amps representing all lights.
** Transitions to 10" round available. (see accessory section on page 13)

Replacement bulbs:
Fluorescent: F14T12/SW (Soft White) Any F14T8 or F14T12 15" long preheat fluorescent lamp will fit.
Heat Lamps: 250-Watt, R40 Infrared (Bulbs and lamps not included).

ECLIPSE®...see page 5

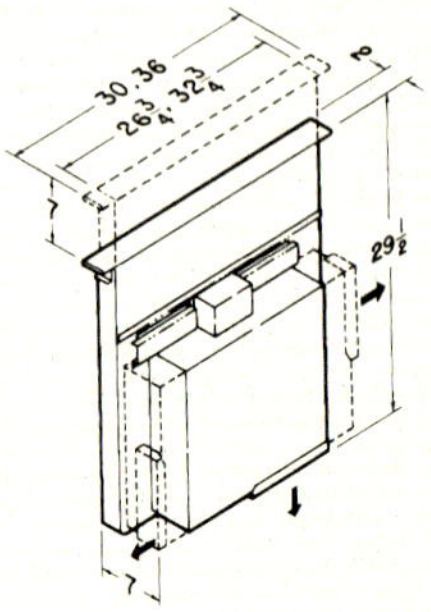

With 500 CFM interior blower

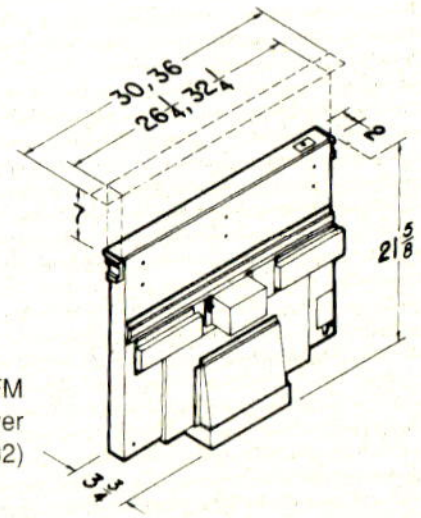

With 900 CFM exterior blower (Model 332)

To Fit Nominal Cooktop Size	Model	Description	Cover Color
30"	273003	Interior Blower Unit	Stainless Steel
36"	273603	Interior Blower Unit	Stainless Steel
30"	283003	Exterior Blower Unit*	Stainless Steel
36"	283603	Exterior Blower Unit*	Stainless Steel
30"	273001C	Optional Cover	White
36"	273601C	Optional Cover	White
30"	273023C	Optional Cover	Black
36"	273623C	Optional Cover	Black

* Exterior unit utilizes Model 332 Exterior-Mounted Blower, available separately.

Specifications**

Model	Volts	Amps	CFM	Vent
27000	120	4.0	500	3-1/4" x 10"
28000	120	4.0	900	3-1/4" x 10"

** Cooktops, countertops and cabinets vary in dimension and support systems depending upon manufacturer. These factors may impact the Eclipse's ability to fit with every worktop/cabinet combination. Specifications subject to change without notice.

SILHOUETTE®...see page 5

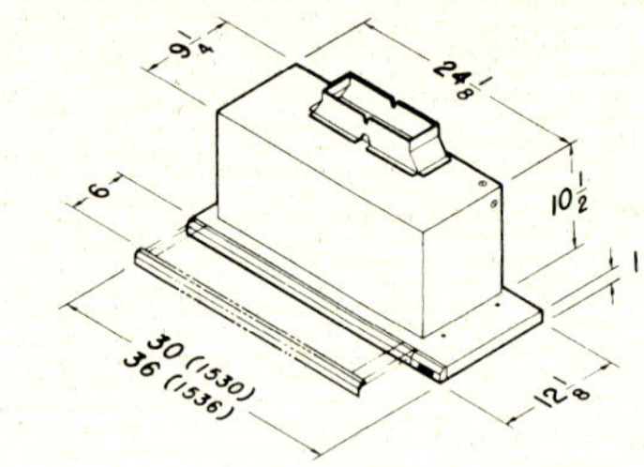

Width	White	Black
30"	153001	153023
36"	153601	153623

Allow 18 inches minimum from cooking surface to bottom of hood.

Specifications

Volts	Amps	Sones	CFM	Vent
120	3.7	4.5	300	3-1/4" x 10" (vertical)

Fluorescent Tube - 24", F20T12 (not included).

EXTERIOR BLOWERS...see page 13

For use with Rangemaster and Eclipse models.

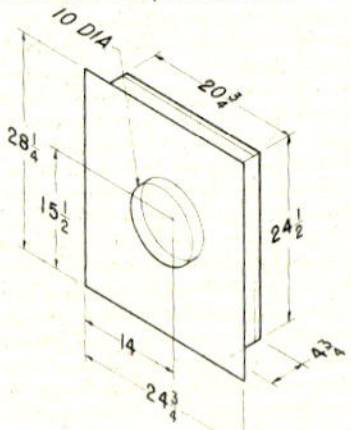

Specifications

Model	Volts	Amps	CFM	Vent
331	120	2.3	600	10" round
332	120	5.8	900	10" round

90000 SERIES...see page 6

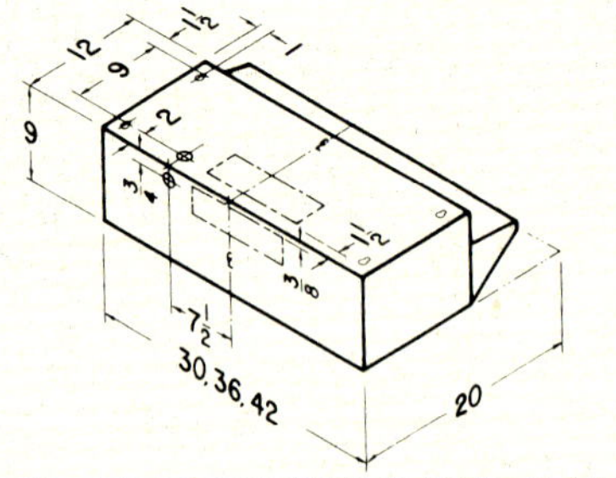

Width	White	Almond	White on White	Black	Stainless
30"	903001	903008	903011	903023	903004
36"	903601	903608	903611	903623	903604
42"	904201	904208	904211	904223	904204

Order Microtek® System IV filter 97007662 for vent-free operation.

Specifications

Volts	Amps	Sones Ver.	Sones Hor.	CFM Ver.	CFM Hor.	Vent-Free RHP Index	Vent
120	4.5	5.5	6.0	360	350	59.09	3-1/4" x 10"

89000 SERIES...see page 7

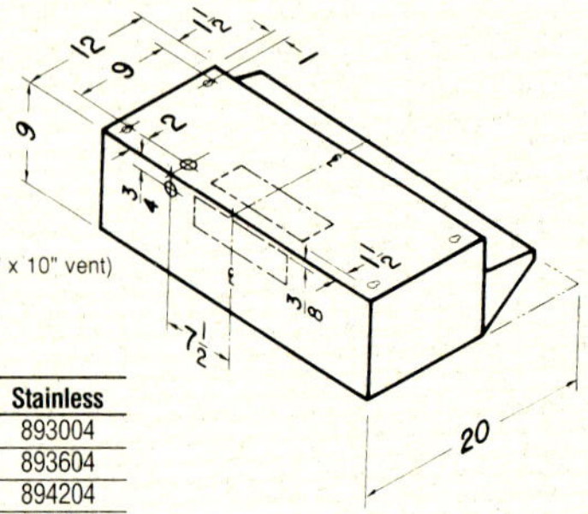

(3-1/4" x 10" vent)

Width	Stainless
30"	893004
36"	893604
42"	894204
48"	894804

Specifications

Volts	Amps	Sones Ver.	Sones Hor.	CFM Ver.	CFM Hor.	Vent
120	6.0	6.0	7.0	460	440	3-1/4" x 10"

88000 SERIES...see page 7

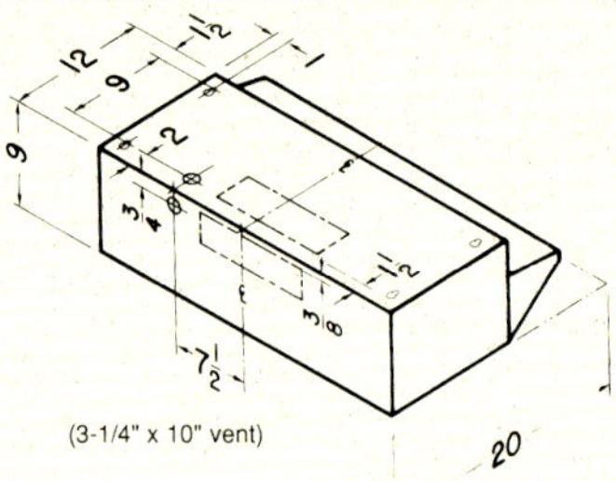

(3-1/4" x 10" vent)

Width	White	Almond	White on White	Black	Stainless
30"	883001	883008	883011	883023	883004
36"	883601	883608	883611	883623	883604
42"	884201	884208	884211	884223	884204

Also available in Harvest, Avocado and Coffee.

Specifications

Volts	Amps	Sones Ver.	Sones Hor.	CFM Ver.	CFM Hor.	Vent-Free RHP Index	Vent
120	4.5	5.5	6.0	360	350	59.09	3-1/4" x 10"

76000 SERIES...see page 8

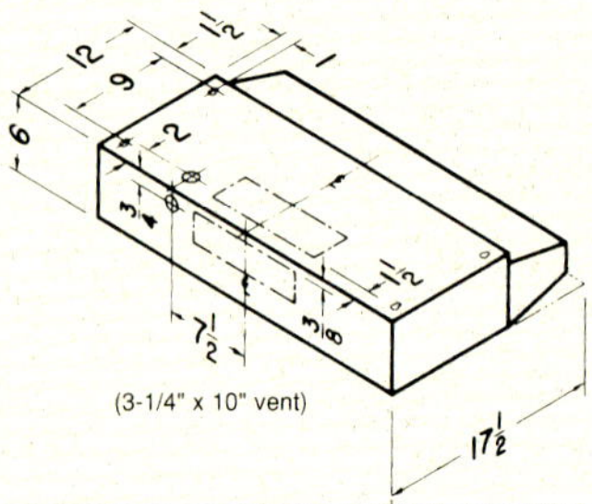

(3-1/4" x 10" vent)

Width	White	Almond	White on White	Black	Stainless
24"	762401	762408	762411	762423	762404
30"	763001	763008	763011	763023	763004
36"	763601	763608	763611	763623	763604
42"	764201	764208	764211	764223	764204

Also available in Harvest, Avocado and Coffee.

Specifications

Volts	AMPS	Sones Ver.	Sones Hor.	CFM	Vent-Free RHP Index	Vent
120	3.0	5.5	6.0	200	22.73	3-1/4" x 10"

75000 SERIES...see page 9

Width	White	Almond	Stainless
30"	753001	753008	753004
36"	753601	753608	753604
42"	754201	754208	754204

Specifications

Volts	AMPS	Sones Ver.	Sones Hor.	CFM	Vent-Free RHP Index	Vent
120	3.6	6.5	6.0	250	25.0	3-1/4" x 10"

68000 SERIES...see page 9

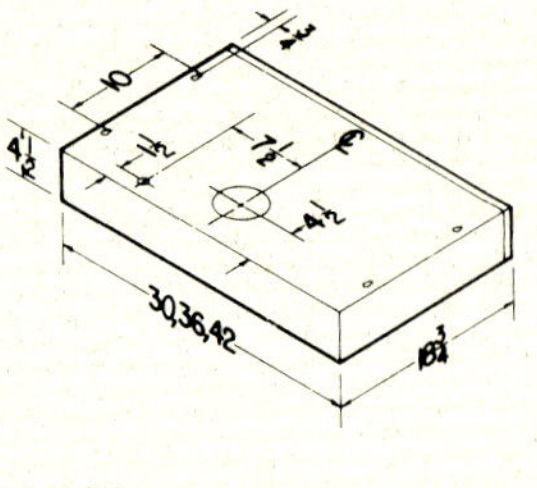

7" Round Vent

Width	White	Black
30"	683001	683023
36"	683601	683623
42"	684201	684223

Specifications

Volts	AMPS	CFM	Sones
120	2.5	230	7.0

67000 SERIES...see page 9

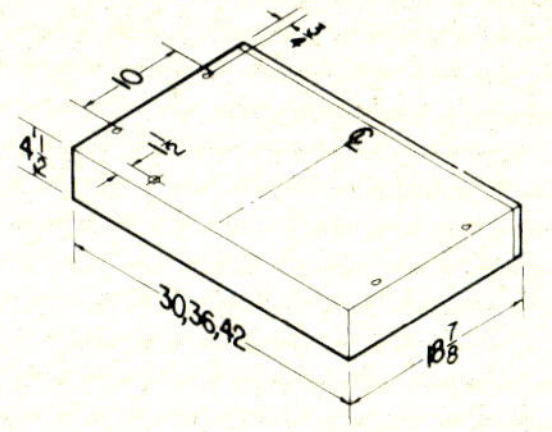

Vent-Free

Width	White	Black
30"	673001	673023
36"	673601	673623
42"	674201	674223

Specifications

Volts	AMPS	CFM	Sones
120	2.0	Vent-Free	Vent-Free

48000 SERIES...see page 9

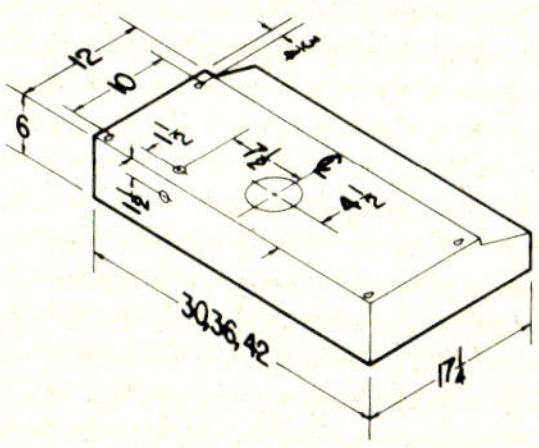

7" Round Vent

Width	White	Almond	Stainless
30"	483001	483008	483004
36"	483601	483608	483604
42"	484201	484208	484204

Specifications

Volts	AMPS	CFM	Sones
120	2.5	230	7.0

47000 SERIES...see page 9

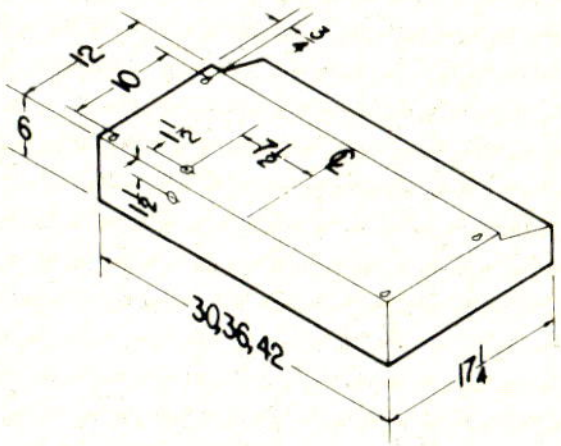

Vent-Free

Width	White	Almond	Stainless
30"	473001	473008	473004
36"	473601	473608	473604
42"	474201	474208	474204

Specifications

Volts	AMPS	CFM	Sones
120	2.0	Vent-Free	Vent-Free

FINESSE...see page 3

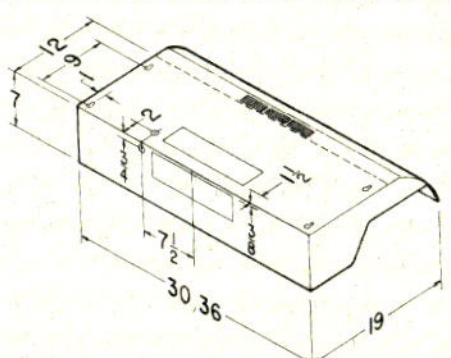

81000 Series (250 CFM)

Width	White	Almond	Black	Stainless
30"	813011	813018	813025	813004
36"	813611	813618	813625	813604

83000 Series (400 CFM)

Width	White	Almond	Black	Stainless
30"	833011	833018	833025	833004
36"	833611	833618	833625	833604

46000 SERIES...see page 10

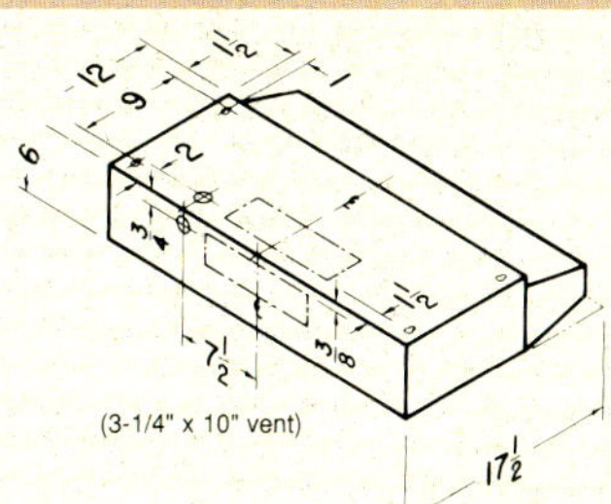

(3-1/4" x 10" vent)

Width	White	Almond	Stainless
30"	463001	463008	463004
36"	463601	463608	463604
42"	464201	464208	464204

Also available in Harvest, Avocado and Coffee.

Specifications

Volts	AMPS	Sones Ver.	Sones Hor.	CFM	Vent-Free RHP Index	Vent
120	2.5	7.0	6.5	230	7.0	3-1/4" x 10"

42000 SERIES...see page 11

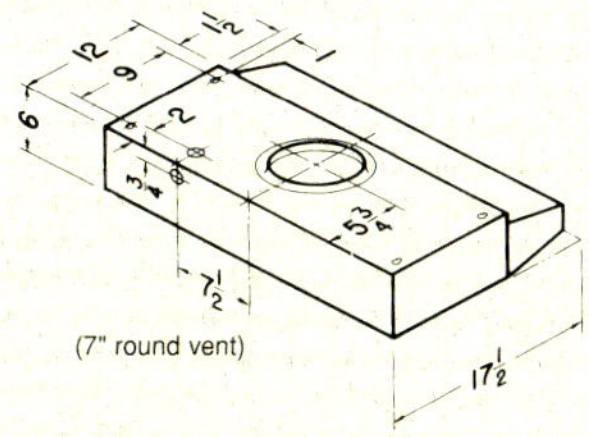

(7" round vent)

7" Round Vent

Width	White	Almond	Stainless
30"	423001	423008	423004
36"	423601	423608	423604

Also available in Harvest, Avocado and Coffee.

Specifications

Volts	AMPS	Sones Ver.	Sones Hor.	CFM	Duct-Free RHP Index	Vent
120	2.5	5.5	–	190	–	7" Round

Economy hoods are not convertible.

41000/40000 SERIES...see page 11

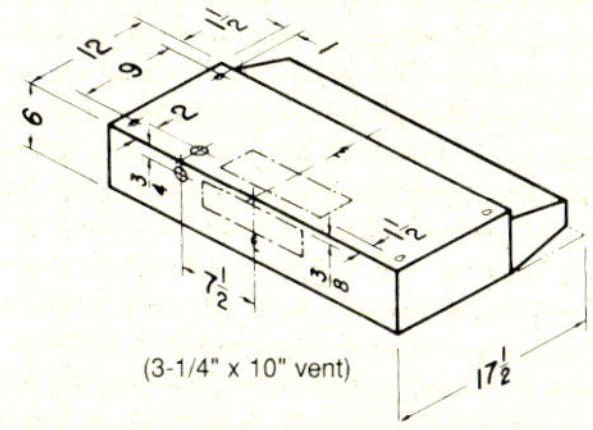

(3-1/4" x 10" vent)

41000 Vent-Free

Width	White	Almond	Stainless
24"	412401	412408	412404
30"	413001	413008	413004
36"	413601	413608	413604

Also available in Harvest, Avocado and Coffee.

41000 Specifications

Volts	AMPS	Sones Ver.	Sones Hor.	CFM	Vent-Free RHP Index
120	2.0	Vent-Free		Vent-Free	8.70

40000 Vented

Width	White	Almond	Stainless
24"	402401	402408	402404
30"	403001	403008	403004
36"	403601	403608	403604

Also available in Harvest, Avocado and Coffee.

40000 Specifications

Volts	AMPS	Sones Ver.	Sones Hor.	CFM	Vent-Free RHP Index	Vent
120	2.0	5.5	6.5	160	–	3-1/4" x 10"

Economy hoods are not convertible.

HIDEAWAY-Model 113023...see page 12

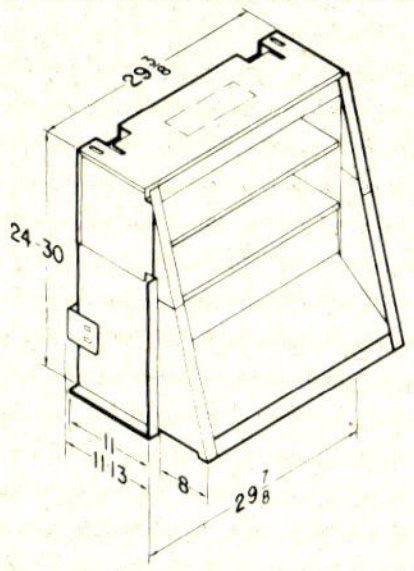

Specifications

Volts	Amps	Sones	CFM	Vent
120	3.7	4.5	360	3-1/4" x 10"

WOOD HOOD-Model 103023...see page 12

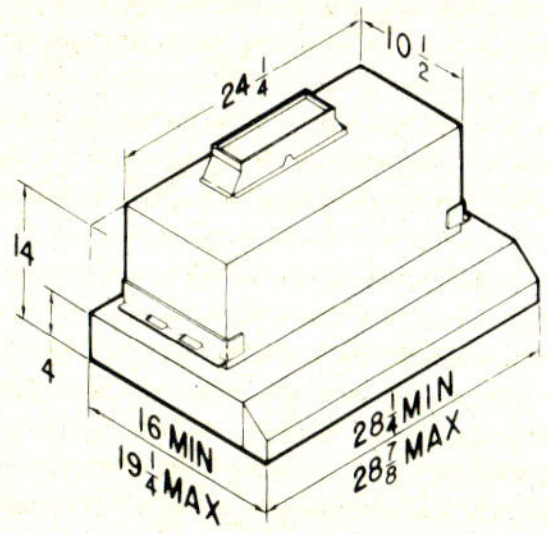

Specifications

Volts	Amps	Sones Ver.	Sones Hor.	CFM	Vent
120	3.7	5.0	4.5	360	3-1/4" x 10"

MICROMATE™-120000 Series...see page 13

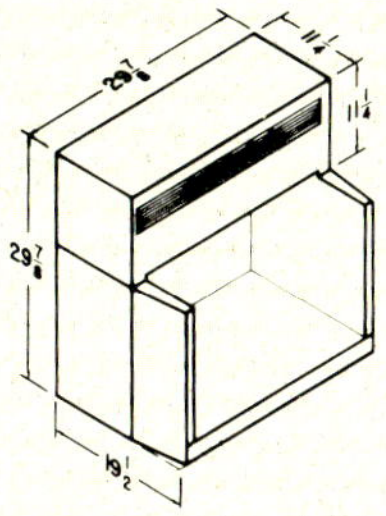

Specifications

Volts	Amps	Sones	CFM	Vent-Free RHP Index	Vent
120	2.7	4.5	300	9.8	3-1/4" x 10"

11000 SERIES...see page 13

Traditional Wall Canopy Hood

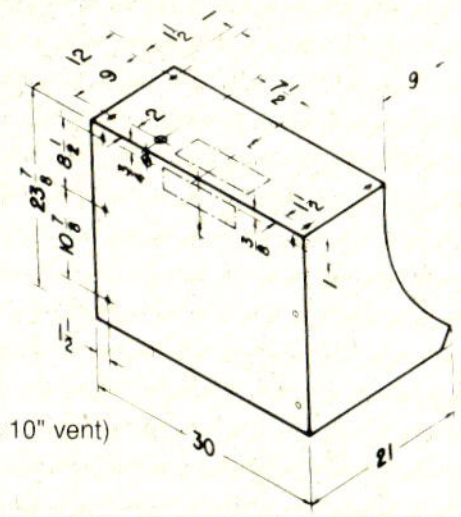

(3-1/4" x 10" vent)

11000 Series

Width	Hammered White	Hammered Almond	Hammered Harvest	Hammered Avocado	Hammered Coffee
30"	113036	113042	113047	113048	113049

Specifications

Volts	AMPS	Sones Ver.	Sones Hor.	CFM Ver.	CFM Hor.	Vent-Free RHP Index	Vent
120	3.0	6.0	6.5	190	200	9.80	3-1/4" x 10"

BROAN®

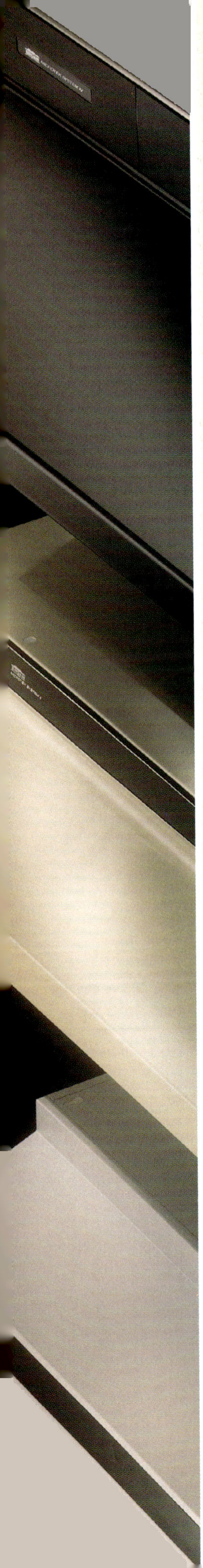

Broan delivers what customers want in kitchen ventilation.

Product: Broan offers the largest selection of range hoods in North America. Choose from Premium, Deluxe, Intermediate, Economy or Specialty models in more styles, sizes and colors than any other manufacturer.

Quality: All painted parts and weldments are inspected to assure a quality finish. All dimensional specifications are verified electronically to assure a quality fit and feel. And all shipments are inspected to be certain you receive the quality product you ordered, the way you ordered it. No shortcuts. No exceptions.

Value: State-of-the-art manufacturing and a continuing commitment to innovation ensure customers always receive the quality, reliability and performance they want, in every price category.

Performance: Exclusive features, available on a wide variety of products, allow you to turn prospects into customers:

- Heat Sentry™ – Automatically turns blower to high speed when excess heat is detected.
- AutoTemp – Monitors cooking conditions and automatically adjusts blower to appropriate ventilation levels.
- Blower Memory – Returns fan speed to the last setting used, so your customers don't have to reset the control.

Marketing support that works for you.

National Consumer Advertising: Broan is the leading residential range hood advertiser, with more than 415 million impressions each year in leading shelter magazines.

Public Relations: Broan maintains direct contact with more than 230 consumer and trade publications, ensuring that information on our range hood innovations gets to consumers.

In-Store Displays: Broan designs and builds custom range hood displays in our own

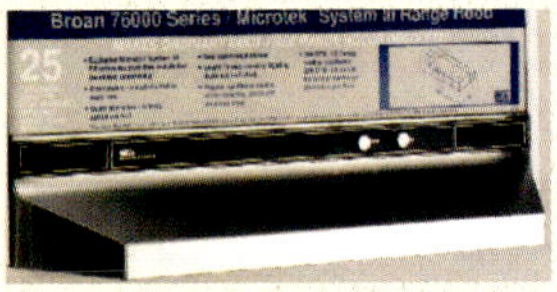

fully-equipped display department, so you can demonstrate our products for maximum exposure and sales.

Merchandising Support: Broan range hood ad slicks and logo sheets help you compose ads and fliers, and our instruction sheets are written to make installation especially easy.

Microtek® Filters: Broan Microtek replacement filters are a built-in sales and profit opportunity. Order in convenient, prepacked shipper displays.

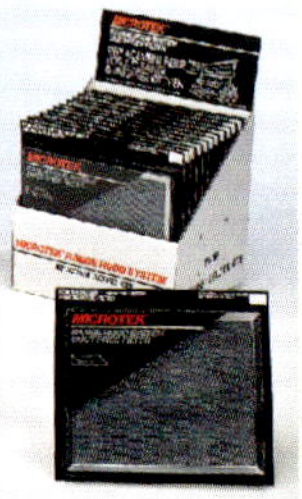

Service: Broan sales and merchandising experts help you plan orders and promotions to maximize sales and profits. Our customer service representatives are available to help you between 7:30AM and 6:00PM Central Time. Call 1-800-558-1711.

BROAN®
A NORTEK COMPANY
P.O. Box 140, Hartford, WI 53027 **1-800-548-0790**
In Canada: Broan Limited **905-670-2500**

ALL THE COMFORTS OF HOME™

Printed in the U.S.A.
99850148E
B69

BLUE CREEK™

BY JENN-AIR®

C502
11452/JEN
BuyLine 5769

JENN-AIR PRODUCT INFORMATION

Designer Line

Pro-Style™

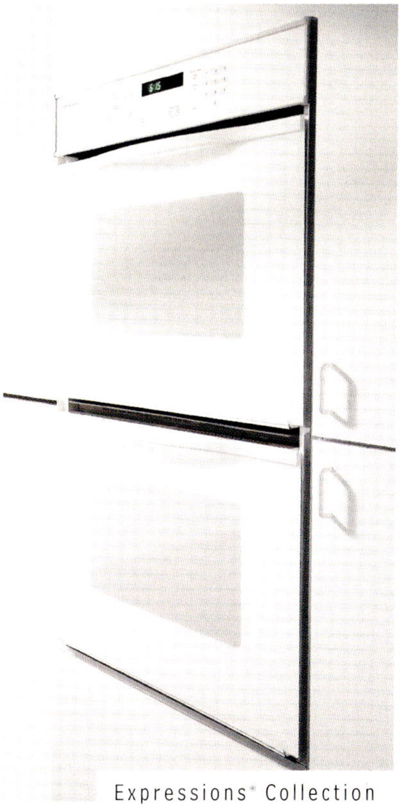

Expressions® Collection

JENN-AIR

THE SIGN OF A GREAT COOK®

Blue Creek™

By Jenn-Air®

It's time to say hello to color—thanks to a bright line of professional-style products from Jenn-Air Appliances.

The Blue Creek WaterColors Collection offers a full palette of brilliant, colorful appliances to let you make a dramatic change.

Pick one color for all your appliance choices. Or mix and match. Blue Creek gives you the freedom to create just the effect you want.

27" DOUBLE ELECTRIC WALL OVEN
(model WW27430P)
The Electric Double Wall Oven features an upper dual speed convection oven for even baking on up to three racks and superb roasting results, along with a lower bake/broil oven. Both ovens are self-cleaning.

Also available: 30" Single Electric Wall Oven (model W30400P) Self-cleaning dual speed convection and bake/broil oven.

48" Triple-Bay Gas Downdraft Cooktop

(model CVG4380P)

48" Triple-Bay Gas Downdraft Cooktop, shown here in gleaming Bordeaux Red, gives you practically unlimited options in both style and function. Professional-style knobs enhance the distinctive look of this versatile cooktop.

Dual-Fuel™ Range

(model SVD48600P)

Dual-Fuel™ Range, shown in shimmering Jade with optional backsplash, adds bold drama to any decor. Range features a modular gas cooking surface with self-cleaning electric dual speed convection and bake/broil oven. Comes with interchangeable grill and 2 two-burner modules.

Choose from this impressive palette of colors from the WaterColors Collection

Bordeaux Red

Copper

Jade

Sapphire Blue

Champagne Gold

BLUE CREEK™

by Jenn-Air

For fresh new ideas in kitchen appliances, look to Blue Creek. For more information, call **800-244-1491.**

Counter Depth Side-By-Side Refrigerator

(model JRSD209T)
This counter depth side-by-side refrigerator offers a built-in look while its striking color stands out to give your kitchen a totally creative look. Spill proof, roll-out shelves, humidity-controlled fresh produce crispers and crescent cubed/crushed ice and water convenience center make it totally convenient.

Ultimate Quiet Dishwasher

(model DW861UQ)
Shown in striking Sapphire Blue, this Ultimate Quiet Built-In Dishwasher has pizazz and practicality. This model features a deep Flex-Rack loading system and triple level quiet action fan-jet wash system for outstanding performance.

BLUE CREEK™

by Jenn-Air

For fresh new ideas in kitchen appliances, look to Blue Creek. For more information, call **800-244-1491.**

SUNCAST SERIES™ COOKTOPS

CRESCENT

(model CCE9300)
The shape of the Crescent cooktop is ideal for both traditional and corner applications. The versatile, flush-to-the-counter design of Crescent features three Ultra Quick-Start™ radiant elements, and one Ultra Quick-Twin™ dual radiant element for fast start-up and even heating.

PROFORM

(model CCE9100)
The ProForm cooktop extends beyond the counter profile for a unique look. Side-mounted recessed controls keep a low profile for a perfect blend of form and function.

The Suncast Series™ explores a full spectrum of choices in cooktops with a fascinating array of rich natural-looking textures and colors. Each works with virtually any cabinet or countertop material imaginable. Cooktop material is cool to the touch, thanks to a specially engineered surface material that dissipates heat.

BLUE CREEK™

by Jenn-Air

For fresh new ideas in kitchen appliances, look to Blue Creek. For more information, call **800-244-1491.**

Expressions® Collection

With its award-winning flush design and appealing features, the Jenn-Air Expressions® Collection is perfect for those who appreciate great style as well as great cooking. Let's begin with the Expressions modular cooktop system. It enables you to design your own personal cooktop by mixing and matching a variety of innovative cooking cartridges. The smooth lines and top performance of Expressions wall ovens and refrigerators round out the collection to create a beautifully coordinated look for the kitchen. No matter how you serve it up, the Expressions Collection is the ideal choice for today's home.

30" Dual-Fuel™ Pro-Style™

(model SVD48600P)
(shown with optional 30" lighted A518S backsplash)

The 30" Pro-Style™ range combines the versatility of a gas cooktop with the performance of a self-cleaning electric dual speed convection (convect bake/convect roast) and bake/broil oven. The modular design allows you to customize your cooking surface. And our downdraft ventilation system lets you grill right in your kitchen.

MOST PREFERRED CONVECTION OVEN*

Ultimate Quiet Series Pro-Style™

(model DW861UQP)
The Ultimate Quiet Series Dishwasher combines superb cleaning power with virtually silent operation. The UQ Insulation System and Quiet Liner™ Tub ensure years of quiet performance. And the Quiet Action Jet Wash system can handle anything you dish out.

48" Pro-Style™ Triple Gas

(model CCGP2820P) (shown with optional 12" A509S backsplash)
This Pro-Style cooktop offers versatility and style with its six sealed gas burners, electric griddle and drop-down extendible control panel with over-size knobs. Two 15,000 BTU burners allow high heat cooking while the Excalibur® nonstick griddle finish makes clean-up easy. Optional stainless steel backsplash and hood complete the professional look.

**Based on brand preference surveys; homeowners prefer Jenn-Air over leading brands.*

Excalibur® is a registered trademark of Whitford Corp.

For the most current specification sheets, call Dimension Express from your fax machine at (702)833-3600. Enter code #9018 for Jenn-Air products. You will receive information on how to use the system, along with the corresponding model code numbers. Or, for a complete Jenn-Air full line catalog, call 1-800-JENN-AIR.

Designer Line

*The Jenn-Air® Designer Line offers a full selection of appliances featuring sophisticated design and innovative features. From convertible cooktop systems to high-performance wall ovens and ranges to feature-rich refrigerators and dishwashers, the Jenn-Air Designer Line has it all. Turn to the Designer Line for incomparable versatility and streamlined good looks. With Jenn-Air reliability and innovation built into every model, the Designer Line is sure to be a perfect fit for any kitchen. Looking at our unique cooking products, you can understand why Jenn-Air is the #1 preferred brand of cooking appliances.**

** Based on consumer surveys.*

For superb convection results, look for the Most Preferred Convection Oven symbol and expect juicy meats and evenly-browned baked goods on every rack! Our unique dual-speed convection system features two fan speeds and a convection plate that circulate hot air evenly inside the oven for excellent cooking results. Jenn-Air has led the way in convection cooking innovation since 1975, and it shows.

MOST PREFERRED CONVECTION OVEN*

30"/27" Expressions® Collection Double Electric

(models WW30430 and WW27430)

MOST PREFERRED CONVECTION OVEN*

The Double Electric Wall Oven features upper dual speed convection which lets you choose between Convect Bake and Convect Roast, as well as conventional baking, roasting and temperature-controlled broiling. The lower oven offers bake/broil capabilities. Large Panaview™ oven windows give you a clear look at what's cooking inside.

30"/27" Expressions® Collection Microwave/Electric Combo

(models WM30460 and WM27460)

MOST PREFERRED CONVECTION OVEN*

This Combination Wall Oven features a sleek outline backed by effortless efficiency, all in one versatile package. Electronic touch controls, curved handles and flush design give this combo its streamlined appearance, while upper microwave and lower dual speed convection oven with temperature probe help streamline its performance as well.

**Based on brand preference surveys; homeowners prefer Jenn-Air over leading brands.*

For the most current specification sheets, call Dimension Express from your fax machine at (702)833-3600. Enter code #9018 for Jenn-Air products. You will receive information on how to use the system, along with the corresponding model code numbers. Or, for a complete Jenn-Air full line catalog, call 1-800-JENN-AIR.

30" Expressions® Collection Single Electric

(model W30400)
*(shown with **model CCG2423** gas cooktop)*
The sleek, flush design of the 30" Single Electric Wall Oven is designed for the consumer who demands that an appliance look as good as it performs. The curved designer handle and electronic touch controls complete the look. Extra-large, dual speed convection and bake/broil oven ensures top performance. Choose in-wall or under-counter installation.

27" model W27400 also available.

MOST PREFERRED CONVECTION OVEN*

30 15/16" Expressions® Collection Double Electric

(model CVEX4720W)
This electric cooktop features the Expressions® Collection award-winning flush-to-the-counter design with side-mounted, backlit controls. Energy-Saver grill with Jenn-Air's Excalibur® non-stick finish grill grates makes grilling indoors easy and enjoyable anytime of the year. Shown with optional cartridge.

34 1/8" Expressions® Collection Double Gas

(model CVGX2423)
Flush-to-the-counter design offers a smooth appearance enhanced by the low contour of its backlit controls. Four sealed burners with porcelain-enameled cast-iron burner grates make clean-up easy. Downdraft ventilation eliminates the need for a hood. Add a single Expressions® Collection grill to either side to increase your cooking options.

Excalibur® is a registered trademark of Whitford Corp.

**Based on brand preference surveys; homeowners prefer Jenn-Air over leading brands.*

For the most current specification sheets, call Dimension Express from your fax machine at (702)833-3600. Enter code #9018 for Jenn-Air products. You will receive information on how to use the system, along with the corresponding model code numbers. Or, for a complete Jenn-Air full line catalog, call 1-800-JENN-AIR.

20 cu. ft. Expressions® Collection Counter Depth Side-by-Side

(model JRSD209T)

This 20 cubic foot refrigerator offers a sleek, counter depth design for built-in look without a built-in price. The extended front door panel with concealed hinge and factory installed perimeter door trim extends up to 1/4" to easily accept custom wood and decorator panels to suit any decor. Spill-proof shelves roll out for convenience.

For the most current specification sheets, call Dimension Express from your fax machine at (702)833-3600. Enter code #9018 for Jenn-Air products. You will receive information on how to use the system, along with the corresponding model code numbers. Or, for a complete Jenn-Air full line catalog, call 1-800-JENN-AIR.

P R O - S T Y L E™

The Pro-Style™ Collection gives you the best of both worlds—the sleek styling of professional appliances plus the innovative features of Jenn-Air appliances.

Our self-cleaning ovens, modular downdraft cooktops and convection baking system are but a few of the Pro-Style Collection offerings. And best of all, the professional look of the Pro-Style Collection is available without the professional price.

24 CU. FT. PRO-STYLE™ REFRIGERATOR
(model JRSD2490T)
This side-by-side crushed ice/chilled water dispenser model accepts optional custom stainless steel panels that give it the same sleek, professional look as the rest of the Pro-Style™ Collection. Its Crystal White interior features spill-proof roll-out shelves to afford you easy access.

30"/27" PRO-STYLE™ DOUBLE ELECTRIC WALL OVEN
(model WW30430P/WW27430P)
The Pro-Style™ Double Electric Wall Ovens feature an upper dual speed convection (convect bake/convect roast) oven and lower bake/broil oven. Both ovens are self-cleaning with electronic touch controls with keypad entry. It's no wonder more people have chosen Jenn-Air convection ovens for their homes over any other brand.

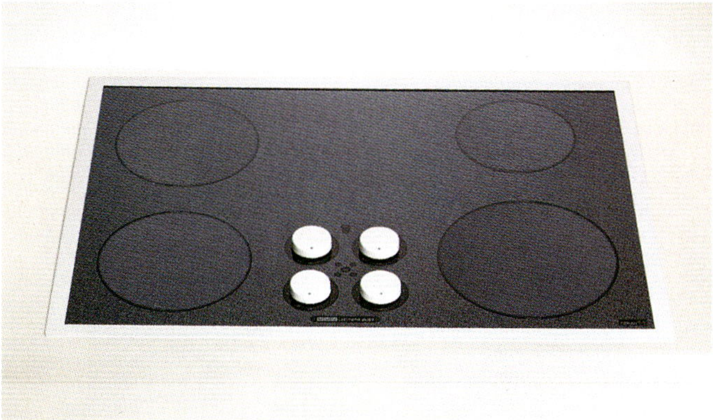

30" Designer Line Conventional Magnetic Induction and Ultra Quick-Start™ Radiant

FASTEST
Temperature Response with Induction

(model CCE3450)
This 30" Designer Line Cooktop features two Ultra Quick-Start™ radiant elements, and two magnetic induction elements for the fastest response. Induction's precise temperature control takes a boil-over to a simmer in an instant.

36" Designer Line Frameless Radiant Cooktop

(model CCE3531)
The unique frameless design of this Jenn-Air Cooktop smooths the way to performance and style. Ultra Quick-Start™ radiant elements make cooking easy, while smooth, polished radiused edges and glass-ceramic surface make clean-up a breeze.

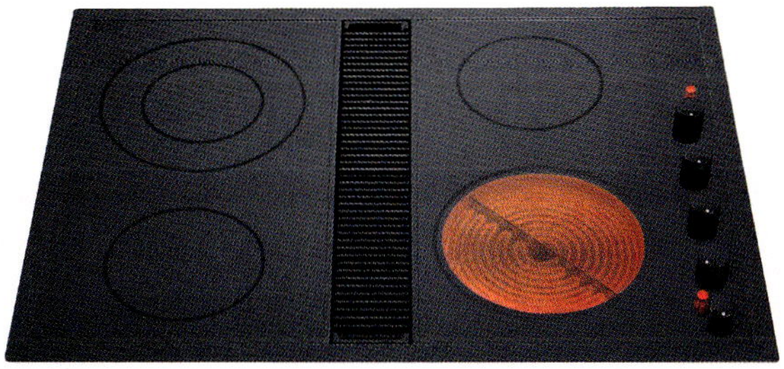

30" Designer Line Downdraft Electric

(model CVE3400)
30" Downdraft Electric Cooktop features a variable-speed fan that pulls steam and odors down and out for a fresher, cleaner kitchen. Ultra Quick-Twin™ dual radiant element, and three Ultra Quick-Start™ radiant elements make cooking easy.

48" Designer Line Downdraft Triple Gas

(model CVG4380)
The Downdraft Triple Gas Cooktop offers the ultimate in flexibility for creative cooking. Three bays can accommodate up to six burners and accepts gas accessories. E-ven Heat™ grill and two-speed downdraft ventilation continue Jenn-Air's tradition of excellence in indoor grilling.

For the most current specification sheets, call Dimension Express from your fax machine at (702)833-3600. Enter code #9018 for Jenn-Air products. You will receive information on how to use the system, along with the corresponding model code numbers. Or, for a complete Jenn-Air full line catalog, call 1-800-JENN-AIR.

30" Electric

MOST PREFERRED CONVECTION OVEN*

(model SVE47600) (shown with optional A122W radiant element cartridge)

Designed for countertop, island or peninsula installation, the slide-in range provides the elegant built-in look that today's consumers prefer. With its sleek, electronic keypad controls, extra-large dual speed convection and bake/broil oven, and Energy Saver grill, it's the natural choice.

30" Dual-Fuel™

MOST PREFERRED CONVECTION OVEN*

(model SVD48600)

The Dual-Fuel™ Range combines a modular gas cooking surface with electric dual speed convection and bake/broil oven for maximum versatility. Along with Jenn-Air's extra-large 3.8 cu. ft. oven size, you'll find that no other range gives you so much performance in so little space.

30" Radiant

MOST PREFERRED CONVECTION OVEN*

(model SCE30600)

Jenn-Air ranges serve up the perfect combination—contemporary designer styling and a variety of creative cooking features. Like this model's three Ultra Quick-Start™ radiant elements, the Ultra Quick-Twin™ dual radiant element, and a dual speed convection and bake/broil oven.

**Based on brand preference surveys; homeowners prefer Jenn-Air over leading brands.*

30" Free-Standing Electric Radiant

MOST PREFERRED CONVECTION OVEN*

(model JER8850)

Jenn-Air free-standing ranges offer electronic oven controls with keypad entry, extra-large self-cleaning oven and a large Panaview™ window. The dual-speed convection oven offers a dehydration feature for drying aromatic herbs and flowers or delicious fruits right in your kitchen. A high-quality mesh drying rack is included.

For the most current specification sheets, call Dimension Express from your fax machine at (702)833-3600. Enter code #9018 for Jenn-Air products. You will receive information on how to use the system, along with the corresponding model code numbers. Or, for a complete Jenn-Air full line catalog, call 1-800-JENN-AIR.

24 cu. ft. Designer Line

(model JRSD2490T)
This 24 cubic foot refrigerator gives you more of what every kitchen needs—space. With three spill-proof roll-out cantilevered shelves, a temperature-controlled cold storage drawer, lift-out storage trays and deep storage shelves, you can always make room for more. Comes with perimeter door trim which extends to 1/4" to easily accept custom wood and decorator panels to suit any decor.

27" Designer Line Microwave/ Electric Combo

(model WM27260)
The 27" Wall Oven/Microwave Electric Combo brings microwave and oven together in a streamlined design. The lower dual speed convection and bake/broil oven means superb baking and roasting results, while the upper microwave offers the perfect match in Designer Line styling and convenience.

MOST PREFERRED CONVECTION OVEN*

Ultimate Quiet Series

(model DW961UQ)
The Ultimate Quiet Series dishwasher brings you the quiet efficiency of Jenn-Air's UQ insulation system, along with all the features you depend on for easy loading and clean, sparkling dishes every time.

27" Designer Line Single Electric

(model W27200) MOST PREFERRED CONVECTION OVEN*
The 27" Single Electric Wall Oven features a self-cleaning dual speed convection oven with electronic controls and Panaview™ window for easy viewing of what's cooking inside. Under-counter or in-wall installation adds stylish versatility.

**Based on brand preference surveys; homeowners prefer Jenn-Air over leading brands.*

For the most current specification sheets, call Dimension Express from your fax machine at (702)833-3600. Enter code #9018 for Jenn-Air products. You will receive information on how to use the system, along with the corresponding model code numbers. Or, for a complete Jenn-Air full line catalog, call 1-800-JENN-AIR.

Cartridges and Accessories

Customize your Jenn-Air modular cooktop or range with these cartridges and accessories.
(Expressions® Collection models shown, except for solid element, gas module and cooker-steamer)

Solid Element

Gas Two-Burner Module

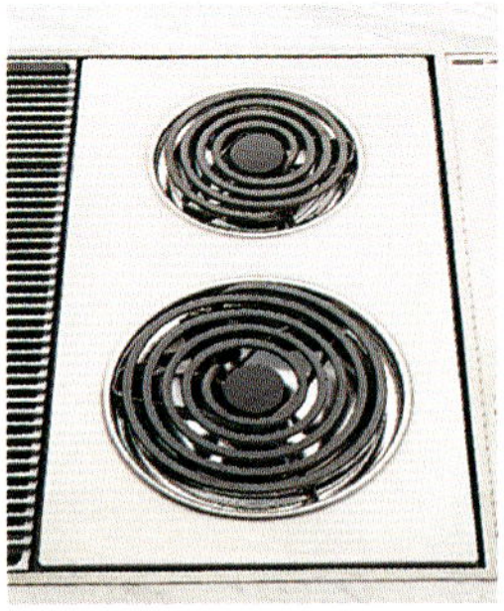

Conventional Coil

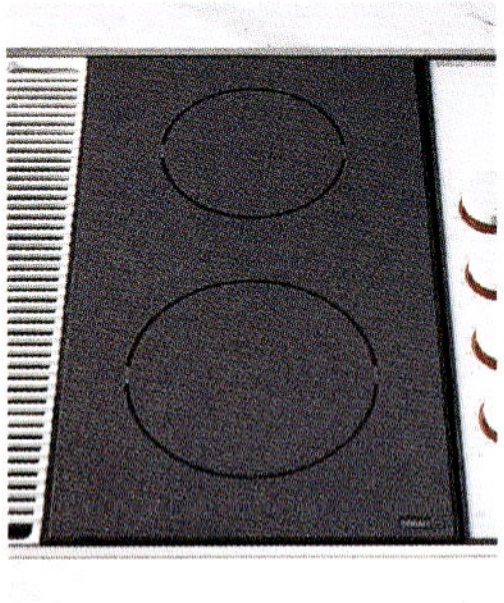

Halogen Element

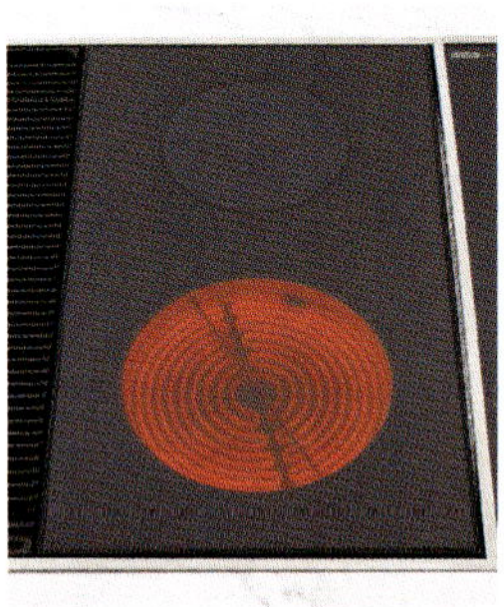

Radiant Element

Energy Saver Grill Assembly

Griddle

Wok

Rotiss-Kebab

Cooker-Steamer

Excalibur® Finish Grill Grates

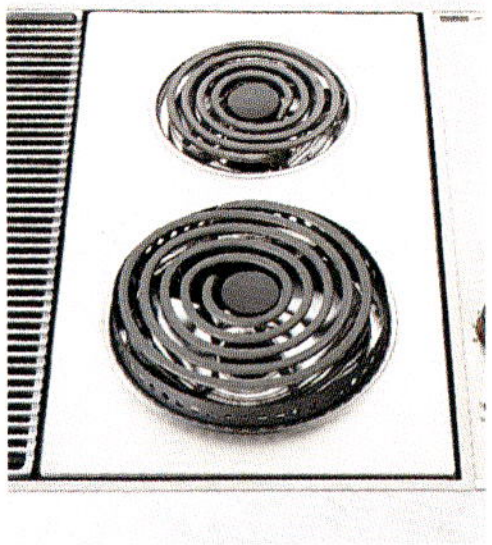

Big Pot Element

Grill Cover Designer Line

Grill Covers Expressions® Collection

Excalibur® is a registered trademark of Whitford Corp.

JENN-AIR

The Sign of a Great Cook®

C507
11452/May
BuyLine 7564

YOUR HELPFUL GUIDE TO

KITCHEN DESIGN

MAYTAG

WELCOME

The kitchen is truly the hub of activity for the family of the '90s. Besides being the primary spot where household meals are prepared, the kitchen is the place family members plan their day, where kids tackle homework, where Mom often pays the bills, and where Dad and daughter discuss the fundamentals of T-ball.

Such a special room needs a versatile design—one that will allow family members ample room to move around, that offers surfaces of different heights to accommodate all who use it, and that brings many functions into a central space without feeling crowded.

Planning the ideal kitchen requires information that is dependable, that you can count on. We at Maytag—the dependability people—understand your concerns, and we're here to help. We know that for many of you, your home is your greatest investment. As one of the most recognized brand name appliances in North America, Maytag and its full line of appliances add to the value of your investment, just as they add to the quality of your life. So, if you're considering building a new house or remodeling your current kitchen, plan to customize your kitchen to fit your family needs—and plan to use Maytag appliances to add lasting value.

Your Helpful Guide to Kitchen Design provides an imaginative array of exciting, inspirational ideas to help you meet that goal. It also offers two bonus sections: one on planning a utility room that will do more than just meet your laundry needs, and one on the latest in kitchen trends and technology.

We at Maytag want to help you—and the kitchen professionals you choose—create the ideal plan for your family's needs and lifestyle.

C507
11452/May
BuyLine 7564

MAYTAG

Your Helpful Guide to Kitchen Design

Table of Contents

The Right Stuff: Designing a Kitchen that Works for You 2

25 Proven Tips for Smart Kitchen Design 4

What's Amiss in Your Present Kitchen 6

The Work Triangle Revisited 8

Getting the Most for Your Remodeling Dollar 10

Utilizing the Utility Room 12

What's Hot 16

Published for Maytag by Meredith Publishing Services, a division of Meredith Corp.

YOUR HELPFUL GUIDE TO KITCHEN DESIGN

TWO

C507
11452/May
BuyLine 7564

THE RIGHT STUFF

Designing a Kitchen that Works for You

As the nerve center of the home, the kitchen is the place you and your family play together, work together, eat together and ponder some of life's biggest decisions. It's where your kids struggle with algebra problems, where friends gather to share a cup of coffee and neighborhood news and where holiday meals are created.

For all its uses, the kitchen needs to be the most accommodating room in your house. It should encourage fluid movement, offer dependable appliances and suggest an atmosphere that buoys your spirits.

If you're dreaming of a new kitchen or a new home, read on. You'll learn how to plan your project so that when the sawdust has been swept away, you can relax at the table knowing there's nothing you would change.

Smart design ideas in the kitchen shown opposite include appliances from Maytag—your full-line kitchen manufacturer. A microwave is located conveniently close to the refrigerator and dishwasher and opposite the island sink. The oven lies outside the main work area.

WHAT'S IN IT FOR ME?

Start by holding a heart-to-heart talk with family members. Ask how each person uses the kitchen—and how each person *wants* to use the kitchen. Kitchen designers recommend that your kitchen be a series of activity areas rather than one free-for-all space.

Don't forget to think about your future, too. Will an elderly parent likely be living with you down the road? Are your kids leaving home in the next few years? Imagine what lifestyle changes might lie ahead, and how the kitchen layout and features you plan today can help accommodate those lifestyle changes now and in the future.

As you draw up your plan, think about how you move around the kitchen as you prepare meals. Typically, a cook moves from the refrigerator to the sink to cooking and serving areas. Arrange major appliances so you will be able to move smoothly from one point to the next without backtracking.

GO WITH THE FLOW

Think also about your family's traffic flow through the kitchen. You won't want family members—as much as you love them—trooping through your work space at the busiest stage of meal preparation. Consider adding a small second sink where the children can get a drink of water, or purchase a refrigerator with an ice and water dispenser in the door. Either way, place it on the outside edge of the work core.

Plan doorways carefully, and route traffic around the work core with an island or

continued on page five

The all-Maytag kitchen above serves as heart of the home by offering a cozy, intimate table where two can share a meal. A wing chair nearby can be pulled up for a third person or can simply provide a cozy planning spot.

25 Proven Tips for Smart Kitchen Design

Time-tested tips to help you plan your dream kitchen.

1. Before you start, figure out how much you can spend.
2. Work with a certified kitchen designer who can help you best utilize your space while staying within your budget.
3. Consider the needs of the entire family to create a kitchen that functions well and fits your lifestyle.
4. Involve all members of the family in planning. Consider how each person uses the kitchen.
5. Share ideas; make a list of your priorities.
6. Aim for a kitchen that is attractive, efficient, comfortable, labor-saving and well-equipped—not just big.
7. Avoid gadgets and fads that add expense but don't simplify day-to-day life.
8. Create the look of custom cabinetry while saving money. Use stock cabinetry in imaginative ways or mix stock with custom cabinetry.
9. Spend the money saved on cabinetry to buy appliances that save time and energy.
10. Don't scrimp on counter space or adequate storage; they make a kitchen function well. Plan to have stretches of continuous countertop.
11. Store items as near the appliance or spot where you will use them most often.
12. Store heavy items at a height between your hip and shoulder and light articles above your head.
13. Install vertical pullouts, roll-outs and lazy Susans on full extension slides for maximum accessibility.
14. Plan counters and work stations of different heights according to the tasks to be performed there and the height of the user.
15. Shield the cooking area from the eating area by installing a multilevel island.
16. For a safer kitchen, use non-skid flooring.
17. Choose surface materials that are easy to maintain and aren't likely to chip or dent.
18. Replace outdated appliances with newer, energy-efficient models to save on utility bills.
19. To avoid back strain, situate dishwashers 6 to 18 inches above the floor.
20. Install ovens at convenient heights.
21. Position your dishwasher close to dish storage for easier unloading.
22. Add a second microwave at a height accessible to children.
23. Incorporate a recycling center.
24. Plan to locate your laundry in or near your kitchen.
25. Be sure to include enough electrical outlets for smaller appliances.

Unload your dishwasher with ease while doing your back a favor. When installing your Maytag dishwasher, raise it from 6 to 18 inches off the floor, as shown above.

C507
11452/May
BuyLine 7564

continued from page three

peninsula. If you include a countertop in your island or peninsula, other family members can chat with you, do homework, have a snack or engage in other activities without getting in your way.

Define an Open Plan

If you're planning a kitchen that's adjacent to the family room, consider the following solutions to problems you could encounter:

Too gaping? Break up open spaces with angled walls, alcoves or nooks.

Monotonous? Vary the heights of ceilings and floors to add visual interest and define parameters.

Losing identity? Create a feel of separate areas with columns, pocket doors and partial walls.

Jumbled? Install separate lighting systems for each activity area. Then you'll be able to turn out your sink lights, for example, so you're not spotlighting dirty dishes.

continued on page seven

Install a Maytag stacked washer and dryer next to the recycling center, top, to make good use of space. The desk below offers a place to work; the built-in Maytag microwave in the background saves space.

The side-by-side Maytag refrigerator, left, is conveniently near the kitchen table. The Maytag cooktop, below, is located at a convenient height for a person in a wheelchair.

MAYTAG

WHAT'S AMISS
IN YOUR PRESENT KITCHEN

Early in the planning process, use this checklist to pinpoint major and minor problems in your present kitchen. Taking this step will ensure that these problems do not reappear in your new kitchen. Also, keep notes about the features you dislike most in your existing kitchen.

- ❒ Inadequate countertop space
- ❒ Broken-up space
- ❒ Counter space in wrong locations
- ❒ Inadequate lighting
- ❒ Cabinetry too dark
- ❒ Room decorated in dark colors
- ❒ Appliances outdated aesthetically
- ❒ Appliances outdated functionally
- ❒ Insufficient storage
- ❒ Cabinets scratched, gouged and worn
- ❒ Sink chipped or difficult to clean
- ❒ Traffic aisles too narrow
- ❒ Not enough room for extra cooks
- ❒ No room to socialize in kitchen
- ❒ Countertop worn or color no longer appropriate
- ❒ Poor use of floor and wall space
- ❒ Doors and windows poorly located
- ❒ Too many doors and windows
- ❒ Ventilation nonexistent or inadequate
- ❒ Family dining area too small or nonexistent
- ❒ Electrical outlets inadequate
- ❒ Dishwasher does poor job or no dishwasher
- ❒ Not enough daylight
- ❒ It's seen better days
- ❒ It's ugly
- ❒ Floor covering outdated or worn
- ❒ Cook isolated from family
- ❒ Poor work triangle
- ❒ Doors interfere with work counters
- ❒ Too few drawers
- ❒ No efficiency/convenience features
- ❒ No recycling center
- ❒ No landing counter next to refrigerator
- ❒ No landing counter next to oven
- ❒ No good location for microwave
- ❒ Traffic goes through work area

❒ NUMBER OF ITEMS CHECKED

SCORING

Total up the number of checked items.

SCORE 5 OR LESS
You have a pretty good kitchen.

SCORE 6-14
Can use improvement, but not a disaster.

SCORE 15-24
You should start remodeling your kitchen now.

SCORE 25-30
Gut the kitchen and start from scratch.

SCORE 31-36
Evacuate. Your kitchen is hazardous to your health.

continued from page five

Put Appliances in Their Place

Avoid hassles and enjoy your kitchen more by thoughtfully deciding where to place appliances. Here are a few tried-and-true tips.

Dishwasher

Designers are beginning to realize that the dishwasher doesn't have to be located under a counter. Consider placing yours 6 to 18 inches above the floor to minimize bending when you load and unload. You can plan cabinets or drawers above and below. Since you lose counter space when you raise the dishwasher, leave at least 18 inches of counter space between the sink and the raised dishwasher so you'll have a landing spot for dirty and just-cleaned dishes. In any installation, you'll probably want the dishwasher no more than 36 inches from the edge of a sink.

Because so many important activities take place in your kitchen, shop around for a dishwasher that is designed to work quietly.

Also consider whether a dishwasher is easy to load, what its capacity is and how it performs. A good dishwasher will clean your

continued on page nine

As you plan, think about how you live and cook. In the kitchen at left, an island offers an additional landing pad for hot dishes from the nearby Maytag wall ovens. In the kitchen below, kids can snack at the table and help themselves to water from the Maytag refrigerator without bothering the cook.

The Work Triangle Revisited

The classic foundation of kitchen design has been the work triangle—the three points being the refrigerator, cooktop (or range) and sink.

The old rules no longer dictate—but instead serve as starting points for creating a customized kitchen.

But as appliances get better and better and lifestyles get busier and busier, the evolution of kitchen design has speeded up. While traditional design principles remain valuable tools, designers are adding new twists to target the needs of individual homeowners. The old rules are no longer dictates—but instead serve as starting points for creating a customized kitchen.

Conventional wisdom has long held that the distance from refrigerator to cooktop to sink should total 12 to 22 feet. Any less, the kitchen will feel cramped; any more, extra mileage will be added to kitchen chores. Standard distances in the triangle: four to seven feet from refrigerator to sink, four to six feet from sink to cooktop and four to nine feet from cooktop to refrigerator.

Using these rules as a springboard, kitchen designers now encourage families to consider their own needs and shape the kitchen accordingly. For example:

✗ Consider designing a kitchen within a kitchen. On weekdays, when you're making quick, simple meals, you'll use the scaled-down space. On weekends, when you cook for a crowd, you'll use the entire kitchen.

✗ If two members of your family like to work in the kitchen simultaneously, you could create two separate work triangles. Both might include the refrigerator, but don't overlap or you'll likely be in one another's way. The secondary triangle might include a microwave oven and small sink.

✗ Kitchen islands are especially useful in large kitchens, because they can keep the work triangle down to a manageable size.

✗ Today's dishwasher, which can be plumbed directly into the water line and can handle unrinsed dishes, does not have to be right next to the sink, though you'll probably still want a sink nearby. But for easier loading, consider putting the dishwasher a few steps closer to the dining area—perhaps in a peninsula.

✗ Dual appliances may be worth the investment. For example, consider a second microwave under a countertop near the eating area so the kids can make popcorn and other snacks. If you entertain on a large scale, two wall ovens will help you cook for a crowd. If you entertain often or have a large family, consider one dishwasher near the sink and another near the table to make after-meal clean-up more efficient.

✗ You may want to incorporate a stacked washer and dryer into your kitchen design. For busy people and those with limited mobility, this is an efficient way to bring major household tasks to a central location.

✗ Place a wall oven, which may be used infrequently, outside your main work space to save prime locations for your workhorses: the microwave oven and cooktop.

If you're busy and like to combine tasks, or if you have limited mobility and want to avoid stairs, include a Maytag stacked washer and dryer, right, in or near the kitchen.

continued from page seven

dishes without prerinsing, once large food scraps have been removed.

Refrigerator/Freezer

Place your refrigerator/freezer so that it's near the kitchen area but also as close to the table as possible. You'll have to decide between a side-by-side or a top-freezer unit. Side-by-side models offer freezer access to children and to people in wheelchairs; top freezers usually cost less.

Microwave Oven

Microwave ovens are used frequently, so place them in the main work area. Because their doors hinge left, plan counter space to the right of your microwave. For children, it's safest to install the microwave oven at countertop level or lower.

Wall Oven

It's a kitchen staple. But designers often place it outside the main work area because most people don't use the oven daily. For safety's sake, a wall oven should be installed in an area where its open door is three inches below the user's bent elbow and won't hinder passersby.

Another rule of thumb: Install a single wall oven so the bottom is at countertop level or about 36 inches off the floor. With two wall ovens, the top one should open at countertop height; the second oven should be placed directly below the top oven.

Range or Cooktop

It's one of the most used kitchen appliances, and should be placed for easy access next to the microwave oven and the refrigerator, the kitchen's other hard-working equipment. Make sure you plan at least 12 inches of counter space on either side of the

continued on page eleven

In the white kitchen, below left, a Maytag wall oven is located outside the main work triangle. This arrangement makes the second Maytag oven available for parties, but leaves the prime space to meet the demands of everyday living.

A Maytag drop-in range, below, serves as one point in the traditional triangle.

GETTING THE MOST FOR YOUR REMODELING DOLLAR

A rolling island with recessed wheels can double as a serving counter or an extra work surface wherever it's needed.

Don't be afraid to dream of creating your fantasy kitchen, even if your building or remodeling budget is modest. With creativity and wise planning, you can hold down costs. The money you save can buy design touches, wonderful appliances and other items you've longed for.

Here are some inside tips from today's top designers:

With creativity and planning, you can hold down costs. The money you save can buy design touches, wonderful appliances and other items you've longed for.

✘ Save on cabinetry, which can account for more than half the cost of a major kitchen remodeling project, by finding someone who can add a few details to customize sturdy, ready-made cabinets. You could add a plate rack, display nook or perhaps decorative cutouts to fashion a great look while holding costs down.

✘ Ask your builder for the cost of creating a built-in pantry. Building one may cost less than a cabinetry pantry unit.

✘ Fit an island with recessed wheels so it can double as a serving counter or be moved to provide an extra work surface anywhere in the kitchen.

✘ If you're trying to add storage space on a budget, consider the space between studs. It's about 3½ inches deep and can house spices and canned goods. You can create a pantry that's about 30 inches wide if you remove a stud and add a header and full-width storage shelves. Finish off with face frame and doors to match other cabinets.

✘ Place wall cabinets on the back or far side of an island. The cabinets will provide foot-deep storage, and if you use 42-inch-high units behind a 36-inch-high island, they will conceal the work area.

✘ To create a recycling center, place two wastebaskets in one pull-out cabinet.

✘ Combine two inexpensive mouldings to create the look of high-end decorative moulding.

✘ Create the clean look of a built-in refrigerator by pulling adjacent base cabinets forward to match the front line of the refrigerator. This provides extra-deep countertops as a bonus. You also can build an enclosure for the refrigerator with plywood panels.

✘ Another way to make your refrigerator look like a built-in is to bump it into the wall behind it, if it's not a weight-bearing interior wall. To do this, remove the drywall behind the refrigerator and frame the area. Then remove the studs between the frame and install a new header. Move the refrigerator into the recess and install cabinetry around it. This is far less expensive than purchasing special cabinetry and a shallower built-in appliance.

C507
11452/May
BuyLine 7564

continued from page nine

cooktop to make room for pan handles and to serve as landing areas for hot pots.

Finishing Touches

The colors, patterns and materials you choose will set the tone in your kitchen. If you don't know where to start, try letting a lovely set of dishes or a favorite picture inspire the color scheme.

Cabinets have a major impact on a kitchen's look. Choose a set that's compatible with your home's overall design.

Select materials that unify the design and make your kitchen inviting. To lend continuity, repeat a design element, material or motif from elsewhere in your home—perhaps a few items from a set of collectibles displayed in your living room can be shown off in your new kitchen.

Exhibit an item or two near and dear to your heart to complement the warmth your family brings to this very special room.

Tucking a Maytag microwave above the range, top right, frees up precious counter space and gives the kitchen a custom look. To complete the custom look, make your Maytag side-by-side refrigerator, top left, look like a built-in by recessing it into stud space. For a kitchen that doesn't have space for a side-by-side, consider a Maytag refrigerator with a top freezer and an outside ice and water dispenser, bottom right. Add interest to a traditional galley kitchen with some gentle angles, bottom left, to create a zig-zag effect.

C507
11452/May
BuyLine 7564

Utilizing the Utility Room

Imagine a first-floor room near the kitchen in which you could do your laundry, store soft drinks, work on a special hobby, drop off muddy boots, locate a recycling center and stow bulk food items. Imagine having places for your roasting pans and serving platters and a handy spot for mops and brooms.

If you find this appealing, you're not alone. Yesterday's laundry room is evolving into the ultimate utility room.

Center of Attention

When located near the kitchen, such a room centralizes work areas near the hub of home activity. It enables working parents to tackle laundry chores in the evening hours without sacrificing family time. And being next to the kitchen offers the money-saving benefit of tapping into existing plumbing lines.

Every laundry room should include a few basics. Besides the washer and dryer, you'll need adequate storage space for detergents and dirty laundry. You will want places to hang up your damp clothes and garments fresh from the dryer. The utility room will need a drain and plumbing line, and the dryer will need to be vented to the outdoors.

Your Dreams Are the Limits

But there's no reason to stop with the basics when the room can do so much more to accommodate your family. Consider these additional ideas:

- **Plan for the storage space of your dreams.** Use it for paper goods purchased in bulk, large pots, party goods, platters, roasting pans, soft drinks and snacks.
- **Establish a recycling center.** You can simply plan floor space for stackable plastic bins, or design a more elaborate cabinetry system with containers on pull-out shelves.
- **Include space for a large freezer.** Stocks of frozen foods are a great convenience.

continued on page fourteen

A stacked Maytag washer and dryer, opposite page, leaves plenty of room for storage and counter space for bathroom necessities. A rolling worktable near the Maytag pair, above, offers a landing pad for freshly folded clothes. Or it can be scooted off to be used as a hobby table or work surface.

continued from page thirteen

✗**Make way for work or play.** Incorporate a sewing or hobby table, a desk for paying bills or a place for your computer.

✗**Raise the dryer.** Position it 15 inches off the floor to reduce back strain. A drawer below offers additional storage space.

✗**Keep the noise down.** Consider Maytag's Quiet-Pak™ feature, especially in an open plan or if you'll be using the utility room as a home office. Offered to lessen the level of sound emitted by appliances, it's available on all Dependable Care™ "Plus" washers and dryers.

✗**Aim for the right height.** Install cabinets, shelves and countertops that accommodate your height.

✗**Figure on a folding zone.** Consider including easy-to-clean countertop or tabletop space for folding. You could also locate a shelf below to hold laundry baskets; label with each family member's name to simplify putting clothes away.

✗**Store cleaning agents away from little hands.** If you have young children, you'll want wall cabinets to keep detergents and bleach out of their reach.

✗**Shelve it.** Open shelving, pull-out drawers or tilt bins will simplify laundry collection and sorting.

✗**Designate a drip-dry area.** Plan a place for drip-drying clean clothes as well as wet snow gear and swimwear. Include a drip pan or drain.

Stacked Maytag washers and dryers make efficient use of space in these utility rooms. A pull-out ironing board adds to an efficient laundry center at top right. The room at bottom left doubles as a sewing and potting center. The raised Maytag dryer in the cheery room at bottom right eliminates stooping.

✗**Include an entry door from the garage or yard.** That way, you and your kids can peel off wet or muddy clothes as you enter the house and toss them right into the washer.

✗**Short on space? Install stacked washer and dryer units.** They use about 27 inches of floor space instead of the 54 inches needed for installation of traditional side-by-side models.

✗**Try a wandering worktable.** A worktable on casters can be positioned where you need it most. Roll it near the dryer for folding clothes, place it beside the desk when doing computer work or roll it into the kitchen to transport groceries or soft drinks to the refrigerator.

✗**Hide the ironing corner.** Consider installing an ironing board that pulls down or slides out.

✗**Create a place for potting plants.** Add a deep pull-out drawer for your potting tools and include racks for wet items.

✗**Isolate the laundry.** If you're planning a utility room that's adjacent to your kitchen, be sure to shield the laundry function from direct contact with the area where food is prepared. A folding door, a standard door or a peninsula can help accomplish that separation.

Remember the days when doing the laundry meant descending to a shadowy basement? In contrast, the room above, featuring a stacked Maytag washer and dryer, suggests a summer garden—a delightful place to start a load of laundry, catch up on ironing or spend some time sewing.

WHAT'S HOT

A dishwasher that does the thinking for you, an oven that improves the quality of your food while letting you cook more of it, a grill that allows you to enjoy the taste of outdoor cooking in the dead of winter, gas burners that won't let the boilover seep down—and more!

ADVANCED BUT SIMPLE

The Maytag IntelliSense™ Plus dishwasher, directly below, simplifies your life by choosing the right settings for each load it washes. It's the first dishwasher that makes a mental note of your dishwashing habits, and then does the thinking for you, adjusting water temperature, cycle times, even drying time with each load. And, the IntelliSense dishwasher saves you up to 21 percent in energy, 27 percent in water and 19 percent in wash time.

CONVECTION EASE

The Dependable Bake™ Plus Convection Oven, bottom left, is available as a wall oven or a freestanding electric range. The freestanding unit comes in monochromatic white, almond or black. It circulates hot air over, under and around food, improving the quality of food and increasing the quantity you can bake at one time.

ISLAND COOKING

Maytag's grill-range, bottom right, lets you enjoy the flavor of outdoor cooking without leaving the comfort of your kitchen. The grill-range's powerful surface-ventilation system eliminates the need for an overhead exhaust hood, so you can install the grill-range in a freestanding island.

C507
11452/May
BuyLine 7564

The Built-In Look

Get the look of a built-in refrigerator without paying the price of one. Maytag's counter-depth, side-by-side refrigerator, top left, is shallower than standard models, so it doesn't stick out beyond standard cabinets. But its 20-cubic feet of storage space provides ample room. Available in monochromatic white or black, it offers two sealed humidity controlled crisper drawers, temperature adjustable meat and cheese drawer, adjustable easy-glide Spill-Catcher™ sealed shelves, covered dairy compartment and deep door bins.

Step-Saving Laundry

In a two-story home, an upstairs laundry eliminates the chore of lugging clothes from floor to floor. The washer and dryer at left are tucked neatly into an upstairs alcove.

The Dishwasher Gets a Raise

Reduce the amount of stooping you do when unloading the dishwasher by installing it 6 to 18 inches off the floor, as shown top right.

A Hot New Option: Sealed Gas Burners

"Boilovers" won't seep under the gas burners shown below because they're sealed into the cooktop. The newest technological and design advancement in gas cooking, they save you from the task of cleaning the burner box.

Mrs. Gampl has always had the same husband and washer, but only one gives her any trouble.

Mrs. Ruth Gampl of McHenry, Illinois, can remember the day she began what has turned out to be a truly wonderful relationship. In all the years since that special day, she's raised a family, moved that family three times and, of course, done thousands and thousands of loads of laundry.

She has no regrets about that choice she made all those years ago. The fact is, during all that time, for better and for worse, through thick and through thin, she's hardly had a single problem.

And you will be happy to hear that, like her washer, Mrs. Gampl's marriage is still going as strong as ever.

We can't promise your Maytag washer will last as long as Mrs. Gampl's, but we vow to build every one of our washers to last longer and need fewer repairs.

So when you're ready to make a long-term commitment, make your next washer a Maytag. Chances are, like Mrs. Gampl, you'll end up spending many happy years together.

MAYTAG
THE DEPENDABILITY PEOPLE ™

Form No. 44PR

C509
11452/NUT
BuyLine 8633

NuTone®

800-543-8687

An Overview of Selected Ventilation, Electronic and Bath Products

NuTone Exhaust Fans

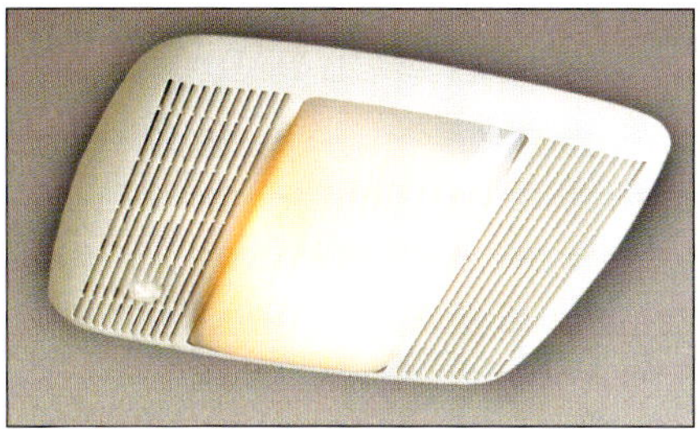

SmartSense™ Fans
Internal sensors trigger automatic activation, providing convenience while protecting walls from humidity damage. 5 models. Available in fan and fan/light combinations, with manual override. For bathrooms up to 105 Sq. Ft.; 90 - 110 CFM; 1.5 - 2.0 sones. 5 year warranty.

Ultra-QuieTTest™ Fans
Powerful ventilation at sone levels that can hardly be heard. Highly energy-efficient, consuming 50% less energy. Perfect for continuous ventilation applications. Gracefully curved, rounded grilles. 3 models. For bathrooms up to 95 Sq. Ft.; 50 - 110 CFM; 0.3 - 1.5 sones. Guaranteed for as long as you own your home.

QuieTTest™ Fans & Fan-Lights
Quiet operation for any room in the house. Six models approved for tub/shower use. Lighted models come with 100/7 watt light/night light. 3 Fan-Light models and 7 Fan only models. For bathrooms up to 280 Sq. Ft.; 80 - 300 CFM; 1.0 - 4.5 sones. Guaranteed for as long as you own your home.

Deluxe Fan-Lights
High performance triple-function provides ventilation, light & night light. 100 watt bulb or 26 watt fluorescent models. Grilles: white, polished metal or wood framed. 8 models. For bathrooms up to 95 Sq. Ft.; 100 CFM; 3.5 sones. Guaranteed for as long as you own your home.

Deluxe Exhaust Fans
Ideal for bath or dressing areas and rooms with an existing light source. A variety of models and grilles, including ceiling, through-the-wall, and room-to-room. 6 models. For bathrooms up to 105 Sq. Ft.; 80 - 220 CFM; 2.5 - 6.0 sones. Guaranteed for as long as you own your home.

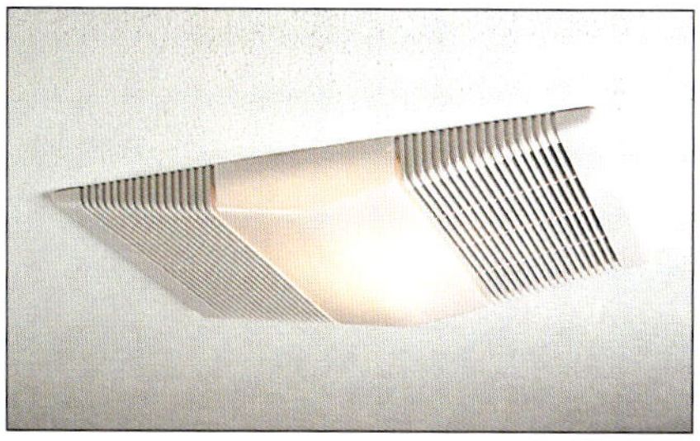

ValueTest™ Exhaust Fan-Lights
Efficient ventilation and bright ceiling light in one easy installation. Incandescent or fluorescent lamps available. Two-function wall switch allows independent operation of fan and light. 6 models. For bathrooms up to 65 Sq. Ft.; 50 - 70 CFM; 2.5 - 4.5 sones. 1 year warranty.

ValueTest™ Exhaust Fans
Ideal for bath, utility and recreation rooms; ceiling or wall installation. Ducted and non-ducted types. 6 models. For bathrooms up to 105 Sq. Ft.; 50 - 110 CFM; 2.5 - 6.0 sones. 1 year warranty.

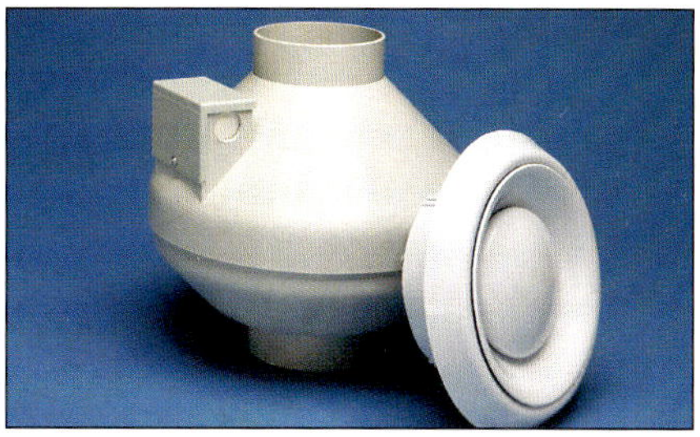

In-Line Fans
Remote-mounted in-line fans provide maximum installation versatility. Install fan in attic to minimize noise, ducting to ventilation area(s). Ideal for multi-port ventilation from two or more locations, venting a new room without ductwork, dryer booster and more. 6 models. For bathrooms up to 450 SF and other rooms up to 660 Sq. Ft.; 110 - 530 CFM. 5 year warranty.

NuTone offers an unmatched selection of exhaust fans in a variety of sizes, styles and functions. From builder models to automatic fan / light units, NuTone has a fan for any residential / light commercial application. Fans are UL Listed and HVI certified. Many are suitable for tub / shower installation with GFI circuiting.

HVI UL®

NuTone Heaters

QuieTTest™ Heat-A-Ventlite®
Four benefits in one simple installation! 1500W Fan-forced heat, powerful ventilation, incandescent bright ceiling light, night light. Available in polished brass (QT9093BR), chrome (QT9093CH) and white (QT9093WH) finishes. 110 CFM, 2.5 sones. Also available, 9093 series, 70 CFM, 3.5 sones, Polished brass (9093BR), chrome (9093CH) and white (9093WH) finishes. Fluorescent model, 9093FWH provides energy saving, high light output and 10,000 hour life. Each Heat-A-Ventlite includes a wall switch with separate controls for all functions. Guaranteed for as long as you own your home

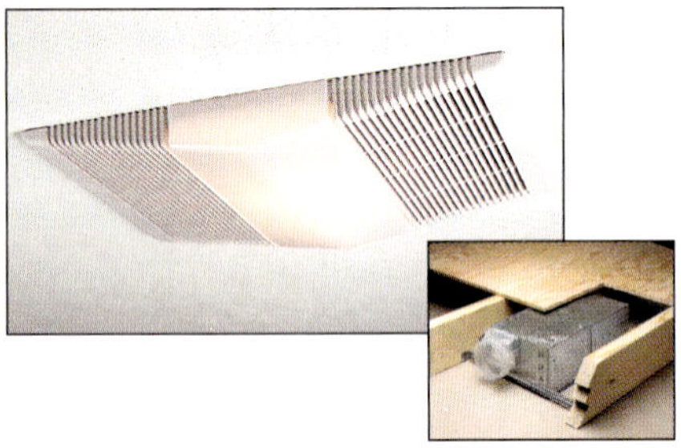

ValueTest™ Electric Heaters
Engineered to reduce installation time. Fits into 2" x 6" beam. Ground lead for connection, Color coded wiring, Hanger bar locks position after securing unit to rafters.
665P: Heat-A-Ventlite®. 1500W heat, 70 CFM fan, 100W ceiling light.
665SP: Same as 665P, includes 3-way switch
665F: Same as 665P but with fluorescent light
605P: Heat-A-Vent®. 1500W heat
660P: Heat-A-Lite®. 1500W heat, 100W light

Deluxe Heaters - Combination Units
Choose the combination to meet your needs. Heat/Vent/Light, Heat/Light, Heat/Vent.
9965F: Fluorescent Heat-A-Ventlite® offers energy-saving light, night light, 1500W fan-forced heat and 70 CFM ventilation.
9965: Same features with incandescent light.
9960 Heat-A-Lite®: 1500W fan-forced heat, light and night light.
9905: Heat-A-Vent®: 1500W fan-forced heat and 70 CFM fan. All models Guaranteed for as long as you own your home

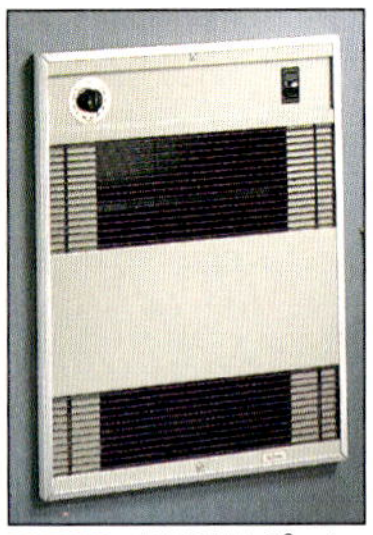

Auxiliary Wall Heaters
9840: Fan-forced heat, 240V, 2000W or 4000W with built-in switch. 14" x 18½" x 3½", Almond
9810: 1000W, 10½" x 12½" x 3⅜", white or brown
9815: 1500W, 10½" x 12½" x 3⅜", white or brown
9819: 1920W, 10½" x 12½" x 3⅜", white or brown
9376N: 1250W, 8 9/16" x 12 9/16" x 4", Aluminum
9356/9358: 1200W/1500W infrared heater, 10 1/16" x 16" x 3½", Aluminum

Register Heaters
Inconspicuous style. Select 750W or 1500W at installation with plug-in elements.
11" x 8⅛" x 3⅜", Almond
9315T: 120V
9315XT: 240V

Bulb Heaters – UL Listed Type IC
9427P: Two-bulb Heat-A-Vent® 500W heat with 70 CFM vent. Can use one heat lamp and one incandescent lamp. Mount in 2" x 8" joists.
9422P: Two-bulb Heat-A-Lamp® 500W heat. Mounts in 2" x 6" joists.
9417DN: One-bulb Heat-A-Vent®. 250W heat with 70 CFM vent. Adjustable socket for ceilings up to 1" thick. Adjustable hanger bars.
9412DN: One-bulb Heat-A-Lamp®. 250W heat. Adjustable socket for ceilings up to 1" thick. Adjustable hanger bars. Recessed bulb heaters have automatic reset thermal protection and are Guaranteed for as long as you own your home.

Surface Mount Bulb Heater –
UL Listed Type IC
H910W: One-bulb Heat-A-Lamp®. 250W heat or light only. Swivel base lets you direct heat as desired. Mounts to standard junction box.

Surface Mount Radiant Heaters
9294T: 1250W heat. Mounts to 3" or 4" junction box, 14⅜" diameter, extends 3¼" from ceiling.
9297T: Same as above except 10⅞" diameter, extends 3" from ceiling.

Kickspace Heater
Fit under bathroom vanity, kitchen cabinet. Select 750W or 1500W at installation with plug-in elements.
17⅛" x 12⅛" x 3⅝", Black
9515: 120V **9515X**: 240V

NuTone Attic Ventilation

Aluminum Roof Fans
Energy-saving, quiet PSC motor, Heavy gauge aluminum, 14½" diameter roof cutout, Guaranteed for as long as you own your home
RF-68HRPSC: 1530 CFM for attics to 2200 sq ft
RF-69NR: 1250 CFM for attics to 1800 sq ft

Plated Steel Roof Fans
Durable plated steel, Brown or Black, 14½" diameter roof cutout, 5 Year warranty
RF-85R: 1500 CFM for attics to 2200 sq ft, PSC motor
RF-59NRPSC: 1250 CFM for attics to 1800 sq ft, PSC motor
RF-49NR: 1020 CFM for attics to 1400 sq ft

Plastic Dome Roof Fans
Tough polymeric, Gray, 14½" diameter roof cutout, 1 Year warranty
RF-79P: 1400 CFM for attics to 2200 sq ft
RF-59P: 1250 CFM for attics to 1800 sq ft
RF-49P: 1020 CFM for attics to 1400 sq ft

Gable Fans
WF-37: 2090 CFM for attics to 2200 sq ft, includes louvers, Wall cutout 17¾" diameter, Guaranteed for as long as you own your home
WF-57NR: 1500 CFM for attics to 2200 sq ft, includes louvers, Wall cutout 17¾" diameter, Guaranteed for as long as you own your home
GF-1200N: 1200 CFM for attics to 1800 sq ft, 5 year warranty
GF-900N: 900 CFM for attics to 1400 sq ft, 1 year warranty

NuTone Range Hoods

Specialty Range Hoods

Downdraft Range Hood

RDD Series: Telescopic style Downdraft hood rises to 7" over cooktop surface. Hides from view when not in use. Available with or without interior blower. Interior blower delivers 510 CFM. Available in 30" or 36" widths, White or Black. Five Year warranty

High-Performance Range Hood

HCH Series: Twin Blowers: 430 CFM (HVI test at .1 Wg). Excellent for all cooking (woks, other cooktop frying). Twin Oil Collectors, Patented Twin Oil-Trapping Cones with Filters. Front Steam Baffle. 6" Round or 3¼" X 10" Duct. 30" width, White, Almond, Stainless Steel, Five year warranty

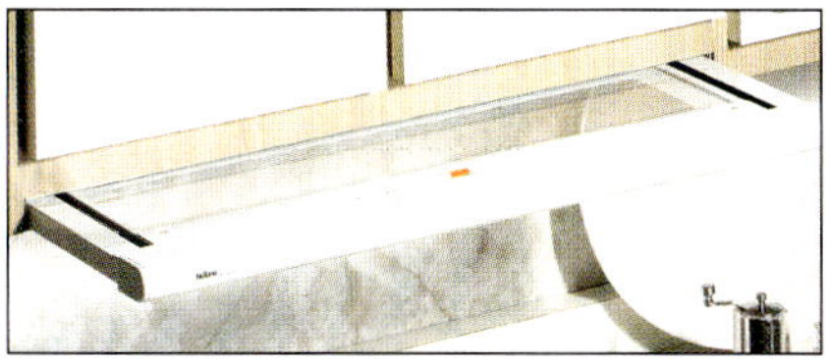

Slide-Away Range Hood

SH-1000: Installs in cabinet – pull out tempered glass visor to turn on, slide back into cabinet to turn off. 320 CFM. Variable speed controls. Cooking light or Night Light. 30" or 36" width, White finish

Deluxe Range Hoods

Designer Range Hood

V-91 Series: Seamless, textured design. Low 8" profile. Variable speed, microprocessor touchpad controls, Light and programmable night light. Twin Blowers: 400 CFM, 7" round or 3¼" x 10" ducting. Quiet, energy-efficient PSC motor, 30" or 36" width, All White, White w/black trim, All Almond, Almond w/black trim and Black, Guaranteed for as long as you own your home

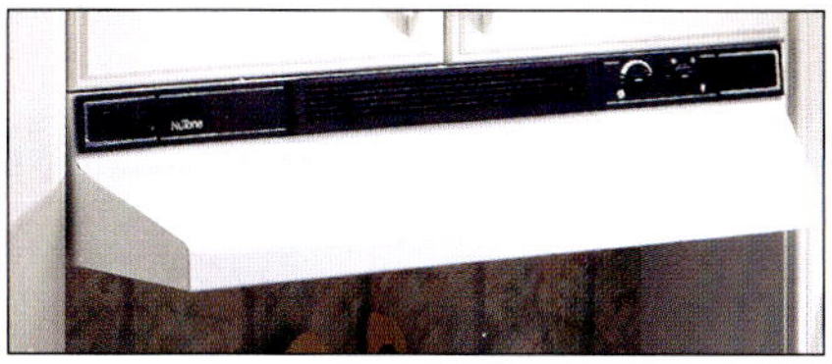

Deluxe Range Hood

TN Series: Twin Blowers: 250 CFM, Solid state infinite speed control, Light/night light, 3¼" X 10" Duct or non-duct, 30" or 36" width, All White, White w/black trim, All Almond, Almond w/black trim, Black and Stainless Steel, Guaranteed for as long as you own your home

Shell Only

V-90: Shell only, Available as shell only or with built-in 410 CFM power unit. Light and night light, Ducts horizontally or vertically, built-in damper and duct collar, 30" or 36" width, All White, White w/black trim, Almond w/black trim, Black and Stainless Steel, Guaranteed for as long as you own your home

11452/NUT
BuyLine 8633
NuTone®
800-543-8687

Decorator Range Hoods

Decorator Range Hood

SM Series: Variable speed, Light and night light. Convertible - 7" round, 3¼" x 10" or non -ducted. 190 CFM vertical, 200 CFM horizontal, 220 CFM round, Plug-in motor, 30", 36" or 42" width, All White, White w/black trim, All Almond, Almond w/black trim, Black and Stainless Steel, Guaranteed for as long as you own your home

Value Range Hoods

Value Range Hood

RL Series: Convenient rocker switches, Light, Two-speed plug-in motor, Available in 24", 30", 36" and 42" widths, All White, White w/black trim, Almond w/black trim, Black and Stainless Steel

RL-6100 series: 3¼" x 10" ducting.

RL-6200 series: Non-ducted.

RL-6300 series: 7" round ducting.

Convertible kit (RL FK series)-3¼" x 10", 7" round or non-ducted with all components in one box, All White, All Almond, Black and Stainless Steel, 24", 30", 36" and 42" widths,

Exterior Power Units

RF-1N

RF-1N: Centrifugal blower wheel with ⅛ HP motor. All-aluminum housing with 24" self-flange, Uses 8" round duct, 620 CFM

WF-1N

WF-1N: Centrifugal blower wheel with ⅛ HP motor. All-aluminum housing with stainless steel fittings, Includes rain shield, Uses 8" round duct, 650 CFM

WF-35/RF-35

WF-35: Wall Fan, **RF-35** Roof Fan: Enamel on zinc-coated steel, Uses 7" round duct, Built-in aluminum damper, 270 CFM

All Exterior units guaranteed for as long as you own your home

Custom Hood Shells and Interior/Exterior Power Units

Shell Only

VS-92: Shell only, Same features of V-91, 30" and 36" width, same finishes as V-91, Guaranteed for as long as you own your home

VP-400

VPU-400

Interior Power Units

VP-400: Use with SO-9100 shell only. 400 CFM, Twin blowers, horizontal or vertical mount, Plug-in motor, automatic thermal reset.

VPU-400: Use with custom hood enclosures. Twin blowers, 400 CFM, Solid state rotary control, light, plug-in motor, horizontal or vertical mount, includes duct collar and damper, 22¾" x 7⅝" x 11$\frac{9}{16}$"

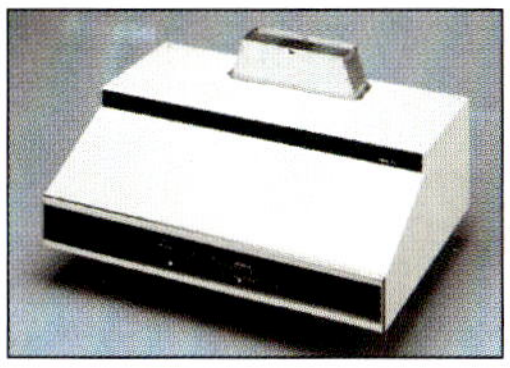

Commercial-Style Shell

SO-9100: Select-A-Matic commercial-style shell, Infinite speed control, wide collection area, Light and night light. Duct horizontally or vertically, Use with VP-400 interior power unit, 30", 36" or 42" width, All White, White w/black trim, Almond w/black trim and Stainless Steel, Guaranteed for as long as you own your home

NEW! NuTone ACS-2000 Central Air Cleaning System

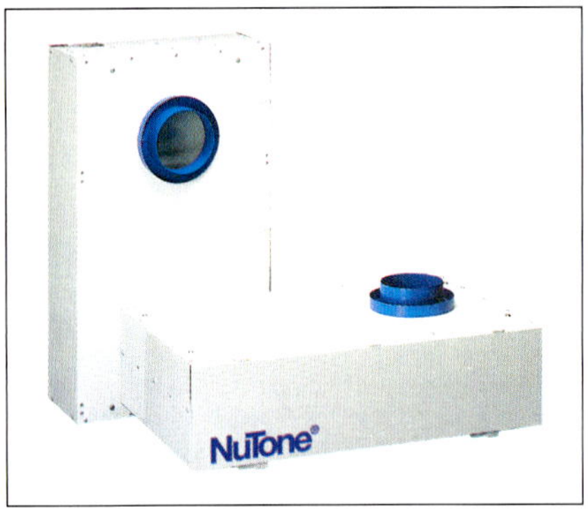

NuTone's ACS-2000 offers peak efficiency air cleansing that does not deteriorate over time because it utilizes the revolutionary Turbulent Flow Precipitator system.

Turbulent Flow Technology prevents the particle build-up and subsequent particle pass-thru common with conventional filtering systems. This build-up compromises filtration performance and air flow.

The ACS-2000 design consists of **two air spaces** instead of the usual single flow area: The **upper space** is contiguous with the duct. Velocity fluctuations in the air flow - turbulent flow eddies - cause particles to drop into the lower chamber where they are trapped.

The baffled **lower chamber** creates a no-flow zone that allows particles to remain trapped.

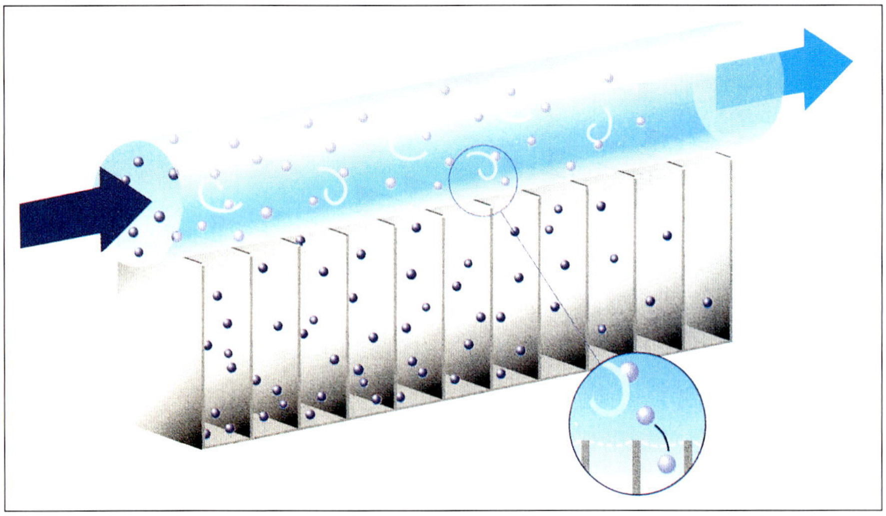

Once trapped, particles cannot reenter the airstream or be recirculated.

The ACS-2000 features a 90% removal rate for airborne particles greater than .5 microns (pollen, dust mites, mold spores, bacteria).

The ACS-2000 delivers maximum performance without interruption, frequent attention or loss of effectiveness. Inspect collectors annually to determine replacement schedule (typical replacement 1-2 collectors / year). 110 Watt, 120 V AC power consumption allows economical full-time use for maximum benefits.

Flexible Mounting

- Mount to system ductwork
- Can be used with HRV or as stand-alone
- Units typically mount to joists and are ducted to furnace/air conditioner

NEW! NuTone HRV - Heat Recovery Ventilator

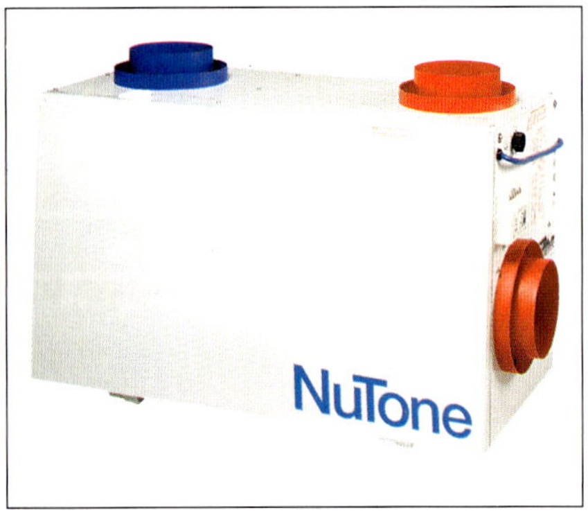

The NuTone Heat Recovery Ventilator is a fan-assisted heat exchanger used to temper incoming outside air with the heat recovered from return indoor air. **The HRV permits significant amounts of fresh air to be economically introduced into the home environment.**

Problem: Today's "air-tight" homes trap indoor air pollutants. These pollutants can cause drowsiness and headaches and create unpleasant smelling odors.

Solution: NuTone's HRV exchanges trapped indoor air with fresh, outdoor air.

Benefits: Continuous HRV operation helps:

- Prevent the build-up of gases such as carbon dioxide, formaldehyde, radon and cleaning solvents.
- Prevent build-up of odors from cooking, bathroom, tobacco and fireplace.
- Prevent build-up of solvent fumes from paints, adhesives, plastics, cleaning compounds, furnishings and carpets.

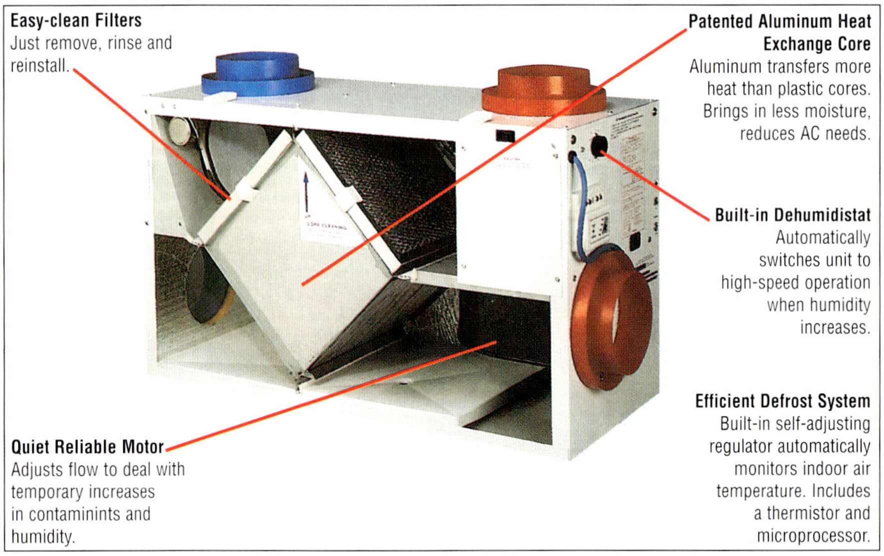

Operation

Two separate streams of air - incoming outdoor and outgoing indoor return - pass on either side of the patented aluminum core without mixing. The core transfers 80% of the heat energy from the outgoing to the incoming air. Once the energy has been extracted, outgoing pollutant-laden air is exhausted to the exterior. The tempered incoming air is moved through the (optional ACS-2000 Air Cleaner) heating / cooling system for final distribution throughout the house.

Use the HRV with the ACS-2000 Air Cleaning System to maximize indoor air quality.

Power Consumption and Warranty

- Operational costs are very low - equivalent to less than a 100 watt light bulb.
- 5 speed 120V/60HZ motor unit
- 5 year warranty

Accessory Options

Include programmable controls, electronic and manual timers and air quality monitors.

NuTone Central Cleaning Systems

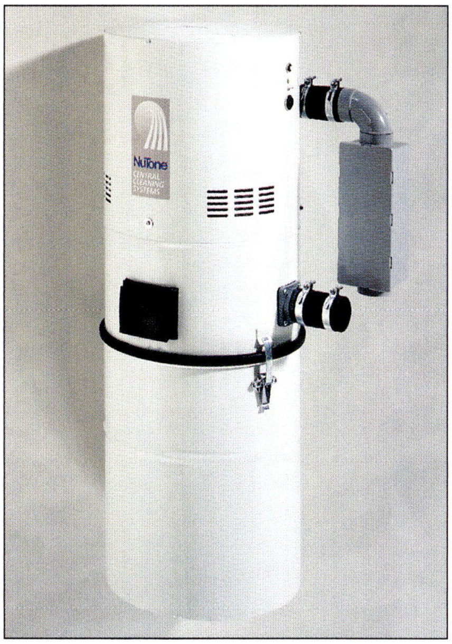

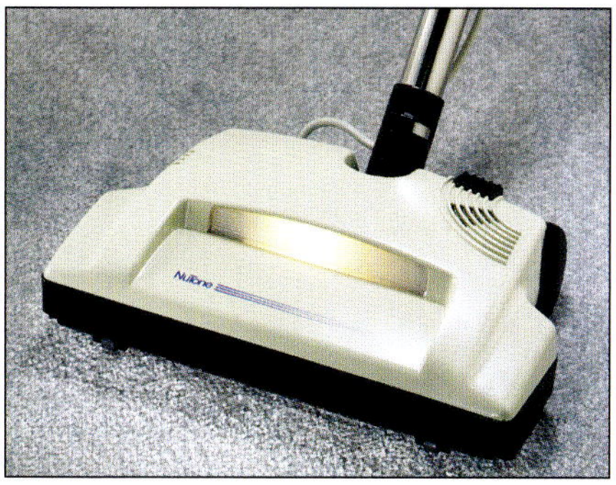

11452/NUT
BuyLine 8633
NuTone®
800-543-8687

TODAY'S MOST EFFICIENT WAY TO CLEAN

NuTone Central Cleaning Systems offer time-saving convenience and value for today's busy lifestyles.

The power unit, the heart of the system, installs in any area away from normal living areas, such as utility room, basement or garage.Tubing from the power unit connects through the walls, under the floor or through the attic to inlets placed conveniently throughout the house. As few as two or three inlets can take care of an average size home.

Inserting the lightweight, flexible hose into the inlet turns the system on automatically; the strong vacuum power is instantaneous. Removing the hose turns the system off and seals the inlet. The long hose enables movement from room to room, even up and down stairways.

THE CENTRAL CLEANING ADVANTAGE

More Cleaning Power

- Pulls more dirt and dust out of the house because the motor is so powerful – more powerful than most portables
- Better dust pick-up – dust less often, spend less time cleaning

Better Dust Filtration

- Dual filtration system within the power unit traps dirt and dust away from living environment – great for those who suffer allergies

Built-In Convenience

- Easy-to-use – built-in power unit means no lugging around a heavy vacuum cleaner

Quieter

- Remote power unit minimizes noise in the living area of the home; Quiet Series power units available for reduced sound levels at the power unit location
- Can be vented to the outside

A Good Investment

- Can be installed in new or existing construction
- Adds to the resale value of the home

Central Cleaning Systems are an important part of Total Indoor Air Quality…solutions for today's lifestyles!

A wide selection of tools and accessories are available from NuTone to maximize the versatility of the Central Cleaning System. Motor-driven power brushes, turbine brushes, deluxe cleaning hoses, a variety of tool sets and optional accessories maximize the efficiency and convenience of the system for cleaning at the floor and above-the-floor surfaces.

NuTone Central Cleaning Systems offer a variety of well-built components and fittings to allow for easy, efficient system installation and to assure a long, reliable performance. Whatever the home layout, a NuTone Central Cleaning System can be planned to meet the cleaning needs. And for most homes, installation can be completed in a day or less.

Several of the NuTone Central Cleaning System power units are Maximum Performance Products (MPP) and therefore are guaranteed for as long as you own your home.

A VacPan™ Automatic Dustpan Inlet adds daily convenience as an inlet mounted directly at floor level. Great for kitchens, laundry rooms, mud rooms and more!

NuTone Built-in Ironing Centers

Build in time-saving convenience and added value to any home with a NuTone Ironing Center. They are designed to install easily in new construction or existing homes. Recessed cabinets fit in wood frame construction where studs are at least 16" o.c. Surface-mounting is available.

The NuTone Deluxe model (shown) features a sturdy steel cabinet and is fully electric. Unit comes prewired with work light and convenience outlet for iron. 42" heavy-gauge vented steel board swivels full 180° and adjusts to three heights. Storage shelf stores iron and other supplies. UL Listed.

Choose door separately: solid core wood, raised-panel oak, or mirrored door. Unfinished wood doors can be painted or stained.

Other cabinet styles and models are available. See NuTone catalog for complete selection.

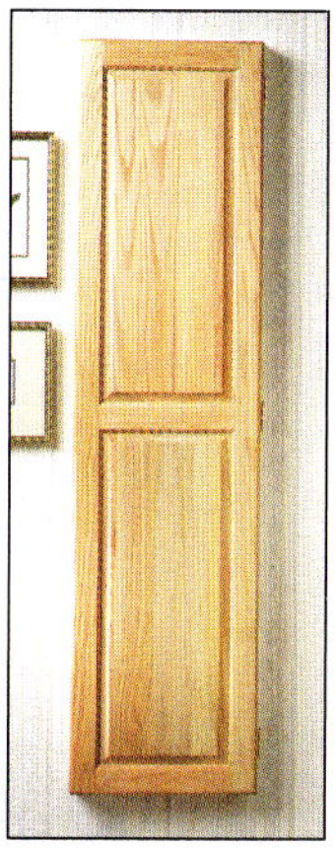

Board folds up, stores neatly out of sight, yet is always conveniently ready. Just open the door and lower the board. Great for touch-ups!

NuTone Door Chimes & Pushbuttons

Door Chimes & Pushbuttons

Since 1936, NuTone Door Chimes have been announcing visitors to homes across the country. Today, NuTone provide the finest selection of Door Chimes to builders, contractors and homeowners ... more style, more features plus more quality - guaranteed.

Choose from wired, wireless or electronic chimes and a wide array of decorative pushbuttons to create a complete system. Chime styles range from traditional to contemporary, with a variety of chime sounds.

LA-169WH

LA-167GN

LA-165SA

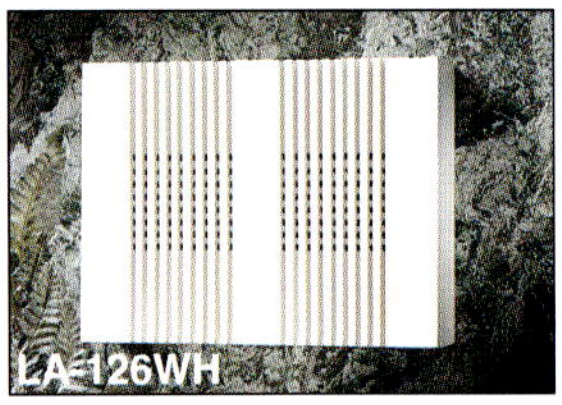
LA-126WH

LA-139WH

LA-140WH

NuTone Intercom Systems

NuTone Intercom Systems

The NuTone IM-3303WH (shown to the top right) provides the latest in intercom technology. It offers cleaner, crisper vocal and musical transmission, clean styling, and the convenience of hands free answering from the master Up to 13 speakers and three door speakers can be combined in a single system.

The IM-3303WH system allows monitoring, listening in, radio operation from remote speakers and convenient door answering.

IM-3303WH

IM-4406

NuTone Intercom Systems

The IM-4406 (shown to the bottom left) provides superior quality in intercom technology. A CD player and AM/FM radio are built into the intercom master and can be controlled from any of the 9 remote stations.

The IM-4406 system allows 'hands free' answering at all stations, monitoring, "wake to music" feature, and door answering from any station.

NuTone has intercom systems available in every size and price range available for your customers. Each system is designed with its own unique set of features and benefits to meet the needs of today's homeowner.

NuTone Video Door-Answering System

Video Door Answering System VS-1100

The security of video surveillance can be combined with the step saving convenience and entertainment value of the NuTone radio-intercom systems. Interior and exterior surveillance cameras and video monitors allow you to identify callers or monitor areas visually day or night.

The video door answering system is easy to operate and offers an exceptionally clear black and white picture on the 4" (102 mm) video screen.

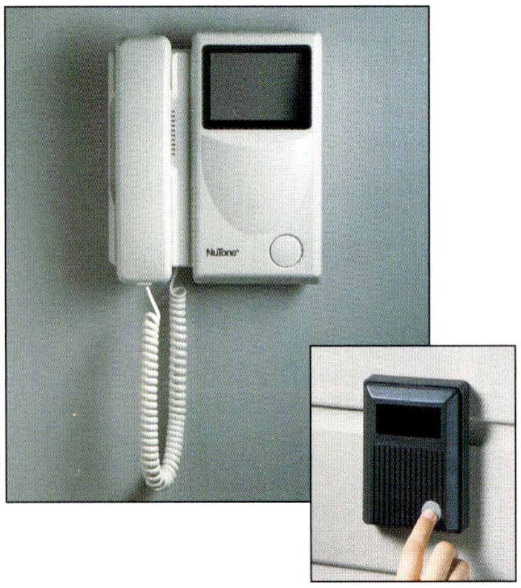

VS-1100 Video Door Answering System

NuTone

NEW! NuTone SenSonic™ Speaker System

11452/NUT
BuyLine 8633
NuTone®
800-543-8687

For 60 years, NuTone has stood for excellence in built-in systems for the home. Now you can experience that same level of confidence in every speaker system you install by specifying NuTone SenSonic speakers and accessories. There's a SenSonic speaker for virtually every application - in-wall, ceiling, surface mount and indoor/outdoor speakers.

Every speaker is guaranteed for five years of reliable service. Installation is easy, configurations are flexible, cost is affordable and the sound is exceptional.

NuTone offers several pre-designed "builder packages" that contain the speakers necessary for multiple room music distribution or home entertainment applications.

Call NuTone today for additional information or for the name of the nearest representative for guidance when developing in-home theater applications for the SenSonic Speaker Systems and to see first-hand how the SenSonic Speaker System can enhance your next project.

SENSONIC
SPEAKER SYSTEMS

MS-825 Two-Way, In-Wall, Inside Speaker, 5¼" woofer, 40-23,000 Hz +/- 3db frequency response; 80 watts. Infinite baffle woofer, ¾" dome tweeter. Swivel dome tweeter; 15° from a flush position and swivels 360°. Includes adjustable tweeter audio level control. Paintable grille. Polyswitch tweeter protection. Rough-ins available on Model MS825K. White

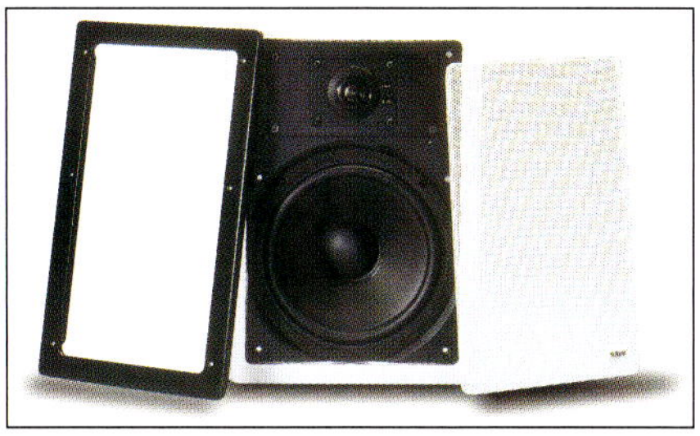

MS-828 Two-Way, In-Wall, Inside Speaker, 8" woofer, 35-23,000 Hz +/- 3db frequency response; 120 watts. Infinite baffle woofer, ¾" dome tweeter. Swivel dome tweeter; 15° from a flush position and swivels 360°. Includes adjustable tweeter audio level control. Paintable grille. Polyswitch tweeter protection. Rough-ins available on Model MS828K. White

MS-838K Three-Way, In-Wall, Inside Speaker, 8" woofer, 35-23,000 Hz +/- 3db frequency response; 120 watts. Infinite baffle woofer, 2 ½" midrange, ¾" dome tweeter. Swivel dome tweeter; 15° from a flush position and swivels 360°. Adjustable tweeter audio level control. Paintable grille. Polyswitch tweeter protection. White

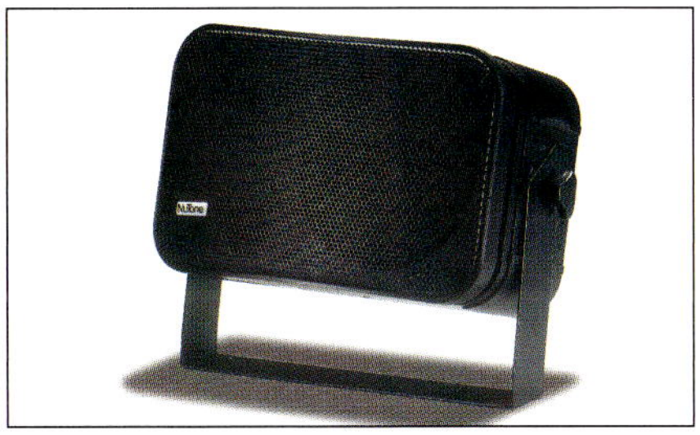

MS-525BL (black) and **MS-525WH** (white) Surface Mount, Indoor or Outdoor Use, 5¼" woofer, 45-22,000 Hz +/- 3db frequency response; 70 watts. Bass reflex, ½" dome tweeter. Wall / surface mount.

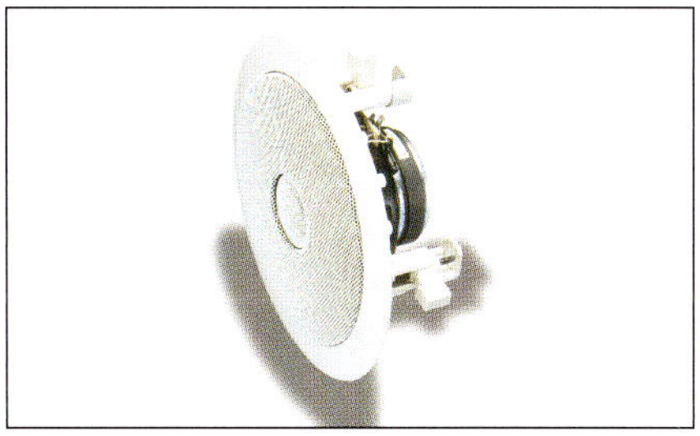

MS-626 Ceiling Speaker, Inside Speaker, 6½" woofer, 40-23,000 Hz +/- 3db frequency response; 100 watts. Infinite baffle woofer, 3/4" dome tweeter with capability of 15° swivel from a flush position and 360° swivel on axis. Does not require rough-in. White

MS-625 Ceiling Speaker, Inside Speaker, 5¼" woofer, 45-22,000 Hz +/- 3db frequency response; 70 watts. Infinite baffle woofer, ½" dome tweeter with capability of 15° swivel from a flush position and 360° swivel on axis. Does not require rough-in. White

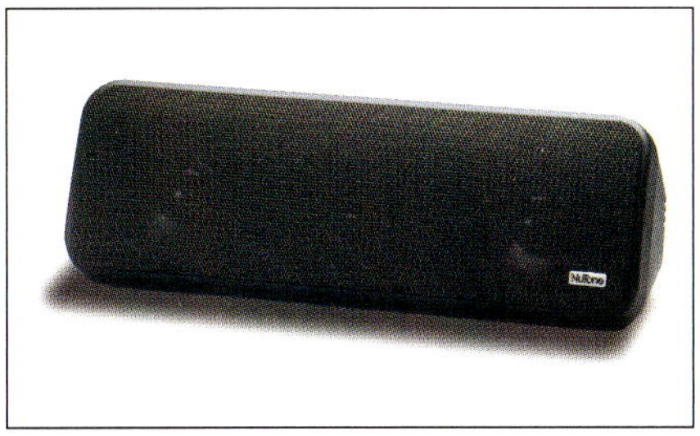

MS-725 Center Channel Speaker, Inside Speaker, Two 4" woofers, 50-22,000 Hz +/- 3db frequency response; 35 watts. ½" dome tweeter, for home theater use. Unique cabinet design allows installation either above or below television, magnetically shielded to eliminate TV picture distortion. Black.

MS-418 Floor Standing Speaker, Inside Speaker, 8" woofer, 30-250 Hz +/- 3db frequency response; 100 watts. Dual port band pass design, twin voice coil. Overload protected. Can be positioned vertically or horizontally. Black.

SenSonic™ System Accessories

Switches & Controls

SP-6 Stereo Speaker Selector
360 watts, connects 6 pairs of speakers to 2 independent audio sources

SW-AB-1 Speaker Selector
250 watts per channel, connects 1 pair of speakers to 2 independent audio sources

SW-AB-2 Speaker Selector
100 watts per channel, connects 2 pairs of speakers to 1 audio source

SW-AB-3 Speaker Selector
100 watts per channel, connects 2 pairs of independent speakers to 2 independent audio sources

Stereo Volume Controls

SVC-101 Auto transformer Type 75 watts
SVC-102 Auto transformer Type 150 watts

NuTone Bath Cabinets

Custom Match™ Bath Mirrors & Cabinets

NuTone has invented a revolutionary concept that allows the homeowner to design a custom cabinet in minutes. It's perfect for new home construction or a bathroom remodeling project!

By installing the cabinet first, the rest of the bathroom construction can continue without any damage to the mirror. After cleanup the homeowner can choose from a wide selection of mirrors to fit their style. It's as easy as 1-2-3!!

1 Select a Body

Wood, Metal or Plastic

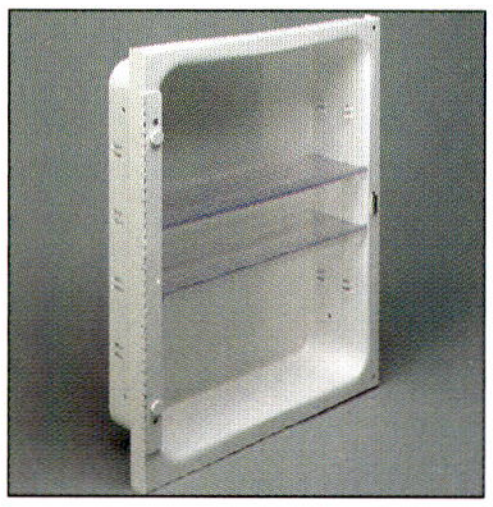

2 Select a Mirror

40 styles to choose from!

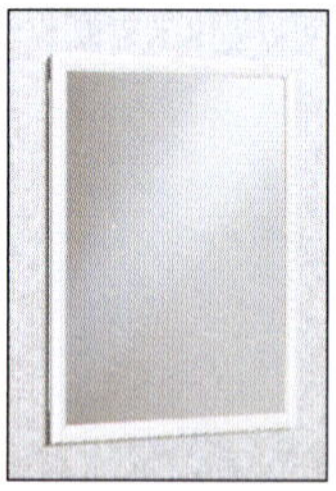
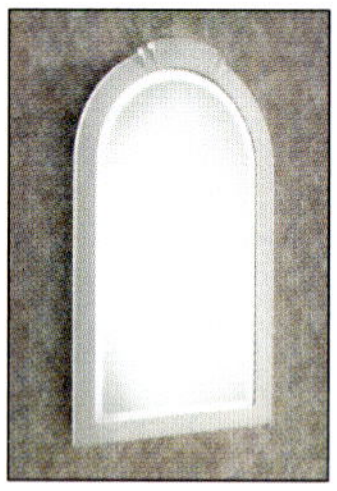

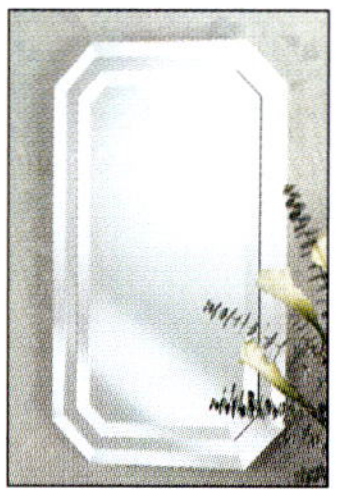

3 Create a Cabinet

A unique new hinge lets you attach the mirror to the cabinet body in just minutes!

NuTone Bath Hardware

Sovereign II Collection - HM500PB/PC Series. (shown at right) Solid Brass, available in Polished Brass or Chrome finishes.
Coronado Collection - HM600PCN Series. Cast Zamak, Polished Chrome or Bright White finishes.
Metropolitan Collection - HM700PBN/PCN Series. Concealed mount, cast Zamak, available in Polished Brass or Polished Chrome.
Tempo Collection - HM800PC Series. Exposed screw mount, cast Zamak in Polished Chrome finish
Grab Bars - HM360PCN Series. Polished Chrome

The first choice in kitchens of distinction

In remodeling and new construction, the look of distinction in kitchens begins with the beauty of built-in appliances and built-in refrigeration by Sub-Zero. That's why leading custom kitchen designers choose Sub-Zero first. Classic in styling and unequaled for storage, convenience and quality, Sub-Zero true built-ins are the ultimate in elegant home refrigeration.

Enjoy the elegance of built-in refrigeration

Sub-Zero home refrigeration is designed to enhance the beauty of any decor by blending compatibly with other kitchen furnishings. This is possible because of its simple design . . . removable decorative panels and the fact it is the same 24″ depth as most base kitchen cabinets. A Sub-Zero is designed with a minimum of external hardware, making it hardly noticeable when built into a kitchen. It also has an exclusive toe-base feature, important in kitchen appliances, which lines up with kitchen cabinets.

All units are constructed with the 24″ depth which enables the face to fit flush with most standard base cabinets. A typical free-standing refrigerator protrudes into the room 4 to 6 inches beyond cabinets, creating an unsightly appearance and takes up valuable space in the room.

Sub-Zero built-ins are designed to accept removable exterior panels of any material on the front and sides. In doing so, the unit practically disappears into the overall kitchen, blending completely into the decor instead of dominating the kitchen appearance, as a free-standing unit does. And, because the panels are removable, they can be changed, should the room decor change.

These true built-in features mean your home refrigeration need not be an unattractive standout but can now complement the over-all style of the kitchen and function as an integral part of the total kitchen design. They allow individual styling and expression of your personal taste.

Built-in work savers

Truly an accent to the kitchen of distinction, Sub-Zero built-in refrigeration offers all of the time and work saving features that today's lifestyles require...like convenient usable storage, easy up-keep, simplified cleaning, automatic defrosting and automatic ice maker.

The shallow depth makes it easier to find what you are looking for, eliminating the need to search for items that have found their way to the back shelf area (as in other refrigerators). This, along with the fact that all shelves are fully adjustable, gives even greater flexibility for storage arrangements.

Easy up-keep is achieved because of the quality materials and craftsmanship used in the construction of a Sub-Zero. ...interior, exterior and mechanical.

Cleaning is simplified because of two reasons: First the unit's built-in feature eliminates cracks and crevices that would normally collect dust and also eliminates the chore of pulling the refrigerator out to clean behind it.

Secondly, all shelves in Sub-Zero full-size units are removable to allow for ease of cleaning.

The automatic defrost feature is standard on all full-size models as well as the undercounter models (except 249R). This eliminates the need to shut down the refrigerator to defrost and clean the unit.

Model 550

Another standard feature of the full-size units is the automatic ice maker which produces an adequate supply of ice automatically without the need to handle awkward ice trays.

Many models to choose from

Whatever your space or usage requirements, Sub-Zero offers a selection of over 12 models to fit your needs and specifications. Choose from the popular side-by-side, the over-n-under (freezer on the bottom), the all-freezer and all-refrigerator units, compact undercounter refrigerators and an ice maker. Ranging in width from 18″ to 48″, Sub-Zero units offer capacities to 30.0 cubic feet. The combination all-refrigerator and all-freezer together provide as much as 40.0 cubic feet of food storage.

Sub-Zero 12-Year Protection Plan

Sub-Zero has always backed what it has manufactured, and offers a warranty package no one can match — the Sub-Zero 12-Year Protection Plan. From the day your Sub-Zero is installed, you have a full five-year (parts and labor) warranty and limited sixth through twelfth-year (parts) warranty on the sealed system, consisting of the compressor, condenser, evaporator, drier and all connecting tubing. You also have a full two-year (parts and labor) warranty on the entire product. (See warranty for non-residential use and other exceptions). Sub-Zero stands behind every refrigerator and freezer they manufacture, ensuring you of the finest in service and trouble-free maintenance.

Outstanding performance and craftsmanship

Sub-Zero is a leader in the industry in engineering functional refrigeration. Because Sub-Zero full-size units use a refrigerant in both the refrigerator and freezer compartments, proper and even temperatures are maintained more consistently throughout. This is the same type system used in some commercial refrigerators and is a standard feature in Sub-Zero home units, to insure top performance and operation. Complete factory testing of every Sub-Zero unit is your assurance of quality workmanship.

More than just refrigeration, Sub-Zero quality craftsmanship is a tradition, custom designed to enhance the value and elegance of your home for years to come.

C514

BuyLine 8639

Built-in Home Refrigeration Designed for Beauty and Performance

SUB-ZERO®

specifications:

MODEL	R-1492, R-1491, R-1490	R-1482, R-1481, R-1480	R-1852, R-1851, R-1850	R-930AK, R-930AW	R-530BS
OVEN CAPACITY	1.4 cu. ft.	1.4 cu. ft.	1.1 cu. ft.	1.5 cu. ft.	1.8 cu. ft.
COOKING UNIFORMITY	Turntable or stirrer system; 13" diameter glass turntable	Turntable or stirrer system; 13" diameter glass turntable	Turntable or stirrer system; 13" diameter ceramic turntable	Carousel Turntable system; 15 3/8" diameter porcelain enamel turntable	Carousel Turntable system; 16" diameter glass turntable
DISPLAY	7-digit Interactive	7-digit Interactive	7-digit Interactive 2-color	7-digit Interactive 2-color	2-line, 12-digit interactive
CONVECTION OVEN TEMPERATURE CONTROL			100°, 150°, 275°-450° F in 25° increments	100°, 150°, 275°-450° F in 25° increments	
DESIGN	R-1492: Almond-on-almond R-1491: White-on-white R-1490: Black-on-black	R-1482: Almond-on-almond R-1481: White-on-white R-1480: Black-on-black	R-1852: Almond-on-almond R-1851: White-on-white R-1850: Black-on-black	R-930AK: Metallic charcoal cabinet; black front R-930AW: White-on-white	Stainless steel front; Silver painted cabinet
OUTPUT POWER	950W	950W	850W	900W	1100W
OUTSIDE DIMENSIONS (W x H x D)	29 15/16" x 16 3/8" x 15 1/4"*	29 15/16" x 16 3/8" x 15 1/4"*	29 15/16" x 16 11/32" x 15 9/32"	24 5/8" x 14 7/8" x 18 3/4"	23 15/16" x 13 7/16" x 19 1/4"
OVEN DIMENSIONS (W x H x D)	20 1/4" x 8 3/16" x 14 1/2"	20 1/4" x 8 3/16" x 14 1/2"	17 1/8" x 8 1/16" x 13 13/16"	16 1/8" x 9 5/8" x 16 1/8"	16 13/16" x 10 1/16" x 18 5/8"
OVEN INTERIOR	Acrylic with light	Acrylic with light	Stainless steel with light	Stainless steel with light	Acrylic with light
APPROX. WEIGHT	Net: 55 lbs. Shipping: 63 lbs.	Net: 55 lbs. Shipping: 63 lbs.	Net: 71 lbs. Shipping: 81 lbs.	Net: 60 lbs. Shipping: 68 lbs.	Net: 41 lbs. Shipping: 46 lbs.
AC LINE VOLTAGE	All models: 120V, single phase, 60Hz, AC only				
AC POWER REQUIRED	1.7kW, 14.3A	1.7kW, 14.3A	1.6kW, 13.2A	1.55kW, 13.0A	1.65kW, 14.0A
SAFETY COMPLIANCE	All models: FCC, DHHS, UL listed				
SUPPLIED ACCESSORIES	RK-230 Charcoal Filter for non-ducted installations+	RK-230 Charcoal Filter for non-ducted installations+	High and low racks	High and low racks	
OPTIONAL ACCESSORIES (AVAILABLE AT EXTRA COST)			RK-220 Charcoal Filter for non-ducted installations+	R-930AK: Built-in Kit RK-66A (black) R-930AW: Built-in Kit RK-66WB (white) for in-the-wall installation+	30" Built-in Kit RK-51S30 (Stainless look) 27" Built-in Kit RK-51S27(Stainless look) for in-the-wall installation+

Specifications subject to change without notice. +Refer to Operation Manual for installation recommendations. Output wattage based on IEC-705 1988 Test Procedure. Models R-930AK/AW have UL approval to build-in over General Electric brand 27" electric wall oven models JKP18BW/WW/AW. Model R-530BS has UL approval to build-in over General Electric brand 30" electric wall oven model ZET837SYSS, Thermador 30" electric wall oven model CT130S, or Thermador 27" electric wall oven model CT127NS.

* Depth Dimension excludes handle.

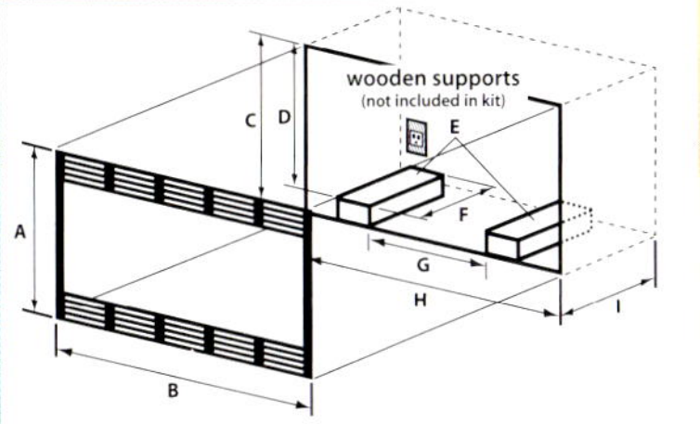

Your Sharp Microwave Oven can be built into your kitchen wall or cabinet using the appropriate Sharp Built-in Kit. Complete hardware and easy-to-follow instructions are included. Prepare cabinet or wall opening according to the illustration at left, providing access to a separate 3-pronged, 120V AC outlet, 15 amps. or larger.

	A	B	C	D	E	F	G	H	I
RK-66A, RK-66WB	19 7/8"	26 7/8"	17 1/8" (+ ht. of wood)	17 1/8"	nominal 2" x 2"; actual 1 9/16" x 1 9/16" x 15"	15"	18 3/8" ± 1/8"	25 1/4" ± 1/8"	min. 19 1/2"
RK-51S27	18 1/8"	26 11/16"	16 7/8" ± 1/8"	—	not used	—	—	24 1/2" ± 3/16"	min. 20"
RK-51S30	18 1/8"	29 11/16"	16 7/8" ± 1/8"	—	not used	—	—	24 1/2" ± 3/16"	min. 20"

To receive the most current specifications, call Dimension Express at (702) 833-3600 from a fax machine. Enter code 9026 for instructions and a directory of Sharp microwave oven products.

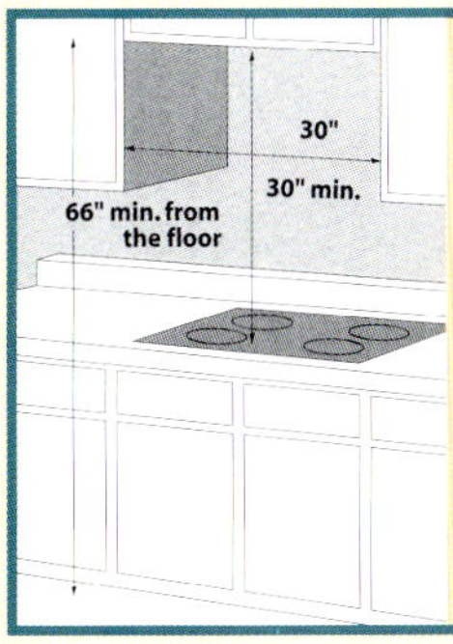

Each Sharp Over The Range microwave oven can be easily adapted for either outside ventilation (vertical or horizontal) or nonvented, ductless recirculation. Make sure top of oven will be at least 66" from the floor and at least 30" from the cooking surface. A separate 15 amp. or greater electrical receptacle must be located in the cabinet directly above the microwave oven.

LIMITED WARRANTY **(R-930AK, R-930AW, R-530BS):** 5 years on magnetron tube, 1 year on all other parts, 1 year on related labor and carry in service.* See Operation Manual or your dealer for complete details.

*1 year in-home service will be provided when built-in using applicable Sharp Built-in Kit.

LIMITED WARRANTY **(R-1492, R-1491, R-1490, R-1482, R-1481, R-1480)** 7 years on magnetron tube, 1 year on all other parts, 1 year on related labor and in-home service. See Operation Manual or your dealer for complete details.

LIMITED WARRANTY **(R-1852, R-1851, R-1850)** 7 years on magnetron tube, 2 years on all other parts, 2 years on related labor and in-home service. See Operation Manual or your dealer for complete details.

SHARP

FROM SHARP MINDS
COME SHARP PRODUCTS™

Sharp Electronics Corporation
Sharp Plaza, Mahwah, NJ 07430-2135
For more information call: 1-800-BE-SHARP
http://www.sharp-usa.com

MW-06-053

C512
11452/SHA
BuyLine 8637

R-930AK R-930AW

THE BROWNING, BAKING, BROILING, CRISPING, MICROWAVING

All-In-One INTERACTIVE SYSTEM.

It's everything anyone could want in a convection microwave oven...and more. Available in metallic charcoal (R-930AK) and white-on-white (R-930AW), with a stainless steel interior, this oven may be used as a countertop unit or installed as a wall oven with optional Built-in Kits. Both incorporate Sharp's advanced Interactive Cooking System with a 2-Color Display that provides easy-to-follow cooking steps and programming instructions. The large 1.5 cu. ft. capacity with 15 3/8-inch diameter porcelain enamel turntable can easily handle a wide range of conventional and microwave cooking needs. It's the most convenient way to create everything from cakes and casseroles to steaks and roasts to potatoes and popcorn. Output power: 900 watts.

R-930AK

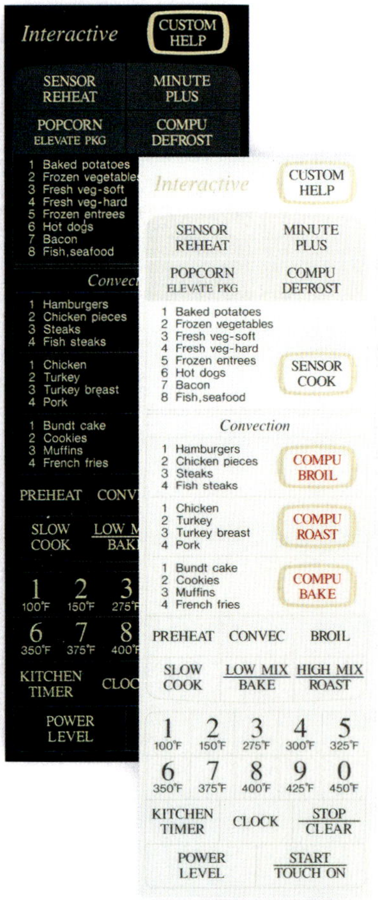

R-930AW

R-930AK

R-930AW

features:

4-WAY SYSTEM
browns, bakes, broils, crisps. Two combination settings for roasting and baking are included. Broil key automatically preheats oven, signals when ready.

SMART & EASY SENSOR
eliminates guesswork by automatically determining microwave cooking/reheating times and setting power levels for 8 different food categories.

COMPUBROIL, COMPU-ROAST, COMPUBAKE
automatically compute broiling, roasting, and baking times/temperature settings. High and low racks satisfy multiple cooking needs.

7-DIGIT TWO-COLOR INTERACTIVE DISPLAY WITH CUSTOM HELP KEY
provides easy-to-read programming steps, cooking hints, and special options.

Many time and worksaving extras include:

SLOW COOK, LOW MIX/BAKE, HIGH MIX/ROAST, COMPUDEFROST, 10 VARIABLE POWER LEVELS, REHEAT & POPCORN SENSORS, MINUTE PLUS, TIMER.

R-1850 R-1851 R-1852

CONVECTION MICROWAVE: THE *Ultimate* IN COOKING *Versatility.*

With these Over the Range convection microwave ovens, Sharp brings new meaning to multifunctional convenience. Now consumers can brown, bake, broil, crisp, and roast with microwave, convection, combination, and broil options. One oven does it all, without taking up a lot of space. They even come in a choice of designer colors: R-1850 (black-on-black), R-1851 (white-on-white), and R-1852 (almond-on-almond)– to suit any decor. A generous 1.1 cu. ft. stainless steel interior easily handles a variety of cooking needs and 850 watts offer cooking power to spare.

R-1850

R-1851

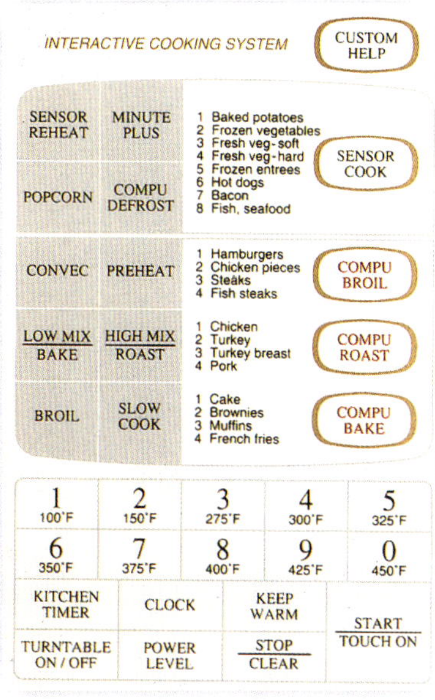

R-1851

features:

LARGE 13-INCH DIAMETER CERAMIC TURNTABLE

with **ON/OFF** flexibility to handle oversized or oblong-shaped dishes or containers.

BUILT-IN EXHAUST SYSTEM

offers horizontal or vertical discharge or ductless recirculation. Comes with hood light and powerful fan.

7-DIGIT, TWO-COLOR INTERACTIVE DISPLAY

spells out programming steps on a lighted easy-to-read display. **CUSTOM HELP** key offers helpful cooking hints and step-by-step instructions for special features such as Child Lock and Auto Start.

SMART & EASY SENSOR

settings automatically determine and se cooking or reheating times and power levels for a variety of popular foods including baked potatoes, frozen entree vegetables, hot dogs, bacon, fish/seafoo

COMPUBROIL™, COMPUROAST™, COMPUBAKE™

settings provide a new level of automat ease. Broil a steak, roast a chicken, bak a cake to perfection at the touch of a k

HIGH RACK

included for two-level baking.

LOW RACK

may be used for baking, roasting, or broiling.

C512
11452/SHA
BuyLine 8637

R-1480 R-1481 R-1482

THE BEAUTY OF *High Performance.*

One look at these stunning Over the Range Carousel microwave ovens and it's easy to see what makes them so appealing. Three sophisticated matte finishes: R-1480 (black-on-black), R-1481 (white-on-white), and R-1482 (almond-on-almond)–beautifully complement any environment. And the uniquely curved handles reflect the latest in modern design. Aesthetics aside, it's the incredible performance that attracts so much attention. With high-speed cooking power of 950 watts and a capacity of 1.4 cu. ft., they can handle a wide range of microwaving needs. And with an impressive line-up of timesaving automatic features, mistake-proof microwaving is guaranteed. And the work light and night light are handy additions.

R-1480

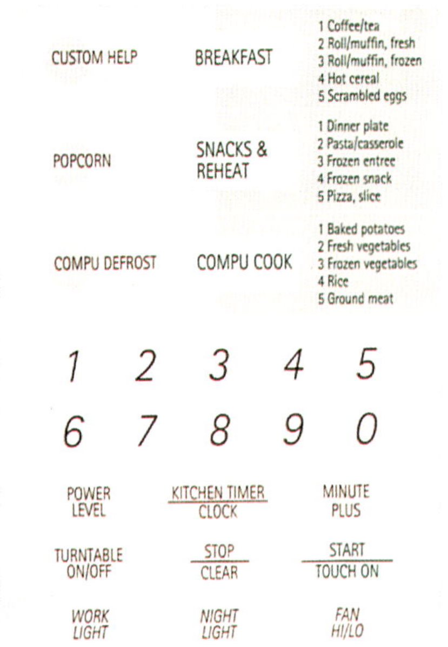

R-1481

features:

POWERFUL 300 CFM VENTILATION SYSTEM
offers three convenient venting options. Comes **READY-TO-RECIRCULATE** with the charcoal filter provided, making it easier than ever to install. May also be ducted to the outside, either vertically or horizontally.

INTERACTIVE COOKING SYSTEM WITH 7-DIGIT DISPLAY
makes programming special options easy for anyone. Easy-to-follow instructions guide user through the cooking process in English, Spanish or French.

TURNTABLE ON/OFF SETTING
enables user to put large 13" turntable in "OFF" position when using oversized, up to 4-quart, 10"x15" oblong-shaped dishes. Makes it easier to cook for a crowd.

CUSTOM HELP
key provides user assistance with cooking hints and programming options such as Child Lock, Auto Start, English, Spanish or French language/weight options.

COMPUCOOK, BREAKFAST, SNACKS & REHEAT
settings automatically prepare 15 of your favorite foods.

R-1490 R-1491 R-1492

STYLE TRANSCENDS MERE *Fashion*, SUBSTANCE TRANSCENDS MERE *Function*.

Sharp's new 1.4 cu. ft. capacity Over the Range Carousel microwaves represent the latest in innovative design and advanced technology. Gracefully curved handles and elegant colors set them apart visually. Available in 3 matte finishes, R-1490 (black-on-black), R-1491 (white-on-white), R-1492 (almond-on-almond), they feature a 13-inch diameter turntable plus 950 watts of high-speed cooking power. The powerful ventilation system has a 2-speed fan to quickly remove smoke and steam. Installation, whether to the outside or recirculating, is easier than ever. And a convenient work light and night light are also included.

R-1491

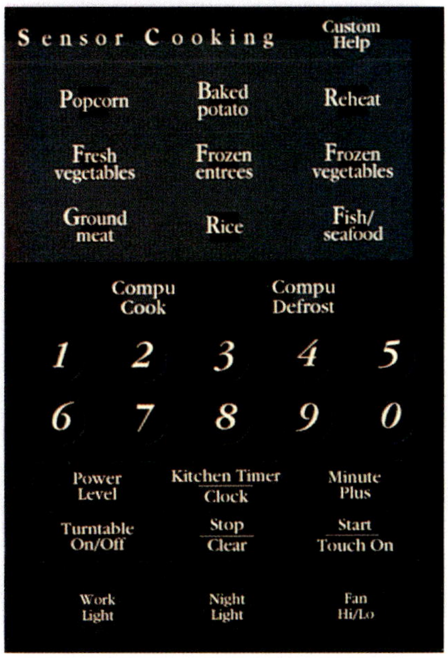

R-1490

features:

TURNTABLE ON/OFF SETTING
enables user to put turntable in "OFF" position when using oversized, up to 4-quart, 10"x15" oblong-shaped dishes. Makes it easier to cook for a crowd.

POWERFUL 300 CFM VENTILATION SYSTEM
offers three convenient venting options. Comes **READY-TO-RECIRCULATE** with the charcoal filter provided, making it easier than ever to install. May also be ducted to the outside, either vertically or horizontally.

12 SMART & EASY SENSOR SETTINGS
automatically select optimum cooking times and power levels for popular foods including Popcorn and Reheat.

INTERACTIVE COOKING SYSTEM WITH 7-DIGIT DISPLAY
makes programming special options a no-brainer. Guides user through the cooking process and offers a variety of helpful hints in English, Spanish and French.

CUSTOM HELP™ KEY
helps users customize oven at a touch with options such as Child Lock, Auto Start, and English, Spanish or French language/weight options.

COMPUCOOK™ and COMPUDEFROST™
provide automatic cooking and defrosting for many different food categories. Specific programs for each defrost category ensure consistent results.

R-530BS

THE DISTINCTIVE *Beauty* OF STAINLESS STEEL.

Finally, a beautiful, well-designed stainless steel microwave packed with advanced features to meet every cooking and entertaining need. Designed to address the growing popularity of professional-type equipment, the look of stainless steel seems to say there's some serious cooking going on here. The R-530BS microwave enhances its stunning appearance with intelligent timesaving features that eliminate cooking and programming guesswork. A generous 1.8 cu. ft. capacity, an extra-large 16-inch turntable, and 1100 watts of high-speed cooking power create unlimited possibilities. The R-530BS works as a countertop or built-in model (using optional RK-51S27 or RK-51S30 stainless Built-in Kits). So it not only looks good in any kitchen, it makes anyone using it look like an expert.

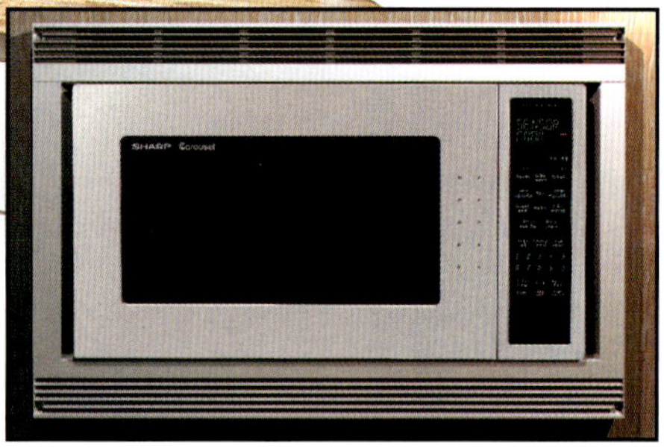

R-530BS

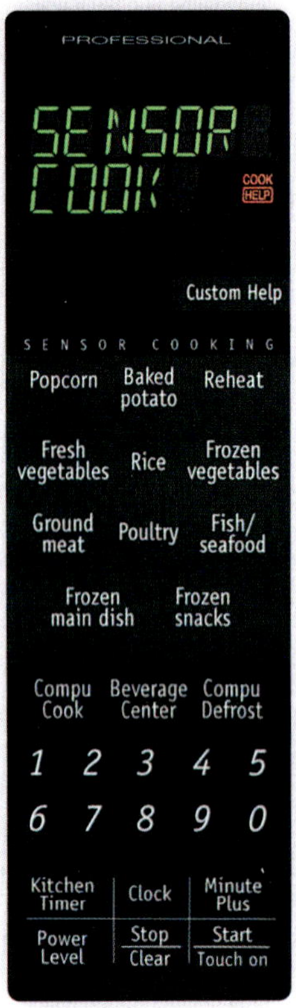

R-530BS

features:

14 SMART & EASY SENSOR SETTINGS

automatically determine and set cooking times and power levels for such popular foods as popcorn, baked potatoes, rice, seafood, frozen main dishes, and more.

NEW! 2-LINE 12-DIGIT 2-COLOR INTERACTIVE DISPLAY

provides clear word prompts to help the user get optimum cooking results. With 2 lines, communication is faster to read and easier to follow.

EXTRA-LARGE 16-INCH DIAMETER TURNTABLE

can hold up to a 9"x13" oblong dish. Perfect for entertaining or large family needs.

INTERACTIVE COOKING SYSTEM

offers step-by-step instructions to guide user through programming steps, special options, and cooking tips.

CUSTOM HELP™

key makes it easy to program special options such as Child Lock, audible signal elimination, Auto Start, language/weight options - in English, Spanish or French.

COMPUCOOK™

automatically cooks 6 categories of the most frequently microwaved foods.

COMPUDEFROST™

automatically thaws 6 food categories including meats and poultry, casseroles and soups.

THE PERFECT MARRIAGE OF *Intelligence* AND *Good Looks.*

[WITH NONE OF THE USUAL COMPROMISES.]

microwave ovens

Sharp's Over the Range Carousel® microwave ovens answer both the demand for superior performance and the desire for great style and value. Known for uncompromising quality, innovative design, and easy-to-use technology, these defining qualities are what set Sharp apart. And now, they are more in evidence than ever, in the latest Over the Range models from Sharp. Sharp has long been the leading innovator in the industry. Beginning with its development of the first turntable system to its Smart & Easy™ Sensor technology, Interactive Displays, and unique designs, no one has been able to duplicate Sharp's ingenuity. Which is probably why Sharp has been the #1 selling brand of microwave ovens for so many years. And why every Sharp Carousel microwave oven delivers exceptional styling and performance, without having to compromise either.

Details. Details. Details.

Great attention has been given to include thoughtful, intuitive touches that consumers will appreciate – work lights and night lights, for example, and new design innovations such as an elegantly-curved handle. Upon closer inspection, users will find that the Carousel turntable has an "OFF" position to accommodate virtually any oversized dish. What's more, the oven's powerful ventilation system comes assembled for the recirculation mode, making it easier than ever to install.

More than a new look, a new attitude.

Further confirmation of Sharp's design leadership can be seen in its innovative new adaptation of stainless steel – available for the first time in its large capacity model. It's a look so professional, so modern, it makes these the first microwave ovens that are perfectly in sync with today's high-tech kitchens.

Convection microwave – it's easier to ask "What can't it do?"

Everything your customers love about conventional cooking plus the convenience of a microwave – all in one space-saving oven. With a Sharp convection microwave, users have unlimited cooking flexibility to brown, bake, broil, crisp, and roast with microwave, convection, combination, and broil options.

So advanced, it's easier than ever.

Sharp's engineers keep raising the bar of excellence as they continue to expand Sharp's Smart & Easy Sensor technology. Now Sensor cooking and reheating convenience is available for more food categories than ever before. And the user-friendly Interactive Displays are larger and easier to read.

SHARP

C512
11452/SHA
BuyLine 8637

Carousel® microwave *ovens*

NEW STYLING AND

Performance PUT

Over the Range

OVER THE TOP

Maximum storage with the 500 SERIES Models 501R and 501F

For large families or those people who need maximum storage, Sub-Zero offers the convenience of its new Eurostyled all-refrigerator (Model 501R) and all-freezer (Model 501F) with a total storage capacity of 40 cubic feet. The "all-refrigerator's" 20 cubic foot capacity makes this exclusive unit the largest built-in all-refrigerator on the market. One of the advantages of these units is the flexibility of planning your kitchen. The units can be installed side-by-side or with a convenient counter between them or at opposite ends of the room, depending on your kitchen layout. Adjustable shelving in both the refrigerator and freezer gives even more storage versatility. The 501F has an automatic ice maker. The "all-refrigerator" Model 501R is also ideal for people who have existing freezer storage. **Separate detailed specification sheets on models 501R and 501F available upon request.**

501F

501R

ALL FREEZER
Model 501F—Automatic defrost. Freezer is equipped with automatic ice maker.
ALL REFRIGERATOR
Model 501R—Automatic defrost refrigerator.

Model	501F	501R
Capacity	20.0 cu. ft.	20.0 cu. ft.
Dimensions	Height 73″ Width 36″ Depth 24″	Height 73″ Width 36″ Depth 24″
Finished Roughing-In Dimensions	35 1/2″x72 3/4″	35 1/2″x72 3/4″
Weight (lbs.)	363 crated	376 crated

*Additional shelves available at extra cost.

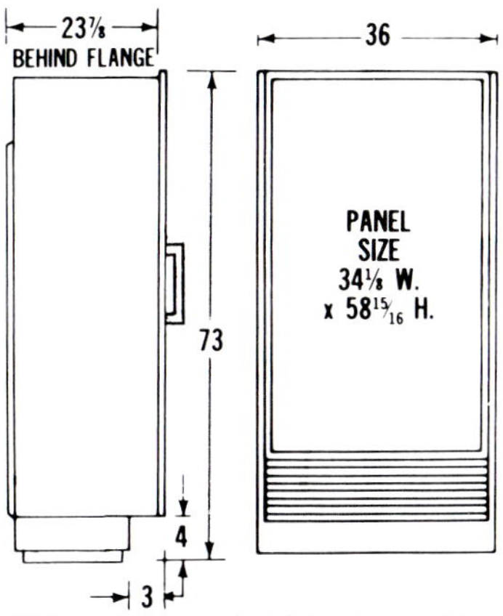

Minimum height required (when levelers in) is 72 7/16″

NOTE: Roughing-in width is 71 1/2″ when these models are installed side by side. If mullion is used to separate cabinets, add mullion width to 71 1/2″ dimension. Filler must be used when installed hinge to hinge.

One 115 volt, 60 cycle single phase, 15 amp. wall outlet must be provided.

Refer to 500 series "Installation Instruction" booklet for detailed installation and panel requirements.

Model 561

Model 561 Interior

SUB-ZERO®

Side by Side Combination
Models 561 and 532

The new 500 series incorporates exciting engineering innovations, with built-in beauty and elegant Eurostyled interiors. This series also features the new satin-brushed aluminum exterior trim and simplicity of design. The elegant combination of white and clear interiors, together with the built-in appearance, offers breathtaking beauty.

Sub-Zero's model 561 features an 8.9 cu. ft. freezer and 12.5 cu. ft. refrigeration in convenient top-to-bottom, side-by-side storage. Its two compressors provide independent temperature control of the freezer and refrigerator compartments. The freezer compartment has four pull-out storage baskets, automatic ice maker with removable ice storage drawer and adjustable door storage.

Model 561

COMBINATION REFRIGERATOR-FREEZER
Model 561 — Automatic defrost model. Freezer compartment equipped with automatic ice maker.

Capacity:	12.5 cu. ft. Refrigerator 8.9 cu. ft. Freezer
Dimensions:	Height 84″ Width 36″ Depth 24″
Finished Rough-In Dimensions	35 1/2″ x 83 3/4″
Weight (lbs.):	480 lbs. crated

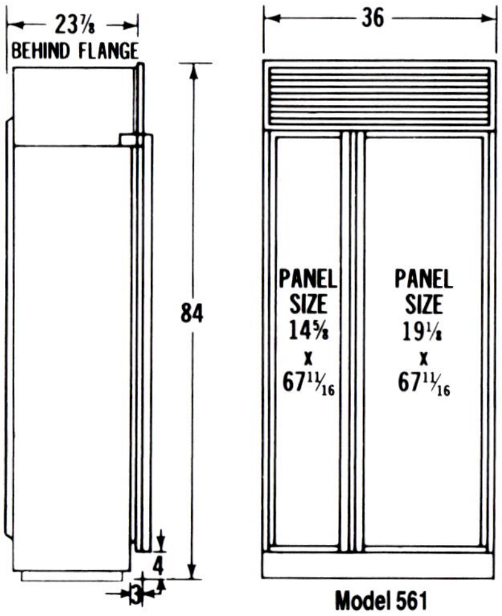

Model 561

One 115 volt, 60 cycle single phase, 15 amp. wall outlet must be provided.

Minimum height required (when levelers in) is 82 7/8″ (smaller grille recommended).

Refer to 500 series "Installation Instruction" booklet for detailed installation and panel requirements.

Model 532

Model 532 Interior

Sub-Zero's huge 30 cu. ft. combination refrigerator/freezer model 532 is one of the largest home built-in units made. It incorporates new engineering innovations and Eurostyled interior. It has an 11.2 cu. ft. freezer and 18.8 cu. ft. refrigerator with convenient top-to-bottom storage.

The freezer compartment has four pull-out storage baskets, an automatic ice maker with roll-out removable ice storage drawer and adjustable door storage. The refrigerator has four self-sealing crispers, each with independent humidity control. It also features an adjustable roll-out utility drawer, adjustable door storage shelves and adjustable glass shelves. This model also has two compressors to provide independent temperature control in both the freezer and refrigerator compartments.

This unit is available in the 48 inch format with water and ice dispensed through the refrigerator door. This is not an optic but another addition to our full line called the Model 590.

Detailed specification sheets on model 532, 561 and 590 are available on request.

Optional solid panel grilles that accept matching panels are available for 532 and 561. The panel grille i standard on the 590. Detailed specification sheets on the three units and grilles available upon request.

Model 532

COMBINATION REFRIGERATOR-FREEZER

Model 532—Automatic defrost model Equipped with automatic ice maker.

Capacity:	18.8 cu. ft. Refrigerator 11.2 cu. ft. Freezer
Dimensions:	Height 84″ Width 48″ Depth 24″
Finished Rough-In Dimensions:	47 1/2″x83 3/4″
Weight (lbs.):	563 crated

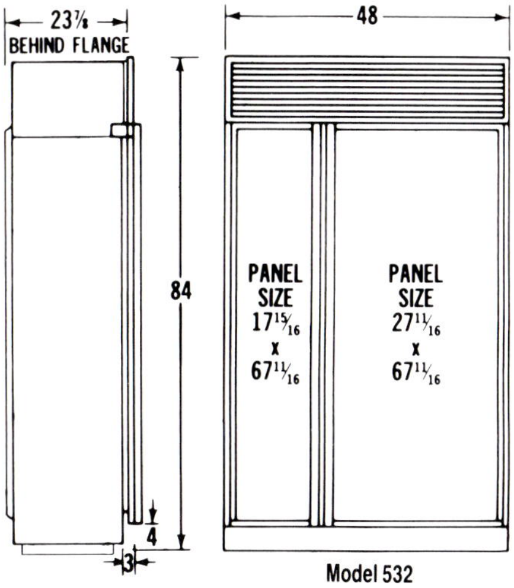

Model 532

One 115 volt, 60 cycle single phase, 15 amp. wall outlet must be provided.

Minimum height required (when levelers in) is 82 7/8″ (smaller grille recommended).

Refer to 500 series "Installation Instruction" booklet for detailed installation and panel requirements.

Model 550

Model 550 Interior

SUB-ZERO®

Over-N-Under (freezer on bottom)
Models 550 and 511

For those who prefer, Sub-Zero offers a convenient arrangement with freezer on the bottom. This design was prompted by the fact that the refrigerator section is used more often than the freezer, thereby providing the greatest convenience and best accessibility. The refrigerated top half offers full width storage on adjustable shelves while frozen foods below are easily accessible with a pull-out drawer.

The over-n-under units in the 500 series also incorporate exciting engineering innovations with built-in beauty and elegant Eurostyled interiors. These units also feature the new satin-brushed aluminum exterior trim and simplicity of design.

Sub-Zero's 22.1 cu. ft. model 550 over-n-under combination unit has a 6.4 cu. ft. slide-out, double-tier freezer drawer in the

Model 550

COMBINATION REFRIGERATOR-FREEZER
Model 550 — Automatic defrost model. Freezer compartment equipped with automatic ice maker.

Capacity:	15.7 cu. ft. Refrigerator 6.4 cu. ft. Freezer
Dimensions:	Height 84″ Width 36″ Depth 24″
Finished Rough-In Dimensions	35½″x83¾″
Weight (lbs.):	468 crated

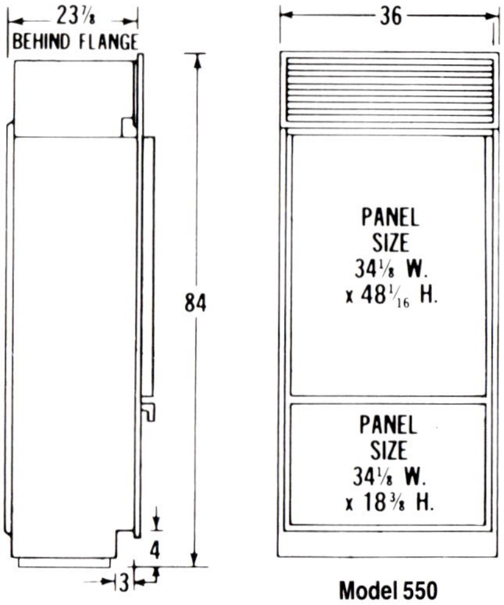

One 115 volt, 60 cycle single phase, 15 amp. wall outlet must be provided.

Minimum height required (when levelers in) is 82⅞″ (smaller grille recommended).

Refer to 500 series "Installation Instruction" booklet for detailed installation and panel requirements.

Model 550

(Optional panel grille shown) Model 511

Model 511 Interior

bottom. The freezer has an automatic ice maker with removable ice storage container. The top pull freezer handle and double-tier design provide easy access. The refrigerator has two self-sealing crispers, each with independent humidity control. It has a roll-out utility drawer, adjustable glass shelves and fully adjustable door storage.

The model 511 features a 5.2 cu. ft. slide-out double-tier freezer drawer and a 12.7 cu. ft. refrigerator compartment. Again the freezer has an automatic ice maker with removable ice storage container. Like the model 550, easy freezer access is provided by top pull handle and roll-out double-tier design.

These over-n-under models are extremely versatile for kitchen designs used alone or in various combinations, such as the kitchen shown on the cover of this brochure.

Both units have two compressors which provides independent temperature control in both the refrigerator and freezer compartments. These units are backed by Sub-Zero's exclusive Twelve-Year Protection Plan.

Optional solid panel grilles that accept matching panels also available. Specification sheet available upon request. Detailed specification sheets on models 550 and 511 are available upon request.

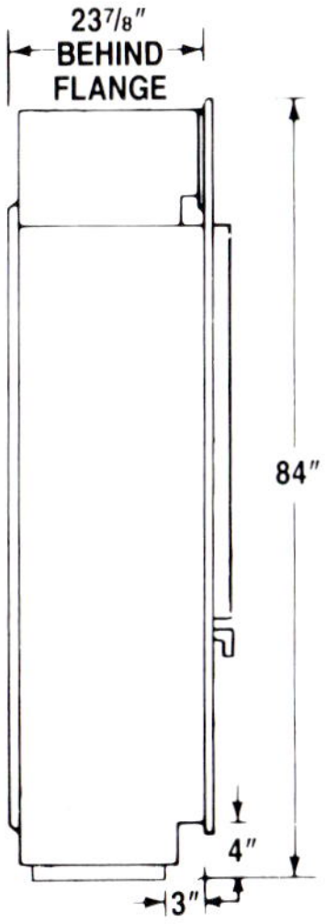

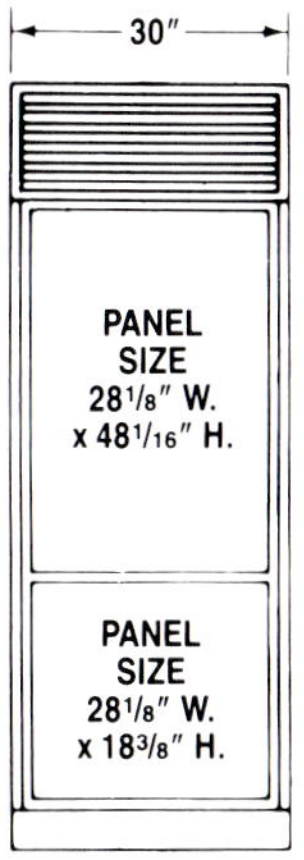

Model 511

One 115 volt, 60 cycle single phase, 15 amp. wall outlet must be provided.

Minimum height required (when levelers in) is 82 7/8" (smaller grille recommended).

Refer to 500 series "Installation Instruction" booklet for detailed installation and panel requirements.

COMBINATION REFRIGERATOR-FREEZER

Model 511 — Automatic defrost model. Freezer compartment equipped with automatic ice maker.

Capacity:	12.7 cu. ft. Refrigerator 5.2 cu. ft. Freezer
Dimensions:	Height 84" Width 30" Depth 24"
Finished Rough-In Dimensions	29 1/2" x 83 3/4"
Weight (lbs.):	375 crated

Model 511

SUB-ZERO®

Features of full-size, built-in units

1. Convenient Storage

All Sub-Zero units are 24″ in depth to conform to most kitchen base cabinet units. This not only improves appearance of finished installation but provides more accessible storage on interior shelves.

2. Sub-Zero 12-Year Protection Plan

Full five-year (parts and labor) warranty and limited sixth through twelfth-year (parts) warranty on the sealed system, consisting of the compressor, condenser, evaporator, drier and all connecting tubing; and a full two-year (parts and labor) warranty on the entire product from the date of installation. (Does not include installation.) (See warranty for non-residential use and other exceptions.)

3. Automatic Ice Maker

Makes and stores crescent-shaped ice pieces. Although several conditions affect the amount of ice that is produced in a given period of time, an adequate supply is provided. (Model 532 and 561 icemaker shown)

4. Automatic Defrosting

Automatically eliminates frost accumulation in both refrigerator and freezer sections.

5. Accepts Removable Decorative Door Panels

Front panels of virtually any material, not exceeding 1/4″ in thickness are easily installed. Raised panels may also be used when perimeter edge does not exceed 1/4″. **(We recommend routing, recessing or optional extended handles for finger clearance when using raised panels.) Refer to Installation Instruction Guide for detailed information. Only colored and stainless steel panels are available from the factory. (50# per door panel weight limit.)**

6. Side Panels

Unit is made to accept side panels if sides are exposed. Only colored and stainless steel panels are available from the factory.

7. Front-Vented

Allows for true built-in installation and eliminates over heating.

8. Removable and Adjustable Shelves

Cantilever type glass shelves in the refrigerator and wire shelves in the freezer for easy cleaning and flexible storage.

9. Deluxe Crispers

Spacious, self-sealing crispers have easy-glide roller design and adjustable, independent humidity control to assure food freshness.

10. Interiors

Award-winning Eurostyled white and clear interior.

11. Magnetic Door Gasket

Surrounds entire door with a pull that assures a positive seal. **NOTE** — Because of a perfect seal, allow a slight delay before reopening door.

12. Right or Left Door Swing

Available, when specified, on all over-n-under and single door units (all side-by-side units are hinged on outside). Doors are not reversible.

13. Portable Egg Trays

Convenient and versatile, they may be carried to the table or preparation area.

14. Adjustable Dairy Compartment

Versatile, positive sealing compartment for dairy items.

15. Adjustable Utility Basket

Adjustable roll-out refrigeration basket offers handy storage for small items.

16. Clean Trim

No visible screws.

17. Colored Panels

Decorator front and side steel panels are available from Sub-Zero in the following colors: Harvest Gold, Almond, Avocado, Coffee, Stainless Steel and White.

18. Grilles

Standard grille height is 11″. Other available grille heights range from 10″ to 15″ in 1″ increments. Optional decorative, solid panel grilles that accept matching panels also available in these sizes.

Panel grille

19. Toe Space Base

Integral part of cabinet. Inset is 4″ high by 3″ deep — meeting specifications of American Institute of Architects and conforming with most bases of kitchen cabinets.

20. Door Handles

Standard as shown in photographs throughout this literature.

21. Door Closers

All models equipped with door closers.

22. Door Stops

Although most installations do not require a door stop (door opens to 130°), an optional kit is available if needed. The Door Stop Kit allows the door to open to 90°.

23. Rollers

Unit has rollers and convenient leveling system for ease of installation.

24. Additional Shelves

Available at additional cost.

IMPORTANT: For proper operation and use, the door must open at least a full 90°. A minimum 2″ filler should be used in corner installations to assure a 90° door opening. Remember to allow enough clearance in front of unit for full door swing.

Undercounter models

Sub-Zero undercounter refrigerators, freezers, combinations and ice makers are ideal for the bar, den, family room, yacht or office. They are designed to be installed under a counter. However, some may also be used as free-standing units.

All under-counter models are self-venting, have foamed-in-place insulation, have durable ABS easy to clean interiors and accept front door panels of practically any material to harmonize with cabinets or other equipment. They also have right to left door swings which are interchangeable in the field (kit required except model 245). All of these features and more are backed by Sub-Zero's 12-Year Protection Plan – providing a full five-year (parts and labor) warranty and limited sixth through twelfth year (parts) warranty on the sealed system, consisting of the compressor, condenser, evaporator, drier and all connecting tubing; and a full two year (parts and labor) warranty on the entire product from the date of installation. (Does not include installation.) (See warranty for non-residential use and other exceptions.)

The Sub-Zero combination model 245 provides automatic defrost, refrigerator storage, freezer storage and automatic ice making.

Sub-Zero also offers "all-refrigerator" and "all-freezer" undercounter units. The model 249RP "all-refrigerator" features automatic defrost, door storage and adjustable compartment shelving. Our model 249FF "all-freezer" features automatic defrost, adjustable compartment shelving and can be equipped with an automatic ice maker, but it must be installed at the factory.

A unit for those who desire primarily refrigerator storage with some freezer storage is the model 249R. This unit is a manual defrost, with a small full-width freezer, door storage and adjustable compartment shelving.

Model 249R

We also offer a built-in ice maker for those who entertain in style. Requirements for clear ice can be satisfied with the model 506, which provides an abundance of crystal-clear cubes in a unit that requires only an 18″ width. Featuring a drop-down hopper-type door, this unit stores up to 35 pounds of 3/4″ cubes. This unit requires a drain or pump.

Separate specification sheet on each undercounter model is available upon request.

Undercounter Model	249R	249RP	249FF	245	506
Capacity	4.4 cu. ft. Refrigerator .7 cu. ft. Freezer	4.9 cu. ft. Refrigerator	4.6 cu. ft. Freezer	3.0 cu. ft. Refrigerator 1.9 cu. ft Freezer	Stores 35 lbs. of ice
Unit Dimensions [Levelers in] (H x W x D in inches)	33 13/16 x 23 7/8 x 24	33 13/16 x 23 7/8 x 24	33 13/16 x 23 7/8 x 24	34 x 23 7/8 x 24	34 13/32 x 17 7/8 x 23 7/8
Weight (lbs.)	120 crated	117 crated	135 crated	139 crated	110 crated

Note: Refer to "Installation Instruction" booklet for detailed water, electrical and other installation requirements.

Model 249R

Model 249RP

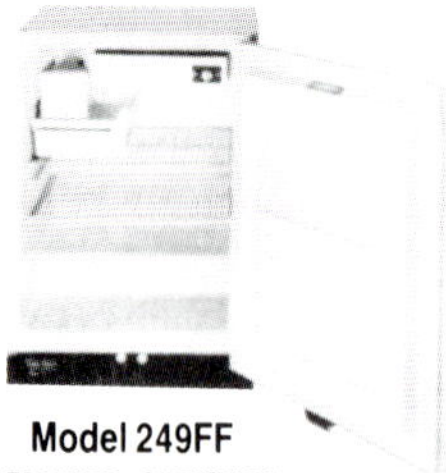

Model 249FF
(ICEMAKER OPTIONAL)

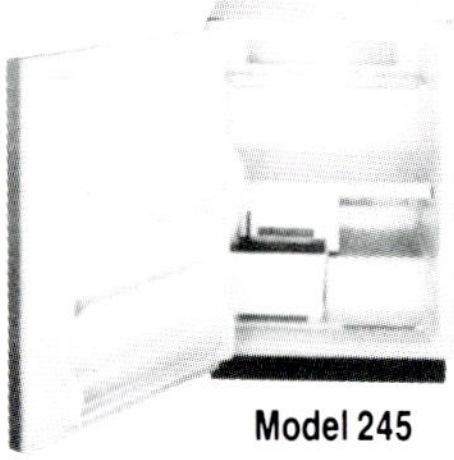

Model 245

Model 506

Installation specifications

Following are the installation specifications for all Sub-Zero full-size and undercounter models. The dimensions shown in the chart correlate with the schematic drawings. For further details refer to the **Installation Instruction Booklet.**

Wood grille not available from Sub Zero.

Schematic drawing

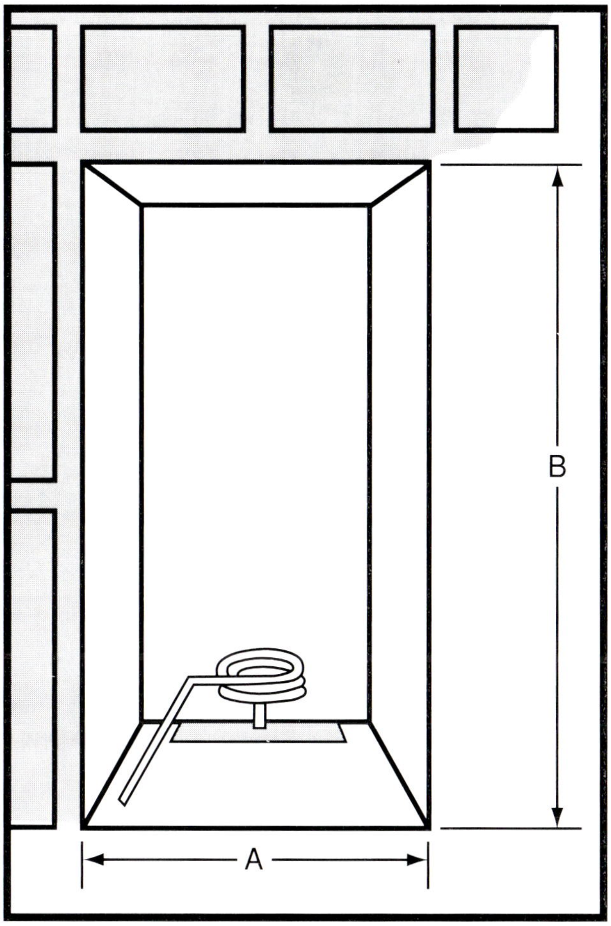

Door Clearance Schematic Drawing Top View

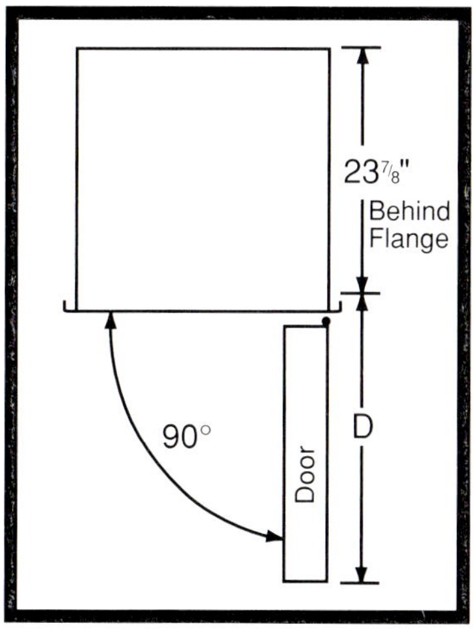

Model No.	Finished Rough Opening Dimensions A	Finished Rough Opening Dimensions B	Door Panel Dimensions (width x height) C	Minimum Door Clearance Requirement at 90° D
550	35 1/2″	83 3/4″	34 1/8″ x 48 1/16″ & 34 1/8″ x 18 3/8″	36 1/16″
511	29 1/2″	83 3/4″	28 1/8″ x 48 1/16″ & 28 1/8″ x 18 3/8″	30 1/8″
561	35 1/2″	83 3/4″	14 5/8″ x 67 11/16″ & 19 1/8″ x 67 11/16″	20 3/4″
532	47 1/2″	83 3/4″	17 15/16″ x 67 11/16″ & 27 11/16″ x 67 11/16″	29 1/4″
501R	35 1/2″	72 3/4″	34 1/8″ x 58 15/16″	36 1/16″
501F	35 1/2″	72 3/4″	34 1/8″ x 58 15/16″	36 1/16″
590	47 1/2″	83 3/4″	15 1/8″ x 67 11/16″ & 20 9/16″ x 67 11/16″	29 1/4″
245	24″	34 1/2″	23 1/2″ x 28 1/8″	25 13/16″
249R	24″	34 1/2″	23 5/8″ x 30″	25 3/8″
249RP	24″	34 1/2″	23 5/8″ x 30″	25 3/8″
249FF	24″	34 1/2″	23 5/8″ x 30″	25 3/8″
506	18″	34 1/2″	17″ x 13 3/16″ & 17″ x 11 15/16″	11 3/4″

(Optional panel grille shown)

How to buy

Sub-Zero home refrigeration can be seen and purchased at top custom kitchen dealers and appliance stores in all major cities across the United States and many Canadian cities. If not available in your area, feel free to contact Sub-Zero direct for the distributor nearest you. Call 800-222-7820.

Service

There are hundreds of authorized service centers throughout the country to provide warranty service and perform other service functions. These centers maintain a stock of Sub-Zero approved parts and a staff of qualified repair technicians. The service center nearest you may be found in the yellow pages or by contacting the dealer you purchased the unit from. If service cannot be found, contact Sub-Zero direct: 800-356-5826.

SUB-ZERO®

SUB-ZERO FREEZER CO., INC.
Post Office Box 44130
Madison, Wisconsin 53744-4130
608/271-2233

C515
BuyLine 8660

SUB-ZERO®

Model 590

Ice & Water Refrigerator-Freezer

Innovative Excellence

SUB-ZERO®

Sub-Zero has led the built-in home refrigeration industry for years with product enhancements which have set trends. Sub-Zero continues to redefine the art of built-in refrigeration for the 90's with the introduction of the distinctive Model 590 with its innovative version of ice and water through the refrigerator door.

The convenient placement and inconspicuous appearance of the ice and water dispenser and its controls were designed with you in mind.

And the ability to match your kitchen design has been assured with the Model 590. Like all Sub-Zero units, the Model 590 will fit flush with virtually all 24-inch cabinets and accept decorative side and front panels. Another exclusive feature of the Model 590 is the complementary color handle trim panels and glasswells which are offered at no charge.

Ice & Water Dispenser with Night Light.

Craftsmanship, a Sub-Zero trademark, is also built into each of these features:

- **Ice & Water Dispenser**– designed and practically placed for your convenience. A new industry feature, the water is constantly chilled within its huge 51 oz. reservoir.
- **Bulk Ice Dispenser**– conveniently located inside the refrigerator door when larger quantities are needed. This new industry feature is activated at the touch of a button.
- **Two Refrigeration Systems** – ensures independent, accurate freezer and refrigerator temperature control.
- **Decorative Door Panels** – front panels of virtually any material not exceeding 1/4" perimeter thickness are accommodated. Only color and stainless steel panels are available from the factory. (50# per door panel weight limit)
- **Automatic Defrosting** – freezer and refrigerator have own systems.
- **Adjustable Shelves** – cantilever type, easy to move and clean.
- **Spacious Crispers with Humidity Control** – four self-sealing crispers have clear view and individual controls.
- **Adjustable Door Shelves** – easy to adjust shelves provide complete flexibility on both doors.
- **Automatic Ice Maker** – an adequate supply of cresent-shaped ice is ensured.
- **Dairy Module** – a moveable, sealed environment for freshness.
- **Master Switch** – quick practical access is offered to shut unit off.
- **Rollers** – provides easy installation.
- **Positive Sealing Doors** – magnetic gaskets guarantee a tight seal.
- **Brushed Satin Trim** – offers clean design so there's no distraction from the beauty of your kitchen.
- **Portable Egg Containers** – easy access and convenient storage.
- **Panel Grille** – 11"panel grille is standard. Other sizes from 10" to 15" are available in one inch increments.
- **Solid Toe Plate** – allows custom finishing.

Refrigeration System Control and Bulk Ice Dispenser.

Model 590 shown with optional bright white handle trim panel and glasswell.

Sub-Zero 12 Year Protection Plan— full five-year (parts and labor) warranty and limited sixth through twelfth-year (parts) warranty on the sealed system, consisting of the compressor, condenser, evaporator, drier and all connecting tubing; a full two-year (parts and labor) warranty on the entire product from the date of installation. (Does not include installation. See warranty for other exceptions.)

Beauty — our award-winning interior is beautiful to the eye, but more importantly it is spacious with nearly 30 cubic feet of flexible storage for all your needs.
Refrigerator – 18.2 cubic feet.
Freezer – 11.2 cubic feet.

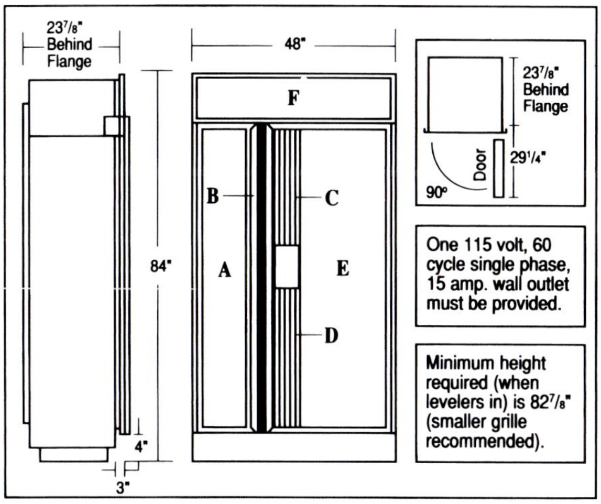

Capacity: Refrigerator 18.2 cu. ft. Freezer 11.2 cu. ft.	**Dimensions: Height 84" Width 48" Depth 24"**
Two Compressors	**Finished Roughed-in Dimensions: 47 1/2 x 83 3/4**

Weight: 598 lbs. crated

Door Panel Dimensions: **A** 15 1/8 w x 67 11/16 h **B** 2 9/16 w x 67 11/32 h **C** 6 7/8 w x 25 7/32 h	**D** 6 7/8 w x 31 7/32 h **E** 20 9/16 w x 67 11/16 h **Grille Panel Dimension:** **F** 46 3/16 w x 9 3/16 h

B,C & D may not exceed .050" thickness

Due to our continuous improvement program, models and specifications are subject to change without notice.

Color Selection Guide

for model 590 only

Complete Flexibility

Your Sub-Zero Model 590 will be shipped with handsome pin-striped pewter gray handle trim panels and glasswell. But an exclusive feature from Sub-Zero allows you to change this color scheme to accent your kitchen.

Model 590 shown with standard pin-striped pewter gray handle trim panels and glasswell.

Ask your local dealer about specific color combinations. The eight glasswell and laminate handle trim panel alternatives we offer at no charge are:

P1/G1	Bright White
P2/G2	Almond Buff
P3/G3	Camel
P4/G4	Adobe
P5/G5	Pewter Gray
P6/G6	Smoke Gray
P7/G7	Charcoal
P8/G8	Port Brown
P9/G9	Black Slate

**The colors illustrated here are only meant to give you an idea of the shades available and you should contact your dealer for more accurate color combinations and shading.*

Note: Metal handle trim panels to match Sub-Zero supplied metal door and side panels are also available in white, almond, avocado, coffee, harvest gold and stainless steel at no charge.

Sales

In addition to the Model 590, Sub-Zero features a full line of built-in home refrigeration units with side-by-side, over-and-under and undercounter models which vary in size from 4.5 to 30 cubic feet of storage. For the dealer near you look in the yellow pages or call Sub-Zero at **800/222-7820** for your nearest distributor.

Service

Sub-Zero has an extensive service network throughout the United States and Canada to meet your needs. You can find them in the yellow pages or call us at **800/356-5826.**

SUB-ZERO ®

SUB- ZERO FREEZER CO., INC.
P.O. Box 44130
Madison ,WI 53744 - 4130
(608) 271- 2233

It takes vision to create
a revolutionary new
system of refrigeration.

SUB-ZERO

Ponder it, just for a mom

The convenience of stor

your vegetables in a dra

by the sink. Fresh fish

Under the cooktop. Ne

the table. In the island. N

the question isn't whe

can you put a refrigerat

But rather, where can't y

another drawer near t

cooktop. Milk, juice a

last night's leftovers in

▲ **Spice cabinets. China cabinets. Now Sub-Zero introduces orange juice and pork chop cabinets.**

Tuck a freezer into the ▶ island and you'll never be stranded there.

cabinet by the kitchen table. And a separate reezer drawer near the back door for the kids. The advantages of our ntegrated refrigerators and freezers go well beyond aesthetics. easuring just 27 inches de, they allow you to put refrigeration in places never before possible. stead of being limited to a single, centralized refrigerator, you can now utilize several. (Hence, when your teenager complains there's nothing good in the refrigerator, you can reply, "Which refrigerator?") With five different configurations, you can mix and match our tall units with additional base units. Or use them to supplement a 500 Series Sub-Zero. (In fact, who says you have to limit them to the kitchen? Imagine hiding a refrigerator in the living room, bedroom or entertainment area.) And rest assured, each features Sub-Zero's legendary, uncompromising craftsmanship. Which is why we're confident enough to back them with the 12-Year Sub-Zero Protection Plan. So the only unknown you will ever face with our new refrigerators is how many places to put them.

How's this for a reminder to wash the fruits and vegetables? Store them near the sink.

With its inconspicuous looks, you could misplace the refrigerator. But thanks to its brilliant halogen lighting,

Its advanced features are fresher than anything you are likely to put inside it.

you'll never misplace the food inside. All units also feature a microprocessor control panel that lets you program specific temperatures. In one tall refrigerator, for instance, you could store fresh meat at 30 degrees, while storing your vegetables at the optimal 32 degrees — and the milk and leftovers at 38 degrees. Leave any door or drawer ajar and an alarm will sound. (It can be disengaged for loading groceries.) And like all Sub-Zeros, our tall units offer the ultimate in adjustable, drip-proof shelving.

▲ A see-through, humidity controlled crisper cover provides easy access to fresh fruits and vegetables.

◄ The tall unit comes with spill-proof shelves and a deli drawer for handy storage.

▲ The microprocessor control panel uses "fuzzy logic," which helps save energy by continuously adapting to usage and climates.

All the doors and compartment shelves are adjustable, providing exceptional flexibility. ►

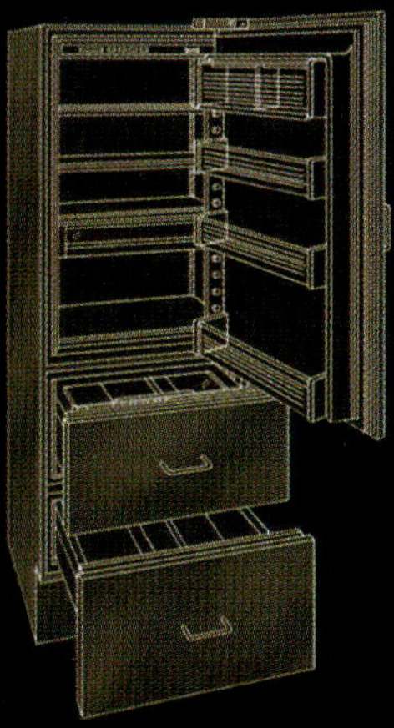

700TR-All Refrigerator

DIMENSIONS
H 80" W 27" D 24"
Door Swing Clearance: 25½"

ENERGY USAGE
553 kwh/$46/Annually*

STORAGE INFORMATION

Refrigerator:
15.0 cu. ft. of Storage
- 9.8 cu. ft. upper cabinet
- 5.2 cu. ft. combined drawers

3 Adjustable Glass Shelves
1 Stationary Glass Shelf
3 Adjustable Door Shelves
1 Adjustable Dairy Compartment
1 Adjustable Deli-Drawer
1 Removable Crisper Cover
2 Removable Drawer Dividers
1 Egg Tray

CRATED WEIGHT
360 pounds

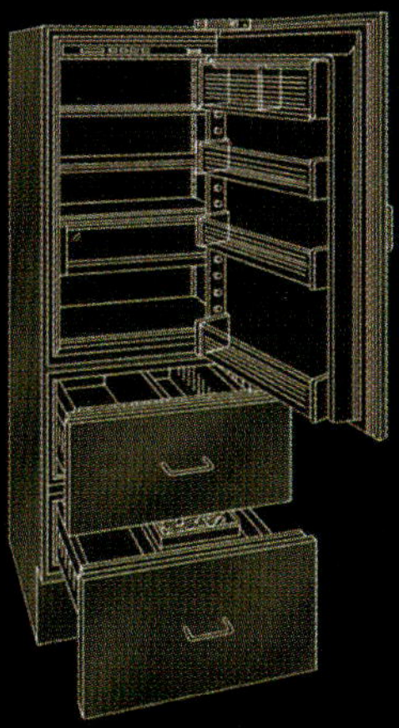

700TC-Refrigerator/Freezer

DIMENSIONS
H 80" W 27" D 24"
Door Swing Clearance: 25½"

ENERGY USAGE
672 kwh/$56/Annually*

STORAGE INFORMATION

Refrigerator (Top Cabinet):
9.8 cu. ft. of Storage
3 Adjustable Glass Shelves
1 Stationary Glass Shelf
1 Adjustable Crisper/Deli Drawer
3 Adjustable Door Shelves
1 Adjustable Dairy Compartment

Freezer (Combined Drawers):
5.4 cu. ft. of Storage
2 Removable Drawer Dividers
(1 Removable Divider when Ice Maker ordered)
Ice Maker Optional (700TCI)

CRATED WEIGHT
360 pounds

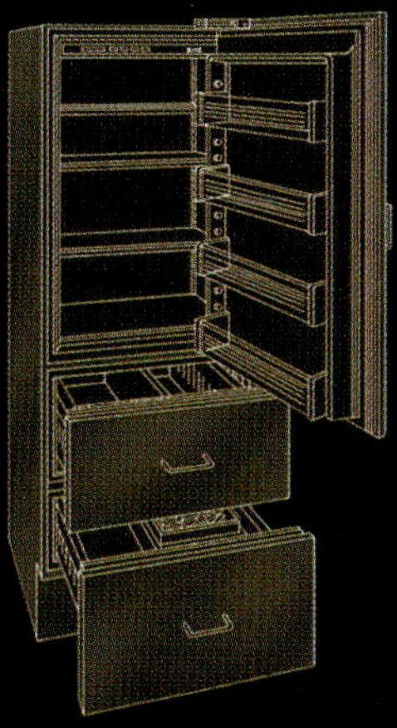

700TF-All Freezer

DIMENSIONS
H 80" W 27" D 24"
Door Swing Clearance: 25½"

ENERGY USAGE
782 kwh/$65/Annually*

STORAGE INFORMATION

Freezer:
15.2 cu. ft. of Storage
- 9.8 cu. ft. upper cabinet
- 5.4 cu. ft. combined drawers

4 Adjustable Door Shelves
3 Adjustable Glass Shelves
1 Stationary Glass Shelf
2 Removable Drawer Dividers
(1 Removable Divider when Ice Maker ordered)
Ice Maker Optional (700TFI)

CRATED WEIGHT
360 pounds

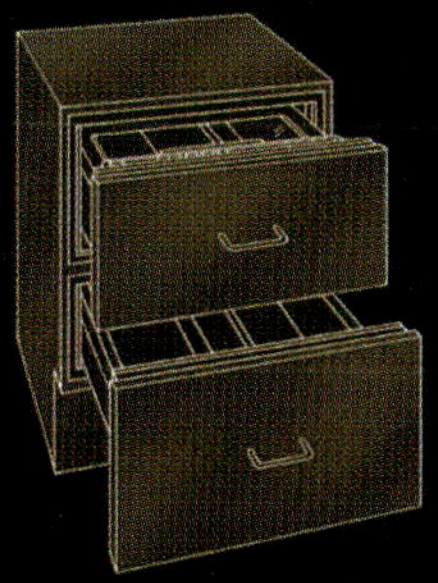

700BR-All Refrigerator

DIMENSIONS
H 34½" W 27" D 24"
Drawer Clearance: 19½"

ENERGY USAGE
449 kwh/$37/Annually*

STORAGE INFORMATION

Refrigerator (Combined Drawers):
4.9 cu. ft. of Storage
2 Removable Drawer Dividers
1 Removable Crisper Cover

CRATED WEIGHT
190 pounds

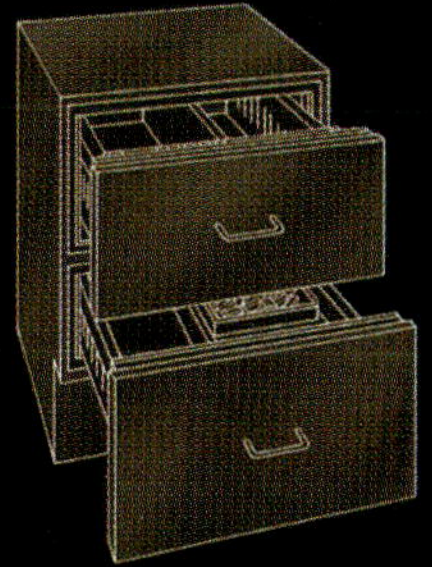

700BF-All Freezer

DIMENSIONS
H 34½" W 27" D 24"
Drawer Clearance: 19½"

ENERGY USAGE
522 kwh/$43/Annually*

STORAGE INFORMATION

Freezer (Combined Drawers):
5.1 cu. ft. of Storage
2 Removable Drawer Dividers
(1 Removable Divider when Ice Maker ordered)
Ice Maker Optional (700BFI)

CRATED WEIGHT
190 pounds

*Annual energy costs are based on 8.3 cents per kilowatt hour.
Consultant: Jerome Caruso Design, Inc.

We've shown you the beautiful exteriors and features. Now take a look at the nuts and bolts.

Our Integrated 700 Series offers five different configurations, to fit any lay-out. In addition to a tall refrigerator/freezer combination unit, we offer both the tall and base models in all-refrigerator or all-freezer models. You also have a choice of left or right-hand door swing, as well as an optional ice maker. And all units can accept most any style of cabinetry panels. Additional accessories, such as stainless steel fronts and handles, are also available. For more details, review our Planning and Installation Guide with your designer, architect or dealer.

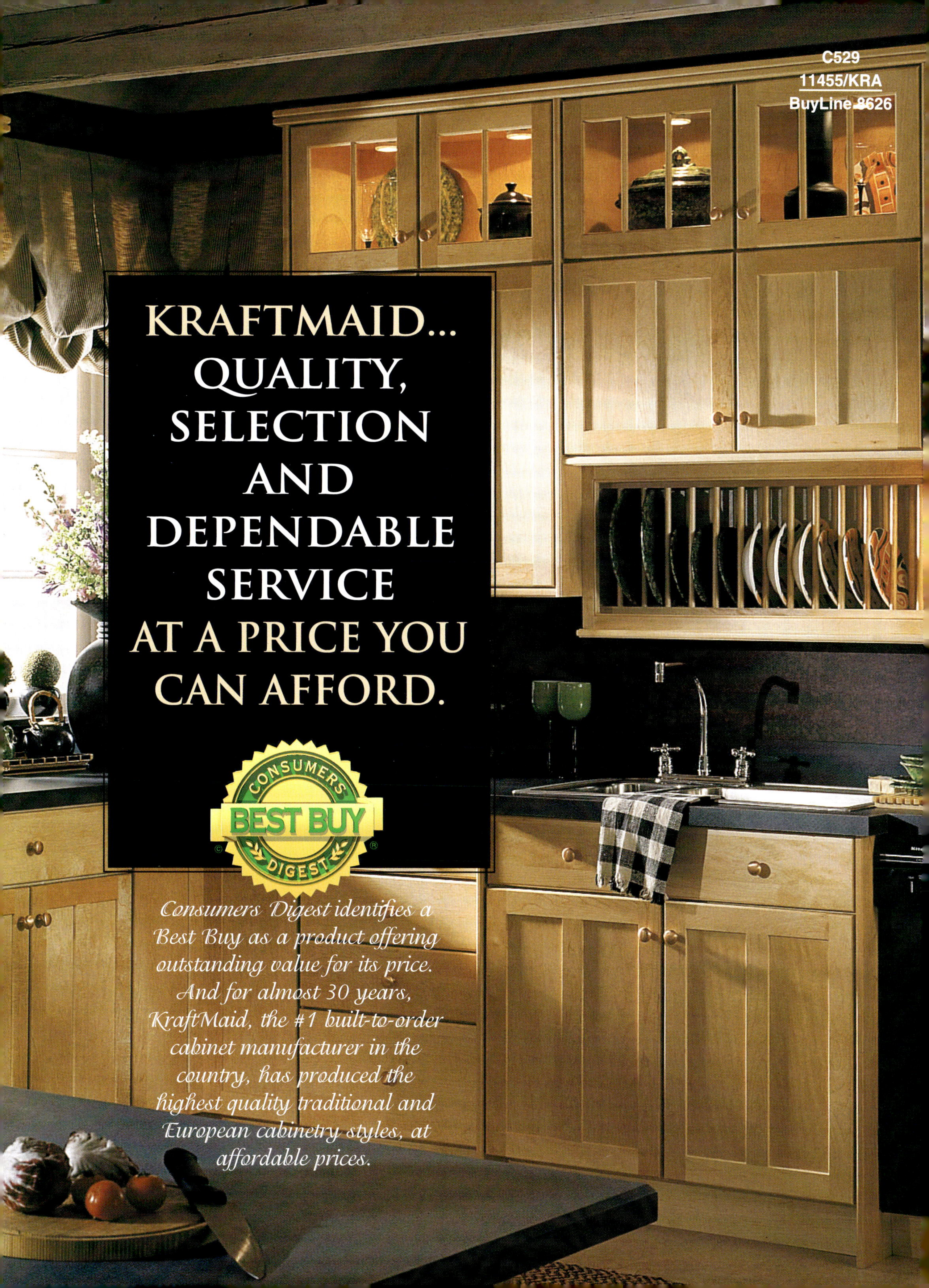
C529
11455/KRA
BuyLine 8626
KRAFTMAID... QUALITY, SELECTION AND DEPENDABLE SERVICE AT A PRICE YOU CAN AFFORD.
CONSUMERS BEST BUY DIGEST
Consumers Digest identifies a Best Buy as a product offering outstanding value for its price. And for almost 30 years, KraftMaid, the #1 built-to-order cabinet manufacturer in the country, has produced the highest quality traditional and European cabinetry styles, at affordable prices.

KraftMaid

C529
11455/KRA
BuyLine 8626

KraftMaid proudly introduces North American poplar, a new wood species for home and office cabinetry. We have successfully developed special sanding techniques and sealers to provide a beautiful look and finish on poplar. By formulating autumn blush and mocha finishes specifically for poplar, KraftMaid can now offer affordable, quality alternatives to expensive cherry and walnut woods.

The most comprehensive line of cabinetry for Universal Design available, KraftMaid's Passport Series cabinetry creates a functional kitchen without sacrificing style. Passport Series is available with all of KraftMaid's construction options, finishes and modifications. Give your customers the beauty and accessibility features of custom cabinetry without custom prices.

KRAFTMAID'S PRODUCTS ARE BUILT TO LAST.

Our construction features not only surpass industry requirements, but are standard in all of KraftMaid's cabinetry.

• *Exclusive 14-step furniture finish process with DuraKraft catalyzed topcoat provides the industry's finest finish.*

• *Exclusive PermaSet bumpers are pre-drilled to stay in place forever.*

•*3/4" solid wood drawer box and concealed undermount suspension system offer lifetime guarantees.*

• *3/4" shelving material is 20 - 50% thicker than industry standards, increases shelf load capacity and reduces sagging.*

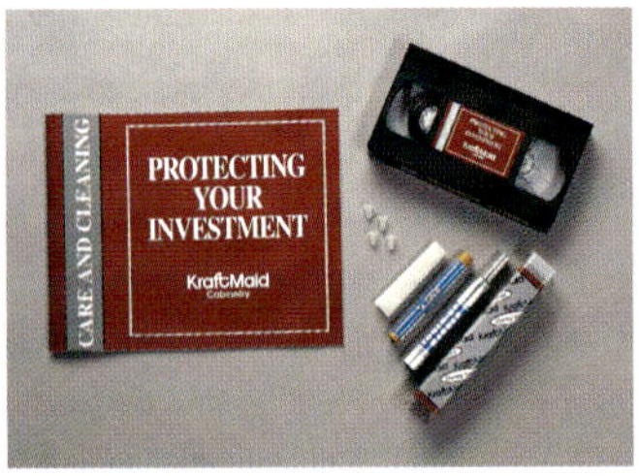

• *The only cabinetry company to offer a free care and cleaning kit, to protect your client's investment, with each cabinetry purchase.*

• *Full-depth base shelves provide up to 50% more storage space.*

• *Multi-adjustment hinges feature lifetime guarantees and corrosion-free performance.*

And we still make sure it gets to you when needed with our one week production program, the only one in the semi-custom cabinet industry.

These are the qualities that you look for in a cabinetry company and the reasons why you and Consumers Digest choose KraftMaid.

CONSUMERS DIGEST BEST BUY

KraftMaid
Cabinetry

Middlefield, OH 44062
440/632-5333
www.kraftmaid.com

C536

11455/WEL

BuyLine 6292

WELLBORN CABINET, INC.

THE WOODCRAFT SERIES

All Wood Cabinetry

Nothing Could Be More Natural

The Woodcraft Series

1 Matching Finished Veneer Exterior Plywood End Panels in Oak, Maple, Cherry or Hickory

Matching finished end panels eliminate the cost and labor of adding finished skins to cabinet ends, saving time and money during installation.

2 ½" Thick Plywood End Panels

Plywood end panels provide a strong foundation for cabinetry construction and is the highest quality.

Lifetime limited **warranty**
- Solid Wood Drawers
- Drawer Guides
- Door Hinges

3 ¾" Thick Solid Wood Drawer Sides

Natural finished solid wood drawer sides, sub-front and back easily wipe clean and carry a Lifetime Warranty.

4 Dovetail Drawer Construction

Dovetail construction has always been recognized as the strongest, most durable method of assembly and creates a beautiful, long lasting drawer.

5 Undermount Drawer Guides

Epoxy coated captive self-closing drawer guides have positive stops to prevent spills and slide shut with just a slight touch. The drawer has a 75 lb. capacity and carries a Lifetime Warranty.

6 ¼" Thick Finished Plywood Drawer Bottom

The drawer bottom locks into the dadoed sides and are glued and stapled into place. The finished interior is easy to clean.

7 Adjustable Drawer Front

Four screws attach the drawer front to the drawer sub-front providing easy adjustment.

Than All Wood!

C536
11455/WEL
BuyLine 6292

¾" Thick Plywood Hanging Rails 8

Hanging rails are built-in at the top and bottom of wall and base cabinets to secure installation and add strength.

½" Thick Plywood Tops and Bottoms 9

Tops and bottoms lock into the dadoed hanging rails and face frames and are glued and stapled into place for extra strength.

3/16" Thick Plywood Backs 10

Backs are locked into a step groove within the hanging rails and are glued and stapled into place.

¾" Thick Fully Adjustable Laminated & Edgebanded Furniture Board Shelves 11

Cabinet shelves and interiors are covered in a natural colored wood grain laminate which easily wipes clean and is resistant to most household chemicals.

¾" Thick Solid Oak, Maple, Cherry or Hickory Face Frames 12

All face frames joints are precisely aligned with blind mortise and tenon joints. The frames are then machined squared and glued and stapled at each joint to assure tightness.

¾" Thick Natural Finished Plywood Toe Space 13

Captive toe space is fully enclosed featuring a rodent proof design.

¾" Thick Plywood Shipping Brace 14

The shipping brace provides extra security to the end panels during shipping and handling.

WELLBORN
CABINET, INC.

15 Solid Oak, Maple, Cherry or Hickory Drawer Fronts

Solid wood drawer fronts are attached to the hardwood sub-front with four screws for complete adjustability.

16 Solid Oak, Maple, Cherry or Hickory Doors

A large selection of door styles are constructed of solid wood. No wood substitutes are used.

Nothing Can Match Our Latest Technology!

17 WellGuard Finishing System

Combining Time Tested Finishing Techniques with today's technology has resulted in the 18 steps Wellborn uses to create the furniture-like luster that shines deep from within the wood. Hand sanding prepares surfaces, end grain sanding protects edges and hand rubbing stains deep into the wood grain produces the highest quality finish. Research has proven Wellborn's oven cured and melamine rich sealers and top coats to be strong and tough to last for years of beauty.

18 WellGrip Corner Brace

High impact polystyrene material resists shock and is stapled to the cabinet to produce a strong corner brace. Pilot holes prevent splitting during countertop installation and the WellGrip Corner Brace features a smooth flat surface to provide a secure level bond to countertop surfaces. This material is proven stronger than wood.

19 Unique Step Down Groove Construction

End Panels are joined to the face frame with a step down groove for added strength.

20 WellLock Shelf Clips

Positive locking shelf clips in a natural color blend with the interior. They lock shelves in place to prevent tipping and are simple to release to adjust shelf height.

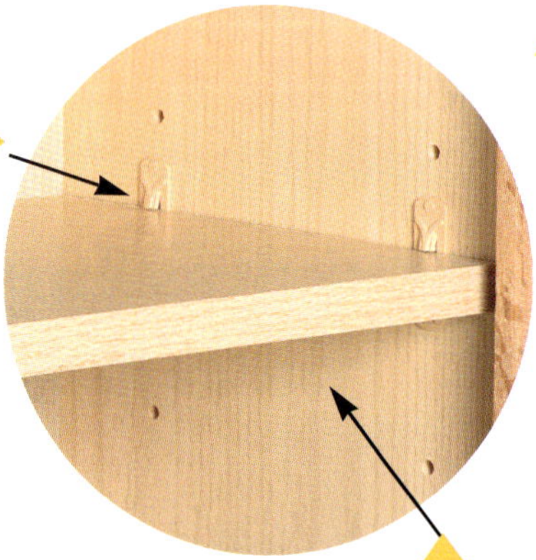

21 Natural Wood Grain Laminated Interior

Laminated interiors are easy-to-wipe clean and resistant to most household chemicals. Enjoy the natural wood grain interior look and eliminate shelf paper forever.

22 WellLine Hinges

Hinges can be adjusted both vertically and horizontally to maintain perfect alignment and carry a Lifetime Warranty.

5 year limited warranty

Lifetime limited warranty
• Solid Wood Drawers •
• Drawer Guides •
• Door Hinges •

National Kitchen NKBA & Bath Association

Kitchen Cabinet KCMA Manufacturers Association

WELLBORN CABINET, INC.
38669 Hwy 77 • P.O. Box 1210
Ashland, Alabama 36251
(205) 354-7151 • Fax (205) 354-7022

The Finishing Touches

C561
15410/OPE
BuyLine 6942

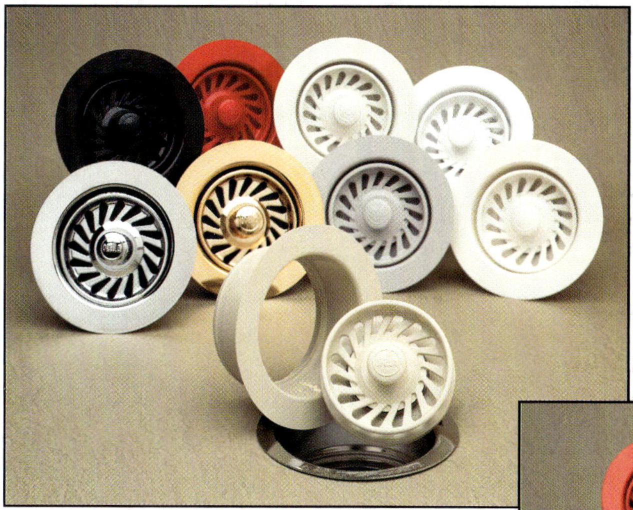

Disposer Waste Assembly: DWA

Color coordinate your kitchen decor with these designer kitchen accessories made of Celcon®, guaranteed not to crack, chip or peel.

Strainer Waste Assembly: STW

Soap Lotion Dispenser: SLD

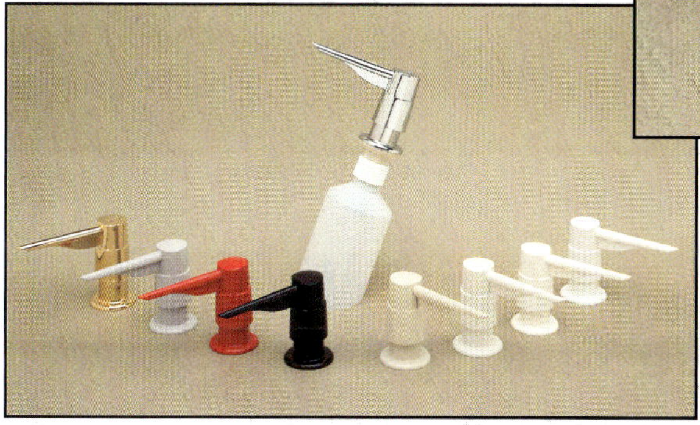

Remote Control Strainers: STR 1 or STR 2

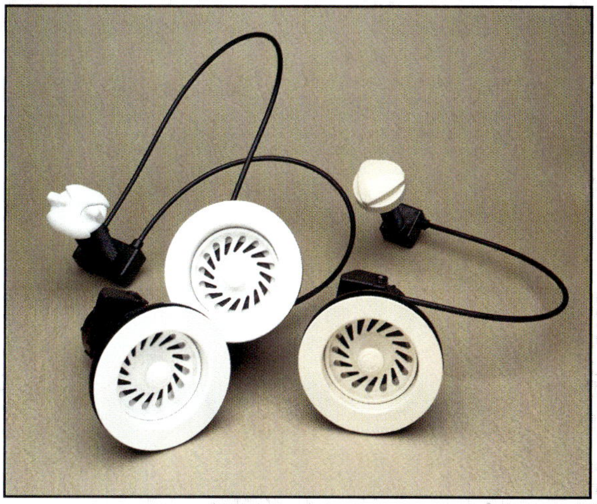

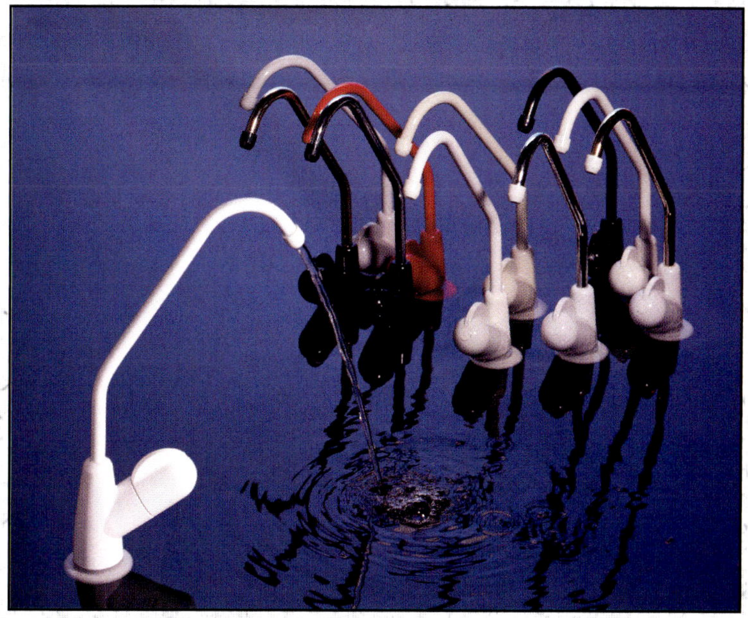

Drinking Dispenser Faucet: DDF
Also available: DDF with an Air Gap: ADF

Also available for the complete kitchen or bath: Pop-up Waste, Air Gap, Hole Covers, Sprayer Hose, Aerators and more.

OPELLA, Inc. For information on our complete line, call us at (800) 969-0339 Fax (800) 867-3552

This sleek contemporary European designed faucet makes a bold statement in any surrounding. Our solid brass kitchen or bar faucet with single lever hot and cold cartridge will provide years of dependable service and is available with a matching solid brass sprayer.

OPELLA®

SUPERGRIF

Arcadia Kitchen

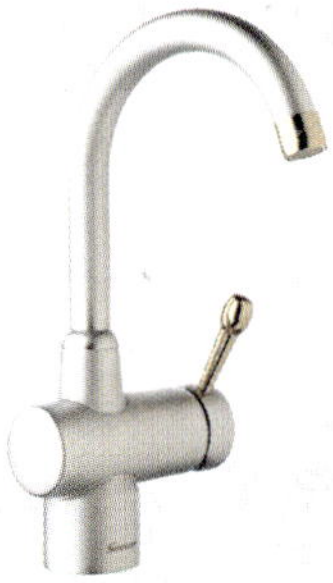

Arcadia Bar

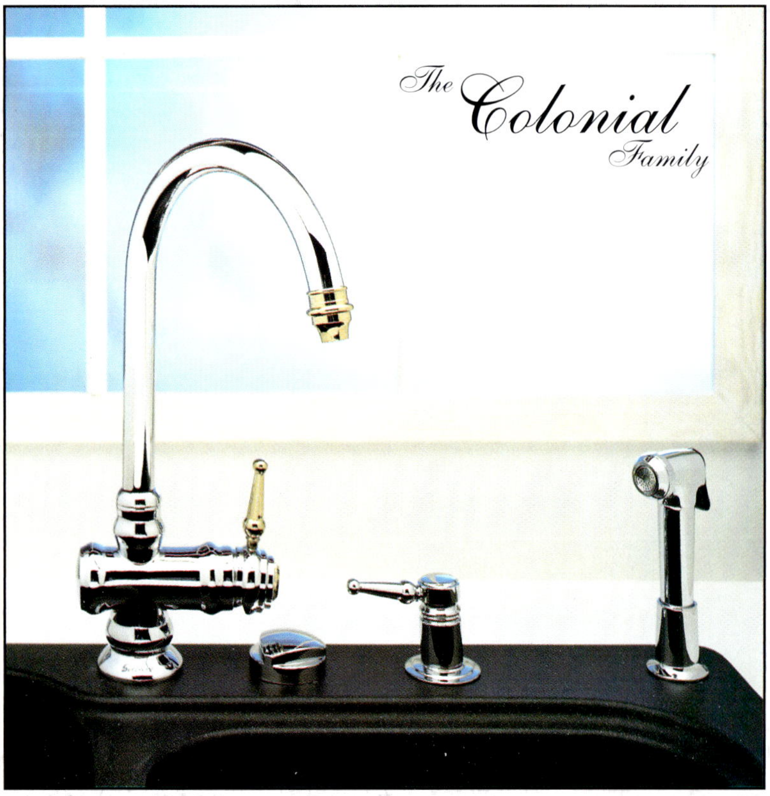

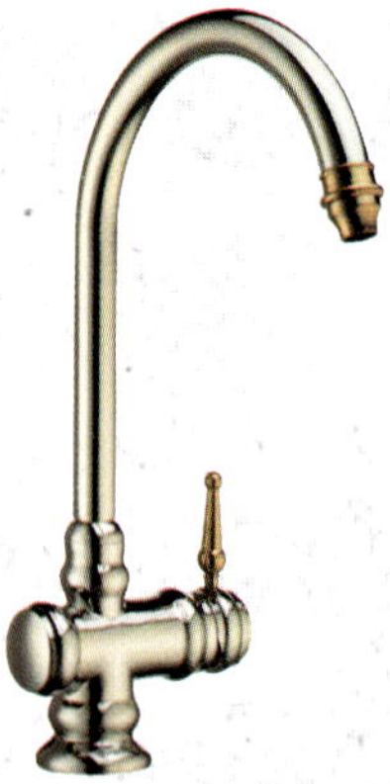

Colonial Kitchen

Colonial Bar

Classic elegance to complement any decor with the old world style of the Colonial family. These single lever hot and cold, bar and kitchen faucets are offered in 12 different finishes and are available with matching soap lotion dispenser and sprayer.

C564B

® 15426/MOG

BuyLine 0751

MOEN®

Buy it for looks. Buy it for life.®

PureTouch™

The Filtering Faucet System

Great Tasting Filtered Water
With Just One Touch™

PureTouch™

The Filtering System Reduces Impurities

Fresh, great tasting water with just the push of a button. The PureTouch filtering system is the latest innovation in water filter technology. In fact, its replaceable MicroTech filter cartridge was designed by Culligan®, the leader in water quality. This advanced filtering cartridge effectively reduces common impurities and delivers great tasting, cleaner water on demand.

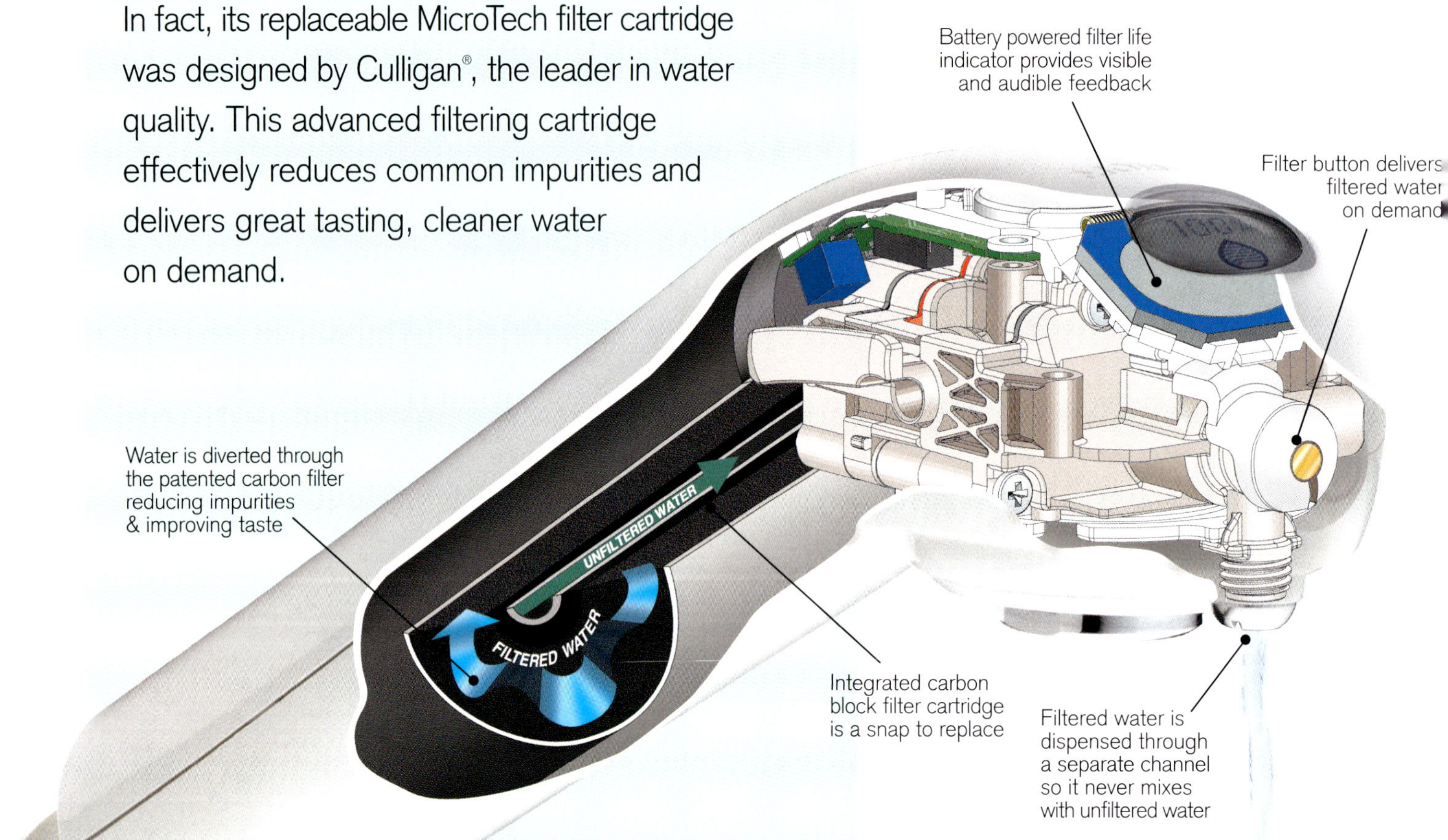

Comes Complete with MicroTech 5000 Filter

- Removes Chlorine (93.3%)
- Removes lead (99.5%)
- Removes Cryptosporidium & Giardia (99.98%)
- Does not remove beneficial fluoride
- Improves taste, reduces odor
- Each cartridge filters approximately 200 Gallons (3 months average use)

Nearly three out of four Americans are concerned about the taste and smell of their drinking water. Source: The Water Quality Association's 1997 National Consumer Water Quality Survey

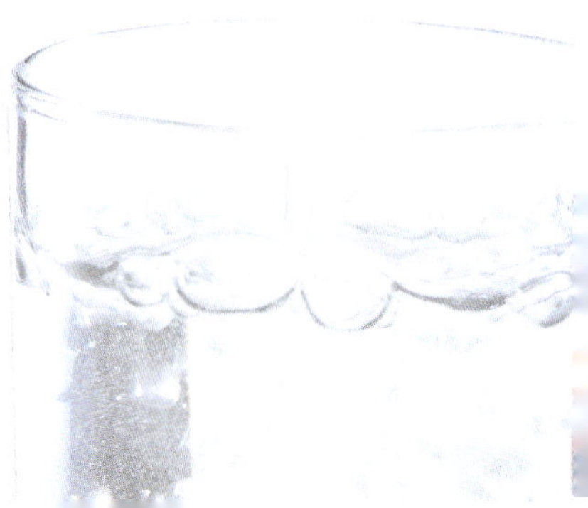

MOEN®
Buy it for looks. Buy it for life.®

• Improves Taste • Eliminates Odors

C564B
15426/MOG
BuyLine 0751

Filters Water Instantly Right From The Tap

- Delivers great tasting, cleaner water on demand
- Select either filtered or unfiltered water flow

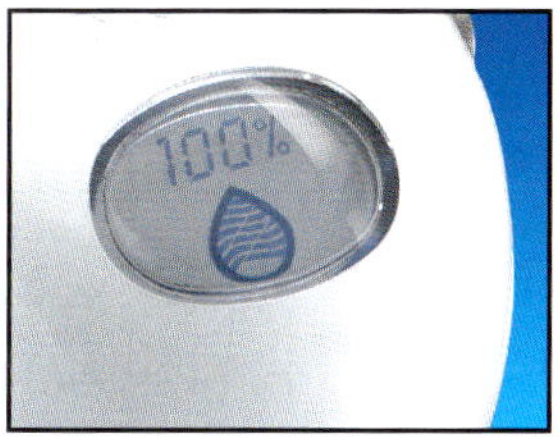

Electronic Filter Life Indicator

- Provides visual and audible feedback
- Indicates remaining filter life
- Shows water is being filtered
- Monitors battery strength

MicroTech™ Filter Cartridge

- Patented Culligan® carbon block filter traps impurities
- Three filter options available (see box below)
- Improves the taste of water for drinking and cooking
- Economical and convenient
- Does not remove beneficial fluoride

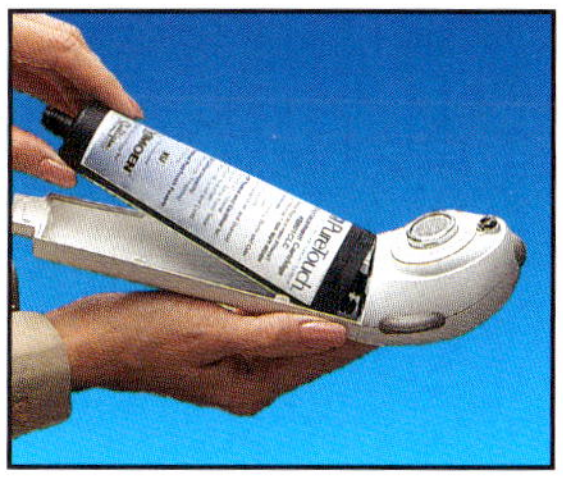

Easy-To-Change Filter Cartridge

- Quick and simple replacement
- Snaps into place
- Average filter life of 3 months

MicroTech Replacement Filter Options

MicroTech 1000 Filter Cartridge
Reduces chlorine taste and odor

MicroTech 3000 Filter Cartridge
Also reduces lead

MicroTech 5000 Filter Cartridge
All the benefits of MicroTech 3000 **plus** reduces cysts (cryptosporidium and giardia)

The contaminants or other substances removed or reduced by this filter are not necessarily in all users' water.

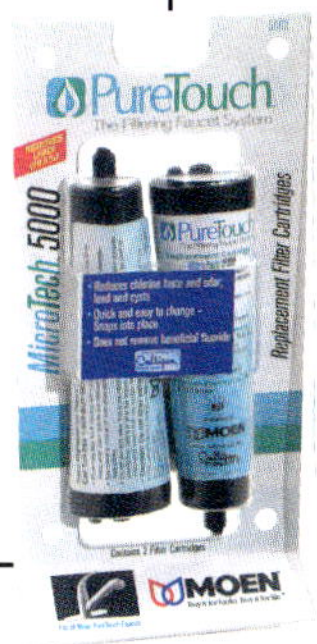

Replacements available in single and two packs

PureTouch™

The Faucet Designer Styling • Adde

Sleek lines create a style never before seen in a kitchen faucet. With its contoured pullout spout, the PureTouch filtering system is easy to hold and easy to use. The tapered spout puts control right at the user's fingertips.

- Beautiful designer styling complements any decor
- Pullout spout with flexible hose for easy cleaning and filling large containers
- Spray pattern option for rinsing vegetables or cleaning up around the sink
- Tapered spout fits hand comfortably
- Smooth surfaces for easy cleaning

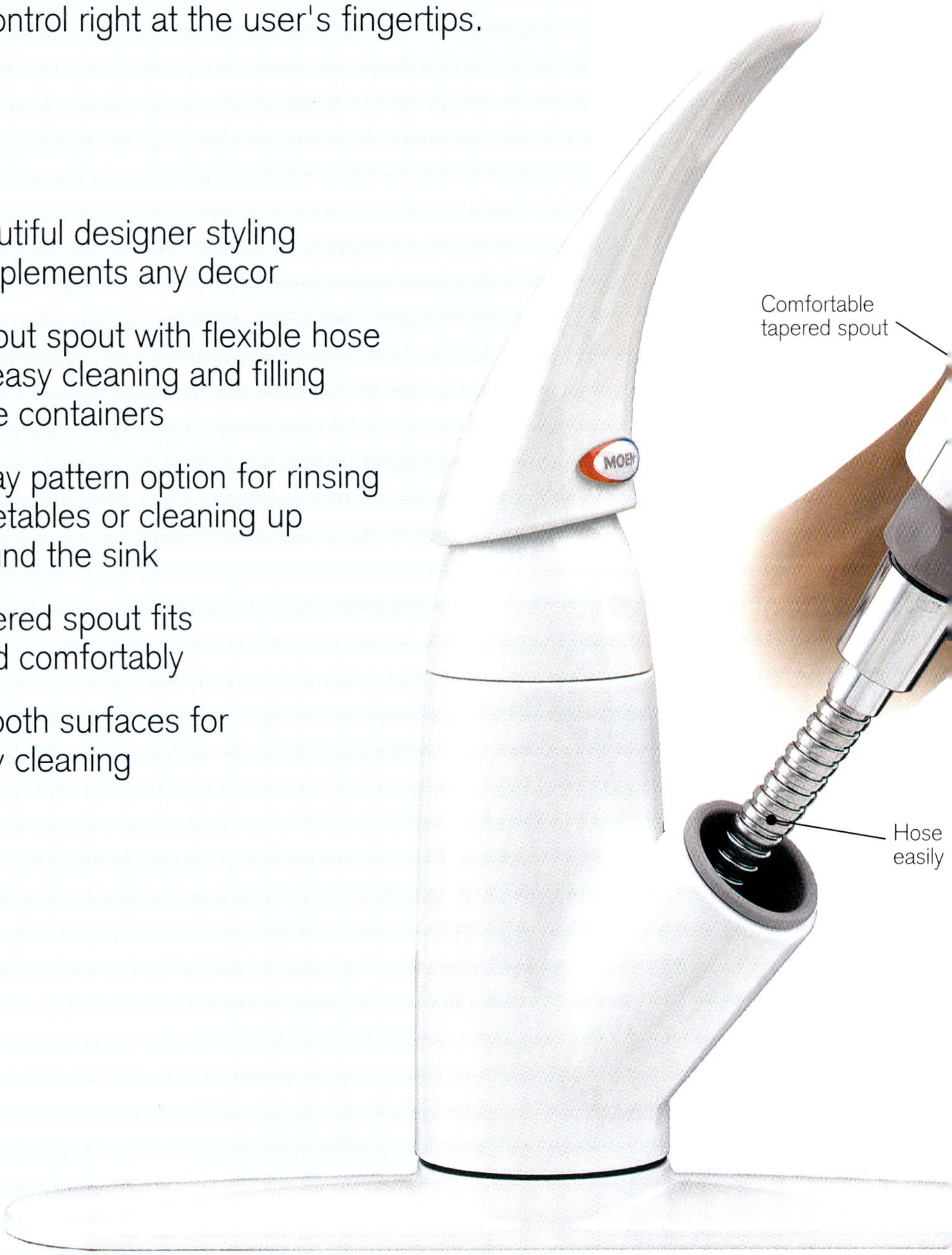

Even if water leaving a utility meets Clean Water Act standards, by the time it reaches the homeowner's tap it may have picked up lead and other contaminants.

Buy it for looks. Buy it for life.®

C564B
15426/MOG
BuyLine 0751

Convenience • Versatile Performance

Convenient 3-Way Operation

Aerated Stream
For everyday kitchen use

Wide Forceful Spray
Makes kitchen cleanup fast

Filtered Water
Common impurities reduced

PureTouch™

The Filtering Faucet System

Product Models

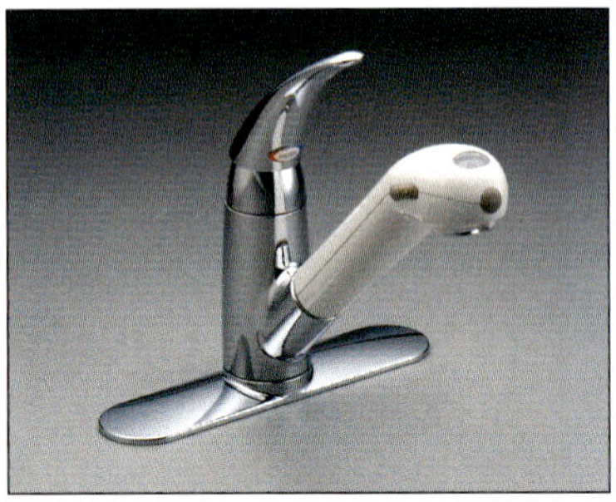

PureTouch 7850

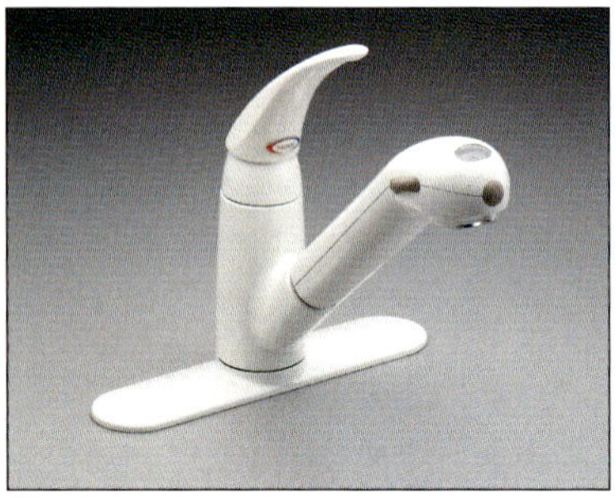

PureTouch 7850W

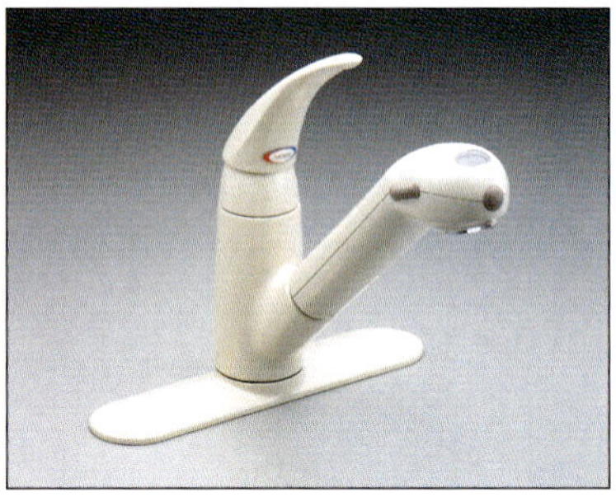

PureTouch 7850S

Tested and Certified by NSF

Products bearing the NSF International mark are tested and certified to applicable national consensus standards and comply with many stringent requirements.

MicroTech **5000** filter cartridges have been tested and certified by NSF to ANSI/NSF Standard 53 for lead reduction (99.5% at 8.5 pH) and cyst reduction (99.98%) and ANSI/NSF Standard 42, Class 1 for chlorine reduction (93.3%) and taste and odor reduction.

Filtering Technology by Culligan® Water for life.™

Culligan Filter Technology

The *MicroTech* replaceable carbon block filters are designed and manufactured by Culligan®, America's leader in water quality.

MOEN®

Buy it for looks. Buy it for life.®

Moen Incorporated
25300 Al Moen Drive
North Olmsted, Ohio 44070-8022
1-800-BUY-MOEN
Visit our website at www.moen.com

MF-2673-1/98-75M-GLL

MOEN®
Buy it for looks. Buy it for life.®

C564B
15426/MOG
BuyLine 0751

Featuring the NEW LifeShine™ Finish

The New Look For Today's Lifestyles

INTRODUCING MONTICELLO® FAUCETS FOR THE KITCHEN

7700 Series

MONTICELLO®

WITH CATHEDRAL™ SPOUT

7730W. Glacier faucet with designer hose spray.

C564B
15426/MOG
BuyLine 0751

Innovation and Elegance...Designed into Every Faucet

The Monticello with Cathedral Spout represents an artistic blend of style and function. Its graceful curves make a dramatic statement. With its compelling array of innovative features and functions, it sets a new standard for kitchen convenience.

Dramatic Style with Function and Convenience

Cathedral 11" Spout
No more struggling with pitchers, planters or over-sized pots. Our graceful 11" spout gives consumers the height and reach they need for most kitchen jobs.

Designer Hose Spray
Our new hose spray is designed to feel natural and comfortable in your hand while it delivers a forceful spray pattern for quick cleaning and rinsing.

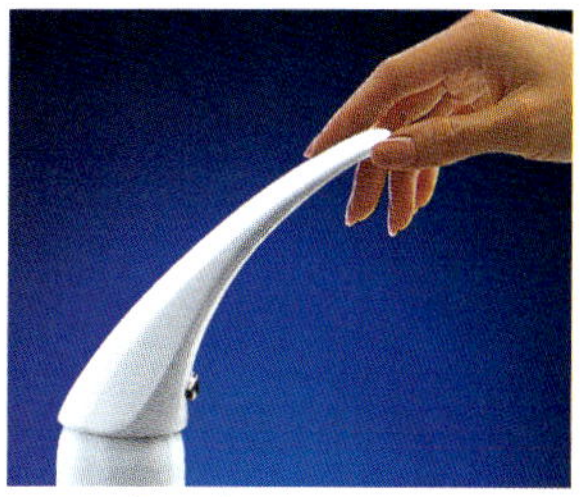

Smooth and Precise Handle Control
The elegant, natural shape of the handle allows smooth, fingertip control. Hot and cold indicators are provided for easy temperature reference.

- *Cathedral 11" high & 10" reach Spout*
- *Designer Hose Spray*
- *Smooth and Precise Handle Control*
- *Easier to Clean Smooth, Curved Surfaces*
- NEOPERL® *Features Neoperl Cascade® Aeration*
- *Stylish Aerator*
- *Up to 2" Thick Deck Installation*
- *Durable Copper and Brass Components*
- *Washerless Moen 1225® Cartridge*
- *Loop and Solid Handle Options*
- *Lifetime Limited Warranty*

LIFE SHINE™ Finish

Won't tarnish. Guaranteed for Life.
Your faucet will have the shine of a lifetime if it's a Moen faucet with the LifeShine finish. Because of the LifeShine finish, your faucet won't tarnish, corrode, or discolor, and can be cleaned with most household cleaners. Based on the advanced technology used to protect the space station, Moen's LifeShine is the only finish developed with NASA specifically to stand up to years of faucet use.

7730P. Polished Brass finish faucet with hose spray.

7730. Chrome faucet with designer hose spray.

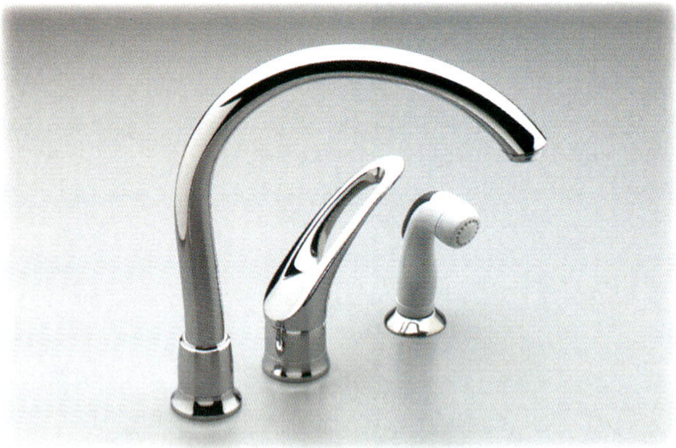

7750. Chrome loop-handle faucet with designer hose spray.

7750W. Glacier loop-handle faucet with designer hose spray.

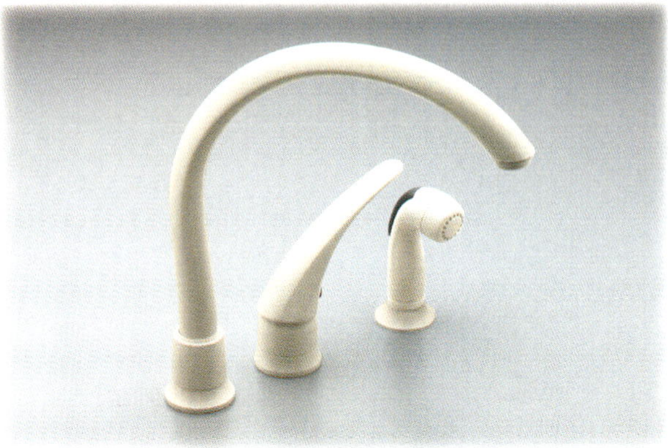

7730S. Sand faucet with designer hose spray.

7630P. Polished Brass finish faucet with designer hose spray.
7630. Chrome faucet with designer hose spray. (not shown)

7630CP. Chrome/Polished Brass designer hose spray.

7652. Chrome loop-handle faucet with designer hose spray.
7652W. Glacier loop-handle faucet with designer hose spray. (not shown)

7637. Chrome faucet with desigr
7637W. Glacier faucet with desig
(not shown)

C564B
15426/MOG
BuyLine 0751

Designed for Homeowners Who Demand More

Monticello®

7600 Series

7645. Chrome loop-handle faucet.

Monticello has been designed with the decorating style and functional features that make it easy for homeowners who demand more. These faucets make life easier in the kitchen while complementing any decor with their sleek elegance.

A Complete Package of Function and Convenience

Longer-Reach 10" Spout
Our elegant and sleek 10" spout reaches all bowls of even the largest sinks.

Stylish Aerator
Our streamline aerator enhances the sleek beauty of our faucets.

Designer Hose Spray
Our new hose spray is designed to feel natural and comfortable in your hand while it delivers a forceful spray pattern for quick cleaning and rinsing.

- *Longer-Reach 10" Spout*
- *Designer Hose Spray*
- *Smooth and Precise Handle Control*
- *Easier to Clean Smooth, Curved Surfaces*
- *Single-Bolt Installation*
- *Stylish Aerator*
- *Durable Copper and Brass Components*
- *Washerless Moen 1225® Cartridge*
- *Loop and Solid Handle Options*
- *Lifetime Limited Warranty*

th

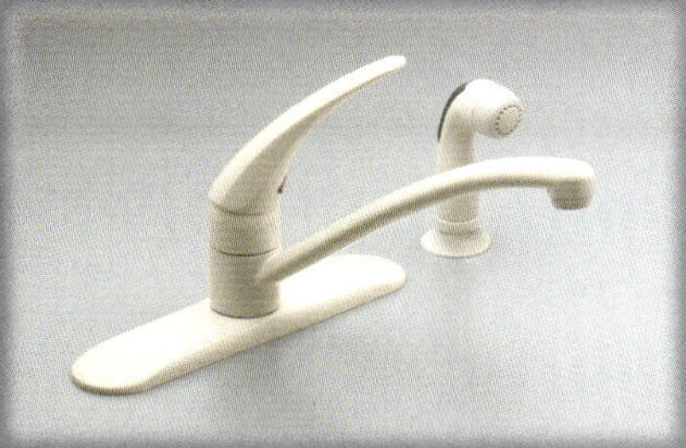

7630S. Sand faucet with designer hose spray.
7630W. Glacier faucet with designer hose spray. (not shown)

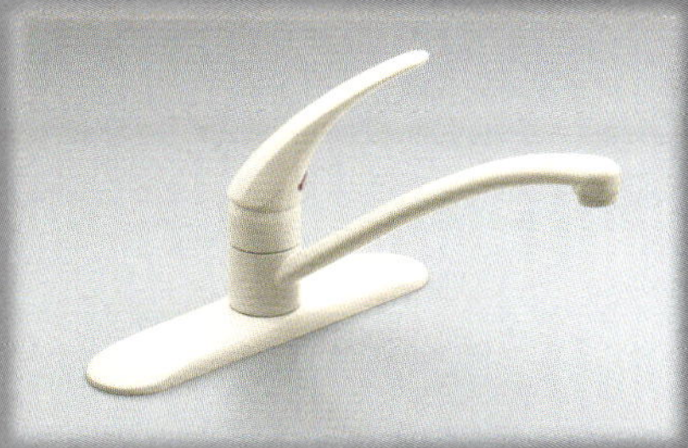

7625S. Sand faucet.
7625W. Glacier faucet.(not shown)
7625. Chrome faucet.(not shown)

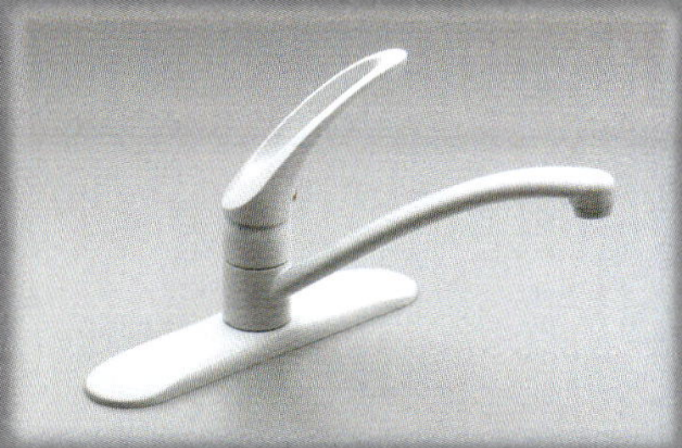

7645W. Glacier loop-handle faucet.
7645. Chrome loop-handle faucet. (not shown)

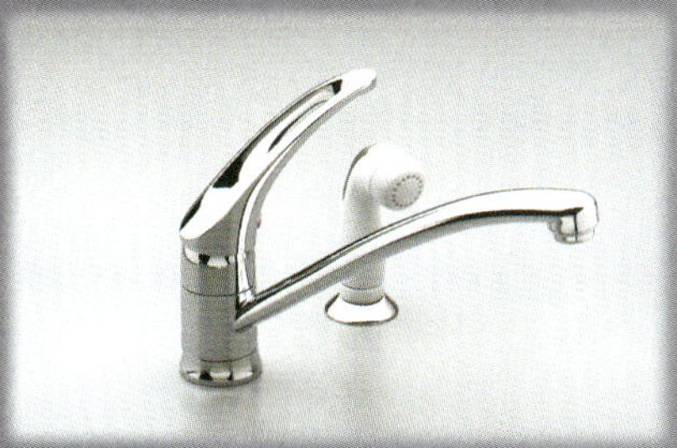

7657. Chrome single-mount, loop-handle faucet with designer hose spray.

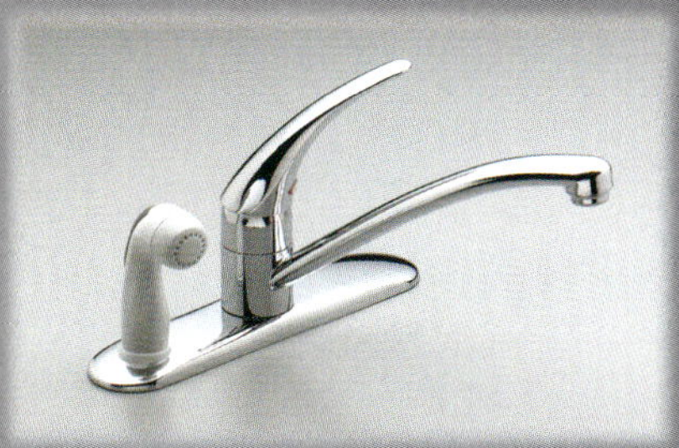

7634. Chrome faucet with designer hose spray in deck plate.

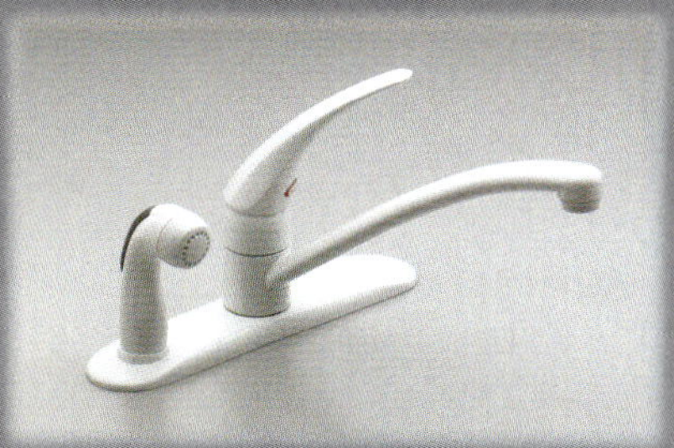

7634W. Glacier faucet with designer hose spray in deck plate.
7634S. Sand faucet with designer hose spray in deck plate. (not shown)

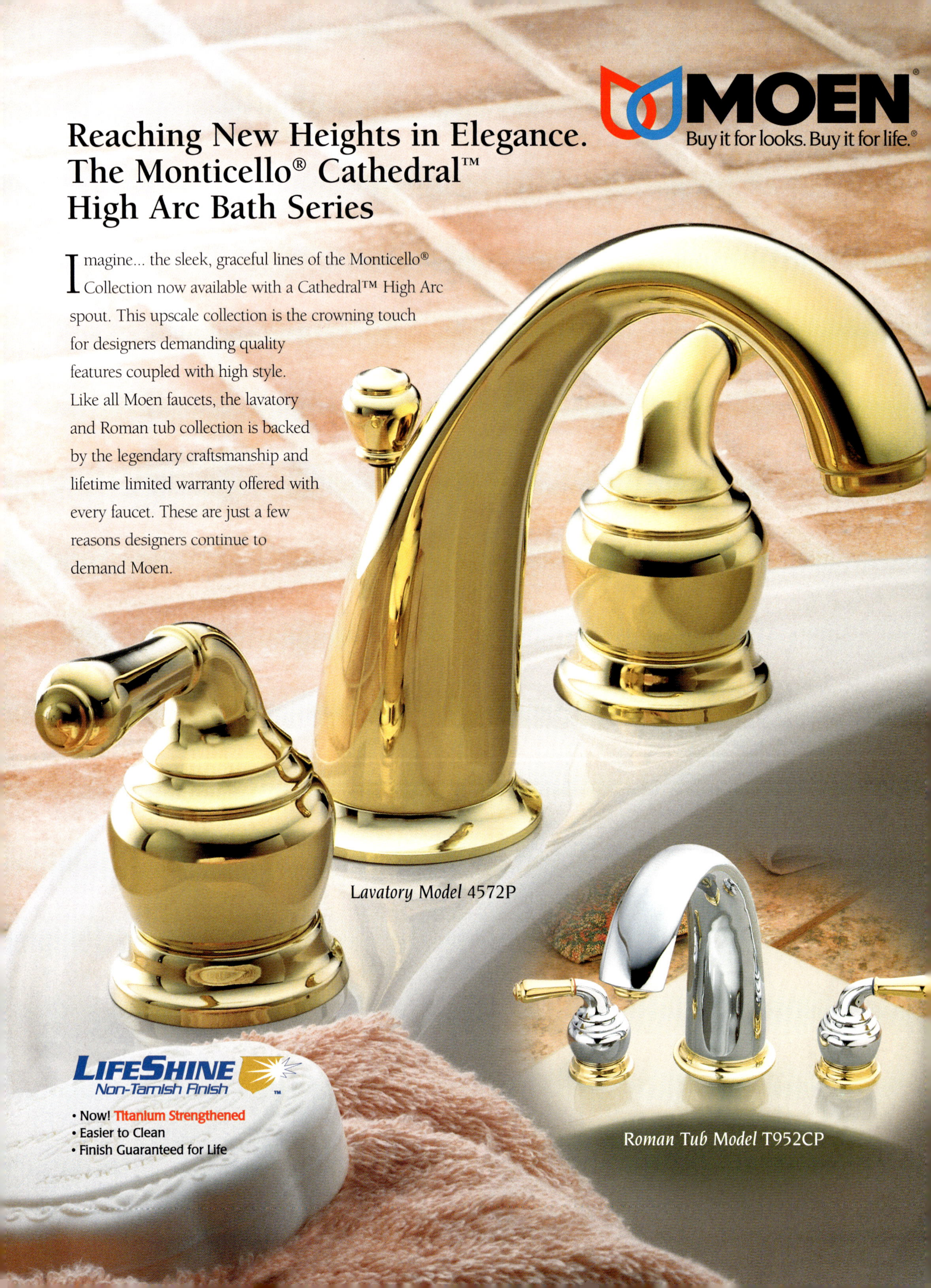
MOEN®
Buy it for looks. Buy it for life.®
Reaching New Heights in Elegance.
The Monticello® Cathedral™
High Arc Bath Series
Imagine... the sleek, graceful lines of the Monticello® Collection now available with a Cathedral™ High Arc spout. This upscale collection is the crowning touch for designers demanding quality features coupled with high style. Like all Moen faucets, the lavatory and Roman tub collection is backed by the legendary craftsmanship and lifetime limited warranty offered with every faucet. These are just a few reasons designers continue to demand Moen.
Lavatory Model 4572P
Roman Tub Model T952CP
LIFESHINE Non-Tarnish Finish™
• Now! Titanium Strengthened
• Easier to Clean
• Finish Guaranteed for Life

C565A
15410/ACM
BuyLine 3015
One of the most dramatic shower scenes since "Psycho."
Peninsula/right angle shower enclosure
Total installation time: 1 hour 50 minutes
Economical, easy-installing glass block shower enclosures from
IBP glass block grid system™
WINDOWS
WALLS • SKYLIGHTS • FLOORS
DOORS
SHOWERS

Turn corners. Turn heads. All without mortar or costly labor.

Execute breathtaking shower designs with the IBP Glass Block Grid System™.

Glass block adds drama to any shower enclosure, but the difficulties of conventional mortared installation often add extra costs and occasional callbacks as well. Now for the first time, these exciting accents are as practical as they are beautiful—with IBP Glass Block Grid System Shower Enclosures.

The IBP shower enclosure system replaces mortar with a combination of three elements:

- a precision-engineered aluminum grid
- closed-cell foam tape around each block
- Dow Corning TradeMate™ silicone sealant

Together, these elements provide a degree of versatility, strength, and safety unmatched by other glass block installation methods. By eliminating the need for highly skilled trades, the system also saves builders money.

IBP technology has been proven in more than 45,000 window, wall, floor, door, and skylight installations. In adapting the grid system for shower enclosures, IBP's design team has developed a number of features that allow easy attachment to a standard shower curb (see back page) using standard construction methods:

Notice the dramatic difference that an IBP Shower Enclosure adds to the corner of a bath.

- **Aluminum corner extrusions in 22½° increments:** These corner pieces easily snap together with aluminum grid wall sections to produce a clean, symmetrical joint without mortar or grout. You can construct corners of 22½°, 45°, 67½°, and 90° with ease.

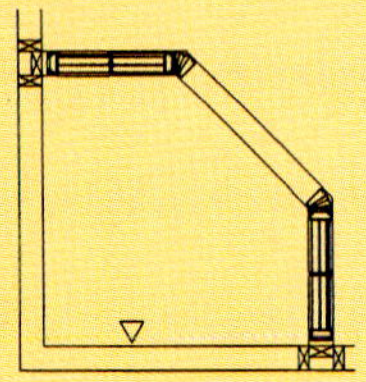

corner/neo-angle

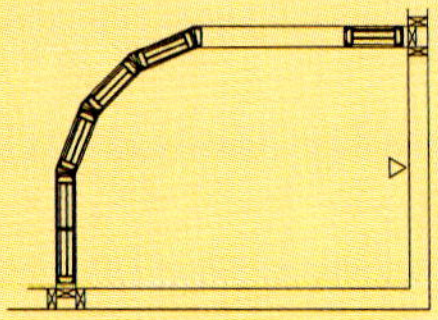

corner/radius

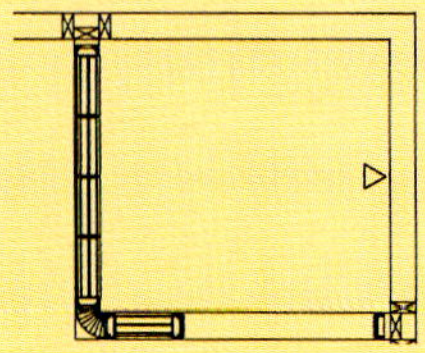

corner/right angle

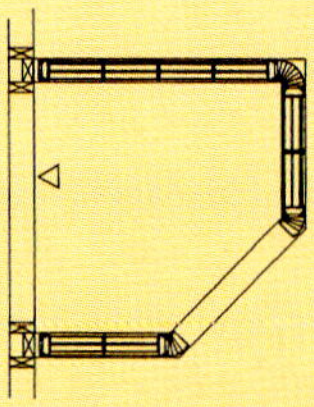

peninsula/neo-angle

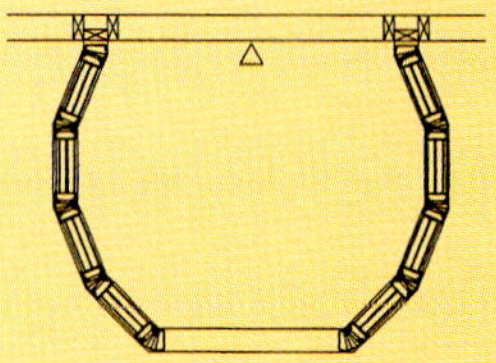

peninsula/radius

Even for designs like the buttress-style enclosure pictured below, IBP shower installations are simple. They call only for common tools and conventional construction skills—which saves money and reduces the chance of callbacks.

- **Flush aluminum finishing pieces that encase the grid system:** This innovative feature allows for easy shower door attachment and simple installation to adjoining walls and shower bases.
- **Glass block door headers that eliminate the need for lintels:** Conventional glass block shower enclosures are typically designed without headers, which usually entails some trade-off between support and appearance. IBP's unique header design is self-supporting.

The result is a watertight, aesthetically pleasing, virtually callback-free installation—often accomplished in two hours or less.

Total installation time is approximately two hours. To complete your decorative scheme, IBP also offers matching glass block window grids.

Choose colors and patterns to complement any decor.

The grid system and corner extrusions are available in white, black, red, gold, and silver finishes. However, with six weeks' advance notice, IBP can custom-match your color sample.

A wide selection of glass block patterns and colors provides design choices to strike the perfect balance of ambiance and privacy.

Another benefit of the grid system is that you can easily view different combinations of glass block colors and patterns before siliconing the installation. Also, block can be removed and replaced in the future to fit remodeling color schemes or plans.

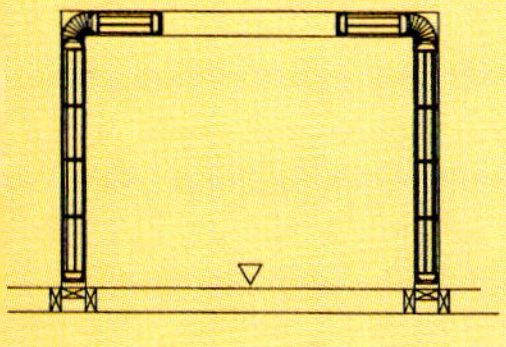

peninsula/right angle

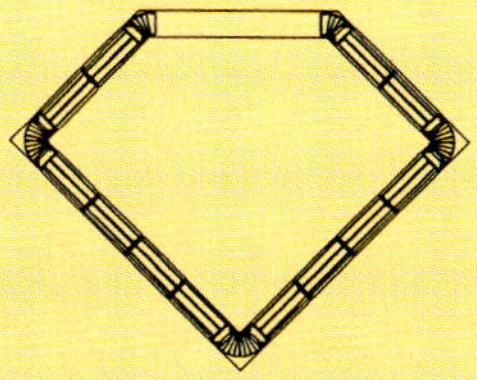

island neo-angle

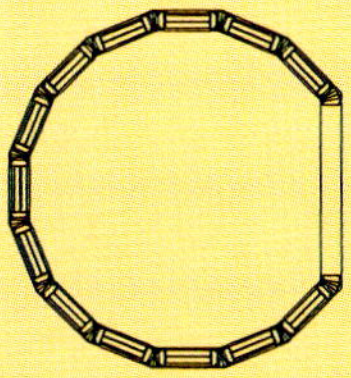

island/radius

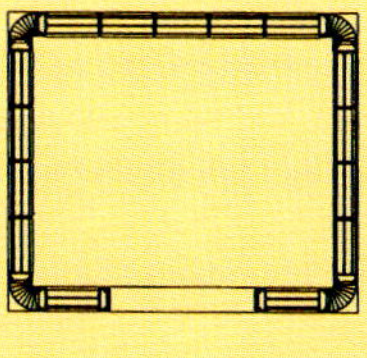

island/right angle

traditional in-line

Use IBP's technical assistance to multiply your design options.

Ten examples of typical shower installations are illustrated inside, but these are merely suggestions. The final design is literally up to you. IBP offers free design service for all Glass Block Grid System products. IBP detail drawings and installation details are also available in AutoCad® Release 12 format.

Other exciting IBP applications include skylights, windows, walls, floors, doors, and more. Simply call toll-free for additional information: **1-800-932-2263**. Add drama and economy to your next bath with the IBP Glass Block Grid System.

Zero to 90 in Seconds Flat

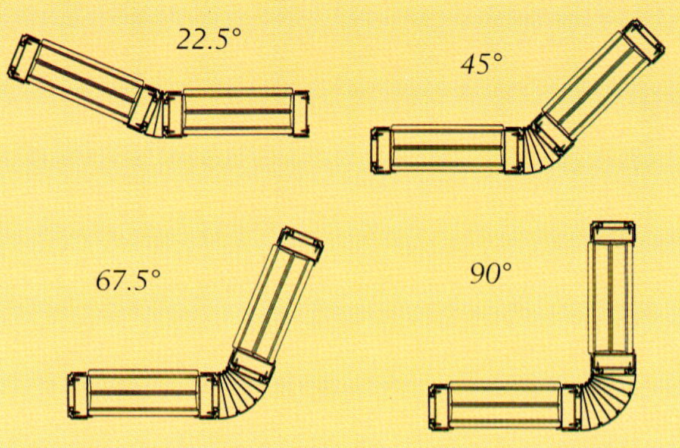

IBP corner extrusions snap together in 22.5° increments, to turn corners with precision.

Engineered for Trouble-Free Installation

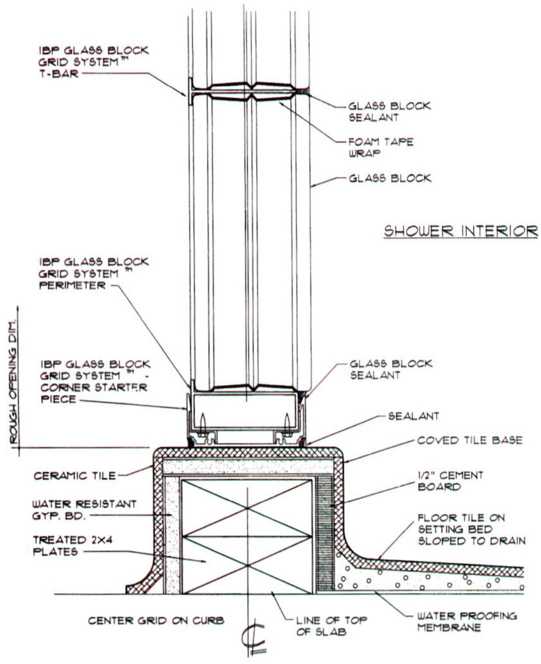

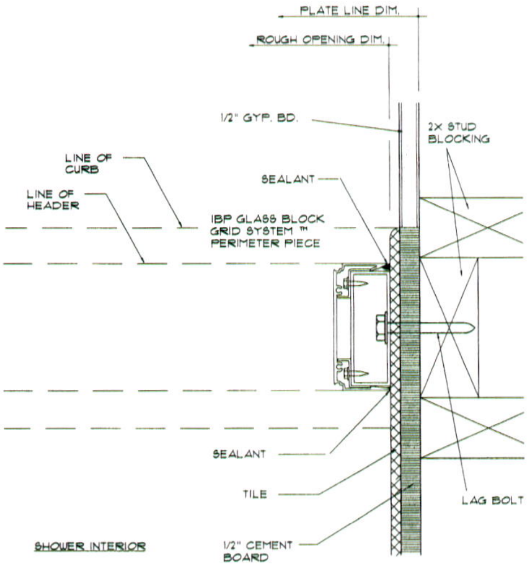

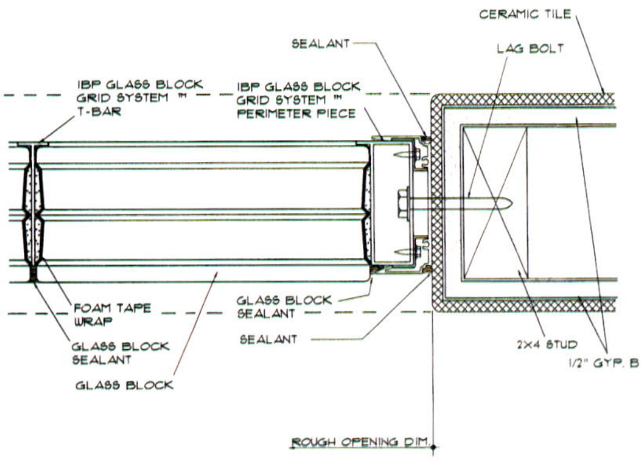

Details shown here are for shower curb (above), shower door at wall (upper right), and shower jamb at wall (right). For a complete set of detailing sheets, call 1-800-932-2263.

ACME BRICK
Since 1891

Acme Brick Company • P.O. Box 425 • Fort Worth, TX 76101 • 1-800-932-2263

IBP-SWR-A1-4/95

C566B
BuyLine 7535

The most fun you can have without a barrel.

Clarion's whirlpool and soaker tub collection offers both acrylic and fiberglass models.

President's Series acrylic models are vacuum formed from a one-piece solid sheet of cast acrylic to provide years of care free use. Each whirlpool is engineered and manufactured to meet the most demanding specifications. Clarion's acrylic is the tub of choice for many families. Clarion's gel-coated fiberglass whirlpools and soaker tubs are manufactured with the same exacting standards as our acrylic products.

Multiple laminates of fiberglass and 16-18 mills of gel-coat make our products among the strongest in the industry. All whirlpools are manufactured using custom formed PVC pipe, 3/4 H.P. motors with a 5 year warranty, and matching trim. The air control, suction outlet, and on/off switch are all factory installed. Clarion pressure water tests each whirlpool before it is delivered. A host of options such as 6 jets, brass or chrome trim, mood lites, and heaters are among some of the upgrades available for your new whirlpool.

ACRYLIC

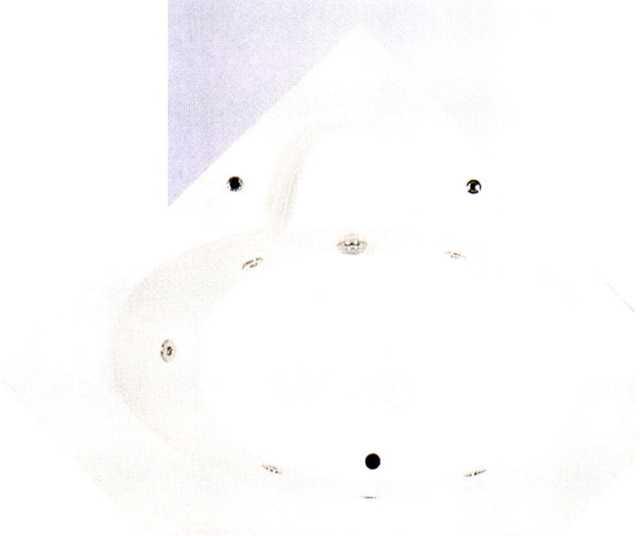

MODEL# AC6060SO
$59\frac{1}{2}$" x $59\frac{1}{2}$" x $26\frac{1}{2}$" x $26\frac{1}{2}$" x $21\frac{3}{4}$"H

VAN BUREN

ACRYLIC

MODEL# AC7236SO
$71\frac{1}{2}$"L x 36"W x $21\frac{1}{2}$"H

BUCHANON

ACRYLIC

MODEL# AC7242SO
70 3/4"L x 41 1/2"W x 21 1/2"H

LINCOLN

ACRYLIC

MODEL# AC7248SO
71 3/4"L x 47 3/4"W x 21 1/2"H

TAFT

ACRYLIC

MODEL# AC6036SO
60 1/2"L x 36"W x 21 1/2"H

WASHINGTON I

ACRYLIC

MODEL# AC6032SO
60"L x 31 3/4"W x 21 1/2"H

WASHINGTON II

Lucite XL

Clarion Bathware uses LUCITE XL cast acrylic sheet in all of its acrylic modules. LUCITE XL is beautiful, durable and will not mildew and stain. Its hard, non-porous surface is scratch resistant. Its rich colors go all the way through the thickness of the material to ensure color fastness and its high gloss finish wipes to a shine without scrubbing. LUCITE XL, easy to maintain with common household non-abrasive cleaning products, is your assurance of quality.

Freight Information

Clarion ships product on our own fleet of air-ride trailers with new tractors and company drivers. Assisted care products ship on Clarion's trucks or on any number of LTL companies contracted with CFM.

Limited Warranty

Clarion Bathware offers a Three-Year Limited Warranty against defects in material and workmanship on fiberglass and acrylic products. Whirlpool systems carry a Full Three-Year Limited Warranty.

For More Information

For sales information, service, technical support or ordering information call your Clarion Bathware distributor or the corporate office below.

CFM, Inc.

Corporate and Sales Office

Clarion Bathware

205 Amsler Avenue
Shippenville, PA 16254

Phone 814-226-5374
Fax 814-226-5568

Manufacturing Plant

Clarion Bathware

Star Route Box 20
Marble, PA 16334

Phone 814-782-3011
Fax 814-782-3434

THE BOLD LOOK OF KOHLER

C574

BuyLine 0775

A BOLD LOOK AT

KITCHEN &

BATH PRODUCTS

Welcome *to the beautiful world of*

Whether you are building your dream home, remodeling or just keeping up with what is new, Kohler will get you started in the right direction. Kohler offers exciting new products, innovative designs, and a full palette of colors to match your personal style. But before you begin, there are some important factors you and your family should consider:

TABLE OF CONTENTS

4 **Suites and Collections**

8 **BodySpa Systems**

10 **Whirlpools and Baths**

12 **Showers & Enclosures**

14 **Lavatories**

16 **Artist Editions**

18 **Toilets and Bidets**

20 **Faucets, Bath and Kitchen**

22 **Kitchen and Entertainment Sinks**

On the Cover:
Memoirs 24" Pedestal Lavatory with classic design shown in Jersey Cream.

Style

What type of style are you trying to capture for your home? Traditional, contemporary, nostalgic or a little bit of everything? KOHLER suites and collections explore design themes to their fullest. Each offers fixtures, faucets and accessories with coordinated styling to bring continuity to your decor. Or, create your own look by mixing and matching complementary product lines.

Gracious Living...

Now, you're ready to continue! Sit back and enjoy this brochure. It's designed to give you an overview of the many products Kohler has to offer. For a more complete listing, please visit your nearest Kohler Registered Showroom or refer to the back cover for more information.

Size & Shape

Got a tight spot? Kohler offers a range of choices for small, medium and large kitchen and baths. However, please make sure the product you fall in love with will fit into your space requirements and especially through the front door!

Kohler also carries a wide selection of shapes and sizes. Ever see a hexagon-shaped lavatory? Flip through our Bath & Powder Room brochure and you'll find more than one.

Materials

What type of material do you prefer? Kohler offers a wide variety of premium materials such as **KOHLER** CAST IRON, vitreous china, fireclay, stainless steel, fiberglass, acrylic and many more. Our **KOHLER** CAST IRON –a premium material for plumbing fixtures–is as good as it gets! It is "fire polished" to obtain its vivid color, deep gloss,

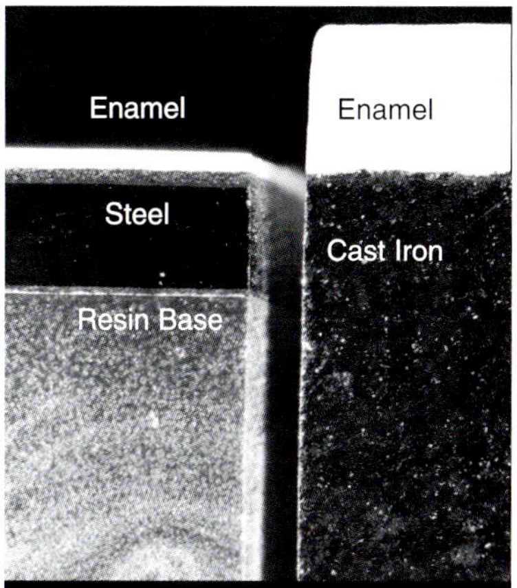

Plastic Reinforced Enameled Steel | KOHLER Cast Iron

and provides protection against chips, dents and abrasions. **KOHLER** CAST IRON construction assures long-lasting durability against everyday wear and tear. You can actually see the difference!

Color

Kohler offers the widest selection in color. Choose from soft dreamy pastels, warm neutrals, bold dramatic blues and greens, and stone textures. Any way you look at it, our colors are timeless and let you explore your creative side.

You're going to love what we can bring to your home. Discover

THE BOLD LOOK OF **KOHLER**.

A The **Memoirs™ Above-counter Lavatory** adds a contemporary edge to a traditional look. Resting above the vanity or countertop, it creates a strong visual focal point.

B The **Memoirs Collection** exudes the warmth and gentility of generations past. A selection of coordinated pieces blend to create a personal haven that welcomes you home.

SUITES AND COLLECTIONS

Fixtures, faucets and accessories styled and coordinated to bring a custom look to your decor.

C The **Folio Suite** offers a contemporary blending of lines, arcs, curves and planes, bringing a refreshing simplicity to your decor.

D The **Vintage™ Suite** combines the nostalgic look of yesterday with the technology of today. Smooth design and generous curves reflect the charm of traditional styling in **KOHLER** CAST IRON.

A The charm of traditional styling is captured in the **Portrait™ Suite**. Designed to accommodate both large and small baths.

B The **Portrait Wall-mount Lavatory** attaches to the wall at any height and is practical where space is at a premium. (Includes matching pipe shroud.)

C Unwind in the **Portrait 5' Bath Whirlpool** as five adjustable flexjets deliver waves of relaxation where you need it most. An optional removable apron provides easy access to pump.

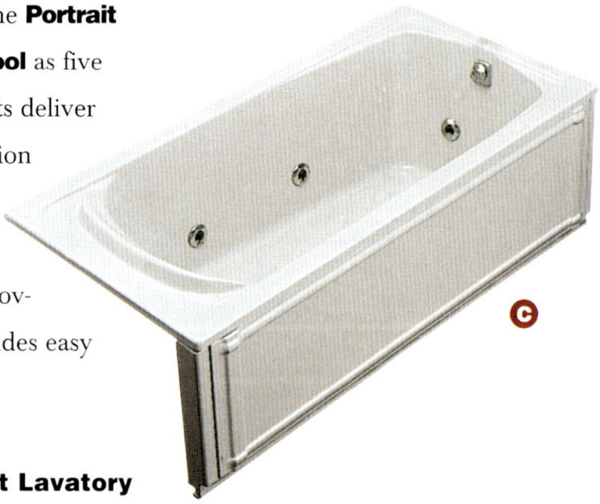

D The **Portrait Lavatory Shelf** adds the finishing touch for your Portrait Suite. $21\frac{5}{8}$" x $4\frac{3}{4}$"

E The **Portrait Self-rimming Lavatory** has a choice of 8", 4" or single-hole faucet drillings to accommodate virtually any faucet.

F The **Revival™ Collection** blends classic design with a modern viewpoint. It has an extensive selection of fixtures, faucets and accessories.

G

G The **Revival Pedestal Lavatory with Traditional Pedestal** has a wide ledge to accommodate your grooming products. It's also offered with a transitional pedestal as well.

I

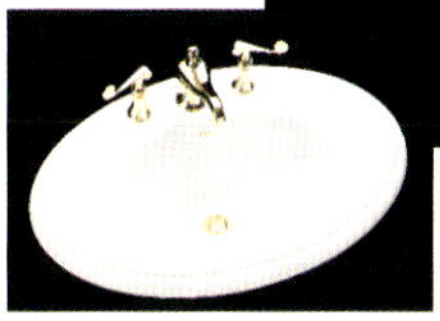

J

H The **Revival One-piece Toilet**. The **Revival Two-piece Toilet** is shown above in the set shot.

H

I Relax in the **Revival 6' Bath Whirlpool** and let its eight adjustable flexjets penetrate your tired muscles.

J The **Revival Self-rimming Lavatory** features a large rim area to minimize splashing and is made from **KOHLER** CAST IRON.

A Using less water than a 5' whirlpool, the **BodySpa™ Personal Hydro-massage System** heats, propels and recirculates every drop of water up to two times a minute. The result: up to 80 gallons per minute of supercharged hydro-power. That's more than the combined delivery of 25 standard showerheads.

BODYSPA SYSTEMS

Customize your experience with a ***Solid-State Control Panel****. Adjust the flow from a gentle stream to an ultra-intense rush of water, for just the right degree of hydro-massaging action.*

Invigoration! There is no other word to describe it! A series of whirlpool jets are arranged vertically in a shower-like enclosure. Instead of pushing water through water—as in a whirlpool, BodySpa propels it through the air. So it's just you and the force of the bodyjets.

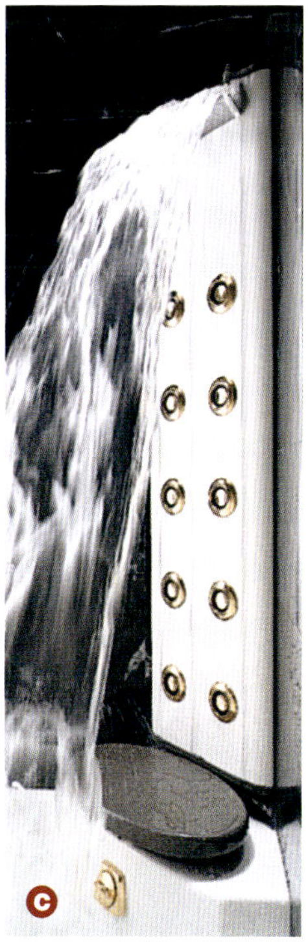

B The **BodySpa 8-Jet Tower** has six body-level jets and two head/neck-level jets that can be selected by banks, and adjusted for high or low flow. Coax tired muscles and mind back into the flow.

C The **BodySpa 10-Jet Tower** starts with a sensual, soothing waterfall cascading over your head and shoulders.

D Then activate the body-level jets. Hear the rush of the water and succumb to the pounding waves.

Stress relief. Relaxation.

Spiritual renewal.

Bring the rejuvenating effects of warmth and water into your home with KOHLER® whirlpool systems and baths.

WHIRLPOOLS AND BATHS

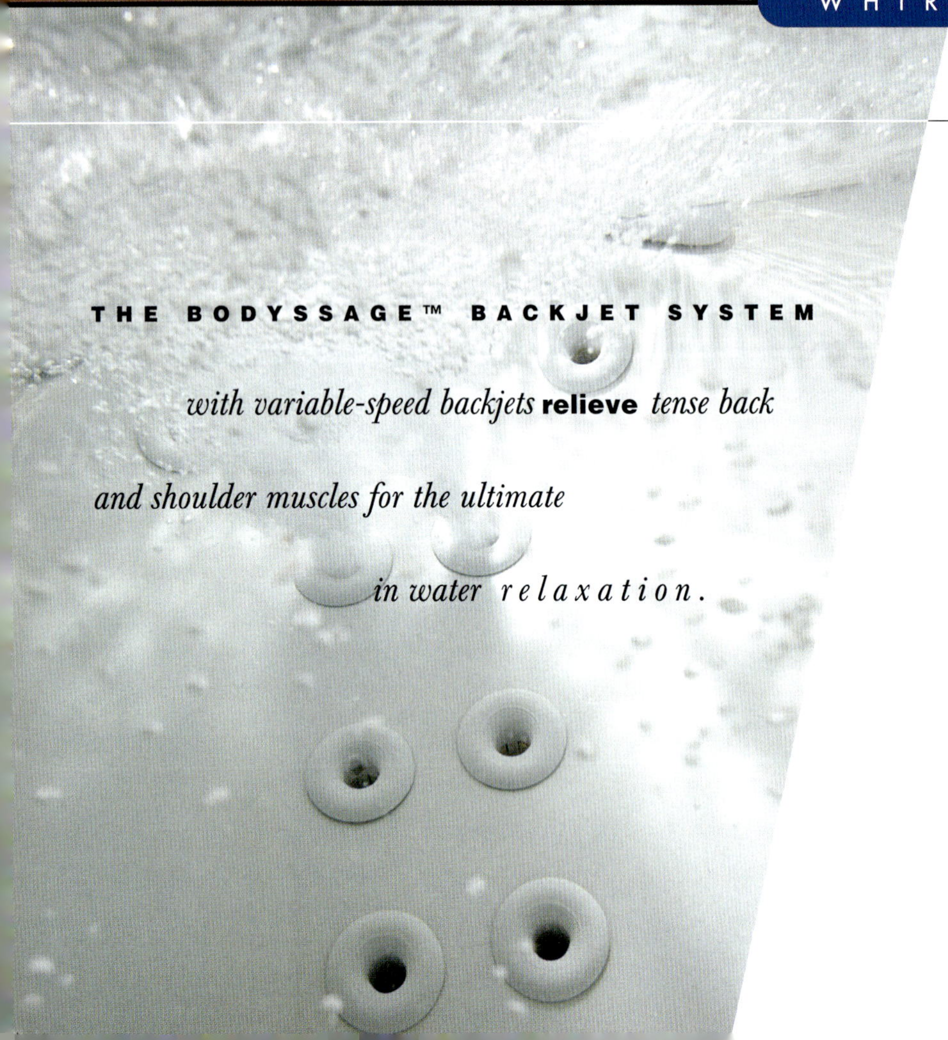

THE BODYSSAGE™ BACKJET SYSTEM

with variable-speed backjets **relieve** *tense back and shoulder muscles for the ultimate in water relaxation.*

A The **Vigora™ Whirlpool** features Bodyssage variable-speed backjets that sequence up the back and across the shoulders like the soothing hands of a master masseuse.

Muscle soreness results when acids build up in the muscle, or when muscle contraction restricts the normal flow of blood and oxygen. Massage improves circulation without putting extra strain on the heart.

C From top to bottom, the traditional **Vintage Bath** looks great either free-standing or recessed. Accent your bath with a wood base and towel rail of solid white ash in a choice of Natural Ash, Golden Oak, or Dark Walnut finish. Part of the Vintage Suite.

B With contoured armrests and lumbar back support, the 5' and 6' **Mariposa™ Whirlpools** are styled for comfort, easy-to-install and affordably priced.

D The exclusive KOHLER **Pulsating Neckjet Pillow** features two integral jets that pulse alternately from left to right at the base of the neck. A standard feature on most KOHLER System III whirlpools.

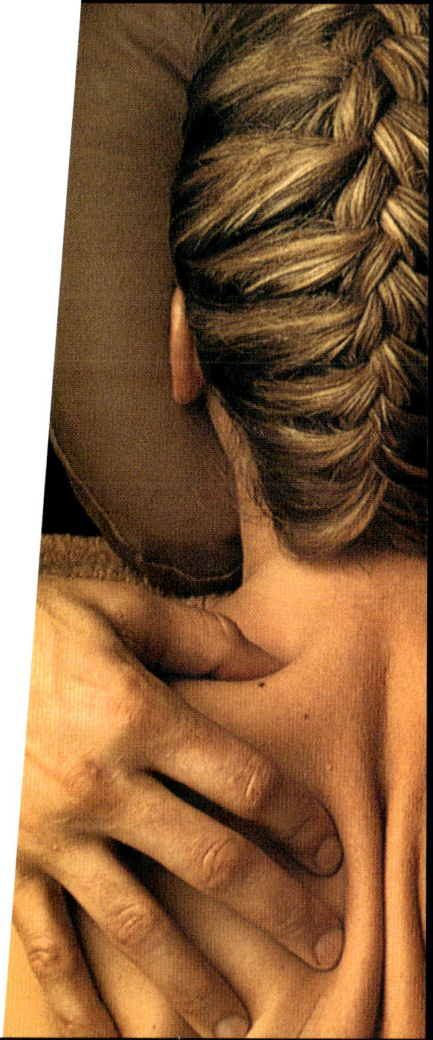

Indulge yourself with

STEAM THERAPY

Let the hectic work day melt away

as you drift to your private escape.

Feel the **warm, relaxing steam air**

penetrate your tired muscles and your soul.

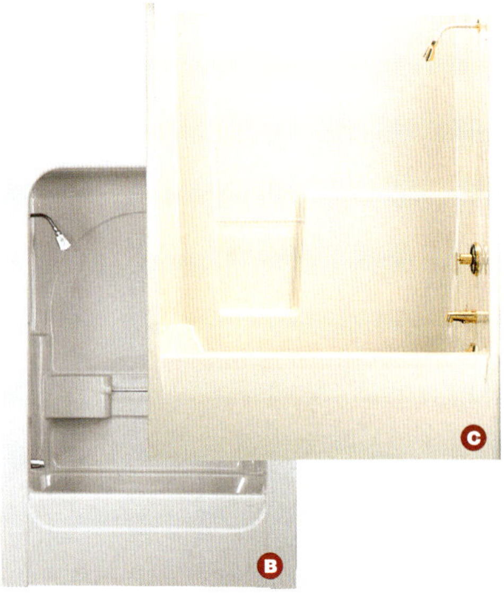

SHOWERS AND ENCLOSURES

B The **Sonata® Bath and Shower Module** is available as a single or multi-piece unit with dome ceilings, sculpted ledges and integral grab bar. Sonata can also be converted into a steam shower.

C The **Veracruz™ Bath & Shower Module** is available in a single unit for new construction or a two-piece unit for remodeling.

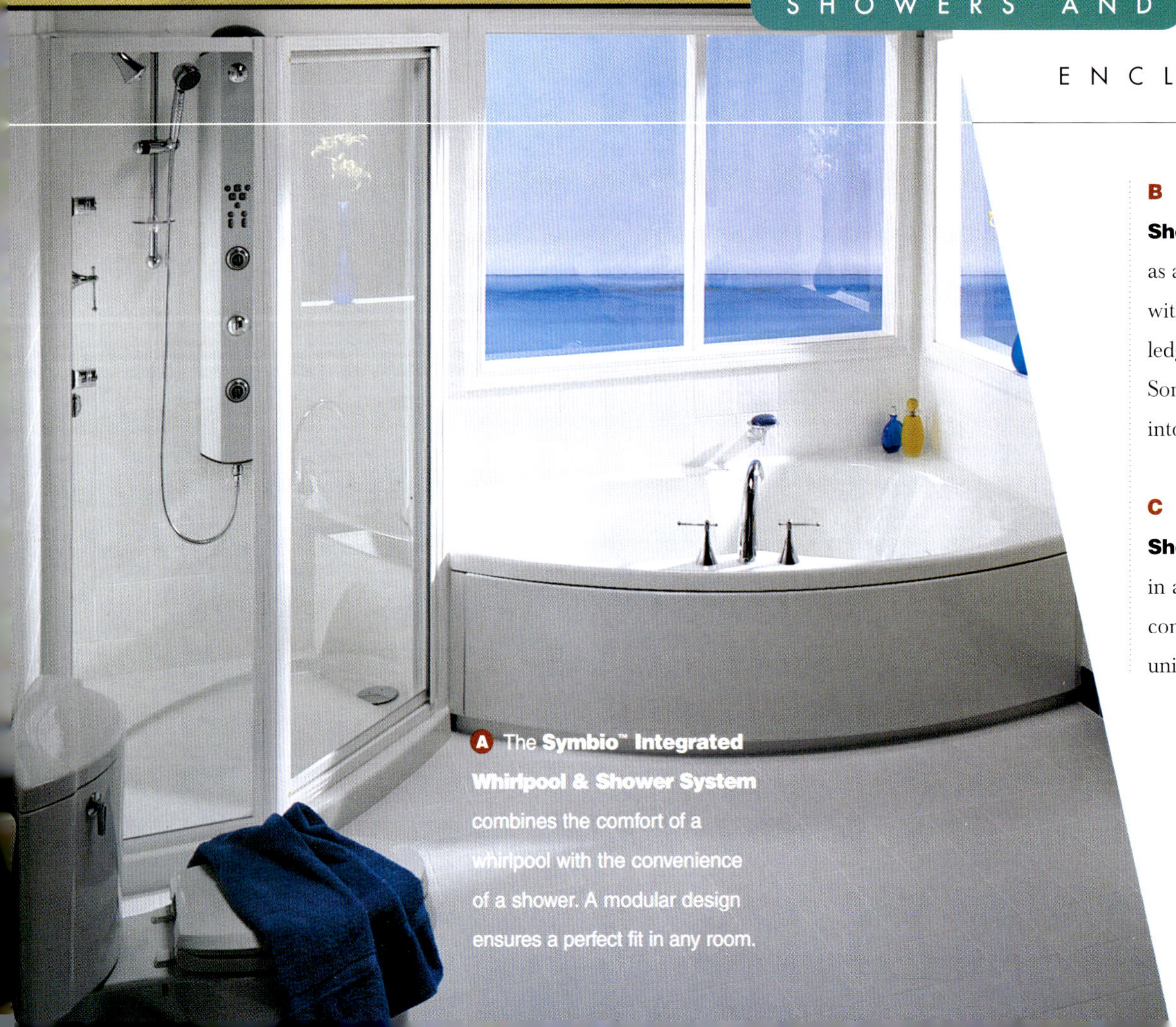

A The **Symbio™ Integrated Whirlpool & Shower System** combines the comfort of a whirlpool with the convenience of a shower. A modular design ensures a perfect fit in any room.

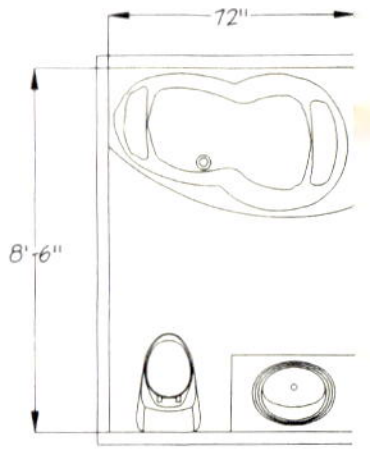

D

No longer just an addition to the bathtub, the shower is an essential part of today's active lifestyle. And no one gives you more shower choices than Kohler.

D Forum™ Bypass Shower Doors feature a detachable bottom guide for easy cleaning and an anti-derailing mechanism for added safety.

The Symbio Integrated Whirlpool & Shower System *will fit almost any bathroom, large or small. Use the whirlpool and shower components together as an integrated system, or install them independently to fit your floorplan.*

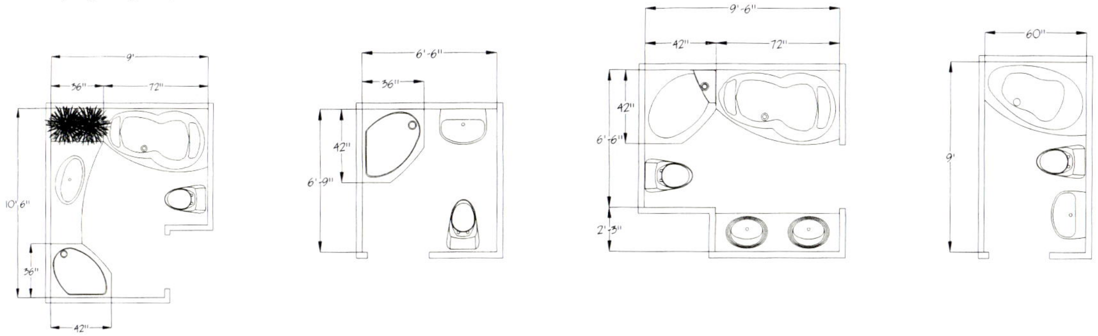

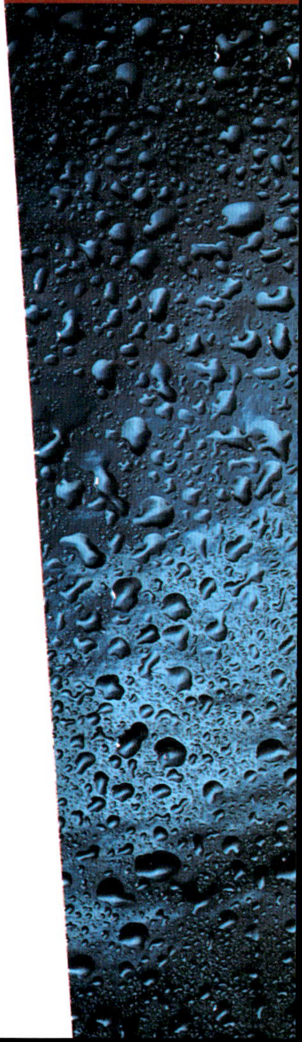

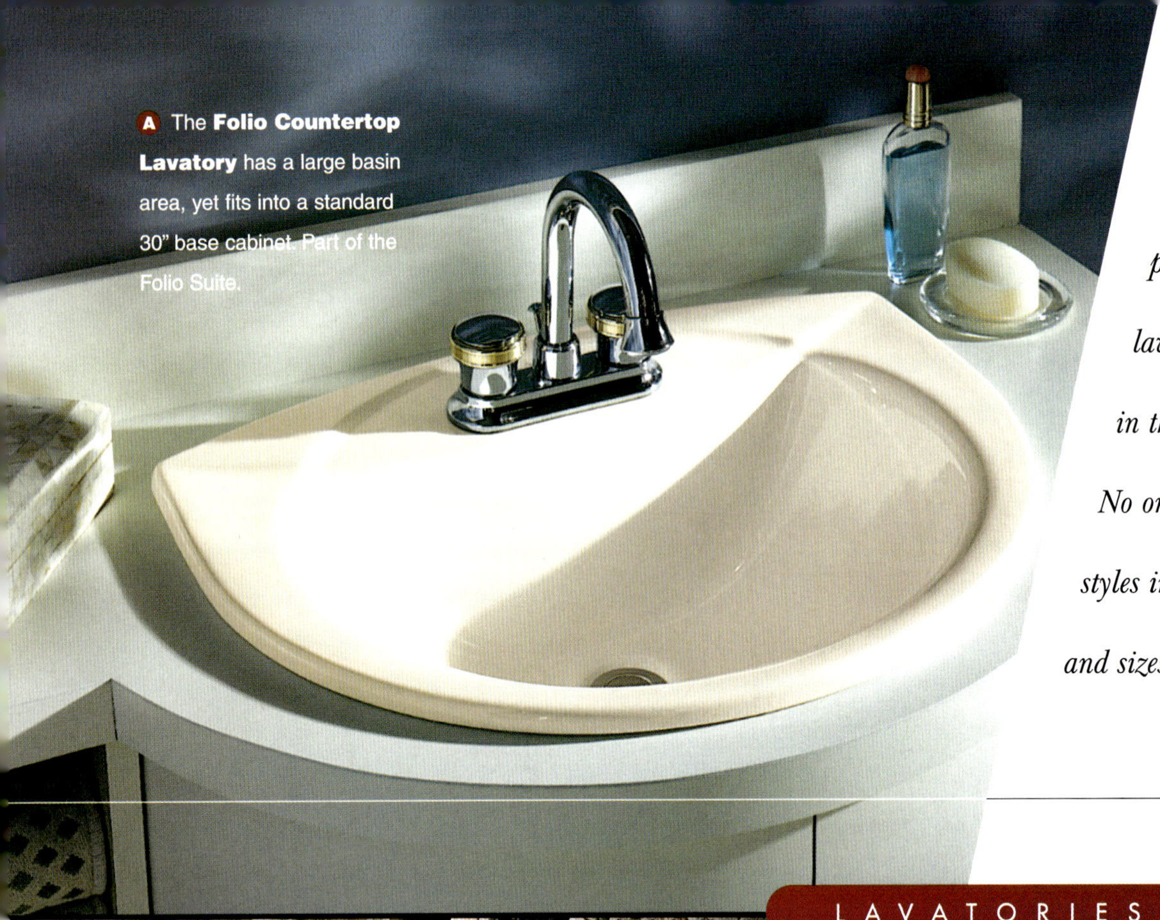

A The **Folio Countertop Lavatory** has a large basin area, yet fits into a standard 30" base cabinet. Part of the Folio Suite.

More than simply a place to wash, today's lavatories are a focal point in the bath or powder room. No one offers more lavatory styles in a wider array of colors and sizes than Kohler.

LAVATORIES

B **Vessels™ Turnings**
Three new stone finishes add a softened, natural option. Offered on select vitreous china products, they will bring warmth and charm to your bathroom decor.

C The **Memoirs 30" Pedestal Lavatory**, part of the Memoirs Collection, provides ample room for your personal grooming items.

D KOHLER Vessels like this **Vessels Hex Strata,** represent the next bold step in lavatory styling.

When selecting a lavatory, be sure that it is compatible with your chosen faucet. KOHLER lavatories are drilled to accommodate a wide variety of KOHLER faucets.

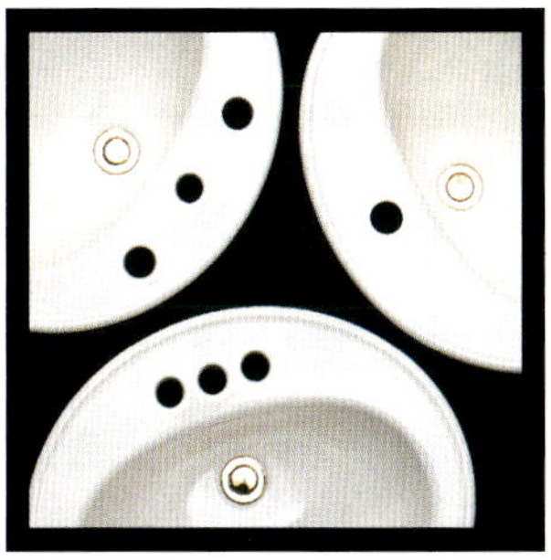

E The **Revival Self-rimming Lavatory** features a large rim area to minimize splashing and and is part of our Revival Collection.

F The larger basin of the **Thoreau™ Self-rimming Lavatory** still fits nicely into a 30" cabinet.

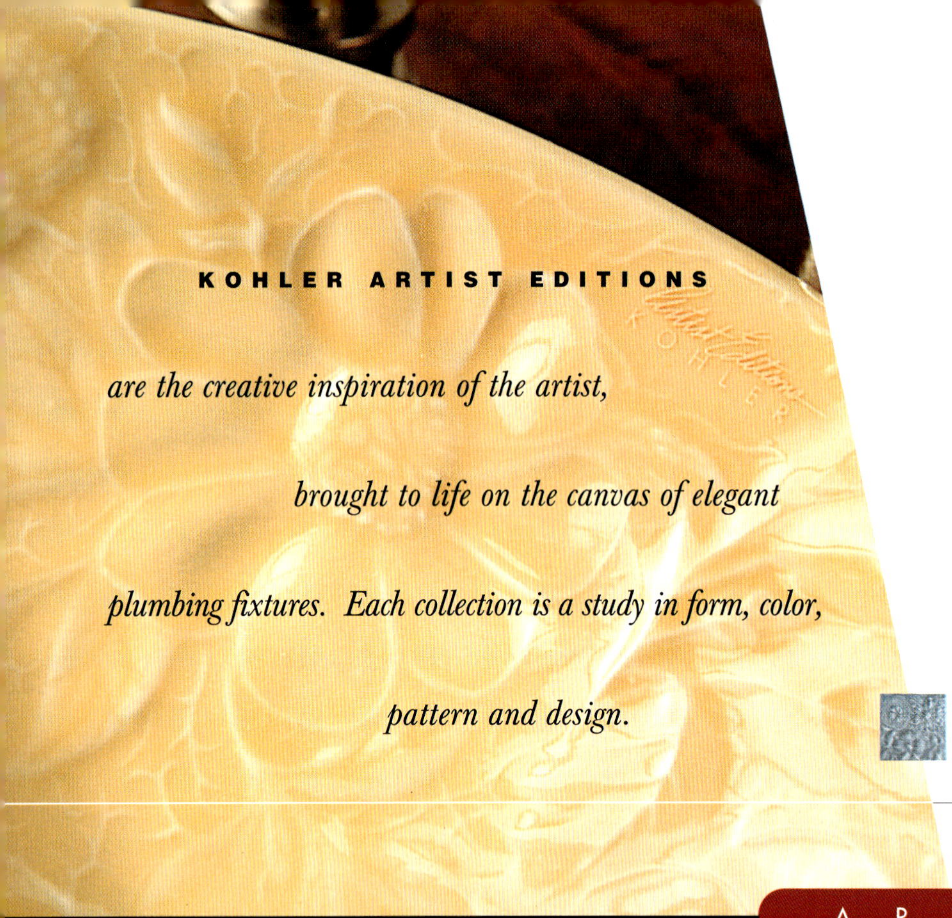

KOHLER ARTIST EDITIONS

are the creative inspiration of the artist, brought to life on the canvas of elegant plumbing fixtures. Each collection is a study in form, color, pattern and design.

A **Water's Grove™** is reminiscent of hand-crafted pottery from the American Arts & Crafts era. A relief pattern of clematis, hibiscus and roses are highlighted with a translucent glaze.

A R T I S T

E D I T I O N S

B The **Peonies & Ivy** design on **Cantata™ Self-rimming Lavatory & Antique™ Faucet** was inspired by traditional Victorian floral imagery. Biscuit vitreous china is adorned with peony blossoms and ivy.

C The **Peonies & Ivy** design on **Couture™ Toilet**. Includes a **Vintage Oak Toilet Seat** and features a powerful 1.6 gallon flush.

D The **English Trellis** design was inspired by the legacy of English chintz patterns. A light floral on white reminiscent of hand touched engravings.

A **Decorative Pitcher**, 17" **Round Platter**, and **Decorative Tile** extends the **Life in the Country** motif throughout your kitchen.

E Life in the Country™ Undercounter Sinks celebrate the rituals of country living in warm, natural hues, with scenes rendered in the tradition of Delft tile. The basins can be installed individually or in multiples.

A The **Revival Toilet** features an elongated bowl and a polished chrome or polished brass lift knob to deliver powerful flushing action. The **Revival Bidet** compliments the toilet design.

KOHLER® toilets and bidets combine outstanding function and performance with style.

TOILETS AND BIDETS

B When you're looking for the best in flushing performance, there's one undisputed leader–Kohler. For more than 60 years, the KOHLER **Wellworth™ Toilet** has been the benchmark for both innovation and excellence. A 2" trapway (26% larger than the 1½" ANSI industry standard), Wellworth can pass an object the size of a handball, while the ANSI trapway could only pass a golf ball.

C The one-piece **San Raphael™ Toilet** features an elongated bowl with a French Curve seat and cover. Both the toilet and the **San Tropez™ Bidet** are shown in Mexican Sand, part of our warm neutral color collection.

D Finally, potty training made fun! Designed with the needs of young children in mind, KOHLER **Primary™ Toilet Seats** are wider and the opening is smaller to keep little bottoms from slipping into the bowl. The scalloped edges are molded to form hand grips which help children feel more stable and secure.

27" 29"

ROUND VS. ELONGATED

Toilet bowls are offered in two designs. Round front bowls require less space and are a nice size for children. When space permits, a toilet with an elongated bowl is recommended. The extended rim length is designed for comfortable use by adults.

D

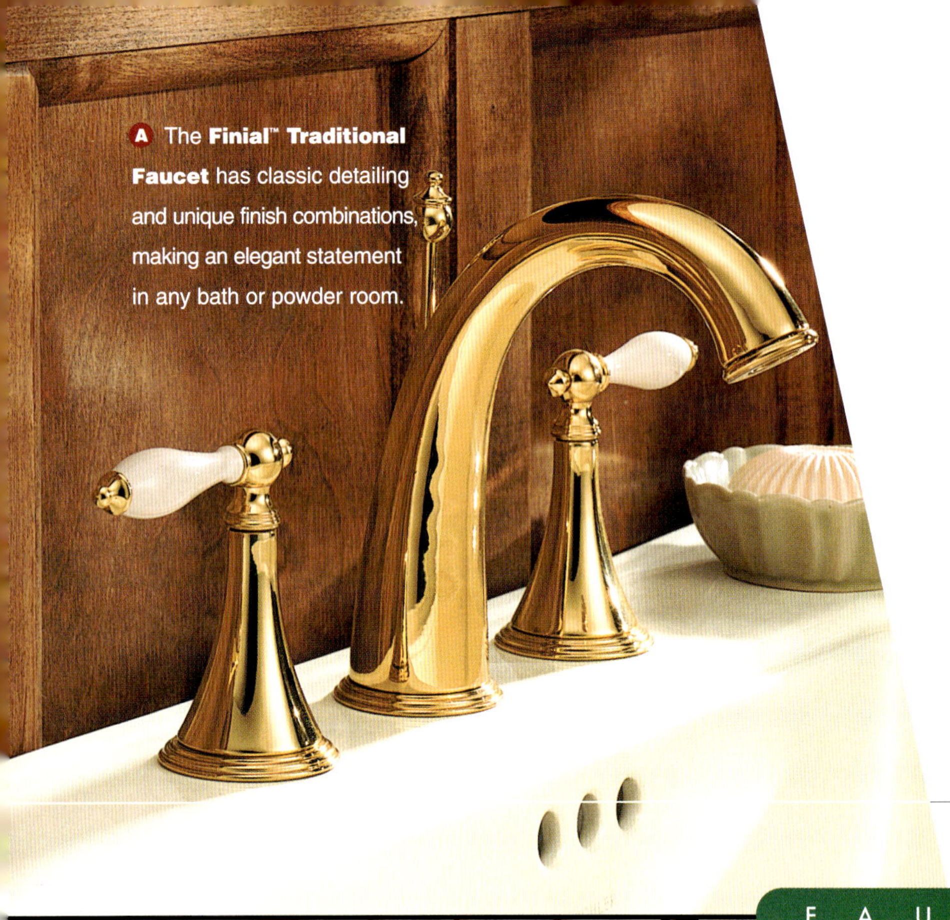

A The **Finial™ Traditional Faucet** has classic detailing and unique finish combinations, making an elegant statement in any bath or powder room.

C

C Revival Widespread Lavatory Faucets blend European style with early American influences. Curved spouts flow into pedestal bases. Scroll lever, traditional lever or faceted dome handles provide added appeal.

FAUCETS

BATH AND KITCHEN

B Falling Water™ Wall-mount Faucets are striking in their simplicity; smooth and serene with total functionality.

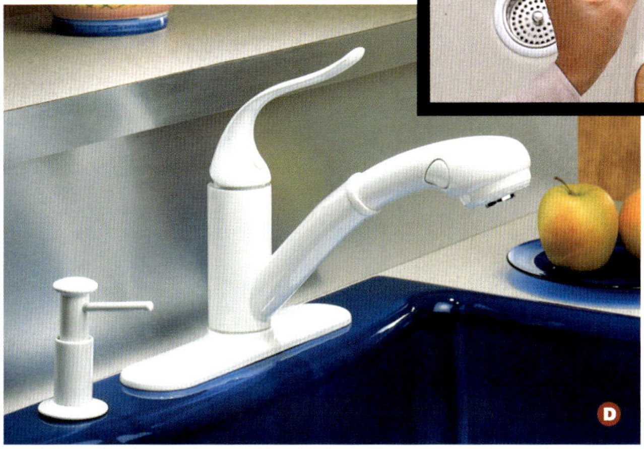

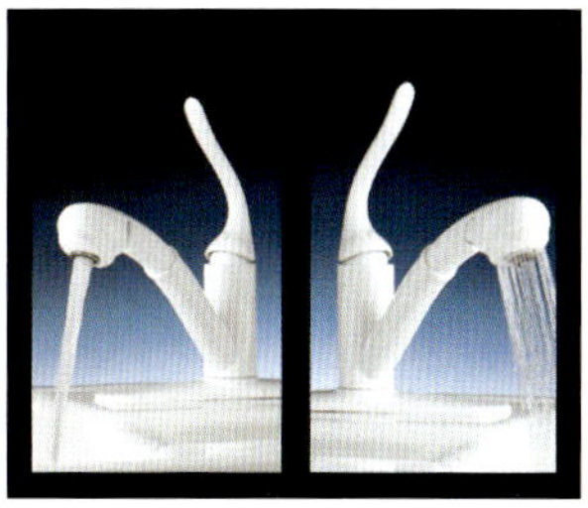

The beauty of a KOHLER faucet goes far beyond its appearance. Each is precision engineered and constructed of premium quality materials. A wide selection of faucets offer long-term performance for a lifetime of use.

D The new **Coralais™ Decorator Pull-out Spray Faucet** features the popular palm spray found on KOHLER Avatar faucets. Designed to fit the natural motion of the hand and wrist, the palm spray is both comfortable and convenient.

The Coralais Pull-out Spray Faucet *combines single-control operation, a retractable sprayhead and an integral vacuum breaker for outstanding convenience.*

E Coralais Decorator Single-control Kitchen Sink Faucet with lever handle in polished chrome.

F Revival Faucets from the Revival Collection bring traditional style to your kitchen.

G Antique Faucets add a nostalgic touch to your kitchen.

A The **Galleon™ Self-rimming Kitchen Sink** has a large left sink compartment and a large right disposal basin.

B Create a custom food preparation, dishwashing or multi-function area with **Iron/Tones™ Sinks.**

KITCHEN AND ENTERTAINMENT SINKS

C The **Cilantro™ Kitchen Sink** in Iron Cobalt is sure to attract attention in your kitchen. Its main basin accommodates even the largest pots and pans, yet the sink fits into a standard 36" base cabinet. A custom hardwood cutting board fits in front of the unique circular disposal basin. The **Napa Self-rimming Entertainment Sink** provides another work area for busy kitchens.

No other work area in your kitchen is used as much as the sink. Unmatched in style and diversity, KOHLER® kitchen and entertainment sinks, when used alone or in combination,

ARE PRACTICAL WORK CENTERS

that offer quality and convenience.

D The **Ravinia™ Sink** features contemporary styling with soft, rounded curves in 18-gauge stainless steel.

E The **Executive Chef™ Tile-in Kitchen Sink** offers two large compartments and square corners for a flush fit.

F Shown in bold Timberline, the **Bakersfield™ Self-rimming Kitchen Sink** has a spacious single basin.

G The **Lakefield™ Kitchen Sink** features a left disposal basin and a right sink comparment.

H The **Brookfield™ Kitchen Sink** offers two equal sized functional basins. The front edge of the sink is angled for ergonomic support of the wrists and forearms.

H

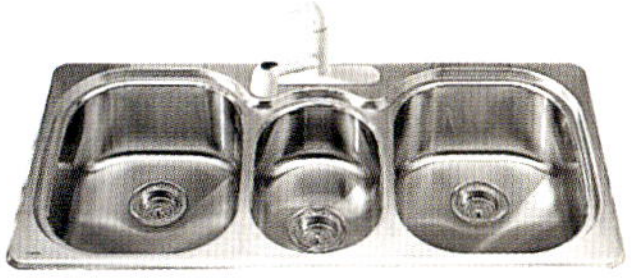

D

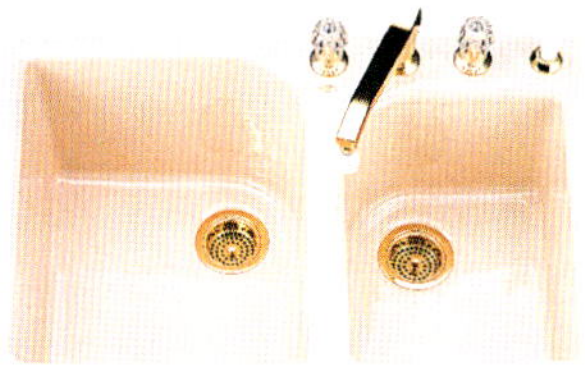

E

F

G

ADDITIONAL LITERATURE AVAILABLE

Bath & Kitchen Ideas from Kohler Coordinates

170177-AA (magazine)
170185-AA (hardcover)

Whirlpools, Baths & BodySpas

170150-AA

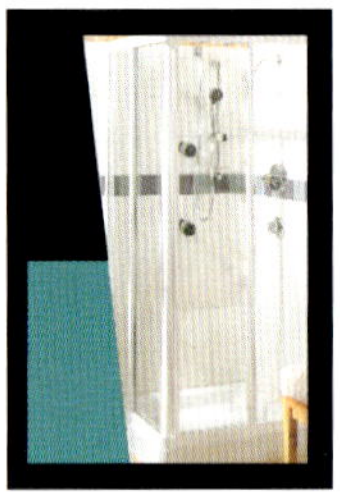

Showers, Enclosures and MasterShower

170151-AA

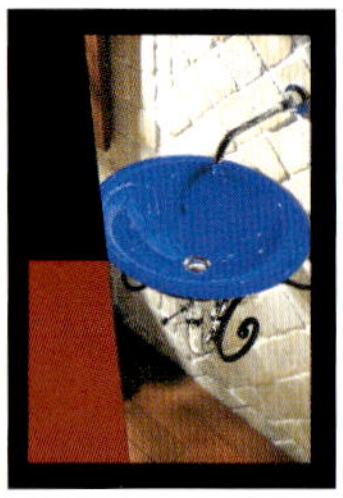

Lavatories, Artist Editions, Vanities & Console Tables

170152-AA

Toilets & Bidets

170153-AA

Kitchen & Entertainment Sinks & Faucets

170154-AA

Bath & Powder Room Faucets

170155-AA

THE BOLD LOOK OF **KOHLER**.

Form 170149-AA 4/97

KOHLER, WISCONSIN 53044

Printed in U.S.A.

www.kohlerco.com

For more information see your KOHLER Registered Showroom or call: 1-800-4-KOHLER

C575
15410/PRA
BuyLine 7787

World Leader In Accessible Bathware

AQUARIUS™

AQUARIUS™

More Choices, Better Products, Better Value

11 Reasons Why Aquarius is the World Leader in Accessible Bathware

Originator – We set the *industry standard* with the *First ADA Compliant Acrylic Bathware*. For the past 20 years we've continued to lead the way with innovative products of unmatched quality.

Experience – Our manufacturing team draws on *over 100 years of combined experience* in bathware manufacturing.

First Choice – Aquarius is *the choice of architects and engineers*, specified by more professionals where accessible bathware is required than any other line in the industry.

Variety – Aquarius has the *largest variety* of special needs acrylic and gelcoat units in the world. Our core units range from the *Hospital/Nursing Home* Commercial Line through the *Lifestyles Series* and *Universal Design Series*

Options – We offer the *widest array* of available options such as *a Unique 3/4" Threshold* that provides ease of entry and easy installation on an existing slab. We also offer *a Unique 4" Threshold* for the rapidly expanding *Assisted Living* market. Over 50 other available options make our bathware versatile.

Flexibility – *Create your own environment* with the most flexible modification capabilities in the industry. We can modify drain location, bar placement, backing for future bar placement (HUD), depth of unit, soap dish location... anything you can imagine. Our unique engineering process can create a mold for any large project.

Superior Craftsmanship – Aquarius uses the *finest raw materials on the market. Our Acrylic is the highest grade material available*, made from a .187mil continuous cast acrylic sheet molded into a seamless one-piece unit. The non-porous one-piece design allows for easier cleaning versus tile showers. It produces a *more sanitary unit*, making it easier to *eliminate dirt, bacteria and mildew*. Our Gelcoat *units use only sanitary-grade*, hand-sprayed gelcoat. *Balsawood* and other solid wood products are used as reinforcements, *not cardboard*. We also mix our own resin to ensure consistent quality.

Attention to Detail – Our operation is a *"Craftory,"* the practice of crafting materials on a large factory scale. The result is a product produced using old-world craftsmanship.

Service – Aquarius prides itself on *willingness to listen* and ability to respond. You'll get straight talk with real people. Our customer service department has over 30 years of experience and is eager to help obtain your objective. If a problem does develop, our field service representatives will respond quickly to avoid delays.

Aesthetic Appeal – *Traditional designs*, not trendy fads, ensure your project will remain in good taste for decades to come. Add *colorful HEWI® support bars* to create a *home-like environment* in any setting.

Affordability – Our *Dynamic Bathware* line provides years of virtually *maintenance-free* enjoyment, all at a competitive price.

VARIETY TO FIT ANY NEED

15410/PRA
BuyLine 7787

Hotel / Motel Series

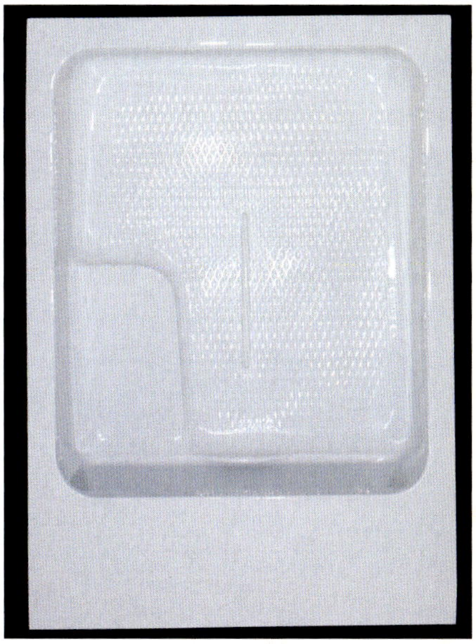

A 1000 TS
60 L x 34 W x 84 H

Over 10 elegant models available in Acrylic or Gelcoat. Designer colors and whirlpool options are available.

"Whirlwind" Series

The "Whirlwind" Series offers more than 20 luxurious models. Available in Acrylic or Gelcoat. Options include designer colors and matching trim.

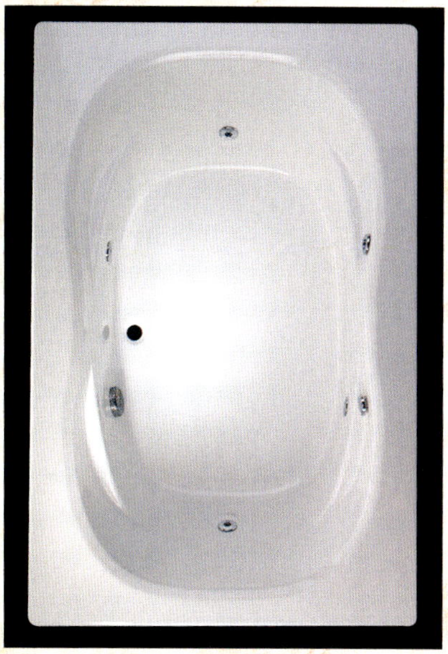

A 7248 CW
72 L x 48 W x 25 H

Lifestyle Series Universal Design

Our Lifestyle Series combines the unparalleled strength of our special needs units with the aesthetic appeal of the famed HEWI® bar and seats. The beauty of our Universal Design units provide a homelike environment in any setting.

S 6436 BF with HEWI® Accessories
64 L x 36 W x 84 H

Over 60 distinctive models available in Acrylic or Gelcoat. A wide variety of options are available

Special Needs Series

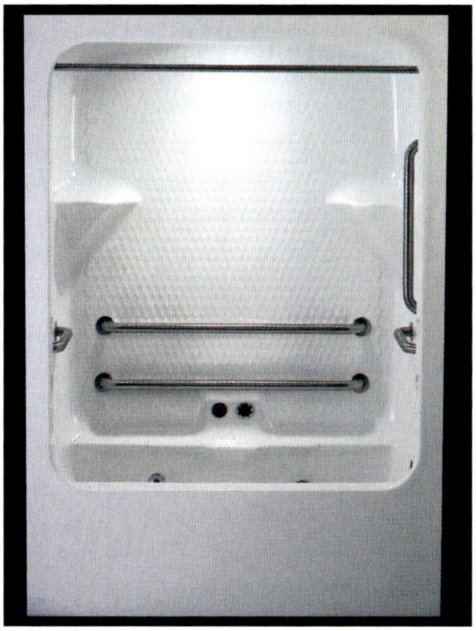

H 6032 TS Whirlpool
60 L x 32 W x 84 H

More than 50 Special Needs models available in Acrylic or Gelcoat. Create your own environment with our large array of options and colors. Therapeutic whirlpool system available in all special needs tub shower models as shown in the H 6032 TS.

Commercial & Residential Series

A 7236 TS
72 L x 36 W x 84 H

AQUARIUS - S 4136 BF ADA Acrylic

The Originator - The first ADA compliant tub

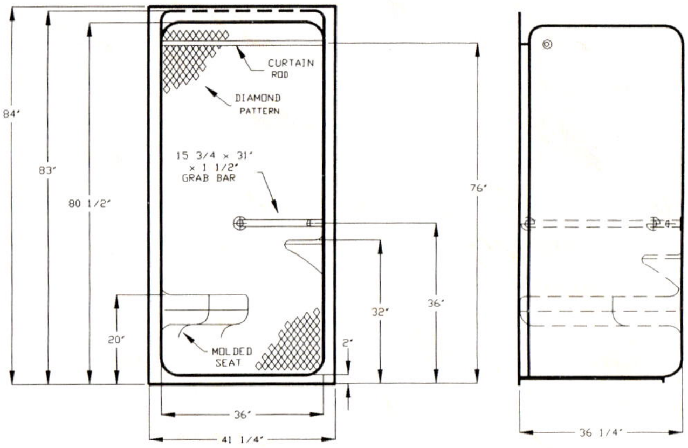

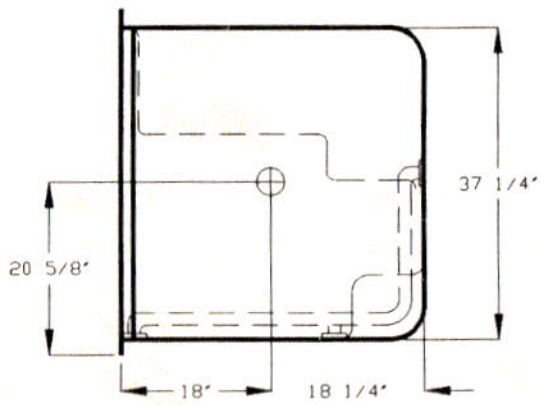

The **Aquarius S 4136 BF** is a Transfer Type Barrier Free Shower available in right or left. The unit is vacuum-formed from a cross-linked, continuous cast acrylic sheet with a minimum thickness of .187 mills and a finished cured Barcol hardness of 94-104 as tested by ASTM D-2583 standards. The unit has a reinforced fiberglass coating with a 15% minimum fiberglass content. It meets ANSI 117.1, ANSI Z 124.2 and ADA requirements, has a backside fire rating of "A" and a flame spread of less than 25. The base is attached to the sump of the unit in such a way to form an integral part with an inner and outer coating of reinforced polyester resin. It meets requirements for Universal Plumbing Code administered by IAPMO, HUD, BOCA, NAHB and Southern Building Code.

AQUARIUS - S 6436 BF ADA Acrylic

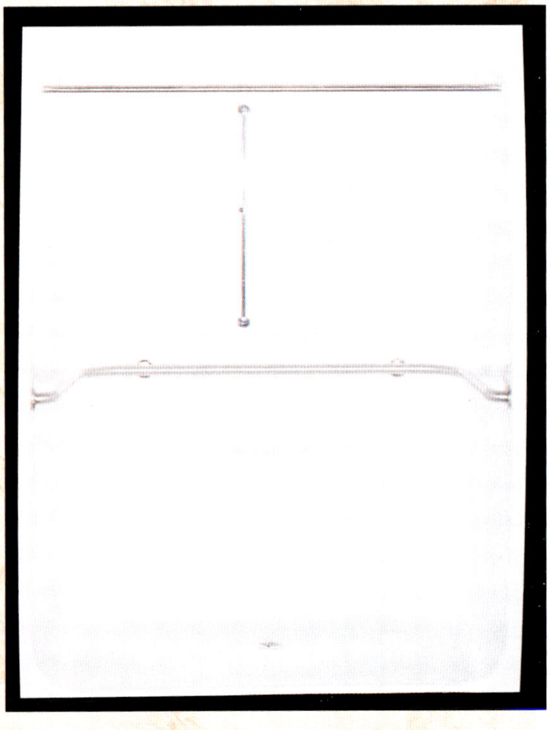

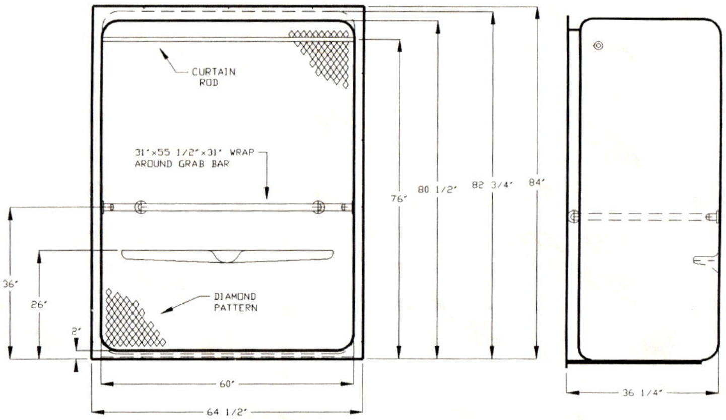

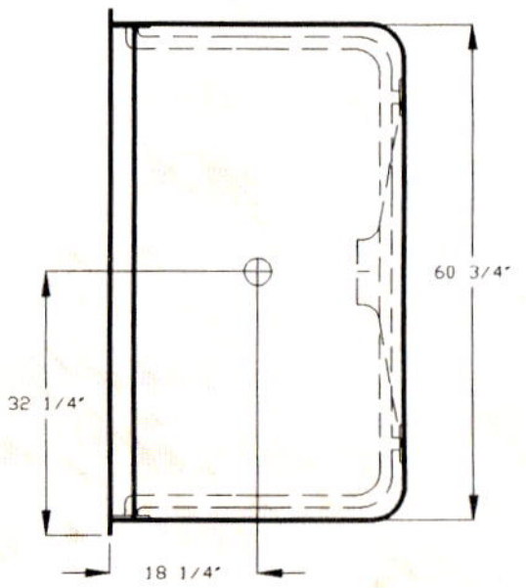

The **Aquarius S 6436 BF** is a Barrier-Free Accessible Shower available in right or left. The unit is vacuum-formed from a cross-linked, continuous cast acrylic sheet with a minimum thickness of .187 mills and a finished cured Barcol hardness of 94-104 as tested by ASTM D-2583 standards. The unit has a reinforced fiberglass coating with a 15% minimum fiberglass content. It meets ANSI 117.1, ANSI Z 124.2 and ADA requirements, has a backside fire rating of "A" and a flame spread of less than 25. The base is attached to the sump of the unit in such a way to form an integral part with an inner and outer coating of reinforced polyester resin. It meets requirements for Universal Plumbing Code administered by IAPMO, HUD, BOCA, NAHB and Southern Building Code.

AQUARIUS - S 6032 TS ADA ACRYLIC

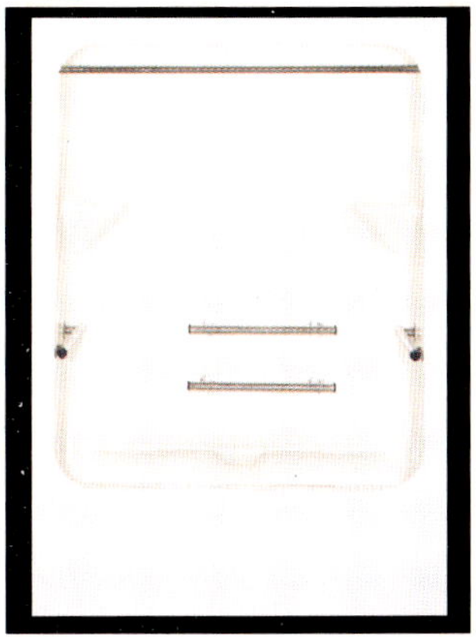

The Aquarius S 6032 B is a Transfer Type Tub Shower available in right or left. The unit is vacuum-formed from a cross-linked, continuous cast acrylic sheet with a minimum thickness of .187 mils and a finished cured Barcol hardness of 94-104 as tested by ASTM D-2583 standards. The unit has a reinforced fiberglass coating with a 15% minimum fiberglass content. It meets ANSI 117.1, ANSI Z 124.2 and ADA requirements, has a backside fire rating of "A" and a flame spread of less than 25. The base is attached to the sump of the unit in such a way to form an integral part with an inner and outer coating of reinforced polyester resin. It meets requirements for Universal Plumbing Code administered by IAPMO, HUD, BOCA, NAHB and Southern Building Code.

AQUARIUS - S 7236 TS ADA ACRYLIC

The **Aquarius S 7236 TS** is a Transfer Type Tub Shower available in right or left. The unit is vacuum-formed from a cross-linked, continuous cast acrylic sheet with a minimum thickness of .187 mills and a finished cured Barcol hardness of 94-104 as tested by ASTM D-2583 standards. The unit has a reinforced fiberglass coating with a 15% minimum fiberglass content. It meets ANSI 117.1, ANSI Z 124.2 and ADA requirements, has a backside fire rating of "A" and a flame spread of less than 25. The base is attached to the sump of the unit in such a way to form an integral part with an inner and outer coating of reinforced polyester resin. It meets requirements for Universal Plumbing Code administered by IAPMO, HUD, BOCA, NAHB and Southern Building Code.

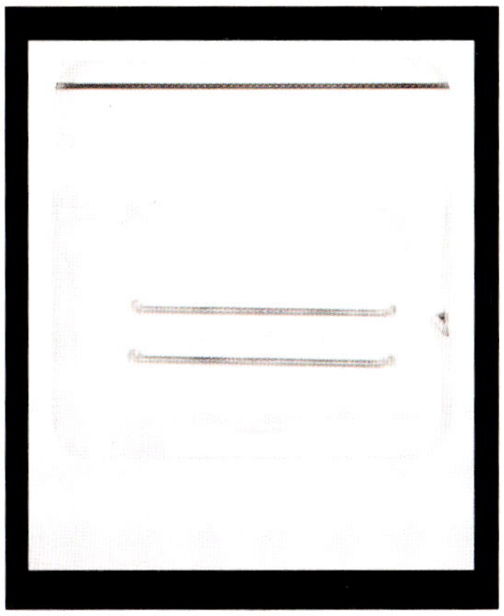

AQUARIUS - CA 4248 BF ACRYLIC

The **Aquarius CA 4248 BF** is a Transfer Type Barrier Free Shower Stall available in right or left. The unit is vacuum-formed from a cross-linked, continuous cast acrylic sheet with a minimum thickness of .187 mills and a finished cured Barcol hardness of 94-104 as tested by ASTM D-2583 standards. The unit has a reinforced fiberglass coating with a 15% minimum fiberglass content. It meets ANSI 117.1, ANSI Z 124.2 and has a backside fire rating of "A" and a flame spread of less than 25. The base is attached to the sump of the unit in such a way to form an integral part with an inner and outer coating of reinforced polyester resin. It meets requirements for Universal Plumbing Code administered by IAPMO and California Title 24.

AQUARIUS - G 4248 BF ADA GELCOAT

The **Aquarius G 4248 BF** is a Transfer Type Barrier Free Shower available in right or left. The finished surface consists of a sanitary-grade polyester gelcoat exhibiting a minimum thickness of 15 dry mills and a finished cured Barcol hardness of 80-90 as tested by ASTM D-2583 standards. Constructed of molded fiberglass resin with a 15% minimum fiberglass content, the unit is reinforced by hand-laying multiple layers of fiberglass and resin. It meets ANSI 117.1, ANSI Z 124.2 and ADA requirements. The unit is constructed of a fire-retardant gelcoat with a Class A Flame Spread Rating of 25 or less. It meets requirements for Universal Plumbing Code administered by IAPMO and California Title 24.

15410/PRA

BuyLine 7787

Standard Features "*"
Optional Features "•"

		G 4248 BF (ADA)	CA 4248 BF	S 7236 TS (ADA)	S 6032 BF (ADA)	S 6436 BF (ADA)	S 4136 BF (ADA)
See Below	1		*	*	*	*	*
See Below	2	*					
2" Dia drain	3			*	*		
3-3/8" Dia Drain	4	*	*			*	*
See Below	5	*	*	*	*	*	*
Textured bottom	6	*	*	*	*	*	*
Anti Flex floor with support	7	*	*	*	*	*	*
See Below	8			*	*		
1" Dia stainless steel curtain rod	9	*	*	*	*	*	*
Diamond pattern on back wall	10		*	*	*	*	*
Molded soap trays	11		*	*	*	*	*
Molded seat opposite valve	12		*	*			*
2" Threshold	13		*			*	*
3/4" Threshold	14					•	•
4" Threshold	15						
Fold-up seat - Padded cushion	16	•	•			•	•
Fold-up seat - Phenolic slotted	17	•	•			•	•
Fold-up seat - Tech wood	18	•	•			•	•
Removable Phenolic slotted	19				•		
See Below	20	•	•	•	•	•	•
Hand held shower set	21	•	•	•	•	•	•
See Below	22	•	•	•	•	•	•
Pressure balance valve	23	•	•	•	•	•	•
Green antibacterial curtain and hooks	24	•	•	•	•	•	•
White shower curtain with hooks	25	•	•	•	•	•	•
Stainless steel soap dish	26	•	•	•	•	•	•
Dome light	27		•	•	•	•	•
Nurse's call box	28	•	•	•	•	•	•
See Below	29	•	•	•	•	•	•
Smooth back	30	•	•	•	•	•	•
See Below	31	•	•	•	•	•	•
Painted textured floor	32		•	•	•	•	•
Rough In Dimensions		45 L x 51-3/8 W x 78-1/4 H	46 L x 49-1/2 W x 84 H	70 L x 37 W x 84 H	59 L x 34 W x 84 H	62-3/4 L x 37-1/4 W x 84 H	38-1/4 L x 37-1/4W x 84H
Inside Dimensions		42 L x 48 W x 77 H	42 L x 48 W x 81-3/4 H	68-1/2 L x 35 W x 81-1/2 H	59 L x 30 W x 81-1/2 H	60 L x 36 W x 81-1/2 H	36 L x 36 W x 81-1/2 H
Outside Dimensions		45 L x 51 W x 78-1/4 H	48 L x 48-3/4 W x 84 H	72 L x 36-1/4 W x 84 H	60 L x 32-1/2 W x 84 H	64-1/2 L x 36-1/4 W x 84 H	41-1/4 L x 36-1/4 W x 84 H

1-One piece, cross-linked continuous cast acrylic sheet of .187 mil min. thickness, reinforced and laminated for superior rigidity.
2-Gelcoat, Fiber reinforced & laminated for superior rigidity
5-ADA compliant grab bar caulked and sealed in place
8-Above floor rough-in, waste and overflow
20-Galvanized steel stiffeners; one piece stiffeners support side and back
22-Slide bar for hand held shower mounted in place with stainless steel plates and bolts
29-Predrill valve at recommended height
31-Two mounted wall brackets for hand held shower

Standard Features "*"
Optional Features "•"

	G 6094 BF (ADA)	G 3694 BF (ADA)	G 6092 TS (ADA)	G 6017 TS (ADA)	G 3637 BF 3 piece SH	G 6037 BF 3 piece SH	G 3896 Neo angle BF	G 4242 Neo angle SH
1 See Below								
2 See Below	*	*	*	*	*	*	*	*
3 2" Dia drain			*	*				
4 3-3/8" Dia Drain	*	*			*	*	*	*
5 See Below	*	*	*	*	*	*	*	*
6 Textured bottom	*	*	*		*	*	*	*
7 Anti Flex floor with support	*	*	*	*	*	*	*	*
8 See Below			*	*				
9 See Below	*	*	*	*	*	*	*	*
10 Diamond pattern on back wall								
11 Molded soap trays				*			*	*
12 Molded seat opposite valve								*
13 2" Threshold	*	*			*	*	*	*
14 3/4" Threshold								
15 4" Threshold								
16 See Below	•	•			•	•	•	
17 Fold-up seat - Phenolic slotted	•	•	•	•	•	•	•	
18 Fold-up seat - Tech wood	•	•	•	•	•	•	•	
19 Removable Phenolic slotted			•	•				
20 See Below	•	•	•	•	•	•	•	•
21 Hand held shower set	•	•	•	•	•	•	•	•
22 See Below	•	•	•	•	•	•	•	•
23 Pressure balance valve	•	•	•	•	•	•	•	•
24 See Below	•	•	•	•	•	•	•	•
25 See Below	•	•	•	•	•	•	•	•
26 Stainless steel soap dish	•	•	•	•	•	•	•	•
27 Dome light								
28 Nurse's call box	•	•	•	•	•	•	•	•
29 See Below	•	•	•	•	•	•	•	•
30 Smooth back	*	*	*	*	*	*	*	*
31 See Below	•	•	•	•	•	•	•	•
32 Painted textured floor	•	•	•	•	•	•	•	•

	Outside Dimensions	Inside Dimensions	Rough in Dimensions
G 6094 BF (ADA)	65 L x 39-1/2 W x 80 H	61 L x 36 W x 78 H	65 L x 39-1/2 W x 80 H
G 3694 BF (ADA)	41 L x 39-1/2 W x 78-1/2 H	36 L x 36 W x 78 H	41 L x 39-1/2 W x 78-1/2 H
G 6092 TS (ADA)	60 L x 32 W x 78 H	56-1/2 L x 30 W x 75 H	60 L x 32-1/2 W x 78 H
G 6017 TS (ADA)	60 L x 32-1/2 W x 80-1/4 H	56-1/4 L x 30 W x 77 H	60 L x 32-1/2 W x 80-1/4 H
G 3637 BF 3 piece SH	39 L x 38 W x 78-1/2 H	36 L x 36 W x 75-1/4H	39 L x 38 W x 78-1/2 H
G 6037 BF 3 piece SH	60 L x 37 W x 78 H	57 L x 35 W x 76 H	60 L x 37 W x 78 H
G 3896 Neo angle BF	38 L x 36 W x 79 H	33 L x 31 W x 77 H	38 L x 36 W x 79 H
G 4242 Neo angle SH	42 L x 42 W x 78 H	41 L x 41 W x 76 H	42 L x 42 W x 78 H

1-One piece, cross-linked continuous cast acrylic sheet of .187 mill min. thickness, reinforced and laminated for superior rigidity.
2-Gelcoat, Fiber reinforced & laminated for superior rigidity
5-ADA compliant grab bar caulked and sealed in place
8-Above floor rough-in, waste and overflow
9-1" Dia stainless steel curtain rod
16-Fold-up seat - Padded cushion
20-Galvanized steel stiffeners; one piece stiffeners support side and back
22-Slide bar for hand held shower mounted in place with stainless steel plates and bolts
24-Green antibacterial curtain and hooks
25-White shower curtain with hooks
29-Predrill valve at recommended height
31-Two mounted wall brackets for hand held shower

AQUARIUS - G 6094 BF ADA GELCOAT

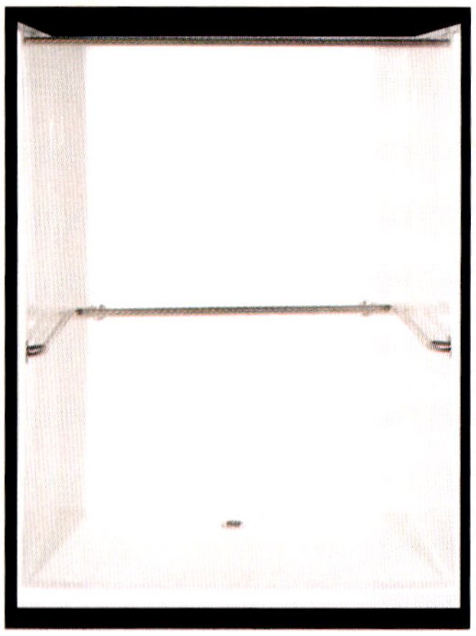

Handicapped Shower Stall

Model G 6094 BF offers the choice of right, left or center and is made with a finished surface of sanitary-grade polyester Gelcoat exhibiting a minimal thickness of 15 dry mils, and a finished cured Barcol hardness of 80-90 as tested with ASTM D-2583. The unit is constructed of molded reinforced fiberglass with a 15% minimum fiberglass content. Outside dimensions of the unit are 65" x 39 1/2" x 80". The base is attached to the sump of the unit in such a way to form an integral part with an inner and outer coating of reinforced polyester resin. The unit meets ANSI 124.2, FHA, HUD, BOCA, NAHB, UPC and Southern Building Code.

AQUARIUS - G 3694 BF ADA GELCOAT

Handicapped Shower Stall

Model G 3694 BF offers the choice of right or left and is made with a finished surface of sanitary-grade polyester Gelcoat exhibiting a minimal thickness of 15 dry mils, and a finished cured Barcol hardness of 80-90 as tested with ASTM D-2583. The unit is constructed of molded reinforced fiberglass with a 15% minimum fiberglass content. Outside dimensions of the unit are 41" x 39 1/2" x 78 1/2". The base is attached to the sump of the unit in such a way to form an integral part with an inner and outer coating of reinforced polyester resin. The unit meets ANSI 124.2, FHA, HUD, BOCA, NAHB, UPC and Southern Building Code.

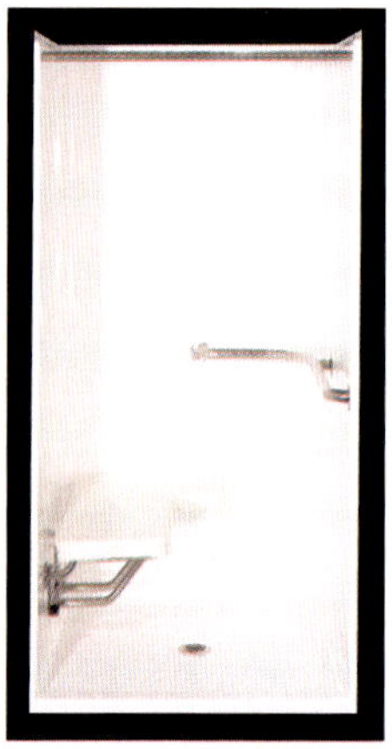

AQUARIUS - G 6092 TS ADA GELCOAT

The **Aquarius G 6092 TS** is a Special Need Tub Shower available in right or left. The finished surface consists of a sanitary-grade polyester gelcoat exhibiting a minimum thickness of 15 dry mils and a finished cured Barcol hardness of 80-90 as tested by ASTM D-2583 standards. Constructed of molded fiberglass resin with a 15% minimum fiberglass content, the unit is reinforced by hand-laying multiple layers of fiberglass and resin. It meets ANSI 117.1, ANSI Z 124.2 and ADA requirements. The unit is constructed of a fire-retardant gelcoat with a Class A Flame Spread Rating of 25 or less. It meets requirements for Universal Plumbing Code administered by IAPMO, HUD, BOCA, NAHB and Southern Building Code.

AQUARIUS - G 3637 BF ADA GELCOAT

The **Aquarius G 3637 BF** is a three piece unit available in right or left. The finished surface consists of a sanitary-grade polyester gelcoat exhibiting a minimum thickness of 15 dry mils and a finished cured Barcol hardness of 80-90 as tested by ASTM D-2583 standards. Constructed of molded fiberglass resin with a 15% minimum fiberglass content, the unit is reinforced by hand-laying multiple layers of fiberglass and resin. The outside dimensions of the unit are 39" x 38" x 78-1/2". It meets ANSI Z 124.2 and ADA requirements. It meets requirements for Universal Plumbing Code administered by IAPMO, HUD, BOCA, NAHB and Southern Building Code.

AQUARIUS - Universal Design / Lifestyles Series Acrylic

ADA Handicapped Shower Stall

Aquarius Model S 6436 BF is an acrylic unit molded from a single sheet so as not to have any joints or seams. It meets ANSI A117.1 and ANSI Z124.2 requirements, has a backside fire rating of "A" and a flame spread of less than 25. It meets ADA, FHA, HUD, BOCA, NAHB, UPC and most state and national standards on design for the disabled as well as Southern Building Code. Inside dimensions of the unit are 60" x 36" x 80 1/2". Outside dimensions of the unit are 64 1/2" x 36 1/4" x 82 3/4".

AQUARIUS - H 4836 SH Assisted Living 4" Threshold Acrylic

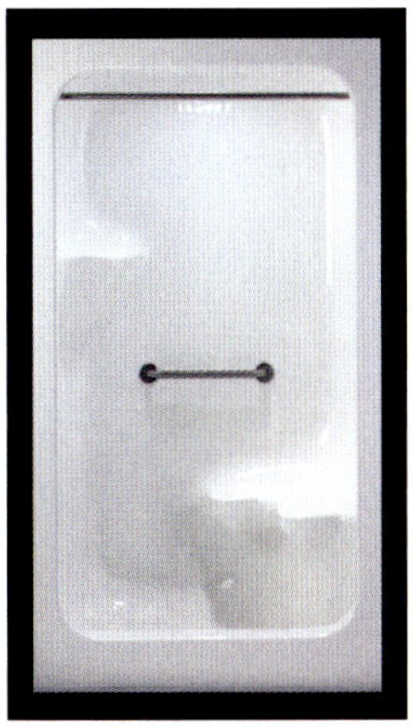

Acrylic 4" Threshold

Handicapped Shower Stall

Model H4836 SH is an acrylic unit molded from a single sheet so as not to have any joints or seams. It meets ANSI Z124.2 requirements, has a backside fire rating of "A" and a flame spread of less than 25. It meets FHA, HUD, BOCA, NAHB and most state and national standards on design for the disabled as well as Southern Building Code. Outside dimensions of the unit are 48" x 36" x 84".

AQUARIUS - G 6096 SH Assisted Living Gelcoat

Gelcoat 4" Threshold

Model G 6096 SH offers the choice of right or left and is made with a finished surface of sanitary-grade polyester Gelcoat exhibiting a minimal thickness of 15 dry mils, and a finished cured Barcol hardness of 80-90 as tested with ASTM D-2583. The unit is constructed of molded reinforced fiberglass with a 15% minimum fiberglass content. Outside dimensions of the unit are 60" x 36" x 74" with a 4" threshold. The base is attached to the sump of the unit in such a way to form an integral part with an inner and outer coating of reinforced polyester resin. The unit meets ANSI 124.2, FHA, HUD, BOCA, NAHB, UPC and Southern Building Code.

AQUARIUS - G 3636 SH Assisted Living Gelcoat

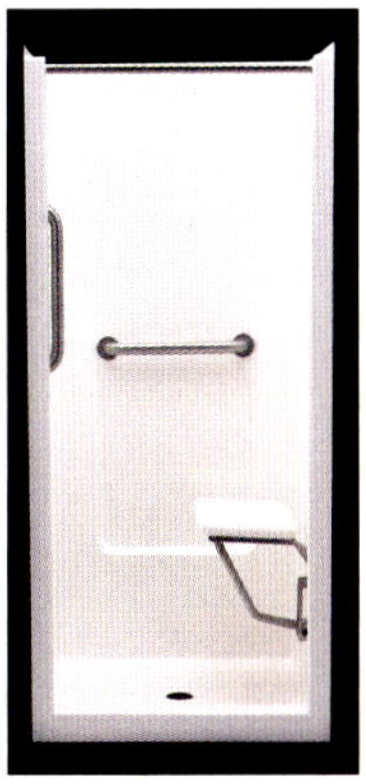

Gelcoat 4" Threshold

Handicapped Shower Stall with Fold-Up Seat

Model G 3636 SH offers the choice of right or left and is made with a finished surface of sanitary-grade polyester Gelcoat exhibiting a minimal thickness of 15 dry mils, and a finished cured Barcol hardness of 80-90 as tested with ASTM D-2583. The unit is constructed of molded reinforced fiberglass with a 15% minimum fiberglass content. Outside dimensions of the unit are 35 3/4" x 37 1/4" x 77 1/2". The base is attached to the sump of the unit in such a way to form an integral part with an inner and outer coating of reinforced polyester resin. The unit meets ANSI 124.2, FHA, HUD, BOCA, NAHB, UPC and Southern Building Code.

15410/PRA

BuyLine 7787

Standard Features "*"
Optional Features "•"

		G 3636 SH	G 4894 SH	G 6096 SH	H 6036 SH	H 4136 SH	H 4836 SH	S 4136 BF (ADA)	S 6436 BF (ADA)
See Below	1				*	*	*	*	*
See Below	2	*	*	*					
2" Dia drain	3								
3-3/8" Dia Drain	4	*	*	*	*	*	*	*	*
See Below	5	*	*	*	*	*	*	*	*
Textured bottom	6				*	*	*	*	*
Anti Flex floor with support	7	*	*	*	*	*	*	*	*
See Below	8			*	*	*	*		
See Below	9	•	•	•	*	*	*	*	*
Diamond pattern on back wall	10				*	*	*	*	*
Molded soap trays	11	*	*	*	*	*	*	*	*
Molded seat opposite valve	12		*	*				*	
2" Threshold	13							*	*
3/4" Threshold	14							•	•
4" Threshold	15	*	*	*	•	•	•		
See Below	16	•			•	•	•	•	•
See Below	17	•			•	•	•	•	•
Fold-up seat - Tech wood	18	•			•	•	•	•	•
Removable Phenolic slotted	19								
See Below	20	•	•	•	•	•	•	•	•
Hand held shower set	21	•	•	•	•	•	•	•	•
See Below	22	•	•	•	•	•	•	•	•
Pressure balance valve	23	•	•	•	•	•	•	•	•
See Below	24	•	•	•	•	•	•	•	•
See Below	25	•	•	•	•	•	•	•	•
Stainless steel soap dish	26	•	•	•	•	•	•	•	•
Dome light	27				•	•	•	•	•
Nurse's call box	28	•	•	•	•	•	•	•	•
See Below	29	•	•	•	•	•	•	•	•
Smooth back	30	*	*	*	•	•	•	•	•
See Below	31	•	•	•	•	•	•	•	•
Painted textured floor	32	•	•	•	•	•	•	•	•
Rough in Dimensions		35-1/4 L x 37-1/4 W x 77-1/2 H	47-1/2 L x 36-1/4 W x 78 H	60 L x 36 W x 73 H	59 L x 37 W x 84 H	37-1/4 _x 37 W x 84 H	46-1/2 L x 36-1/2 W x 84 H	38-1/4 L x 37-1/4 W x 84 H	62-3/4 L x 37-1/4 W x 84 H
Inside Dimensions		33 L x 35 W x 76 H	44-1/2 L x 32-1/2 W x 76-1/2 H	57 L x 34 W x 72 H	56-1/4 L x 35-1/2 W x 81-1/2 H	36 L x 35-1/4 W x 81-1/2 H	46 L x 34-1/2 W x 81-1/2 H	36 L x 36 W x 81-1/2 H	60 L x 36 W x 81-1/2 H
Outside Dimensions		35-1/4 L x 37-1/4 W x 77-1/2 H	47-1/2 L x 36-1/4 W x 78 H	60 L x 36 W x 73 H	60 L x 36 W x 84 H	41-1/4 L x 36 W x 84 H	48 L x 35-1/2 W x 84 H	41-1/4 L x 36-1/4 W x 84 H	64-1/2 L x 36-1/4 W x 84 H

1-One piece, cross-linked continuous cast acrylic sheet of .187 mill min. thickness, reinforced and laminated for superior rigidity.
2-Gelcoat, Fiber reinforced & laminated for superior rigidity
5-ADA compliant grab bar caulked and sealed in place
8-Above floor rough-in, waste and overflow
9-1" Dia stainless steel curtain rod
16-Fold-up seat - Padded cushion
17-Fold-up seat - Phenolic slotted
20-Galvanized steel stiffeners; one piece stiffeners support side and back
22-Slide bar for hand held shower mounted in place with stainless steel plates and bolts
24-Green antibacterial curtain and hooks
25-White shower curtain with hooks
29-Predrill valve at recommended height
31-Two mounted wall brackets for hand held shower

Standard Features "*"
Optional Features "•"

#	Feature	H 7236 BF	H 6036 BF	H 4848 BF	H 4836 BF	H 4136 SH	H 1836 SH corner shower	H 3632 SH	H 6032 TS
1	See Below	*	*	*	*	*	*	*	*
2	See Below								
3	2" Dia drain								*
4	3-3/8" Dia Drain	*	*	*	*	*	*	*	
5	See Below	*	*	*	*	*	*	*	*
6	Textured bottom	*	*	*	*	*	*	*	*
7	Anti Flex floor with support	*	*	*	*	*	*	*	*
8	See Below					*	*	*	*
9	See Below	*	*	*	*	*	*	*	*
10	Diamond pattern on back wall	*	*	*	*	*	*	*	*
11	Molded soap trays	*	*	*	*	*	*	*	*
12	Molded seat opposite valve				*				
13	2" Threshold	*	*	*	*				
14	3/4" Threshold		•		•				
15	4" Threshold					•		•	
16	See Below	•	•	•	•	•	•	•	
17	Fold-up seat - Phenolic slotted	•	•	•	•	•	•	•	
18	Fold-up seat - Tech wood	•	•	•	•	•	•	•	
19	Removable Phenolic slotted								•
20	See Below	•	•	•	•	•	•	•	•
21	Hand held shower set	•	•	•	•	•	•	•	•
22	See Below	•	•	•	•	•	•	•	•
23	Pressure balance valve	•	•	•	•	•	•	•	•
24	See Below	•	•	•	•	•	•	•	•
25	See Below	•	•	•	•	•	•	•	•
26	Stainless steel soap dish	•	•	•	•	•	•	•	•
27	Dome light	•	•	•	•	•	•	•	•
28	Nurse's call box	•	•	•	•	•	•	•	•
29	See Below	•	•	•	•	•	•	•	•
30	Smooth back	•	•	•	•	•	•	•	•
31	See Below	•	•	•	•	•	•	•	•
32	Painted textured floor	•	•	•	•	•	•	•	•

Model	Outside Dimensions	Inside Dimensions	Rough in Dimensions
H 7236 BF	72 L x 36-1/2 W x 84 H	68-1/2 L x 36 W x 81-1/2 H	71 L x 37-1/4 W x 84 H
H 6036 BF	60 L x 36 W x 84 H	56-1/4 L x 35-1/2 W x 81-1/2H	59 L x 37 W x 84 H
H 4848 BF	53 L x 48-1/4 W x 84 H	48 L x 48 W x 81-1/2 H	52 L x 49-1/4 W x 84 H
H 4836 BF	48 L x 35-1/2 W x 84 H	46 L x 34-1/2 W x 81-1/2 H	46-1/2 L x 36-1/2 W x 84 H
H 4136 SH	41-1/4 L x 36 W x 84 H	36 L x 35-1/4 W x 81-1/2 H	37-3/4 L x 37 W x 84 H
H 1836 SH corner shower	42-1/2 L x 36 W x 84 H	35 L x 35 W x 81-1/2 H	42-1/2 L x 36 W x 84H
H 3632 SH	36 L x 32 W x 84 H	31-1/2 L x 31-1/2 W x 81-1/2H	32 L x 32 W x 84 H
H 6032 TS	60 L x 33 W x 84H	59 L x 30 W x 81-1/4 H	59 L x 34 W x 84 H

1-One piece, cross-linked continuous cast acrylic sheet of .187 mill min. thickness, reinforced and laminated for superior rigidity.
2-Gelcoat, Fiber reinforced & laminated for superior rigidity
5-ADA compliant grab bar caulked and sealed in place
8-Above floor rough-in, waste and overflow
9-1" Dia stainless steel curtain rod
16-Fold-up seat - Padded cushion
20-Galvanized steel stiffeners; one piece stiffeners support side and back
22-Slide bar for hand held shower mounted in place with stainless steel plates and bolts
24-Green antibacterial curtain and hooks
25-White shower curtain with hooks
29-Predrill valve at recommended height
31-Two mounted wall brackets for hand held shower

AQUARIUS - H 1836 SH Special Needs Corner Shower

Handicapped Corner Shower Stall
Model H 1836 SH is an acrylic unit molded from a single sheet so as not to have any joints or seams. It meets ANSI Z124.2 requirements, has a backside fire rating of "A" and a flame spread of less than 25. It meets FHA, HUD, BOCA, NAHB and most state and national standards on design for the disabled as well as Southern Building Code. Dimensions of the unit are 42" x 35 1/2" x 80 1/2" with outside dimensions of 42 1/2" x 36" x 84".

AQUARIUS - H 4136 SH Special Needs Shower

Handicapped Shower Stall
Model H 4136 SH is an acrylic unit molded from a single sheet so as not to have any joints or seams. It meets ANSI Z124.2 requirements, has a backside fire rating of "A" and a flame spread of less than 25. It meets FHA, HUD, BOCA, NAHB and most state and national standards on design for the disabled as well as Southern Building Code. Dimensions of the unit are 36" x 36" x 80 1/2" with outside dimensions of 41 1/4" x 36 1/4" x 84".

AQUARIUS - H 6036 BF Special Needs Barrier Free Shower

The **Aquarius H 6036 BF** is a Transfer Type Barrier Free Shower available in right, left or center. The unit is vacuum-formed from a cross-linked, continuous cast acrylic sheet with a minimum thickness of .187 mils and a finished cured Barcol hardness of 94-104 as tested by ASTM D-2583 standards. The unit has a reinforced fiberglass coating with a 15% minimum fiberglass content. It meets ANSI 117.1 and ANSI Z 124.2 requirements, has a backside fire rating of "A" and a flame spread of less than 25. The base is attached to the sump of the unit in such a way to form an integral part with an inner and outer coating of reinforced polyester resin. It meets requirements for Universal Plumbing Code administered by IAPMO, HUD, BOCA, NAHB and Southern Building Code.

AQUARIUS - H 4848 BF Special Needs Barrier Free Shower

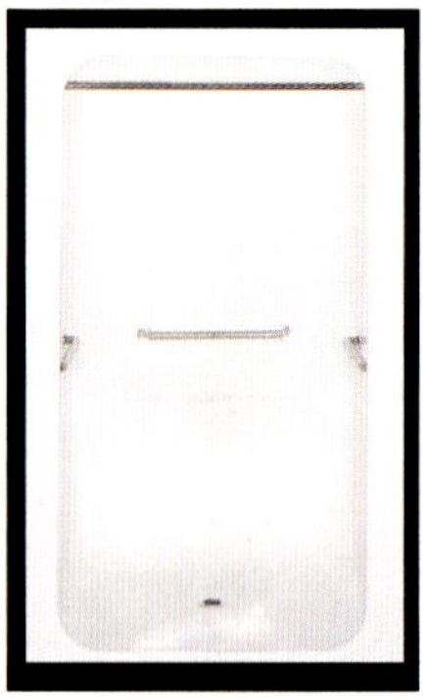

The **Aquarius H 4848 BF** is a Transfer Type Barrier Free Shower available in right, left or center. The unit is vacuum-formed from a cross-linked, continuous cast acrylic sheet with a minimum thickness of .187 mils and a finished cured Barcol hardness of 94-104 as tested by ASTM D-2583 standards. The unit has a reinforced fiberglass coating with a 15% minimum fiberglass content. It meets ANSI 117.1 and ANSI Z 124.2 requirements, has a backside fire rating of "A" and a flame spread of less than 25. The base is attached to the sump of the unit in such a way to form an integral part with an inner and outer coating of reinforced polyester resin. It meets requirements for Universal Plumbing Code administered by IAPMO, HUD, BOCA, NAHB and Southern Building Code.

AQUARIUS™

AQUARIUS™

Praxis Industries, Inc.
Route 1, Box 46 D
Industrial Park
Savannah, TN 38372
(800) 443-7269
FAX (901) 925-4290

C584
15445/STR
BuyLine 8653

Strom Plumbing

P0150

P0146

P0461

BY

Sign of the Crab

Sign of the Crab, Ltd.
3756 Omec Circle, Dept. 214
Rancho Cordova, CA 95742

Telephone (916) 638-2722
FAX (916) 638-2725

SIGN OF THE CRAB specializes in solid brass plumbing and decorative accessories. Through years of product development, our products include authentic reproduction items and new, designer-oriented products. Also available is the service that is necessary to see your project through to completion. We have custom made many items to include stainless steel and brass products for the Sheraton Palace Hotel in San Francisco and the Beverly Wilshire Hotel in Beverly Hills.

Enclosed is a sampling of some of our items. Please write to us or call us for our complete catalog available at no charge to the trade. We welcome you to the world of STROM PLUMBING.

P0462

P0460

C584
15445/STR
BuyLine 8653

This photograph indicates how towel bars and other bath accessories can be modified with different escutcheons to create a bath "suite", thereby coordinating an entire room with matching faucets and accessories.

P0034 – Leg Tub Shower Enclosure Set.

Includes: P0006, P0008, P0009, P0010.

P0006 – Leg Tub Faucet with Diverter. Porcelain handles marked "Hot", "Cold" and "Shower", 33/8″ centers.

P0008 – Shower Enclosure with Adjustable Ceiling 36″ and Wall 12″ Braces. 5/8″ (1/4″ IPS) heavy gauge polished brass tubing, 45″ long, 25″ wide.

P0009 – Shower Riser (2 piece). 3/8″ brass pipe size, 5′ total height, 1/2″ iron pipe size shower head fitting extends 9″ from vertical.

P0010 – Shower Head. Polished brass, 47/8″ diameter, 1/2″ IPS connection.

All items may be purchased separately.

P0034P – Leg Tub Enclosure Set. *Same as P0034, but with P0051 porcelain shower head instead of P0010.*

For gooseneck spout order P0400 faucet or P0403 enclosure set

P0034 – Shower Enclosure
P0034P – Shower Enclosure with P0051 Porcelain Shower Head

P0008-1 – C Clamp only.

Extra braces include c-clamp, brace & escutcheon:

P0008 – 12
P0008 - 24
P0008 - 36
P0008 - 48

C584
15445/STR
BuyLine 8653

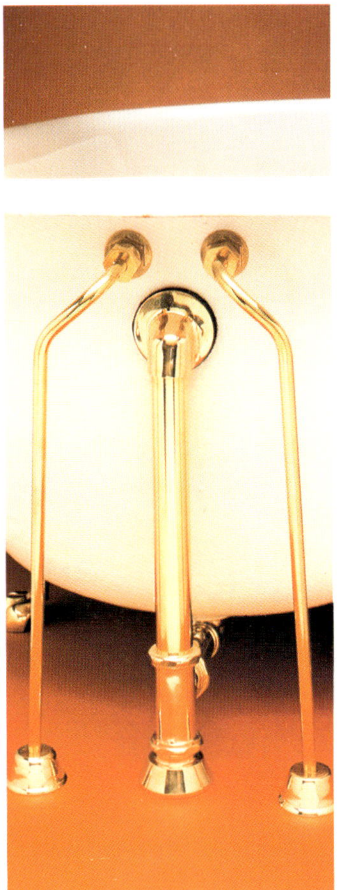

P0011 – Shown with P0007

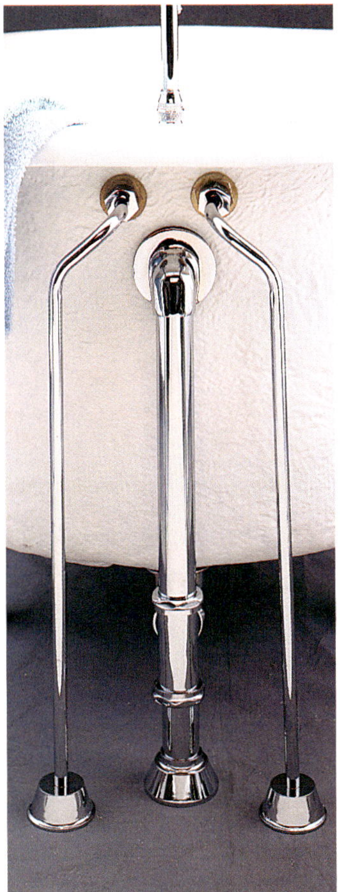

P0011C – Shown with P0007C

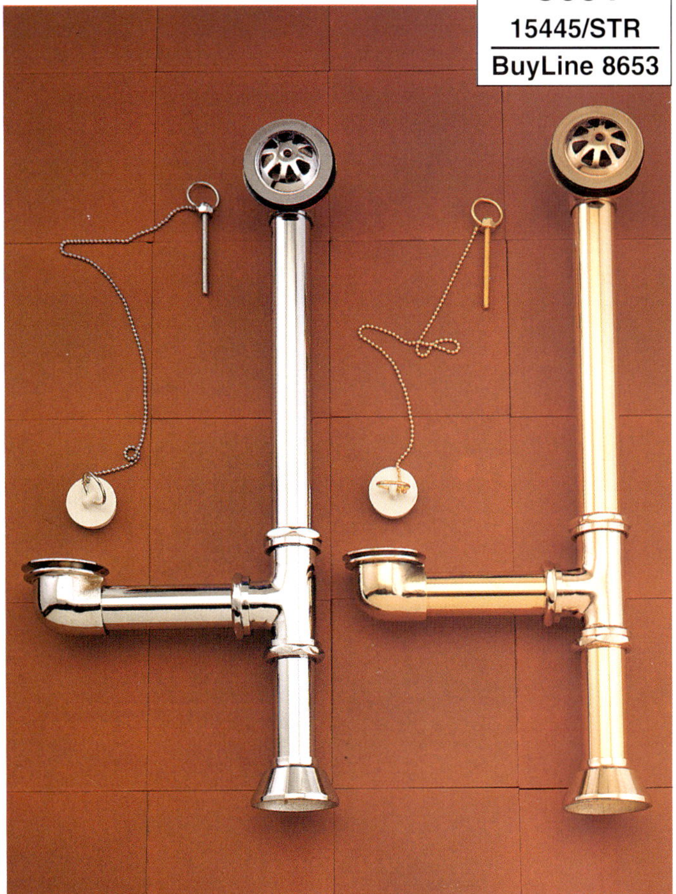

P0007C

P0007

P0149-1 and P0398

P0398

P0146 and P0398

P0140

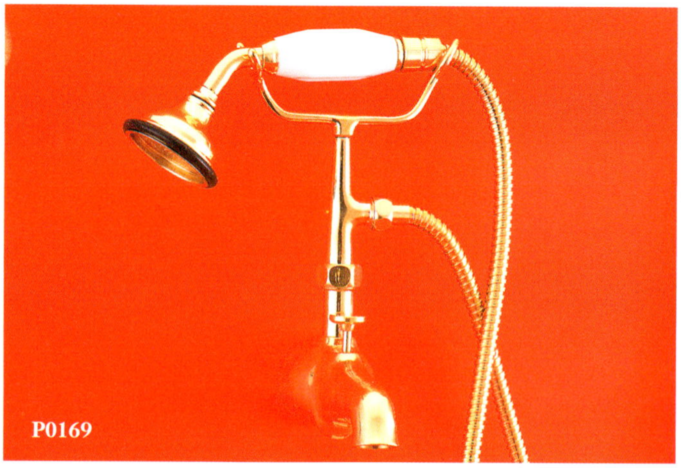

P0169

P0402

P0400C

P0499C

P0460

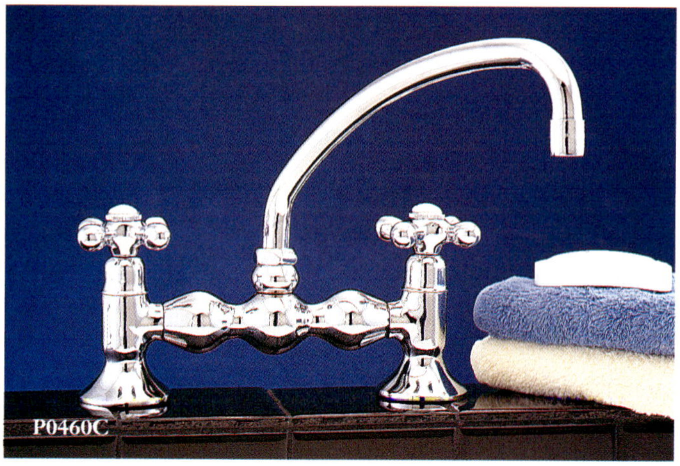

P0460C

C584
15445/STR
BuyLine 8653

P0353C

P0354C

P0355C

P0356C

P0357C

P0353C on P0081 Pedestal Lav

P0359C – Roman Tub Set
P0362C – Roman Spout Only

P0360C – Tub & Shower Set
P0408C – Tub Only Set
P0409C – Shower Only Set

P0188

P0188C

P0188X

P0188XC

P0317 – Tub & Shower Set
P0449 – Tub Only Set
P0450 – Shower Only Set

P0317C – Tub & Shower Set
P0449C – Tub Only Set
P0450C – Shower Only Set

P0444

P0445 – Tub & Shower Set
P0446 – Tub Only Set
P0447 – Shower Only Set

C587
BuyLine 8659

BROAN®

Medicine Cabinets & Lighting

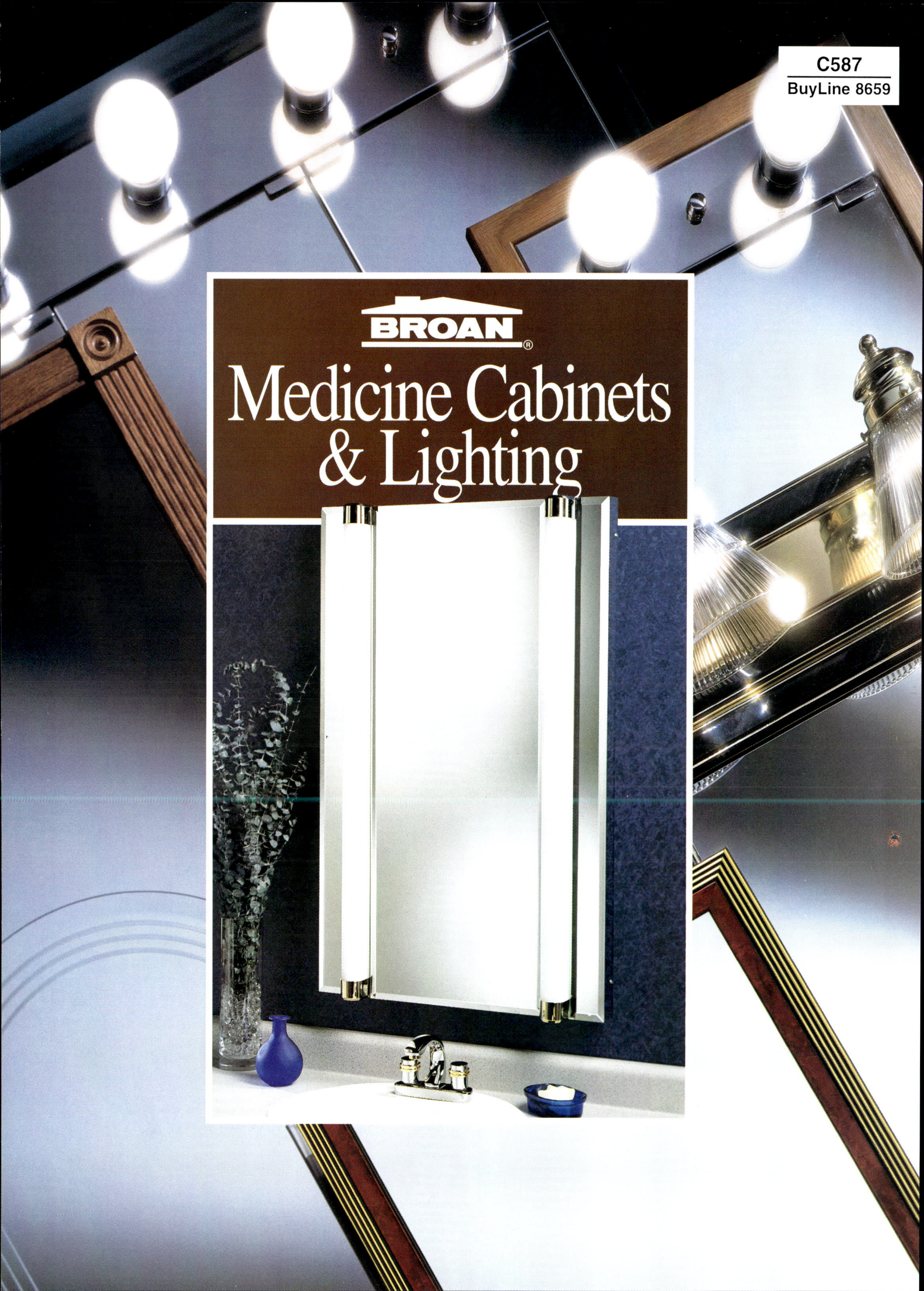

Introducing this streamlined, elegant new look for your bath from Broan...

Contents

FRAMELESS 4-10

METAL TRIMMED MIRRORS . . 11

DECORATOR FRAMES . . . 12-15

WOOD FRAMES 16-22

WOOD BODY CABINETS . . 23-24

SPECIALTY CABINETS . . . 25-30

SPECIFICATIONS 31-35

Welcome to the world of Broan Medicine Cabinets and Lighting. This catalog includes a unique variety of lighting, mirrors and storage options for your bathroom. To help you review our large selection, we have divided the catalog into sections by product similarities, and included a detailed specification list at the back, making it easy for you to choose the right models to meet your individual needs.

Throughout our product line, Broan prides itself on quality and craftsmanship. From genuine oak frames to the jewel-like finish of our beveled-edge mirrors, no detail is overlooked. We use premium float glass mirrors for distortion-free viewing and all lighting products are UL listed so they can be installed with confidence. In each design and with all of our materials, we strive to balance timeless beauty with the decorative trends of today and the enduring quality construction that our customers demand.

Broan selection, quality and value... a nice reflection on you!

BROAN®

Luminary (See page 5)

The Luminary is the newest look in bathroom lighting from Broan. Designed to capitalize on the trend toward taller cabinets, the 24-inch wide mirror is perfect for side-by-side installation in a his-and-her, dual vanity. The cabinet has a soft grey interior and is perfect for color-corrected bulbs that cast a natural glow over skin tones for ideal cosmetic lighting, as well as energy savings. Crafted of premium float glass, the mirror has sealed, beveled edges for an elegant finish–and the quality and style you always expect from Broan.

The Frameless group of cabinets offers the beauty of mirrored panels that multiply the available light for an increased sense of space.

Cabinet PRC1148; PRL1048 Soffit Light

Cabinet LBC10

PRIMEVÉRE *Expressions*

Tasteful design on a grand scale, our leader in luxury options features a polished-edge, clear tri-view mirror framed with beveled mirror trim in clear finish. The accompanying 8" diameter magnifying mirror can be mounted on the inside of the cabinet door at the height of your choice. Matching soffit light with mirror trim sold separately; features instant-on, warm-tone, color-correct fluorescent light (included). Parabolic diffuser softens the light for a decidedly elegant atmosphere.

Style	Model	Overall Size W H D	Wall Opening W H D
Tri-View Built-In Cabinets	PRC1148 PRC1160	48 x 37⅜ 60 x 37⅜	36⅞ x 32⅞ x 3⅞ 48⅞ x 32⅞ x 3⅞
Tri-View Wall Mount Cabinets	PRC1148SM PRC1160SM	48¼ x 37⅜ 60¼ x 37⅜	– –
Matching Soffit Lights for Tri-View Wall Mount or Built-In Cabinets	PRL1048 PRL1060	48 x 4¼ x 5⅜ 60 x 4¼ x 5⅜	– –

LE BACCARAT *Expressions*

Like fine cut crystal, Le Baccarat brings the bath to life with a rich kaleidoscope of light. This arched-top, beveled mirror is framed in clear finish mirror mosaic trim with a clear mirrored single-door in the center. Matching wall mirrors echo the arched motif and the mosaic beveled glass design. The accompanying 8" diameter magnifying mirror can be mounted on the inside of the cabinet door at the height of your choice.

Style	Model	Overall Size W H D	Wall Opening W H D
Single-Door Built-In Cabinet	LBC10	24 x 35⅜	16½ x 25¼ x 3⅞
Wall Mirror Only	LBM15	24 x 35⅜	–

Models on this page are handcrafted. Please allow time for these special orders.

FRAMELESS

For a contemporary look with an elegant note, the Luminary is the newest introduction from Broan.

Cabinet 658BC

Cabinet 658BC

LUMINARY

Perfect for side-by-side installation, the Luminary is designed to capitalize on the trend toward taller cabinets. Color-corrected bulbs (not included) cast natural light while saving energy. The high quality float glass mirror has sealed 1/2" beveled edges for an elegant finish.

Style	Model	Overall Size W H D	Wall Opening W H D
Single-Door Built-In Cabinet	658BC	24 x 37⅜	14¼ x 34¼ x 3½
Single-Door Wall Mount Cabinet	652BC	24 x 37⅜ x 7¼	–

Chrome lens caps available on request. Part # 90714216

See pages 31-35 for detailed specifications.

Cabinet 655236

SATURN

The distinctive look of the industry's first 1/2" beveled-edge, tri-view mirror designed for new warm-tone fluorescent light tubes (not included). These lights provide true-color reflections making them ideal for cosmetic lighting, while offering substantial energy savings over incandescent bulbs. Electrical outlets inside cabinet add convenience and glass shelves add elegance.

Style	Model	Overall Size W H D	Wall Opening W H D
Tri-View Built-In Cabinets	655036 655048	36 x 30 48 x 30	33¾ x 24¾ x 3½ 45¾ x 24¾ x 3½
Tri-View Wall Mount Cabinets	655236 655248	36 x 30 48 x 30	– –

Chrome lens caps available on request. Part # 90714216

Cabinet 5528; Lights 73591

TORINO

Beveled-edge and frosted cut-glass teardrop designs are ideal for use with a "his-n-hers" vanity or pedestal sinks. Matching side light fixtures feature beveled-edge mirror backplates and frosted glass shades.

Style	Model	Overall Size W H D	Wall Opening W H D
Single-Door Built-In Cabinets	5520 5528	16½ x 34½ 16½ x 34½	14 x 18 x 3½ 14 x 24 x 3½
Side Lights for Single-Door Built-In Cabinets	73591*	5⅜ x 13¾ x 6½	–

*Packed in pairs.

See pages 31-35 for detailed specifications.

Cabinet 1350

Cabinet 1454; Lights 73190

Cameo Oval Bevel

This cabinet features the tailored elegance of a classic cameo oval mirrored door. Frameless, 1" beveled-edge float glass mirror is supported by heavy-gauge steel construction. Adjustable shelves. Reversible.

Style	Model	Overall Size W H D	Wall Opening W H D
Single-Door Built-In Cabinets	1350 1358	21 x 31 24 x 35	14 x 18 x 3½ 14 x 24 x 3½

Mirage

Faceted like a gemstone, this octagonal, 1/2" beveled-edge mirror cabinet teams nicely with side lights featuring beveled-edge mirror backplates and smoked glass shades.

Style	Model	Overall Size W H D	Wall Opening W H D
Single-Door Built-In Cabinets	1454 1456	18 x 27 17⅜ x 32	14 x 18 x 3½ 14 x 24 x 3½
Side Lights for Single-Door Built-In Cabinets	73190*	5 x 12 x 6½	–

*Packed in pairs. (Globes are smoked glass and accommodate slim line 60w bulbs.)

Sonata

Graceful top and bottom curves on this 1/2" beveled-edge cabinet and lights make an elegant and unusual ensemble in a single-door design. Matching side light fixtures feature beveled-edge mirror backplate and distinctive frosted glass shades with grey accent and chrome-plated fittings.

Style	Model	Overall Size W H D	Wall Opening W H D
Single-Door Built-In Cabinet	258	16 x 32	14 x 24 x 3½
Side Lights for Single-Door Built-In Cabinet	72052*	5 x 17½ x 6⅛	–

*Packed in pairs.

Cabinet 258; Lights 72052

FRAMELESS

Cabinet 1420FL; Light 735FL

Cabinet 1418; Light 73290

Decorah

Beveled-edge mirror with a soft gold-tone and soft white floral design lends a unique decorator touch that beautifully completes an overall floral motif.

Style	Model	Overall Size W H D	Wall Opening W H D
Single-Door Built-In Cabinet	1420FL	16 x 26	14 x 18 x 3½
Top Light for Single-Door Built-In Cabinet	735FL	16 x 4⅜ x 2	–

Aurora

Deep-cut, 1/2" beveled-edge design mirrors fill the bath with shimmering reflections, adding a new dimension to a classic style.

Style	Model	Overall Size W H D	Wall Opening W H D
Single-Door Built-In Cabinet	1418	16 x 26	14 x 24 x 3½
Top Light for Single-Door Built-In Cabinet	73290	16 x 4½ x 2	–

Mirror-on-Mirror

Stunning 1/2" beveled-edge, mirror-on-mirror designs create a sophisticated, upscale look even in small-space environments. Each features a clear center mirror with contrasting grey smoke background mirror for an all-glass, picture-frame effect.

Style	Oval Model	Rectangular Model	Overall Size W H D	Wall Opening W H D
Single-Door Built-In Cabinets	1452 1457	1450BC 1458	16 x 26 16 x 26	14 x 18 x 3½ 14 x 24 x 3½
Top Light for Single-Door Built-In Models	73290	73290	16 x 4½ x 2	–
Side Lights for Single-Door Built-In Models	73190*	73190*	5 x 12 x 6½	–

*Packed in pairs. (Globes are smoked glass and accommodate slim line 60w bulbs.)

Cabinet 1450BC; Lights 73190

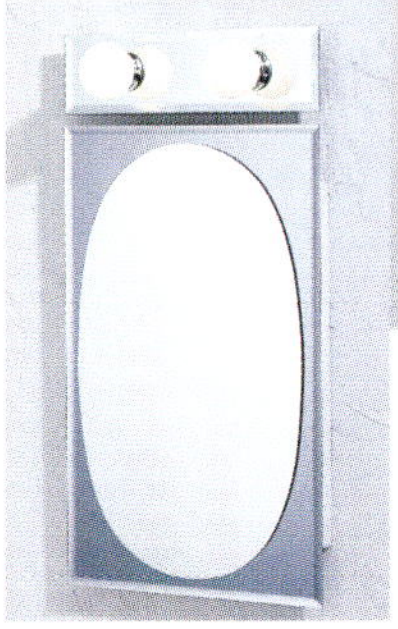

Cabinet 1452; Light 73290

Cabinet 255236; Light HO33690

Cabinet 1451; Light 73290

HORIZON

Our most popular style, the Horizon features the understated elegance of beveled-edge design. A wide selection of tri-view and single-door models and optional matching light bars means this classic is right at home in any size bath.

Style	Model	Overall Size W H D	Wall Opening W H D
Tri-View Built-In Cabinets	255024	24 x 24	21¾ x 20⅞ x 3½
	255030	30 x 28¼	27¾ x 25⅛ x 3½
	255036	36 x 28¼	33¾ x 25⅛ x 3½
	255048	48 x 28¼	45¾ x 25⅛ x 3½
Tri-View Wall Mount Cabinets	255224	24 x 24 x 5¼	–
	255230	30 x 28¼ x 5¼	–
	255236	36 x 28¼ x 5¼	–
	255248	48 x 28¼ x 5¼	–
Top Lights for Tri-View Built-In Cabinets	HO42490	24 x 4½ x 2¼	–
	HO43090	30 x 4½ x 2¼	–
	HO43690	36 x 4½ x 2¼	–
	HO44890	48 x 4½ x 2¼	–
Top Lights for Tri-View Wall Mount Cabinet	HO32490	24 x 4½ x 5⅞	–
	HO33090	30 x 4½ x 5⅞	–
	HO33690	36 x 4½ x 5⅞	–
	HO34890	48 x 4½ x 5⅞	–
Single-Door Built-In Cabinets	1451	16 x 26	14 x 18 x 3½
	1459	16 x 26	14 x 24 x 3½
	1453†	16 x 20	14 x 18 x 2½
Side Lights for Built-In Cabinets	73190*	5 x 12 x 6½	–
Top Light for Single-Door Built-In Cabinets	73290	16 x 4½ x 2	–

*Packed in pairs — See page 7 for picture.
†Molded body.
(See page 29 for stainless steel body cabinets.)

Cabinet 295230

FOCUS

Simple, clean polished-edge design enables this tri-view mirror with built-in top lights to complement a diverse range of decorating styles.

Style	Model	Overall Size W H D
Tri-View Wall Mount Cabinets	295224	24 x 30 x 5¼
	295230	30 x 34 x 5¼

See pages 31-35 for detailed specifications.

Cabinet 455248

QUANTUM

Beveled-edge elegance with a softened radius corner design. Quantum is ideal for the curvaceous, flowing lines of many of today's vanity tops and bath fixtures.

Style	Model	Overall Size W H D
Tri-View Wall Mount Cabinets	455230	30 x 36½ x 5¼
	455236	36 x 36½ x 5¼
	455248	48 x 36½ x 5¼

LAFAYETTE

A choice of beveled-edge mirror cabinets to suit your decorating tastes. Both square corner and radius corner styles feature built-in top lights.

Style	Model	Overall Size W H D
Single-Door Wall Mount Cabinets	1402	18⅛ x 32⅜ x 6
	1462	18⅛ x 28⅜ x 6

Cabinet 1462

Cabinet 1402

Broan's Metal Trimmed line is styled to emphasize a modern functionality with a flair all its own.

Cabinet 155130; Light SB23129

VIENNA

Our most economical steel body tri-view cabinet, the Vienna features contemporary elegance trimmed in polished chrome finish. Matching top light has polished stainless steel faceplate.

Style	Model	Overall Size W H D
Tri-View Wall Mount Cabinets	155124 155130	24 x 26 x 5½ 30 x 26 x 5½
Top Lights for Tri-View Wall Mount Cabinets	SB22529 SB23129	24 x 4 x 5½ 30 x 4 x 5½

Cabinet 565

STYLELINE 2

The Styleline 2 has stainless steel trim top and bottom, with polished vertical edges. Built-in top light features stainless steel faceplate.

Style	Model	Overall Size W H D
Single-Door Wall Mount Cabinet	565	18 x 28 x 6

See pages 31-35 for detailed specifications.

Broan's Decorator Frames series offers unique patterns, designs and colors to accessorize your bath or powder room.

A duo with neo-classical timelessness, the Classico medicine cabinet and matching fixture are available in Honey Oak Burl with gold trim or Mahogany Burl with black trim.

Cabinet 3890; Light 715M

Cabinet 3870; Light 715K

CLASSICO

Smart, neo-classical styling adds flavor to bathroom decor. Available in two finishes: Honey Oak Burl with Gold Accent, or Mahogany Burl with Black Accent. Both have plate glass mirror and heavy gauge steel construction. Matching top light fixtures feature glass shades, brass fittings, brass faceplate and use standard 60 watt bulbs.

Style	Oak Model	Mahogany Model	Overall Size W H D	Wall Opening W H D
Single-Door Built-In Cabinets	3870 3878	3890 3898	18 1/16 x 28 1/16 18 1/16 x 28 1/16	14 x 18 x 3 1/2 14 x 24 x 3 1/2
Single-Door Wall Mount Cabinets (almond body)	3872	3892	18 1/16 x 28 1/16	–
Top Lights for Single-Door Built-In Cabinet	715K	715M	18 5/8 x 8 x 7	–
Top Lights for Single-Door Wall Mount Cabinet	716K	716M	18 1/16 x 8 x 9 3/4	–

See pages 31-35 for detailed specifications.

Cabinet 3910; Light 711FG

With the exquisitely elegant look inspired by the artistry of Florentine craftsmen, the Florentine medicine cabinet and light fixture are the perfect addition to the classic bath.

FLORENTINE

With classic Italian-style details finished in simulated gold leaf for the traditional American home, this style has 3/4" beveled-edge float glass mirrors, and heavy gauge steel construction. Matching light fixture features glass shades, brass fittings, mirror faceplate, and uses standard 60 watt bulbs.

Style	Model	Overall Size W H D	Wall Opening W H D
Single-Door Built-In Cabinets	3910 3918	17 15/16 x 27 15/16 17 15/16 x 27 15/16	14 x 18 x 3½ 14 x 24 x 3½
Single-Door Wall Mount Cabinet (almond body)	3912	17 15/16 x 27 15/16	–
Top lights for Built-In Cabinet Light	711FG	17 15/16 x 8 x 6 15/16	–
Top Lights for Wall Mount Cabinet	712FG	17 15/16 x 8 x 9 15/16	–

Cabinet 6120; Light 761WH

The beauty of the flowering Hibiscus is captured in the Art Nouveau look of this distinctive cabinet and complementary light fixture.

Almond

Forest Green

HIBISCUS

Dramatic Art Nouveau styling accents matching cabinets and light fixtures with 3-dimensional floral carving. Available in 3 high-gloss lacquer finishes: White, Almond, and Forest Green. The white and almond models can be painted to further customize them to your bathroom color scheme. Float glass mirrors. Heavy-gauge steel storage cabinets. Light fixtures use G-25 bulbs.

Style	White Model	Almond* Model	Green* Model	Overall Size W H D	Wall Opening W H D
Single-Door Built-In Cabinets	6120	6130	6140	18½ x 27½	14 x 18 x 3½
Single-Door Wall Mount Cabinets	6122	6132	6142	18½ x 27½	–
Top Lights for Built-In Cabinets	761WH	761AL	761GR	18½ x 6¾ x 3	–
Top Lights for Wall Mount Cabinets	762WH	762AL	762GR	18½ x 6¾ x 5½	–

*Please allow extra time for customization.

Cabinet 350WH (3); Light 745WH (3)

SPECTRUM WITH MATCHING LIGHTING

Spectrum single door medicine cabinets feature a white "Enduro" frame with "hardshell" acrylic finish on a molded core which offers long life in the high moisture atmosphere of a bathroom. Matching top light fixtures feature bright chrome faceplate.

Style	Model	Overall Size W H D	Wall Opening W H D
Single-Door Built-In Cabinets	350WH 358WH	18 x 27½ 18 x 27½	14 x 18 x 3½ 14 x 24 x 3½
Top Light for Single-Door Built-In Cabinets	745WH	18 x 6½ x 3	–

SPECTRUM TRI-VIEW

Tri-view cabinets with matching top light are available in gloss white and are constructed using the same Enduro frame material as other styles.

Style	Model	Overall Size W H D	Wall Opening W H D
Tri-View Wall Mount or Built-In Cabinets	3230WH 3236WH	30 x 30 x 4½ 36 x 30 x 4½	27½ x 27 x 3½* 33½ x 27 x 3½*
Top Lights for Tri-View Wall Mount Cabinets	SP132WH SP133WH	30 x 6½ x 5¼ 36 x 6½ x 5¼	– –

*Optional Wall Opening.

Cabinet 3236WH; Light SP133WH

SPECTRUM WITH BUILT-IN LIGHTING

This model, also in white, features a look similar to the other Spectrum models, but with a built-in light for a compact, space-saving look and easy installations.

Style	Model	Overall Size W H D	Wall Opening W H D
Tri-View Wall Mount or Built-In Cabinets w/Built-In Top Light	3330WH 3336WH	31 x 30⅜ x 5 37 x 30⅜ x 5	28¾ x 27½ x 3½* 34¾ x 27½ x 3½*
Single-Door Wall Mount or Built-In Cabinet w/Built-In Top Light	2009WH	19⅛ x 32¼ x 5	16¾ x 28¾ x 3½

*Optional Wall Opening.

Cabinet 3336WH

Cabinet 2009WH

VERONA

Reflective, glossy metallic-framed mirror in fixture-matching brass finish. Molded frame core is designed for the bath.

Style	Model	Overall Size W H D	Wall Opening W H D
Single-Door Built-In Cabinets	310BR 318BR 313BR†	17¼ x 27¼ 17¼ x 27¼ 16 x 20	14 x 18 x 3½ 14 x 24 x 3½ 14 x 18 x 2½
Top Light for Single-Door Built-In Cabinets	747BR	17¼ x 5½ x 3	

†Molded body.

Cabinet 318BR; Light 747BR

VICEROY

Bright brass metallic-look framing on a molded core complement today's bathroom accessories.

Style	Model	Overall Size W H D	Wall Opening W H D
Single-Door Wall Mount or Built-In Cabinet w/Built-In Top Light	2012BR	18 x 31 x 5	16¾ x 29 x 3½*

*Optional Wall Opening.

Cabinet 2012BR

See pages 31-35 for detailed specifications.

This Wood Frame series uses natural and painted hardwoods to achieve a warm look matching or complementing your bathroom decor.

Cabinet 820; Light 70323

Cabinet 870, Light 70373

BAKER STREET

Charming Victorian detail lends a distinctive period touch to practical bathroom storage. Choose from classic colonial white painted hardwood or warm, honey-finish solid oak frames. Matching light fixtures feature frosted glass shades and bright brass fittings.

Style	Colonial White Model	Honey Oak Model	Overall Size W H D	Wall Opening W H D
Tri-View Wall Mount Cabinets	842230 842236	– –	30 x 28½ x 5½ 36 x 28½ x 5½	– –
Top Lights for Tri-View Wall Mount Cabinets	BS84023 BS84623	– –	30 x 6 x 6½ 36 x 6 x 6½	– –
Single-Door Built-In Cabinets	820 828	870 878	18 x 27 18 x 27	14 x 18 x 3½ 14 x 24 x 3½
Single-Door Wall Mount Cabinets	822	872	18 x 27 x 5	–
Top Lights for Single-Door Built-In Cabinets	70323	70373	18 x 8 x 9	–
Top Lights for Single-Door Wall Mount Cabinets	70223	70273	18 x 8 x 13½	–

Cabinet 842236; Light BS84623

Cabinet 8570; Light 76378

CANTERBURY

This traditional cathedral arch design is available in solid oak with honey oak finish and matching finish sides. Matching top lights feature clear ribbed prismatic glass shades and bright brass fittings for a warm, inviting look.

Style	Model	Overall Size W H D	Wall Opening W H D
Single-Door Built-In Cabinet	8570	18¼ x 27¼	14 x 18 x 3½
Single-Door Wall Mount Cabinet	8572	18¼ x 27¼ x 5½	–
Top Light for Single-Door Built-In Cabinet	76378	18 x 8 x 8	–
Top Light for Single-Door Wall Mount Cabinet	76478	18 x 8 x 11½	–

See pages 31-35 for detailed specifications.

Cabinet 562230; Light WH53023

Cabinet 5622; Light 708WH

WHITE MARBLE

Solid oak frame with honey oak finish has white onyx cultured marble inlay. White accent brightens the room; oak frame blends with most wood vanities. Also looks great over a white pedestal sink. Matching wood-tone sides.

Style	Model	Overall Size W H D	Wall Opening W H D
Tri-View Wall Mount Cabinet	562230	30 x 28½ x 5¼	–
Top Light for Tri-View Wall Mount Cabinet	WH53023	30 x 7¼ x 12¼	–
Single-Door Wall Mount Cabinet	5622	17⅛ x 27⅛ x 5½	–
Top Light for Wall Mount Cabinet	708WH	17⅛ x 7¼ x 10⅛	–

Cabinet 8120; Light 70928

PRAIRIE

Painted hardwood frame with traditional detailing is simply elegant in colonial white. Matching top light fixtures feature clear prismatic glass shades and bright brass finish fittings.

Style	Model	Overall Size W H D	Wall Opening W H D
Single-Door Built-In Cabinets	8120 8128	18 x 27½ 18 x 27½	14 x 18 x 3½ 14 x 24 x 3½
Single-Door Wall Mount Cabinet	8122	18 x 27½ x 5	–
Top Light for Single-Door Built-In Cabinets	70928	18 x 8 x 8	–

Note: The Prairie can also be special ordered in two tri-view sizes featuring a blonde oak finish frame.

Style	Model	Overall Size W H D	Wall Opening W H D
Tri-View Wall Mount Cabinets	8199703 8199704	30 x 28⁵⁄₁₆ 36 x 28⁵⁄₁₆	– –
Top Lights for Tri-View Wall Mount Cabinets	OK8199705 OK8199706	30 x 8 x 8 36 x 8 x 8	– –

AUTUMN

Warm solid oak, honey finish frame with matching wood-tone sides. Canopy design shields bulbs and provides close-up make-up light, yet delivers plenty of subdued lighting for the whole bath.

Style	Model	Overall Size W H D	Wall Opening W H D
Tri-View Wall Mount or Built-In Cabinets	197230 197236	30 x 29 x 5½ 36 x 29 x 5½	28¾ x 27½ x 3½* 34¾ x 27½ x 3½*

*Optional Wall Opening.

Cabinet 197236

See pages 31-35 for detailed specifications.

Grand Oak II

Solid oak frame, honey finish tri-view cabinet for wall mounting or built-in installation. Top light has matching frame and oak finish faceplates. Light is designed for use with wall mount cabinet.

Style	Model	Overall Size W H D	Wall Opening W H D
Tri-View Wall Mount or Built-In Cabinets	277924 277930 277936 277948	24 x 25 29 x 28⅞ 35 x 28⅞ 47 x 28⅞	22¼ x 23 x 3½* 27½ x 27 x 3½* 33½ x 27 x 3½* 45½ x 27 x 3½*
Top Lights for Tri-View Wall Mount Cabinets	SG32479 SG33079 SG33679 SG34879	24 x 5⅝ x 4¾ 29 x 5⅝ x 4¾ 35 x 5⅝ x 4¾ 47 x 5⅝ x 4¾	– – – –
Wood Tone Trim Kit for Wall Mount Application	97014099	–	–

*Optional Wall Opening.

Cabinet 277930; Light SG33079

Grant

Solid oak, honey finish frame cabinet has top light with matching frame and oak finish faceplate.

Style	Model	Overall Size W H D	Wall Opening W H D
Single-Door Built-In Cabinets	8770 8778 8773† 973BC†	16¼ x 24¼ 16¼ x 26¼ 16¼ x 22 16 x 20	14 x 18 x 3½ 14 x 24 x 3½ 14 x 18 x 2½ 14 x 18 x 2½
Single-Door Wall Mount Cabinet	8772	16¼ x 24¼ x 5½	–
Top Light for Single-Door Built-In Cabinets	74279	16¼ x 5½ x 3	–

†Molded body.

Cabinet 8778; Light 74279

Cabinet 2072

Oakdale

This cabinet, in solid oak with a honey oak finish, features attached lighting for one-step installation.

Style	Model	Overall Size W H D	Wall Opening W H D
Single-Door Wall Mount or Built-In Cabinet	2072	18 x 31 x 5½	16¾ x 28¾ x 3½*

*Optional Wall Opening.

Dunhill

Solid oak oval with honey finish frames your face in cameo style.

Style	Model	Overall Size W H D	Wall Opening W H D
Single-Door Built-In Cabinet	1370	21 x 31	14 x 18 x 3½

Cabinet 1370

See pages 31-35 for detailed specifications.

Cabinet 8278

Cabinet 8378; Light 71829

Chapel Hill

Honey oak finish mirror frame has contemporary rounded-edge styling.

Style	Model	Overall Size W H D	Wall Opening W H D
Single-Door Built-In Cabinet	8278	17¼ x 27¼	14 x 24 x 3½

Kingston

Solid wood, honey oak mirror frame with beveled-edge mirror has a shadow box effect.

Style	Model	Overall Size W H D	Wall Opening W H D
Single-Door Built-In Cabinets	8370 8378	16½ x 26½ 16½ x 26½	14 x 18 x 3½ 14 x 24 x 3½
Top Light for Single-Door Built-In Cabinets	71829	16½ x 5½ x 2¼	–

Oakhill

Classically shaped edges on this solid oak, honey finish frame make it a traditional style. Attached top lights make wall mounting or built-in installation easier.

Style	Model	Overall Size W H D	Wall Opening W H D
Tri-View Wall Mount or Built-In Cabinets w/Built-In Top Lights	177924 177930 177936 177948	23¼ x 29⅝ x 4¼ 30 x 29⅝ x 4¼ 36 x 29⅝ x 4¼ 48 x 29⅝ x 4¼	22¾ x 27½ x 3½* 28¾ x 27½ x 3½* 34¾ x 27½ x 3½* 46¾ x 27½ x 3½*

*Optional Wall Opening.

Cabinet 177930

The Prestique Wood Body cabinets feature beautiful woods in a variety of classic designs with ample storage capacities.

Cabinet 907236; Light CR93679

Cabinet 902236; Lights CR93629

Solid Oak or White Frame

Our most popular wood body tri-view cabinet features solid oak or white painted hardwood frames with matching finish cabinet body. Matching top light for the oak model has brass finish faceplate and white model has bright chrome finish faceplate.

Style	Solid Oak Model	White Model	Overall Size W H D
Tri-View Wall Mount Cabinets	907224 907230 907236 907248	902224 902230 902236 –	24 x 26 x 4¾ 30 x 30 x 4¾ 36 x 30 x 4¾ 48 x 30 x 4¾
Top Lights for Tri-View Wall Mount Cabinets	– CR93079 CR93679	CR92429 CR93029 CR93629	24 x 5⅞ x 5½ 30 x 5⅞ x 5½ 36 x 5⅞ x 5½
Bulk Pack Tri-View Cabinet			
(24 - bulk pack)	907224BP*	–	24 x 26 x 4¾
(20 - bulk pack)	907230BP*	–	30 x 30 x 4¾

*Bulk pack models have open face cartons with top and bottom banded carton caps.

Prestique Bathroom Cabinets

Our Prestique Series features:
- Cabinet-maker wood box styling
- Sturdy glue-and-nail butt-joint construction
- Classic designs at affordable prices

Cabinet 905236; Light CR93690

Frameless Beveled-Edge

This frameless, tri-view cabinet has beveled-edge glass mirrors and matching, mirrored light fixture.

Style	Model	Overall Size W H D
Tri-View Wall Mount Cabinets	905224 905230 905236 905248	24 x 26 x 4¾ 30 x 30 x 4¾ 36 x 30 x 4¾ 48 x 30 x 4¾
Top Lights for Tri-View Wall Mount Cabinets	CR92490 CR93090 CR93690 CR94890	24 x 5⅞ x 5½ 30 x 5⅞ x 5½ 36 x 5⅞ x 5½ 48 x 5⅞ x 5½

See pages 31-35 for detailed specifications.

Wood Frame with Built-in Top Light

All-in-one frame style offers upscale look in a value-priced cabinet. Available in tri-view and single-door models in oak or white finish. Lights have bright chrome finish faceplate.

Style	Oak Model	White Model	Overall Size W H D
Tri-View Wall Mount Cabinets	947224 947230 947236	942224 942230 942236	24 x 28⅞ x 4⅛ 30 x 28⅞ x 4⅛ 36 x 28⅞ x 4⅛
Single-Door Wall Mount Cabinets	9472	9422BC	15¾ x 23⅝ x 4⅛

Cabinet 9472

Cabinet 947230

Perfume & Medicine Cabinets

Add color and variety to any bath with one of Broan's distinctive two-compartment cabinets. The narrow compartment features a clear, beveled-edge glass window with a delicate stenciled pattern and three shelves. It's perfect for displaying today's elegant designer fragrances and colorful health and beauty product packaging. The larger compartment has a framed, beveled-edge mirror door and two shelves.

Style	Oak Model	White Model	Overall Size W H D
2-Door Wall Mount Cabinets	977225	972225	25½ x 28 x 4¾

Cabinet 977225

Cabinet 972225

Wood Frame Cabinets

These value-priced, wood frame cabinets are standardized on a 25½" height and are available in oak or white finish.

Style	Oak Model	White Model	Overall Size W H D
Tri-View Wall Mount Cabinets	967224 967230 967236	– – –	24 x 25½ x 4¾ 30 x 25½ x 4¾ 36 x 25½ x 4¾
Single-Door Wall Mount Cabinets	902 982	902WH 982WH	16 x 20 x 4¾ 16 x 26 x 4¾
Bulk Pack (38 - bulk pack)	902BP	–	16 x 20 x 4¾

Cabinet 967224

Cabinet 902WH

Cabinet 902

Prestique Bathroom Cabinets

Our Prestique Series features:
- Cabinet-maker wood box styling
- Sturdy glue-and-nail butt-joint construction
- Classic designs at affordable prices

Broan's Specialty Cabinets offer unusual sizes and shapes specially designed to meet your unique needs.

Cabinet 629

ILLUSION

Auxiliary storage with frameless, polished, sealed-edge mirror doors, this special low-profile style (1/4" projection from wall) fits flush with adjacent 1/4" wall mirrors.*

Style	Model	Overall Size W H D	Wall Opening W H D
Built-In Cabinets	629	15 x 36	14 x 34 x 3½
	639BC	13 x 36	12 x 34 x 3½

Hide cabinet storage in a flat wall mirror area.

*Surrounding mirrors not included.

See pages 31-35 for detailed specifications.

Avanti Corner Cabinet

Triangular shape ideal for 3-way viewing with a simple wall mirror makes small corner areas look larger.

Style	Model	Trim	Overall Size W H D
Wall Mount Corner Cabinet	631	Stainless Steel	13 x 36 x 7¼

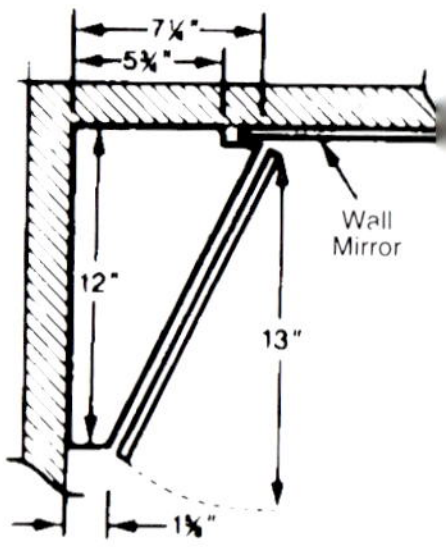

Triangular Shaped

Cabinet 631 (2); Mirror PEM3636 (see pg. 30)

Centered Corner Cabinet

For use over a corner vanity, this corner cabinet is perfect for small spaces.

Style	Model	Trim	Overall Size W H D
Wall Mount Corner Cabinets	672 672SS	Oak Stainless Steel	19½ x 33½ x 10½ 17¼ x 31 x 9⅞

Cabinet 672

Bel Aire Auxiliary

Ideal in combination with a wall mirror and light strips, this model provides extra storage and 3-way viewing. Stainless steel trim top and bottom with polished vertical mirror edges.

Style	Model	Overall Size W H D	Wall Opening W H D
Built-In Cabinet	625	13 x 36	11¼ x 33½
Wall Mount Cabinet	626	13 x 36 x 4¼	–

Cabinet 626 (2); Mirror PEM3036 (see pg. 30)

Cabinet 625

Stainless Steel Body

This easy to clean, rust-resistant single-door cabinet features high luster type 304 stainless steel with bright #4 satin finish and choice of two mirror styles. One-half inch beveled-edge mirror looks like Horizon Series on page 9. Stainless steel looks like Styleline on page 29.

Style	Model	Trim	Overall Size W H D	Wall Opening W H D
Built-In Cabinets	1448	Beveled-Edge	16 x 26	14 x 24 x 3½
	448BC	Stainless Steel Frame	16 x 26	14 x 24 x 3½

Cabinet 1448

Modular Shelf

Our unique cabinet design provides maximum storage capacity. Six modular half-shelves can be positioned in a number of configurations utilizing four snap-in center posts. This flexible design means shelves can quickly be adjusted without tools to accommodate various container sizes.

Style	Model	Trim	Overall Size W H D	Wall Opening W H D
Built-In Cabinet	468MOD	Stainless Steel Frame	16 x 26	14 x 24 x 3½

468MOD

Focus

Polished-edge mirror features simplicity and supreme functionality.

Style	Model	Overall Size W H D	Wall Opening W H D
Single-Door Built-In Cabinets	1430	16 x 22	14 x 18 x 3½
	1438	16 x 26	14 x 24 x 3½
	1433†	16 x 20	14 x 18 x 2½

†Molded body.

Cabinet 1430

See pages 31-35 for detailed specifications.

Oak Hollywood

Solid, honey oak frame and matching wood-tone sides has built-in incandescent top light, grounded outlet, on-off switch and gold-tone door pulls.

Style	Model	Overall Size W H D
Wall Mount Cabinets	2471IL 2871IL	24¾ x 24½ x 9 28¾ x 24½ x 9

Cabinet 2471IL

Beauty Glide

Stainless steel shadow box frame with chrome door pulls features grounded outlet and on-off switch. Models with built-in top light include fluorescent tube.

Style	Model	Overall Size W H D	Wall Opening W H D
Built-In Cabinets Unlighted	SD15 SD41	24 x 18¾ 27½ x 19¼	21½ x 17 x 3½ 26¼ x 17¼ x 3½
Built-In Cabinet w/Top Light	SDL82	27½ x 22	26¼ x 18¼ x 3½

Cabinet SDL82

Ensign

Stainless steel trim with built-in incandescent light includes convenient grounded outlet and on-off switch.

Style	Model	Overall Size W H D
Wall Mount Cabinets	124LP 128LP	24 x 23½ x 8¼ 28 x 23½ x 8¼

Cabinet 128LP

Flair

Our economy leader, this model has incandescent built-in top light, stainless steel trim and on-off switch.

Style	Model	Overall Size W H D
Wall Mount Cabinets	323LP 327LP	24 x 19½ x 8 28 x 19½ x 8

Cabinet 323LP

CABINET 455FL

This one-piece steel storage cabinet has attached fluorescent side lights (tubes included), grounded outlet and on-off switch.

Style	Model	Overall Size W H D	Wall Opening W H D
Built-In Storage Cabinet	455FL	20⅜ x 22¼ x 7⅜	14 x 19 x 3½

Cabinet 455FL

Cabinet 555IL

CABINET 555IL

This surface mounted steel cabinet has a stainless steel frame and trim with built-in light, grounded outlet and on-off switch.

Style	Model	Overall Size W H D
Wall Mount Cabinet	555IL	16 x 24 x 8

STYLELINE

This classic, one-piece mirrored storage cabinet comes in a variety of sizes. Steel or molded body.

Style	Model	Overall Size W H D	Mirror Glass Thickness	Wall Opening W H D
Built-In Cabinets Molded	401ADJ† New! '97	16 x 20	3/32	14 x 18 x 3½
	449BC†	16 x 22	3/32	14 x 18 x 3½
	407ADJ† New! '97	16 x 22	3/32	14 x 18 x 3½
Bulk Packs	405BP	(407BC in a 2-Pack)		
	405BP27	(407BC in a Bulk Pack of 30)		
Built-In Steel Cabinets	410BC	16 x 22	3/32	14 x 18 x 3½
	420BC	16 x 22	1/16	14 x 20 x 3½
	421BC	16 x 22	1/16	14 x 20 x 3½
	458	16 x 26	⅛	14 x 24 x 3½
	468	16 x 26	3/32	14 x 24 x 3½
	468MOD*	16 x 26	1/16	14 x 24 x 3½
	490	18 x 24	3/16	16 x 21½ x 3½
	478FS**	16 x 26	⅛	14 x 24 x 3½
	495	20 x 30	3/16	17¼ x 26¼ x 3½
Wall Mount Steel Cabinets	412SM	16 x 22 x 4¾	3/32	–
	422SM	14 x 20 x 5	3/32	–
	452SM	16 x 22 x 4¾	3/32	–

†Molded body
*Modular storage. See page 27 for details.
**Meets Federal spec #WW-P-541/8B
(For stainless steel body cabinets see page 27.)
ADJ = Adjustable shelves.

Cabinet 407ADJ

WHITE FRAME

Molded polystyrene body with white finish molded frame.

Style	Model	Overall Size W H D	Wall Opening W H D
Built-In Cabinet	313WH	16 x 20	14 x 18 x 2½

Cabinet 313WH

See pages 31-35 for detailed specifications.

These medicine cabinets offer practical style with an emphasis on storage and function.

HIDEAWAY

Steel single-door can be wallpapered to blend with wall for hidden storage and is reversible for left- or right-hand opening. Door has tension latch.

Style	Model	Overall Size W H D	Wall Opening W H D
Single-Door Built-In Cabinet	622	17⅛ x 21½	14 x 18 x 3½

Cabinet 622

Combination VM230M

Light IL30; Mirror PEM3024; Cabinet V30

COMMODORE

Choose the convenient combination unit or match individual components to suit your needs. Components channeled for easy installation. Light fixture includes grounded outlet and switch. Mirrors feature polished edges and copper backing. Stainless steel trim.

Style	Model	Mirror Door Model	Styrene Door Model	Overall Size W H D
Combination Mirror & Cabinet	–	VM224M	VM224P	24¼ x 32 x 4⅛
	–	VM230M	VM230P	30¼ x 32 x 4⅛
		VM236M	VM236P	36¼ x 32 x 4⅛
Storage Cabinets	–	V24	–	24¼ x 8¾ x 4¼
	–	V30	–	30¼ x 8¾ x 4¼
	–	V36	–	36¼ x 8¾ x 4¼
	–	V48	–	48¼ x 8¾ x 4¼
Incandescent Light Fixtures	IL24	–	–	24 x 4 x 7½
	IL30	–	–	30 x 4 x 7½
Wall Mirrors	PEM2424	–	–	24 x 24
	PEM3024	–	–	30 x 24
	PEM3624	–	–	36 x 24
	PEM4824	–	–	48 x 24
	PEM3036	–	–	30 x 36
	PEM3636	–	–	36 x 36
	PEM4836	–	–	48 x 36
	PEM6036	–	–	60 x 36

Cabinet 602

Cabinet 603

Cabinet 606

LOUVER DOOR

Versatile auxiliary cabinets for added storage are available in white molded polystyrene or unfinished pine which can be painted or stained.

Style	Model	Overall Size W H D	Wall Opening W H D
Arch Top Door (Unfinished) Built-In Cabinets	602	16 x 24	14 x 18 x 3½
	605ADJ†	16 x 24	14 x 18 x 2½
Flat Top Door (Unfinished) Built-In Cabinets	606	16 x 22	14 x 18 x 3½
	609	16 x 26	14 x 24 x 3½
	607ADJ†	16 x 22	14 x 18 x 2½
White Molded Door Built-In Cabinet	603†	16 x 22¼	14 x 18 x 2½

†Molded body.

See pages 31-35 for detailed specifications.

MEDICINE CABINET SPECIFICATIONS

Page	Model No.	Style Name	Frame	Style T-Tri-View B-BiView S-Single SB-Slide-by L-Light WM-Wall Mirror	Overall Size W H D	Mount Type WM-Wall Mount B-Built-In B/WM-Built-In or Wall Mount M-Mirror	Wall Opening W H D	Hinge Type P-Piano C-Con. L-Leaf PN-Pin B-Butt	Single Door Hinge L-Left R-Right RV-Rev.	Cabinet Body S-Steel SS-Stainless P-Polystyrene W-Wood	Shelves			Matching Light Fixture	Recommended Bulbs Qty-Type
											Quantity *	G-Glass S-Steel P-Polystyrene AL-Aluminum	F-Fixed A-Adjustable		
28	124LP	Ensign	Stainless Steel Trim	SB	24x23½x8¼	WM	-	-	-	S	1	S	F	Built-In	4-60W Std. MB
28	128LP	Ensign	Stainless Steel Trim	SB	28x23½x8¼	WM	-	-	-	S	1	S	F	Built-In	4-60W Std. MB
7	1350	Cameo Oval Bevel	Frameless Bevel	S	21x31	B	14x18x3½	P	RV	S	2	P	A	-	-
7	1358	Cameo Oval Bevel	Frameless Bevel	S	24x35	B	14x24x3½	P	RV	S	3	P	A	-	-
21	1370	Dunhill	Solid Oak, Honey	S	21x31	B	14x18x3½	P	RV	S	2	P	A	-	-
10	1402	Lafayette	Frameless	S	18⅛x32⅜x6	WM	-	P	R	S	3	S	F	Built-In	3-60W G25/G40
8	1418	Aurora	Frameless	S	16x26	B	14x24x3½	P	RV	S	3	P	A	73290	-
8	1420FL	Decorah	Frameless	S	16x26	B	14x18x3½	P	RV	S	2	P	A	735FL	-
27	1430	Focus	Frameless	S	16x22	B	14x18x3½	P	RV	S	2	P	A	-	-
27	1433	Focus	Frameless	S	16x20	B	14x18x2½	P	RV	P	2	P	F	-	-
27	1438	Focus	Frameless	S	16x26	B	14x24x3½	P	RV	S	3	P	A	-	-
27	1448	Stainless Steel	Frameless	S	16x26	B	14x24x3½	P	RV	SS	2	G	A	-	-
8	1450BC	Mirror-on-Mirror	Frameless	S	16x26	B	14x18x3½	P	RV	S	2	P	A	See pg. 8	-
9	1451	Horizon	Frameless	S	16x26	B	14x18x3½	P	RV	S	2	P	A	73290	-
8	1452	Mirror-on-Mirror	Frameless	S	16x26	B	14x18x3½	P	RV	S	2	P	A	73290	-
9	1453	Horizon	Frameless	S	16x20	B	14x18x2½	P	RV	P	2	P	F	73290	-
7	1454	Mirage	Frameless	S	18x27	B	14x18x3½	P	RV	S	2	P	A	73190	-
7	1456	Mirage	Frameless	S	17⅜x32	B	14x24x3½	P	RV	S	3	P	A	73190	-
8	1457	Mirror-on-Mirror	Frameless	S	16x26	B	14x24x3½	P	RV	S	3	P	A	See pg. 8	-
8	1458	Mirror-on-Mirror	Frameless	S	16x26	B	14x24x3½	P	RV	S	3	P	A	See pg. 8	-
9	1459	Horizon	Frameless	S	16x26	B	14x24x3½	P	RV	S	3	P	A	73290	-
10	1462	Lafayette	Frameless	S	18⅛x28⅜x6	WM	-	P	R	S	3	S	F	Built-In	3-60W G25/G40
11	155124	Vienna	Chrome Finish Trim	T	24x26x5½	WM	-	L	-	S	2	S	F	SB22529	-
11	155130	Vienna	Chrome Finish Trim	T	30x26x5½	WM	-	L	-	S	2	S	F	SB23129	-
22	177924	Oakhill	Solid Oak, Honey	T	23¼x29⅝x4¼	B/WM	22¾x27½x3½	PN	-	S	2	S	F	Built-In	3-60W G25/G40
22	177930	Oakhill	Solid Oak, Honey	T	30x29⅝x4¼	B/WM	28¾x27½x3½	PN	-	S	2	S	F	Built-In	4-60W G25/G40
22	177936	Oakhill	Solid Oak, Honey	T	36x29⅝x4¼	B/WM	34¾x27½x3½	PN	-	S	2	S	F	Built-In	5-60W G25/G40
22	177948	Oakhill	Solid Oak, Honey	T	48x29⅝x4¼	B/WM	46¾x27½x3½	PN	-	S	2	S	F	Built-In	6-60W G25/G40
19	197230	Autumn	Solid Oak, Honey	T	30x29x5½	B/WM	28¾x27½x3½	PN	-	S	2	S	F	Built-In	4-60W Std. MB
19	197236	Autumn	Solid Oak, Honey	T	36x29x5½	B/WM	34¾x27½x3½	PN	-	S	2	S	F	Built-In	5-60W Std. MB
15	2009WH	Spectrum	Molded Acrylic Fin.	S	19⅛x32¼x5	B/WM	16¾x28¾x3½	PN	R	S	3	S	F	Built-In	3-60W G25/G40
15	2012BR	Viceroy	Molded Brass Finish	S	18x31x5	B/WM	16¾x29x3½	PN	R	S	3	S	F	Built-In	3-60W G25/G40
21	2072	Oakdale	Solid Oak, Honey	S	18x31x5½	B/WM	16¾x28¾x3½	PN	R	S	3	S	F	Built-In	3-60W G25/G40
28	2471IL	Oak Hollywood	Solid Oak, Honey	SB	24¾x24½x9	WM	-	-	-	S	1	S	F	Built-In	4-60W Std. MB
9	255024	Horizon	Frameless	T	24x24	B	21¾x20½x3½	C	-	S	2	S	A	HO42490	-
9	255030	Horizon	Frameless	T	30x28¼	B	27¾x24¾x3½	C	-	S	2	S	A	HO43090	-
9	255036	Horizon	Frameless	T	36x28¼	B	33¾x24¾x3½	C	-	S	2	S	A	HO43690	-
9	255048	Horizon	Frameless	T	48x28¼	B	45¾x24¾x3½	C	-	S	2	S	A	HO44890	-
9	255224	Horizon	Frameless	T	24x24x5¼	WM	-	C	-	S	2	S	F	HO32490	-
9	255230	Horizon	Frameless	T	30x28¼x5¼	WM	-	C	-	S	2	S	F	HO33090	-
9	255236	Horizon	Frameless	T	36x28¼x5¼	WM	-	C	-	S	2	S	F	HO33690	-
9	255248	Horizon	Frameless	T	48x28¼x5¼	WM	-	C	-	S	2	S	F	HO34890	-
7	258	Sonata	Frameless	S	16x32	B	14x24x3½	P	R	S	3	P	A	75052	-
20	277924	Grand Oak II	Solid Oak, Honey	T	24x25	B/WM	22¼x23x3½	PN	-	S	2	S	F	SG32479	-
20	277930	Grand Oak II	Solid Oak, Honey	T	29x28⅞	B/WM	27½x27x3½	PN	-	S	2	S	F	SG33079	-
20	277936	Grand Oak II	Solid Oak, Honey	T	35x28⅞	B/WM	33½x27x3½	PN	-	S	2	S	F	SG33679	-
20	277948	Grand Oak II	Solid Oak, Honey	T	47x28⅞	B/WM	45½x27x3½	PN	-	S	2	S	F	SG34879	-
28	2871IL	Oak Hollywood	Solid Oak, Honey	SB	28¾x24½x9	WM	-	-	-	S	1	S	F	Built-In	4-60W Std. MB
9	295224	Focus	Frameless	T	24x30x5¼	WM	-	C	-	S	2	S	F	Built-In	3-60W G25/G40
9	295230	Focus	Frameless	T	30x34x5¼	WM	-	C	-	S	2	S	F	Built-In	4-60W G25/G40
15	310BR	Verona	Brass Finish	S	17¼x27¼	B	14x18x3½	P	RV	S	2	P	A	747BR	-
15	313BR	Verona	Molded, Brass Finish	S	16x20	B	14x18x2½	B	RV	P	2	P	F	747BR	-
29	313WH	White Frame	Molded, White Finish	S	16x20	B	14x18x2½	B	RV	P	2	P	F	-	-
15	318BR	Verona	Molded, Brass Finish	S	17¼x27¼	B	14x24x3½	P	RV	S	2	P	A	747BR	-
28	323LP	Flair	Stainless Steel Trim	SB	24x19½x8	WM	-	-	-	S	1	S	F	Built-In	4-60W Std. MB
14	3230WH	Spectrum	Molded, Acrylic Fin.	T	30x30x4½	B/WM	27½x27x3½	PN	-	S	2	S	F	SP132WH	-

*Cabinet bottom always provides an additional storage level.
Note: Unless so stated, bulbs not included.

**3 shelves in each side.

MEDICINE CABINET SPECIFICATIONS

Page	Model No.	Style Name	Frame	Style T-Tri-View B-BiView S-Single SB-Slide-by L-Light WM-Wall Mirror	Overall Size W H D	Mount Type WM-Wall Mount B-Built-In B/WM-Built-In or Wall Mount M-Mirror	Wall Opening W H D	Hinge Type P-Piano C-Con. L-Leaf PN-Pin B-Butt	Single Door Hinge L-Left R-Right RV-Rev.	Cabinet Body S-Steel SS-Stainless P-Polystyrene W-Wood	Shelves Quantity *	Shelves G-Glass S-Steel P-Polystyrene AL-Aluminum	Shelves F-Fixed A-Adjustable	Matching Light Fixture	Recommended Bulbs Qty-Type
14	3236WH	Spectrum	Molded, Acrylic Fin.	T	36x30⅜x4½	B/WM	33½x27x3½	PN	-	S	2	S	F	SP133WH	-
28	327LP	Flair	Stainless Steel Trim	SB	28x19½x8	WM	-	-	-	S	1	S	F	Built-In	4-60W Std. MB
15	3330WH	Spectrum	Molded, Acrylic Fin.	T	31x30⅜x5	B/WM	28¾x27½x3½	PN	-	S	2	S	F	Built-In	4-60W G25/G40
15	3336WH	Spectrum	Molded, Acrylic Fin.	T	37x30⅜x5	B/WM	34¾x27½x3½	PN	-	S	2	S	F	Built-In	5-60W G25/G40
14	350WH	Spectrum	Molded, Acrylic Fin.	S	18x27½	B	14x18x3½	P	RV	S	2	P	A	745WH	-
14	358WH	Spectrum	Molded, Acrylic Fin.	S	18x27½	B	14x24x3½	P	RV	S	3	P	A	745WH	-
12	3870	Classico	Oak Burl	S	18 1/16x28 1/16	B	14x18x3½	P	RV	S	2	P	A	715K	2-60W
12	3872	Classico	Oak Burl	S	18 1/16x28 1/16	WM	-	P	RV	S	3	P	F	716K	2-60W
12	3878	Classico	Oak Burl	S	18 1/16x28 1/16	B	14x24x3½	P	RV	S	3	P	A	715K	2-60W
12	3890	Classico	Mahogany	S	18 1/16x28 1/16	B	14x18x3½	P	RV	S	2	P	A	715M	2-60W
12	3892	Classico	Mahogany	S	18 1/16x28 1/16	WM	-	P	RV	S	3	P	F	716M	2-60W
12	3898	Classico	Mahogany	S	18 1/16x28 1/16	B	14x24x3½	P	RV	S	3	P	A	715M	2-60W
13	3910	Florentine	Simulated Gold Leaf	S	17 15/16x27 15/16	B	14x18x3½	P	RV	S	2	P	A	711FG	2-60W
13	3912	Florentine	Simulated Gold Leaf	S	17 15/16x27 15/16	WM	-	P	RV	S	3	P	F	712FG	2-60W
13	3918	Florentine	Simulated Gold Leaf	S	17 15/16x27 15/16	B	14x24x3½	P	RV	S	3	P	A	711FG	2-60W
29	401ADJ	Styleline	Stainless Steel	S	16x20	B	14x18x3½	B	RV	P	2	P	A	-	-
29	405BP	Styleline	Stainless Steel	S	16x22	B	14x18x2½	B	RV	P	2	P	F	-	-
29	405BP27	Styleline	Stainless Steel	S	16x22	B	14x18x2½	B	RV	P	2	P	F	-	-
29	407ADJ	Styleline	Stainless Steel	S	16x22	B	14x18x3½	B	RV	P	2	P	A	-	-
29	410BC	Styleline	Stainless Steel	S	16x22	B	14x18x3½	P	RV	S	2	P	A	-	-
29	412SM	Styleline	Stainless Steel	S	16x22x4¾	WM	-	P	RV	S	2	S	F	-	-
29	420BC	Styleline	Stainless Steel	S	16x22	B	14x20x3½	P	RV	S	2	P	A	-	-
29	421BC	Styleline	Stainless Steel	S	16x22	B	14x20x3½	P	RV	S	2	P	A	-	-
29	422SM	Styleline	Stainless Steel	S	14x20x5	WM	-	P	RV	S	2	P	F	-	-
27	448BC	Styleline	Stainless Steel	S	16x26	B	14x24x3½	P	RV	SS	3	SS	A	-	-
29	449BC	Styleline	Stainless Steel	S	16x22	B	14x18x3½	B	RV	P	2	P	F	-	-
29	452SM	Styleline	Stainless Steel	S	16x22x4¾	WM	-	P	RV	S	2	S	F	-	-
29	455FL	Cabinet 455FL	Stainless Steel	S	20⅜x22¼x7⅜	B	14x19x3½	P	R	S	2	P	A	Built-In	Fluorescent (incl.)
10	455230	Quantum	Frameless	T	30x36½x5¼	WM	-	C	-	S	2	S	F	Built-In	4-60W G25/G40
10	455236	Quantum	Frameless	T	36x36½x5¼	WM	-	C	-	S	2	S	F	Built-In	5-60W G25/G40
10	455248	Quantum	Frameless	T	48x36½x5¼	WM	-	C	-	S	2	S	F	Built-In	6-60W G25/G40
29	458	Styleline	Stainless Steel	S	16x26	B	14x24x3½	P	RV	S	3	P	A	-	-
29	468	Styleline	Stainless Steel	S	16x26	B	14x24x3½	P	RV	S	3	P	A	-	-
27, 29	468MOD	Modular Shelf	Stainless Steel	S	16x26	B	14x24x3½	P	RV	S	6†	P	A	-	-
29	478FS	Styleline	Stainless Steel •	S	16x26	B	14x24x3½	P	RV	S	3	A	A	-	-
29	490	Styleline	Stainless Steel	S	18x24	B	16x21½x3½	P	RV	S	3	P	A	-	-
29	495	Styleline	Stainless Steel	S	20x30	B	17¼x26¼x3½	P	RV	S	3	P	A	-	-
6	5520	Torino	Frameless	S	16½x34½	B	14x18x3½	P	R	S	2	P	A	73591	-
6	5528	Torino	Frameless	S	16½x34½	B	14x24x3½	P	R	S	3	P	A	73591	-
29	555IL	Cabinet 555IL	Stainless Steel	S	16x24x8	WM	-	P	R	S	2	S	F	Built-In	2-60W
18	5622	White Marble	Solid Oak & White	S	17⅛x27⅛x5½	WM	-	P	RV	S	3	S	F	708WH	-
18	562230	White Marble	Solid Oak & White	T	30x28½x5¼	WM	-	L	-	S	2	S	F	WH53023	-
11	565	Styleline 2	Stainless Steel	S	18x28x6	WM	-	P	R	S	3	S	F	Built-In	3-60W G25/G40
30	602	Louver Door	Unfinished Pine	S	16x24	B	14x18x3½	B	R	S	2	P	A	-	-
30	603	Louver Door	White Molded	S	16x22¼	B	14x18x2½	P	RV	P	2	P	F	-	-
30	605ADJ	Louver Door	Unfinished Pine	S	16x24	B	14x18x2½	P	R	P	2	P	A	-	-
30	606	Louver Door	Unfinished Pine	S	16x22	B	14x18x3½	B	RV	S	2	P	A	-	-
30	607ADJ	Louver Door	Unfinished Pine	S	16x22	B	14x18x2½	P	RV	P	3	P	A	-	-
30	609	Louver Door	Unfinished Pine	S	16x26	B	14x24x3½	P	RV	S	3	P	A	-	-
13	6120	Hibiscus	Floral, White	S	18½x27½	B	14x18x3½	P	RV	S	2	P	A	761WH	2-G25
13	6122	Hibiscus	Floral, White	S	18½x27½	WM	-	P	RV	S	3	P	A	762WH	2-G25
13	6130	Hibiscus	Floral, Almond	S	18½x27½	B	14x18x3½	P	RV	S	2	P	A	761AL	2-G25
13	6132	Hibiscus	Floral, Almond	S	18½x27½	WM	-	P	RV	S	3	P	A	762AL	2-G25
13	6140	Hibiscus	Floral, Green	S	18½x27½	B	14x18x3½	P	RV	S	2	P	A	761GR	2-G25

*Cabinet bottom always provides an additional storage level. † Modular half shelves. • Meets federal spec., see page 29.

Page	Model No.	Style Name	Frame	Style T-Tri-View B-BiView S-Single SB-Slide-by L-Light WM-Wall Mirror	Overall Size W H D	Mount Type WM-Wall Mount B-Built-In B/WM-Built-In or Wall Mount M-Mirror	Wall Opening W H D	Hinge Type P-Piano C-Con. L-Leaf PN-Pin B-Butt	Single Door Hinge L-Left R-Right RV-Rev.	Cabinet Body S-Steel SS-Stainless P-Polystyrene W-Wood	Shelves Quantity *	Shelves G-Glass S-Steel P-Polystyrene AL-Aluminum	Shelves F-Fixed A-Adjustable	Matching Light Fixture	Recommended Bulbs Qty-Type
13	6142	Hibiscus	Floral, Green	S	18½x27½	WM	-	P	RV	S	3	P	A	762GR	2-G25
30	622	Hideaway	Steel Door	S	17⅛x21½	B	14x18x3½	P	RV	S	2	P	A	-	-
26	625	Bel Aire Auxiliary	Stainless Steel Trim	S	13x36	B	11¼x33¼x3½	P	RV	S	3	S	A	-	-
26	626	Bel Aire Auxiliary	Stainless Steel Trim	S	13x36x4¼	WM	-	P	RV	S	3	P	F	-	-
25	629	Illusion	Frameless	S	15x36	B	14x34x3½	C	RV	S	3	S	A	-	-
26	631	Avanti Corner	Stainless Steel Trim	S	13x36x7¼	WM	-	P	RV	S	3	G	F	-	-
25	639BC	Illusion	Frameless	S	13x36	B	12x34x3½	C	RV	S	3	S	A	-	-
5	652BC	Luminary	Frameless - ½" Bevel	S	24x37⅜x7¼	WM	-	C	-	S	3	G	A	Built-In	2-25W Fluor.
6	655036	Saturn	Frameless	T	36x30	B	33¾x24¾x3½	C	-	S	2	G	A	Built-In	2-17W Fluor.
6	655048	Saturn	Frameless	T	48x30	B	45¾x24¾x3½	C	-	S	2	G	A	Built-In	2-17W Fluor.
6	655236	Saturn	Frameless	T	36x30	WM	-	C	-	S	2	G	A	Built-In	2-17W Fluor.
6	655248	Saturn	Frameless	T	48x30	WM	-	C	-	S	2	G	A	Built-In	2-17W Fluor.
5	658BC	Luminary	Frameless - ½" Bevel	S	24x37⅜	B	14¼x34¼x3½	C	-	S	3	G	A	Built-In	2-25W Fluor.
26	672	Centered Corner	Solid Oak, Honey	S	19½x33½x10½	WM	-	PN	RV	S	3	S	F	-	-
26	672SS	Centered Corner	Stainless Steel	S	17¼x31x9⅞	WM	-	PN	RV	S	3	S	F	-	-
16	70223	Baker Street	Hardwood, White	L	18x8x13½	For WM Cab.	-	-	-	-	-	-	-	-	2-60W Std. MB
16	70273	Baker Street	Solid Oak, Honey	L	18x8x13½	For WM Cab.	-	-	-	-	-	-	-	-	2-60W Std. MB
16	70323	Baker Street	Hardwood, White	L	18x8x9	For B Cab.	-	-	-	-	-	-	-	-	2-60W Std. MB
16	70373	Baker Street	Solid Oak, Honey	L	18x8x9	For B Cab.	-	-	-	-	-	-	-	-	2-60W Std. MB
18	708WH	White Marble	Solid Oak & White	L	17⅛x7¼x10⅛	For WM Cab.	-	-	-	-	-	-	-	-	2-60W Std. MB
19	70928	Prairie	Hardwood, White	L	18x8x8	For B Cab.	-	-	-	-	-	-	-	-	2-60W Std. MB
13	711FG	Florentine	Gold Leaf	L	8x17 15/16x6 15/16	B	-	-	-	-	-	-	-	-	2-60W Std. MB
13	712FG	Florentine	Gold Leaf	L	8x17 15/16x9 15/16	WM	-	-	-	-	-	-	-	-	2-60W Std. MB
12	715K	Classico	Oak	L	18⅝x8x7	B	-	-	-	-	-	-	-	-	2-60W Std. MB
12	716K	Classico	Oak	L	18 1/16x8⅛x9¾	WM	-	-	-	-	-	-	-	-	2-60W Std. MB
12	715M	Classico	Mahogany	L	18⅝x8x7	B	-	-	-	-	-	-	-	-	2-60W Std. MB
12	716M	Classico	Mahogany	L	18 1/16x8⅛x9¾	WM	-	-	-	-	-	-	-	-	2-60W Std. MB
22	71829	Kingston	Solid Oak, Honey	L	16½x5½x2¼	For B Cab.	-	-	-	-	-	-	-	-	3-60W G25/G40
7	72052	Sonata	Frameless	L▲	5x17½x6⅛	For B Cab.	-	-	-	-	-	-	-	-	2-75W Std. MB
7,8,9	73190	Mirage	Frameless	L▲	5x12x6½	For B Cab.	-	-	-	-	-	-	-	-	2-60W Slim Line
8,9	73290	Horizon	Frameless	L	16x4½x2	For B Cab.	-	-	-	-	-	-	-	-	2-60W Std. MB
6	73591	Torino	Frameless	L▲	5⅜x13¾x6½	For B Cab.	-	-	-	-	-	-	-	-	2-75W Std. MB
8	735FL	Decorah	Frameless	L	16x4⅜x2	For B Cab.	-	-	-	-	-	-	-	-	2-60W G25/G40
20	74279	Grant	Solid Oak, Honey	L	16¼x5½x3	For B Cab.	-	-	-	-	-	-	-	-	2-60W G25/G40
14	745WH	Spectrum	Molded, Acrylic Fin.	L	18x6½x3	For B Cab.	-	-	-	-	-	-	-	-	3-60W G25/40
15	747BR	Verona	Molded, Brass Fin.	L	17¼x5½x3	For B Cab.	-	-	-	-	-	-	-	-	3-60W G25/40
13	761WH	Hibiscus	Floral, White	L	18½x6¾x3	B	-	-	-	-	-	-	-	-	2-G25
13	761AL	Hibiscus	Floral, Almond	L	18½x6¾x3	B	-	-	-	-	-	-	-	-	2-G25
13	761GR	Hibiscus	Floral, Forest Green	L	18½x6¾x3	B	-	-	-	-	-	-	-	-	2-G25
13	762WH	Hibiscus	Floral, White	L	18½x6¾x5½	WM	-	-	-	-	-	-	-	-	2-G25
13	762AL	Hibiscus	Floral, Almond	L	18½x6¾x5½	WM	-	-	-	-	-	-	-	-	2-G25
13	762GR	Hibiscus	Floral, Forest Green	L	18½x6¾x5½	WM	-	-	-	-	-	-	-	-	2-G25
17	76378	Canterbury	Solid Oak, Honey	L	18x8x8	For WM Cab.	-	-	-	-	-	-	-	-	2-60W Std. MB
17	76478	Canterbury	Solid Oak, Honey	L	18x8x11½	For WM Cab.	-	-	-	-	-	-	-	-	2-60W Std. MB
19	8120	Prairie	Hardwood, White	S	18x27½	B	14x18x3½	P	RV	S	2	P	A	70928	-
19	8122	Prairie	Hardwood, White	S	18x27½x5	WM	-	P	RV	S	3	P	F	71028	-
19	8128	Prairie	Hardwood, White	S	18x27½	B	14x24x3½	P	RV	S	3	P	A	70928	-
19	8199703**	Prairie	Solid Oak, Blonde	T	30x28 5/16	WM	14x24x3½	P	RV	S	3	P	A	OK8199705	-
19	8199704**	Prairie	Solid Oak, Blonde	T	36x28 5/16	WM	14x24x3½	P	RV	S	3	P	A	OK8199706	-
16	820	Baker Street	Hardwood, White	S	18x27	B	14x18x3½	P	RV	S	2	P	A	See p. 16	-
16	822	Baker Street	Hardwood, White	S	18x27x5	WM	-	P	RV	S	3	P	F	See p. 16	-
22	8278	Chapel Hill	Solid Oak, Honey	S	17¼x27¼	B	14x24x3½	P	RV	S	3	S	F	75719	-
16	828	Baker Street	Hardwood, White	S	18x27	B	14x24x3½	P	RV	S	3	P	A	See p. 16	-
22	8370	Kingston	Solid Oak, Honey	S	16½x26½	B	14x18x3½	P	RV	S	2	S	A	71829	-
22	8378	Kingston	Solid Oak, Honey	S	16½x26½	B	14x24x3½	P	RV	S	3	S	A	71829	-
16	842230	Baker Street	Hardwood, White	T	30x28½x5½	WM	-	L	-	S	2	S	F	BS84023	-

*Cabinet bottom always provides an additional storage level. ▲ Packed in pairs. **Special Order

MEDICINE CABINET SPECIFICATIONS

Page	Model No.	Style Name	Frame	Style T-Tri-View B-BiView S-Single SB-Slide-by L-Light WM-Wall Mirror	Overall Size W H D	Mount Type WM-Wall Mount B-Built-In B/WM-Built-In or Wall Mount M-Mirror	Wall Opening W H D	Hinge Type P-Piano C-Con. L-Leaf PN-Pin B-Butt	Single Door Hinge L-Left R-Right RV-Rev.	Cabinet Body S-Steel SS-Stainless P-Polystyrene W-Wood	Shelves Quantity *	Shelves G-Glass S-Steel P-Polystyrene AL-Aluminum	Shelves F-Fixed A-Adjustable	Matching Light Fixture	Recommended Bulbs Qty-Type
16	842236	Baker Street	Hardwood, White	T	36x28½x5½	WM	-	L	-	S	2	S	F	BS84623	-
17	8570	Canterbury	Solid Oak, Honey	S	18¼x27¼	B	14x18x3½	P	R	S	2	P	A	76378	-
17	8572	Canterbury	Solid Oak, Honey	S	18¼x27¼x5½	WM	-	P	R	S	3	P	F	76478	-
16	870	Baker Street	Solid Oak, Honey	S	18x27	B	14x18x3½	P	RV	S	2	P	A	See p. 16	-
16	872	Baker Street	Solid Oak, Honey	S	18x27x5	WM	-	P	RV	S	3	P	F	See p. 16	-
20	8770	Grant	Solid Oak, Honey	S	16¼x24¼	B	14x18x3½	P	RV	S	2	P	A	74279	-
20	8772	Grant	Solid Oak, Honey	S	16¼x24¼x5½	WM	-	P	RV	S	2	P	F	-	-
20	8773	Grant	Solid Oak, Honey	S	16¼x22	B	14x18x2½	B	RV	P	2	P	F	74279	-
20	8778	Grant	Solid Oak, Honey	S	16¼x26¼	B	14x24x3½	P	RV	S	3	P	A	74279	-
16	878	Baker Street	Solid Oak, Honey	S	18x27	B	14x24x3½	P	RV	S	3	P	A	See p. 16	-
24	902	Prestique	Wood, Oak Finish	S	16x20x4¾	WM	-	B	RV	W	1	Wood	F	-	-
24	902BP	Prestique	Wood, Oak Finish	S	16x20x4¾	WM	-	B	RV	W	1	Wood	F	-	-
24	902WH	Prestique	Wood, White Finish	S	16x20x4¾	WM	-	B	RV	W	1	Wood	F	-	-
23	902224	Prestique	Hardwood, White	T	24x26x4¾	WM	-	L	-	W	2	Wood	F	CR92429	-
23	902230	Prestique	Hardwood, White	T	30x30x4¾	WM	-	L	-	W	2	Wood	F	CR93029	-
23	902236	Prestique	Hardwood, White	T	36x30x4¾	WM	-	L	-	W	2	Wood	F	CR93629	-
23	905224	Prestique	Frameless	T	24x26x4¾	WM	-	C	-	W	2	Wood	F	CR92490	-
23	905230	Prestique	Frameless	T	30x30x4¾	WM	-	C	-	W	2	Wood	F	CR93090	-
23	905236	Prestique	Frameless	T	36x30x4¾	WM	-	C	-	W	2	Wood	F	CR93690	-
23	905248	Prestique	Frameless	T	48x30x4¾	WM	-	C	-	W	2	Wood	F	CR94890	-
23	907224	Prestique	Solid Oak, Honey	T	24x26x4¾	WM	-	L	-	W	2	Wood	F	-	-
23	907224BP	Prestique	Solid Oak, Honey	T	24x26x4¾	WM	-	L	-	W	2	Wood	F	-	-
23	907230	Prestique	Solid Oak, Honey	T	30x30x4¾	WM	-	L	-	W	2	Wood	F	CR93079	-
23	907230BP	Prestique	Solid Oak, Honey	T	30x30x4¾	WM	-	L	-	W	2	Wood	F	CR93079	-
23	907236	Prestique	Solid Oak, Honey	T	36x30x4¾	WM	-	L	-	W	2	Wood	F	CR93679	-
23	907248	Prestique	Solid Oak, Honey	T	48x30x4¾	WM	-	L	-	W	2	Wood	F	CR94879	-
24	942224	Prestique	Wood, White Finish	T	24x28⅞x4⅛	WM	-	PN	-	W	2	Wood	F	Built-In	3-60W G25/G40
24	9422BC	Prestique	Wood, White Finish	T	15¾x23⅝x4⅛	WM	-	PN	R	W	2	Wood	F	Built-In	2-60W G25/G40
24	942230	Prestique	Wood, White Finish	T	30x28⅞x4⅛	WM	-	PN	-	W	2	Wood	F	Built-In	4-60W G25/G40
24	942236	Prestique	Wood, White Finish	T	36x28⅞x4⅛	WM	-	PN	-	W	2	Wood	F	Built-In	5-60W G25/G40
24	9472	Prestique	Wood, Oak Finish	S	15¾x23⅝x4⅛	WM	-	PN	R	W	2	Wood	F	Built-In	2-60W G25/G40
24	947224	Prestique	Wood, Oak Finish	T	24x28⅞x4⅛	WM	-	PN	-	W	2	Wood	F	Built-In	3-60W G25/G40
24	947230	Prestique	Wood, Oak Finish	T	30x28⅞x4⅛	WM	-	PN	-	W	2	Wood	F	Built-In	4-60W G25/G40
24	947236	Prestique	Wood, Oak Finish	T	36x28⅞x4⅛	WM	-	PN	-	W	2	Wood	F	Built-In	5-60W G25/G40
24	967224	Prestique	Wood, Oak Finish	T	24x25½x4¾	WM	-	L	-	W	2	Wood	F	-	-
24	967230	Prestique	Wood, Oak Finish	T	30x25½x4¾	WM	-	L	-	W	2	Wood	F	-	-
24	967236	Prestique	Wood, Oak Finish	T	36x25½x4¾	WM	-	L	-	W	2	Wood	F	-	-
20	97014099	Grand Oak II	Trim Kit for 2779 Series				-	-	-	-	-	-	-	-	-
24	972225	Prestique	Wood, White Finish	2-Door	25½x28x4¾	WM	-	**	RV	W	5	Wood	F	-	-
20	973BC	Grant	Solid Oak, Honey	S	16x20	-	14x18x2½	B	RV	P	2	P	F	74279	-
24	977225	Prestique	Wood, Oak Finish	2-Door	25½x28x4¾	WM	-	**	RV	W	5	Wood	F	-	-
24	982	Prestique	Wood, Oak Finish	S	16x26x4¾	WM	-	B	RV	W	2	Wood	F	-	-
24	982WH	Prestique	Wood, White Finish	S	16x26x4¾	WM	-	B	RV	W	2	Wood	F	-	-
16	BS84023	Baker Street	Hardwood Wh. Paint	L	30x6x6½	For WM Cab.	-	-	-	-	-	-	-	-	3-60W Std. MB
16	BS84623	Baker Street	Hardwood Wh. Paint	L	36x6x6½	For WM Cab.	-	-	-	-	-	-	-	-	4-60W Std. MB
23	CR92429	Prestique	Hardwood, White	L	24x5⅞x5½	For WM Cab.	-	-	-	-	-	-	-	-	3-60W G25/G40
23	CR92490	Prestique	Frameless	L	24x5⅞x5½	For WM Cab.	-	-	-	-	-	-	-	-	3-60W G25/G40
23	CR93029	Prestique	Hardwood, White	L	30x5⅞x5½	For WM Cab.	-	-	-	-	-	-	-	-	4-60W G25/G40
23	CR93079	Prestique	Solid Oak, Honey	L	30x5⅞x5½	For WM Cab.	-	-	-	-	-	-	-	-	4-60W G25/G40
23	CR93090	Prestique	Frameless	L	30x5⅞x5½	For WM Cab.	-	-	-	-	-	-	-	-	4-60W G25/G40
23	CR93629	Prestique	Hardwood, White	L	36x5⅞x5½	For WM Cab.	-	-	-	-	-	-	-	-	5-60W G25/G40
23	CR93679	Prestique	Solid Oak, Honey	L	36x5⅞x5½	For WM Cab.	-	-	-	-	-	-	-	-	5-60W G25/G40
23	CR93690	Prestique	Frameless	L	36x5⅞x5½	For WM Cab.	-	-	-	-	-	-	-	-	4-60W G25/G40
23	CR94890	Prestique	Frameless	L	48x5⅞x5½	For WM Cab.	-	-	-	-	-	-	-	-	6-60W G25/G40
9	HO32490	Horizon	Frameless	L	24x4½x5⅞	For WM Cab.	-	-	-	-	-	-	-	-	3-60W G25/G40
9	HO33090	Horizon	Frameless	L	30x4¼x5⅞	For WM Cab.	-	-	-	-	-	-	-	-	4-60W G25/G40

*Cabinet bottom always provides an additional storage level.
**Semi concealed, self closing hinge.

Page	Model No.	Style Name	Frame	Style T-Tri-View B-BiView S-Single SB-Slide-by L-Light WM-Wall Mirror	Overall Size W H D	Mount Type WM-Wall Mount B-Built-In B/WM-Built-In or Wall Mount M-Mirror	Wall Opening W H D	Hinge Type P-Piano C-Con. L-Leaf PN-Pin B-Butt	Single Door Hinge L-Left R-Right RV-Rev.	Cabinet Body S-Steel SS-Stainless P-Polystyrene W-Wood	Shelves Quantity *	 G-Glass S-Steel P-Polystyrene AL-Aluminum	 F-Fixed A-Adjustable	Matching Light Fixture	Recommended Bulbs Qty-Type
9	HO33690	Horizon	Frameless	L	36x4¼x5⅞	For WM Cab.	-	-	-	-	-	-	-	-	4-60W G25/G40
9	HO34890	Horizon	Frameless	L	48x4½x5⅞	For WM Cab.	-	-	-	-	-	-	-	-	5-60W G25/G40
9	HO42490	Horizon	Frameless	L	24x4½x2¼	For B Cab.	-	-	-	-	-	-	-	-	3-60W G25/G40
9	HO43090	Horizon	Frameless	L	30x4½x2¼	For B Cab.	-	-	-	-	-	-	-	-	4-60W G25/G40
9	HO43690	Horizon	Frameless	L	36x4½x2¼	For B Cab.	-	-	-	-	-	-	-	-	4-60W G25/G40
9	HO44890	Horizon	Frameless	L	48x4½x2¼	For B Cab.	-	-	-	-	-	-	-	-	5-60W G25/G40
30	IL24	Commodore	Stainless Steel Trim	L	24x4x7½	ForWM Cab.	-	-	-	-	-	-	-	-	4-60W MB
30	IL30	Commodore	Stainless Steel Trim	L	30x4x7½	ForWM Cab.	-	-	-	-	-	-	-	-	4-60W MB
4	LBC10	Le Baccarat	Frameless	S	24x35⅜	B	16½x25¼x3⅞	C	R	SS	3	G	A	-	-
4	LBM15	Le Baccarat	Frameless	WM	24x35⅜	M	-	-	-	-	-	-	-	-	-
19	OK8199705**	Prairie	Solid Oak, Blonde	L	30x8x11	ForWM Cab.	-	-	-	-	-	-	-	-	3-60W Std. MB
19	OK8199706**	Prairie	Solid Oak, Blonde	L	36x8x11	ForWM Cab.	-	-	-	-	-	-	-	-	4-60W Std. MB
30	PEM2424	Commodore	Frameless	WM	24x24	WM	-	-	-	-	-	-	-	-	IL24
30	PEM3024	Commodore	Frameless	WM	30x24	WM	-	-	-	-	-	-	-	-	IL30
30	PEM3036	Commodore	Frameless	WM	30x36	WM	-	-	-	-	-	-	-	-	IL30
30	PEM3624	Commodore	Frameless	WM	36x24	WM	-	-	-	-	-	-	-	-	-
30	PEM3636	Commodore	Frameless	WM	36x36	WM	-	-	-	-	-	-	-	-	-
30	PEM4824	Commodore	Frameless	WM	48x24	WM	-	-	-	-	-	-	-	-	-
30	PEM4836	Commodore	Frameless	WM	48x36	WM	-	-	-	-	-	-	-	-	-
30	PEM6036	Commodore	Frameless	WM	60x36	WM	-	-	-	-	-	-	-	-	-
4	PRC1148	Primevère	Frameless	T	48x37⅜	B	36⅞x32⅞x3⅞	C	-	SS	3	G	A	PRL1048	-
4	PRC1148SM	Primevère	Clear Mirror	T	48¼x37⅜	WM	-	C	-	SS	3	G	F	PRL1048	-
4	PRC1160	Primevère	Clear Mirror	T	60x37⅜	B	48⅞x32⅞x3⅞	C	-	SS	3	G	A	PRL1060	-
4	PRC1160SM	Primevère	Clear Mirror	T	60¼x37⅜	WM	-	C	-	SS	3	G	F	PRL1060	-
4	PRL1048	Primevère	Clear Mirror	L	48x4¼x5⅜	For B/WMCab.	-	-	-	S	-	-	-	-	Fluorescent (Incl.)
4	PRL1060	Primevère	Clear Mirror	L	60x4¼x5⅜	For B/WMCab.	-	-	-	S	-	-	-	-	Fluorescent (Incl.)
11	SB22529	Vienna	Chrome Trim	L	24x4x5½	ForWM Cab.	-	-	-	-	-	-	-	-	3-60W G25/G40
11	SB23129	Vienna	Chrome Trim	L	30x4x5½	ForWM Cab.	-	-	-	-	-	-	-	-	4-60W G25/G40
28	SD15	Beauty Glide	Stainless Steel Trim	SB	24x18¾	B	21½x17x3½	-	-	S	1	S	A	-	-
28	SD41	Beauty Glide	Stainless Steel Trim	SB	27½x19¼	B	26¼x17¼x3½	-	-	S	1	S	A	-	-
28	SDL82	Beauty Glide	Stainless Steel Trim	SB	27½x22	B	26½x18¼x3½	-	-	S	1	S	A	Built-In	Fluorescent (Incl.)
20	SG32479	Grand Oak II	Solid Oak, Honey	L	24x5⅝x4¾	For B/WMCab.	-	-	-	-	-	-	-	-	3-60W G25/G40
20	SG33079	Grand Oak II	Solid Oak, Honey	L	29x5⅝x4¾	For B/WMCab.	-	-	-	-	-	-	-	-	4-60W G25/G40
20	SG33679	Grand Oak II	Solid Oak, Honey	L	35x5⅝x4¾	For B/WMCab.				-	-	-	-	-	5-60W G25/G40
20	SG34879	Grand Oak II	Solid Oak, Honey	L	47x5⅝x4¾	For B/WMCab.	-	-	-	-	-	-	-	-	6-60W G25/G40
14	SP132WH	Spectrum	Molded, Acrylic Fin.	L	30x6½x5¼	For B/WMCab.	-	-	-	-	-	-	-	-	4-60W G25/G40
14	SP133WH	Spectrum	Molded, Acrylic Fin.	L	36x6½x5¼	For B/WMCab.	-	-	-	-	-	-	-	-	5-60W G25/G40
30	V24	Commodore	Stainless Steel Trim	SB	24¼x8¾x4¼	WM	-	-	-	Cosmetic Box, Mirrored Door					
30	V30	Commodore	Stainless Steel Trim	SB	30¼x8¾x4¼	WM	-	-	-	Cosmetic Box, Mirrored Door					
30	V36	Commodore	Stainless Steel Trim	SB	36¼x8¾x4¼	WM	-	-	-	Cosmetic Box, Mirrored Door					
30	V48	Commodore	Stainless Steel Trim	SB	48¼x8¾x4¼	WM	-	-	-	Cosmetic Box, Mirrored Door					
30	VM224M	Commodore	Stainless Steel Trim	SB	24¼x32x4⅛	WM	-	-	-	Cosmetic Box & Mirror, Mirrored Door					
30	VM224P	Commodore	Stainless Steel Trim	SB	24¼x32x4⅛	WM	-	-	-	Cosmetic Box & Mirror, Styrene Door					
30	VM230M	Commodore	Stainless Steel Trim	SB	30¼x32x4⅛	WM	-	-	-	Cosmetic Box & Mirror, Mirrored Door					
30	VM230P	Commodore	Stainless Steel Trim	SB	30¼x32x4⅛	WM	-	-	-	Cosmetic Box & Mirror, Styrene Door					
30	VM236M	Commodore	Stainless Steel Trim	SB	36¼x32x4⅛	WM	-	-	-	Cosmetic Box & Mirror, Mirrored Door					
30	VM236P	Commodore	Stainless Steel Trim	SB	36¼x32x4⅛	WM	-	-	-	Cosmetic Box & Mirror, Styrene Door					
18	WH53023	White Marble	Solid Oak & White	L	30x7¼x12¼	ForWM Cab.	-	-	-	-	-	-	-	-	3-60W MB

*Cabinet bottom always provides an additional storage level.

**Special Order

BROAN®

There really is a difference with Broan. It's in the details.

P.O. Box 140, Hartford, WI 53027 • 1-800-558-1711
In Canada: Broan Limited • 1-905-670-2500

0 26715 08097 7

99850013J
C 79

C588

BuyLine 8620

COLLECTIONS

LUXURY BATHROOM FAUCETS AND ACCESSORIES

By JADO

Dear JADO friends,

We are pleased to present you with this showcase of continuing refinements in our line of luxury bath fixtures. The products featured in this brochure once again demonstrate JADO's commitment to provide you with the highest quality available in the industry in both design and performance.

JADO remains at the forefront in the development of new design. The addition of Wynd 816 Series and Telluride Series represent our latest achievements in coordinated design. Our latest innovation is Diamond Finish, the PVD process that guarantees these brass products will never tarnish. The Crystal Collection offers design versatility with the radiance of crystal levers. A brilliant silver finish, with our lifetime warranty against tarnishing, is now available in the Platinum Nickel Collection. As always, the beauty of our design is complemented by JADO's precision engineering to make sure the beauty lasts.

We invite you to visit an authorized JADO dealer to fully appreciate the beauty and craftsmanship of our luxury bath plumbing and hardware. We are confident you will agree that JADO's commitment to the finest in design and engineering continue to be unmatched in the industry.

Dennis D. Dickover
President
JADO, U.S.A.

Available Finishes

Gold

Diamond Finish®

Polished Chrome

Brushed Nickel

Platinum Nickel

Brushed Nickel/ Gold

SiNi/Gold

19 Custom Finishes
Now available with 1 year warranty against manufacturers defects

Available Finishes Not Pictured:
Polished Chrome/Gold
Polished Chrome/UltraBrass®

Warranties

JADO Bathroom & Hardware Manufacturing Corp. provides the finest warranties in the industry.

A LIFETIME MECHANICAL WARRANTY is provided against defects in materials and workmanship.

The GENERAL FINISH WARRANTY is a full 10 years from the date of purchase, against manufacture related defects in materials and workmanship.

OUR LIFETIME WARRANTY AGAINST TARNISHING FEATURED IN:

PLATINUM-NICKEL
DIAMOND FINISH
ULTRABRASS

JADO warranties carry the normal limitations regarding proper installation, abuse or mishandling. Contact your authorized JADO dealer who has all the details and conditions on JADO plumbing and hardware warranties. JADO means integrity throughout the world.

C588
BuyLine 8620

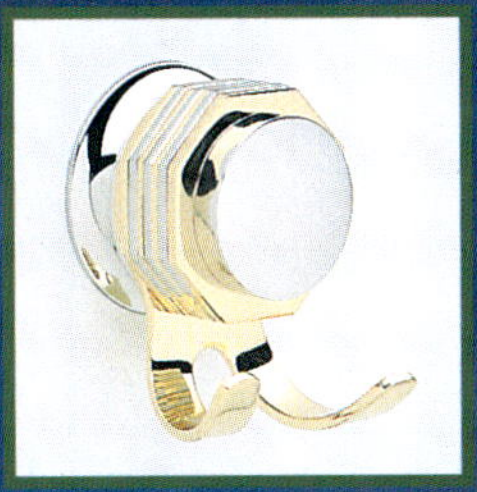
030/010
Robe hook

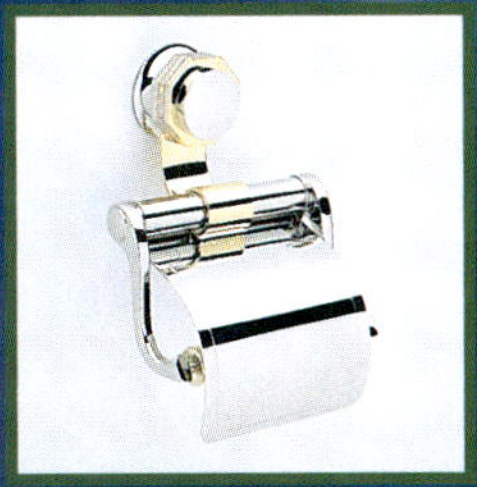
030/145
Tissue holder with cover

030/133
Soap dish

030/150
Towel ring 6"

030/141
Tumbler clear

Series TELLURIDE

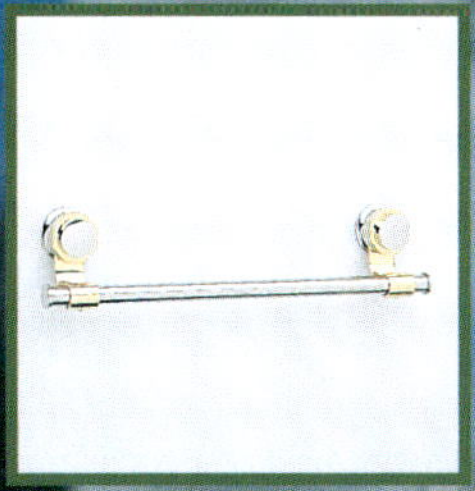
030/600
Towel bar 24"

833/018
Widespread lavatory set - flat spout

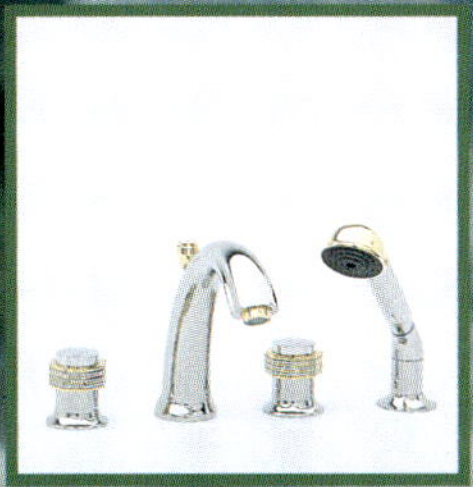
834/448
Roman tub set with hand shower

833/008 Widespread lavatory set

027/141
Tumbler clear

027/612
Clear shelf 24"

027/150
Towel ring 6"

027/600
Towel bar 24"

027/911
Toilet brush set
wall mounted

027/132
Soap dish clear

807/875
Roman tub set
with hand shower

027/145
Tissue holder
with cover

807/003 Widespread lavatory set

SERIES AMADEA

501/150
Towel ring 6"

501/600
Towel bar 24"

501/145
Tissue holder with cover

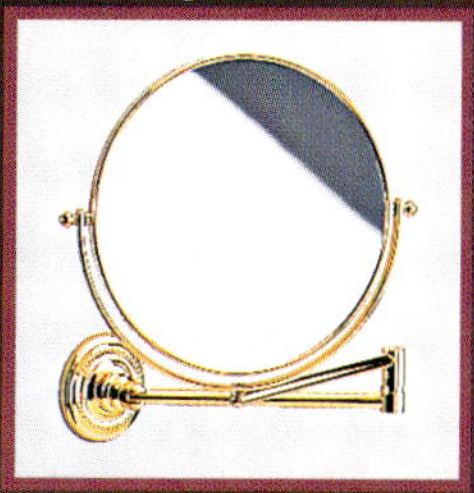

501/185
Shaving mirror

Series *Perlrand*

893/902 Widespread lavatory set

Swan

896/302 Roman tub set

Rhapsody crystal lever handle selection

Solid knob handle selection

Curved handle selection

862/102
Wet Bar faucet

Crystal knob
handle selection

033/145
Tissue holder
with cover

891/650
Pressure balanced
shower set

033/150
Towel ring 6"

Series Oriental

891/903
Single hole
lavatory set

033/141
Tumbler clear

033/600
Towel bar 24"

894/933
Roman tub set
with hand shower

893/933 Widespread lavatory set

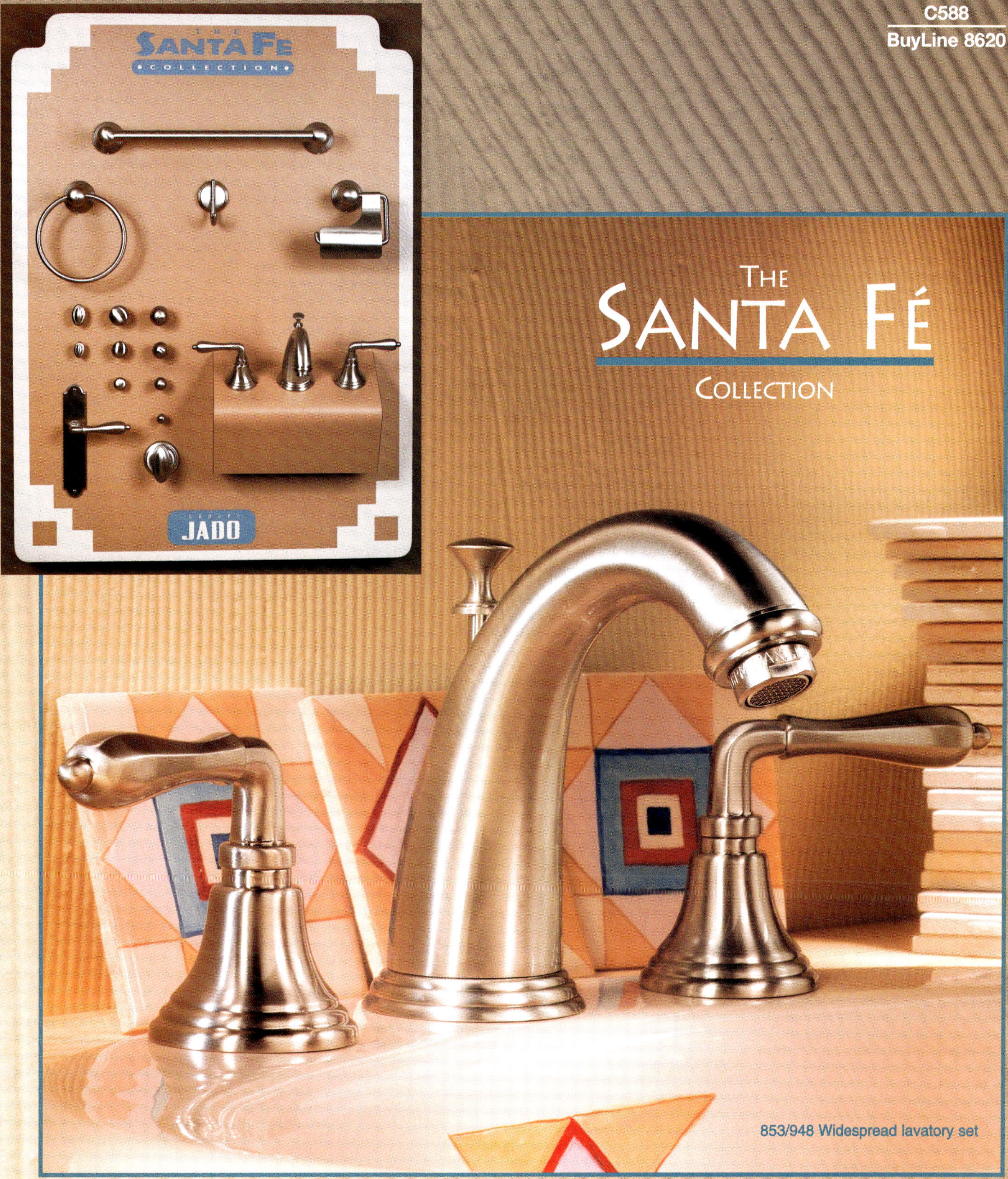

853/948 Widespread lavatory set

Series

Evergreen

853/907 Widespread lavatory set

Lever handle selection

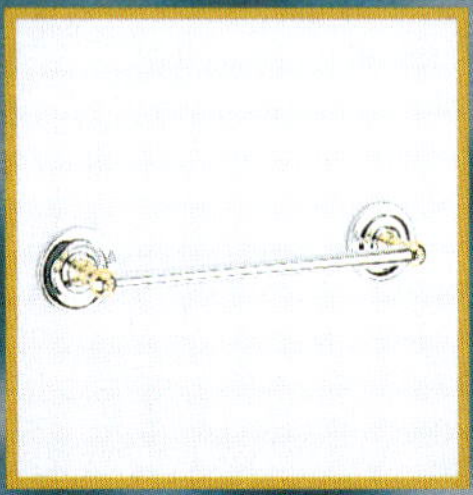

014/600
Towel bar 24"

855/927
Roman tub set with hand shower

853/997
Widespread lavatory set

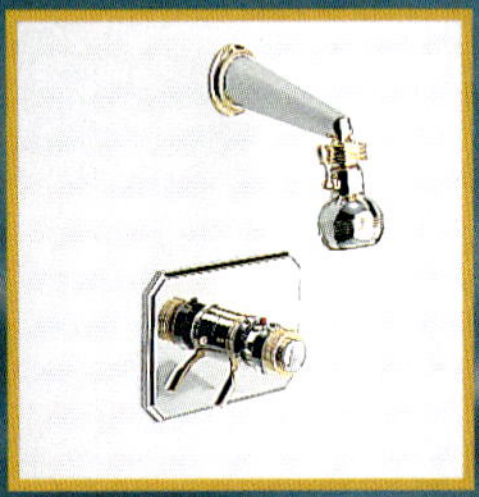

875/907
Single control thermostatic shower set

016/145
Tissue holder with cover

016/911
Toilet brush set - wall mounted

016/121
Soap dish - clear

016/150
Towel ring 6"

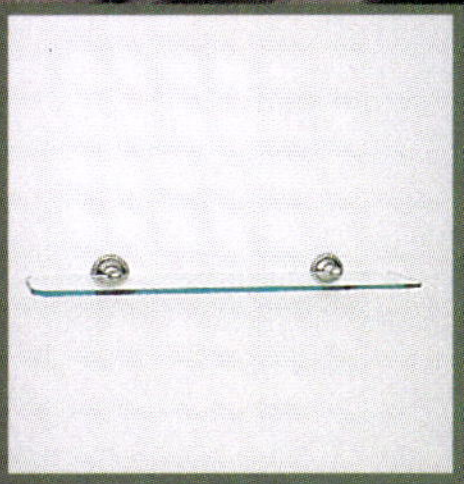
016/612
Clear shelf 24"

016/010
Robe hook

016/600
Towel bar 24"

016/141
Tumbler clear

816/003 Widespread lavatory set

Cross handle selection

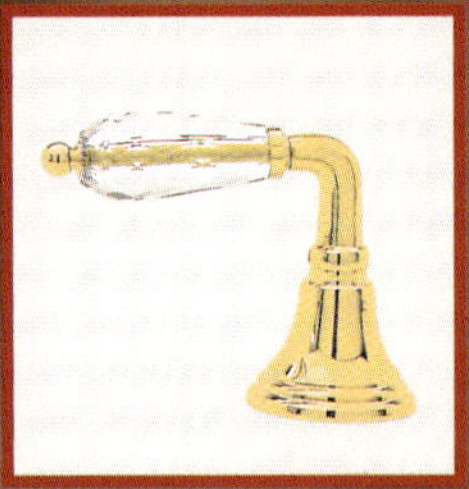

Crystal handle selection

Curved lever handle selection

Porcelain handle selection

853/948 Widespread lavatory set

820/751
Mirror

508/010
Robe hook

508/146
Tissue holder

855/948
3-Valve tub and shower set

033/141
Tumbler clear

033/140
Tissue holder

Lever handle
selection

033/010
Robe hook

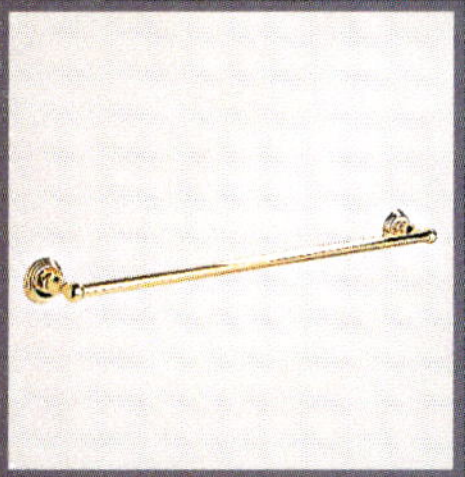

033/600
Towel bar 24"

875/908
Single control thermostatic
shower set

Series
Colonial

853/998 Widespread lavatory set

892/928
3-Hole bidet set

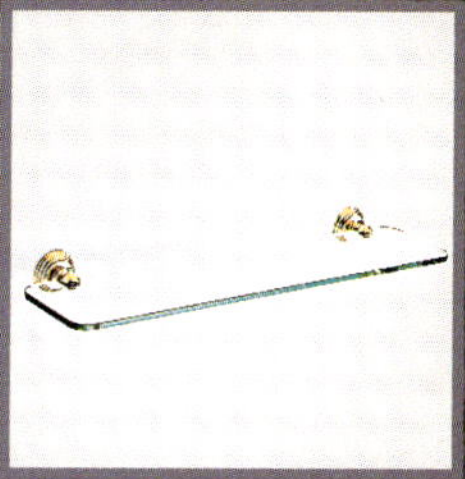

033/612
Clear shelf 24"

New Finishes
and Designs
by JADO.
New Haven
Widespread
Cross handle
Classic/Colonial
Viala
Viala/Caprice
JADO®

Luxury Bathroom Faucets and Accessories Forged from Brass

Products Available

Single Hole LAV Sets
Widespread LAV Sets
Wet Bar Faucets
Single Hole Bidet Sets
3-Hole Bidet Sets
Roman Tub Sets
Roman Tub with Hand Shower
Pressure Balanced Tub and Shower Sets
Pressure Balanced Shower Sets
3 Valve Tub and Shower Sets
2 Valve Shower Sets
Single Control Thermostatic Shower Sets
3/4" Thermostatic Mixing Valve Sets
5-Port Diverters
4-Port Diverters
1/2" and 3/4" Wall Valves
Body Sprays
Wall Angle Stops
Hand Shower Systems
Robe Hooks
6" Towel Rings
8" Towel Rings
12" Towel Rings
18" Towel Bars
24" Towel Bars
30" Towel Bars
Tissue Holders
Tumbler Holders
Soap Dish Holders
24" Shelves
Mirrors
Facial Tissue Box
Waste Paper Baskets
Wire Soap Trays

1/4 Turn Ceramic Disc Cartridge-LIFETIME WARRANTY

For further information call:
Phone 805 482 2666
FAX 805 484 4799

JADO®
P.O. BOX 1329 CAMARILLO, CA 93011

Introducing JADO® Custom Finish Program... an exciting selection of nineteen distinctive new finishes to satisfy discriminating design tastes from classical to contemporary and beyond. All cataloged JADO® and TopLine™ plumbing, bath accessories, door hardware and cabinet hardware are available in the new finishes, with few exceptions.

Our Custom Finish Program raises the standards of the industry again with a selection of finishes matching the unmistakable beauty and craftsmanship of JADO®. All finishes carry a one-year warranty against manufacturer's defects, and all products carry a limited lifetime warranty on parts against defects in materials and workmanship.

All custom finish orders are non-cancellable and non-refundable.

JADO®

P. O. Box 1329, Camarillo, CA 93011
For further information call:

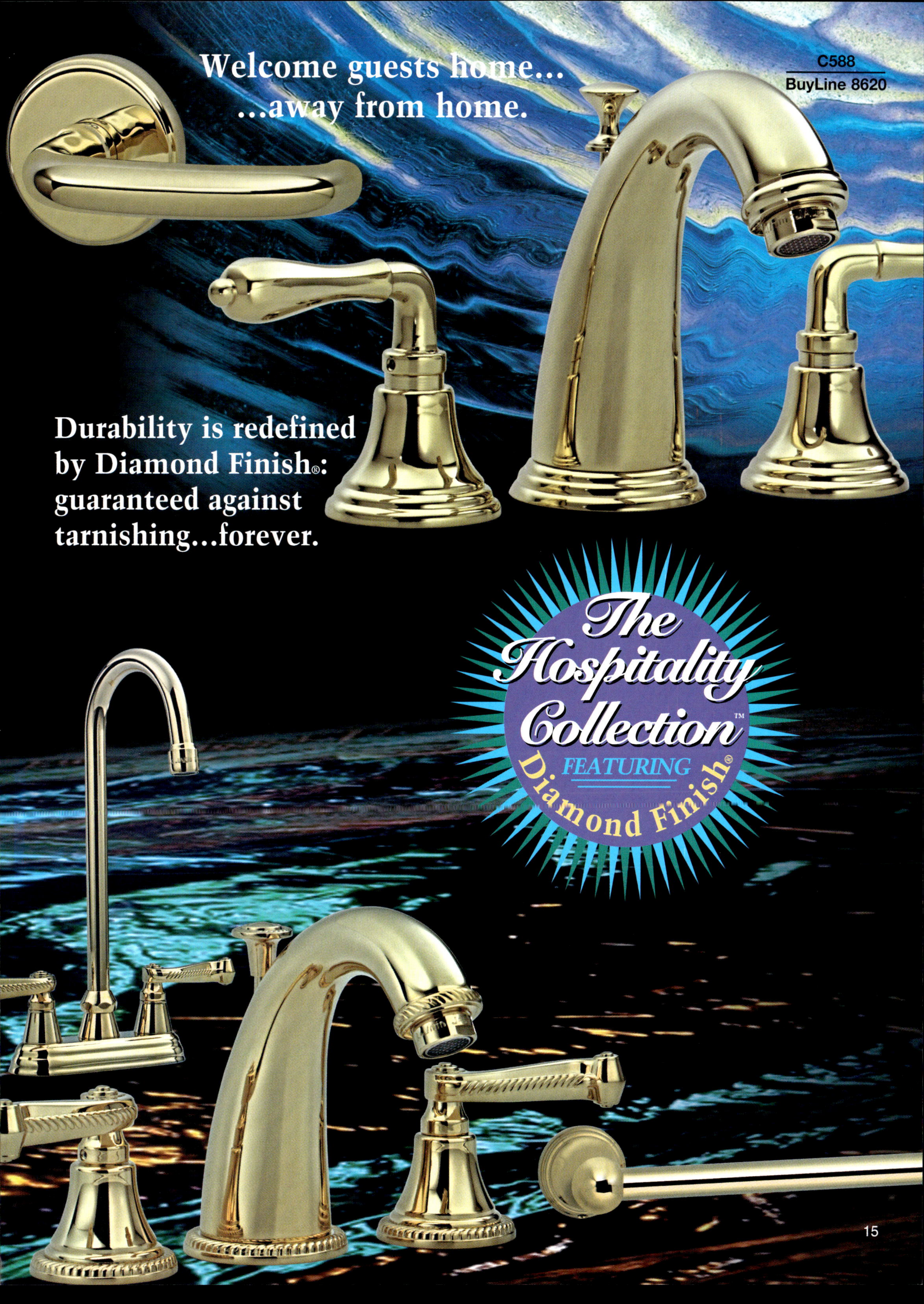

C588
BuyLine 8620
Welcome guests home...
...away from home.
Durability is redefined by Diamond Finish®: guaranteed against tarnishing...forever.
The Hospitality Collection™
FEATURING
Diamond Finish®

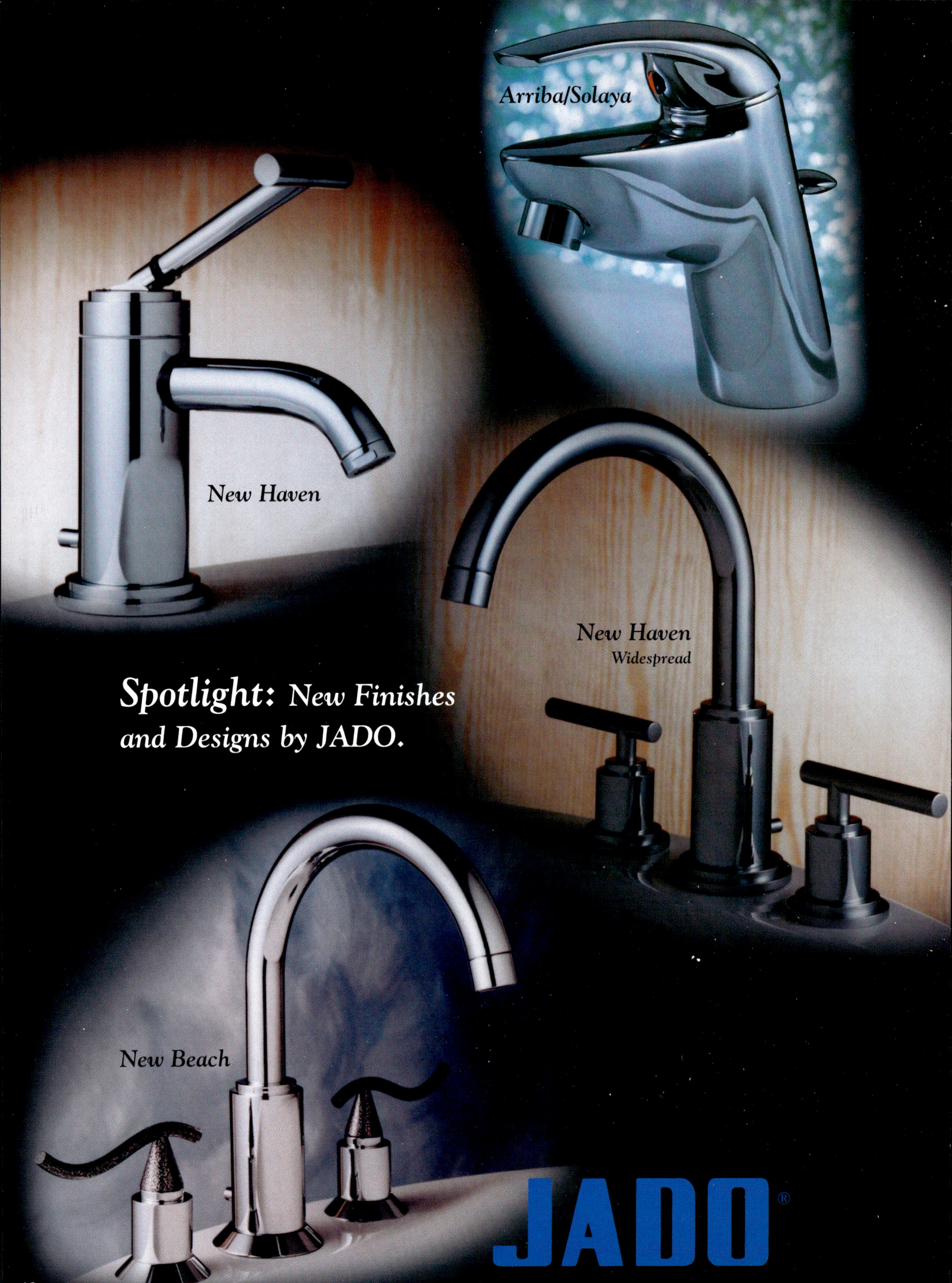
Arriba/Solaya
New Haven
New Haven
Widespread
Spotlight: New Finishes and Designs by JADO.
New Beach
JADO®

Diamonds Don't Earn Their Reputation By Being Soft.

Only from the precise combination of the elements, physics and master craftsmanship comes such flawless beauty that stands against time.

The Finish of the Future is Diamond Tough™

Diamond Finish® by JADO®

Diamond Finish® By JADO®

The Look of Brass, the Durability of Chrome

JADO's new *Diamond Finish* brings you the bright, warm look of brass without the worry of tarnishing, corrosion or scratching. The traditional maintenance problems associated with brass are simply gone.

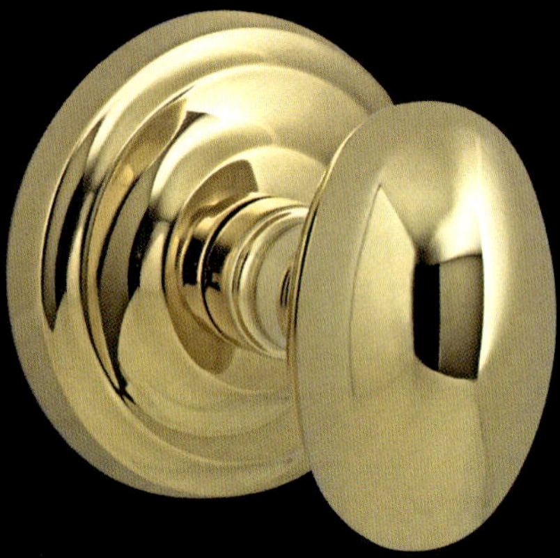

The Beauty and Performance You Expect from JADO

You asked us to combine the look of brass with the performance of a more durable finish such as chrome—and we listened. With the development of *Diamond Finish*, JADO once again delivers the product you want while setting new industry standards.

Plumbing and Hardware for Completely Coordinated Design

Diamond Finish is available throughout our Classic, Colonial and WYND 816 Series of faucet sets, pressure balanced shower sets, tub and shower sets, Roman tub sets and bar faucets. For truly coordinated design in *Diamond Finish* we also offer a complete bath accessory collection of towel bars, towel rings, robe hooks and tissue holders, as well as perfectly matching hardware, in *Diamond Finish*.

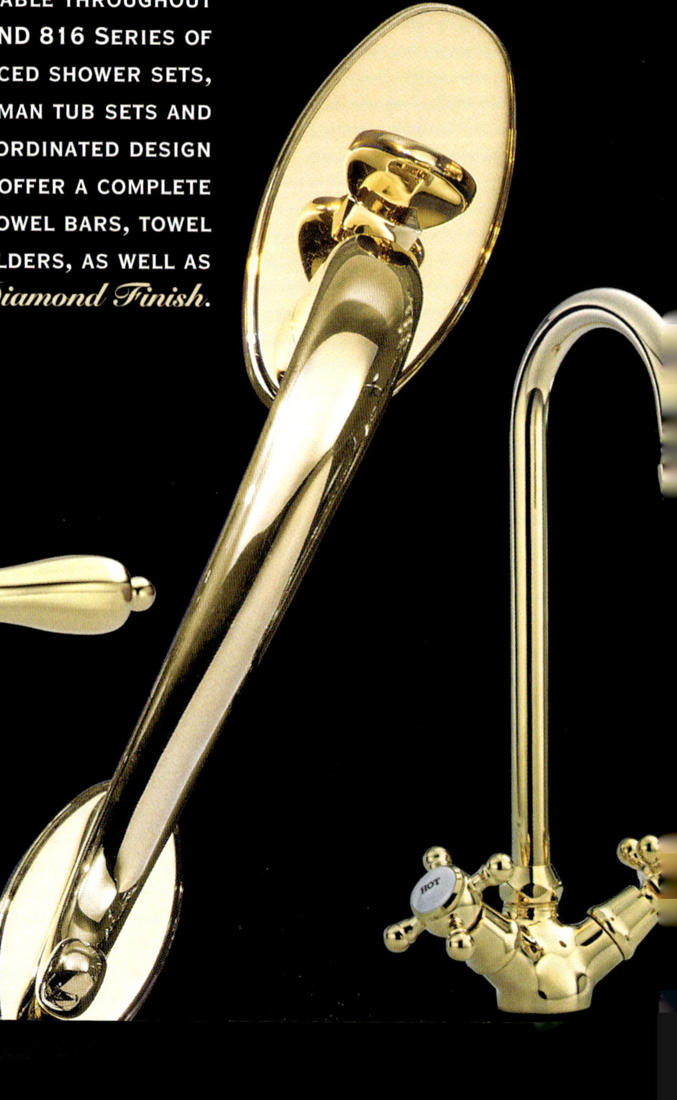

PVD and JADO Technology: The Finish of the Future

Diamond Finish is an exclusive process that begins with the highest quality brass available. Through a special forging and plating technique using Physical Vacuum Deposition (PVD) Technology, the brass is encased in extra thick layers of protection that offer the durability of chrome while retaining the natural look of polished brass.

JADO®
CERTIFIED
PVD
Diamond Finish®

Look for the Seal that guarantees it's Certified JADO PVD Technology.
Diamond Finish....The Finish of the Future™

PVD Technology Plus JADO's Design and Quality

In addition to the impressive durability of the PVD *Diamond Finish*, all products in the *Diamond Finish* collection are manufactured using JADO's precision engineering and world-class design. The result is the beautiful look of polished brass with a lifetime of reliability.

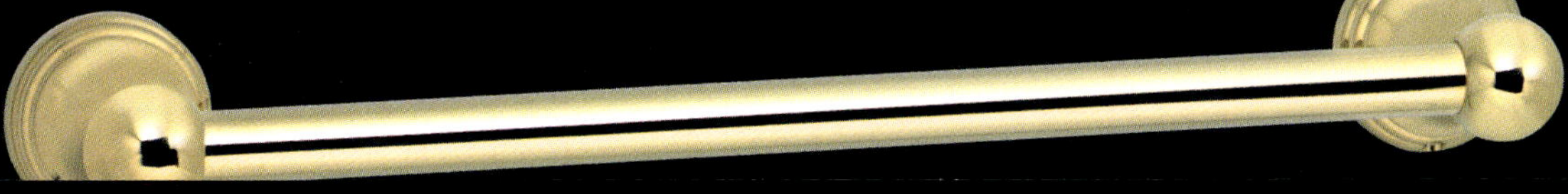

The Look of Brass—Guaranteed Not to Tarnish

JADO's exclusive PVD *Diamond Finish* carries a lifetime warranty against tarnishing. The *Diamond Finish* collection also carries a JADO standard lifetime warranty against defects in materials and workmanship. Now you can have the beautiful look of brass, guaranteed against tarnishing...forever.

The Maintenance Worries of Brass are Gone...

...nearly 100 standard cleaning products have been tested on *Diamond Finish* without harm. In fact, the use of liquid cleanser and steelwool did not damage the finish! Simply avoid cleaners that contain acids or other caustic agents such as toilet bowl cleaners or those that are formulated specifically to remove rust or tarnish.

JADO® CERTIFIED PVD *Diamond Finish*

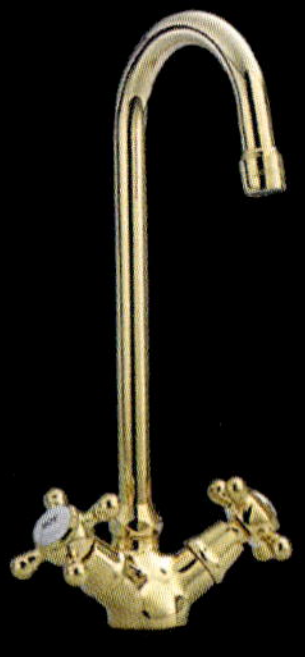

862/108/167

816/002/167

853/948/167

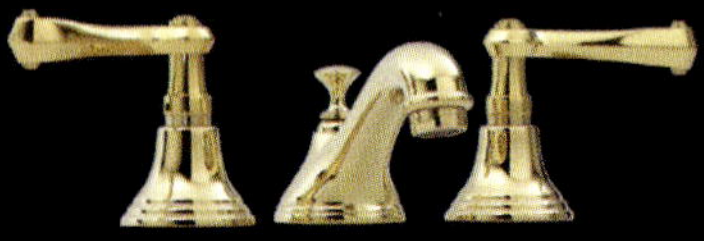

853/918/167

816/213/167

901/946/767

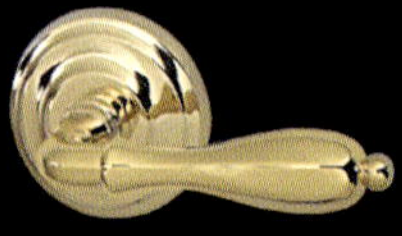

933/946/767

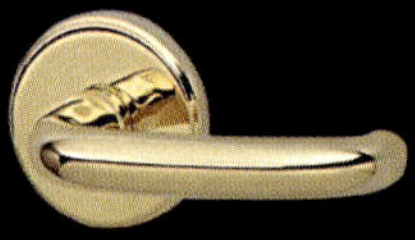

939/947/767

455/946/767

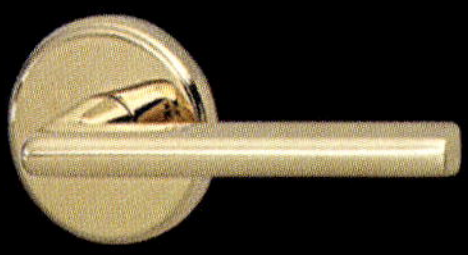

926/947/767

450/195/067

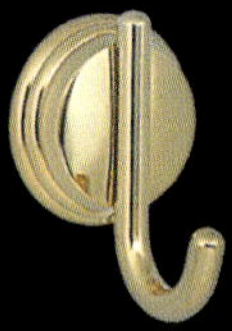

508/010/167

853/651/167

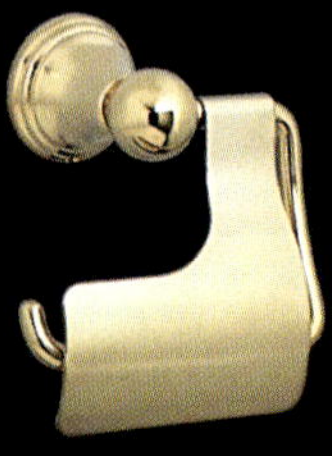

508/145/167

508/460/167

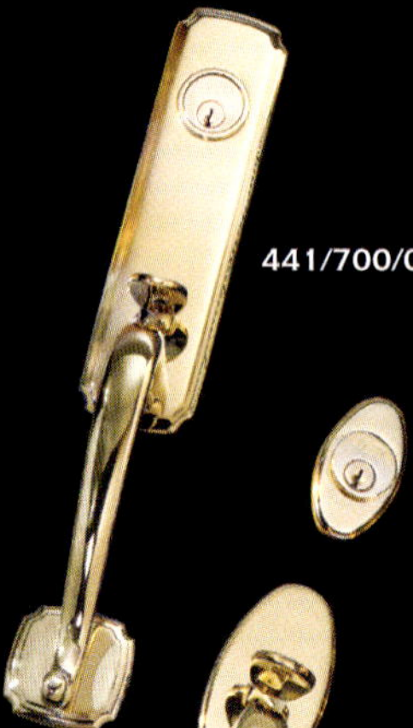

441/700/067

440/700/067

901/951/467E

JADO®

P. O. Box 1329, Camarillo, CA 93011
For further information call:
Phone 805-482-2666
Fax 805-484-4799

C588
BuyLine 8620

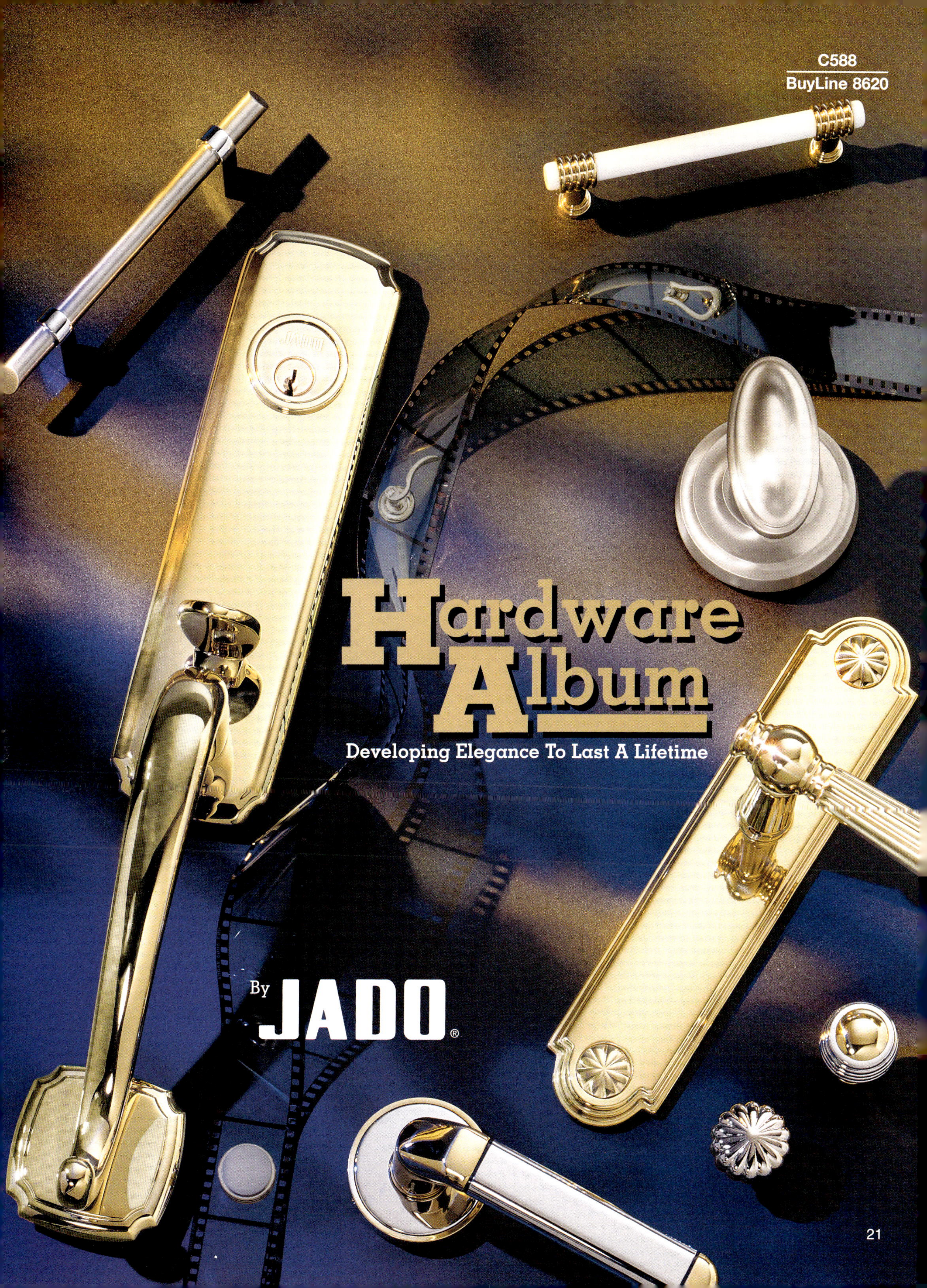

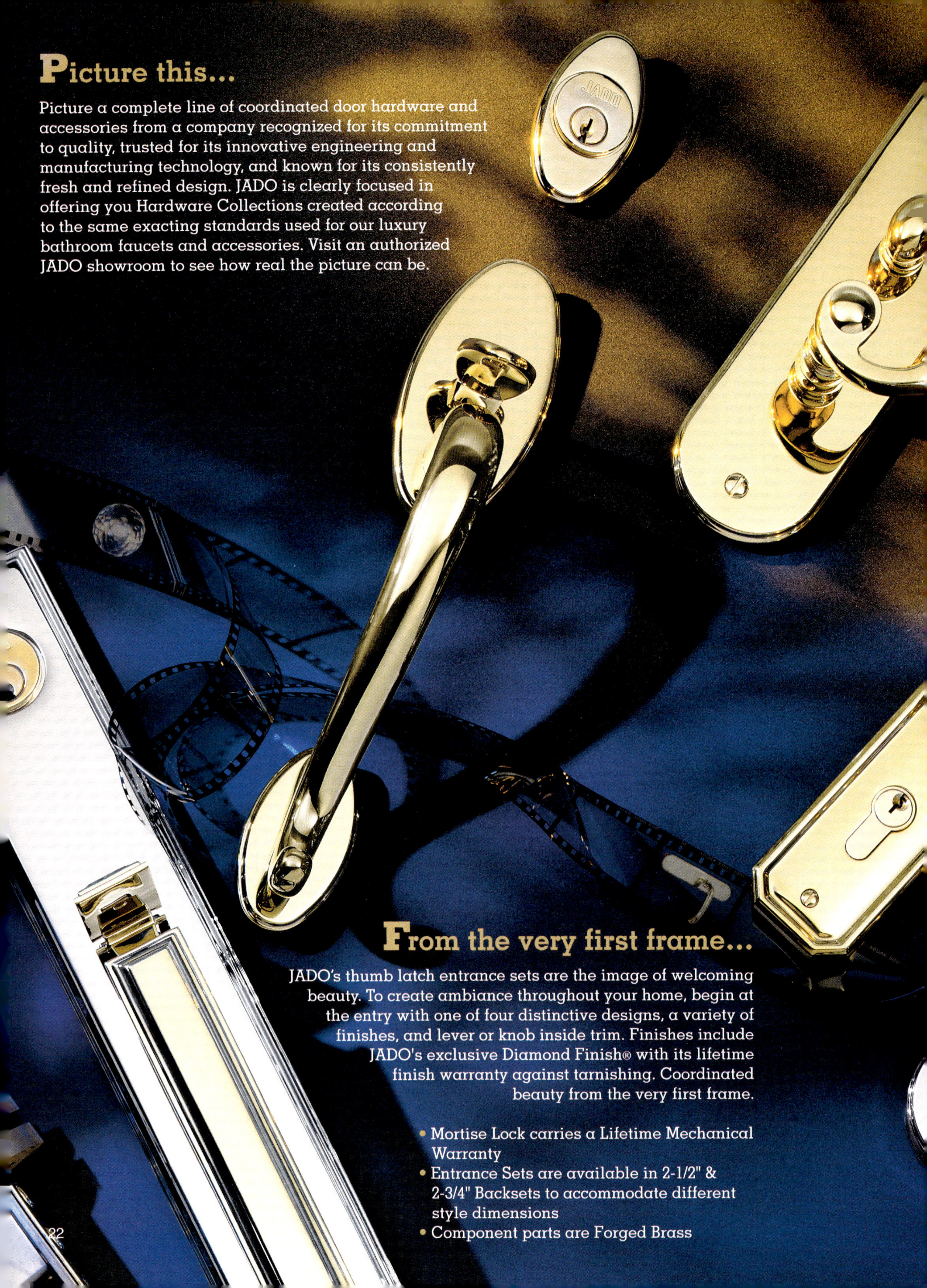

Picture this...

Picture a complete line of coordinated door hardware and accessories from a company recognized for its commitment to quality, trusted for its innovative engineering and manufacturing technology, and known for its consistently fresh and refined design. JADO is clearly focused in offering you Hardware Collections created according to the same exacting standards used for our luxury bathroom faucets and accessories. Visit an authorized JADO showroom to see how real the picture can be.

From the very first frame...

JADO's thumb latch entrance sets are the image of welcoming beauty. To create ambiance throughout your home, begin at the entry with one of four distinctive designs, a variety of finishes, and lever or knob inside trim. Finishes include JADO's exclusive Diamond Finish® with its lifetime finish warranty against tarnishing. Coordinated beauty from the very first frame.

- Mortise Lock carries a Lifetime Mechanical Warranty
- Entrance Sets are available in 2-1/2" & 2-3/4" Backsets to accommodate different style dimensions
- Component parts are Forged Brass

JADO Custom Finishes

Introducing the JADO® Custom Finish Program... an exciting selection of nineteen distinctive new finishes to satisfy discriminating design tastes from classical to contemporary and beyond. All cataloged JADO® and TopLine™ plumbing, bath accessories, door hardware and cabinet hardware are available in the new finishes, with few exceptions.

Our Custom Finish Program raises the standards of the industry again with a selection of finishes matching the unmistakable beauty and craftsmanship of JADO®. All finishes carry a one-year warranty against manufacturer's defects, and all products carry a limited lifetime warranty on parts against defects in materials and workmanship.

All custom finish orders are non-cancellable and non-refundable.

Topline TAMARAC

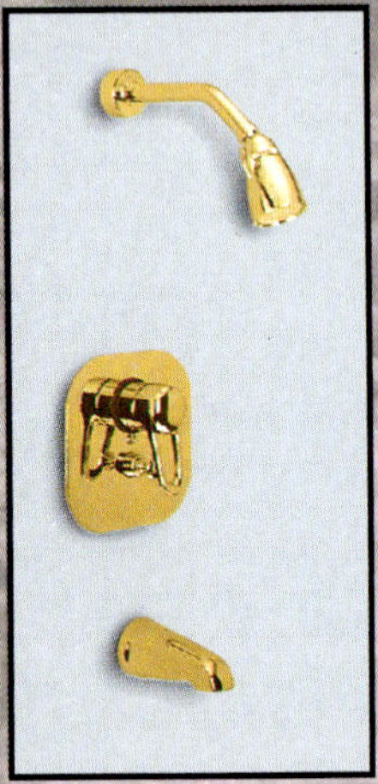

Topline Tamarac, finished in gleaming chrome or polished brass, is timeless and traditional with its understated elegance and choice of cross or lever handles. Coordinating a complete JADO look are accessories that include a robe hook, towel ring, tumbler holder, shower set and single-control tub and shower combination.

A truly striking subject...

JADO's single and double cylinder function dead bolts are precision engineered to give years of reliable security. A variety of finishes and designs coordinate JADO's door hardware to give you peace of mind without detracting from appearance.

- 2-3/8" or 2-3/4" backsets
- Adapter ring for 2-1/8" pre-drilled doors available
- Single & Double Cylinder function
- Two designs are available: Standard & Classic

Radiant beauty under any light...

JADO hardware is available in a wide selection of finishes to accommodate the preferences of design professionals and discerning homeowners alike. From the soft luster of Brushed Nickel to the radiant tones of Polished Brass, Polished Chrome or Luxurious Gold, JADO has a finish to match your decor. Also available is UltraBrass®, which has a lifetime warranty against tarnishing from ultraviolet rays and humidity, and Patina Collection®, which is guaranteed to wear naturally and develop highlights unique to your touch. Regardless of the finish you choose, it's guaranteed to look beautiful.

Positively stunning...

JADO Diamond Finish® achieves new standards for enduring beauty and quality. The beauty of this exclusive finish is its resistance to tarnishing and corrosion. We back all Diamond Finish products: thumb latch entry sets, dead bolts and selected interior sets, with a lifetime finish warranty against tarnishing. JADO Diamond Finish...
...simply brilliant.

1:27 LATCH SYSTEM™

It's About Time...

...In fact it is about installation time–
One minute, 27 seconds to install a complete set.

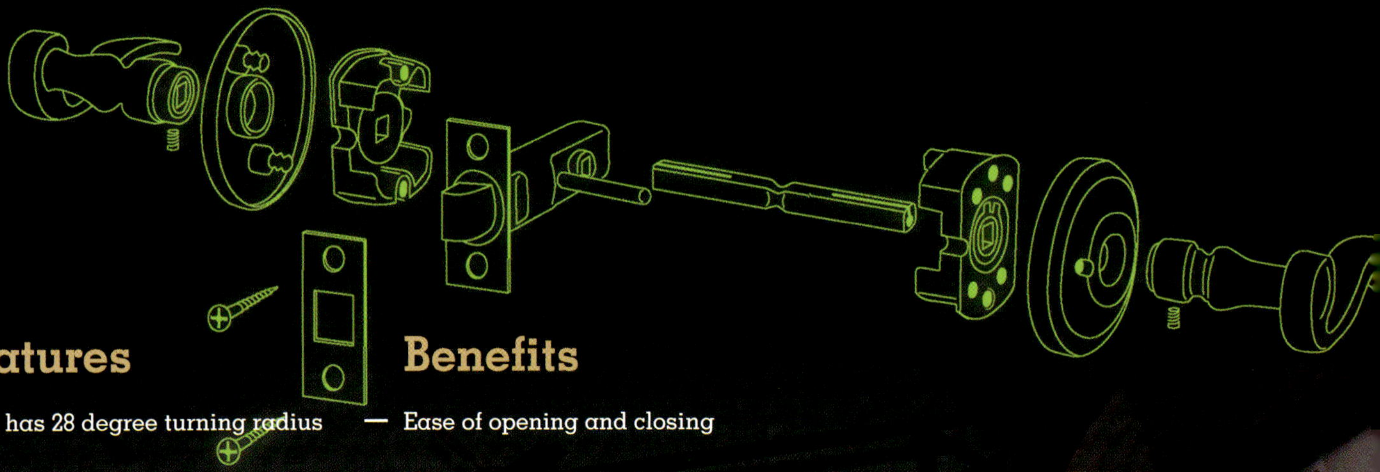

Features		Benefits
Latch has 28 degree turning radius	—	Ease of opening and closing
Two piece bracing is made to fit into a 2-1/8" prepped door	—	Bracing supports the latch to prevent rosette movement and lever sagging REDUCES INSTALLATION TIME
Bracing has additional assist spring for lever function	—	Assist spring adds life to the latch and gives a European mortise lock feel
Mounting screws for the bracing are pre-installed by the factory	—	Ready to mount out of the carton, eliminates misplacement of mounting screws REDUCES INSTALLATION TIME
Same bracing is used for passage and privacy functions and 2-3/8" or 2-3/4" backset installations	—	Reduces inventory requirements
Rosettes are conceal mounted	—	Enhances the look of the hardware, no matter which side of the door you view REDUCES INSTALLATION TIME
Rosettes are self-aligning	—	Eliminates any chance of binding REDUCES INSTALLATION TIME
Rosettes (passage & privacy) are not handed	—	Reduces inventory requirements REDUCES INSTALLATION TIME
Privacy latch is not handed, simply turn latch bolt to achieve proper handing	—	Reduces inventory requirements REDUCES INSTALLATION TIME

Our latest development...

With JADO's revolutionary 1:27 door latch and bracing system, adding beauty and quality to your home has never been easier. The 1:27 LATCH SYSTEM™, featured in all of our interior door sets, installs on any 2-1/8" prepped door in less than one and one-half minutes using only a Phillips screwdriver and an Allan wrench.

It's About Time...for JADO.

JADO®

An ISO 9001 Certified Corporation

P.O. Box 1329, Camarillo, CA 93011
Phone: 805.482.2666 FAX: 805.484.4799

THE PATINA COLLECTION

"Naturally Aging Finish"
THE
·PATINA·
COLLECTION™
JADO
The Patina Collection is the original "Naturally Aging Finish" manufactured exclusively by JADO. Its dramatic design is true to the heritage of quality craftsmanship that is JADO's world-wide trademark. As the newest member of the TopLine Series, the Patina Collection is competitively priced, yet unmistakably JADO.
Patina's precision craftsmanship is backed by a lifetime mechanical warranty. Known by many as JADO's personal seal of approval, this warranty is by far the most respectable in the industry.
JADO's Patina Finish is guaranteed to age gracefully. Classic warmth and elegance combine to make this one of the most sought after finishes in the country. The Patina Collection entry set is accompanied by a wide variety of passage and dummy sets, as well as cabinet hardware.
To learn more about all the precision engineering and incomparable design of JADO hardware and plumbing products, we invite you to visit an authorized JADO designer showroom.
The Patina Collection by JADO
JADO®
P.O. Box 1329, Camarillo, CA 93011
For further information call:
Phone 805 482 2666
FAX 805 484 4799

Topline II

422/446

423/446

426/446

Topline

- Historical Reproduction
- Mortise and Tenon Construction
- Fine Hardwoods
- 100% Custom-Sized
- Fully Assembled or D.I.Y.
- Commercial and Residential
- Interior and Exterior
- Operable and Fixed Louvers
- Raised and Flat Panels
- Full Hardware Selection

Website: http://www.DIYShutters.com

Kestrel Manufacturing

Specify authenticity; specify Kestrel.

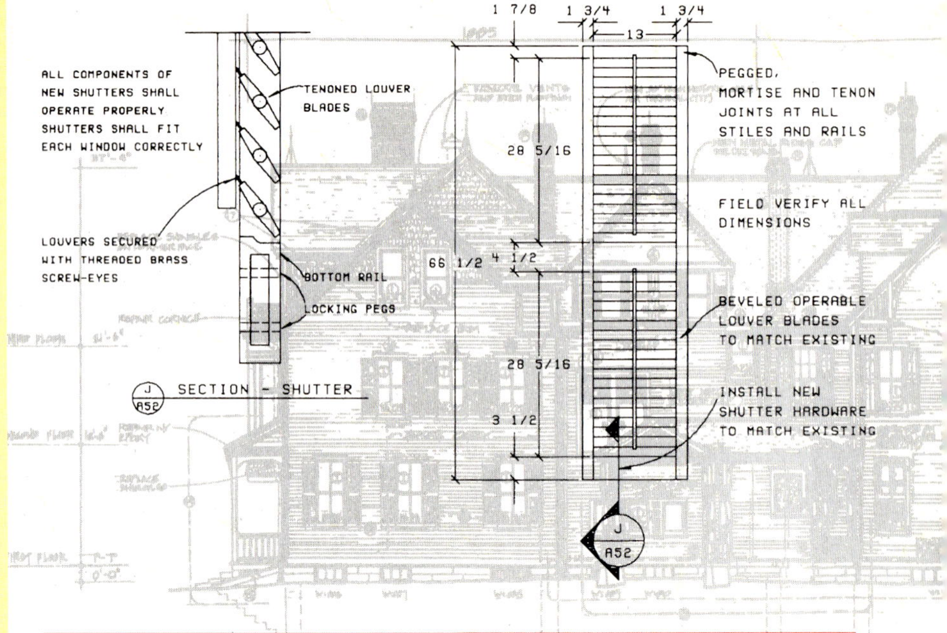

Introduction

Since 1989 Kestrel Shutters have been supplied to the finest commercial and residential sites worldwide. Hand-crafted for both interior and exterior applications, Kestrel Shutters maintain quality in appearance, design and durability.

Manufactured here in the rolling hills of southeastern Pennsylvania, Kestrel Shutters are available in an array of styles, each made to order to the exact size required. Only the finest quality materials are used. Frame components are milled to precise tolerances and then joined with Old World techniques; true pegged, deep pocket mortise and tenon joints ensure strength and longevity for generations to come. Kestrel's selection of hardware provides the final complimenting finish.

Remember, combined knowledge, experience and dedication to quality make Kestrel Shutters sparkle with a difference found no where else... Our signature of quality and careful attention to detail.

Historic Reproduction/Custom Work

Sometimes projects both historic and new require the shutters to match exactly to what was or what is in mind... We fill your needs. From the shape of the louver blades to the sizing of individual rails and stiles we will produce shutters to meet your specifications. We can work from your shop drawings or send us the original shutters to be reproduced.

Interior

Kestrel Interior Shutters are made to look and perform beautifully. Manufactured with clear basswood the soft warm tones of this lightweight hardwood readily accepts both paint, stain and natural oil finishes. Our pegged, deep pocket mortise and tenon shutters will stand up to all the thumps and bumps of real living environments while still maintaining the original furniture quality. Louver and panel shutters will help insulate against the extreme temperatures outdoors while protecting interior furnishing and floor coverings from UV light. Kestrel Interior Shutters are available in all of our styles both pre-assembled and our exclusive D.I.Y. shutter kits.

Exterior

Kestrel Exterior Shutters are made to hold up to nature's wear and tear while providing the exterior facade with style and elegance. Manufactured with clear Spanish Cedar, this reddish-brown tight grained wood will take both paint and stain beautifully. And unlike other cedars Spanish Cedar is an extremely durable hardwood which when combined with our pegged, deep-pocket mortise and tenon construction provides you with lasting protection and sound security. Kestrel Exterior Shutters are available in all of our styles both pre-assembled and our exclusive D.I.Y. shutter kits.

The Anatomy of a Kestrel Shutter

True pegged mortise-and-tenon frame joints.
A stronger, longer-lasting joinery technique that out-performs dowels, splines or screws.

Balanced louvers.
Produces smooth, positive movement and keeps louvers in position, once adjusted.

Smooth, clean surfaces and outer edges slightly rounded to protect against splintering.
Because they're hand-sanded and made of the finest grade hardwoods, Kestrel shutters take a beautiful finish.

100% custom sized to your dimensions.
Your shutters will look proportional and provide the perfect fit.

True milled louver tenons that are actual, strong extensions of the blade...making a stronger and historically correct shutter.

Louvers properly secured to the operating tilt-rod with solid brass threaded screw-eyes, which will not pull out.

Furniture-grade quality throughout.
A better-looking and better-performing shutter.

Garden Screen™

This versatile screen can virtually hold anything, anywhere, both indoors and out. Designed as a portable shelving system, it's uses range from starting bedding plants to store displays, buffet and hotel serving stations. Verandas, lobbies and poolsides are accented beautifully by the rich Spanish Cedar tones and available inserts of fabric, lattice, bead board and louvers provide screening if need be. Kestrel's four section Garden Screen™ is fitted with double action hinges and can be folded up for compact storage. Other folding screens designed for fabric and glass inserts are also available.

Cabinet, Closet & Entranceway Doors

Kestrel Shutters are made to measure for cabinet, closet and entranceway doors. With the options of operable and fixed louvers, as well as raised and flat panels, you can customize every door to match your shutters.

Do-It-Yourself operable and fixed louver inserts are also available to easily fit within your own stile and rail assembly for retrofitting existing doors or creating new. Kestrel cabinet and closet doors are available in all of our styles both pre-assembled and our exclusive D.I.Y. shutter kits.

The Original D.I.Y. Shutter™ Kit

The first ever of its kind, Kestrel's Do-It-Yourself Shutter Kit lets you build premium quality shutters while providing cost savings and personal satisfaction. Kestrel D.I.Y. kits are a knock-down version of our pre-assembled shutters; all you have to do is the simple hand assembly. Each shutter can be completed at home or on the job site with nothing more than needlenose pliers, clamps and glue. And with Kestrel D.I.Y. shutters, paint and stain can easily be applied prior to assembly. We also provide a complete selection of D.I.Y. Shutter components.

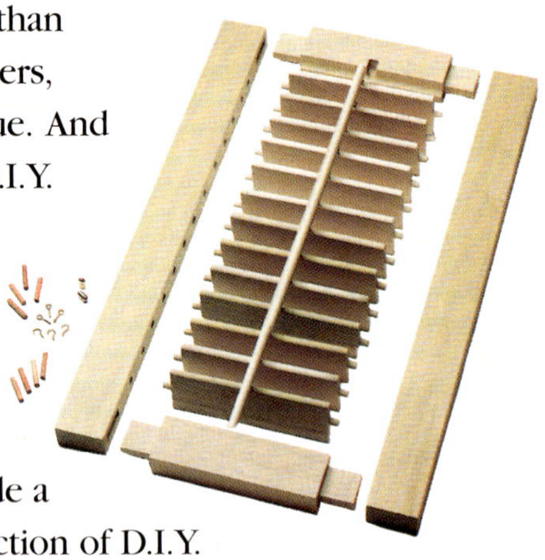

Interior & Exterior Hardware

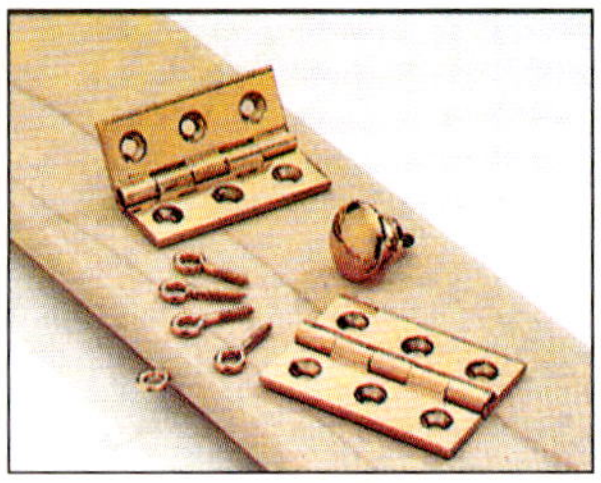

Strong, elegant & durable, Kestrel's range of hardware compliments your shutters, doors and cabinetwork while providing lasting functionality. We provide a selection of the finest interior solid brass hardware which is produced in Pennsylvania and England. Exterior hardware from Pennsylvania Foundries is available in several traditional and period designs fabricated from either steel, wrought iron or cast iron.

Interior & Exterior Shutter Styles

Kestrel Shutters both pre-assembled and D.I.Y. are offered in all of the above styles.
Louvered shutters are available with both fixed and operable blades.
Operable louver blades are 1.7/8", 2.1/2" or 3.1/2" wide. Fixed louver blades are 1.7/8" wide.
Panel shutters are available with both Colonial raised and flat panels, each with optional cutouts.

Please contact us concerning your specific architectural and historical requirements.

Kestrel Manufacturing

Specify authenticity; specify Kestrel.

Post Office Box 12, Saint Peters, Pennsylvania 19470-0012
Telephone: 800-494-4321 or 610-326-6679
Telefax: 610-326-6779
http://www.DIYShutters.com

Photographs: Caroline Caldwell, Architect - Shutters installed in private residence, St. John USVI

ZOELLER PUMP CO.

"QUALITY PUMPS SINCE 1939"

C908

15130/ZOE

BuyLine 8646

Qwik Jon Sewage Removal Systems

INSTALL A QWIK JON JUST ABOUT ANYWHERE.

- Designed to accommodate a toilet, lavatory and a bathtub
- Use with a variety of toilet styles (1.6 Gallon residential flush; other installations should use over 3 gallon flush)
- Perfect for basements, family rooms, warehouse, factories, room additions.
- No need to destroy concrete floors.
- Reduces construction cost.
- Pumps any direction.
- Fits just about anywhere.

MODELS:

Model 100 UL Listed 264 Pump
Model 102 UL Listed 266 Pump
Patent No. 5,038,418

TYPICAL INSTALLATIONS

Versatile installation enables the pump compartment and piping to be concealed by the installation of a wall.

NOTE: Access must be maintained to the pump compartment.

NOTE: The Qwik Jon is designed to fit flush with any elevated floor made of standard 2" x 6" material (actual dimensions 1½" x 5½"). And you can add a Lavatory - Bathtub - Shower with the installation of the 2" adapt-a-flex seal (provided). Tub or shower requires built in installation. See Installation Instructions.

BOCA ES™

UPC FOUNDED 1926 IAPMO®

Built In Installation
Toilet, Fixtures and
Piping Not Included

Basic Installation
Toilet, Fixtures and
Piping Not Included

TECHNICAL INFORMATION . . .

Code approved (Consult factory)

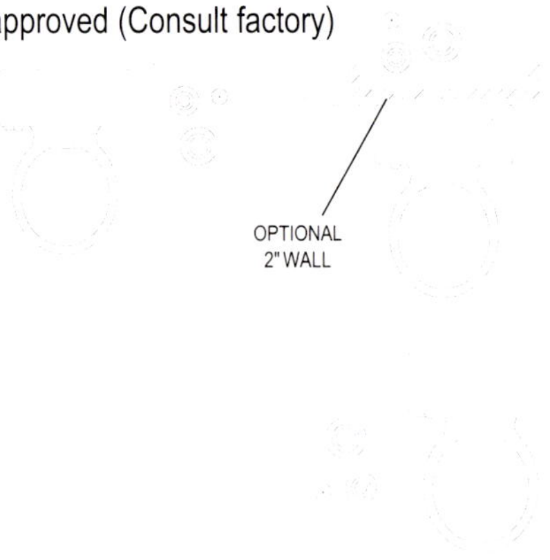

QWIK JON SYSTEMS INCLUDE:

Sewage Pumps

MODEL 100
Model WM 264 Pump
.4 HP 115V 9.4 amps
P.S.C. Motor
UL Listed

MODEL 102
Model WM 266 Pump
1/2 HP 115V 10.4 amps
Split Phase Motor
UL Listed

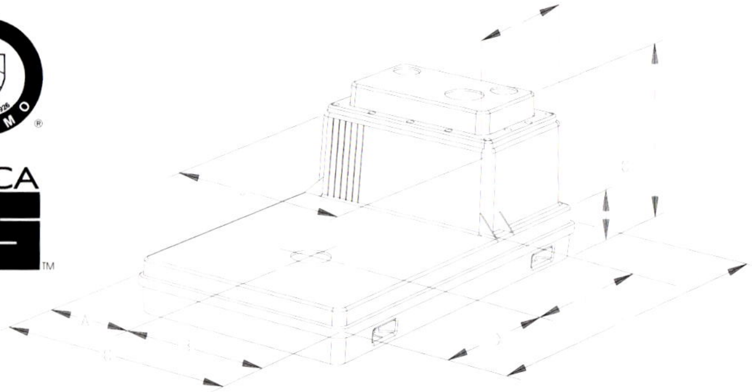

FEATURES:

- Automatic level control switch.
- Thermal overload protected motor.
- Stainless steel screws, bolts & handle.
- Non-clogging vortex impeller.
- Passes 2" solids (sphere).
- UL listed 3-wire neoprene 10 ft. cord & plug.
- Maximum temperature rating - 130° F. (54° C).

Tank

MODEL 100/102 (Patented)

- Poly Structural Foam
- Lt. gray finish, black base
- Lightweight
- Wt. 27 lbs.

2" Back Flow Device and Union

- 2" back flow device (check local codes) required to prevent backflow of water and sewer gas.
- No threading of pipe required.
- Fits ABS, PVC and steel pipe.
- Weight: 2 lbs.

ALL IN ONE CARTON

- Tank, lid & gasket.
- .4 HP or ½ HP sewage pump.
- Back flow device (check local codes).
- 2" Discharge & 3" Vent with adapt-a-flex seals.
- 2" adapt-a-flex seal for additional fixtures.
- Floor flange extender kit for ½" & ⁵/₈" thick floors.
- Hardware pack.
- Installation instructions.
- Shipping weight:
  100 System - 94 lbs.
  102 System - 96 lbs.

ITEMS NEEDED BY INSTALLER

- Supply fittings & waste pipe.
- Toilet fixture and/or other fixtures.
- Electrical source with ground fault interrupter protected receptacle.
- Water source.
- Tools.

MODEL NO.	A	B	C	D	E
100/102	12 ¼	12 ¼	5 ½	13 ¼	14 ⅛
	F	G	H	I	J
100/102	42 ³/₁₆	24 ½	17	13 ½	20 ½

Model		264 (100)		266 (102)	
Feet	Meters	Gal.	Ltrs.	Gal.	Ltrs.
5	1.52	102	386	100	379
10	3.05	60	227	72	273
15	4.57	11.5	44	34	129
Lock Valve:		16 ft.		18.4 ft.	

NOTE:

Recommended for installations up to 16′ total dynamic head. Consult factory if installation is above 15′ vertical height in 2" pipe.

NOTE:

Sewage Pumps WM264 & WM266 are designed for use in Qwik Jon units only. They are not designed for use in any other application.

CAUTION

All installation of controls, protection devices and wiring should be done by a qualified licensed electrician. All electrical and safety codes should be followed including the most recent National Electric Code (NEC) and the Occupational Safety and Health Act (OSHA).

ZOELLER PUMP COMPANY

MAIL TO: P.O. BOX 16347 • Louisville, KY 40256-0347
SHIP TO: 3649 Cane Run Road • Louisville, KY 40211-1961
(502) 778-2731 • 1 (800) 928-PUMP • FAX (502) 774-3624

VISIT OUR INTERNET SITE AT *http://www.zoeller.com*

C915

BuyLine 7948

Unmistakably Powerful *even before you turn it on.*

Rangemaster® by Broan *the leader in home ventilation.*

Ballista™

450 cfm centrifugal blower

3-speed slide control

two 20-watt halogen lights

Stainless steel.

Seamless corners for easy cleaning.

Telescopic flue fits 8′ to 10′ ceilings.

A flawless look. A lasting impression.

450cfm centrifugal blower

touch controls

two 20-watt halogen lights

Seamless underside with recessed lighting.

Easy-clean, seamless corner design.

Telescopic flue fits 8′ to 10′ ceilings.

Dramatically unites stainless steel and hand-blown glass.

Mirage™

Provisa™

900 cfm centrifugal blower

3-speed control

four 20-watt halogen lights

Stainless steel.

Seamless corners for easy cleaning.

Telescopic flue fits 8′ to 10′ ceilings.

Designed to draw the eye from every vantage point.

600 or 900cfm external blower

600 or 1200cfm internal blower

infinite speed control

Available in stainless, white or black.

Twin infrared food-warming lamps.

Three 20-watt halogen lights.

The design says professional, the detail pure perfection.

Rangemaster Original™

Rangemaster Original™ 60000

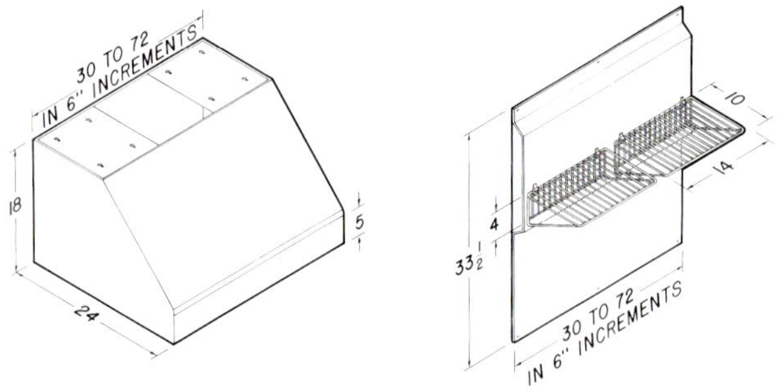

Ballista™ 61000

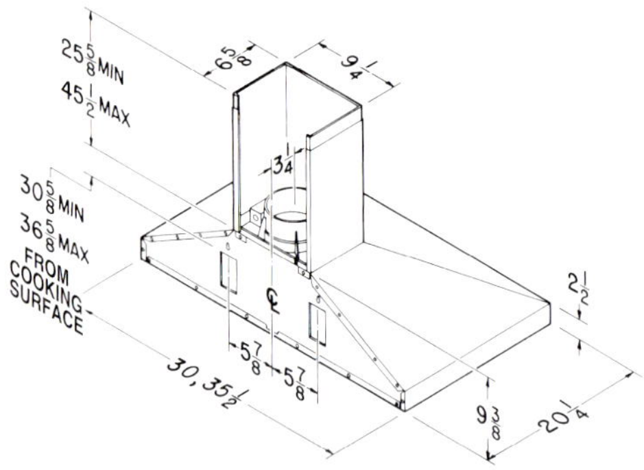

Mirage™ 62000

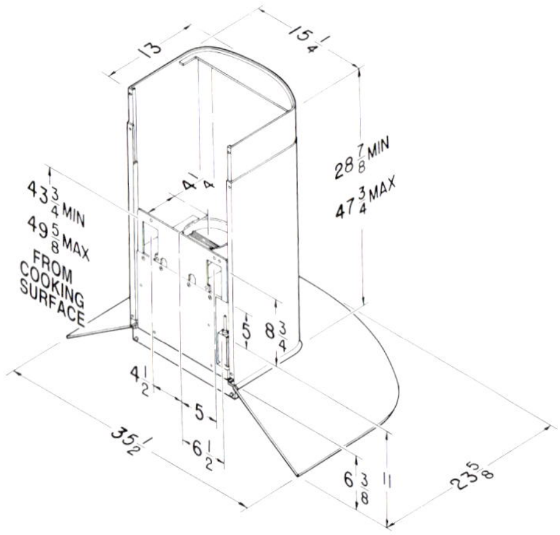

Provisa™ 63000

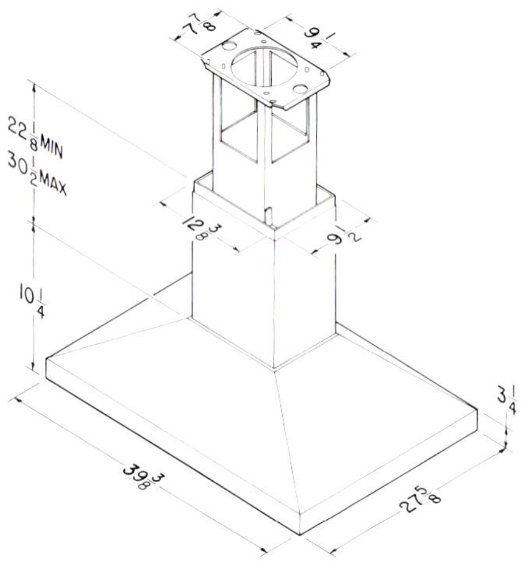

Model	Available Widths
Rangemaster Original 60000	30"/36"/42"/48"/54"/60"/66"/72"
Ballista 61000	30" or 90cm (35 7/16")
Mirage 62000	90cm (35 7/16")
Provisa 63000	70cm x 100cm (27 9/16" x 39 3/8")

Options for Rangemaster Original

Model	Description
325	600 cfm Internal Blower
326	1200 cfm Internal Blower
331	600 cfm External Roof or Wall Mount Blower Requires 332K rough-in kit.
332	900 cfm External Roof or Wall Mount Blower Requires 332K rough-in kit.
RN	Soffit Chimney for 60000–12" high
RP	Backsplash with fold down shelves. Can be used with all Rangemaster Hoods.

Rangemaster range hoods are a perfect combination of power and style for your professional-look kitchen. Ask about matching stainless steel backsplashes, which are available as options, to complete your wall-mounted Rangemaster ensemble.

BROAN®
A NORTEK COMPANY

99850531A Printed in the U.S.A.

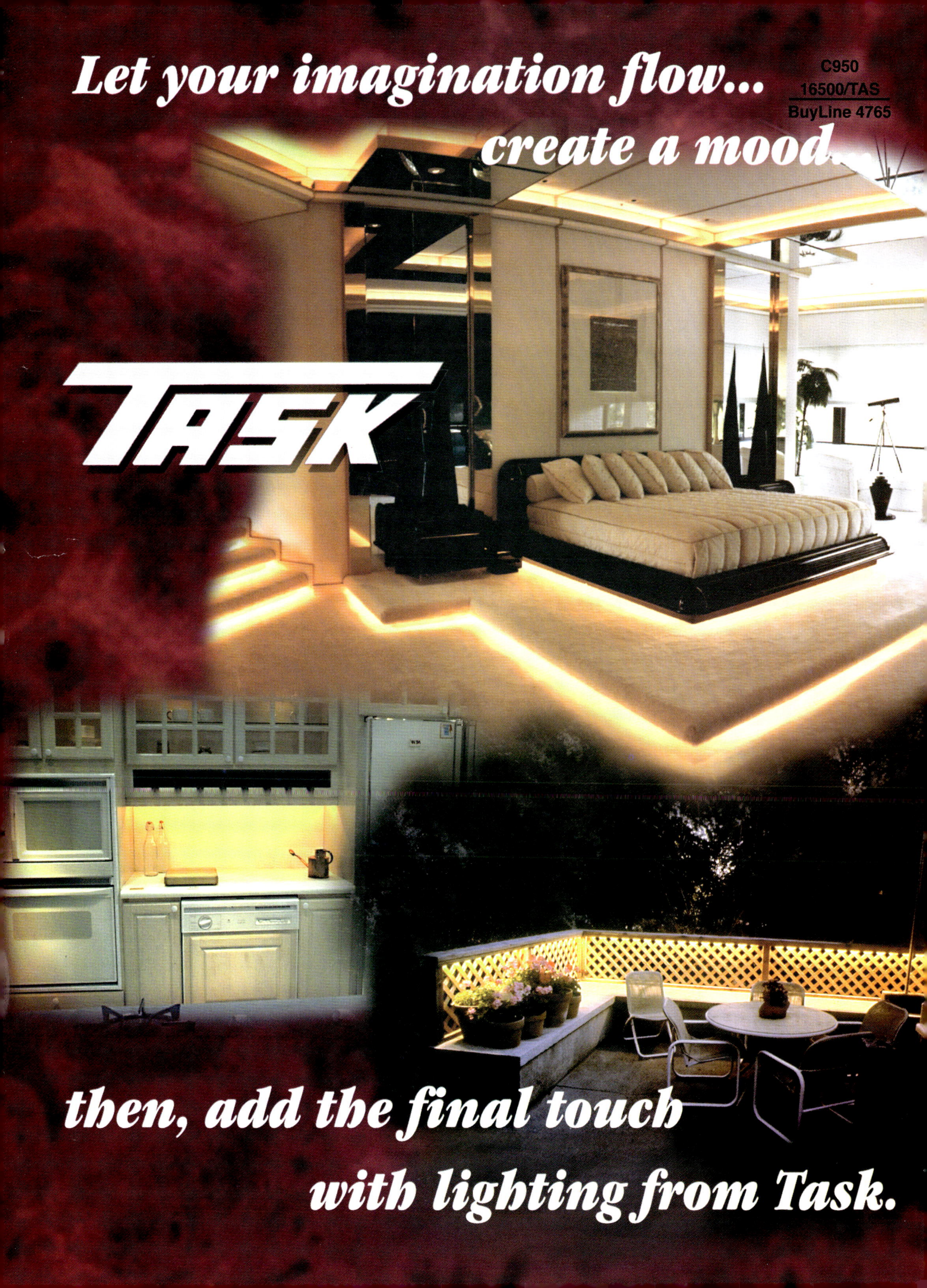
Let your imagination flow...
C950
16500/TAS
BuyLine 4765
create a mood...
TASK
then, add the final touch
with lighting from Task.

Executive Office

Commercial Installations

Custom Fixtures for Air Traffic Control Center

Founded in 1985, Task Lighting Corporation has been a pioneer in the field of low voltage task and accent lighting. Company recognitions include inclusion in the IES Progress Report as well as the "Blue Chip Award" for small businesses.

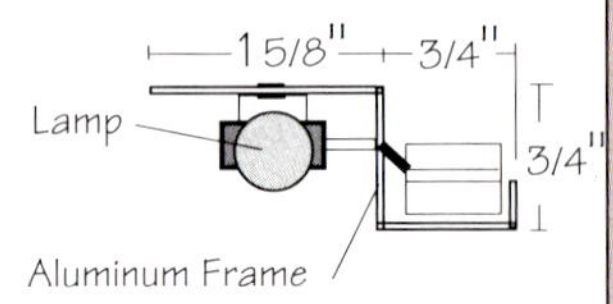

KC Series

UL LISTED

69X5

c UL LISTED

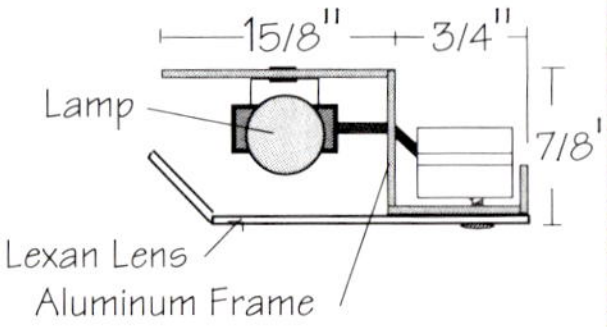

LX Series

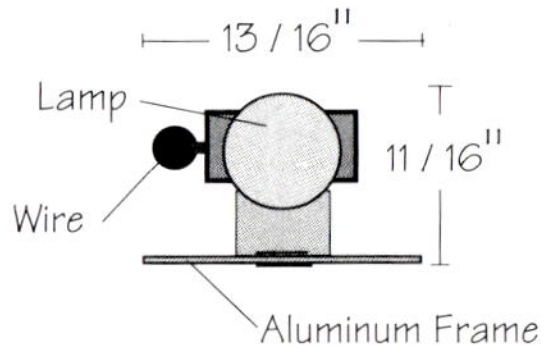

TS Series

Create a mood ...

Task Lighting's Luche & Lumere lighting systems are for creative people who design spaces for beauty, function & feeling. The UL Listed systems are ideal for providing continuous, uninterrupted lighting, from under and inside cabinets to cove moldings, deck rails and steps. Designed to illuminate and enhance, all fixtures are small enough to conceal behind a one inch valance - so you see the effect of the light, not the source. Lumere & Luche are available in standard incandescent lamps for a warm quiet light or Xenon lamps for a brighter, whiter light. With lamp life ranging from 9,000 hours to 24,000 hours, maintenance is minimal.

With Task Lighting

Without Task Lighting

Luche Fixture Guide

C950
16500/TAS
BuyLine 4765

- KC & LX Series fixtures are suited for undercabinet applications.
- TS Series is used in toe kick, open soffit & cove applications.
- All dimming devices must be low voltage rated.
- Twelve gauge wire must be used on the low voltage side of the transformer.
- Locate transformer in accessible, ventilated area within 20' of fixtures.

KC Series

Designed for undercabinet use to light countertops & work areas. The compact size allows fixture to be installed behind front rail of most cabinets & not be seen. Uses 5 watt incandescent lamps. Average lamp life is 9,000 hours. Fixture is dimmable.

Luche KC Series

Length	Series	Total Watts
5"	KC	10
7"	KC	20
9"	KC	20
15"	KC	30
21"	KC	40
24"	KC	50
30"	KC	60
36"	KC	70

LX Series

Also designed for undercabinet use. This fixture, with 6 watt Xenon lamps, produces approximately 35% more light than standard incandescent. It is brighter & whiter, has an average lamp life of 11,600 hours and may be dimmed. Removable Lexan lens.

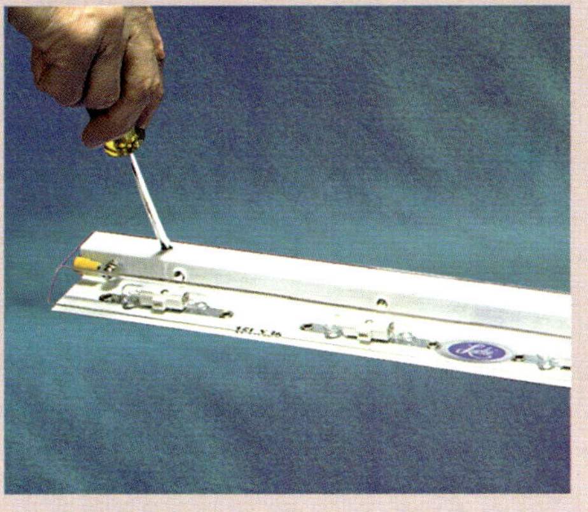

Luche LX Series

Length	Series	Total Watts
5"	LX	12
7"	LX	24
9"	LX	24
15"	LX	36
21"	LX	48
24"	LX	60
30"	LX	72
36"	LX	84

TS Series

Available with 4 lamp wattages for different effects- 3 watt, 5-watt incandescent, 4 watt and 6 watt Xenon. All fixtures are 48" long and may be field cut. Double sockets are 6" on center. Mounting is easy with double faced tape or screws.

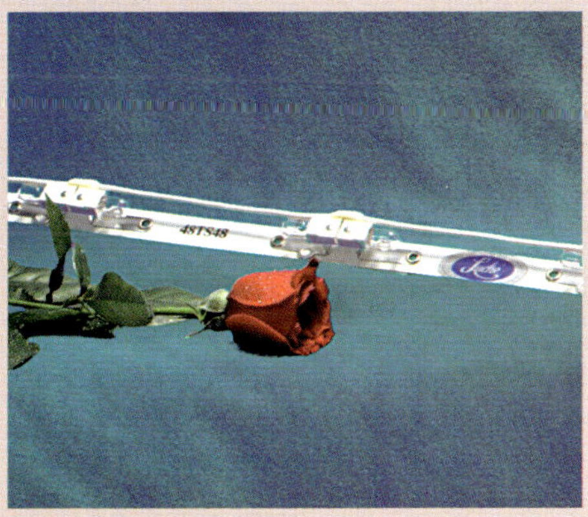

Luche TS Series

Length	Series	Total Watts
48"	TS	48
48"	TS	80
48"	TS	64X
48"	TS	96X

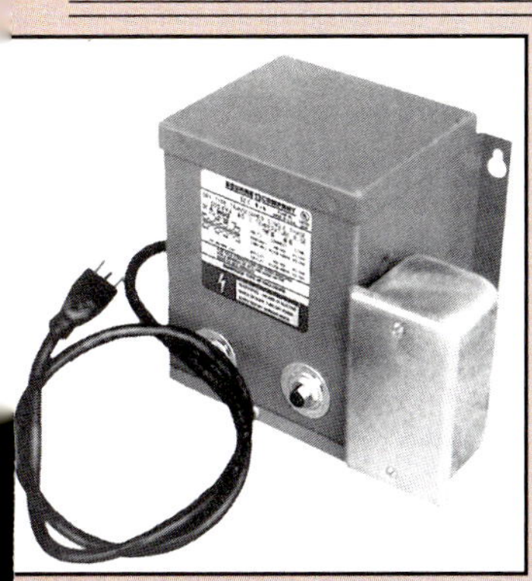

CBT Series power supplies come in four sizes; CBT-50 / 50 watts, CBT-150 / 150 watts, CBT-250 / 250 watts, CBT-500 / 500 watts. Also available with an electrostatic shield for applications designated as "damp locations". Circuit breakers protect the low voltage circuits with easy external reset buttons. The 3' grounded power cord plugs into a switched outlet. Transformer may be remotely located up to 20 feet away from lights.

Lumere Quick Reference

- Lumere is a patented modular lighting system.
- The 4" module makes Lumere adaptable to almost any lighting configuration.
- Gap connectors allow for turning corners and custom spacing.
- Combined modules available with single reflector.
- All dimming devices must be low voltage rated.

4LM6 (2-3 watt lamps)
4LM10 (2-5 watt lamps)
4LM8X (2-4 watt Xenon lamps)
4LM15X (2-6 watt Xenon lamps)

Modules, Starter & Gap Connectors

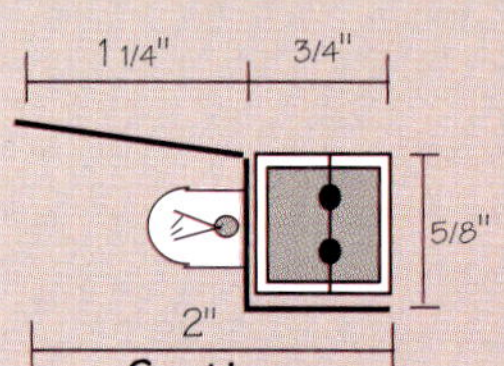

Section

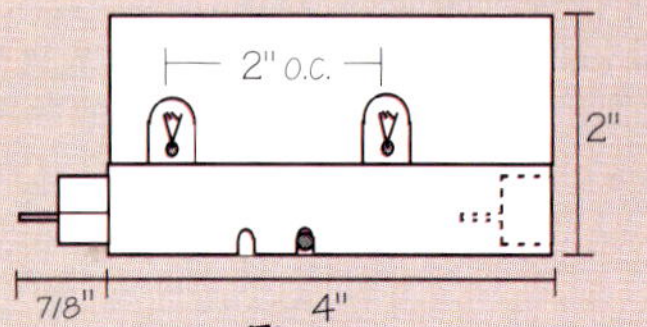

Fixture
Patent # 4,639,841

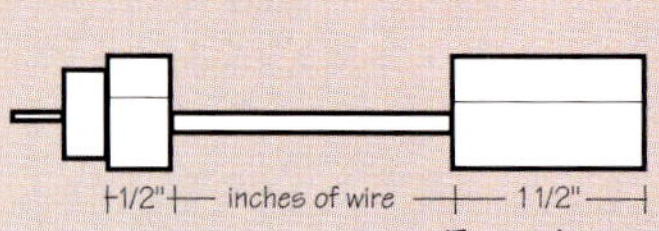

Male end Female end

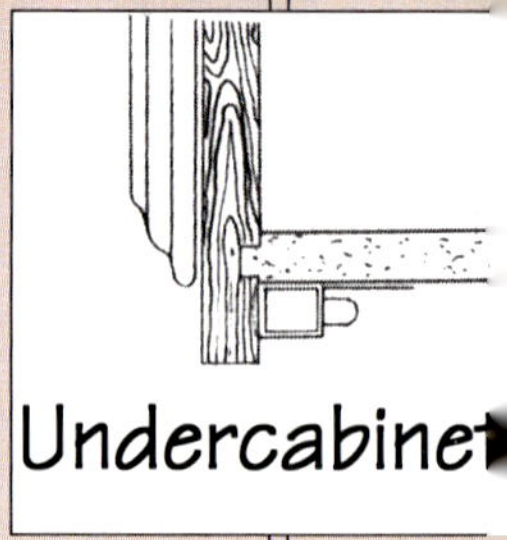

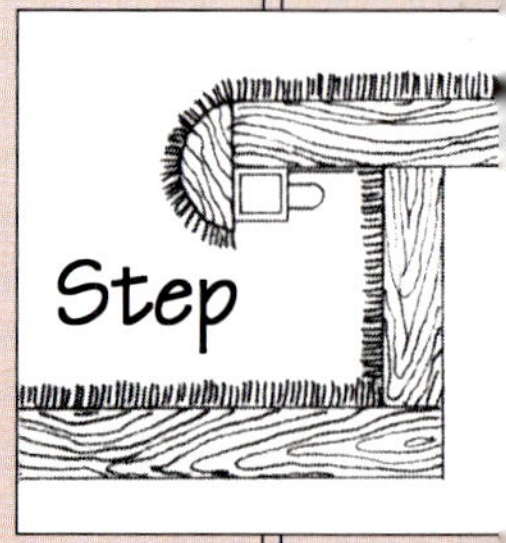

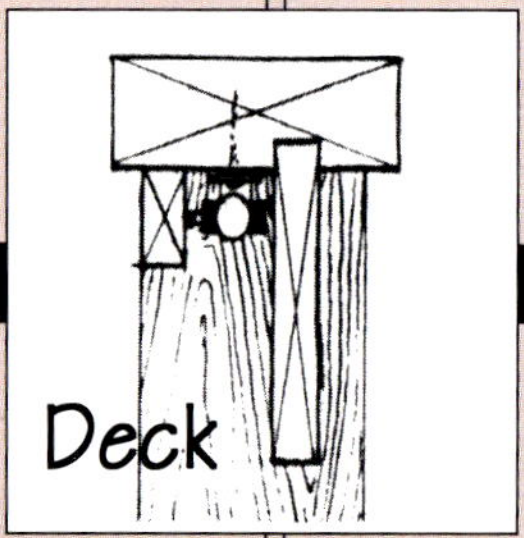

C UL LISTED

UL LISTED
69X5

800-445-6404
P.O. Box 1090
Kearney, NE 68848-1090
Fax 308-234-9401

TASK
Lighting Corporation

http://www.tasklighting.com e-mail: task@worldnet.att.net

Tu es Victor et tu es venu visiter un site archéologique avec tes parents. Dans ces grottes, tu vas découvrir les peintures réalisées par les hommes qui vivaient à l'âge de glace. Tu pourras également voir des restes d'outils et des ossements que les guides commenteront.

Il fait beau, les visiteurs sont nombreux... et l'un d'entre eux attire ton attention. Il vient de s'introduire dans une galerie dont l'accès est pourtant interdit. De plus, on dirait qu'il porte une torche : sa lumière danse sur les parois, tu en es certain !

N'écoutant que ton courage, tu décides d'aller voir...

Et te voilà transporté à l'âge de glace, au milieu des chasseurs de mammouths !

Tu vas devoir partir à la rencontre du mammouth sacré et te lancer à la poursuite du voleur de feu. Surtout, ne le perds pas de vue : à chaque page, il faudra retrouver sa trace.

Pour parvenir au bout de cette aventure, tu devras éviter les nombreux dangers, échapper aux griffes des fauves, apprendre à fabriquer tes armes, retrouver le grand mammouth et obtenir son aide.

Souviens-toi : il t'est interdit de revenir en arrière, à moins que cela ne te soit expressément indiqué.

Bonne chance !

Livre-Jeu

50 surprises au temps des Mammouths

Texte de Jean-Luc Bizien - Illustrations de Emmanuel Chaunu

GRÜND

Tu t'avançais dans l'entrée de la caverne... et te voilà revenu au temps des chasseurs de mammouths !

Cette famille a installé son igloo dans la plaine gelée. Le papa est catastrophé : un étranger est venu et a volé leur feu, sans lequel ils ne pourront pas survivre très longtemps. Toute la famille te demande de l'aide.

– Tu dois retrouver le mammouth sacré, t'explique le chasseur. Il est le seul à pouvoir apaiser la nature et empêcher que des tempêtes se lèvent et détruisent nos abris. Mais il faut faire vite !

Ta décision est prise : tu vas partir à la recherche de l'animal magique. Mais par où commencer ?

Si tu choisis de traverser la plaine gelée, marche jusqu'à la **Page 20**.
Si tu préfères aller inspecter les abords de l'igloo, rends-toi **Page 14**.
En te dirigeant vers les montagnes, tu arriveras **Page 28**.

Mais avant tout, observe le décor : 5 adversaires vous épient. Repère-les tous et signale leur présence au chasseur, qui les fera fuir avec ses flèches !

Attiré par la lumière à l'entrée de cette grotte, tu découvres que trois chasseurs s'y sont déjà installés. Ils t'invitent à les rejoindre auprès du feu.

Aide-les à réparer leurs armes, en signalant tous leurs défauts. En échange, ils t'autoriseront à te reposer au chaud.

Ensuite, observe les peintures sur la paroi. Le mammouth sacré y est représenté : repère-le et garde-le bien en mémoire, si tu veux le reconnaître quand tu le croiseras.

Tu n'auras plus qu'à attendre le matin pour poursuivre ton chemin jusqu'à la **Page 40**.

Ce bébé mammouth appelle à l'aide : une partie de la banquise s'est détachée et l'entraîne au milieu des vagues. Si tu ne trouves pas le moyen de le ramener auprès de sa maman, il va dériver jusqu'à l'ours...

Tu as sûrement un moyen de sauver le petit, avant que l'ours se décide à plonger pour l'attraper. Observe bien le décor et va vérifier à la page des solutions que tu as trouvé.

Quand tu y seras parvenu, tu pourras suivre le bébé et sa maman jusqu'à la Page 22.

Ces tigres à dents de sabre sont des animaux très impressionnants !
Ils approchent, sûrs de leur force...

Que vas-tu faire ?
Si tu montes dans les collines pour leur échapper, tu atteindras la **Page 32**.
Si tu les laisses approcher, il te faudra caresser le chef de meute.
C'est le seul d'entre eux qui n'a pas de jumeau. Si tu ne te trompes pas,
il se montrera gentil avec toi et tu pourras repartir vers la **Page 26**.

Mais attention !
Il faut faire le bon choix, si tu ne veux pas retourner **Page 6**.

Cette femelle renard argenté a bien des soucis : lors de la dernière tempête de neige, elle a voulu réunir ses petits dans cet abri, mais elle vient de s'apercevoir que tous les bébés ne sont pas les siens.

Identifie les intrus afin que chacun puisse retourner chez soi.

Quand tu auras terminé, poursuis ton chemin jusqu'à la Page 20.

Tu as enfin trouvé le mammouth sacré !
Malheureusement, il semble bien mal en point...

Vois-tu pourquoi il est si faible ?

Soulage vite le pauvre animal, qui doit souffrir.

Ensuite, trouve un moyen de le guérir et de lui faire retrouver toutes ses forces. Puis indique-lui tous les adversaires qui le cernent - ils sont six, prêts à l'attaquer.
S'il les repère grâce à toi, ils n'oseront pas bouger.

Si tu trouves comment soigner le mammouth sacré, son esprit te raccompagnera jusqu'à l'igloo et tu pourras aider la famille du chasseur à refaire du feu, en passant par la Page 34.

Dans le cas contraire, ton aventure s'achève ici et tu dois repartir Page 6...

Malheur ! Il ne fallait pas s'élancer au hasard, comme tu l'as fait : tu n'as pas vu la crevasse qui s'ouvrait sous tes pieds et tu es tombé au fond !

Ton aventure s'achève ici, car tu as perdu l'occasion de retrouver le mammouth sacré.

Pour retourner **Page 6**, tu dois d'abord sortir de ce piège en escaladant la paroi. Tu n'es pas le premier à tomber ici : d'autres que toi sont parvenus à construire un escalier de fortune, mais il manque des appuis.

Choisis sur le sol les objets nécessaires et observe bien la forme des failles. Si tu trouves les morceaux qui correspondent, tu pourras rejoindre la surface.

Ce grand élan est magnifique ! Ses bois somptueux t'impressionnent.

L'animal choisit de ne pas charger, il te laisse approcher en t'observant. Sa voix résonne dans ta tête :

– Eh bien, Victor ! Tu as encore un long chemin avant de trouver le mammouth sacré. Tu devrais, comme les chasseurs, faire appel aux esprits de la nature pour guider tes pas.

Regarde-le avec attention : tu devrais voir les visages de six esprits qui le protègent. Si tu les trouves tous, ils te viendront en aide, et te guideront jusqu'à la **Page 8**.

Ces mammouths se déplacent à la recherche d'une vallée qui les abritera. Vois-tu parmi eux le mammouth sacré ? S'il n'est pas là, tu peux toujours leur demander de t'aider à le trouver. Mais avant cela, il te faut agir : cinq graves menaces planent sur le troupeau... Les vois-tu ?

Va vérifier à la page des solutions que tu les as bien repérées, et n'oublie pas de prévenir tes amis mammouths. Ils t'indiqueront comment rejoindre la Page 30.

Ce chasseur s'installe devant un trou dans la banquise. Il y dépose des lignes et guette les poissons qu'il peut chasser au harpon... mais il risque d'avoir des problèmes, s'il ne fait pas attention !

Indique-lui le seul endroit où il pourra chasser sans avoir à combattre un adversaire. En récompense, il t'expliquera comment atteindre au plus vite la page 36.

Aïe ! Tu observais le vol de l'aigle géant et tu n'as pas vu approcher cet ours qui s'est lancé à ta poursuite !

Comble de malheur, te voilà dans un labyrinthe de glace, dont tu dois trouver la sortie, si tu ne veux pas servir de dîner à l'ours blanc.

Si tu y parviens, tu peux aller **Page 38**.

Dans le cas contraire, c'est la **Page 6** qui t'attend pour une nouvelle aventure !

Ces deux ours n'ont pas l'air agressifs, mais il faut toujours se méfier des animaux sauvages...

Que vas-tu faire ? Tu peux t'enfuir et filer à travers la plaine glacée, en espérant leur échapper. Dans ce cas, cours jusqu'à la **Page 18**.

Tu peux aussi rester calme, et les observer attentivement. Tu devrais noter leurs sept différences. Si tu les trouves et les leur montre, ils seront si occupés à les vérifier que tu pourras repartir sans risque jusqu'à la **Page 20**.

Tu es entré te mettre à l'abri dans cette caverne, tu y as trouvé des braises dans les restes du feu de camp de ses anciens occupants. Tu as réuni des brindilles, tu as soufflé, le feu a repris... et les flammes ont révélé la présence de monstres dont tu vois les ombres !

Pointe-les tous du doigt pour les faire fuir, puis ramasse sur le sol de quoi fabriquer une lance.

Quand tu auras chassé tous les animaux de la grotte, repose-toi un moment, car il te faudra des forces pour relever le défi
de la **Page 42** !

Hélas ! Tu as perdu du temps à gravir la colline et tu aperçois, dans le lointain, le mammouth sacré qui s'éloigne…

Ton aventure s'achève ici.

Pour retourner **Page 6** et retenter ta chance, tu dois dévaler la pente à bord de cette luge. Pour cela, tu dois d'abord démêler les lanières de cuir et trouver la seule qui te permettra de la diriger.

Ces loups t'ont surpris. Pour le moment, le chef de meute, qui t'observe avec curiosité, intime aux autres de garder leurs distances mais sois bien attentif à chacun de ses mouvements, il pourrait décider de lancer l'attaque ! Repère-le bien, c'est le seul qui n'a pas de jumeau.

Seul, tu ne peux pas leur échapper, mais si tu aperçois un allié, trouve un moyen de l'appeler à l'aide.

Si tu y arrives, il t'emmènera Page 44.

Cette chamane passe d'une tribu à une autre pour exercer ses pouvoirs magiques. Elle peut soigner les hommes et les animaux, sur simple demande.

En échange, on lui donne à manger et on l'abrite quelque temps.

En essayant un nouveau pouvoir, elle s'est trompée de formule et voilà le résultat ! Pour mettre fin à ce sortilège, il te suffit de nommer un à un tous les animaux qui sont mélangés dans cette terrible créature.

Si tu y parviens, la sorcière te promettra de t'aider, si tu en as besoin un jour.

Tu n'auras plus qu'à aller **Page 12**.

Horreur ! Tu as échappé à l'ours affamé, mais l'aigle géant a piqué sur toi. Il t'a emporté dans les airs, jusqu'à ce repaire inaccessible où il élève ses petits.

Si tu ne veux pas qu'il t'offre en repas aux oisillons géants, trouve vite quelque chose à lui offrir... L'aigle appréciera sûrement de recevoir un totem sacré assurant la protection de son nid face aux éléments. Quand tu as fait ton choix, trouve un moyen de récupérer l'objet !

Ensuite, pour amadouer les aiglons, cherche un instrument de musique. Il y en a un, dans ce nid, qui possède des pouvoirs magiques : en jouant de cet instrument, tu peux appeler le rapace géant quand tu le souhaites, et endormir ses petits.

En échange de tes efforts, l'aigle te proposera de t'emmener sur son dos jusqu'à la Page 16.

Alors que tu t'avançais dans la plaine, un grondement terrible s'est fait entendre... et voilà qu'un troupeau d'aurochs arrive en chargeant !

Que vas-tu faire ? Tu peux courir au hasard à travers la plaine, tu arriveras **Page 18**.

Si tu décides de rester, trouve au plus vite un moyen d'effrayer les aurochs pour qu'ils te contournent. Sinon, tu seras piétiné et tu devras retourner **Page 6** pour une nouvelle aventure.

Va vérifier à la page des solutions que tu as fait le bon choix et, si tel est le cas, tu peux poursuivre jusqu'à la **Page 10**.

En inspectant ta caverne, tu as longé une galerie... et tu as glissé sur ce toboggan naturel. Te voilà obligé de traverser le gouffre pour ressortir de l'autre côté, car derrière toi, la pente est trop abrupte !

Tu vas devoir marcher en équilibre sur les colonnes, en faisant bien attention de ne pas prendre appui sur celles qui sont fragiles.

Si tu tombes, tu devras retourner **Page 6**.

Choisis avec soin ton parcours.

Si tu parviens de l'autre côté, tu arriveras **Page 24**.

Tu peux aussi longer ton côté de la falaise et aller jusqu'à la **Page 36**.

Victoire ! Tu as échappé aux loups grâce à ton ami l'aigle géant. Les pouvoirs du mammouth sacré t'ont permis de redonner le feu aux habitants de l'igloo et tu as regardé un moment les flammes qui s'élevaient vers le ciel...

Elles se sont transformées et tu t'es retrouvé nez à nez avec ce spéléologue, très surpris de te découvrir dans une galerie interdite au public !

– Elle n'est pas encore ouverte aux visiteurs, t'explique-t-il. Je vérifie que tout est en place. Viens avec moi !

Il te fait découvrir les parois des galeries, sur lesquelles tu observes de nombreuses peintures. Un mammouth géant, des tigres à dents de sabre, un aigle, un igloo...

Peut-être n'as-tu pas tout rêvé, finalement ?

Le meilleur moyen d'en décider, c'est de regarder tout autour de toi, quand tu quittes la grotte avec le spéléologue. Tu devrais identifier de nombreux personnages de cette aventure qui sont venus te saluer une dernière fois !

SOLUTIONS DES JEUX

Pages 6-7 : Les cinq adversaires sont : l'ours derrière l'arbre en bas à droite de l'image, le loup derrière l'entrée de l'igloo, le loup derrière l'igloo près de la peau tendue et les deux autres loups cachés dans les montagnes à droite de la tornade.

Pages 8-9 : Deux lances sont mal ficelées, il manque des pics à la massue, la pointe de l'une des flèches en bas à droite est détachée et la corde de l'arc à droite est défaite. Le mammouth sacré est le dernier dessin sur la gauche : l'une de ses défenses est cassée.

Pages 10-11 : Il faut attacher la pierre à la corde à gauche de l'image et l'utiliser pour ramener le morceau de banquise où est le bébé mammouth vers sa maman.

Pages 12-13 : Le chef de meute est le tigre en haut de l'image, celui qui n'a ni rayures sur le dos ni taches sous l'oreille.

Pages 14-15 : Les intrus sont : l'ourson, le bébé tigre à dents de sabre, le singe, le crocodile, le chaton, la tortue et l'œuf en train d'éclore.

Pages 16-17 : Pour soigner le mammouth, il faut retirer la lance et la flèche de sa patte avant et demander à la chamane, qui se trouve en haut à gauche, de le guérir. Les adversaires sont : le chasseur derrière la défense du mammouth et les deux loups, les deux autres chasseurs et le tigre à dents de sabre qui se cachent parmi les arbres.

Pages 18-19 : Pour remonter à la surface, il faut insérer dans les encoches les morceaux de bois dont la forme correspond.

Pages 20-21 : Les esprits se dissimulent dans les bois de l'élan : il y en a trois de chaque côté.